ALEXANDER THE GREAT

A Reader

Edited by
Ian Worthington

Routledge
Taylor & Francis Group

LONDON AND NEW YORK

First published 2003
by Routledge
2 Park Square, Milton Park, Abingdon, Oxon, OX14 4RN

Simultaneously published in the USA and Canada
by Routledge
270 Madison Ave, New York, NY 10016

Routledge is an imprint of the Taylor & Francis Group, an informa business

© 2003 selection and editorial matter Ian Worthington;
individual contributions, the contributors

Reprinted 2004, 2006, 2007

Typeset in Garamond by
Florence Production Ltd, Stoodleigh, Devon

Printed and bound in Great Britain by
TJ International Ltd, Padstow, Cornwall

British Library Cataloguing in Publication Data
A catalogue record for this book is available from the British Library

Library of Congress Cataloging in Publication Data
A catalog record for this book has been requested

ISBN 13: 978–0–415–29186–6 (hbk)
ISBN 13: 978–0–415–29187–3 (pbk)

CONTENTS

Preface ix
Ancient sources and modern books xi
Alexander's reign: the main events xiii
Map of Alexander's empire xiv
Special notes and abbreviations xvi
Alexander in quotes xvii

1 THE SOURCES 1

Sources 1–13 2

Introduction: some basic principles   *A.B. Bosworth* 7
From *From Arrian to Alexander* (Oxford 1988), 1–15

2 ALEXANDER'S BACKGROUND 17

Sources 14–16 18

The language of the Macedonians   *N.G.L. Hammond* 20
From *The Macedonian State* (Oxford 1989), 12–15

The king and the Macedones   *N.G.L. Hammond*
From *Alexander the Great: King and Commander* (Bristol 1989), 13–18 23

The Legacy of Philip   *A.B. Bosworth* 28
From *Conquest and Empire: the reign of Alexander the Great*
(Cambridge 1988), 5–19

3 ALEXANDER'S AIMS 42

Sources 17–19 43

The aims of Alexander   *P.A. Brunt* 45
From *Greece and Rome* 12 (1965), 205–15

On the final aims of Philip II   *E.A. Fredricksmeyer* 54
From W.L. Adams and E.N. Borza (eds), *Philip II, Alexander the Great,
and The Macedonian Heritage* (Lanham MD 1982), 85–98

4 ALEXANDER AND THE GREEKS   65

   Sources 20–32   66

   Macedonian domination: the Peace of 338/7 and after   *T.T.B. Ryder*   75
   From *Koine Eirene* (Oxford 1965), 102–9

   Relations with the Greek States   *N.G.L. Hammond* and *F.W. Walbank*   81
   From *A History of Macedonia* 3 (Oxford 1988), 72–83

   The Harpalus Affair and the Greek response to the Macedonian
      hegemony   *Ian Worthington*   90
   From Ian Worthington (ed), *Ventures into Greek History: essays in honour
      of N.G.L. Hammond* (Oxford 1994), 307–330

5 ALEXANDER AND ASIA   106

   Sources 33–58   107

   Alexander and the Macedonian invasion of Asia: aspects of the
   historiography of war and empire in antiquity   *Michel Austin*   118
   From J. Rich and G. Shipley (eds), *War and Society in the Greek World*
   (London 1993), 197–223

   The kingdom of Asia and the Persian throne   *N.G.L. Hammond*   136
   From *Antichthon* 20 (1986), 73–85

6 ALEXANDER, INDIA AND THE FINAL YEARS   148

   Sources 59–84   149

   Alexander and India   *A.K. Narain*   161
   From *Greece and Rome* 12 (1965), 155–65

   The Indian Satrapies under Alexander the Great   *A.B. Bosworth* 170
   From *Antichthon* 17 (1983), 37–46

7 ALEXANDER AS GENERAL   178

   Sources 85–86   178

   Alexander as strategist   *J.F.C. Fuller*   181
   From *The Generalship of Alexander the Great* (New Brunswick 1960),
   284–305

8 ALEXANDER AND THE 'UNITY OF MANKIND'   198

   Sources 87–91   199

   The Susa Wedding   *W.W. Tarn*   202
   From *Alexander the Great* I (Cambridge 1948), 110–111

The Mutiny at Opis   *W.W. Tarn*   203
ibid 115–117

The Policy of fusion   *W.W. Tarn*   205
Ibid 137–8 and 145–8

Alexander and the Iranians   *A.B. Bosworth*   208
From *Journal of Hellenic Studies* 100 (1980), 1–21

9 ALEXANDER AND DEIFICATION   236

Sources 92–100   237

Alexander's deification   *W.W. Tarn*   242
From *Alexander the Great* II (Cambridge 1948), 370–3

Alexander the Great between two thrones and heaven: variations on
an old theme   *E. Badian*   245
From A. Small (ed) *Subject and Ruler: the cult of the ruling power
in Classical Antiquity* = *JRA* suppl, 17 (1996), 11–26

The deification of Alexander the Great: a note   *G.L. Cawkwell*   263
From Ian Worthington (ed), *Ventures into Greek History: Essays in
honour of N.G.L. Hammond* (Oxford 1994), 293–306

10 ALEXANDER AND CONSPIRACIES   273

Sources 101–108   273

Conspiracies   *E. Badian*   277
From A.B. Bosworth and E.J. Baynham (eds), *Alexander the Great
in Fact and Fiction* (Oxford 2000), 50–77

11 ALEXANDER: THE 'GREAT'?   296

Sources 109–112   297

Alexander's personality   *N.G.L. Hammond*   299
From *Alexander the Great: King, Commander and Statesman* (Bristol
1989), 269–73

How 'great' was Alexander?   *Ian Worthington*   303
From *Ancient History Bulletin* 13.2 (1999), 39–55

Alexander the Great today: in the interests of historical accuracy?
  Frank L. Holt   319
From *Ancient History Bulletin* 13.3 (1999), 111–117

Index of primary sources   326
General index   328

PREFACE

Alexander the Great of Macedon is one of the best known and most fascinating figures from antiquity. In his thirteen-year reign (336–323), he defeated the great Persian empire and invaded India, thus establishing a vast Macedonian empire which stretched from Greece in the west to India in the east. His fighting prowess and brilliant strategy were combined with a fierce intellect and appreciation of learning, and he was quick to see the value of integrating Asians into his administration and army. He was the type of man that legends are made of, and therein lies the major problem in any study of Alexander: separating the legendary Alexander from the historical.

In the generations, indeed centuries, after his death stories were written about Alexander which were unhistorical. Some of these, such as the king's dealings with a tribe of headless men, as found in the literary *Alexander Romance*, can easily be dismissed. Others not so, for during Alexander's lifetime and in the generations after his death many works were written about him (primary sources), all with shortcomings and biases, which have not survived in their entirety today. These works were used by the later writers (secondary sources) several centuries after Alexander's death who give us our connected narratives of his reign. The problem is obvious: how reliable are sources written so long after the events they describe, how critically did they evaluate the earlier works (which they probably read in their entirety) and decide which account to prefer over another, and how do their own political, social, and moral backgrounds affect their presentation of Alexander? Indeed, there is no actual evidence that later sources such as Arrian and Plutarch read the primary sources in their entirety, thereby compounding the problem.

Ought we to accept the picture of a dashing king enjoying spectacular successes and establishing a great empire, or should we adopt a more cynical evaluation of him, one based on the downside of his reign, in which we see an Alexander who preferred warfare over long-term administration, who was guilty of drunken, paranoid, acts of murder, who was responsible for the deaths of tens of thousands of people, whose megalomania led him to believe in his own divinity, and whose failure to produce an uncontested heir led to the disintegration of his empire? Does Alexander even deserve to be called 'Great' nowadays?

This book is divided into eleven thematic chapters. The first chapter deals with the problem of the ancient sources, and the last with the 'greatness' of Alexander; the main events of the reign are the focus of Chapters 2 to 10. Each chapter has a brief introduction, which is meant only to set the scene, and a short list of additional readings. The aim of the Routledge Reader series is to provide translations of some of the more inaccessible primary sources, with minimal notes, followed by a selection of modern scholars' works in English. What primary sources we have are quoted in the secondary sources; they are the foundation stones of the later connected histories of the reign and provide valuable information on many aspects of the areas through which Alexander marched. Usually, primary works are passed over in favour of the secondary source, hence this series' format allows readers to consider contemporary evidence and to set it next to the more readily available secondary sources (which need to be read in their entirety). Thus, in this book I give a selection of inscriptional and especially primary literary material. Since completing this Reader, I have become aware of another Alexander reader in preparation, which contains extracts from the secondary source material.

In the selections from the primary sources, I give inscriptional material first (in Chapters 4 and 5) and then literary sources. With the latter, I first give those that deal with areas (geography, customs, general themes, etc.), followed by those that deal with Alexander's actual actions (in chronological order). For ease of reference, the sources are numbered consecutively in the book. Translations of the epigraphical material are my own; translations of the fragments of the Greek historians are those of C.A. Robinson, *The History of Alexander the Great* 1 (Providence: 1953). I am very grateful to Brown University Library for granting permission to reprint.

I have tried where possible to select modern scholars' works that focus on the problems of our ancient source material, as well as give different interpretations of the same topic. My aim is to show that there is no single approach to Alexander, and that there can be substantial disagreement. It is up to the reader, based on his/her critical evaluation of the ancient sources and arguments of modern scholars, to reach his/her own conclusions – as indeed it should be. I know that not everyone will agree with my choices, but if I gave a translation of all sources along with everything that has been written on Alexander, the Reader would probably take up 100 volumes, and I would be criticised for not being selective. There will never be agreement about what a volume on Alexander should contain, and I hope that my critics will see my rationale for what I included, and leave it at that. There have been occasions, especially in Chapter 7 dealing with Alexander's generalship, where I have wanted to reprint more modern works, but the absurdly high reprint fees disallowed that. On pp. ix–x I list the ancient sources and some modern biographies (those who wish to read more as well as works in languages other than English may consult the bibliographies in the modern works cited below and in the chapters).

Acknowledgements

I would like to thank Richard Stoneman for inviting me to compile this Reader and for his willingness to discuss its contents; as an Alexander scholar himself, his expertise was much appreciated. I am indebted to Catherine Bousfield at Routledge, who not only responded to numerous requests promptly but also calmed me down so many times during the thankless task of seeking permissions. I would also like to thank Erin Garvin for compiling the index. Finally, I am grateful to my family, as always, for their support and endurance – more than I (or Alexander) deserve.

Ian Worthington
University of Missouri-Columbia
March 2002

ANCIENT SOURCES
AND MODERN BOOKS

Contemporary inscriptions

M.N. Tod, *Greek Historical Inscriptions* 2 (Oxford: 1948), nos 183–203.
A.J. Heisserer, *Alexander the Great and the Greeks* (Norman: 1980).
L. Moretti, *Inscrizioni Storiche Ellenistiche* (Florence: 1967 and 1976).
P.E. Harding, *From the End of the Peloponnesian War to the Battle of Ipsus* (Cambridge: 1985), nos 102–122.

Collected fragments of the primary sources

F. Jacoby, *Die Fragmente der griechischen Historiker* IIB, nos 117–153 (Berlin: 1927), with a German commentary on them in IID (Berlin: 1927), pp. 403–542, and IIIB pp. 742–743 (Berlin: 1930).
All of the above are translated in C.A. Robinson, *The History of Alexander the Great* 1 (Providence: 1953), pp. 30–276.
See also: L. Pearson, *The Lost Histories of Alexander the Great* (New York: 1960).

Principal secondary sources

Diodorus Siculus, Book 17; Arrian; Quintus Curtius Rufus; Plutarch, *Life of Alexander*; Justin; Strabo, Books 15–17.
The above are translated in the Loeb Classical Library, with the exception of Justin, for which see J.C. Yardley and W. Heckel, *Justin: Epitome of the Philippic History of Pompeius Trogus 1, Books 11–12: Alexander the Great* (Oxford: 1997).

Other sources

The Greek Alexander Romance, translated by Richard Stoneman, Penguin Classics (Harmondsworth: 1991).
Legends of Alexander the Great, translated by Richard Stoneman, Everyman Library (London: 1994).
See also: J. Roisman (ed.), *Alexander the Great: Ancient and Modern Perspectives* (Lexington, MA: 1995), which has translated extracts of the source material, together with some modern views on aspects of Alexander's reign.

Note: A Reader on Alexander, which includes extracts from secondary source material, edited by W. Heckel and J. Yardley, is scheduled for publication in 2004.

Modern biographies and treatments

The bibliography on Alexander is enormous. I list below some biographies and discussions of his reign which are written in English (the bibliographies in many of these works may be consulted for further readings).

A.B. Bosworth, *Conquest and Empire: the Reign of Alexander the Great* (Cambridge: 1988).
—— , 'Alexander the Great', Chapters 16 and 17 in the *Cambridge Ancient History* 6² (Cambridge: 1994), pp. 791–875.
—— , *Alexander and the East* (Oxford: 1996).
A.B. Bosworth and E.J. Baynham (eds), *Alexander the Great in Fact and Fiction* (Oxford: 2000).
D. Engels, *Alexander the Great and the Logistics of the Macedonian Army* (Berkeley and Los Angeles: 1978).
J.F.C. Fuller, *The Generalship of Alexander the Great* (New Brunswick: 1960).
P. Green, *Alexander of Macedon* (Harmondsworth: 1974).
J.R. Hamilton, *Alexander the Great* (London: 1973).
N.G.L. Hammond, *Alexander the Great: King, Commander and Statesman*² (Bristol: 1989).
—— , *The Genius of Alexander the Great* (London: 1997).
W. Heckel, *The Marshals of Alexander's Empire* (London: 1992).
S. Hornblower, *The Greek World, 479–323 BC* (London: 1983), Chapter 18.
R. Lane Fox, *Alexander the Great* (London: 1973).
R.D. Milns, *Alexander the Great* (London: 1968).
J.M. O'Brien, *Alexander the Great: The Invisible Enemy* (London: 1992).
J. Roisman (ed.), *A Companion to Alexander the Great* (Leiden: forthcoming 2003).
W.W. Tarn, *Alexander the Great*, 2 vols (Cambridge: 1948).
U. Wilcken, *Alexander the Great*, translated by G.C. Richards (New York: 1967).
M. Wood, *In the Footsteps of Alexander: A Journey from Greece to Asia* (Berkeley: 1997).
Ian Worthington, *Alexander the Great: Man and God* (London: forthcoming 2003).

Some suggested additional readings are given in each chapter, but the above books should also be consulted on the topics of each chapter.

ALEXANDER'S REIGN

The main events

336   Assassination of Philip II; Alexander succeeds to the throne of Macedon as Alexander III; revolt of the Greeks ended by Alexander

335   Alexander campaigns successfully in the north; revolt of Thebes, which was razed to the ground by Alexander

334   Alexander invades Persia; Battle of the Granicus River

333   Battle of Issus

332   Sieges of Tyre and Gaza

331   Alexander enters Egypt, which surrenders to him; he founds Alexandria and visits the oracle of Zeus Ammon at Siwah; Agis III of Sparta's war against Macedon begins in Greece; Battle of Gaugamela

330   Alexander burns Persepolis; death of Darius III; executions of Philotas and Parmenion; defeat of Agis III by Antipater

329   Crossing of the Hindu Kush and capture of Bessus; revolts of Bactria and Sogdiana

328   Alexander in Bactria and Sogdiana; the murder of Cleitus

327   End of the Bactrian campaign; the attempt to introduce *proskynesis* at Bactra; the Pages' Conspiracy; Alexander marches to India

326   Alexander's army crosses the Indus; Battle of the Hydaspes River; the first army mutiny (at the Hyphasis river)

325   Alexander campaigns against the Malli; the march through the Gedrosian Desert

324   The mass marriage at Susa and the issuing of the Exiles Decree; the second army mutiny (at Opis), followed by the banquet of reconciliation; death of Hephaestion

323   Debate in Greece over Alexander's divinity; 10 June: Alexander dies at Babylon

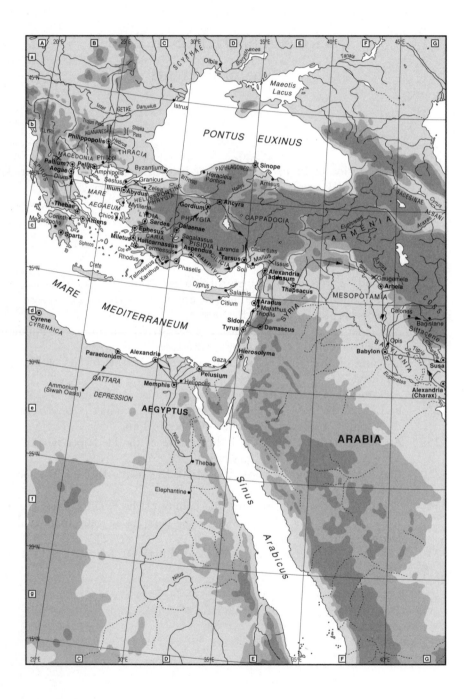

Alexander's empire.

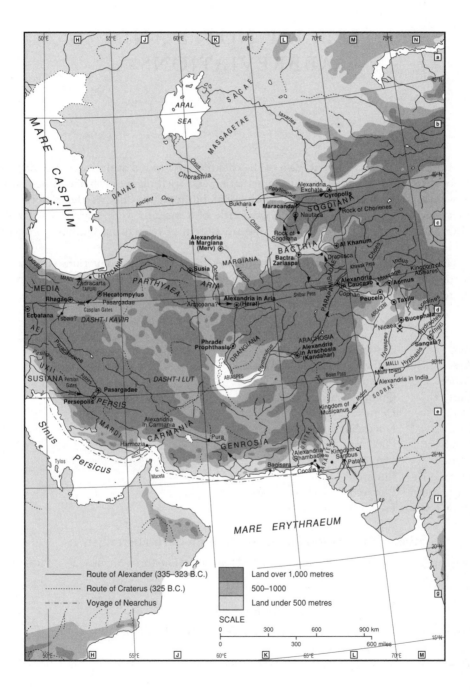

MARE CASPIUM

ARAL SEA

SACAE

MASSAGETAE

Iaxartes

Chorasmia

Oxus

DAHAE

Ancient Oxus

Polytimetus

Alexandria Exchate

Cyropolis

Bukhara

Maracanda

SOGDIANA

Rock of Chorienes

Nautaca

Rock of Sogdiana

Alexandria in Margiana (Merv)

MARGIANA

Susia

BACTRIA

Al Khanum

Bactra Zariaspa

Drapsaca

Ochus

Margus

PARTHYAEA

ARIA

Shibai Pass

Khawak Pass

Indus

Kingdom of Abisares

Zadracarta

HYRCANIA

TAPURI

MEDIA

Hecatompylus

Pasargadae

Artacoana?

Alexandria in Aria (Herat)

PARAPAMISADAE

Alexandria in Caucaso

Massaga

Aornus

Rhagae

Caspian Gates

Cophan

Peucela

ASSACENI

Taxila

Ecbatana

Tsbae?

DASHT-I KAVIR

Nicaea

Bucephala

Hydaspes

AEI

Phrade Prophthasia

DRANGIANA

ARACHOSIA

Hyrotes

Acesines

Chenab

Pasitigris

Alexandria in Arachosia (Kandahar)

Sangala?

UXII

ABIASPES

Etymandrus

MALLI

Hyphasis

SUSIANA

Persian Gates

DASHT-I LUT

Malli town

Araxes

Bolan Pass

Alexandria in India

Persepolis

Pasargadae

SODRAE

PERSIS

MARDI

Kingdom of Musicanus

Indus

Alexandria in Carmania

Sinus

Harmozia

CARMANIA

Pura

GENROSIA

Alexandria Rhambacie

Kingdom of Sambous

Persicus

Tylos

Bagisara

Patala

C. Maceta

Cocala

MARE ERYTHRAEUM

——— Route of Alexander (335–323 B.C.)

············· Route of Craterus (325 B.C.)

—·—·— Voyage of Nearchus

Land over 1,000 metres

500–1000

Land under 500 metres

SCALE

0   300   600   900 km

0   300   600 miles

SPECIAL NOTES AND ABBREVIATIONS

The modern scholars' works in each of the chapters are printed as they were published, hence they will have differences in punctuation and spelling (English and American), as well as style of referencing. An individual bibliography follows those works in which an author has used an abbreviated title of a modern work that is not immediately obvious to the reader or the Harvard system of referencing (author + year of publication) in the notes.

The abbreviations below are used in my own notes on the introductions and translated sources as well as by most scholars whose works are reprinted; some use different abbreviations for ancient authors, but these are easily recognisable (see below).

Ancient sources

Aes.	Aeschines
Arr.	Arrian, *Campaigns of Alexander*
Athen.	Athenaeus
Curt.	Quintus Curtius Rufus
Dem.	Demosthenes
Din.	Dinarchus
Diod.	Diodorus
Hyp.	Hyperides
Plut.	Plutarch
Plut. *Alex.*	Plutarch, *Life of Alexander*
[Plut.] *Mor.*	Pseudo-Plutarch, *Moralia*

Other abbreviations used in some modern abstracts:

A – Arrian; C – Quintus Curtius Rufus; D *or* DS – Diodorus Siculus; P – Plutarch; J – Justin

Modern works

FGrH	F. Jacoby, *Die Fragmente der griechischen Historiker*
IG	*Inscriptiones Graecae*
Tod	M.N. Tod, *Greek Historical Inscriptions* 2

Journals cited in the notes of articles usually have the same abbreviation as given in *L'Année Philologique.*

ALEXANDER
IN QUOTES

Of the three philosophers remaining, the one who was asked how someone might become a god from being a man said: 'By doing what is impossible for a man to do.'

(Plut. *Alexander* 64.9)

Demades urged [the Athenians] to pay no heed to the report [of Alexander's death], since, had it been true, the whole world would long ago have been filled with the smell of the body.

(Plut. *Phocion* 22.3)

Tranio: Alexander the Great and Agathocles, so I've heard say, were the two foremost champion wonder-workers of the world. Why shouldn't I be a third; aren't I a famous and wonderful worker?

(Plautus, *The Ghost Story* 775–778)

The storie of Alisaundre is so commune
That every wight that hath discrecioun
Hath herd somwhat or al of his fortune

(Chaucer, *The Monk's Tale* 2361–2363)

Alexander was fortunate in his death. His fame could hardly have increased; but it might perhaps have been diminished. For he died with the real task yet before him. He had made war as few have made it; it remained to be seen if he could make peace.

(W.W. Tarn, *Alexander the Great* 1, p. 121)

Alexander has often been worshipped, by biographers ancient and modern, for virtues he lacked. He deserves greater credit for those he possessed.

(E. Badian, 'The Administration of the Empire',
Greece and Rome[2] 12 (1965), p. 182)

Alexander was in most things a Macedonian through and through . . . and primarily a man of war whose genius is seen most clearly on the field of battle.

(N.G.L. Hammond, *Alexander the Great*, p. v)

The king's name and image were invoked as his conquests were renounced and dismembered. The debate over legitimacy lasted a mere generation. After that Alexander was a symbol and nothing else. For subsequent ages he typified the world conqueror, and his territorial acquisitions were a standing inspiration and challenge to successive dynasts.

(A.B. Bosworth, *Conquest and Empire*, p. 181)

Determined to astound contemporaries and awe future generations with his unique *arete*, Alexander exploited mankind and god with relentless perseverance. In the process, his *hybris* offended a deity capable of revealing and expiating mortal deficiencies with artful brutality. Dionysus chose wine as the vehicle through which he would unveil and magnify the defects of a brilliant man who was spiritually blind.

(J.M. O'Brien, *Alexander the Great*, pp. 229–230)

... when evaluating Alexander it is essential to view the 'package' of king as a whole; i.e., as king, commander and statesman. All too often this is not the case. There is no question that Alexander was spectacularly successful in the military field, and had Alexander only been a general his epithet may well have been deserved. But he was not just a general; he was a king too, and hence military exploits form only a percentage of what Alexander did, or did not do – in other words, we must look at the 'package' of him as king as a whole.

(Ian Worthington, 'How "Great" was Alexander?',
Ancient History Bulletin 13 (1999), p. 39)

1

THE SOURCES

Introduction

The study of Alexander is challenging and frustrating because of the source material. We have only a small number of inscriptions,[1] numismatic evidence, and occasional comments in some of the later Greek orators[2] that are contemporaneous. Although much was written about Alexander during his reign (336–323) and in the generation or two after his death (what may be called primary sources), these works have not survived in their entirety to the present day.[3] What remains of their works are to be found quoted by much later authors in their own histories of Alexander – what are called secondary works (see below). Of those primary sources, we have the most number of fragments from works by Aristobulus of Cassandria (*FGrH* 139), Callisthenes of Olynthus (*FGrH* 124), Chares of Mytilene (*FGrH* 125), Cleitarchus of Alexandria (*FGrH* 137), Nearchus of Crete (*FGrH* 133), Onesicritus of Astypalaea (*FGrH* 134), and Alexander's general Ptolemy, son of Lagus (*FGrH* 138). All the primary authors raise problems: did each one deal with the reign in full or did some concentrate on aspects of it or on the person of the king, for example? We cannot answer this question, but just because what we have quoted from, say, Baeton's work (*FGrH* 119) does not mean that he was only concerned with geographical and social matters.

We also have information on aspects of Alexander's reign in other sources, of which the most important are Strabo (first century BC) and Athenaeus (second/early third century AD). These sources also furnish valuable information on such things as the topography, culture, wealth, fauna, natural resources, and the peoples of the areas through which Alexander marched.[4] Three other sources may also be mentioned. First, the *Ephemerides* (*FGrH* 117), supposedly a daily journal kept throughout the reign, but apart from a fragment about Alexander's hunting practices what survives today tells of Alexander's excessive drinking habits and the manner of his death (Arr. 7.25.1–26.3, Plut. *Alex.* 76–77.1; see below, and Source 109). Second, *On the Fortune or Virtue of Alexander*, a treatise attributed to Plutarch which depicted Alexander as a warrior king and philosophical idealist. Third, the *Alexander Romance*, a mostly fictitious account of Alexander's reign which began its life in the third or second century BC and was reworked and expanded for many centuries to come.

It is not until several centuries after the king's death that we get a connected narrative of the reign by Diodorus Siculus (first century BC), Quintus Curtius Rufus (first century AD), Arrian (second century AD), and Justin (third century AD), who epitomized Pompeius Trogus' history of the world (first century AD). To these may be added Plutarch's biography of Alexander, and to a lesser extent his biographies of

1

Demosthenes and Phocion (second century AD). Our knowledge of what the earlier sources said is derived from the secondary sources, all of which used and cited primary works. Whether they had access to these sources in their entirety is unknown, but presumably they had more to read than we do today. For example, Nearchus' account of his voyage around India was used extensively by Arrian and Strabo, Ptolemy's essentially unromantic and military account of Alexander's reign lay at the heart of Arrian's account, and Cleitarchus was the principal source for Diodorus, Curtius, and Plutarch. Athenaeus quoted many earlier accounts, though he is less interested in facts and more in anecdotes (not a surprise since his work was set at a banquet at which guests discussed various intellectual and artistic matters).

As already stated, the primary accounts need to be viewed with caution, not just because we do not have them in their entirety. Additionally, for example, as the official court historian Callisthenes was biased towards Alexander, and Ptolemy and Aristobulus exaggerated their own roles and achievements during the reign (cf. Sources 5 and 6), in the process embellishing those of Alexander − for their own as well as his sake (cf. Source 2). Moreover, the primary sources are often in dispute with each other; for example, over the numbers of Alexander's invasion force in 334 (cf. Sources 18 and 45), or on matters of geography (cf. Sources 35–36, 59–61) or on matters affecting conspiracies (cf. Sources 102–107).[5] Caution needs also to be exercised towards the *Ephemerides*, *On the Fortune or Virtue of Alexander*, and the *Alexander Romance*. Although Arrian and Plutarch cited the *Ephemerides* for Alexander's last days, their authenticity is disputed − although the reports of Alexander's excessive drinking appear in many sources and are not likely to be inaccurate. *On The Fortune or the Virtue of Alexander* is essentially a rhetorical exercise, much influenced by the background, especially philosophical, in which it was written. Finally, the *Alexander Romance* is riddled with exploits attributed to Alexander that are unhistorical. Some of these may be dismissed without hesitation, such as Alexander's encounter with the tribe of headless men, but others not so − did Alexander meet the Amazons and have sex with their queen, Thalestria, for example? The primary sources are divided on this event (see Source 3).

The shortcomings of the primary sources clearly affect the secondary writers. We can only presume that they had access to the accounts of the primary authors, whereas we do not, but if so, then how accurately did the later authors interpret the earlier material? How and why did they decide that one account was to be preferred over another (cf. Source 1)? On what was their selectivity of earlier sources based? To what extent did they impose their own social, political, and moral backgrounds on their subject matter? How the sources are interpreted has affected many generations of modern scholars, whose images of Alexander range from the philosophical idealist to a cynical and pragmatic king.

Ancient sources

1 How Alexander constructed his bridge over the River Indus is explained neither by Aristobulus nor Ptolemy (*FGrH* 138 F 19), authors whom I usually follow (Aristobulus, *FGrH* 139 F 34 = Arr. 5.7.1).

2 Many false notions were also added to the account of this sea (the Hyrcanian) because of Alexander's love of glory; for, since it was agreed by all that the Tanais separated Asia from Europe, and that the region between the sea and the Tanais, being a considerable part of Asia, had not fallen under the power of the Macedonians, it was resolved to manipulate the account of Alexander's expedition so that in fame at least he might be credited with having conquered those parts of Asia too. They therefore united Lake Maeotis, which receives the Tanais, with the Caspian Sea, calling this too a lake and asserting that both were connected with one another by an underground passage and that each was a part of the other. Polycleitus goes on to adduce proofs in connection with his belief that the sea is a lake (for instance, he says that it produces serpents, and that its water is sweetish); and that it is no other than Maeotis he judges from the fact that the Tanais empties into it. From the same Indian mountains, where the Ochus and the Oxus and several other rivers rise, flows also the Iaxartes, which, like those rivers, empties into the Caspian Sea and is the most northerly of them all. This river, accordingly, they named Tanais; and in addition to so naming it they gave as proof that it was the Tanais mentioned by Polycleitus that the country on the far side of this river produces the fir tree and that the Scythians in that region use arrows made of fir wood; and they say that this is also evidence that the country on the far side belongs to Europe and not to Asia, for, they add, Upper and Eastern Asia does not produce the fir tree. But Eratosthenes says that the fir tree grows also in India (Polycleitus, *FGrH* 128 F 7 = Strabo 11.7.4).

3 Here the queen of the Amazons came to see him as most writers say, among whom are Cleitarchus (*FGrH* 137 FF 15–16), Polycleitus (*FGrH* 128 F 8), Onesicritus, Antigenes (*FGrH* 141 F 1), and Ister; but Aristobulus (*FGrH* 139 F 21), Chares the royal usher (*FGrH* 125 F 12), Ptolemy (*FGrH* 138 F 21), Anticleides (*FGrH* F 12), Philo the Theban, and Philip of Theangela, besides Hecataeus of Eretria, Philip the Chalcidian, and Duris of Samos, say that this is a fiction. And it would seem that Alexander's testimony is in favour of their statement. For in a letter to Antipater which gives all the details minutely he says that the Scythian king offered him his daughter in marriage, but he makes no mention of the Amazon (Onesicritus, *FGrH* 134 F 1 = Plut. *Alex.* 46.1–3).

4 The whole of the naval force was under the command of Nearchus; but the pilot of Alexander's ship was Onesicritus, who, in the narrative which he composed of Alexander's campaigns, falsely asserted that he was admiral, while in reality he was only a pilot (Onesicritus, *FGrH* 134 F 27 = Arr. 6.2.3).

5 Cleitarchus, as well as Timagenes, represents Ptolemy, who was subsequently a sovereign,[6] to have been present at this assault (at a town of the Sudracae);[7] but Ptolemy, truly no detractor from his own glory, relates that he was absent (*FGrH* 138 F 26 = Source 6), detached on an expedition (Cleitarchus, *FGrH* 137 F 24 = Curt. 9.5.21).

6 Moreover, in regard to those who covered Alexander with their shields in his peril,[8] all agree that Peucestas did so; but they no longer agree in regard to Leonnatus or Abreas, the soldier in receipt of double pay for his distinguished services. Some say that Alexander, having received a blow on the head with a piece of wood, fell down in a fit of dizziness; and that having risen again he was wounded with a dart through the corselet in his chest. But Ptolemy, son of Lagus, says that he received only this wound in the chest. However, in my opinion, the greatest error made by those who have written the history of Alexander is the following. There are some who have recorded that Ptolemy, son of Lagus, in company with Peucestas, mounted the ladder with Alexander, that Ptolemy held his shield over him when he lay wounded, and that he was called Soter on that account. And yet Ptolemy himself has recorded that he was not even present at this engagement, but was fighting battles against other barbarians at the head of another army. Let me mention these facts as a digression from the main narrative, so that the correct account of such great deeds and calamities may not be a matter of indifference to men of the future (Ptolemy, *FGrH* 138 F 26a = Arr. 6.11.7–8).

7 There was a report about Alexander ... that he did not drink much, but spent much time over his drink conversing with his friends. Philinus, however, has shown from the *Royal Ephemerides* that such persons talk nonsense, since it is continually and very often written there that 'he slept through the day from drinking' and sometimes 'the next day too' (*Ephemerides, FGrH* 117 F 2c = [Plut.] *Mor.* 623e).

8 Alexander also drank a very great deal, so that after the spree he would sleep continuously for two days and two nights. This is revealed in his *Ephemerides* written by Eumenes of Cardia and Diodotus of Erythrae (*FGrH* 117 F 2b = Athen. 10.434b).[9]

9 But Alexander, after returning from the funeral pyre[10] and assembling many of his friends and officers for supper, proposed a contest in drinking neat wine, the victor to be crowned. Well, then, the one who drank the most, Promachus, got as far as four pitchers; he took the prize, a crown of a talent's worth, but lived only three days afterwards. And of the rest, according to Chares, forty-one died of what they drank, a violent chill having set in after their debauch (Chares, *FGrH* 125 F 19b = Plut. *Alex.* 70.1–2).

10 And Nicoboule, or whoever ascribed to her the compilation, says that when Alexander was dining with Medeius of Thessaly he pledged the health of everyone at the dinner, there being twenty in all, and accepted the same number of toasts from all; he then left the party and soon after went to sleep (Nicoboule, *FGrH* 127 F 1 = Athen. 12.434c).

11 But Nicoboule says, that 'while he was at supper all the morris dancers and athletes studied to amuse the king; and at his very last banquet, Alexander, remembering an episode in the *Andromeda* of Euripides, recited it in a declamatory manner, and then drank a cup of unmixed wine with great eagerness, and compelled all the rest to do so' (Nicoboule, *FGrH* 127 F 2 = Athen. 12.537d).

12 Moreover, in the *Ephemerides* there are recorded the following particulars regarding his sickness. On the eighteenth of the month Daesius he slept in the bathing-room because he had a fever. On the following day, after his bath, he removed into his bed-chamber and spent the day at dice with Medius. Then, when it was late, he took a bath, performed his sacrifices to the gods, ate a little, and had a fever through the night. On the twentieth, after bathing again, he performed his customary sacrifice; and lying in the bathing-room he devoted himself to Nearchus, listening to his story of his voyage and of the great sea. The twenty-first he spent in the same way, and was still more inflamed, and during the night he was in a grievous plight, and all the following day his fever was very high. So he had his bed removed and lay by the side of the great bath, where he conversed with his officers about the vacant posts in the army, and how they might be filled with experienced men. On the twenty-fourth his fever was violent and he had to be carried forth to perform his sacrifices; moreover he ordered his principal officers to tarry in the court of the palace, and the commanders of divisions and companies to spend the night outside. He was carried to the palace on the other side of the river on the twenty-fifth, and got a little sleep, but his fever did not abate. And when his commanders came to his bedside, he was speechless, as he was also on the twenty-sixth; therefore the Macedonians made up their minds that he was dead, and came with loud shouts to the doors of the palace, and threatened his companions until all opposition was broken down; and when the doors had been thrown open to them, without cloak or armour, one by one, they all filed slowly past the couch. During this day, too, Python and Seleucus were sent to the temple of Serapis to enquire whether they should bring Alexander thither; and the god gave answer that they should leave him where he was. And on the twenty-eighth (Daesius), towards evening, he died. Most of this account is word for word as written in the *Ephemerides* (*FGrH* 117 F 3b = Plut. *Alex.* 76–77.1; cf. Arr. 7.25.1–26.3).

13 Neither Aristobulus nor Ptolemy has given an account differing much from the preceding. Some authors, however, have related that his Companions asked him to whom he left his kingdom; and that he replied: 'To the best.' Others say, that in addition to this remark, he told them that he saw there would be a great funeral contest held in his honour. I am aware that many other particulars have been related by historians concerning Alexander's death, and especially the poison that was sent to him by Antipater (Ptolemy, *FGrH* 138 F 30 = Arr. 7.26.3).

Modern works

In the following modern extract, A.B. Bosworth, Professor of Classics at the University of Western Australia, discusses some of the problems associated with the nature of the ancient sources. A.B. Bosworth, *From Arrian to Alexander* (Oxford: 1988), pp. 1–15.[11]

Additional reading

E. Baynham, *The Unique History of Quintus Curtius Rufus* (Ann Arbor: 1998).

E.N. Borza, 'An Introduction to Alexander Studies', in U. Wilcken, *Alexander the Great*, transl. G.C. Richards (New York: 1967), pp. ix–xxviii.

A.B. Bosworth, *From Arrian to Alexander* (Oxford: 1988).

——, *Alexander and the East* (Oxford: 1996), Chapters 1 and 2.

P.A. Brunt, *Arrian, History of Alexander*, Loeb Classical Library 1 (Cambridge, MA and London: 1976), pp. xviii–xxxiv.

N.G.L. Hammond, *Three Historians of Alexander the Great* (Cambridge: 1983) – for Diodorus, Curtius, and Justin.

——, *Sources for Alexander the Great* (Cambridge: 1993) – for Arrian and Plutarch's *Alexander*.

J.M. Mossman, 'Tragedy and Epic in Plutarch's *Alexander*', *Journal of Hellenic Studies* 108 (1988), pp. 83–93.

K.S. Sacks, 'Diodorus and his Sources: Conformity and Creativity', in S. Hornblower (ed.), *Greek Historiography* (Oxford: 1994), pp. 213–232.

R. Stoneman, '*The Alexander Romance*: From History to Fiction', in J.R. Morgan and R. Stoneman (eds.), *Greek Fiction: The Greek Novel in Context* (London: 1994), pp. 117–129.

Notes

1 See Sources 20–25, 33, and 34, a selection of more important inscriptions that deal with Alexander.

2 For example, Dem. 18.270 (wide-ranging power of Philip and Alexander), Aes. 3.133 (fate of Thebes in 335 and of Spartan hostages after Agis III's war of 331–330 being sent to Alexander), 3.160–164 (Alexander's first few years as king and that Demosthenes hoped that he would be defeated at the battle of Issus in 333), 3.165 and Din. 1.34 (mistakenly say that Alexander was in India during Agis III's war).

3 For information on where these sources are collected, see p. ix.

4 See Chapters 5 and 6.

5 Cf Arr. *Preface* 2: 'Different authors have given different accounts of Alexander's exploits, and there is no one about whom more have written, or more at variance with each other', Strabo 11.5.5:

> The stories that have been spread far and wide with a view to glorifying Alexander are not accepted by all; and their fabricators were men who cared for flattery rather than truth. For instance, they transferred the Caucasus into the region of the Indian mountains and of the eastern sea which lies near those mountains from the mountains which lie above Colchis and the Euxine; for these are the mountains which the Greeks named Caucasus, which is more than thirty thousand stades distant from India; and here it was that they laid the scene of the story of Prometheus and of his being put in bonds; for these were the farthermost mountains towards the east that were known to writers of that time. And the expedition of Dionysus and Heracles to the country of the Indians looks like a mythical story of later date, because Heracles is said to have released Prometheus one thousand years later. And although it was a more glorious thing for Alexander to have subdued Asia as far as the Indian mountains than merely to the recess of the Euxine and to the Caucasus, yet the glory of the mountain, and its name, and the belief that Jason and his followers had accomplished the longest of all expeditions, reaching as far as the neighbourhood of the Caucasus, and the tradition that Prometheus was bound at the ends of the earth on the Caucasus, led writers to suppose that they would be doing the king a favour if they transferred the name Caucasus to India.

6 He founded the Ptolemaic dynasty in Egypt, and ruled there as Ptolemy I from 323 to 283.

7 Against the Malli; see Source 6.

8 At the siege of Malli, when an enemy arrow punctured Alexander's lung: see Sources 71 and 72.

9 On drinking, see also Sources 68, 103 and 109.

10 Of Calanus, the Indian philosopher: see Sources 66–69.

11 © A. B. Bosworth 1988, Reprinted by permission of Oxford University Press.

INTRODUCTION:
SOME BASIC PRINCIPLES

A.B. Bosworth

The period of Alexander the Great is at first sight well attested.[1] There is an apparent abundance of narrative material: full-length histories of the reign by Arrian and Curtius Rufus, a formal biography by Plutarch, a whole book of Diodorus Siculus' *Bibliotheca*, two books of Justin's epitome of Pompeius Trogus, and substantial passages in the latter books of Strabo's *Geography*. This wealth of documentation is misleading, for all the primary sources are late. The earliest of our extant authorities, Diodorus, composed his work in the third quarter of the first century BC. Strabo wrote in the late Augustan period, Curtius at a still undefined date in the early Empire,[2] Plutarch and Arrian in the second century AD, and Trogus' work, composed under Augustus, is known through the third-century epitome of Justin. There is, then, a hiatus of close to three centuries between the death of Alexander in June 323 and the first connected narrative of the reign. The problem of transmission therefore becomes acute. What sources did our extant authorities use and how faithfully did they report the substance of what they read? Both questions are clearly important. A careless and perfunctory epitome by a secondary author can be as rich a source of historical error as conscious mendacity and distortion in a contemporary historian. On the other hand a derivative history based on reliable authorities, carefully selected and meticulously reported, may be more trustworthy than any single first-generation source.

The main thrust of modern scholarship has been to attempt to isolate the contemporary or near-contemporary historians of Alexander and to reconstruct as far as possible the outline and characteristics of each work. This approach has had major and permanent results. Its most tangible product is the two hundred pages of fragments of lost Alexander historians which Felix Jacoby compiled in his monumental *Fragmente der griechischen Historiker*.[3] We have a fair knowledge of the names and the general sequence of the primary historians and a sample, largely random, of the content of their work. Contemporary history began in the king's lifetime, with Anaximenes' work *On Alexander*[4] and, more importantly, the *Deeds of Alexander* by Callisthenes of Olynthus, who lived at court from the beginning of the campaign in Asia until his dramatic death in 327 and gave a first-hand narrative of events down to 330 at least.[5] Callisthenes' work was the only history known to be exactly contemporaneous with the events, but after the king's death there was a great efflorescence of memoirs by senior and not-so-senior members of his staff. Onesicritus and Nearchus wrote early in the period of the Successors, and at some indeterminate date before his own death (in 283 BC) came the work of Ptolemy.[6] Some time after the battle of Ipsus (301) the ageing Aristobulus of Cassandreia composed his history of the reign, and during the first generation after Alexander (so it is now generally agreed[7]) Cleitarchus of Alexandria wrote what was probably the most widely read of the early histories of the reign. There was also less formal material: pamphlets of differing political persuasions, such as the treatises on the deaths of Alexander and Hephaestion by Ephippus of Olynthus, and works of a documentary or pseudo-documentary nature like the *stathmoi* of the Royal surveyors and the Royal *Ephemerides* which Eumenes allegedly compiled.[8] These sources, contemporary or near-contemporary, provided a rich field for the historian of antiquity, and it is tempting to trace their effect on the extant tradition, using the preserved fragments as a basis. The method is to examine the texts and testimonia and extrapolate characteristic attitudes and biases which can then be identified in the secondary tradition. It is an approach which can be fertile when one has some external evidence for the sources used,[9] as is the case with Arrian, but there are major drawbacks when the identification is merely speculative

The principal and besetting problem is that the majority of Alexander's early historians are only known through brief citations, and it is rare that one can examine any single author *in extenso*. Nearchus is the chief exception to the rule. His account of his voyage from South India to Susa is the narrative base for the second half of Arrian's *Indike*, and we have a fair idea of the content of his work in outline and detail. For some passages, Strabo acts as a control source and provides an independent record of the original.[10] As a result portions of Nearchus' work are well attested and capable of analysis. The same is true, to a more limited degree, of Aristobulus,[11] but there is no extended extract which can compare with Arrian's digest of Nearchus. Most often the lost histories are known from a scattering of citations, usually short, indirect, and uncharacteristic. The vast majority of the verbatim quotations come from the *Deipnosophistae* of Athenaeus of Naucratis, but their value is largely impaired by the content, which, thanks to Athenaeus' avowed interests, is concentrated upon the pleasures of the flesh and the table and cannot be expected to give a representative sample of the authors cited. In some cases, such as the pamphlets of Ephippus and Nicobule, the rather lurid passages quoted by Athenaeus may indeed be characteristic of those productions, but it is hard to think that his excerpts from the works of Alexander's surveyors (a comment on the Tapurians' addiction to wine and descriptions of the natural produce of the East) are in any sense typical of their general tenor.[12] Other authors are no less selective in their citation, and usually they are not concerned to reproduce the wording of their original. In any case the sources are usually named because there is something suspect in what is recorded. Ancient writers tend to refer to their authorities by name primarily to criticize – to point out falsehood or to indicate information the veracity of which they are not prepared to guarantee. As a result the preserved citations naturally highlight the colourful and the erroneous. Material which was sober and informative would be exploited without comment.

Callisthenes of Olynthus makes an interesting case study. One would naturally expect him, as Alexander's first historian, to have been widely used and cited, but there are no more than a dozen identifiable references to his *Deeds of Alexander*. Those references are a scattered bunch. Observations on the mythology of Asia Minor, reported by Strabo, comprise the majority.[13] Otherwise there is a Homeric scholion citing his description of the Pamphylian Sea doing obeisance before Alexander (F 31), two vignettes from his account of Gaugamela, retailed by Plutarch (F 36–7), and finally the two major fragments. Both these fragments are critical. Polybius examines his description of the battle of Issus, concentrating on the figures he gives for both sides and proving their incompatibility with the terrain as described.[14] The passage is designed to prove Callisthenes' incompetence, and indeed Polybius does isolate real faults in his account – gross exaggeration of Persian numbers and a eulogistic bias towards Alexander and his Macedonians.[15] But on the other hand much of Polybius' criticism is demonstrably wrong-headed, vitiated by the false assumption that all

Alexander's infantry was contained in his phalanx and by the equally false conviction that the phalanx at Issus was as clumsy and inflexible as the phalanx of his own day.[16] Polybius' attempt to convict Callisthenes of ignorance and military incompetence largely fails, and most of the details he singles out have been taken as axioms for modern reconstructions of the battle-site.[17] We should be grateful for Polybius' minuteness of criticism, for all its petty-mindedness. Had he merely stigmatized the description as false without argument, his statement would have been unhesitatingly accepted, and had he quoted the Persian numbers out of context Callisthenes would surely have been dismissed as worthless. As it is, the detail given helps rectify the criticism and allows a broad, if sketchy, reconstruction of Callisthenes' narrative. In most cases we have a single detail, isolated from its context, and there is no way of telling whether or not it is characteristic of the author, or even correctly reported.

The other major fragment concerns the journey to Siwah. Once again the context of the citation is critical. Strabo refers to Callisthenes' narrative as a classic example of historical flattery. The motif of adulation first occurs with the story of the two ravens acting as guides to the oasis, and Strabo states that it persists throughout the consultation of the oracle. There was an equally suspect sequel in the report of the formal delivery at Memphis of oracles from Branchidae and Erythrae.[18] Now Strabo is not pretending to give a full reproduction of Callisthenes' narrative. He is emphasizing details which he considered biased to flatter Alexander, and there is every indication that he was retailing standard criticisms. Plutarch also singled out the episode of the guidance by ravens,[19] and long before, early in the third century, Timaeus of Tauromenium had arraigned Callisthenes as an example of unphilosophical adulation for his concentration on ravens and frenzied women (i.e. the Sibyl of Erythrae).[20]

Callisthenes' account of the consultation of Ammon was clearly a well-known passage and regularly cited as an illustration of partial and interested writing. It fell within the wider context of his general picture of the king, which was widely denounced as flattery. Both Timaeus and Philodemus[21] stated that his historical work amounted to an apotheosis of Alexander, and several of the fragments illustrate the theme. Plutarch highlights his prayer to Zeus at Gaugamela.[22] The Homeric scholia depict the Pamphylian sea offering *proskynesis* to its new lord (F 31). Most importantly, Strabo's passage on the visit to Siwah is an extended essay on the subject, culminating in the priest's statement that Alexander was son of Zeus and appending the oracles from Asia Minor which also declared his divine sonship. This was a genuine and undeniably important feature of Callisthenes' work,[23] but it was only one feature. Polybius' critique of his description of Issus reveals that he gave quite detailed statements of numbers and movements which, coming from a contemporary and eyewitness, have every likelihood of being correct.[24] But this is not the material for which Callisthenes is quoted. Such facts were absorbed into the secondary historical tradition without acknowledgement, and the named citations concentrate upon the eulogistic and the bizarre.

As a result Callisthenes' work is totally lost for us. His style, like that of most of the prose writers of his day, was reprobated by later generations as inflated and clumsy, and he had no chance of survival as a literary model. But he certainly influenced the early tradition of Alexander history. The main lines of his description both of Issus and of the Siwah visit were repeated and developed by later writers. Even the exaggerations were echoed and embellished.[25] The same must have been true of his narrative as a whole, but the vast bulk of his work is irretrievable. One facet alone is preserved for us in a sharp and lurid light.

The problem is especially acute in the case of Cleitarchus. It is clear that he was a popular author in the Roman period, the only historian between Ephorus and Timagenes to be included in Quintilian's canon.[26] He is cited by a wide range of authorities, and he may have been the most generally read of all the Alexander historians. Unfortunately, the thirty-six fragments which Jacoby accepts as authentic deal exclusively with trivialities. The most extensive come from Aelian of Praeneste, who excerpted several of Cleitarchus' descriptions of the animal curiosities of India,[27] and Strabo (probably echoing the strictures or Eratosthenes) comments critically on the geographical errors in his description of Central Asia.[28] Indeed most of the citations are critical. Demetrius focuses on his stylistic impropriety (F 14), Curtius Rufus on exaggeration and invention (F 24–5), Cicero on rhetorical mendacity (F 34). The general impression conveyed by the fragments alone is therefore far from favourable. It suggests a taste for the tawdry and colourful, a predilection for sensationalism, a preoccupation for rhetoric which encouraged exaggeration and preferred imaginative fiction to sober truth.[29] Unfortunately we have no easy way of testing these criticisms. The handful of verbatim quotations that survive amounts to five lines in all and can scarcely be representative. There is no extensive appreciation of any part of his work, nothing comparable to Polybius' detailed critique of Callisthenes.

The general impression conveyed by the fragments may be correct, as far as it goes, but it is unlikely to be the whole story. If, for instance, our knowledge of Herodotus were limited to the citations in Athenaeus and Plutarch's essay *On the Malice of Herodotus,* we should have a much larger body of testimony than exists for Cleitarchus and it would give the same general impression, a sensational and trivial concentration on curiosities and a penchant for bias and historical deformation. The extant criticisms of Cleitarchus may be similarly misleading. It would certainly be erroneous to conclude that everything he wrote was sensational, biased, or fictional. What is needed is a more extensive sample of Cleitarchus' work than that provided by the named fragments.

That sample is probably provided by the so-called 'vulgate tradition'. One of the few established results of the source-criticism of the Alexander period has been the extrapolation of a common tradition at the root of several of the extant sources. It is undeniable that large segments of Diodorus and Curtius Rufus run parallel, retailing the same information and supplementing each other to a degree that is only explicable if both authors were ultimately working from the same source.[30] The same material is detectable in Justin's epitome of Trogus and in the *Metz Epitome* (a late compilation following roughly the same tradition as Curtius but extant only for the campaign between Hyrcania and South India). There is obviously a common tradition, and the term 'vulgate', despite a certain clumsiness, is a useful shorthand. It is sometimes misunderstood,[31] and for the reader's convenience I should state that when I refer to the 'vulgate tradition' I am referring to the body of material which is multiply attested (in Diodorus and Curtius and often in Justin and the *Metz Epitome*) and can reasonably be attributed to a common source. 'Vulgate sources' is perhaps a more questionable expression, but once again it can be useful shorthand to denote the sources which *on a given occasion* reflect the common tradition. There is no implication that these sources use the vulgate and nothing else. Plutarch, for instance, is eclectic.[32] He may follow the common tradition of Diodorus and Curtius but more often he uses material that is quite distinct. What is denoted as the vulgate may come from different sources at different times, but the nucleus is usually agreement in Diodorus and Curtius, corroborated, as the case may be, by one or more other sources. 'Vulgate' nicely encapsulates the idea of a shared tradition without begging the question of its authorship.

But there is a very strong probability that the vulgate tradition is based ultimately on Cleitarchus. The key passage is provided by Curtius (ix. 8. 15), who refers to Cleitarchus as his source for the number of Indians killed during Alexander's campaign in the kingdom of Sambus. The information is no variant. It is a figure taken out of the general narrative and comes in a context that is exactly paralleled in Diodorus.[33] We therefore have an instance of a common tradition with a direct attribution to Cleitarchus. That establishes a strong probability that the rest of the shared tradition goes back ultimately to the same source. The other alternative, that Diodorus and Curtius used two or more common sources independently, is far less plausible and founders on what is known of Diodorus' approach to historical composition. Where cross-comparison is possible, it is demonstrable that Diodorus followed a single source for chapters on end, transferring only when he came to the end of his subject-matter.[34] There are occasional inserts from other sources, but such inserts are largely digressions, short and limited in scope. Within each book Diodorus tends to change sources as he moves from area to area, particularly when he reverts to the history of his native Sicily, and he adds chronographic material from a separate date-table.[35] But Book xvii is unusually homogeneous. The narrative focus is exclusively on Alexander and there is no material on the history of the Greek west, nor is there any chronographic information.[36] It is overwhelmingly probable that his material derives from a single major source and that there is a single source for the tradition shared with Curtius.

Now Diodorus himself takes us back to Cleitarchus. In a digression in Book ii he gives Cleitarchus' figures for the dimensions of the walls of Babylon and presents them as a variant, contrasting with the description of his main source, Ctesias.[37] This information is paralleled in Curtius' description of Babylon, which otherwise corresponds to Diodorus' narrative in Book xvii.[38] It looks as though Diodorus extrapolated the material relating to the city walls and used it in his mythological exordium, to set off the information in Ctesias. There may well be a similar digression later. After describing the death of Themistocles, following his main source for Greek affairs in Book xi, Diodorus adds a variant from an unnamed source (ἔνιοι ... τῶν συγγραφέων).[39] That variant is the story of Themistocles drinking bull's blood, an episode which we know was rhetorically treated by Cleitarchus.[40] Once more, it looks as though Diodorus has drawn upon his general knowledge of Cleitarchus to embellish his earlier historical narrative.[41]

In that case it can hardly be doubted that Cleitarchus provided the narrative base for his account of Alexander, and that Cleitarchus is the ultimate source of the vulgate tradition. The attribution has, of course, been challenged, largely on the ground that several of the extant fragments of Cleitarchus are not found in any of the so-called vulgate sources. In fact the points of detail contained in the fragments are in general so trivial that their omission is only to be expected. The two most striking absences (the Roman embassy and the story of Ptolemy's presence at the Malli town) are more difficult to explain,[42] but given Diodorus' extreme selectiveness it is not too surprising that he passed over both incidents. On the other hand there is a reasonably strong correlation between many of the preserved fragments and the common tradition of Diodorus and Curtius; and it remains the strongest probability that the vulgate tradition in general and Diodorus' account in particular is derived ultimately from the single source, Cleitarchus.

In that case there is a large corpus of material which can be traced back to Cleitarchus, and in theory the broad characteristics of his work should be capable of reconstruction. That is easier said than done. The material in the vulgate covers a wide spectrum, from wild and colourful zoological fantasy to sober and apparently well-informed campaign reports. A recent analysis has concluded that there is not a single common source for Diodorus and Curtius but two, a baroque and sensation hungry author, hostile to Alexander and his Macedonians (Cleitarchus), and a better-informed, more impartial historian, not prone to sensationalism and fiction (Diyllus?).[43] It is perhaps more profitable to ask whether the same source cannot be both Jekyll and Hyde, capable both of objective reporting and emotional bathos (one need only reflect on the almost infinite variety of material in Herodotus).

A more pertinent question is the amount of distortion that has taken place in transmission. All the extant sources of the vulgate tradition are highly erratic and second-rate authors, and they may be assumed to have altered their material for the worse. Contraction is a serious problem. Cleitarchus' work was fairly voluminous. In Book xii he described the Indian ascetics and their disregard for death.[44] That presumably came in the context of Calanus' self-immolation in Persis late in 325. The period to Alexander's death, one assumes, would have required several more books. By contrast Diodorus covers the entire reign in a single book (admittedly of unusual length) and Justin is even more grossly abridged. Given such a drastic précis it is not surprising that some episodes in Diodorus are abbreviated to near gibberish, and the distortion in Justin is such that one often needs other texts to infer even what was in his immediate exemplar, Trogus.[45] There is also the problem of embellishment and exaggeration in the immediate source. That is a particular danger with Curtius Rufus, whose work is deeply infused with rhetoric.[46] His narrative is punctuated by a running commentary, with highly subjective attributions of motive, and there is no doubt that his source material is reworked, often a mere vehicle for descriptive rhetoric or moralizing comment. Even Diodorus is prone to impose his own personality. The style of his original is watered down and reduced to flat monotony. More seriously, he has an eye for the sensational and has favourite themes, usually banalities such as epic pictures of slaughter and fighting in relays.[47] That accounts for the unbalanced nature of such episodes as the battle of the Granicus. Diodorus' interest is attracted by the single combat between Alexander and the Persian commanders and he spends a disproportionate amount of his battle narrative expatiating upon it. The remaining details are scattered and drastically abbreviated, so as to obscure the strategy and defy any rational reconstruction of the engagement.[48] There is no control source, and we cannot assume that Diodorus' original was as unbalanced as his epitome of it.

Cleitarchus, then, is elusive. Is he also irretrievable? My feeling is that it *is* possible to reconstruct something of his work, but the exercise of doing so is particularly arduous. One must begin with an appreciation of the methods of the major extant sources. In the case of Diodorus this is not too difficult, for there is an abundance of material for comparison outside Book xvii. Curtius is far more difficult, for his work is confined to the Alexander period, the text is lacunose and often corrupt, and there are no extant sources to provide a direct check on his methods of excerpting. One can only rely on cross-comparison, where the material is attested in other contexts. That is the crux. The starting-point should be examination of extended passages which are reported by Diodorus and Curtius (preferably other sources as well).[49] Then one can build up a composite narrative and gain some idea of what is omitted or distorted in each individual writer. The more focuses that can be brought to bear on the vulgate, the more illumination of the common base will accrue. But the illumination will come from the continuous narrative of the extant works, not from the scattered and unrepresentative 'fragments' to which Cleitarchus' name is explicitly attached.

The importance of Arrian is now clear. His work is the most complete and the most sober account of Alexander's reign and at the same time it provides explicit information about the sources used. The seven-book *History of Alexander* was based on Ptolemy son of Lagus and Aristobulus son of Aristobulus. That is stated explicitly in the Preface and confirmed by the narrative which refers repeatedly to the authority of both men.[50] From Book vi the narrative range is expanded by the inclusion of Nearchus and there are explicit borrowings from the geographical work of Eratosthenes. The companion work, the *Indike*, dealing with the natural curiosities of India and the voyage of Alexander's fleet in the southern Ocean, is equally candid about its use of sources: the material comes from Eratosthenes, Megasthenes, and Nearchus.[51] In the case of Arrian we have the entire range of primary sources spelt out for us, and they are exciting and contemporary. Ptolemy, Nearchus, and Aristobulus were all eyewitnesses of the campaigns, and the first two at least were major actors in the great events they described. It is not surprising that the primary sources have occupied the centre stage of research. The text of Arrian is often read as though it were practically the same as Ptolemy, and Ptolemy/Arrian is a traditional shorthand used to characterize that part of Arrian's narrative that is commonly believed to be based on Ptolemy. Ernst Kornemann even subjected Arrian's text to a detailed stylistic analysis, extrapolating what he thought were distinctive thumb-prints of Ptolemaic phraseology.[52] The assumption, usually implicit, is that one may go direct from Arrian to his sources and that Arrian himself may be disregarded, a simple solider who paid his tribute to the memory of Alexander by selecting the best possible sources and reproducing them with patient fidelity.

The object of this exercise is wholly commendable. Arrian's sources *are* of fundamental importance, far more so for the modern historian than Arrian himself. In particular Ptolemy's picture of Alexander is of consuming interest, an account of the reign by one of its great architects and beneficiaries. But whatever results are obtained, they are necessarily distorted unless they are based on a careful study of Arrian as a writer. It is obvious from the most perfunctory reading of Arrian and the most superficial study of his career that he was a sophisticated and experienced writer, with the highest claims to stylistic excellence. To put it mildly, he is unlikely to have transcribed his sources without reshaping them and adding his own comments. The methodology outlined for approaching Cleitarchus will therefore hold good for Arrian's sources also. Arrian's pretensions as a historian need to be elucidated, in particular his aims in composing a history of Alexander. His modes of citing sources should also be studied and, where possible, his version should be contrasted with other writers' use of the same source material. Finally his own contribution should be delineated, the degree to which he comments on his material, whether parenthetically or in formal digressions and set speeches. That is the object of this book and explains its somewhat pretentious title. One cannot examine the history of Alexander without a study of the primary sources and the primary sources themselves are embedded in secondary and derivative works like those of Arrian.

Notes

1 For modern bibliography the two surveys by Jakob Seibert are indispensable: *Alexander der Grosse* (Erträge der Forschung 10; Darmstadt, 1972); *Das Zeitalter der Diadochen* (Erträge der Forschung 185; Darmstadt, 1983). Both volumes present an exhaustive survey of modern literature from the middle of the nineteenth century and obviate the need for extensive references to secondary works. I shall attempt to limit my annotations to what is most important or most recent.

2 The controversy about the date is unresolved and continuing. J. E Atkinson, *A Commentary on Q, Curtius Rufus' Historiae Alexandri Magni Books 3 and 4* (Amsterdam, 1980) 19–57, has presented the strongest case yet for the reign of Claudius (see further, Syme, *HSCP* 86 [1982] 197f.), and there are more arguments in support of the Claudian dating in H. Bodefeld's dissertation, *Untersuchungen zur Datierung der Alexandergeschichte des Q. Curtius Rufus* (Düsseldorf, 1982). The problem is far from settled (for some counter-arguments see *CP* 78 [1983] 151–4), but it is largely irrelevant to the study of Alexander. Most scholars would concede that Curtius was later than Diodorus and earlier than Plutarch or Arrian.

3 Jacoby, *FGrH* ii.B 618–828 (nos 117–53; commentary ii.D 403–542). A few additional fragments, mostly insignificant, are printed at *FGrH* iii.B 742–3 and in H. J. Mette, *Lustrum* 21 (1978) 18–20. For a sensible and readable appraisal of the principal fragments see L. Pearson, *The Lost Histories of Alexander the Great* [*LHA*]. There is also a recent compendium by P. Pédech, *Historiens campagnons d'Alexandre* (Paris, 1984), which deals extensively with Callisthenes, Onesicritus, Nearchus, Ptolemy, and Aristobulus.

4 *FGrH* 72 F 15–17, 29. The work is too scantily attested to support any conclusions on its nature or purpose.

5 *FGrH* 124. The last datable fragments (F 36–7) deal with Gaugamela, late in 331. See further Jacoby, *RE* x. 1674–1707 (still fundamental); Pearson, *LHA* 22–49 (cf. Badian, *Studies in Greek and Roman History* 251–2); Pédech (above, n. 3) 14–69.

6 The date is elusive. For a sceptical survey of arguments for both early (post 320) and late (*c*.285) dates see J. Roisman, *CQ* 34 (1984) 373–85.

7 Cf. Schachermeyr, *Aleexander in Babyon* 211–24; Badian, *PACA* 8 (1965) 1–8.

8 Cf. *FGrH* 126 (Ephippus), 119–23 (surveyors [βηματισταί]), 117 (*Ephemerides*). On the latter see ch. 7 [in Bosworth, *Arrian to Alexander*].

9 The best example of the genre is probably Hermann Strasburger's early monograph, *Ptolemaios und Alexander* (Leipzig, 1934 = *Studien zur alten Geschichte* [Hildesheim, 1982] 83–147).

10 Arr. *Ind.* 18–42 = *FGrH* 133 F 1 (Jacoby interweaves seven extracts from Strabo).

11 See ch. 2. [in Bosworth, *Arrian to Alexander*].

12 Athen. x. 442B = Baeton, *FGrH* 119 F 1; ii. 67A, xi. 5ood = Amyntas, *FGrH* 122 F 4, 1. See also Brunt, *CQ*30 (1980) 485–6 on the extant fragments of Chares of Mytilene (*FGrH* 125).

13 *FGrH* 124 F 28–30, 32–3, 38(?).

14 Polyb. xii. 17. 1–22. 7 = *FGrH* 124 F 35. There are detailed commentaries by P. Pédech, *Polybe xii* (Budé 1961), 104 ff. and Walbank, *HCP* ii. 364 ff.

15 On the exaggerated numbers (of cavalry and mercenaries) see Polyb. xii. 18. 2 ff., and for exaggeration of the difficulties of the terrain to enhance the Macedonian achievement see particularly 18. 11–12.

16 Cf. xii. 19. 1–4, 21. 2–10 (calculation of phalanx numbers); 20. 6–8, 22. 4 (criticism of phalanx movements).

17 xii. 17. 4–5. For the modem literature see Seibert, *Alexander der Grosse* 98–102; *HCArr.* i. 198 ff. For the adaptation and embellishment of Callisthenes in the later tradition see *Entretiens Hardt* 22 (1976) 25–32.

18 Strabo xvii. 1. 43 (814) = *FGrH* 124 F 14a. For some of the specific problems of the passage see Pearson, *LHA* 33–6 and my own observations in *Greece & the E. Mediterranean* 68–75.

19 Plut. *Al*. 27. 4 = *FGrH* 124 F 14b.

20 Polyb. xii. 12b. 2 = *FGrH* 566 F 155.

21 Philod. π. κολακ. i².4 = *FGrH* 124 T 21.

22 Plut. *Al*. 33. 1 = *FGrH* 124 F 36. See further *Greece & the E. Mediterranean* 57–60.

23 For Callisthenes' view of his own importance (which was not unlike Arrian's own) see Arr. iv. 10.2. On his panegyric tendencies see Jacoby, *RE* x. 1701–4.

24 Polyb. xii. 19. 1–2, 5–6, 20. 1.

25 For details see *Entretiens Hardt* 22 (1976) 26 f.; *HCArr* i. 31, 212, 217, 272–3.

26 Quint. *Inst*. x. 1. 74 = *FGrH* 137 T 7. Cf. Jacoby, *RE* xi. 654: 'In Rom war er . . . im 1. Jhdt. v. Chr. die grosse Mode.'

27 *FGrH* 137 F 18–19, 21–2.

28 F 13, 16.

29 For thoroughgoing condemnation see Tarn, *Alexander* ii. 54–5; Hammond, *Three Historians*, esp. 25–7. Jacoby, *RE* xi. 645, was (typically) more measured and judicious.

30 A list of parallels, far from complete, was compiled by Eduard Schwartz (*RE* iv. 1873f.). For a survey of modern literature see Seibert, *Alexander der Grosse* 26–8 and J. R. Hamilton, *Greece & the E. Mediterranean* 126–46 (additional parallels 127 n. 7).

31 For criticisms of the use of the term see Hammond, *Three Historians*, esp. 2.

32 See the excellent appreciation by Hamilton, *Plut. Al*. xlix–lii. Hammond, *Three Historians* 170 n. 5. has taken me to task for inconsistency in references to Plutarch, including him sometimes in the vulgate, sometimes not. All the references which include him as a vulgate source are instances where he corroborates the shared tradition of Diodorus and Curtius. Where he stands apart from that shared tradition, he cannot be classed as part of the vulgate. The same is of course true of Curtius. He is to a great extent dependent on the common tradition, but he undeniably uses a multiplicity of other sources.

33 Diod. xvii. 102. 5–7. Diodorus gives 80,000 as the number of victims, whereas the manuscripts of Curtius vary between 800 and 800,000. Given the general concordance, it is usually assumed that the numerals in Curtius are (as so often) corrupt. The common source is not in doubt.

34 The most illuminating segment of narrative is Diod. iii. 12–48, where the source is Agatharchides of Cnidus (cf. iii. 11. 2). The same material is digested by Photius (*Bibl.* cod. 250), and there is impressive agreement both in economy and vocabulary. For parallel texts see Müller, *GGM* i. 123–93 and, for discussion, D. Woelk, *Agatharchides von Knidos: Über das Rote Meer* (diss. Bamberg, 1966); J. Hornblower, *Hieronymus of Cardia* 27–32. See further, Seibert, *Das Zeitalter der Diadochen* 30–2.

35 These passages are usefully listed by Schwartz, *RE* v. 666–9.

36 The same is true of Book xviii, which is largely (if not wholly) based on Hieronymus of Cardia. Sicilian history resumes emphatically at XIX. 1 with the tyranny of Agathocles (cf. xviii. 1. 6, 75.3); notes on Roman history continue from XIX. 10. 1, and the chronographic information emerges again in Book xx.

37 Diod. ii. 7.3 = *FGrH* 137 F 10.

38 Curt. v. 1. 10–45 (esp. 26); cf. Diod. xvii. 64. 3–6. Hammond (*Three Historians* 190 n. 25) mentions only the figure of 365 stades for the circuit of the walls, which he suggests might have been reported by sources other than Cleitarchus. He omits the rest of the correspondences which make the hypothesis of a common source compelling. See, however, Hamilton, in *Greece & the E. Mediterranean* 138–40.

39 Diod. xi. 58. 2–3.

40 Cic. *Brut*. 42–3 = *FGrH* 137 F 34.

41 This was suggested by Schwartz, *RE* v. 684 and accepted by Jacoby, *FGrH* ii.D 497.

42 See ch. 4 [in Bosworth, 1988].

43 Hammond, *Three Historians*, esp. 12–51. See now the critical observation of Badian, *EMC* n. s. 4 (1985) 461–3.

44 Diog. Laert. i. 6 = *FGrH* 137 F 6. The other book numbers are unhelpful. The sack of Thebes came (as we would expect) in Book i (F 1), the Sardanapalus saga (perhaps a digression based

on Alexander's visit to Anchiale in 333) in Book iv (F 2), the Adonis cult at Byblus (332?) in Book v, and a dissertation on the upright tiara in Book x (F 5). The book number in F 4 is contracted and possibly corrupt. One can hardly reconstruct the outlines of Cleitarchus' history, but its volume is not in doubt.

45 For some examples see *HCArr*. i. 358 (on Justin xii. 4. 12); *Antichthon* 17 (1983) 42 (on Justin xiii. 4. 20).

46 Cf. Atkinson (above, n. 2) 67–73, with my comments in *CP* 78 (1983) 157–9. W. Rutz, *Hermes* 93 (1965) 370–82.

47 On this, see R. K. Sinclair, *CQ* 16 (1966) 249–55. For a general appreciation of Diodorus see Hornblower (above, n. 34) 22 ff.

48 The *aristeia* monopolizes the narrative from xvii. 20. 1 to 21. 3. The rest of the narrative is a series of commonplaces, the opening sentence (19.3) a celebrated historical crux. For a mordant critique of the tradition see Badian, in *Ancient Macedonia* ii. 272–4. See also Hammond, *JHS* 100 (1980) 73 f., *Three Historians* 16f.

49 The method has been well employed by Hamilton, in *Greece & the E. Mediterranean* 129–35, comparing Curtius ix with Diod. xvii. 89–104.

50 See the exposition in *HCArr*. i. 16–34 for details.

51 See ch. 2 [in Bosworth, 1988].

52 E. Kornemann, *Die Alexandergeschichte des Königs Ptolemaios I. ron Aegspien* (Leipzig, 1934). The method is here at its most extreme and was rightly criticized from the outset (see Strasburger's review in *Gnomon* 13 [1937] 483–92); but its basic assumptions are pervasive in modern scholarship.

References

Entretiens Hardt = E. Badian (ed.), *Alexandre le Grand, Image et Réalité*, Fondation Hardt, *Entretiens* 22 (Geneva: 1976).

Greece & the Eastern Mediterranean = K.H. Kinzl (ed.), *Greece and the Eastern Mediterranean in History and Prehistory: Studies Presented to Fritz Schachermeyr* (Berlin: 1977).

Hamilton, *Plut. Al.* = J.R. Hamilton, *Plutarch Alexander: A Commentary* (Oxford: 1969).

Hammond, *Three Historians* = N.G.L. Hammond, *Three Historians of Alexander the Great* (Cambridge: 1983).

HCArr. = A.B. Bosworth, *A Historical Commentary on Arrian's History of Alexander* (Oxford: 1980–).

Hornblower, J. *Hieronymus of Cardia*

RE = *Realencyclopädie der classischen Altertumswissenschaft*, ed. Pauly, Wisowa, Kroll (Stuttgart: 1893–).

Tarn, *Alexander* = W.W. Tarn, *Alexander the Great* I–II (Cambridge: 1948).

Walbank, *HCP* = F.W. Walbank, *A Historical Commentary on Polybius* I–III (Oxford: 1957–79).

2

ALEXANDER'S
BACKGROUND

Introduction

There was a distinction in the ancient Greek world between those who lived south of Mount Olympus and those who lived to its north, the Macedonians. The proper term for these people was 'Makedones', a name that is Greek in root and ethnic terminations, and may have meant 'highlanders'. However, the Greeks referred to them as 'barbarians' as late as the last quarter of the fourth century (Din. 1.24), perhaps an indication that they did not see them as Greek. Much has been written on the 'ethnicity' of the Macedonians, an issue that will never be solved.

When Philip II was assassinated in 336 Alexander became king at the age of 20.[1] He inherited a Macedonian empire that already controlled Greece and was ready to invade Persia, the legacy of his father Philip II (360–336).[2] The Macedonian kingship was already powerful: the king had semi-divine power, performed certain state sacrifices, sat as final judge in any cases of appeal, and his person was protected at all times. He was, in fact, one half of the government of Macedon. The other half was the Assembly, composed of Macedonian citizens, which among other things met to acclaim a king and to judge cases of treason. While it was a powerful organ, the king had the final say in all matters (cf. Curt. 6.8.25). Yet before Philip there had been disunity between Upper and Lower Macedon, and the people living in the former owed no allegiance to the capital Pella, situated in Lower Macedon.

Philip developed Macedon's mining, agriculture and trade, and changed it from a near feudal tribal type of society into a wealthy, united and powerful state, with a centralized monarchy. He established a dynasty that, contrary to Macedon's previous history, allowed his son to succeed him without problem, and he created a powerful and superbly trained army. His military reforms revolutionized not only the army but also the state, for the army's continued success and the subsequent expansion of Macedonian power created a feeling of national unity and nationalistic pride. Philip's achievements laid the foundations for Alexander's successes: without them, Alexander could not have achieved what he did.

Alexander was born in July 356 (Arr. 7.28.1, Plut. *Alex.* 3.5), the son of Philip's fourth wife Olympias, a princess from Epirus, situated to Macedon's west. When Alexander was 14 in 342 his father hired as his tutor Aristotle (Plut. *Alex.* 7.2–3), who built on Alexander's literary accomplishments by probably introducing him to philosophy, rhetoric, zoology and geometry. As a member of the Argead line, Alexander was trained and educated for the day he would become king, and he was called upon to perform duties that we connect with an heir apparent. In 340, at age

16, when his father was away on campaign, Alexander acted as regent (Plut. *Alex.* 9.1), and in 338 he led the left flank of the Macedonian cavalry at the Battle of Chaeronea and annihilated the crack 300-strong Theban Sacred Band (Plut. *Alex.* 9.2; cf. Diod. 16.86.3–4).

Alexander was brought up to believe in the Homeric notion of personal success (*arete*) for the sake of honour (*time*) and glory (*kudos*); he was an avid reader of poetry, tragedy, and historiography, and slept with a copy of the *Iliad* under his pillow (see Source 16). Throughout his life, Alexander emulated his two heroes Heracles and Achilles, both of whom were his ancestors,[3] not to mention trying to outdo the exploits of Dionysus (cf. Source 70). However, his greatest role model was his father. Alexander strove hard to match him and then, as his own reign progressed, to outdo him, but Philip was a hard act to follow.

Ancient sources

14   Be that as it may, Alexander was born early in the month Hecatombaeon, the Macedonian name for which is Lous, on the sixth day of the month, and on this day the temple of Ephesian Artemis was burnt. It was *apropos* of this that Hegesias the Magnesian made an utterance frigid enough to have extinguished that great conflagration. He said, namely, it was no wonder that the temple of Artemis was burned down, since the goddess was busy bringing Alexander into the world. But all the Magi who were then at Ephesus, looking upon the temple's disaster as a sign of further disaster, ran about beating their faces and crying aloud that woe and great calamity for Asia had that day been born. To Philip, however, who had just taken Potidaea, there came three messages at the same time: the first that Parmenion had conquered the Illyrians in a great battle, the second that his race-horse had won a victory at the Olympic Games, while a third announced the birth of Alexander. These things delighted him, of course, and the seers raised his spirits still higher by declaring that the son whose birth coincided with three victories would always be victorious (Hegesias, *FGrH* 142 F 3 = Plut. *Alex.* 3.5–9).

15   Often, too, for diversion, he would hunt foxes or birds, as may be gathered from the *Ephemerides* (*FGrH* 117 F 1 = Plut. *Alex.* 23.4).

16   He (Alexander) was also by nature a lover of learning and a lover of reading. And since he thought and called the *Iliad* a viaticum of the military art, he took with him Aristotle's recension of the poem, called the *Iliad of the Casket*, and always kept it lying with his dagger under his pillow, as Onesicritus informs us; and when he could find no other books in the interior of Asia, he ordered Harpalus to send him some (Onesicritus, *FGrH* 134 F 38 = Plut. *Alex.* 8.2).

Modern works

In the first two extracts, N.G.L. Hammond, formerly Professor of Greek at the University of Bristol, argues that the Macedonians were Greek but spoke a different language to make themselves stand 'apart' from the Greeks. In the second extract, he discusses the powers and role of the Macedonian king, and in the third A.B. Bosworth, Professor of Classics at the University of Western Australia, gives a succinct summary of Philip's reign.

1   N.G.L. Hammond, *The Macedonian State* (Oxford: 1989), pp. 12–15.[4]
2   N.G.L. Hammond, *Alexander the Great: King, Commander and Statesman*[2] (Bristol: 1989), pp. 13–18 and 287 (notes).[5]
3   A.B. Bosworth, *Conquest and Empire: The Reign of Alexander the Great* (Cambridge: 1988), pp. 5–19.[6]

Additional reading

E. Badian, 'Greeks and Macedonians', in B. Barr-Sharrar and E.N. Borza (eds.), *Macedonia and Greece in Late Classical and Early Hellenistic Times* (Washington, DC: 1982), pp. 33–51.

E.N. Borza, 'Greeks and Macedonians in the Age of Alexander: The Source Traditions', in *Transitions to Empire: Essays in Honor of E. Badian*, W. Wallace and E.M. Harris (eds) (Norman, OK: 1996), pp. 122–139.

G.L. Cawkwell, *Philip of Macedon* (London: 1978).

J.R. Ellis, *Philip II and Macedonian Imperialism* (London: 1976).

E.A. Fredricksmeyer, 'Alexander and Philip: Emulation and Resentment', *Classical Journal* 85 (1990), pp. 300–315.

G.T. Griffith, 'The Macedonian Background', *Greece and Rome*[2] 12 (1965), pp. 125–139.

J.R. Hamilton, 'Alexander's Early Life', *Greece and Rome*[2] 12 (1965), pp. 117–124.

N.G.L. Hammond, *Philip of Macedon* (London: 1994).

——— and G.T. Griffith, *A History of Macedonia 2* (Oxford: 1979).

Ian Worthington, 'Alexander, Philip, and the Macedonian Background', in J. Roisman (ed.), *A Companion to Alexander the Great* (Leiden: 2003), pp. 69–98.

Notes

1   Diod. 16.91.1–94.4, Arr. 1.1.1, Plut. *Alex.* 10.6.
2   The start of Philip's reign may be dated to 360 and not 359: M.B. Hatzopoulos, 'The Oleveni Inscription and the Dates of Philip II's Reign', in W.L. Adams and E.N. Borza (eds.), *Philip II, Alexander the Great, and the Macedonian Heritage* (Lanham, MD: 1982), pp. 21–42.
3   The Argead clan traced its ancestry back to Heracles via Temenus, a hero of Argos (Herodotus 5.20, 22, Thucydides 2.99.3, 5.80.2); Achilles and Andromache were ancestors of his mother, Olympias (cf. Plut. *Alex.* 2.1).
4   © N.G.L. Hammond 1989. Reprinted by permission of Oxford University Press.
5   Reprinted by permission of Gerald Duckworth & Co. Ltd.
6   © Cambridge University Press 1988. Reprinted with the permission of Cambridge University Press.

THE LANGUAGE OF THE MACEDONIANS

N.G.L. Hammond

What language did these 'Macedones' speak? The name itself is Greek in root and in ethnic termination. It probably means 'highlanders', and it is comparable to Greek tribal names such as 'Orestai' and 'Oreitai', meaning 'mountain-men'. A reputedly earlier variant, 'Maketai', has the same root, which means 'high', as in the Greek adjective *makednos* or the noun *mēkos*. The genealogy of eponymous ancestors which Hesiod recorded [. . .] has a bearing on the question of Greek speech. First, Hesiod made Macedon a brother of Magnes; as we know from inscriptions that the Magnetes spoke the Aeolic dialect of the Greek language, we have a predisposition to suppose that the Macedones spoke the Aeolic dialect. Secondly, Hesiod made Macedon and Magnes first cousins of Hellen's three sons – Dorus, Xouthus, and Aeolus – who were the founders of three dialects of Greek speech, namely Doric, Ionic, and Aeolic. Hesiod would not have recorded this relationship, unless he had believed, probably in the seventh century. that the Macedones were a Greek-speaking people. The next evidence comes from Persia. At the turn of the sixth century the Persians described the tribute-paying peoples of their province in Europe, and one of them was the 'yauna takabara', which meant 'Greeks wearing the hat'.[1] There were Greeks in Greek city-states here and there in the province, but they were of various origins and not distinguished by a common hat. However, the Macedonians wore a distinctive hat, the *kausia*. We conclude that the Persians believed the Macedonians to be speakers of Greek. Finally, in the latter part of the fifth century a Greek historian, Hellanicus, visited Macedonia and modified Hesiod's genealogy by making Macedon not a cousin, but a son of Aeolus, thus bringing Macedon and his descendants firmly into the Aeolic branch of the Greek-speaking family.[2] Hesiod, Persia, and Hellanicus had no motive for making a false statement about the language of the Macedonians, who were then an obscure and not a powerful people. Their independent testimonies should be accepted as conclusive.

That, however, is not the opinion of most scholars. They disregard or fail to assess the evidence which I have cited,[3] and they turn instead to 'Macedonian' words and names, or/and to literary references. Philologists have studied words which have been cited as 'Macedonian' in ancient lexica and glossaries, and they have come to no certain conclusion: for some of the words are clearly Greek, and some are clearly not Greek. That is not surprising; for as the territory of the Macedonians expanded, they over-laid and lived with peoples who spoke Illyrian, Paeonian, Thracian, and Phrygian, and they certainly borrowed words from them which excited the authors of lexica and glossaries. The philological studies result in a verdict, in my opinion, of 'non liquet'.[4]

The toponyms of the Macedonian homeland are the most significant. Nearly all of them are Greek: Pieria, Lebaea, Heracleum, Dium, Petra, Leibethra, Aegeae, Aegydium, Acesae, Acesamenae; the rivers Helicon, Aeson, Leucus, Baphyras, Sardon, Elpeüs, Mitys; lake Ascuris and the region Lapathus. The mountain names Olympus and Titarium may be pre-Greek; Edessa, the earlier name of the place where Aegeae was founded, and its river Ascordus were Phrygian.[5] The deities worshipped by the Macedones and the names which they gave to the months were predominantly Greek, and there is no doubt that these were not late borrowings.

To Greek literary writers before the Hellenistic period the Macedonians were 'barbarians'. The term referred to their way of life and their institutions, which were those of the *ethnē* and not of the city-state, and it did not refer to their speech. We can see this in the case of Epirus. There Thucydides called the tribes 'barbarians'. But inscriptions found in Epirus have shown conclusively that the Epirote tribes in Thucydides' lifetime were speaking Greek and used names which were Greek.[6] In the following century 'barbarian' was only one of the abusive terms applied by Demosthenes to Philip of Macedon and his people.[7]

In passages which refer to the Macedonian soldiers of Alexander the Great and the early successors there are mentions of a Macedonian dialect, such as was likely to have been spoken in the original Macedonian homeland. On one occasion Alexander 'called out to his guardsmen in Macedonian (*Makedonisti*), as this [viz. the use of 'Macedonian'] was a signal (*symbolon*) that there was a serious riot.' Normally Alexander and his soldiers spoke the standard Greek, the *koinē*, and that was what the Persians who were to fight alongside the Macedonians were taught. So the order 'in Macedonian' was unique, in that all other orders were in the *koinē*.[8] It is satisfactorily explained as an order in broad dialect, just as in a Highland Regiment a special order for a particular purpose could be given in broad Scots by a Scottish officer who usually spoke the King's English.

The use of this dialect among themselves was a characteristic of the Macedonian soldiers (rather than the officers) of the King's Army. This point was made clear in the report – not in itself dependable – of the trial of a Macedonian officer before an Assembly of Macedonians, in which the officer (Philotas) was mocked for not speaking in dialect.[9] In 321 when a non-Macedonian general, Eumenes, wanted to make contact with a hostile group of Macedonian infantrymen, he sent a Macedonian to speak to them in the Macedonian dialect, in order to win their confidence. Subsequently, when they and other Macedonian soldiers were serving with Eumenes, they expressed their affection for him by hailing him in the Macedonian dialect (*Makedonisti*).[10] He was to be one of themselves. As Curtius observed, 'not a man among the Macedonians could bear to part with a jot of his ancestral customs.' The use of this dialect was one way in which the Macedonians expressed their apartness from the world of Greek city-states.

Notes

1 See J. M. Balcer in *Historia* 37 (1988) 7.

2 *FGrH* 4 F 74.

3 Most recently E. Badian in Barr-Sharrar 33–51 disregards the evidence as set out e.g. in *HM* 2. 39–54, when it goes against his view that the Macedonians (whom he does not define) spoke a language other than Greek.

4 The matter is discussed at some length in *HM* 2. 39–54 with reference especially to O. Hoffmann, *Die Makedonen, ihre Sprache und ihr Volkstum* (Göttingen, 1906) and J. Kalléris, *Les Anciens Macédoniens* I (Athens, 1954); see also Kalléris II and R. A. Crossland in the *Cambridge Ancient History* 3. I. 843 ff.

5 For Edessa see *HM* 1. 165 and for the Phrygians in Macedonia 407–14. Olympus occurs as a Phrygian personal name.

6 See Hammond, *Ep* 419 ff. and 525 ff.

7 As Badian, loc. cit. 42, rightly observes: 'this, of course, is simple abuse.'

8 Plu. *Alex.* 51. 6.

9 Curtius 6. 9. 34–6.
10 *PSI* XII 2 (1951) no. 1284: Plu. *Eum.* 14.11. Badian, loc. cit. 41 and 50 n. 66, discusses the former and not the latter, which hardly bears out his theory that Eumenes 'could not directly communicate with Macedonian soldiers', and presumably they with him. Badian says in his note that he is not concerned with the argument as to whether Macedonian was a 'dialect' or 'a language'. Such an argument seems to me to be at the heart of the matter. We have a similar problem in regard to Epirus, where some had thought the language of the people was Illyrian. In Plu. *Pyrrh*, 1. 3 reference was made to 'the local *phonē*', which to me means 'dialect' of Greek: it is so in this instance because Plutarch is saying that Achilles was called 'in the local *phonē* Aspetos'. The word 'Aspetos' elsewhere was peculiar to Greek epic, but it survived in Epirus in normal speech. It is of course a Greek and not an Illyrian word. See Hammond, *Ep.* 525 ff., for Greek being the language of central Epirus in the fifth century BC.

References

Barr-Sharrar = B. Barr-Sharrar and E.N. Borza (eds), *Macedonia and Greece in Late Classical and Early Hellenistic Times* (Washington: 1982).

Hammond, *Ep.* = N.G.L. Hammond, *Epirus* (Oxford: 1967).

HM 1 = N.G.L. Hammond, *A History of Macedonia* 1 (Oxford: 1972).

HM 2 = N.G.L. Hammond and G.T. Griffith, *A History of Macedonia* 2 (Oxford: 1979).

THE KING AND THE MACEDONES

N.G.L. Hammond

Constitutional monarchies were defined by Thucydides as 'hereditary kingships upon stated prerogatives,' and the Macedonian monarchy was a specific example. From the first king of the Temenid house c. 650 BC to the last of the line, Alexander's posthumous son who was murdered in 311 BC, every king was a member of that royal house. It was inconceivable within that time that the Macedonian people would elect anyone else to the throne. This was made clear at Babylon after Alexander's death, when the army, acting as the Macedonian people under arms, elected his half-brother Arrhidaeus, 'rejoicing that the strength of authority would remain in the same house and the same family, and that one of the royal stock would assume the hereditary authority, since the people were accustomed to honour and worship the very name, and no one assumed it unless born to be king' (C. 10.7.15). All sons of Philip were potential kings, and the choice between them lay with the people when Philip was assassinated.

At the demise of a king a leading Macedonian might declare his own preference by putting on his breastplate and moving to the side of his preferred candidate, but it was the Macedonian people, the Macedones under arms, who decided the election, 'clashing their spears against their shields as a sign that they would take with satisfaction the blood of any pretender who had no right to the throne.' The first duties of the newly elected king were the purification of the people, which was achieved by a ceremonial march of the entire army between the two halves of a disembowelled dog, and the obsequies of the dead king, who was buried with some emblem of his kingship.

Another duty of the king was to maintain the security of the throne by acting as prosecutor in any case of treason before the Assembly of the Macedones, which alone gave and executed the verdict. Such a case arose at once if the previous king had died by assassination. The new king had to ensure the succession by begetting heirs as soon as possible and by training them in the dangerous schools of hunting and war. To this end many Macedonian kings were polygamous. Philip, for instance, 'had by his various marriages many other sons [besides Alexander and Arrhidaeus], all legitimate in accordance with the royal custom, but they died, some by chance, others in action' (J. 9.8.3). Despite advice, Alexander left the begetting of heirs too late for the security of the realm. It was his greatest mistake. Wives were chosen by the king for himself and for his children. According to Satyrus (fr. 4), Philip himself married 'with an eye to war' (and territorial expansion too); for considerations of state were much involved in royal matches. Thus when the Persians were in Europe the Macedonian king married his daughter to a Persian grandee, and Philip agreed to marry his son Arrhidaeus to the daughter of a Persian satrap.

The chief function of the king in a state which lacked a professional priesthood was religious. He began each day with sacrifice. Alexander, for instance, carried out 'the prescribed sacrifices' daily, even during his last illness as long as his strength lasted. The king in person conducted sacred festivals and contests of various kinds. In ceremonial sacrifice he was accompanied by the male members of the royal house, and there were special attendants who interpreted the omens which were revealed then or on other occasions. The king stood on a higher plane than other men in relation to the gods; for he himself was descended from Zeus both as a Temenid and as head of the Macedones. In state justice, which affected relations with the gods and the safety of the realm, the king held the place of the trained judiciary in a modern society. He was sole and final judge in certain cases, some involving the capital sentence. The wise judgements of Philip and the concentration of Alexander in the hearing of cases were proverbial (P. 42.2; cf. 23.3). Further, every subject had the right of appeal to the king against an act of his representative, even against an act of Alexander's 'General in Europe,' Antipater, in the last year of Alexander's life (P. 74.4–6).[1]

The powers of the king in secular matters were almost absolute. He conducted foreign policy, declaring war and making peace, for instance, at his own discretion. He was sole commander of the Macedonian forces. On campaign he issued orders of all kinds, and he exercised strict discipline, sentencing soldiers to flogging or execution as he thought fit. In battle he led the foremost troops, whether infantry or cavalry, and he himself fought at the point of greatest danger; for this was a warrior kingship as in the epic society which Homer had described. He also led the royal hunt on horseback, in pursuit not of the fox but of lions, aurochs, bears, and boars which were native to the virgin forests of Macedonia. He owned all deposits of gold, silver, copper, and iron, and all forests in his kingdom; he had large hunting reserves and considerable estates; and he raised taxes of various kinds from his subjects. He issued his own coinage, recruited and equipped and paid his own troops, and administered his own property and the state finances. He was himself the government. Because the safety of the realm depended upon him, any step taken to safeguard his life was justified on the principle 'salus regis suprema lex esto.' Whatever the rights and wrongs of the quarrel between Alexander and Cleitus, once Alexander thought his life was threatened, no Macedonian questioned his right to defend himself by killing Cleitus on the spot.

To assist him the king called upon his male relations in the royal house and upon 'Friends' and 'Companions' whom he selected himself. For instance, when Perdiccas II made a treaty with Athens, the oath was taken by the king, his relations and then his Friends. These assistants acted as officers, envoys, governors, generals, treasurers, estate-managers, and so on, and they were rewarded with gifts in land, money or kind by the king, whose generosity was on an epic scale. If the king wished, he summoned his assistants to give advice on matters of policy or government or war, but it was he who made the decision. The same persons formed the king's court; they attended him in public, fought at his side in war, protected him in the hunt, escorted him on ceremonial parades, and enjoyed his confidence and affection. It was a rare thing for a king to shut himself up in his tent alone, as Alexander was to do on some occasions; for a king's success depended much upon his personal relations with his friends, and he lived most of the time in their company, feasting and drinking in the epic manner.

Another department of court was formed by the royal pages, who were selected by the king from his own relations and from the sons of his Friends and Companions at the age of fourteen. They served as the personal attendants of the king, sitting with him at table, guarding him at night, aiding him in the hunt, handling his horse while he mounted, and fighting near him in war. It was natural that these pages, when they were men, often became the closest friends and companions of the one among them who was elected king, as Hephaestion did of Alexander.

In this man-centered monarchical system the women of the royal house played little part in public life. They were not present at banquets and drinking parties, though courtesans might be, and their role was usually that of the housewife, making the menfolk's clothes, grinding corn, and baking bread. They might become influential in court intrigues and in matters of the succession to the throne, especially when they were queen mothers or queen grandmothers; this happened particularly when the heir was an infant. Even in the personal life of the court the women had less influence on a king and his friends than the men and the boys who shared so many interests in peace and war. It is not surprising that Alexander was as closely attached to Hephaestion as Achilles was to Patroclus; but such an attachment did not exclude love for Roxane and love for Briseis. Attachments between men and boys were more liable to lead to love affairs than attachments between contemporaries, and some conspiracies against the king were attributed to jealousy or chagrin over such affairs.

In writing about the Macedonians we have to be on our guard against using modern terms which imply modern standards of outlook and criticism. Thus it is too easy to label the powers of a Macedonian king as tyrannical, whereas they were in historical fact constitutional; to condemn Philip as profligate for taking a seventh wife in the hope of another heir, unless we recall that the only competent heir, Alexander, had led the cavalry charge at Chaeronea and was expected to lead others in Asia; to select one wife as queen and call the others prostitutes, as Greek writers did; and to speak of divorce between Philip and Olympias, the mother of Alexander, when she withdrew to the Molossian court in Epirus.

Again it is erroneous to call the Friends and Companions of Alexander 'Macedonian nobles' or 'barons.' For the first implies a nobility of birth, a hereditary aristocracy of the English kind, which did not exist at all among the Macedones of Lower Macedonia; and even in Upper Macedonia where such an aristocracy had existed, it was absorbed by Philip into his entourage without any special privileges. Rather there was equality of opportunity to rise in the king's service, and the choice of Friends and Companions was made by the king alone on grounds not of family lineage but of personal quality. When a father and a son, say Parmenio and Philotas, served a king or kings well, we may say that the family of Parmenio was a leading family in Macedonia; but that was by merit. The term 'baron' implies a special, mediaeval form of nobility, in which a Great Baron, holding a hereditary domain and recruiting his personal army from his retainers, might challenge the king himself; but in the Macedonia of Philip and Alexander no Friend or Companion had his own troops and there was no possibility of any commoner challenging the king.

The key to the unity of the Macedonian state under Philip and Alexander is to be found in the devotion of the Macedonian people to their king. When Curtius described Alexander's recovery from a serious illness on a campaign, he wrote as follows. 'It is not easy to say – quite apart from the reverence which is innate in that people towards their kings – how much they were devoted to this particular king in their admiration, indeed in their ardent affection' (C. 3.6.17). However, their attitude was not servile or obsequious. On addressing the king in the Assembly a soldier bared his head, but he spoke openly and frankly, whatever his rank. Indeed there was truth in the paradoxical statement that the Macedonians 'being accustomed to the rule of a king lived with a greater sense of freedom than any other people' (C. 4.7.31).

To this extent the monarchy was a democratic monarchy. The royal house in its attitude to the people had benefited from three centuries of accumulated experience, and its princes inherited a sense of dedication to their subjects and showed an almost instinctive capacity for rule from an early age; so much so that four kings in succession – Alexander II, Perdiccas III, Philip II, and Alexander himself – ruled in their early twenties with assurance, initiative, and authority. The separateness of the royal house from all other Macedonians enhanced its self-awareness and its reputation. Its founder, Perdiccas I, had not been a native of Macedonia but had come from the Greek city of Argos in the Peloponnese as a member of the ruling house there, the Temenidae, which was descended from Heracles, son of Zeus. The foreign origin of the dynasty, like that of the dynasty in modern Greece, set it apart from any indigenous family and above traditional feuds. It was also valuable in diplomatic contacts with the Greek city-states; for a Macedonian king was a Greek, as well as a Macedonian.

While the Macedonian kingship resembled other warrior kingships in the Balkans, the organisation of the Macedones proper, the conquerors of Lower Macedonia, was peculiar to them. Full citizenship, indicated by the title 'Macedon,' was held only by men under arms in the service of the king,[2] and their citizenship was further defined by residence in relation to a city, as we have seen. For example, a man is defined in an inscription as 'Machatas, son of Sabbataras, a Macedon of Europos,' or in a text as 'Peucestas, a Macedon of Mieza.' When Upper Macedonia was incorporated fully into the realm, each man who attained citizenship there was defined by his canton, so that one might be called 'Alexander, a Macedon of Lyncus,' and another 'Philarchus, a Macedon of Elimeotis.' Sometimes a town was added, as in the last case, where he was 'a Macedon of Elimeotis from Pythion.' These definitions reflected the system of local government in each area, the city being the civic unit in Lower Macedonia and the canton the civic unit in Upper Macedonia. It is evident that each unit managed its own local affairs, leaving the king and his entourage entirely free to deal with matters of national policy.

We have mentioned the ability of the king to found new towns. The earliest which is known (from excavation only) was founded by Archelaus on land won from Paeonians at Demir Kapu on the north side of the Axius gorge, late in the fifth century. The settlers in these towns were mixed, some drafted from a city of Lower Macedonia and others recruited locally. The town or the territory might be named after a city or a territory of Lower Macedonia; thus the territory above Demir Kapu, having a yellow soil, was named Emathia after the Emathian plain of Lower Macedonia. The most prolific founder of new towns was Philip. He made the men of Upper Macedonia 'dwellers in cities,' and in general 'he transferred at his own discretion peoples and towns, just as shepherds transfer their flocks from winter to summer pastures' (J 8.5.7). Some of the new towns, we are told, were on the frontiers, so as to face an enemy; others were set in distant places; and others were reinforced with women and children captured in war. When Philip added new territory to his kingdom, he extended existing cantons or named new cantons after them. Thus in the southwest it seems that Lyncus was extended to take in the district by Lake Ochrid, and Elimeotis to include a part at least of Ferrhaebia; while the region by Lake Little Prespa was named Eordaea and its river Eordaicus. In the east there were cantons called Astraea and Doberus; some towns were reinforced, such as Philippi, and new towns, like Philippoupolis, were planted. These developments were of the greatest importance, as the young Alexander was in a position to appreciate. For they served the purposes of frontier defence, internal commerce, cultural fusion, agricultural development, and later military recruitment.

Notes

1 The right of appeal is discussed by W.L. Adams in *Anc. Mac.* 4.43–52.
2 And ex-servicemen. For such a restricted citizenship see Arist. *Pol.* 1297 b 1–2 and 13–15 'not only those serving but also those who have served', citing the Malieis as an example. The Spartan state was similar in this as in other respects.

Reference

Anc. Mac. 4 = *Ancient Macedonia* 4, Institute for Balkan Studies (Thessaloniki: 1986).

THE LEGACY OF PHILIP

A.B. Bosworth

The period 336–323 BC is inevitably designated the age of Alexander. It marked a huge expansion of the imperial boundaries of Macedon, a virtually unparalleled outpouring of resources, material and human. *Imperium terris, animos aequabit Olympo.* The prophecy made for Romulus' foundation applies even more appositely to the milieu of Alexander. His empire was in any sense world-wide, his concept of his person and achievements superhuman. From the time of his death his name has been an evocative symbol of worldly glory, alternately eulogised and excoriated as the type of the magnanimous conqueror or the intemperate tyrant; and the history of his reign has all too often been a thinly disguised biography, distorted by the personality and values of its author.[1] This book is an attempt to analyse Alexander's impact on his world without any preconceived model of his personality or motives. *Sine ira et studio* is perhaps an impossible ideal, given the controversial and highly emotive nature of some of the subject matter, but one should at least attempt to base one's interpretation upon the extant sources.[2] Even there we may find prejudice enough, but we have some prospect of identifying and discounting bias, both apologetic and vituperative. Our history of the period can only be fragmentary, based on episodes randomly highlighted in the literary tradition or the scattering of documentary evidence preserved by chance. We may not go beyond the material at our disposal. Alexander the man will always elude us, thanks to the distorting filter of ancient (and modern) judgements and our grossly inefficient documentation, but the events of his reign can be discussed in context and the focus is occasionally clear. That is a sufficiently important theme. The face of the world was changed within a decade, and the events and the forces at work are worth exposition and discussion, even if the personalities of the main actors are irretrievable.

With equal justice the period might be termed the age of Philip. The Macedon that Alexander inherited was the creation of his father. The army he led was forged by Philip. The material resources of the Macedonian throne were acquired by Philip. The system of alliances which turned the Balkans into a virtual annexe of Macedon was Philip's development, and the war against Persia was launched at the end of Philip's reign. In his first years, at least, Alexander was continuing a process begun by his father, and his reign cannot be understood without constant reference to his predecessor. What follows is in no sense a history of Philip, rather a contextual stage setting to introduce the accession of Alexander.

As is well known, Philip came to power in 359 BC, when Macedon was threatened with dissolution, debilitated by a decade of dynastic feuding and crippled by military defeat at the hands of the Illyrians. During the next twenty-three years he made a world power out of that ruined inheritance, creating a political, military and financial basis for empire. On the political front Macedon was welded into a unity, focused on the person of the king. That came about partly by coercion. After his decisive early victory over the Illyrians (358) Philip was able to dominate the turbulent principalities of Upper Macedonia (Lyncestis, Orestis, Elimiotis and Tymphaea) which straddled the Pindus range between the upper Haliacmon and Epirus and had

28

straddled the Pindus range between the upper Haliacmon and Epirus and had tradi-tionally maintained their independence of the monarchy of Macedon proper, based on the lower plains. For the first time they became integral parts of the greater kingdom. Their nobility was absorbed into the court at Pella and achieved distinction under both Philip and Alexander.[3] At the same time they offered a fertile recruiting ground for both infantry and cavalry; no less than three of the original six phalanx battalions of Alexander came from the upper principalities.[4]

The political union was cemented by marriage. Unashamedly polygamous, Philip contracted a sequence of unions, particularly in the early years of his reign. One of his first wives came from Elimiotis (Phila, the sister of Derdas and Machatus), and there is little doubt that the marriage was designed to help the process of annexa-tion. Other wives came from peripheral non-Macedonian areas: Audata from Illyria, Philinna and Nicesipolis from Thessaly and Meda from the Getic North.[5] The most important was the formidable Olympias who came from the royal house of Molossia and was taken to Philip's bed by 357 at latest. This marriage linked together the two dynasties on either side of the Pindus and gave Philip direct influence on the Molossian throne. When he ultimately intervened in Epirus, the reigning king Arybbas was deposed in favour of his nephew, Alexander, the brother of Olympias.[6] These marriages were the linchpins of the great nexus of guest-friends which was to support Philip's interests through the Balkans. At the same time the risk of dynastic conflict which they posed was obviated by the clear superiority that Olympias enjoyed over her fellow consorts.

As the king's network of alliances expanded, the influence of his nobility contracted. Philip increased the élite body of royal Companions (*hetairoi*), attracting immigrants from the wider Greek world. Men who would accept his patronage were given lavish donations of land and status at court. Of Alexander's close circle of boyhood friends three (Nearchus of Crete; Erigyius and Laomedon of Mytilene) were non-Macedonian. Other prominent figures, notably the chief secretary, Eumenes of Cardia, came from abroad. Their loyalty was to the king alone. However intimate and important their functions, they stood apart from the rest of the Macedonian hierarchy, never fully accepted and often resented.[7] Even after Alexander's death Eumenes' foreign extrac-tion was a liability when he commanded troops, and his own Macedonians were finally to turn against him with the bitter gibe, 'plague from the Chersonese' (Plut. *Eum.* 18.1).

Philip's lavishness to his new men was matched by benefactions to the old nobility. The new acquisitions of land in Chalcidice and Thrace were parcelled out to new and old alike. Polemocrates, father of the great marshal Coenus, obtained estates in the hinterland of Olynthus.[8] His primary holdings were in Elimiotis, in Upper Macedonia, and he now had interests, directly conferred by the king, in the new territories. Philip was sharing the advantages of conquest while diversifying the power base of his nobility. He also, it seems, founded the institution of the Pages:[9] the sons of promi-nent nobles received an education at court in the immediate entourage of the king, developing a personal attachment to him while necessarily serving as hostages for the good behaviour of their families. As a result the nobility was simultaneously coerced and rewarded, diluted and diversified. As the frontiers of the kingdom expanded, loyalty to the crown brought tangible rewards, and those rewards involved financial interests and military obligations outside the old baronial centres of power. In the climate of success and expansion there was less incentive to challenge the supremacy of the king at Pella, and even the influx of favoured Companions from beyond the borders was tolerable.

Philip reigned as an autocrat. The political institutions of Macedon were informal and rudimentary, and there were few practical constraints on a strong king. Like his son, Philip presumably consulted an inner council of intimates on major issues of state,[10] but nothing suggests that the council was anything other than advisory. Again, it might be prudential to consult the opinions of the army on various occasions but there was nothing incumbent on the king to hold regular assemblies and he was in no sense bound by popular opinion.[11] It is suggested that by tradition the army exercised capital jurisdiction,[12] but that is a strictly limited area. Even there procedure was apparently fluid and informal, and there was certainly no body of Macedonian statute law. The king operated in a framework of precedent and tradition but, provided that he had the resources and the personality to assert his will, he could do what he liked with the minimum of consultation. That is the constant lament of Demosthenes, that the Greek *poleis* which had public processes of decision-making could not compete with an immensely shrewd autocrat who concealed his actions and policies.[13] For most effective purposes Philip *was* Macedon. He concluded treaties in his own name with sovereign states, sent his own ambassadors to the Amphictyonic Council, and (like his predecessors) struck coins in his own name. Perhaps the best illustration of the advantages of his position is the fate of the hapless Athenian embassy which travelled to Macedon in the summer of 346 to ratify the Peace of Philocrates. Ratification meant the physical presence of Philip, and the ambassadors were forced to wait impatiently at Pella while the king completed his campaigns in Thrace, increasing the territorial possessions which would be confirmed by the peace. The peace was finally accepted at Pherae, on the eve of his attack on Thermopylae, when it was too late for the Athenians to take effective counter-action.[14] Given that he was the only contractual party on the Macedonian side, his initiative was unlimited.

This considerable freedom of action was underpinned by the huge financial resources of Macedon. The mineral reserves of the kingdom, previously centred in the territory east of the River Axios,[15] were vastly expanded when Philip occupied the site of Crenides in 356 and exploited the rich veins of gold and silver in the neighbouring mines of Mt Pangaeum. According to Diodorus (xvi.8.6) this area alone supplied revenues of more than 1,000 talents and Philip extended his mining operations to Chalcidice, exploiting the deposits in the mountainous terrain north of Olynthus. What is more, as the boundaries of the kingdom expanded, so did its fiscal basis: dues upon landed property and extraordinary levies (*eisphorae*).[16] Philip's financial power was comparatively unmatched, except by the Great King, and it gave him invaluable advantages. Diodorus mentions his capacity to keep a formidable mercenary force and to bribe collaborators in the Greek world. Though emotively expressed, the statement is true and important. Philip did attract a large and versatile body of mercenaries which he could use in the most remote theatres of operation and deploy independently of the Macedonian native levy. In 342/1, when the main army was fully engaged in the Thracian hinterland, he was able to send out two separate mercenary forces, under Eurylochus and Parmenion, to intervene in the affairs of Eretria far to the south.[17] His financial reserves ensured that he never suffered the embarrassment of Athenian generals serving in the north Aegean, who were often forced to maintain their mercenaries by subsidiary campaigning for other paymasters or by simple extortion, euphemistically termed 'good will' payments (Dem. VIII.25). His men could be guaranteed continuity of employment and regular payment.

The diplomatic intrigue Diodorus speaks of is equally important. Philip attracted the most prominent figures of the Greek world to Pella, where he entertained lavishly and dispersed huge sums as gifts, in traditional Homeric hospitality. Bribery or guest-friendship, it depended on one's perspective. Philip could buy good-will, encourage political co-operation or even finance dissidents to seize power in their home city. At its starkest the power of money was seen in the Olynthian campaign of 349/8, when Torone, Mecyberna and perhaps Olynthus itself fell through internal treachery and (if we may believe Demosthenes) the Olynthian cavalry was betrayed by its commanders.[18] Not everyone who received Philip's money was disloyal,[19] but few can have been unaffected. Every individual and every community which had the money to do so used it for diplomatic advantage; and the system of *proxenia* ensured that nationals of one city were in honour obliged to promote the interests of another. In this sense Philip's activity was almost orthodox. What was unusual was its scale and complexity. Few Greek cities can have been without citizens who had benefited directly from his largesse, and far more than Greeks were affected. Philip had inaugurated his reign with diplomatic payments to his neighbour, the Paeonian king (Diod. XVI.3.4), and he will have acquired allies in the north by payment as much as by conquest. Even relations with Persia might be affected. Refugees from the court of the Great King, men like Amminapes or even Artabazus, were entertained at Pella,[20] incurring obligations which might be repaid after their rehabilitation. The advantages were great, the expenses colossal. Philip did not merely spend money, alleges the contemporary critic, Theopompus (*FGrH* 115 F 224): he threw it away. His treasury was never flush with excess funds, and Alexander himself is alleged to have been severely embarrassed for ready money on the eve of his invasion of Asia.[21] That is a measure of the expenditure. What is not in doubt is the magnitude of the royal revenues and the financial power of Macedon.

The greatest resource of Macedonia was probably its population. After his incorporation of Upper Macedonia Philip was master of a territory some 20,000 square kilometres in area, comprising some of the richest agricultural land in the Balkans.[22] Its population was necessarily large and was certainly augmented by the internal peace that prevailed in his reign. As always, there are no statistics and no basis for quantification. But for the male population of military age there are some interesting figures. The Macedonian infantry under arms in 334 BC numbered 27,000, and there were ample reserves that could be mustered in subsequent years.[23] The cavalry also was numerous and of high calibre – something over 3,000 at the time of Philip's death. These numbers are formidable, and they comprise only the nucleus of Philip's military resources: his native Macedonian forces. With the allied contingents that would normally take the field with him they amounted to an army without parallel in Greek history. Indeed it can be argued that Philip never needed to mobilise more than a fraction of the forces at his disposal. At the climactic battle of Chaeronea his army is estimated at 30,000 foot and 2,000 horse – and that was an army augmented by numerous allies (Diod. XVI.85.5). His campaigns, numerous though they were, never fully exploited his reserves of manpower, and his military strength, it is safe to say, rose steadily throughout his reign.

Mere numbers are only part of the story. Macedon was populous before Philip but its infantry was a primitive rabble.[24] The mobilisation of the foot soldiers as a political as well as a military force may predate his reign,[25] but it is highly probable that the introduction of the 12-cubit *sarisa* as the fundamental offensive weapon was his innovation.[26] From the beginning of the reign he imposed systematic training, to produce a cohesive and immensely strong formation that could surpass the depth and compactness of the Theban phalanx. This primary striking force was supplemented by light-armed auxiliaries, archers and, in due course, a siege train manned by the finest contemporary military engineers (retained by Philip's gold). The Macedonian cavalry was, as always, superb, and its discipline was sharpened by regular training which evolved the classic tactic of attack in wedge formation. For most of the reign the national army was used on the marches of the kingdom, in relatively brief campaigns against Illyrian or Thracian adversaries. It made few forays into the Greek world proper – to crush the Phocian mercenaries at the Crocus Field (352) and perhaps to finish off the Olynthian campaign. By and large the military profile was as Demosthenes describes it in his *Third Philippic* (IX.49–50): brief opportunistic raids with flexible composite forces of mercenaries, cavalry and light-armed, rather than any large body of heavy infantry. It was generally considered, he says, that Philip could not be compared with Sparta at her prime. Those delusions were rudely shattered by Chaeronea, and even Chaeronea gave an imperfect picture of the true strength of Macedon.

We should also consider the outlying territories, particularly Thessaly and Thrace, which Philip turned into virtual annexes of Macedon. From the beginning of his reign he was involved in the affairs of Thessaly, taking one of his first wives (Philinna) from Larisa, the city traditionally most involved in Macedonian politics.[27] Later, in 353, he intervened in the internecine struggle between the tyrant house of Pherae and the Thessalian League, centred around the old capitals of Pharsalus and Larisa. After his crushing defeat of Pherae in 352 he was elected *archon* of an expanded league which now included all Thessaly. What exactly was meant by this is uncertain, but it did apparently give Philip some revenue from imposts on Thessalian trade and control of the joint military forces of Thessaly.[28] He could and did intervene in conflict between cities; garrisons were imposed, notably at Pherae, and, more drastically, there were mass exiles from the north-western cities of Pharcadon and Tricca (Diod. XVIII.56.5). Inevitably his partisans acquired key positions and he re-established the tetrarchies, the old regional divisions of Thessaly, imposing one of his own men upon each of them as controller.[29] Two of those tetrarchs (Daochus and Thrasydaeus) came from Pharsalus and are named by Demosthenes (XVIII.295) as quislings. Indeed Pharsalus occupied a dominant position in Philip's Thessaly. It provided the representatives to the Amphictyonic Council as well as a cavalry élite which formed a counterpart to the Macedonian royal squadron [. . .] The other cities were relatively depressed, but the relatives of Philip's two wives must have exercised power and influence in and beyond Larisa and Pherae. It proved a stable settlement. Both Philip and Alexander worked with the existing aristocracy of Thessaly (Medeius of Larisa enjoyed high favour as a Companion)[30] and used the traditional cavalry strength of the territory. There was no attempt to mobilise the depressed peasantry into an effective infantry on the Macedonian model. Thessaly remained comparatively weak under its traditional governing circle, now absorbed to some degree in the Macedonian court. It could be mobilised with Macedon but never deployed against the monarchy – as long as Philip's partisans remained stable in power.

His policy in Thrace was not dissimilar. A potential threat if united under a single king, the Thracian lands were renowned in the fifth century for their large popula-tion and financial strength.[31] From Philip's accession what had been a single kingdom under the redoubtable Odrysian Cotys was divided among his three sons, who were unable or disinclined to form a common front against him. The two western king-doms were forced into vassal status, probably by 352, and in his great Thracian campaign of 342/1 he attacked and conquered the Odrysian heartland in the Hebrus valley, deep in modern Bulgaria. As a result the reigning kings, Teres and Cersebleptes, were deposed,[32] and Thrace as a whole came under the control of a Macedonian general. Regional control points were established in the form of new cities, the most important Philippopolis (Plovdiv) and Cabyle, where the motley collection of new settlers formed alien enclaves, necessarily dependent on the favour of the Macedonian king [. . .]. But it was more than mere military occupation. Native princes continued to exercise power locally, and by the end of Alexander's reign the Odrysian Seuthes (Berve 1926, 2 no. 702) had virtually re-established a kingdom – under Macedonian suzerainty. Other princes were attracted to the Macedonian court and later led contingents of their nationals in Alexander's army (the most notorious was Sitalces, who led a unit of javelin-men at Issus and Gaugamela).[33] Like Thessaly, Thrace was neutralised as a potential danger, its peoples ruled by compliant natives under Macedonian patronage and providing auxiliary forces, both cavalry and light infantry. Other peoples in the north enjoyed similar relations with the Macedonian throne. From early in the reign the Paeonians and Agrianians of the upper Strymon valley were subjects of the Macedonian king, their rulers holding power by grace of Philip and their troops swelling the army of Macedon.

By the end of the 340s BC Macedon had become a superpower. Few realised it, certainly not the citizens of the Greek city states which might have been considered Philip's chief rivals. But in fact there was no real challenge. As early as 346 the Athenian orator Isocrates wrote an open letter to the Macedonian king, urging him to unite the four principal powers of Greece (Athens, Argos, Sparta and Thebes) and lead them in a crusade against Persia. These cities, he said in a memorable phrase, were reduced to a common level of disaster (Isocr. V.40). The statement is overstressed for rhetorical purposes, but there is an element of truth in it. No single city state (or even coalition) was a match for Philip. Indeed two of Isocrates' four major powers could be considered anachronisms even in his own day. Argos can never have been considered a significant military power since its catastrophic defeat at the hands of Cleomenes of Sparta in 494 BC, and in more recent years (370) it had been visited by one of the most atrocious examples of Greek political violence, in which a purge of property owners had been followed by reprisals against the democratic leaders (Diod. XV.57.3–58.4). Argos was relatively impotent, of little value for or against Philip.

Much the same could be said of Sparta. The defeat at Leuctra (371) and still more the liberation of Messenia (370/69) had contracted Spartan ambitions and Spartan resources. The male citizen population now dipped below 1,000, and there was no thought of rectifying the situation by enfranchising the subject classes. Spartan society remained in its rigid hierarchical straitjacket, but its territories were confined to old

Laconia and Cythera. The erstwhile helots of Messenia now formed a separate and antipathetic state, its capital on Mt Ithome a formidable fortress. Another fortress, Megalopolis, blocked access to Messenia by the north. It had been founded on Theban initiative in the 360s BC and united the scattered populations of south-west Arcadia into a single great defensive complex. The Spartan leadership was totally recalcitrant, totally incapable of renouncing its traditional claims to hegemony over the Greek world. That hegemony could only be achieved by first destroying and resettling Megalopolis and then attacking Messenia. Only the first step in the programme was ever attempted; Megalopolis was attacked (abortively) in 353/2 and 331/0. Given the scanty military population of Sparta, her political ambitions could only be supported by mercenaries, and the mercenaries could only be retained by campaigning outside Laconia. Spartan kings by necessity became glorified *condottieri*, the great Agesilaus ending his life in the service of Egypt and his son, Archidamus, dying in battle against the Lucanians of southern Italy. That meant that in practice Spartan forces could rarely be deployed in the field, and Sparta was neutral in the great crisis of 338, reserving her forces for the higher end of the conquest of Messenia.

For Philip this attitude was a godsend. It allowed him to befriend and support the leading families of Argos and Messenia, not to mention Megalopolis. His sympathisers were stigmatised as traitors by Demosthenes, but two centuries later the Megalopolitan historian, Polybius, gave a spirited defence: their wooing of Philip ensured local autonomy and security from Sparta.[34] That was justified. Sparta's intentions were naked and threatening, Philip's less so. The Macedonian king supported his partisans financially, militarily and morally, and in 338 the final reward was the partitioning of Spartan borderland to his allies in Messenia, Arcadia and Argos [. . .]. Spartan ambitions were a considerable asset for Philip, who could expand his sphere of influence by espousing the cause of the states directly threatened.

The Thebans were in a similar position. Their period of glory in the 360s was short-lived, abruptly terminated by the unpleasant and ruinously expensive Sacred War with Phocis. Theban hegemonial ambitions had driven the Phocian leaders to occupy the sanctuary at Delphi (356), and the financial resources of the city and its confederation were simply insufficient to match the mercenary armies which Phocis paid from the treasures of Apollo. Like the Spartans, the Thebans sent their hoplite forces to fight for causes overseas. In 353, at the height of the Sacred War, they sent the cream of their army under their premier general, Pammenes, to support the revolt of the Persian satrap Artabazus. A decade later Lacrates with a thousand hoplites formed the spearhead of the Persian invasion of Egypt.[35] The Theban hoplite army still had the greatest military reputation in the Greek world, but numbers were relatively small. Field armies serving outside Boeotia contained no more than 8,000 hoplites from the confederation. At the same time there were bitter international hostilities. The Spartans, the Phocians and the tyrants of Pherae had been inveterate enemies. At Athens the attitude towards Thebes was rarely anything other than chilly; and the drastic fate meted out to dissidents within the confederacy (Plataea, Thespiae and Orchomenus, all destroyed) ensured a plentiful supply of exiles to whom the name of Thebes was anathema. After the Sacred War Thebes was in no position to dominate. Indeed her interests had been eminently served by Philip, who in 346 crushed the power of Phocis in central Greece and confirmed Thebes as mistress of the Boeotian confederacy.

Athens was the most complex of the states of Greece. Firmly democratic since 403 BC, the city had to some degree recovered the power it had lost in the Peloponnesian War. The Athenian navy, on paper at least, was supreme in the contemporary world. Many of the ships in the dockyards were unseaworthy, but navies of over a hundred ships could put out to sea in a crisis.[36] The Second Athenian Confederacy, it is true, had been all but destroyed by the calamitous Social War (357–355). Only a rump of militarily insignificant allies stayed loyal to the city. Fortunately during the naval ascendancy of the 360s the Athenians were able to establish a number of cleruchies (settlements of Athenian citizens overseas). Samos had been occupied in 365; the Chersonese was ceded to Athens in its entirety in 353/2 by the Thracian king Cersebleptes. In the northern Aegean the islands of Imbros, Lemnos and Scyros had become annexes of the Athenian state and (like Samos) received regular officials from the capital. The Athenians were fiercely retentive of these exclaves, which guaranteed a modest competence to citizens who would otherwise have been indigent. Poteidaea, which harboured Athenian cleruchs for a mere five years (361–356), was stubbornly claimed as an Athenian possession, its occupation by Philip denounced as an outrage a decade and more after the event ([Dem.] VII.9–10).

At the same time the domestic revenues of the city increased, from a nadir of 130 talents to some 400 talents by the mid-340s BC.[37] This development went hand in hand with a fundamental change in economic administration. The theoric fund, once responsible only for occasional disbursements at festival time, became the receptacle of all public monies remaining after basic administrative expenses were met. Except in time of war, when Attica was directly threatened, the commissioners of the fund disbursed the proceeds as they thought fit, on public works and direct cash grants to the people.[38] As Demosthenes repeatedly complains, the existence of the fund was a disincentive to rash declarations of war. The *demos*, which profited as a whole from the theoric administration, was generally reluctant to vote for elaborate military adventures. When Athenian interests were conceived as threatened, as in 352/1 when Philip attempted to force Thermopylae and then made a push to the shores of the Propontis, the *demos* might respond vigorously and promptly, but by and large there was little that could be called offensive initiative. Generals (at this period professional generals like Chares and Phocion, who were elected year after year) were assigned to areas of special importance, the Hellespont and Samos, and were expected to retain and maintain mercenaries from local resources.

It did not make for effective military resistance to Philip. Indeed it was only at critical moments, such as the fall of Olynthus, that Philip was conceived as a serious threat to Athenian interests. Even Demosthenes was far from consistent in his crusading fervour and was prepared to countenance peace and alliance between 348 and early 346. There was little sympathy for the Macedonian king. Few Athenians will have forgotten his opportunistic annexation of Amphipolis, Pydna and Methone, not to mention Poteidaea; and the end of the Sacred War in 346 was widely – and rightly – seen as a diplomatic humiliation not to be tolerated. Philip, to his intense annoyance, suffered intense diplomatic pressure from Athens to restore what the *demos* saw as its proper possessions, and his settlement of Phocis was only accepted grudgingly and under coercion. On the other hand the warnings of Demosthenes in the late 340s fell on deaf ears. Few Athenians seriously believed that they would see a Macedonian army in Attica. They would vote for limited campaigns against

Macedonian-backed regimes in Euboea or even military assistance to the threatened area of Acarnania, but full-scale war against Macedon was not seriously envisaged.

Philip's intentions towards Athens are more difficult to assess, given the systematic ambiguity of his actions. It seems unlikely that he would ever have countenanced an ultimate settlement that left the city free of constraints. Athens had played a mischievous role in Macedonian politics at the time of his accession. It had continuously supported the Phocian regime against him. The demands for territory once allegedly Athenian but now his were unremitting and outrageous. If he needed proof of Athenian intransigence, it was amply given in 341, when he was fully engaged in Thrace. Then the Athenian general Diopeithes took advantage of his absence to attack one of his allies, Cardia, and carried hostilities into his Thracian territories. When he complained, his ambassador was arrested by Diopeithes and at Athens Demosthenes successfully argued against the recall of the delinquent general.[39] Ultimately there was little alternative to a military confrontation. It came late in 340 when Philip attacked Byzantium and in the course of the siege captured the entire grain fleet on its way to Athens. This was an intensely hostile act, striking at the very lifeline of Athens, which was notoriously dependent on imported grain. The declaration of war that followed reflected the gravity of the action. Faced with a threat to the grain supply, the *demos* unhesitatingly diverted the administrative surplus from the theoric fund to finance the hostilities.

The final campaign was a little delayed but, once launched, was rapid and decisive. Philip did not seriously contemplate tackling the Athenian fleets in the Propontis, for his own fleet was vestigial and inexperienced. Instead he spent the campaigning year of 339 securing his northern frontiers. Late in the year he moved south, leading yet another Amphictyonic force, in theory to attack Locris. This immediately brought him into conflict with the Thebans, who had come to resent his domination of Central Greece and took advantage of his absence in the north to expel a Macedonian garrison from the mouth of Thermopylae. In the face of the common threat, Athens and Thebes allied themselves and, despite overtures by Philip and his allies, the alliance remained firm. In August 338 came the dénouement. Philip's army, a fraction of his total strength, faced a coalition of roughly equivalent numbers: the Theban and Athenian levies together with a few allied contingents, the most notable from Achaea. It was not an impressive array. The two principals had precious little support from the other Greek states, which were content to wait upon (and profit from) the result.

It was catastrophic. In the plain of Chaeronea the Macedonian phalanx proved its superiority over traditional hoplite forces. The Athenians alone lost 1,000 dead and 2,000 prisoners, and the Boeotians suffered heavy casualties, including the entire Sacred Band. The end of the day saw Philip supreme in Greece. For Thebes it meant the end of her hegemony in Boeotia and the replacement of her moderate democracy by a strictly limited oligarchic junta, comprised mainly of returned exiles.[40] Athens by contrast suffered only the loss of her remaining allies (but not her cleruchies, with the possible exception of the Chersonese) and was compensated by the acquisition of Oropus, territory which since 366 had been part of Boeotia. The price was formal alliance with Macedon. The same applied to the other states of southern Greece which, if they had not done so before, concluded treaties of alliance. The Spartans stood alone. They refused submission in any form, suffered invasion and lost border territories to their embittered neighbours [. . .]. Elsewhere Macedonian garrisons occupied key citadels. They are attested at Thebes, Corinth and Ambracia, and there may have been others. There was also a degree of political subversion, as Philip ensured that his partisans were established in government. In 337 a constitutive meeting of allies was convened at Corinth, and the political system Philip had created was confirmed by a common peace.[41] Its pillars were the freedom and autonomy of all parties (under Macedonian hegemony) and the interdiction of political change and social revolution. It was administered by a *synedrion* of delegates from all allied states and the executive officer was Philip himself. The propaganda was abolition of war and *stasis* under the benign presidency of Macedon; the reality all too often was the preservation of sycophantic and oppressive regimes by the threat of military action. Whatever ideological perspective one takes, the result of the common peace is the same. It entrenched a network of governments largely sympathetic to Philip and guaranteed them stability.

The forum of allies at Corinth also declared war on Persia. This was the climactic act of the reign and was carefully prepared. From the early years of the century the Persian empire had been ripe for attack. Plagued by succession disputes in the royal house and endemic revolts in the satrapies, its whole fabric had been at times threatened with dissolution. In the late 360s practically the entire empire west of the Euphrates was alienated from the Great King at Susa. The Egyptians had asserted their independence as early as 404 and under a series of native pharaohs repelled successive Persian invasions. More seriously, since the impressive display given by Cyrus' mercenaries at Cunaxa, the nucleus of royal armies had regularly been recruited from Greece, and the Great King's interventions in the politics of the Balkans had often been designed to secure a supply of prime troops for his campaigns or to deny them to his antagonists. The most aggressive and successful monarch during the fourth century was Artaxerxes III Ochus (358–338). He was able to crush revolt in Asia Minor after his accession. In Phoenicia he forced Sidon to submission with fire and slaughter and finally (in 343 or 342) he reconquered Egypt and placed the land under a native satrap. This record of achievement is illusory. Sidon had long maintained its independence and only fell through treachery (by the Greek mercenary commander, Mentor of Rhodes). Similarly the conquest of Egypt had been preceded by disastrous failure a decade earlier.[42] The successful invasion was spearheaded by Greek troops with Greek commanders, and on both sides it was the mercenaries who did the effective fighting. They apparently made private treaties with each other and on one occasion Lacrates of Thebes turned against his Persian allies in the interests of the Greek defenders of Pelusium (Diod. XVI.49.4–6). The Persian success depended on the Great King's ability to pay and keep mercenaries. That had long been evident, and the military weakness of the Persian empire was a commonplace by Philip's accession. Isocrates had repeatedly urged a crusade against Persia and the settlement of Greek refugees in the King's lands. On a more practical level the Spartan king, Agesilaus, apparently envisaged the annexation of Asia Minor east of Cilicia, and the Thessalian dynast, Iason of Pherae, also had designs on Persian possessions.[43] The satrapies of Asia Minor were undeniably a natural and lucrative target for aggression.

We cannot date the origins of Philip's ambitions against Persia. There is no literary evidence for them until the latter part of his reign. As late as his *Fourth Philippic*

(341) Demosthenes can only argue on circumstantial evidence that Philip planned to attack the Persian king (Dem. X.31–3).[44] In fact Artaxerxes Ochus rejected Athenian overtures at that juncture and refused subsidies to support operations against Philip (Aesch. III.238). The only Persian involvement against Philip was when Ochus felt his territory threatened by the siege of Perinthus (340) and instructed his generals to co-operate with the defenders (Diod. XVI.75.1). Once the presumed threat to the Propontis receded, his interest in containing Philip also ebbed. Philip, as always, had kept his ultimate intentions secret, deferring them (as was inevitable) until he had imposed a stable and permanent settlement on southern Greece. After Chaeronea the time for a declaration of hostilities was propitious. Shortly before the battle Ochus was assassinated by his vizier, the sinister Bagoas, who then eliminated the immediate family of the deceased king, leaving his youngest son, Arses, to reign as his puppet. The dynastic convulsion provoked revolution in Egypt and Babylon [. . .], and the weakness of the empire was patent to all observers. Accordingly Philip had his allies declare war on Persia, with the avowed intention of avenging the sacrilege of Xerxes and liberating the Greek cities of Asia Minor [. . .]. It was an explicit renewal of the aims of the Delian League, and the Macedonian king was assuming the mantle of Aristeides. He would expand his realm by retaliating for past offences against the Hellenes, and, far from promoting his private interests, he was acting for the entire Greek world. His allies endorsed the declaration of war, fixed the military contributions of each state and passed resolutions forbidding any Hellene to fight on the Persian side. The supreme commander of the combined forces was Philip, at once *hegemon* of the common peace and general in the war of revenge. In the spring of 336 campaigning began in earnest, when a Macedonian expeditionary force 10,000 strong crossed the Hellespont and began the work of liberation (and subjugation) on the coast of Asia Minor. Philip was never able to assume leadership. He was cut down by assassination in the autumn of that same year, and command devolved upon his successor – with fatal results.

Notes

1 Interesting digests of modern views of Alexander are given by Schachermeyr 1973, 609–57 and Badian 1976a. See also (on the German scene) Demandt 1972.

2 See the Bibliography (pp. 295ff. [in Bosworth, *Conquest and Empire*]) for a brief review of the source tradition.

3 Note the list of trierarchs in Arr. *Ind*. 18. 5–6 and the list of domiciles in Berve 1926, 2.445. The most brilliant, Perdiccas and Craterus, were from Orestis.

4 See [Bosworth, *Conquest and Empire*] p. 259, with the literature there cited.

5 On Philip's marriages the prime evidence is a famous fragment of Satyrus the Peripatetic (Athen. 557B–E). On the many problems it presents see Martin 1982, 66–70 and Tronson 1984.

6 Cf. Hammond and Griffith 1979, 2.504–9; *contra* Errington 1975b.

7 On the general antipathy between Greeks and Macedonians see Badian 1982, particularly 39–43.

8 *SIG*[3] 332. On the location see Hammond and Griffith 1979, 2. 338.

9 Arr. IV. 13.1: cf. Hammond and Griffith 1979, 2.401; cf. 167–8 (though there is no evidence of the institution before Philip; nothing indicates that the assassins of Archelaus were Pages).

10 Cf. Arr. I.25.4; Curt. VI.8.1–15, 11.9–10. See further Berve 1926, 1.33–4; Bosworth 1980a, 161–2.

11 See now Lock 1977a; Errington 1978.

12 Curt. VI.8.25; cf. Errington 1978, 86–90. On the most famous instance, the capital trial of Philotas (330 BC), see [Bosworth, *Conquest and Empire*] pp. 101ff.

13 Dem. XVIII.235; cf. I.4, VIII. 11.

14 Note the classic description of Demosthenes XIX. 155–61 (cf. XVIII.32). On the details see Hammond and Griffith 1979, 2.341–5.

15 See Borza 1982, 8–12; Hammond and Griffith 1979, 2.69–73.

16 Arr. I.16.5, on which see Bosworth 1980a, 126.

17 Dem. IX.58 (somewhat earlier a force of 1,000 mercenaries had dismantled the fortifications at Porthmus). For other evidence of Philip's use of mercenaries see Parke 1933, 162–4.

18 Dem. XIX.265–7; cf. Diod. XVI.53.2 with Hammond and Griffith 1979, 2.322–4.

19 For the situation at Athens see [Bosworth, *Conquest and Empire*] pp. 211–13.

20 For Amminapes (Berve 1926, 2 no. 55) see Curt. VI.4.25; for Artabazus (Berve 1926, 2 no. 152) see Diod. XVI.52.3; Curt. V.9.1, VI.5.2.

21 Plut. *Al.* 15.2; cf. Arr. VII.9.6; Curt. X.2.24 with Hamilton 1969, 36–7 *contra* Bellinger 1963, 36ff.

22 See Borza 1982, esp. 12–20, suggesting that the coastal lowlands were malarial (cf. Borza 1979).

23 See [Bosworth, *Conquest and Empire*], pp. 266ff, and, for more documentation, Bosworth 1986.

24 Thuc. IV.124.1; see also (an illuminating passage) II.100.5.

25 This depends on the very vexed interpretation of Anaximenes, *FGrH* 72 F 4; for recent and different approaches to the problem see Brunt 1976, Hammond and Griffith 1979, 2.705–9, Develin 1985.

26 Implied by Diod. XVI.3.1–2. See Hammond and Griffith 1979, 2.421 and, for a different view, Markle 1978.

27 The chronology is vexed, but the marriage must be early. Cf. Hammond and Griffith 1979, 2.225; Martin 1982.

28 For the complex evidence see Hammond and Griffith 1979, 2.285–95.

29 Theopompus, *FGrH* 115 F 208–9; *SIG*³ 274 VIII. Cf. Hammond and Griffith 1979, 2. 533–8; Martin 1985, 104–10; Errington 1986, 55–7. It has often been argued that Philip also organised a coup at Larisa, exiled his former supporters there and imposed a garrison. This theory rests on highly questionable evidence and should be discarded (Martin 1985, 102–4; 255–60).

30 Berve 1926, 2 no. 521 (see [Bosworth, *Conquest and Empire*] p. 171). He was presumably a grandson of Medeius, dynast of Pharsalus in 395 (Diod. XIV.82.5).

31 Hdt. V.3; Thuc. 11.97.5.

32 [Dem.] XII.8; Diod. XVI.71.2. See in general Hammond and Griffith 1979, 2.554–9.

33 Justin XI.5.1; Frontin. *Strat.* II.11.3. On Sitalces see Berve 1926, 2 no. 712.

34 Polyb. XVIII. 14.2–15, *contra* Dem. XVIII.295.

35 Cf. Diod. XVI.34.1; Dem. XXIII.138, with Hammond and Griffith 1979, 2.264–7 (Pammenes); Diod, XVI.44.2, 47.1, 49.1–6.

36 In 357/6 the number of ships in the dockyards is listed as 283 (*IG* II², 1611, line 9); the ships effectively in action at that time are estimated at 120 (Diod. XVI.21.1).

37 Dem. X.37–80; Theopompus. *FGrH* 115 F 166.

38 For a convenient digest of the evidence and recent literature see Rhodes 1981, 514–17.

39 In his speech *On the Chersonese* (Dem. VIII). On the background see Hammond and Griffith 1979, 2.563–6.

40 See now the detailed survey by Gullath 1982, 7–19.

41 For the details see [Bosworth, *Conquest and Empire*] pp. 187ff.

42 Cf. Diod. XVI.48.1, attributing the Egyptian success to their Greek generals, the Athenian Diophantus and the Spartiate Lamius.

43 *Hell.* Ox. 22.4; Xen. IV.1.41 (Agesilaus); Isocr. V.119–20; Xen. *Hell.* VI.I.12 (Iason).

44 Much has been made of the supposed connection between Philip and Hermeias, the dynast of Atarneus in Asia Minor, who died in Persian custody in 341 (for a conservative exposition

of the problem see Hammond and Griffith 1979, 2.518–22). The theory is based on modern speculation and the conviction of the ancient commentators that Hermeias was the agent of Philip obliquely mentioned by Demosthenes (X.32). Even if the identification is correct, Demosthenes is dealing in rumour and innuendo, without knowledge of Philip's intentions. Indeed the tradition on Hermeias has only one explicit statement that he collaborated. Callisthenes (cited by Didymus *in Dem.* col. 6, lines 55–7) says that he died without revealing anything of his agreements with Philip. The context is problematic. Hermeias' death was reported in very different ways and the circumstances were obviously not widely known. Callisthenes at all events spoke of collusion between him and Philip, but what that collusion can have been is a complete mystery.

References

Badian 1976a = E. Badian, 'Some recent interpretations of Alexander', in E. Badian (ed.), *Alexandre le Grand, Image et Réalité*, Fondation Hardt, *Entretiens* 22 (Geneva: 1976), pp. 279–311.

Badian 1982 = E. Badian, 'Greeks and Macedonians', in B. Barr-Sharrar and E.N. Borza (eds.), *Macedonia and Greece in Late Classical and Early Hellenistic Times* (Washington: 1982), pp. 33–51.

Bellinger 1963 = A.R. Bellinger, *Essays on the Coinage of Alexander the Great* (New York: 1963).

Berve 1926 = H. Berve, *Das Alexanderreich auf prosopographischer Grundlage* (Munich: 1926).

Borza 1979 = E.N. Borza, 'Some observations on malaria and the ecology of Central Macedonia in antiquity', *AJAH* 4 (1979), pp. 102–124.

Borza 1982 = E.N. Borza, 'The natural resources of early Macedonia', in W.L. Adams and E.N. Borza (eds.), *Philip II, Alexander the Great, and the Macedonian Heritage* (Lanham MD: 1982), pp. 1–20.

Bosworth 1980a = A.B. Bosworth, *A Historical Commentary on Arrian's History of Alexander* 1 (Oxford: 1980).

Bosworth 1986 = A.B. Bosworth, 'Alexander the Great and the Decline of Macedon', *JHS* 106 (1986), pp. 1–12.

Brunt 1976 = P.A. Brunt, 'Anaximenes and King Alexander I of Macedon', *JHS* 96 (1976), pp. 151–153.

Demandt 1972 = A. Demandt, 'Politische Aspekte in Alexanderbild der Neuzeit', *Archiv für Kulturgeschichte* 54 (1972), pp. 325–363.

Develin 1985 = R. Develin, 'Anaximenes (*FGRHist* 72) F4', *Historia* 34 (1985), pp. 493–496.

Errington 1975b = R.M. Errington, 'Samos and the Lamian War', *Chiron* 5 (1975), pp. 50–57.

Errington 1978 = R.M. Errington, 'The nature of the Macedonian state under the monarchy', *Chiron* 8 (1978), pp. 77–133.

Errington 1986 = R.M. Errington, *Geschichte Makedoniens* (Munich: 1986).

Gullath 1982 = B. Gullath, *Untersuchungen zu Geschichte Boiotiens in der Zeit Alexanders und die Diadochen* (Frankfurt am Main: 1982).

Hamilton 1969 = J.R. Hamilton, *Plutarch, Alexander: A Commentary* (Oxford: 1969).

Hammond and Griffith 1979 = N.G.L. Hammond and G.T. Griffith, *A History of Macedonia* 2 (Oxford: 1979).

Lock 1977a = R.A. Lock, 'The Macedonian Army Assembly in the Time of Alexander the Great', *CP* 72 (1977), pp. 91–107.

Markle 1978 = M.M. Markle, 'Use of the Macedonian Sarissa by Philip and Alexander of Macedon', *AJA* 82 (1978), pp. 483–497.

Martin 1982 = T.R. Martin, 'A phantom fragment of Theopompus and Philip II's first campaign in Thessaly', *HSCP* 86 (1982), pp. 55–78.

Martin 1985 = T.R. Martin, *Sovereignty and Coinage in Classical Greece* (Princeton: 1985).

Parke 1933 = H.W. Parke, *Greek Mercenary Soldiers* (Oxford: 1933).

Rhodes 1981 = P.J. Rhodes, *A Commentary on the Aristotelian Athenaion Politeia* (Oxford: 1981).

Schachermeyr 1973 = F. Schachermeyr, *Alexander der Grosse: das Problem seiner Persönlichkeit und seines Wirkens* (Vienna: 1973).

Tronson 1984 = A. Tronson, 'Satyrus the Peripatetic and the marriages of Philip II', *JHS* 104 (1984), pp. 116–126.

3

ALEXANDER'S AIMS

Introduction

Alexander became king in 336 when Philip II was assassinated.[1] From the outset his aims were apparently clear: to succeed his father as king and hegemon of his League of Corinth,[2] and to fulfil Philip's last plan, the invasion of Persia (Diod. 16.89.2, Arr. 2.14.4, 3.18.12). In order to achieve both, he had to reimpose the Macedonian hegemony of Greece, for the Greeks revolted on Philip's death: this he achieved within a matter of months (Diod. 17.3–4, Arr. 1.1.1–3), and in early spring 334 he left for Persia (Arr. 1.11.3). Although Philip had greatly stimulated Macedon's economy, the need for money and to keep the army on campaign may have been the real purpose of the invasion, for we have reference in the sources to Alexander being hard-pressed for revenue when he invaded Persia (see Sources 17 and 18; *contra* 45). However, the official reason – as put forward by Philip in 337 – was to inflict revenge on the Persians for their sacrilegious looting of Athens in 480 during the Persian War (cf. Source 19) and to liberate the Greek cities under Persian rule in Asia Minor. This was the 'mandate' of the League of Corinth, and it would presumably follow that once Alexander achieved it he would return home. Alexander did not; he intended to bring down the Persian empire (Sources 42, 43 and 48), and afterwards he pressed onwards to India. He would have continued going further had not his army mutinied on him at the Hyphasis river in 326,[3] forcing him to turn back for Greece (Source 77).[4]

Alexander probably did not aim to march as far east as he did. Things changed with the amount of time he spent in Asia and its influence on him.[5] His spectacular military successes were certainly a factor in his continued advance, as Alexander grew to know nothing other than fighting. However, his visit to the oracle of Zeus Ammon at Siwah in 331 (Sources 92–97),[6] at which he had apparently been confirmed as a son of Zeus, was a turning point not only in his attitude to his own divinity but also in his future aims (cf. Source 100). As Alexander continued east, he underwent a drastic transformation, appearing in his dress and manners more like an oriental potentate than a Macedonian warrior king, and his desire to outdo the exploits of his heroic ancestors Heracles and Dionysus is one reason why he decided to invade India (cf. Source 70).[7] However, it appears startling for his empire and his kingship that he developed the aim of moving the capital from Pella to Babylon, or perhaps even Alexandria.

Ancient sources

17   To provision these forces,[8] Aristobulus (*FGrH* 139 F 4 = Source 18) says he had not more than seventy talents; Duris (*FGrH* 70 F 40) speaks of maintenance for only thirty days; and Onesicritus says he owed two hundred talents as well (Onesicritus, *FGrH* 134 F 2 = Plut. *Alex.* 15.2, [Plut.] *Mor.* 327d).

18   [Alexander went to Asia] trusting only to the strength of thirty thousand foot and four thousand horse. For so many there were, by the account which Aristobulus gives; by the relation of King Ptolemy (*FGrH* 138 F 4), there were thirty thousand foot and five thousand horse [. . .] Now the glorious and magnificent sum which Fortune had raised up to supply the necessities [. . .] was no more than seventy talents, according to Aristobulus (Aristobulus, *FGrH* 139 F 4 = Plut. *Alex.* 15.1–2, [Plut.] *Mor.* 327d–e, 342d).[9]

19   Of his campaign against Porus[10] he himself has given an account in his letters. But the Hydaspes, made violent by the storm and dashing high against its bank, made a great breach in it, and a large part of the stream was setting in that direction; and the shore between the two currents gave his men no sure footing, since it was broken and slippery. And here it was that he is said to have cried: 'O Athenians, can you possibly believe what perils I am undergoing to win glory in your eyes?' This, however, is the story of Onesicritus; Alexander himself says that they left their rafts and crossed the breach with their armour on, wading breast-high in water (Onesicritus, *FGrH* 134 F 19 = Plut. *Alex.* 60.1, 5–7).

Modern works

In the following extracts, P.A. Brunt, formerly Camden Professor of Roman History at the University of Oxford, talks of Alexander's invasion of Persia as simply his inheritance from Philip, and his advance to India as something of a natural extension of Alexander's military campaigning and the product of his own growing religiosity. E.A. Fredricksmeyer, formerly Professor of Classics at the University of Colorado, however, argues that Philip had more ambitious plans, which included the establishment of an absolute monarchy in a new empire, and his own deification. If so, then Alexander's inheritance was not a simple invasion of Persia, and his aims were different from what is commonly believed.

1   P.A. Brunt, 'The Aims of Alexander', *Greece and Rome*[2] 12 (1965), pp. 205–215.[11]
2   E.A. Fredricksmeyer, 'On the Final Aims of Philip II', in W.L. Adams and E.N. Borza (eds.), *Philip II, Alexander the Great, and the Macedonian Heritage* (Lanham, MD: 1982), pp. 85–98.[12]

Additional reading

As for Chapters 4–6, 8–9.

Notes

1   Diod. 16.91.1–94.4, Arr. 1.1.1, Plut. *Alex.* 10.6.
2   On this, and on Alexander's dealings with the Greeks, see Chapter 4.

3 Diod. 17.94.3 ff., Arr. 5.25.2 ff., Curt. 9.3.3–5.
4 See Chapter 6.
5 See Chapter 5.
6 Strabo 17.1.43, Arr. 3.3–4, Plut. *Alex.* 27.8–10; cf. Diod. 17.51, Curt. 4.7.25, Justin 11.11.2–12.
7 See Chapter 6.
8 For the invasion of Persia.
9 On numbers see, however, Source 45.
10 The Indian prince, in 326: see Chapter 6.
11 Reprinted with the permission of Oxford University Press.
12 Reprinted with the permission of the author.

THE AIMS OF ALEXANDER[1]

P. A. Brunt

Sir William Tarn wrote that 'the primary reason why Alexander invaded Persia was, no doubt, that he never thought of *not* doing it; it was his inheritance'. The invasion had been planned and begun by Philip. It was, in name, a Panhellenic enterprise, to exact retribution for the devastation wrought by Xerxes in Greece and to liberate the Greeks of Asia Minor.[2] These aims Alexander faithfully fulfilled. From the spoils of the Granicus he dedicated three hundred Persian panoplies to Athens' tutelary goddess; he sent back to Athens the statues of Harmodius and Aristogiton which Xerxes had carried off to Susa; and he excused the burning of Persepolis as a reprisal for the sack of Athens.[3] The Panhellenic war was then over, and Alexander sent the Greek contingents home (A. iii. 19. 5). In general he freed the Greek cities of Asia from the control of satraps; they were to pay no taxes, to receive no garrisons and to live under their own laws.[4] By expelling tyrants or oligarchs and setting up democratic governments, he not only removed the partisans of Persia from power but did homage to the growing tendency in Greece to equate freedom with democracy.[5] The gratitude of the liberated cities was long-enduring; it was here that his cult survived into Roman times.[6] In reality of course they were as much subject to his will as less privileged subjects. And to Greek cities that opposed him he was less accommodating. Halicarnassus and Aspendus, which certainly counted as Greek, were subjected to his satraps.[7] They could be treated as disloyal to the Panhellenic cause, like the captive mercenaries who fought against him at the Granicus and who were sent back in chains to forced labour in Macedon. But Alexander was not always so merciless. He spared the mercenaries who were holding out against him on an island in the harbour of Miletus, and enlisted them in his own army; it would not have been easy to take the island by force.[8] Sentiment and principle gave way to his own interests, as they always did.

Polybius says that Philip launched the crusade against Persia to win goodwill in the Greek world.[9] If he entertained such a hope, it was plainly delusory. The persistent propaganda of Isocrates for a national war against Persia had fallen on deaf ears. Since 412 all the leading Greek cities had vied with each other in seeking Persian subsidies or diplomatic support. None had any reason to fear Persian aggression; like the Romans after Augustus' death, the Persian kings were content with their *fines imperii*; bent on restoring control over Asia and Egypt, they had been very willing to promote internal discords among the Greek cities under the name of 'the freedom and autonomy of every city, great or small'. The sense of natural antagonism between Greeks and barbarians can easily be exaggerated,[10] and in any event to Greeks of the fourth century, even to Isocrates, Macedonians too were barbarians (though the ruling dynasty had a recognized claim to be regarded as Greek),[11] and it was they, not Persia, whose power menaced Greek freedom. Demosthenes and king Agis took Persian gold,[12] and the Thebans in 335 called on their fellow Greeks to fight for liberty in concert with the great king.[13] They were right; in his last year Alexander showed that he meant to be master in Greece. Between 336 and 322 most Greek cities were in arms at one time or another against the Macedonian power.[14] Alexander himself suffered no illusions;[15] he knew that he could not in 334 rely on a Greek fleet to dispute the mastery of the seas with the Persians, and the Greek contingents in his army played only a subordinate role in the fighting, apart from the Thessalians who owed Philip special gratitude for restoring peace and order in their country. The Panhellenic crusade was a fiction for everyone but modern scholars who suppose that Isocrates' pamphlets were widely admired for anything but their languid eloquence.

Even Isocrates had envisaged a war with a different purpose. Retribution for long distant wrongs hardly interested him;[16] he even showed surprisingly little concern for the 'enslaved' Greeks in Asia.[17] In the *Panegyricus* he had urged that it was folly for the Greeks to contend with each other over a few barren acres, when the wealth of the Persian empire was theirs for the taking. In 346 he had recommended Philip to win fame by conquering lands in Asia for the surplus population of Greece. Philip had sufficient power and wealth already; his reward was to be glory, and the material fruits of his victories were to enure to the Greeks.[18] At Pella this can only have evoked ridicule. For attacking Persia Philip had a Macedonian as well as a Panhellenic pretext, that by aiding Perinthus in 340 the Persians had broken a treaty concluded with him,[19] and he surely intended to annex Persian territory himself. Certainly this was Alexander's purpose from the first. As soon as he had won the battle of the Granicus, he appointed satraps and imposed tribute on the king's Asiatic subjects.[20]

We cannot say how far Philip intended to go. Perhaps he could not have said himself. In 332 Darius offered to cede all his territory west of the Euphrates. Parmenio declared that he would close with the offer, if he were Alexander. 'So would I', replied Alexander, 'if I were Parmenio.'[21] It is often supposed that Philip would have agreed with his old general rather than with his son. There is no warrant for this belief. Philip was an opportunist and his ambitions expanded with his successes. Wilcken thought that he would have been content to make his existing possessions secure by conquering the whole or the greater part of the seaboard of the eastern Mediterranean. But the Macedonians were not a maritime or commercial people, and it was natural for their king to entertain continental ambitions. All his contemporaries knew that the Persian empire was weak in everything but money. Outside Iran, where the nobility shared in the imperial government, the king's subjects in general were discontented, or at best indifferent to a change of masters; kings and satraps had depended heavily on Greek mercenaries who might be seduced by Panhellenic propaganda and were in any event not superior to the Macedonian phalanx; the chief strength of native armies lay in the Iranian cavalry, which had threatened the survival of the Ten Thousand and limited the successes of Agesilaus, but which Alexander's Macedonian and Thessalian horse had a good chance of beating easily; and no one with a distant recollection of the triumphs of Cyrus the Great, whose forces were probably no more numerous at first than Alexander's, could assert that the army Alexander inherited from Philip, well-trained, confident, and by ancient standards large, was incapable of doing what Cyrus had once done.

There is then no difficulty in supposing that when Alexander cast a spear on the Asian shore, he meant to symbolize his intention of conquering Asia, that is to say, the whole Persian empire;[22] to Isocrates (v. 76; 100) 'Asia' is a synonym for the king's dominion. The story indeed comes from Diodorus and the source is poor. But it was Aristobulus, a well-informed authority,[23] who told how early in 333 Alexander untied the Gordian knot and offered sacrifice in thanksgiving to the gods for manifesting by this sign that he was destined to rule over Asia. All the evidence suggests that Alexander was a deeply religious man, sedulous in performing the ceremonies sanctioned by custom,[24] and that he came to believe that he was upheld in his victorious career by the favour of the gods.[25] After Gordium then he can have been in little doubt that he was destined to rule over Asia. He proclaimed this aim before Issus, in his negotiations with Darius in 332, and again before Gaugamela. That victory seemed decisive, and he was then apparently acknowledged as king of Asia by the army.[26] A change soon came over his attitude to Darius. In 332 he had castigated him as a usurper; after his death, he paid him respect as the legitimate ruler, and seems to have represented himself in some peculiar way as the heir of the Achaemenids, whose tombs he was zealous to restore.[27] This was natural enough; he had seen the loyalty and courage of the Iranian nobility in defending their king, and he wished to bind them to himself by similar sentiments.

It is not likely indeed that Alexander was guided at any time in his life by purely rational calculations. Devoted to the reading of Homer, he conceived himself as a second Achilles,[28] born

αἰὲν ἀριστεύειν καὶ ὑπείροχον ἔμμεναι ἄλλων.

The spirit of heroic adventure mingled with an insatiate curiosity. The oft-recurring phrase that he was seized with a longing to do or see things that no one or only a few had done or seen before seems to come down from Ptolemy and Nearchus, who were among his most intimate companions.[29] His almost uninterrupted successes engendered in him the conviction that he was permitted to achieve what was denied to ordinary mortals. More than once we are told that the more impracticable a project appeared, the more he was determined to undertake it;[30] though at other times, it is true, he was ready to adopt the prudent courses that caution recommended,[31] this unparalleled audacity served him well by making enemies surrender at the mere terror of his name. In the Indian campaigns a new motif comes to the fore in the emulation of Heracles and Dionysus. The Macedonians, misinterpreting what they heard of local legends, thought that they had found traces that Heracles and Dionysus had preceded Alexander on his march. This idea was very congenial to Alexander. At the rock of Aornus he even found himself able to do what Heracles had failed to do. When he heard of Dionysus' presence at Nysa, and of his foundation of the city, he *wanted* the story to be true and conceived the hope that he might also outstrip the god. Many such stories come from inferior sources and may be disbelieved; but the particular incidents mentioned (and indeed others) were recorded by the best authorities and must be credited.[32] Tarn indeed ridicules the whole tradition on the ground that it makes Alexander into an imitative character.[33] This is a very curious view. To excel the achievements of beings who were thought to have attained to godhead by their terrestrial beneficence was an ambition that could be entertained only by a man conscious of his own transcendent powers, and to Greeks might well have been the basis of a charge of *hybris*. Again, it was Nearchus who told that Alexander sought to outdo Cyrus and Semiramis by traversing the desert of Baluchistan; and this must be believed against the official apologia for an enterprise probably hardly less disastrous than Napoleon's Russian campaign. Here *hybris* was indeed attended by *ate* and *nemesis*.[34]

Long before this, Alexander had been addressed at Siwah by the prophet of Ammon as 'son of Zeus' and, if we may adopt a plausible suggestion of Tarn, had been told within the sanctuary the sense in which he, the new Pharaoh, was of divine filiation.[35] As son of Zeus or Ammon – the identification was not new[36] – he did not cease to be the son of Philip; he never denied his earthly paternity. But he had heard that there was some mystical sense in which he could claim a divine origin too. Perhaps he was not at once convinced; but at Gaugamela he prayed for the help of the gods 'if indeed he was the son of Zeus', and the help came.[37] The prayer is attested by Callisthenes, and (despite his final quarrel with Alexander) that court historian must be supposed to have written either what was true or what he knew would please the king; whichever hypothesis we adopt, we must conclude that the claim to be the son of Zeus was one that Alexander made, if not before the battle, then at least by the time that Callisthenes wrote. Callisthenes also recorded that Apollo at Branchidae and the Sibyl of Erythrae confirmed the prophet of Ammon; we may surmise that Callisthenes gave the interpretation placed officially on ambiguous responses.[38] Probably Alexander's prolonged victories made him more and more certain that he was in some sense divine. There is indeed no proof of this in his unsuccessful attempt to impose *proskynesis* on his Macedonian and Greek entourage; this was an act of respect due in Persian society from inferior to superior, and, living in the country, Alexander cannot have continued to share the mistaken view prevalent in Greece that it was a recognition of divinity. His aim must here simply have been to establish uniformity in court etiquette.[39] But his deification at the end of his reign is another matter. The evidence that he himself demanded acknowledgement of his godhead from the Greeks, slender as it is, seems to me sufficient in the absence of any directly conflicting testimony;[40] and it ought not to be rejected simply on the ground that he had no rational motive for such a demand; Tarn was certainly wrong in holding that as a god a king could have a legitimate excuse for intervening in the affairs of cities whose autonomy he had guaranteed.[41] But the evidence from Greece is powerfully confirmed by what we know of his emulation of Heracles and Dionysus, by the statement of Eratosthenes that the Macedonians were apt to invoke τὸ θεῖον to please Alexander,[42] and above all by the explicit testimony of Aristobulus that Alexander expected to be acknowledged, like 'Dionysus', as a god by the Arabians.[43]

The Greeks did not make the sharp distinction between the divine and the human which we have derived from Jewish thought. But the traditional view that it was proper for mortals θνητὰ φρονεῖν was not extinct; it was only after Alexander that apotheosis became a conventional honour for kings or benefactors in Greece, and in Macedon it was not claimed by later kings. Even if we make the initiative for Alexander's deification come from Greeks who felt gratitude to him or wished to flatter him, it is hard to explain the choice of this still strange mode of doing him honour except on the assumption that it was believed to correspond to his own desires. Arrian's conjecture that he sought apotheosis to enhance his dignity (vii. 29) is not satisfying. A man so devout would hardly have aspired to divinity unless he had felt that he had a religious justification. Long ago Empedocles, one of the most religious of Greek thinkers, had written: 'I go among you as an immortal god, no mortal now, honoured among all as is right, crowned with fillets and flowery garlands.'[44] Why should we not suppose that Alexander too was imbued with a sense of divine inspiration, power and beneficence, sown in his mind by the teaching of Ammon and other oracular responses and confirmed by his superhuman achievements which made him feel himself to be the equal of Dionysus, entitled to the adoration of mankind? He knew of course that he would die, or rather quit this life;[45] but that had been the fate of Heracles and Dionysus. At any rate the belief in his divinity was accepted even by his proud Macedonian officers; for after his death his former secretary, Eumenes, induced them to set up a golden throne in the camp, before which they all did daily sacrifices and obeised themselves to Alexander as a god, taking counsel from his divine will and ever-living spirit.[46] Like Caesar,[47] and unlike any other deified king, Alexander commanded genuine veneration.

To a god upon earth the allegiance of all mankind was rightly due. In India Alexander expected universal submission and treated resistance as revolt,[48] even when he had passed beyond the confines of the empire the Achaemenids had once ruled.[49] Some held that he aimed at reaching the mouth of the Ganges and the encircling Ocean stream.[50] Even on Eratosthenes' later reconstruction of the eastern hemisphere he was not seemingly so far distant from this objective when he had reached the Hyphasis.[51] Here mutiny turned him back; but he had not forsworn conquests, and took his army homewards by a devious route that involved more fighting and brought him to the Ocean at the Indus delta. Certainly he did not (as Tarn holds) abandon any of his Indian acquisitions; the principalities of Porus and Taxilas were still regarded as parts of the empire after his death, and their status was not different in principle from the kingdoms of Cyprus and Phoenicia.[52] After his return to Mesopotamia he was still bent on more wars; he promised his veterans at Opis to give them rewards enough to incite the new Macedonian drafts to be ready to share the same dangers and exertions.[53] His immediate projects comprised the exploration of the Caspian, surely as a prelude to the deferred campaign against the Scyths,[54] and the conquest, not the mere circumnavigation, of Arabia; Aristobulus said that he intended to take possession of the country and found colonies there as part of a design to be 'lord of all'.[55] We are told that he left behind him memoranda for a gigantic plan of conquest in the west that would have taken him along the southern shore of the Mediterranean to the Ocean at Gibraltar (where Heracles once again had preceded him) and then along the northern shore back to Macedon.[56] Arrian has nothing of this, but then he has nothing about *any* plans of Alexander (except for the Caspian and Arabian projects). And Arrian himself had no doubt that Alexander would never have been content with what he had already conquered.[57] The authenticity of Alexander's reputed memoranda has been questioned, but in my view on quite insufficient grounds. The plan attributed to him is in keeping with all that we know of his character. It would have marked a new stage in the attempt to reduce the whole inhabited world, bounded by the Ocean, a world which in the west as in the east appeared much smaller than we know it to be.[58]

A prudent ruler, governed by rational calculations, would clearly not have embarked on such an enterprise. Large tracts of the old Persian empire were still not pacified.[59] Whatever administrative changes in its ramshackle structure be ascribed to Alexander, the conduct of some of his satraps during his long disappearance behind the barrier of the Hindu-Kush had shown that their independence could still, as under the Achaemenids, threaten the stability and unity of the empire. Greece was smouldering with discontent; even the loyalty of Macedon and its vice-gerent, Antipater, who did not comply with Alexander's summons to his court in 324, could not be counted on.[60] To secure the gains he had already made, Alexander needed decades of patient organizing work. It was not enough to remove or punish (as he did) officials whom he suspected of infidelity or oppression. But there is no sign that he had any taste for the humdrum routine of administration.

Not that he lacked statesmanlike views. He sought to turn nomads into settled, peaceful cultivators of the soil,[61] to foster economic development[62] and to create cities as centres of civilization.[63] In some, but not all, of his foundations there were Greek and Macedonian settlers; as, even in these, natives were brought within the walls and the Greeks and Macedonians were no doubt expected to solace themselves with native wives, mixed communities were likely to be formed, in which the culture would surely be Hellenic, as in the older ethnically mixed cities of Ionia,[64] and from which Hellenic ideas would radiate to barbarians, as in fourth-century Caria and Lycia.[65] Alexander himself was devoted to Greek culture, and I suspect that he never thought of his realm as being other than fundamentally Hellenic; it is said that he had Greek taught to Darius' family and to the children his soldiers had had by native women.[66] Not that he despised barbarians. We are told that he rejected Aristotle's advice to treat barbarians as enemies and to behave to them as a master might towards slaves; experience showed him, as indeed it showed Aristotle, that the distinction between natural masters and slaves was not to be equated with that between Greeks and barbarians.[67] Phoenicians, Iranians, Indians, all rendered him valuable services; he needed Orientals to fill the ranks of his army and to administer subjects with whose languages and customs they were familiar. He recognized local laws, left natives to manage local affairs, and even appointed Iranians to satrapies and admitted them to his entourage. To reconcile them to his rule, he progressively adopted Persian dress and court ceremonial. All this aroused opposition among old-fashioned Macedonians. Alexander was prepared to crush it without mercy, but he wished also to effect a genuine union of hearts. The notion of Tarn that he originated the concept of the brotherhood of men is indefensible; the concept was not new and it was not Alexander's.[68] What he prayed for at Opis was harmony between the old ruling class of the Persian empire and the Macedonians; it was *their* lives, customs, and marriages he proposed 'to mix as in a loving-cup'.[69] He approved of his soldiers having children by native women, though they were to be brought up in Macedonian ways.[70] He himself married two Iranian princesses and virtually forced his chief officers to do likewise.[71] Overriding all resentment, he went ahead with plans to incorporate Orientals both in the Companion cavalry and in the phalanx.[72] He always assumed that his invincible will would surmount every obstacle, of sentiment no less than of armed resistance. His colonies illustrate this: established in sites carefully chosen for strategic or commercial value, they were designed to become great cities and by their names to perpetuate his own; for the feelings of conscribed settlers who 'yearned for the Greek way of life and had been cast away in the extremities of the kingdom'[73] he cared nothing. Admirable as these aims were, one may yet feel that he did not possess 'le tact des choses possibles'. But who can say what his iron resolution might not have achieved, if fate had not denied him the long life needed to bring his purposes to fruition?

His early death would have mattered less if he had had an able successor to carry on his work. The rise of Macedon to power had long been retarded by disputes over the succession and by the turbulence of the nobility. Philip had attached the great nobles more closely to the court,[74] but the danger of dynastic quarrels remained, and it was not unreasonable for Demosthenes and other Greeks to hope, after 346 and even after 338, that Macedonian power would disintegrate. Alexander's old advisers, Antipater and Parmenio, had pressed him not to invade Persia before he had married and begotten an heir.[75] He rejected the advice, and at his death he still had no child. Roxane was indeed pregnant, and her unborn son was recognized as the future king. But like all minors who ascended the Macedonian throne, Alexander IV was not suffered to survive for long. The chief Macedonian generals were bent on securing their own power, if necessary at the expense of the unity of the empire; no less independent and ambitious than their ancestors, in the world that Alexander had transformed, they could aim at the acquisition of kingdoms or empires rather than petty principalities. But they had to take more account than Alexander had done of the prejudices of the common soldiers on whose support they relied, prejudices which indeed most of them probably shared; and if some of them adopted his plan of settling Greeks and Macedonians in the east, it was to assure themselves of a supply of fighting men rather than to promote the diffusion of a common and mainly Hellenic culture in their kingdoms, though Hellenization was naturally a result of their policy. The deliberate attempt to found a world-empire based on reconciliation and unity between Macedonians and Iranians faded in their incessant wars.

According to Plutarch Alexander had sought to be 'a governor from God and a reconciler of the world; using force of arms against those whom he failed to bring together by reason, he united peoples of the most varied origin and ordered ... all men to look on the *oikoumene* as their fatherland, the army as their citadel and guardian, good men as kin, and wicked as foreigners; he taught them that the proof of Hellenism lay in virtue and of barbarism in wickedness.'[76] This objective could be achieved only by blood and iron, and by the will of a despot who was prepared to override the sentiments of his subjects; and though the world was to be united in government and culture, there is no concept here of the brotherhood of all men as sons of a common Father, but at best only of those who possessed *arete*. Neither Alexander nor anyone else realized the objective, and it may be doubted if in his own mind it was so clearly defined as in Plutarch's ideal description. But his work tended in this direction and helped to inspire not only perhaps Stoic philosophers but the Romans, who were also to transcend national differences and to conceive that Italy had been marked out to unite scattered empires, to humanise customs, to give mankind a common speech and to become 'una cunctarum gentium in toto orbe patria'.[77]

Notes

1 I thank Professor Badian for comments on an earlier draft; any errors or misinterpretations are my own. I have sought in general to illustrate statements in the text with references to sources that depend on undoubtedly contemporary authorities; this does not imply that I regard the 'inferior' tradition as worthless, or the contemporary authorities such as Ptolemy as reliable at all points. Plutarch is cited from the Loeb edition.
2 Polyb. iii. 6.8 ff.; D. xvi. 89. 2; 91.2; xvii. 24. 1; A. ii. 14. 4.
3 A. i. 16. 7; iii. 16. 7–8; 18. 11–12; vi. 30. 1.
4 Cf. Badian, [*Greece and Rome*[2] 12 (1965)] p. 169.
5 A. H. M. Jones, *The Greek City from Alexander to Justinian* (Oxford, 1940), ch. x.
6 *Inschr. von Priene* 108, 75; *OGIS* 3.
7 A. i. 23. 8; 27. 4. Halicarnassus Greek (*contra* Tarn ii. 218), Hdt. ii. 178; vii. 99.
8 A. i. 16. 6; 19.6.
9 Polyb. iii. 6. 8 ff.

10 The grant of privileges to Sidonians at Athens and the foundation of cults of Isis there (Tod 139; 189) are revealing.

11 Isocr. v. 107–8 (cf. Hdt. v. 20–22; viii. 137–9). Arrian's sources also distinguish Greeks and Macedonians, e.g. *Ind*. 18. 6–7 (Nearchus).

12 Aeschin. iii. 239 ff.; Dinarch. i. 10; 18; Plut. *Dem*. 20; A. ii. 13. 6.

13 D. xvii. 9. 5; cf. 62 (Agis).

14 Some cities saw in Philip or Alexander a protector against powerful and aggressive neighbours, cf. Polyb. xviii. 14; thus Argos and Messene were pro-Macedonian from fear of Sparta, but they too rose against Macedon in the Lamian war, when Sparta was prostrate, as did the Thessalians (D. xviii. 11).

15 A. i. 18. 8; 29. 6; ii. 17, etc.

16 But see iv. 155; 183; 185; v. 124–6 (?).

17 But see iv. 181; xii. 103; *ep*. ix. 8.

18 iv. 131–3; 174; 182; 187; v. 9; 84–85; 107–8; 112; 120–2; 129–45.

19 A. ii. 14. 2.

20 A. i. 17. 1 and 7.

21 A. ii. 25.

22 D. xvii. 17. 2. For another view cf. Badian, [*Greece and Rome*[2] 12 (1965)] pp. 166 ff.

23 Cited in A. ii. 3. 7.

24 A. iii. 16. 9; 25. 1; vi. 3. 1, &c.

25 A. ii. 7. 3; 14. 7; iii. 3. 4; v. 3. 1; 29. 1. The story in Callisthenes (Jacoby, *Fragm. d. griech. Hist.* no. 124) F 31 that the Pamphylian sea miraculously receded to allow Alexander's march past Mount Climax was in all histories of Alexander (Jos. *Ant. Jud.* ii. 348), cf. A. i. 26. 2, and obviously found favour with him.

26 A. ii. 7. 6; 12. 5; 14. 8–9; iii. 9. 6; P. 34.

27 Contrast A. ii. 14. 5 with iii. 22. 1; vi. 29, &c.

28 A. i. 12. 1.

29 V. Ehrenberg, *Alexander and the Greeks* (Oxford, 1938), ch. ii.

30 A. ii. 26. 3; iv. 21. 3; vi. 6. 3; 24. 3.

31 A. i. 18; ii. 17; iii. 9. 1 and 4; but Arrian's own reflections in iii. 10. 3–4 illustrate how Alexander's conduct should *not* be interpreted, in view of the evidence in 10. 2.

32 A. ii. 16; iii. 3; iv. 28; 30. 4; v. 2; 3. 2; vi. 3. 4–5; 14. 2; vii. 20 (all from Ptolemy or Aristobulus or both). Tarn ii. 45 dismisses A. v. 2 as a mere *logos* of the inferior tradition, but wrongly; the first section in *oratio recta* guarantees what follows down to section 7 in *oratio obliqua* as coming from one or both of the main sources (cf. ii. 12. 3–6 for their account in the form of a *logos* in *oratio obliqua*); in section 7 a change of source in explicit.

33 Tarn ii. 51 ff. wrongly ascribing the tradition to Clitarchus.

34 A. vi. 24. 2 f., cf. Strabo xv. 1. 5. On the Gedrosian march cf. H. Strasburger, *Hermes* lxxx (1952), 456 ff. A. vi. 21. 3–22. 3; 23. 1–24. 1; 27. 1 come from an official, apologetic source (presumably Ptolemy) which rationalized Alexander's motives and minimized the disaster; 22. 4–8 from Aristobulus, and 24. 1–26. 5 either from him or, as Strasburger argues, from Nearchus, a reliable source whichever view be adopted, whose account agreed with all others and with modern travellers' descriptions of the desert; Strasburger reckons that Alexander lost three-fourths of the army that went with him.

35 Strabo xvii. 1.43 (Callisthenes), cf. Tarn ii. 353 ff.

36 Tarn's objections (ii. 348 ff.) cannot stand against the texts of Pindar he cites and Hdt. ii. 42; 55. A Greek could not be certain of the true name of Zeus, cf. Aesch. *Agam*. 160 ff.

37 P. 33.

38 Strabo xvii. 1.43.

39 J. P. V. D. Balsdon, *Historia* i (1950), 353 ff.

40 See esp. Dinarch. i. 94; Hyper. *contra Dem*. 31; *epitaphios* 21 (on which cf. E. Bickermann, *Athenaeum* xli (1963), 70 ff.; in my view the present ἀναγκαζόμεθα relates not to Athens, but to Greece generally, or rather cities not yet freed).

41 E. Bickermann, *CPh*. xlv (1950), 43 (review of Tarn).

42 A. v. 3. 1.

43 A. vii. 20. 1; Strabo xvi. 1. 11; cf. L. Pearson, *Lost Histories of Alexander the Great* (New York, 1960), 184.

44 Diels, *Fragm. d. Vorsokratiker* I⁶ B 114.

45 μεταλλάττειν, *OGIS* 4; D. xviii 56. 2.

46 D. xviii. 60–61; Plut. *Eumenes* 13.

47 Suet. *Caes.* 88.

48 A. vi. 15. 5; 17. 1–2, &c.

49 Persian rule had once extended to the Indus (Hdt. iv. 44; A. *Ind.* 1), not beyond; nor in Alexander's time so far (Strabo xv. 1. 26); even the Indus country was no longer known, A. vi. 1; *Ind.* 20; 32.

50 A. iv. 15. 5–6; v. 26 (but the reliability of this speech is called in grave doubt by D. Kienast, *Historia* xiv (1965), 180 ff.).

51 J. O. Thomson, *Hist. of Anc. Geography* (Cambridge, 1948), 135.

52 A. v. 29. 4–5; C. x. 1. 21; D. xviii. 3. 2; 39. 6; xix. 14. 8.

53 A. vii.8. 1.

54 A. vii. 16, cf. iv. 15.

55 A. vii. 19. 3 ff., cf. Strabo xvi. 1. 11.

56 D. xviii. 4; C. x. 1. 17–19. Tarn's criticisms are answered by F. Schachermeyr, *Jahreshefte der österr. arch. Inst.* (1954), 118 ff.

57 A. iv. 7. 5; vii. 1. 4.

58 Thomson, op. cit. 139 ff.

59 Perdiccas conquered Cappadocia after Alexander's death (D. xviii. 16); Armenia remained unsubdued.

60 E. Badian, *JHS* lxxxi (1961), 16 ff.

61 A. *Ind.* 40. 7–8 (Nearchus). For the motive cf. Tac. *Agr.* 21.

62 A. iii. 1. 5 (cf. P. 26); iv. 25. 4; vi. 15. 2; 21. 5; vii. 21; Strabo ix. 2. 18; xvi. 1. 9–11.

63 Jones (op. cit. in n. 5, p. 51), ch. 1. Native towns, e.g. A. ii. 27. 7; iv. 28. 4.

64 Hdt. i. 146.

65 Tod 138 (Caria); A. T. Olmstead, *Hist. of the Persian Empire* (Chicago, 1948), 348–50; 360; 391–2; 405–6 (Lycia).

66 D. xvii. 67. 1; P. 47. 3 (cf. A. vii. 12). For Alexander's culture see P. 4. 1 and 6; 7–8; 10. 4; 11. 6 (= A. i. 9. 10); 26. 1; 29. 1–3 (cf. A. iii. 6. 1); A. i. 12. 1, &c.

67 E. Badian, *Historia* vii (1958), 440 ff.

68 Badian, op. cit. 425 ff.; P. Merlan, *CPh.* xlv (1950), 161 ff.

69 A. vii. 11. 8–9; Plut. *Mor.* 329.

70 A. vii. 12.

71 A. iv. 19; vii. 4.

72 A. vii. 6; 11; 23.

73 D. xviii. 7.

74 e.g. Alexander the Lyncestian, Leonnatus, and Perdiccas (cf. Berve's biographies); see also A. iv. 13. 1.

75 D. xvii. 16.

76 P. 329.

77 Pliny, *NH* iii. 39.

ON THE FINAL AIMS OF PHILIP II

E. A. Fredricksmeyer

Abstract

According to the traditional and prevailing view, the final aims of Philip II, in contrast to those of his son Alexander, were reasonable, cautious, and limited. There is some evidence to indicate, however, that they were in fact much more ambitious. This paper examines the evidence and concludes that there is a good possibility, which must not be discounted, that on the eve of his invasion of Asia Philip hoped to conquer and supersede the Great King, to establish in all parts of his greater empire, as far as possible, an absolute monarchy, and to secure, finally, his own deification. It likely that deification was not merely an end in itself for Philip, for the sake of the glory of it, but that he hoped to establish a theocratic basis for his absolute monarchy, and to institutionalize this new kingship for his successors. If this is correct, Alexander in his policies and ambitions followed Philip's paradeigma more closely than has been hitherto acknowledged. It may well have been the apprehensions on the part of some Macedonian nobles over Philip's final ambitions which led to his assassination in the summer of 336 BC.

Introduction

Philip was assassinated in July 336 BC on the eve of his invasion of the Persian Empire. Officially, as an assignment of the League of Corinth, the war was to be a crusade against the Persians for the injuries inflicted by them on the Greek gods and temples in their invasion of 480–79 BC.[1] Beyond this, Philip harboured ambitions of his own. What were they?

In their assessment of Philip's final aims, historians have been influenced, consciously or unconsciously, by the contrast between Philip and his more dramatic son, Alexander. Alexander is seen as the youthful conquerer of titanic ambitions who won for himself new worlds and changed the course of history. Philip, however, is seen as prudent and cautious, and middle-aged, who pursued a purely national Macedonian policy, and whose final aims against Persia were limited to the annexation of Asia Minor or at most the conquest of the eastern Mediterranean seaboard, to secure his domain in Europe. This perception is given weight by the *auctoritas* of the leading historians in the field, and at present it remains virtually unchallenged. It may well be correct.[2] But it rests entirely on speculation and inference. There exists not a single piece of evidence which directly attributes these goals to Philip. On the other hand, there is some specific evidence to the effect that Philip's aims by the end of his life were considerably more ambitious. The case for this conclusion has occasionally been argued before, at least in part, but without securing acceptance.[3] It deserves further examination. *Audiatur et altera pars.*

The background

First, let us consider whether in Philip's time, say around 338 BC, a war of conquest against the Persian Empire was thought to have a realistic chance of success. The Empire was a heterogeneous entity comprised of many peoples, races, and traditions held together precariously by the dynasty of the Achaemenid kings, who laid claim to absolute dominion by grace of their supreme deity Ahuramazda, that is, by right of conquest. In the fourth century, the Empire was weakened by a series of rebellions and secessionist movements by subject peoples and ambitious satraps. A potential invader out to conquer the Great King could expect, to a considerable extent, mere token resistance or active cooperation, especially in the Western parts of the Empire. And the Persians were known to be militarily inferior to the Greeks. For decades now the Persian kings had succeeded in maintaining or restoring the territorial integrity of the Empire only with the help of Greek mercenaries, who provided the only effective infantry the Persians could muster. The Persians' strength lay in their cavalry, but at Chaeronea Philip proved the superiority not only of the Macedonian infantry over the Greek hoplites but also, by implication, of the Macedonian cavalry over their Persian counterparts.[4]

Moreover, there were on record several attempts, either planned or attempted, to conquer the Great King and seize his kingdom. In 401 BC the younger Cyrus with the help of Greek mercenaries invaded the interior of the Empire with the design of challenging the Great King for the throne of Asia. Cyrus was killed in the battle at Cunaxa near Babylon, but in this battle and in their subsequent retreat to the Black Sea the Greeks demonstrated their superiority over the Orientals.[5] Isocrates expressed the opinion (5.92) that if it had not been for Cyrus, the Greeks "would have overthrown the power of the King." In 396 BC the Spartan king Agesilaus undertook an offensive against the Persians in Asia Minor, and Isocrates claimed (4.144) that "he conquered almost all the territory this side of the Halys river." It was believed that Agesilaus' intention was to march into the interior in order to overthrow the Great King and destroy his Empire.[6] But difficulties in Greece forced him to abandon his plan and return home. Not long afterwards, Jason of Pherae conceived similar ambitions which were, however, brought to naught by his assassination in 370 BC. It was thought that Jason hoped to make himself master of the Balkan peninsula, and then to invade and destroy the Persian Empire.[7] Xenophon quotes him as saying (*Hell* 6.12):

> It is even easier to reduce [the Great King] to subjection than to reduce Greece. For I know that everybody there, save one person, has trained himself to servitude rather than prowess, and I know what manner of force it was – both that which went up with Cyrus and that which went up with Agesilaus – that brought the King to extremities.[8]

In 346 BC Isocrates addressed an open letter to Philip in which he appealed to Jason in urging Philip to unite the Greeks and lead them in a war against the Persians (5.120):

> Now since Jason by use of words alone advanced himself so far, what opinion must we expect the world will have of you if you actually do this thing; *above*

all, if you undertake to conquer, [helein] the whole empire of the King or, at any rate, to wrest from it – to use a current phrase – "Asia from Cilicia to Sinope."

After detailing some of the advantages to be obtained for the Greeks from a conquest of Asia Minor (5.120–23), Isocrates continues (5.123): "If however you do not succeed in these objects [i.e., seizing the whole Empire or Asia Minor], this much you will at any rate easily accomplish, – the liberation of the cities which are on the coast of Asia."

On the eve of Philip's invasion, by mid-summer of 336 BC, this last-stated minimum goal had already been largely achieved, in Philip's sense, by his advance force under Parmenio and Attalus. He would not have launched, with the greatest possible fanfare, the main invasion of Asia only to put the finishing touches to these operations conducted by his subordinates. As for the other two objectives, Isocrates presents the first one, the conquest of the Persian Empire, as the most desirable. But he quickly proceeds to a discussion of the second one, the seizure of Asia Minor, not, as has been thought, because he considered the conquest of the Empire unrealistic, but because he considered the seizure of Asia Minor more profitable for the Greeks. Isocrates thought consistently in terms of Greek, specifically Athenian, interests, and understandably so.[9] At the same time, he hoped to be taken seriously as a counselor of practical policy. We may be reasonably sure that Isocrates considered the conquest of the Persian Empire as feasible, or at least that he expected Philip and a large part of the audience to consider it feasible.[10]

Two years later, in 344 BC, Isocrates wrote again to Philip. After rebuking him for taking unnecessary risks in battles with barbarians (Illyrians), he says (*Ep* 2.11):

> As to the barbarians with whom you are now waging war, it will suffice you to gain the mastery over them only so far as to secure the safety of your own territory, *but the king who is now called Great you will attempt to overthrow [kataluein].*[11]

In 338 BC, after Philip's victory at Chaeronea, Isocrates once again called on Philip to lead the Greeks against the barbarians and to compel them, except for those who would fight on his side, to be subject to the Greeks. And he adds (*Ep*. 3.5): "And to accomplish this from your present status is much easier for you than it was for you to advance to the power and renown you now possess from the kingship which you had in the beginning."[12]

In the fall of 338 BC Philip formalized his domination of Greece achieved at Chaeronea by the establishment of the League of Corinth and then placed before it the proposal of a panhellenic crusade against Persia. Those of the Greeks who would have opposed the plan were in no position to do so, and Philip was elected for the purpose *strategos autokrator*, generalissimo with full powers (Diod. 16.89.2–3). The historian Polybius clearly perceives, however, that Philip's motive was not a desire to punish the Persians for the greater glory of the Greeks, but personal opportunism and the desire for conquest and glory. After stating that Philip was encouraged by the successes of the Ten Thousand and of Agesilaus, Polybius says (3.6.12–13) that Philip

> perceived and reckoned on the cowardice and indolence of the Persians compared with the military efficiency of himself and his Macedonians, and

further fixing his eyes on the splendor of the great prizes which the war promised, he lost no time, once he had secured the good will of the Greeks, but seizing on the pretext that it was his urgent duty to take vengeance on the Persians for the injurious treatment of the Greeks, he bestirred himself and decided to go to war, beginning to make every preparation for the purpose.[13]

The conquest of the Persian Empire

In the spring of 336 BC Philip, according to Diodorus (16.91.2–3), "wanting to enter upon the war with the gods' approval, asked the Pythia *whether he would conquer [kratēsei] the king of the Persians.* She gave him this response: 'The bull stands wreathed. The end is near. The one who will smite him stands ready.' Since the response was ambiguous, Philip accepted it in a sense favorable to himself, namely *that the Persian would be slaughtered like a sacrificial victim.*"[14] After noting that in the end the oracle foretold Philip's own death, Diodorus says (16.91.4):

> In any case, he thought that the gods supported him and he was very happy *that Asia would be made captive [aichmalōtou] under the hands of the Macedonians.*[15]

Diodorus continues (16.91.4–92.3) that Philip thereupon made plans for a great festival and splended sacrifices to the gods. When the occasion arrived, at a state banquet the famous actor Neoptolemus recited several poems which had been commissioned by Philip on the subject of the impending war. In one of them he addressed the great wealth of the Persian king, suggesting that "it could some day be overturned by fortune," and predicting the death of the Great King. After remarking that the remainder of the poem went on in the same vein, Diodorus continues (16.92.4):

> Philip was enchanted with the message and was completely *occupied with the thought of the overthrow [katastrophēn] of the Persian king, for he remembered the Pythian oracle which bore the same meaning as the words quoted by the tragic actor.*

We have seen that Philip took the oracle to mean *that Asia would be made subject (aichmalōtou) to the Macedonians.* Thus the statement that Philip expected the *overthrow (katastrophēn)* of the Persian king appears to mean not that he expected to win some battles and seize some territory but that he expected to take his kingdom from him.

Two years later, Alexander crossed the Hellespont to start the war which Philip had planned. Diodorus, apparently on the authority of Clitarchus, says (17.17.2) that he

> hurled his spear from the ship and fixed it on the ground and then leapt ashore himself the first of the Macedonians, signifying *that he received Asia front the gods as his spear-won [doriktēton] property.*[16]

Two years after this, at Marathus, in northern Syria, Alexander wrote a letter to Darius in which, according to Arrian (2.14.7–9), he called himself *Lord of all Asia* and *King of Asia.* and claimed that *he held the country by gift of the gods.*[17] Although Alexander was painstakingly scrupulous in his dealings with the gods, he apparently did not seek an oracle before the start of the invasion.[18] Why not? And how could he nevertheless both at the Hellespont and again now claim Asia as gift of the gods? At the Hellespont, Alexander claimed to receive Asia from the gods as *doriktētos*, while Philip had interpreted his oracle for the war as signifying that Asia would be *aichmalōtos* under Macedonia. The two words mean virtually the same thing. The conclusion is justified that just as Alexander inherited from Philip the project of the war and its official slogan, so he also applied to himself the oracle which Philip had received for the war, and Philip's interpretation of it, to wit, that he would conquer the Persian Empire.[19]

Absolute monarchy

How would Philip rule over his vast new domain? It was reasonably apparent that it could not be administered easily, if at all, as an appendage of Macedonia. The most feasible, possibly the only, arrangement would be the one which also Alexander aspired to from the beginning, that is, to become the new king of Asia.[20] There is evidence that this is indeed what Philip had in mind. We learn from a fragment of Philodemus (*Rh*. II, 61 ed. S. Sudhaus) that Aristotle

> tried to warn Philip against the [Achaemenid] kingship and the Persian succession (ἐ[κ] βασιλείας παρεκάλει [Φ]ίλιππο[ν] τότ[ε] καὶτῆς Περσικῆς διαδ[ο]χῆς).

This information not only corroborates the belief that Philip aimed to conquer the Persian Empire, but it also indicates that he meant to supersede the Great King, for otherwise there would have been no point for Aristotle to advise against it.

Why would Aristotle advise against it? The Persian kingship, as virtually all rule in the Orient, meant absolute rule. The Orientals knew no other, and any limited rule, even if considered desirable on some theoretical ground, was not practically feasible. The whole Persian Imperial system, from the court ritual to the dynastic religion and art, served above all the enhancement and glorification of the power and majesty of the Great King.[21] Even though Philip probably did not intend to adopt in detail the Persian Imperial system, it was yet clear that his Asiatic kingship would necessarily mean an absolute monarchy over the Asiatics. And it was predictable that this situation would also affect Philip's relationship with the Macedonians and Greeks in Asia, and eventually also his role as king of Macedonia and as Hegemon of the League. No doubt it was the fear that Philip's Achaemenid succession would have a harmful effect on Greece, in particular that his preponderant power as king of (or over) Asia would eventually reduce the Greeks to the status of mere subjects, that moved Isocrates in his address to Philip to propose only *en passant* the seizure of the whole Empire, and that likewise moved Aristotle, like Isocrates a fervent Hellenist, to advise Philip against the Persian kingship. Similarly Aristotle later urged Alexander, perhaps after the latter's proclamation as King of Asia in Oct. 331 BC. (Plut. *Alex* 34. 1). to treat "the barbarians as a despot [*despotikōs*] but the Greeks as a leader [*hēgemonikōs*]" (Plut. *Mor.* 329 B).[22] And in 327 BC Aristotle's nephew, Callisthenes, forfeited his life by opposing Alexander's design to apply his Oriental kingship to the Greeks.[23]

The desire for power was Philip's driving motivation from the beginning of his career, as the record shows, both in his expansionist foreign policy and in his self-aggrandizement at home. Beyond this, it has been shown recently, with some probability, that in the development of his court system and the organization of his kingship, Philip followed to a considerable extent Persian models. In particular the institutions of the court aristocracy recruited in part from foreigners, the Royal Pages, the Hypaspists, the initiation of a harem for political ends, all seem to have been patterned more or less closely on their Persian counterparts.[24] Evidently Philip here followed a carefully designed program. It has been said that in the development of his own supra-national kingdom there was no other model at hand.[25] True. But just as the very soul of the Persian system was the principle of the absolute sovereignty of the Great King, so Philip in imitating this system no doubt also hoped to increase, as much as possible, his own power over the Macedonians. It seems reasonable to conclude that Philip's aim may well have been, after the conquest of the Persian king, to establish an absolute monarchy, as far as possible, in all parts of his empire.

Deification

Beyond this, there is evidence that Philip aspired to the supreme honors. *A priori*, his divine descent from Zeus and Heracles, in addition to his royal rank, placed him in a position of superiority over most mortals.[26] And it appears that, beginning with 359 BC, several Greek cities accorded Philip divine or near-divine honors as benefactor or savior.[27] Moreover, after Chaeronea Philip commissioned the construction at Olympia of a temple that was to house, apparently, a dynastic cult for himself and his family (Paus. 5.20.9–10; cf. 5.17.4).[28] The edifice was completed around the time of Philip's assassination.

On the morning of the assassination, Philip staged a parade into the theatre crowded with people from everywhere. His own entry was preceded in solemn procession by the statues of the Twelve Gods. And accompanying them was Philip's own statue. Diodorus says (16.92.5):

> Along with lavish display of every sort, Philip included in the procession statues of the Twelve Gods wrought with great artistry and adorned with a dazzling show of wealth to strike awe in the beholder, and along with these was conducted a thirteenth statue, suitable for a god, that of Philip himself, so that the king exhibited himself enthroned among the Twelve Gods.

As Philip himself reached the entrance, the assassin struck. Diodorus relates the deed and then comments (16.95.1):

> Such was the end of Philip, who had made himself the greatest of the kings in Europe in his time and because of the greatness of his kingdom had made himself a throned companion of the Twelve Gods.

This information may be taken to mean that through the exhibition of his statue in the procession Philip indicated to the audience that he deserved divine honors, that he deserved them on par, and perhaps in conjunction, with the Twelve Gods, and that he deserved them by virtue of his power as king.[29] Apparently there were those in the audience who were willing to grant these honors on the spot. According to a report preserved by the Macedonian compiler and polymath Ioannes Stobaeus (4.34. 70 p. 846 ed. Wachsmuth-Hense) the tragic actor Neoptolemus, the same who on the preceding day had recited the portentous poetry, was an eye-witness and later commented that he had seen Philip "taking part in the procession and *being invoked* (*epiklēthenta*) *as the thirteenth god*."s There is no reason to doubt the historicity of this information. It provides corroboration for the report of Diodorus.

We may be quite certain that at the end of the procession, in the theatre, sacrifices were planned to the Twelve Gods, and the presence of Philip's statue with theirs in the procession on an equal level must have caused many in the audience to expect that Philip too was to receive a sacrifice. Yet it is difficult to believe that this was really Philip's plan. On this occasion, on the eve of the panhellenic war against Persia, it was important for Philip to court popular good will. His deification, or self-deification, now would surely have provoked as much resentment as approval. It is reasonable to postulate, therefore, that Philip's intention was, after first raising the expectation of his deification, then conspicuously to refrain from it, to demur. Thus he would impress the people with his restraint yet also serve notice, or at any rate suggest, that he deserved the honors and that they might be granted at some time in the future.

At what time? Most modern historians appear to think that the occasion for the procession was the wedding celebration of Philip's daughter and Alexander of Epirus.[30] This is not quite correct. The wedding celebration seems to have been concluded on the previous day. At any rate, certainly the main occasion for this day's activities was the celebration of the imminent invasion of Asia and of the oracle's prediction for it (Diod. 16.91.4).[31] If then at the very celebration of the projected conquest of Persia Philip served notice that he deserved divine honors, but abstained from them at this time, despite the eagerness of some of his partisans, the suggestion was clear that he hoped to obtain them at the time when he would have achieved his goal. Philip commissioned his temple at Olympia on the eve of his proposal to invade Persia, and it was completed, as has been noted, around the time of his assassination. But here too it is difficult to believe that Philip intended to initiate a cult at this time. There certainly is no evidence for it. It is probable therefore that both at Olympia and at Aegae Philip intended the same effect, to serve notice that he expected divine honors after his conquest of the Persian king.

In this light, a statement which Isocrates made in his last address to Philip assumes added significance (*Ep.* 3.5):

> Be assured that a glory unsurpassable and worthy of the deeds you have done in the past will be yours when you shall compel the barbarians – all but those who have fought on your side – to be serfs to the Greeks, and when you shall force the king who is now called Great to do whatever you command. *For then will naught be left for you except to become a god* [*theon genesthai*].

If Philip had already previously received divine honors in several places, including Athens, it is highly probable that Isocrates meant the statement literally, and that he expected others, and Philip himself, to take it literally. We may have here, then,

Isocrates recommending *expressis verbis* what Philip himself at Olympia and Aegae only suggested, namely, deification after the conquest of the Great King.

For what purpose? The cult at Olympia, if instituted, would be a dynastic cult. The suggestion at Aegae was that Philip deserved a cult as king, by virtue of his great power. If, as noted, Philip had already received cults in several individual locales, including Athens, Isocrates' statement that after conquering the Great King Philip "become a god," without limiting qualification, amounted to the suggestion that he receive a universal cult, as ruler of his empire.[32]

This might have been its own end, for the glory of it. But perhaps Philip, forever the pragmatist and politician, wanted more. As for his association with the Twelve at Aegae, it is noteworthy that their cult constituted, or was part of, the state cult at Athens and probably most, or all, other Greek cities, as well as in Macedonia.[33] At Athens, the oaths taken by these gods were officially binding on the city.[34] The same may have held true of other cities. It is quite possible therefore that by association with the cult of the Twelve, perhaps as *Theos Triskaidekatos*, Philip hoped to be acknowledged as an official deity in the Greek communities and even in Macedonia, and thus to acquire there a supralegal and constitutional status.[35] In 324 BC Alexander requested divine honors from the Greek cities,[36] and it is reported in the case of Athens that a cult was proposed for him as *Theos Triskaidekatos* (Ael. *VH* 5.12). The same might have happened elsewhere. Those who made the proposal no doubt knew what Alexander wanted. And Alexander had been present at Philip's procession with the Twelve at Aegae. It is therefore quite likely that Philip on that day at Aegae provided the model for Alexander's design twelve years later.

As for Persia, the Great King did not receive divine honors, but he was nevertheless considered to be of divine descent, to be possessed of a divine quality, and to hold an intermediate position between god and man.[37] In view of this fact, and of Herodotus' statement (1.135) that there was "no nation which so readily adopts foreign ways as the Persians," it would not seem difficult for Philip to introduce his deification in Asia. In 327 BC Alexander attempted to introduce among *all* his subjects, Greeks and Macedonians as well as Asiatics, the Persian *proskynesis*, obeisance.[38] To the Persians, *proskynesis* to the Great King did not mean worship but it nevertheless acknowledged his status as semi-divine.[39] To the Greeks and Macedonians, *proskynesis* meant worship.[40] It has been argued, perhaps correctly, that Alexander on this occasion attempted to introduce his cult as god of his empire.[41] If this is correct, and if this was also Alexander's final aim in 324 BC, we may see here again the influence of Philip.

Conclusion

The possibility should not be discounted that in 336 BC Philip hoped, *deis volentibus*, to conquer and supersede the Great King, to establish in all parts of his greater empire, as far as possible, an absolute monarchy, and to secure, finally, his deification as ruler, to the end of providing a theoretical support for absolute monarchy. As things turned out, it was Alexander who conquered the Persian Empire, and he did so in less than ten years. In 336 BC. Philip may have expected, with longevity apparently running in the family, to live another twenty or even thirty years. If we remember that Cyrus the Great undertook the conquest of his, the Persian, empire from a power-base quite inferior to Philip's at this time, a fact which Philip no doubt appreciated, and that Antigonus Monophthalmus not many years later set out, at age 63, to make himself master of Alexander's empire, it is not difficult to believe that at age 46 Philip harbored comparable ambitions. It may have been the apprehensions on the part of some Macedonian nobles over Philip's final aims that led to his assassination on that fateful day at Aegae in 336 BC.[42]

Notes

1 Diod. 16.89.2; Polyb. 3.6.13. Cf. Arr. 2.14.4; 3.18.12; Polyb. 5.10.8.

2 F. Schachermeyr is representative. He concedes that Philip's aims may have extended to Syria and Egypt. But: "Von grundsätzlicher Bedeutung [ist es] dass Philip über den somit umschriebenen Mittelmeerraum niemals hinausgegriffen hätte, dass ihm also der Radikalismus ferne lag, etwa das gesamte Perserreich zu gewinnen." *Alexander der Grosse* (Vienna 1973) 62. Cf. J. Kaerst, *Geschichte des Hellenismus* I[3] (Leipzig and Berlin 1927) 272 ff.; Ed. Meyer, *Kleine Schriften* (Halle 1910) 245 f., 291, 293 f., 297; G. Radet, *Alexandre le Grand* (Paris 1931) 81; U. Wilcken, *Alexander the Great* (New York 1967; with notes and bibliography by E. Borza) 30; G. Wirth, "Dareios und Alexander," *Chiron* 1 (1971) 143 f.; Ellis, *PMI* 227 ff., 308 n. 72; Griffith, *Hist Macc* II 633 and 691. F. Geyer, *RE* 19 (1938) 2299, grants that he might have gone as far as the Euphrates.

3 Most important, F. Hampl, *Die griechischen Staatsverträge des 4. Jahrhunderts* (Leipzig 1938) 89 ff. See also H. U. Instinsky, *Alexander der Grosse am Hellepont* (Bad Godesberg 1949) 39 f.; H. Berve, *Griechische Geschichte* II (Freiburg 1963) 244. Cf. V. Chapot, "Philippe II de Macédoine," in *Hommes d'état* I, ed. A. B. Duff and F. Galy (Paris 1936) 102; P. Cloché, *Un fondateur d'empire. Philippe II roi de Macédoine* (Saint Etienne 1955) 278. However, note also the view of A. Momigliano, *Filippo il Macedone* (Florence 1934) 166: "Fino a che punto Filippo mirasse di portare la sua conquista dell' Asia nessuno naturalmente sa, e il primo a non saperlo era forse Filippo stesso."

4 For a judicious assessment of the *Machtverhältnisse* at this time, see P. A. Brunt, Loeb *Arrian* I. LXIII–LXVIII, with refs.

5 See, conveniently, H. Bengston, *Griechische Geschichte*[4] (Munich 1969) 262 ff., with refs.

6 Xen. *Hell.* 4.4.41; *Ages.* 1.36; cf. 7.7; Plut. *Ages.* 15.

7 Xen. *Hell.* 6.1.8–12; Isoc. 5.119.

8 This and the following translations from the Greek are from the Loeb editions, with minor changes.

9 U. Wilcken, *Philip II. von Makedonien und die panhellenische Idee* (Sitzungsberichte der Preussischen Akademie der Wissenschaften, Berlin 1929) 296 f. See also S. Perlman, "Isocrates' 'Philippus' – a Reinterpretation," *Historia* 6 (1957) 317, and G. Dobesch, *Der panhellenische Gedanke im 4. Jr. v. Chr. und der "Philippos" des Isokrates* (Österreichisches Archäologisches Institut, Vienna 1968) 144 ff.

10 See also Isoc. 5.124–26, 132, 139, 141. Cf. M. Markle, "Support of Athenian Intellectuals for Philip: A Study of Isocrates' *Philippus* and Speusippus' *Letter to Philip*," *JHS* 96 (1976) 86: "Isocrates understood that, if he was to win the favor of Philip by his pamphlet, he must not be taken for a dreamy intellectual who, though unaware of the means for carrying out his proposal, presumed to advise the world's most successful military leader." Already around 380 BC, in the *Panegyricus*, Isocrates said (4.166): "Whenever we [i.e., the Greeks] transport thither [to Asia] a force stronger than his [the Great King's], which we can easily do if we so will, we shall enjoy in security the resources of all Asia. Moreover, it is much more glorious to fight against the King for his empire than to contend against each other for the hegemony." And in the same speech (4.131) he noted, as well, that it lay in the power of the Lacedaemonians, in cooperation with the Athenians, "to reduce *all* barbarians to a state of subjection to the whole of Hellas." See also 4.154, 186, and G. A. Lehmann, "Die Hellenika von Oxyrhynchos und Isokrates' 'Philippos'," *Historia* 21 (1972) 393. Some allowance, of course, must be made for rhetorical exaggeration in Isocrates.

11 For the date of the letter, see Markle (supra n. 10) 88 n. 15.

12 On the authenticity of the letter, see Markle (supra n. 10) 89 n. 21.

13 Cf. J. G. Droysen, *Geschichte des Hellenismus* I (Berlin 1877) 50: "[Dareios] mochte ahnen, wie sein ungeheures Reich, in sich zerrüttet und abgestorben, nur eines äusseren Anstosses bedürfe, um zusammenzubrechen."

14 Diodorus' sources in the latter part of book 16 remain very much in doubt. See esp. Griffith *Hist Macc* II 459; C. B. Welles, *Diodorus of Sicily* VIII (LCL) 4 f.; N. G. L. Hammond, "The Sources of Diodorus Siculus XVI," *CQ* 31 (1937) 79 ff.; M. Sordi, *Diodori Siculi Bibliothecae Liber XVI* (Florence 1969) XII ff. The information must be taken on its merits. Most historians regard it as historical.

The oracle is cited in identical form by Paus. 8.7.6. H. D. Parke and D. E. W. Wormell consider it authentic: *The Delphic Oracle* (Oxford 1956) I 238; II. no. 266. J. Fontenrose considers it spurious: *The Delphic Oracle* (Berkeley 1978) 67. But it is to be noted that Fontenrose's whole approach in this book seems excessively sceptical and rationalistic. However, if the oracle as quoted is not authentic, but the remainder of Diodorus' account is substantially accurate, we should suppose that Philip doctored it for his own end.

15 "Asia" at this time usually was synonymous with the Persian Empire. See, e.g., P. A. Brunt, "The Aims of Alexander," *G&R* 12 (1965) 208. Sometimes, however, as used by Greek writers, it connotes only "Asia Minor." But in light of Diodorus' statement a little further on (16.92.4) that Philip expected the "overthrow" (*katastrophēn*) of the Persian King, it more probably here means "the Persian Empire."

16 Cf. Just. 11.5.10. See W. Schmitthenner, "Über eine Formveränderung der Monarchie seit Alexander dem Grossen," *Saeculum* 19 (1968) 31 ff.; E. Badian, "Alexander the Great, 1948–67," *CW* 65 (1971) 83.

17 On the letter, no doubt authentic, see esp. Schachermeyr (supra n. 2) 222 ff., and A. B. Bosworth, *A Historical Commentary on Arrian's History of Alexander* I (Oxford 1980) 232.

18 See Parke–Wormell (supra n. 14) I, 240 and 242; II, 110; J. R. Hamilton, *Plutarch Alexander. A Commentary* (Oxford 1969) 34 f.

19 Cf. Instinsky (supra n. 3) 29 ff., Hampl (supra n. 3) 92 ff.; P. A. Brunt (supra n. 15). The oracle was reinforced for Alexander at Gordium and perhaps also at Siwah. See E. A. Fredricksmeyer, "Alexander, Midas, and the Oracle at Gordium," *CP* 56 (1961) 160 ff.

20 With respect to Alexander, see, e.g., H. Berve, "Die Verschmelzungspolitik Alexanders des Grossen," *Klio* 31 (1938) 145, and J. B. Bury, *A History of Greece* (London 1900) 747.

21 See H. H. von der Osten, *Die Welt der Perser* (Stuttgart 1956) 59 ff.; R. Frye, "The Institutions," in *Beiträge zur Achämenidengeschichte*, ed. G. Walser, Historia Einzelschrift 18 (Wiesbaden 1972) 83 ff.

22 E. Badian, "Alexander the Great and the Unity of Mankind," *Historia* 7 (1958) 440–44, dates the advice nearer to Alexander's accession in 336 BC.

23 See esp. Schachermeyr (supra n. 2) 370 ff.

24 D. Kienast, *Philip II. von Makedonien und das Reich der Achämeniden* (Munich 1973). For the Persian models, see Frye (supra n. 21).

25 Kienast (supra n. 24) 33.

26 Hdt. 8.137; Thuc. 2.99; Isoc. 5.105, 127.

27 See Fredricksmeyer, "Divine Honors for Philip II," *TAPA* 109 (1979) 39–61; C. Habicht, *Gottmenschentum und griechische Städte*² (Munich 1970) 12–16 and 245.

28 See Fredricksmeyer (supra n. 27) 52–56. For a different interpretation, see Griffith *Hist Macc* II 691 ff.

29 Fredricksmeyer (supra n. 27) 56–58. Contra Griffith *Hist Macc* II 682 f. and 695.

30 A Schäfer, *Demosthenes und seine Zeit* III (Leipzig 1887) 67, and Ellis *PMI* 223 have it right.

31 I assume therefore that the invasion was to start very soon afterwards, that is, in the late summer or fall of 336 BC. Philip probably intended to use the bases secured by Parmenio as winter quarters and from there start his main push down the coast and inland in the spring of 335 BC.

32 Isocrates did not think of Greece as a potential part of Philip's empire. He considered a monarchical system indispensable for all others, but contrary to the spirit of the Greeks (5.107, 154). Cf. Perlman (supra n. 9) 310 ff.; K. Bringmann, *Studien zu den politischen Ideen des Isokrates, Hypomnemata* 14, Göttingen 1965) 99 ff. But there were those who welcomed the possibility

of Philip's monarchy over Greece. See K. von Fritz, "Die politische Tendenz in Theopomps Geschichtsschreibung," *A&A* 4 (1954) 56 f. Cf. also Markle (supra n. 10) 87 ff.

33 O. Weinreich, in Roscher's *Ausführliches Lexikon der griechischen and lateinischen Mythologie* IV (1924–27) 764 ff.; U. von Wilamowitz-Moellendorff, *Der Glaube der Hellenen* II (Berlin 1932) 351 n. 1; Berve, *Alex* I 87; K. Atkinson, "Demosthenes, Alexander, and Asebeia," *Athenaeum* 51 (1973) 313 ff.

34 Atkinson (supra n. 33) 331 f.

35 *Ibid.* 330

36 E. A. Fredricksmeyer, "Three Notes on Alexander's Deification," *AJAH* 4 (1979) 1 ff.

37 G. Widengren, "The Sacral Kingship of Iran," *Numen*, Supplement 4 (Leiden 1959) 242–57. Cf. R. Frye, *The Heritage of Persia* (London 1962) 95 f.; *id.*, *Persia* (New York 1969) 23.

38 Arr. 4.10.5 ff.; Curt. 8.5.5. ff.; Plut. *Alex.* 54.3. ff.

39 Widengren (supra n. 37)

40 E. Badian (supra n. 16) 43; W. W. Tarn, *Alexander the Great* II (Cambridge 1950) 360.

41 Meyer (supra n. 2) 314 ff.; Tarn (supra n. 40) 359 ff. Cf. L. Edmunds, "The Religiosity of Alexander," *GRBS* 12 (1971) 386 f.

42 I wish to thank my colleagues for valuable criticisms and observations on an earlier version of this paper read at the Alexander Symposium at the Art Institute of Chicago on June 5, 1981, and Professor Erich Gruen, as well as the editors, for carefully reading the manuscript, as a result of which the paper has been further improved. Any remaining faults are entirely my own responsibility. Finally, I wish to take this opportunity to express my appreciation to my brother-in-law, John English, M.D., for the pleasure of many stimulating conversations over the years on Philip and Alexander.

References

Berve, *Alex* = H. Berve, *Das Alexanderreich auf prosopographischer Grundlage* (Munich: 1926).

Ellis, *PMI* = J.R. Ellis, *Philip II and Macedonian Imperialism* (London: 1976).

Griffith, *Hist. Mace.* II = N.G.L. Hammond and G.T. Griffith, *A History of Macedonia* (Oxford: 1979).

4

ALEXANDER
AND THE GREEKS

Introduction

In 337 Philip II had consolidated Macedonian control of the Greeks by means of what is commonly called the League of Corinth, a union of all Greek states, bound together under the hegemony of the Macedonian king and swearing allegiance to the hegemon of the League.[1] The union was called a Common Peace, meaning that a state was forbidden to wage war against another state; if this happened, then all the other states could combine against the aggressor. Matters affecting the Greeks were to be discussed by the League and then implemented on its authority. Thus, when Philip announced his intention to invade Persia on the pretext of avenging the Athenians for what they had suffered during the Persian War (cf. Source 19) and to liberate the Greek cities of Asia Minor, he did so at a meeting of the League of Corinth (Diod. 16.89.2, Arr. 2.14.4, 3.18.12). The Greek states revolted from Macedonian rule when Philip was assassinated in 336, but Alexander quickly subdued them and reimposed the terms of the League of Corinth (cf. Source 20), including the invasion of Persia.[2] In 335 the city of Thebes revolted from Macedon when news came that Alexander had died during a campaign in Illyria (Arr. 1.5.1). The king was far from dead, and far from forgiving: after a brief siege, he razed their city to the ground and either killed or enslaved the population (see Sources 29 and 30).[3] This action was followed up by his demand for several Athenian statesmen (Source 31), although later he relented. Finally, in 334, Alexander departed to Persia, leaving behind Antipater as regent of Greece and deputy hegemon of the League of Corinth (Arr. 1.11.3).

Alexander had little to do with the mainland Greeks while he was on campaign, although inscriptional evidence attests to his dealings with other Greek states, and some examples are given as Sources 21, 22, 23, and 25; Source 24, dated after Alexander's death, attests to a decision he made in the context of his Exiles Decree (see below).[4] Particularly significant are the king's dealings with the return of exiles to some states and the maintenance or creation of a democratic government (Sources 22 to 25). This shows his decision to involve himself in minute matters pertinent only to the state itself, as the details contained in the Mytilene (Source 23) and Tegea decrees illustrate (Source 25).

Antipater was not faced with any major problem until Agis III of Sparta declared war on Macedon in 331.[5] This abortive attempt to free Greece from Macedonian rule had little support, and it ended in 330 with the Spartans' defeat at the hands of Antipater. As might be expected, the League of Corinth debated the punishment of the few states that had supported Agis, but significantly it referred the fate of the Spartans to Alexander himself (cf. Source 32).[6] Sparta seems to have been the only mainland state that refused to join the Common Peace of the League of Corinth, but it is plausible that after Agis' defeat it was forced to join it. Other cities that may also have joined the League were those of Asia Minor and the neighbouring islands, which were liberated from Persian control by Alexander.

After Agis' war Greece remained passive, and may well have come to accept the Macedonian hegemony given the peace and prosperity it provided after decades of fighting and financial exhaustion. Demosthenes had contacts at Alexander's court (Source 27), but these were merely diplomatic and no plan of revolt was hatched. The League of Corinth continued to function, but the Macedonians came to view it, and the autonomy of the Greek states, as less important. The most explicit example of this attitude came in 324 when Alexander issued his Exiles Decree, which ordered that all Greek cities (excluding Thebes) were to receive back those of their exiles who were not wanted for murder or under a curse, and empowered Antipater to force any unwilling city to do so.[7] This unpopular measure was meant to reduce the potential danger of bands of mercenaries in the empire being hired by ambitious satraps or generals against Alexander. The decree was illegal since it flouted the autonomy of the Greek states, and it was resisted. For Athens, the decree meant not only the return of the exiles but also the loss of the island of Samos, then populated by Athenian cleruchs (Source 24). However, it appears that only one state, Tegea, actually received back its exiles (Source 25). To make matters worse, Greece was still recovering from a major famine during which many *poleis* had received donations of corn (Source 26), and the influx of exiles would have caused more economic chaos.

Alexander's divine status was now a matter of discussion among some Greek states, although it is implausible to connect such recognition with the Exiles Decree.[8] At about the same time, Alexander's imperial treasurer Harpalus, together with a significant number of ships and men, and a large amount of money, sought asylum in Athens (Diod. 17.108.6, Curt. 10.2.1). Here was the potential for an Athenian-led full-scale revolt from Macedonian rule. However, no such revolt came – at least not until after Alexander's death in June 323.

Ancient sources

20 ... escort ... will provide corn ... will provide for each man ... however many as may come. But if ... from where the corn will be acquired ... Alexander ... to a hypaspist[9] a drachma and to the ... every day. Will despatch ... may use the troops if any ... having given corn for ten days will despatch ... will erect in Pydna in the (temple of) Athena (Tod, no. 183).

21 King Alexander dedicated the temple of Athena Polias (Tod, no. 184).[10]

22 In the prytany of Deisitheus, from King Alexander to the people of Chios.[11] All the exiles from Chios shall return home and the constitution in Chios shall be a democracy. Law-writers shall be chosen who will write and correct the laws in order that nothing may be contrary to the democracy or to the return of the exiles, and what has been written or corrected shall be referred to Alexander. The Chians shall provide twenty fully-equipped triremes at their own expense, and these shall sail as long as the other fleet of the Greeks sails with us. Of those who betrayed the city to the barbarians,[12] as many as have escaped shall be exiled from all the cities that share in the peace and are to be arrested in accordance with the resolution of the Greeks; all those who were left behind shall be returned and judged in the Council of the Greeks. If a dispute arises between those who have returned and those in the city, those people shall be judged about this before us. Until the Chians are reconciled, there shall be a garrison among them from Alexander the king, of a size that is sufficient; and the Chians shall maintain it (Tod, no. 192).

23 ... let the kings[13] be favourable to the restored exile, for the reason that the one who was previously in the city has been guilty of a fraud.[14] But if anyone of the returned exiles does not follow these reconciliations, let him no longer have any property from the city nor own anything given to him by those who were previously in the city, but let those who were previously in the city who gave them to him regain these properties, and let the generals again transfer the properties to the one who was previously in the city, for the reason that the restored exile has not accepted the reconciliation, and let the kings be favourable to the one who was previously in the city, for the reason that a fraud has been carried out by the restored exile. If anyone brings a lawsuit about these things, the *peridromoi* and the *dikaskopoi*[15] nor any other magistrate shall bring it to court. It shall be the responsibility of the generals and the kings and the *peridromoi* and the *dikaskopoi* and the other officials, if everything does not turn out as has been written in the decree, to condemn the man neglecting any of the terms written in the decree, so that nothing may come between the restored exiles and those who were in the city previously, but all might be reconciled to one another and live in harmony without intrigue and may abide by the inscribed edict and by the reconciliation written in this decree. And the people shall choose twenty men, ten from the returned exiles and ten from those who were previously in the city. Let these men zealously guard and make sure that nothing will be a source of disagreement forever between those who returned and those who were previously in the city, and concerning the contested properties that those who returned shall be reconciled especially with those who were in the city and with one another, but if not, that they will be as just as possible, and that everyone will abide by the reconciliations which the king judged in his edict and will live in the city and the country in harmony with one another. And concerning money, that the reconciliation may be carried out as much as possible, and concerning an oath that the citizens will swear, concerning all these things, the chosen men are to bring before the people whatever they agree among themselves, and the People, upon hearing, if they think it is beneficial, let them deliberate abut accepting what was agreed among themselves as beneficial, just as in the same way it was decreed previously for those who returned in the prytany of Smithinas. If something is lacking in this decree, let the decision about this lie with the Council. When this decree has been ratified by the People, the entire citizen body on the twentieth day of the month after the sacrifice will pray to the gods that the safety and prosperity of all the citizens will be on the reconciliation between those who returned and those who were previously in the city. All of the priests and the priestesses with public authority will open the temples and the people will assemble together for prayer. The sacrifices that the people vowed when it sent the messengers to the king shall be paid by the kings to the gods annually. And there shall be present at the sacrifice the whole citizen body and the messengers who were sent to the king, from those who were in the city and from those who returned. When the treasurers have inscribed this decree on a stone stele, they are to set it up in the temple of Athena[16] (Tod, no. 201).

24   Decreed by the Council and People, Epicurus, son of Dracon, made the motion.[17] Since Gorgus and Minneon the Iasians,[18] sons of Theodotus, have been good and noble towards the Samians in their exile, and since Gorgus, while staying at the court of Alexander, showed much goodwill and zeal concerning the *demos* of the Samians, and worked eagerly so that the Samians might recover their land quickly, and when Alexander proclaimed in his camp that he would return Samos to the Samians,[19] and the Greeks crowned him because of this, and Gorgus crowned him and sent the news to Iasus to the archons that those of the Samians living in Iasus, when they returned to their native land, should carry away their possessions tax-free and transport would be provided to them, the city of the Iasians meeting the cost, and now Gorgus and Minion (*sic*) promise to do whatever good they are able for the *demos* of the Samians, it has been decreed by the *demos* to bestow citizenship on them on fair and equal terms, both to them and to their descendants, and to assign them by lot to a tribe, both a thousand and a hundred and a clan, and to inscribe their names in the clan, whichever one they obtain by the lot, just as also the other Samians, and the five men who have been chosen shall attend to the inscribing, and this decree is to be inscribed on a stone stele and set up in the temple of Hera, and the treasurer will attend to the cost (W. Dittenberger, *Sylloge Inscriptionum Graecorum*[3] [Leipzig: 1915–24], no. 312).

25   ... king Alexander,[20] the edict is to be inscribed in accordance with those terms corrected by the city, that were objected to in the edict.[21] To the returned exiles shall be given the paternal property which they had when they went into exile, and the women the maternal property, as many as were unmarried and held possession of their property and happened not to have brothers. But if it befell any married woman that her brother, both himself and his offspring, has died, she also shall have the maternal property, and it will not be any more. In connection with the houses, each man shall have one in keeping with the edict. And if a house has a garden next to it, let him not take another. But if there is no garden next to the house but there is one nearby within the distance of a *plethron*, let him take the garden. But if the garden is more than a *plethron* away, let him take one half of it, as also it has been written about the other properties. As for the houses, let the price to be recovered for each house be two minas, and the appraisal value of the houses will be whatever the city decides. And double the value shall be recovered for the cultivated gardens than is stipulated in the law. Monetary claims do not involve the city, and it will not settle either with the exiles or with those who previously stayed at home as citizens. In connection with the festivals, from which the exiles have been absent, the city shall deliberate, and whatever the city decides is to be valid. The foreign court[22] is to judge suits for sixty days. All those who do not file suits within sixty days shall not be allowed to have legal recourse about the properties in the foreign court, but in the civic court ever after. If they later discover something (they may present it) within sixty days from the day that the court was established. If a person does not file suit within this time, it will be no longer possible for him to go to court. If later some people return from exile, when the foreign court is no longer convened, let them lay a claim with the generals of the properties within sixty days, and if there is any opposition to them, the court shall be Mantinea. But if they do not file their suits within these days, no longer shall they go to court. In connection with the sacred monies ... the debts, the city will make these right for the Goddess,[23] the one who has the property will give back half to the returned exile just as the others are to do. And all those who are themselves in debt to the Goddess as guarantors or otherwise, if the man holding the property clearly has discharged the debt with the Goddess, let him give back half to the returned exile, just as the others do, omitting nothing. But if he clearly has not discharged his debt with the Goddess, let him give back half to the returned exile and from his half himself discharge the debt. But if he does not wish to settle, let him give back to the returned exile the entire property, and let the man who has received it discharge the whole debt with the Goddess. As many of the wives of the exiles or daughters who stayed at home, married, or were in exile and later (returned and) married in Tegea, and remaining at home obtained their discharge, these shall not be subject to investigation about their paternal or their maternal property, nor their descendants, except that as many who later went into exile through compulsion and are heading back in the opportunity that currently exists, either themselves or their children, those shall be subject to investigation, both themselves and their descendants, concerning their paternal and maternal property in accordance with the edict. I swear by Zeus, by Athena, by Apollo, by Poseidon that I shall be well disposed towards the returned exiles whom it was decided by the city to receive back, and I shall not bear a grievance against any of them for whatever he may have plotted, from the day on which I swore the oath, and I shall not obstruct the safety of the returned exiles, neither in the ... nor in the government of the city ... edict ... towards the returned exiles ... to the city ... the terms that have been written in the edict concerning ... nor shall I plan against anyone (Tod, no. 202).

26 Sosias son of Calliades was priest. The city[24] gave corn to all of these when there was a corn shortage in Greece:[25] One hundred thousand[26] to the Athenians; sixty thousand to Olympias;[27] fifty thousand to the Argives; fifty thousand to the Larisans; fifty thousand to the Corinthians; fifty thousand to Cleopatra; thirty thousand to the Rhodians; thirty thousand to the Sicyonians; twenty thousand to the Meliboeans; twenty thousand to the Megarians; twenty thousand to the Teneans; fifteen thousand to the Lesbians; fifteen thousand to the Theraeans; fifteen thousand to the Oetaeans; fifteen thousand to the Ambraciots; fifteen thousand to the Leucanians; fifteen thousand to the Carystians; twelve thousand six hundred to Olympias;[28] ten thousand to the Atragians of Thessaly; ten thousand to the Cythnians; ten thousand to the Opuntians; ten thousand to the Cydonians; ten thousand to the Coans; ten thousand to the Parians; ten thousand to the Delphians; ten thousand to the Cnosians; ten thousand to the Boeotian Tanagraeans; ten thousand to the Gortynians; ten thousand to the Eleans; ten thousand to the Palaeraeans of Acarnania; ten thousand to the Megarians; eight thousand five hundred to the Meliboeans; eight thousand to the Phliasians; eight thousand to the Hermionians; six thousand four hundred to the Oetaeans; six thousand to the Troezenians; six thousand to the Plataeans; five thousand to the Iulietans of Cos; five thousand to the Aeginetans; five thousand to the Astyphalaeans; five thousand to the Cytherans; five thousand to the Hyrtacinians; five thousand to the Aeginetans; four thousand to the Carthaeans of Cos; three thousand one hundred to the Cytherans; three thousand to the Ceans; three thousand to the Illyrians; three thousand to the Coresians of Cos; one thousand five hundred to the Ambraciots; one thousand to the Icetyrians; nine hundred to the Cnosians (Tod, no. 196).

27 Aristion. Hyperides, *Against Demosthenes*. This man is a Samian or a Plataean, as Diyllus states (*FGrH* 73 F 2), and a friend of Demosthenes from childhood. He was sent by him to Hephaestion for a reconciliation, as Marsyas says (*FGrH* 135 F 2) in the fifth (book) of *Matters Related to Alexander* (Harpocration, *Lexicon*, s.v. Aristion).

28 Margites: used by Aeschines in his speech *Against Ctesiphon*: 'and he gave Alexander the nickname Margites';[29] and Marsyas in the fifth book of his work *On Alexander* writes that Alexander was called Margites by Demosthenes (Marsyas, *FGrH* 135 F 3 = Harpocration, *Lexicon*, s.v. Margites).

29 But Ptolemy, son of Lagus, tells us that Perdiccas, who had been posted in the advanced guard of the camp with his own brigade,[30] and was not far from the enemy's stockade, did not wait for the signal from Alexander to commence the battle; but of his own accord was the first to assault the stockade, and, having made a breach in it, fell upon the advanced guard of the Thebans. Amyntas, son of Andromenes, followed Perdiccas, because he had been stationed with him. This general also of his own accord led on his brigade when he saw that Perdiccas had advanced within the stockade. When Alexander saw this, he led on the rest of his army, fearing that unsupported they might be intercepted by the Thebans and be in danger of destruction. He gave instructions to the archers and Agrianians to rush within the stockade, but he still retained the guards and shield-bearing troops outside. Then indeed Perdiccas, after forcing his way within the second stockade, fell there wounded with a dart, and was carried back grievously injured to the camp, where he was with difficulty cured of his wound. However, the men of Perdiccas, in company with the archers sent by Alexander, fell upon the Thebans and shut them up in the hollow way leading to the temple of Heracles and followed them in their retreat as far as the temple itself. The Thebans, having wheeled round, again advanced from that position with a shout, and put the Macedonians to flight. Eurybotas the Cretan, the captain of the archers, fell with about seventy of his men; but the rest fled to the Macedonian guard and the royal shield-bearing troops. Now, when Alexander saw that his own men were in flight, and that the Thebans had broken their ranks in pursuit, he attacked them with his phalanx drawn up in proper order, and drove them back within the gates. The Thebans fled in such a panic that being driven into the city through the gates they had not time to shut them; for all the Macedonians, who were close behind the fugitives, rushed with them within the fortifications, inasmuch as the walls also were destitute of defenders on account of the numerous pickets in front of them. When the Macedonians had entered the Cadmea,[31] some of them marched out of it, in company with those who held the fortress, along the temple of Amphion into the other part of the city, but others crossing along the walls, which were now in the possession of those who had rushed in together with the fugitives, advanced with a run into the market place. Those of the Thebans who had been drawn up opposite the temple of Amphion stood their ground for a short time; but when the Macedonians pressed hard upon them in all directions, Alexander presenting himself now in one place now in another, their cavalry rushed through the city and sallied forth into the plain, and their infantry fled for safety as each man found it possible. Then indeed the Thebans, no longer defending themselves, were slain, not so much by the Macedonians as by the Phocians, Plataeans and other Boeotians, who by indiscriminate slaughter vented their rage against them. Some were even attacked in the houses (a few of whom turned to defend themselves), and others as they were supplicating the protection of the gods in the temples; not even the women and children being spared (Ptolemy, *FGrH* 138 F 3 = Arr. 1.8).

30 Timoclea. Theagenes the Theban, who held the same sentiments with regard to his country's welfare with Epaminondas, Pelopidas, and the other most worthy Thebans,[32] was slain in Chaeronea,[33] in the common disaster of Greece, even then when he had conquered his enemies and was in pursuit of them. For it was he that answered one who cried out aloud to him, How far wilt thou pursue? Even (saith he) to Macedonia. When he was dead, his sister survived him, who gave testimony that he was nobly descended, and that he was naturally a great man and excellently accomplished. Moreover, this woman was so fortunate as to reap a great benefit by her prowess, so that the more public calamities fell upon her, so much the easier she bore them. For when Alexander took Thebes and the soldiers fell aplundering, some in one part and some in another, it happened that a man, neither civil nor sober but mischievous and mad, took up his quarters in Timoclea's house. He was a captain to a Thracian company, and the king's namesake, but nothing like him; for he having no regard either to the family or estate of this woman, when he had swilled himself in wine after supper, commanded her to come and lie with him. Neither ended he here, but enquired for gold and silver, whether she had not some hid by her; sometimes threatening as if he would kill her, sometimes flattering as if he would always repute her in the place of a wife. She, taking the occasion offered by him, said: 'Would God I had died before this night came, rather than lived to it; that though all other things had been lost, I might have preserved my body free from abuse. But now seeing it is thus come to pass, and Divine Providence hath thus disposed of it that I must repute thee my guardian, lord, and husband, I will not hold any thing from thee that is thine own. And as for myself, I see I am at thy disposition. As for corporeal enjoyments, the world was mine, I had silver bowls, I had gold, and some money; but when this city was taken, I commanded my maids to pack it up altogether, and threw it, or rather put it for security, into a well that had no water in it. Neither do many know of it, for it hath a covering, and nature hath provided a shady wood round about it. Take then these things, and much good may they do thee; and they shall lie by thee, as certain tokens and marks of the late flourishing fortune and splendour of our family.' When the Macedonian heard these things, he stayed not for day, but presently went to the place by Timoclea's conduct, commanding the garden door to be shut, that none might perceive what they were about. He descended in his morning vestment. But the revengeful Clotho brought dreadful things upon him by the hand of Timoclea, who stood on the top of the well; for as soon as she perceived by his voice that he reached the bottom, she threw down abundance of stones upon him, and her maids rolled in many and great ones, till they had dashed him to pieces and buried him under them. As soon as the Macedonians came to understand this and had taken up the corpse, there having been late proclamation that none of the Thebans should be slain, they seized her and carried her before the king and declared her audacious exploit; but the king, who by the gravity of her countenance and stateliness of her behaviour did perceive in her something that savoured of the greatest worth and nobility, asked her first, What woman art thou? She courageously and undauntedly answered: Theagenes was my brother, who was a commander at Chaeronea, and lost his life fighting against you in defence of the Grecian liberty, that we might not suffer any such thing; and seeing I have suffered things unworthy of my rank, I refuse not to die; for it is better so to do than to experience another such a night as the last, which awaits me unless thou forbid it. All the most tender-spirited persons that were present broke out into tears; but Alexander was not for pitying her, as being a woman above pity. But he admired her fortitude and eloquence, which had taken strong hold on him, and charged his officers to have a special care and look to the guards, lest any such abuse be offered again to any renowned family; and dismissed Timoclea, charging them to have a special regard to her and all that should be found to be of her family (Aristobulus, *FGrH* 139 F 2b = [Plut.] *Mor.* 259d–260d).

31 Then straightway[34] Alexander sent to Athens a demand for the surrender to him of ten of their popular leaders, according to Idomeneus and Duris, but according to the most reputable writers, only eight, namely, Demosthenes, Polyeuctus, Ephialtes, Lycurgus, Moerocles, Demon, Callisthenes, and Charidemus. It was on this occasion that Demosthenes told the Athenians the story of how the sheep surrendered their dogs to the wolves, comparing himself and his fellow orators to dogs fighting in defence of the people, and calling Alexander 'the Macedonian arch wolf'. Moreover, he said further: 'Just as grain merchants sell their whole stock by means of a few kernels of wheat which they carry about with them in a bowl as a sample, so in surrendering us you unwittingly surrender also yourselves, all of you.' Such, then, is the account which Aristobulus of Cassandreia has given (Aristobulus, *FGrH* 139 F 3 = Plut. *Demosthenes* 23.4–6).

32 *Homereuontas.* Used by Aeschines in the oration against Ctesiphon, and applied to the Spartans sent up to Alexander. Cleitarchus says in the fifth (?) book that the hostages given by the Spartans were fifty. Hostages are those given by agreement; *homeresai* means 'to come together'; Homer wrote: 'the messenger from the company came together with me' (Cleitarchus, *FGrH* 137 F 4 = Harpocration, s.v. *Homereuontas*).

Modern works

In the first extract, T.T.B. Ryder, formerly Reader in Classics at the University of Reading, discusses the establishment and organization of the League of Corinth. In the second, N.G.L. Hammond, formerly Professor of Greek at the University of Bristol, and F.W. Walbank, Emeritus Professor of Classics at the University of Liverpool, outline Alexander's dealings with mainland Greeks, those of the islands and Asia Minor. In the third extract Ian Worthington, Professor of Greek History at the University of Missouri-Columbia, describes the Harpalus affair and the Exiles Decree in more detail, and argues how the diplomatic reaction to both affects the Greek attitude to Macedonian hegemony.

1 T.T.B. Ryder, *Koine Eirene* (Oxford: 1965), pp. 102–109.[35]
2 N.G.L. Hammond and F.W. Walbank, *A History of Macedonia* 3 (Oxford: 1988), pp. 72–83.[36]
3 Ian Worthington, 'The Harpalus Affair and the Greek Response to the Macedonian Hegemony', in Ian Worthington (ed.), *Ventures into Greek History: Essays in Honour of N.G.L. Hammond* (Oxford: 1994), pp. 307–330.[37]

Additional reading

E. Badian, 'The Administration of the Empire', *Greece and Rome*[2] 12 (1965), pp. 166–182.

—— , 'Alexander the Great and the Greeks of Asia', in E. Badian (ed.), *Ancient Society and Institutions: Studies Presented to V. Ehrenberg* (Oxford: 1966), pp. 37–69.

—— , 'Agis III: Revisions and Reflections', in Ian Worthington (ed.), *Ventures into Greek History: Essays in Honour of N.G.L. Hammond* (Oxford: 1994), pp. 258–292.

A.B. Bosworth, *Conquest and Empire: The Reign of Alexander the Great* (Cambridge: 1988), pp. 187–228 and 250–258.

V. Ehrenberg, *Alexander and the Greeks* (Oxford: 1938).

N.G.L. Hammond and F.W. Walbank, *A History of Macedonia* 3 (Oxford: 1988), pp. 86–94.

A.J. Heisserer, *Alexander the Great and the Greeks* (Norman, OK: 1980).

F. Mitchel, *Lykourgan Athens: 338–322, Semple Lectures* 2 (Cincinnati, OH: 1970).

S. Perlman, 'Greek Diplomatic Tradition and the Corinthian League of Philip of Macedon', *Historia* 34 (1985), pp. 153–174.

Notes

1 Diod. 16.89.1–3, Justin 9.5.1–6; cf. [Dem.] 17.1. For the decree, see Tod, no. 177. On Philip II, see Chapter 2.

2 See Chapter 3. Source 20 is a fragment of a badly mutilated inscription, probably of considerable length if the context is correct.

3 Diod. 17.8.3–14, Arr. 1.7.1–8.8, Plut. *Demosthenes* 23.1–3, Justin 11.3.8.

4 See also Chapter 5, Sources 33 and 34.

5 Aes. 3.165–166, Diod. 17.48.1, 62.6–63.4, 73.5, Curt. 6.1; cf. Arr. 2.13.4, 3.6.3 and 16.10.

6 Aes. 3.133, Diod. 17.63.1–3, 73.5–6, Curt. 6.1.19–21.

7 Hyp. 5.18, Diod. 18.8.2–7, Curt. 10.2.4, [Plut.] *Mor.* 221a, Justin 13.5.2; cf. Plut. *Demosthenes* 9.1 and [Plut.] *Mor.* 845c.

8 See Chapter 9.

9 A member of the special corps of the Macedonian shield-bearing infantry.

10 At Priene, in either 334 or 330.

11 Alexander's letter to the Chians has survived virtually complete, unlike most of the inscriptional evidence from the reign of Alexander. It is not part of the Exiles Decree of 324 (see above), and may be dated to either 334 or 332 (Heisserer, *Alexander the Great and the Greeks*, pp. 83–95).

12 The Persians.

13 Not kings in the sense of monarchs, but probably elected senior officials of the city.

14 This decree concerns returning exiles to Mytilene on the island of Lesbos. It is not part of the context of Alexander's Exiles Decree, as has often been thought (for example, by Tod), but may be dated to 332: Heisserer, *Alexander the Great and the Greeks*, pp. 131–139 and Ian Worthington, 'Alexander the Great and the Date of the Mytilene Decree', *Zeitschrift für Papyrologie und Epigraphik* 83 (1990), pp. 194–214.

15 Officials with legal powers.

16 The end of the decree is missing, and this conclusion has been restored.

17 This decree may be dated to 321.

18 Iasus was south of Miletus on the coast of Asia Minor. See Source 33 for other honours on these brothers.

19 The context is the king's Exiles Decree of 324: see above. However, it was not until 322/1 that the Samian exiles were fully restored, and it was then that they honoured Gorgus and Minneon with citizenship for their efforts.

20 The name of the king is restored here to Alexander, but Cassander, one of the protagonists in the struggles for Macedonian power after the death of Alexander, would also fit here, although

this is unlikely: see Ian Worthington, 'The Date of the Tegea Decree (Tod ii 202): A Response to the *Diagramma* of Alexander III or of Polyperchon?', *Ancient History Bulletin* 7 (1993), pp. 59–64.

21 This decree concerns returning exiles to Tegea, and may be dated to 324 in the context of Alexander's Exiles Decree. The opening indicates that this is the second version of the Tegeans' plan for the return of exiles; clearly, Alexander had found the original plan unacceptable.

22 A foreign court, perhaps from Mantinea since this is cited below.

23 Athena Alea.

24 Cyrene. The inscription is to be dated to the period 331 to 324.

25 Or perhaps sold corn to Athens at less than the market price given the large amounts cited in the inscription.

26 The figures refer to bushels of corn.

27 This was Olympias the mother of Alexander the Great.

28 This was Olympias the half-sister of Alexander the Great.

29 Aes. 3.160; Margites is a nickname associated with stupidity.

30 The context is the revolt of Thebes in 335.

31 The citadel of Thebes.

32 During the so-called Theban hegemony of Greece, from 371 to 362.

33 The battle fought between Philip II and a coalition of some Greek states (notably Athens and Thebes); Philip was victorious and Greek autonomy came to an end.

34 After the razing of Thebes in 335.

35 Reprinted by permission of the author.

36 © Oxford University Press 1988. Reprinted by permission of Oxford University Press.

37 © Ian Worthington 1994. Reprinted by permission of Oxford University Press.

MACEDONIAN DOMINATION:
THE PEACE OF 338/337 AND AFTER

T.T.B. Ryder

Philip's victory at Chaeronea was decisive. He had defeated the combined army of the Athenians, the Thebans and their allies from central Greece and Achaea, and had forced these states to make separate treaties with him. He put garrisons in Thebes, Chalcis and Ambracia, restored the Boeotian cities that the Thebans had destroyed and freed them from Theban control, dissolved the Athenian confederacy and took over the Chersonese. He then entered the Peloponnese, put a garrison on Acrocorinth and reorganized frontiers in favour of his friends in Arcadia, Messene and Argos. The Spartans alone refused to submit. He was now militarily supreme in Greece and his supporters were in power in most of the cities.[1]

It was only at this point that he summoned the representatives of the cities to a meeting at Corinth and laid before them his new adaptation of Common Peace.[2] In organizing the Peace of 338/337, then, Philip was not trying to use the autonomy principle, as the Spartans, Athenians and Thebans had done, in the course of aggrandisement to win over other states outside his political control or to weaken his enemies by detaching their allies;[3] and he was not using it, as the Persians had done, to preserve the *status quo* of a self-cancelling balance of independent states outside his control. The Peace of 338/337 was a different sort of weapon to Philip than any previous Common Peace treaty had been in the hands of its promoters. It did not represent a settlement short of victory, for, as has been said, Philip's victory was complete; and it was not a compromise by which he conceded any real power.

The actual provisions of the treaty show considerable developments from those of previous treaties, mostly at the expense of the sovereignty of individual cities (whom Philip was able to coerce), but likely also to increase the efficacy of the treaty as a means of preventing war.

First, in the guarantee: there was a compulsory guarantee clause of the usual sort binding all to go to the help of the injured party;[4] also a supra-national body, a synhedrion of representatives of the Greeks,[5] was for the first time set up to decide who was the injured party. These representatives were probably not answerable to the individual cities for the decisions of the synhedrion, and were not necessarily chosen by single cities; further, the decrees of the synhedrion were binding on all cities without ratification, though the entrenched clauses of the original treaty, that all cities should be free and autonomous, could not be overthrown;[6] finally, to organize and lead action taken to implement decisions of the synhedrion the office of Hegemon was created.[7] The wars subsequently conducted by Alexander against the Thebans (in 335) certainly,[8] and by his regent Antipater (in 331) probably,[9] were proclaimed as actions of the Greeks in defence of the treaty, and were the first and only punitive actions carried out in defence of a Common Peace treaty by the general body of the signatories after decisions reached by a set procedure.

Second, in the definition of autonomy: there were clauses in the treaty dealing with possible provocative action by one city against another, especially on the sea, which are known here for the first time, but may have occurred in earlier treaties;[10] the important innovation was an attempt to stop indirect interference from without in the domestic politics of a city: the constitution existing in each city at the time of the treaty was guaranteed, and certain types of foreign-assisted subversion were specifically prohibited;[11] this measure left few loopholes for aggression.

Though Macedonian supremacy particularly affected those powerful cities which had tended to lead or control their smaller neighbours, there does not seem to have been any new prohibition on close federations; Theban control of Boeotia and the Athenian confederacy were broken up after the battle of Chaeronea before the general settlement,[12] but there is evidence that under Alexander the Boeotian and Arcadian leagues continued to exist, and 'common meetings' of the Boeotians, the Arcadians and the Achaeans were the subject of some instructions sent by Alexander to Greece in about 324.[13]

Third, in resolving territorial disputes: thanks to Philip's supremacy, some of these had already been settled in the separate agreements which he had made with cities before the general treaty; it is known that Oropus was taken from the Thebans and given to the Athenians, and that Philip settled disputes between the Spartans and their neighbours by force in favour of the latter, perhaps through an arbitrating tribunal,[14] though the Spartans would not recognize its legality and subsequently remained outside the treaty. The synhedrion now existed as a body to which other problems could be referred; an extant inscription records the arbitration at the synhedrion's request of the Argives in a quarrel between Cimolus and Melos.[15]

Seen in isolation then, this Peace was the best of the Common Peace treaties and came nearest to a formulated compromise between city sovereignty and the rule of law. But it had been imposed by a conqueror, and indeed it seemed in many ways to consolidate his supremacy. The reaffirmation of the autonomy principle did not affect the position of Philip's garrisons in Thebes, Chalcis, Corinth and Ambracia or the other arrangements that he had made after Chaeronea; but, administered by the carefully constituted synhedrion, it was likely to diminish still further the power of the larger cities, who were his chief potential enemies, and to win him further support in the smaller cities, who would see in the treaty a protection from the encroachments of the larger. The guarantee of existing constitutions favoured his friends, who had come to power in many cities on the flood-tide of his success. Moreover, the prospect of peace throughout Greece would please those who for one reason or another cared more for stability and quiet than for national independence, while the whole tendency of making the settlement in the now customary Common Peace form, which had been the basis of Greek international relations for most of the past fifty years, was to disguise the supremacy which Philip in fact held. Finally, apart from these intrinsic advantages which the Common Peace arrangement gave to Philip, he received in the treaty, and by immediately subsequent actions of the synhedrion, special guarantees and special powers; the Greeks were made to swear to respect and defend the rule of Philip and his successors in Macedonia,[16] and he was then elected to the office of Hegemon of the Greeks[17] and appointed commanding-general of a war against the Persians.[18]

Whatever the theoretical merits of the Peace of 338/337, there is no escaping the fact that the Common Peace treaty form, which had emerged originally from the principle of city-state independence, had now become the instrument of domination of all city-states by an external power. It might be thought that this was to be the final failure of the Common Peace experiments.

But Common Peace was not finished. The city-state system was enslaved, but not broken up; the wraith of Common Peace, the treaty of 338/337, saw to that, if to nothing else. If Greece became really free again, Common Peace could still be revived; and, if Macedonian rule continued and Philip's successors proved to be more severe, the reinstitution of the settlement of 338/337 remained a price that the Greeks could expect for their valuable co-operation with a master whose position was less sure than that of Philip. Philip had set up his adaptation of the Common Peace treaty form as a standard of liberality for the governing of relations between the Greeks and their Macedonian rulers.

The treaty of 338/337 had been concluded for ever and guaranteed the kingdom of both Philip and his descendants. On Philip's death in 336 the Greeks were inclined to feel that Macedonian power had died too, and Alexander had to move quickly to assert his position. He evidently regarded the office of Hegemon as his rightful inheritance, and his possession of it was recognized severally by the Greek cities; only the command against the Persians, which had been voted to Philip personally, was voted to Alexander at the meeting of the synhedrion which he summoned at Corinth. Philip's settlement was left unaltered.[19]

At first at any rate Alexander, though in no way compromising his supreme power, tried to observe the letter of the treaty. When in 335 the Thebans on his rumoured death laid siege to the Macedonian garrison and tried to rouse the rest of Greece,[20] he made the punitive war an action of the synhedrion, and it was that body which fixed the fatal sentence, when the Thebans surrendered;[21] and it was that body to which he demanded the surrender of ten Athenian orators who had proposed abrogation of the treaty.[22] The fact that he dropped this demand shows where the real decisions were made.

When he crossed to Asia in 334, Alexander had to delegate his powers as Hegemon to Antipater, whom he left as regent of Macedonia; whether this move was formally approved by the synhedrion is not known. As he advanced into Asia, Alexander left the Greek cities autonomous, though it is not clear whether they were enrolled into the Common Peace treaty and sent representatives to the synhedrion;[23] later, when the Chians rebelled in 332 and assisted the Persians, it is likely that he handed over their ringleaders for judgement to the synhedrion, who passed the decision back to him.[24] In Greece in 331 Antipater was faced with a war against the Spartans, who were supported by some of the other Peloponnesian states, and he probably made this too an action of the synhedrion; certainly he was helped by some of the Greek cities, and at the end referred the fate of the Spartans to the synhedrion, who again passed the decision on to Alexander.[25] But, while such actions as these were formally correct, it is fairly clear that in the Greek cities the oligarchic governments installed under Macedonian protection were being less than just to their political opponents, many of whom were driven into exile.[26]

It was probably the problem created by the vast number of these exiles, of whom many had become skilful soldiers in Alexander's mercenary army, that he tried to solve by his so-called Exiles Decree,[27] which has been widely interpreted as a flagrant violation of the treaty.

The literary sources say only that Alexander sent Nicanor to read out at the Olympic festival a proclamation that all exiles save the Thebans and those guilty of sacrilege should return to their own cities, and that Antipater had already been ordered to coerce any city unwilling to co-operate.[28] It is clear, though, from a Tegeate decree regulating the return of exiles that Alexander had sent a *diagramma* containing detailed instructions,[29] perhaps direct to individual cities, though there is no evidence that the synhedrion was ignored. But, if he did act through the synhedrion, he was using it only as a means of publicity and as an inferior executive; the proclamation at Olympia came from him and so, it seems, did the instructions to Antipater.[30] Moreover, whatever the method, the forcible return of exiles, however just it might be said to be, was something against which the cities had been guaranteed in the treaty.[31]

Even so, it would not be safe to say that Alexander had consciously decided to do away with the treaty of 338/337 as the basis of his relations with the Greeks.[32] His distance from Greece and his autocratic position in the East would naturally make him think less of constitutional niceties and it could, no doubt, have been argued that the Exiles Decree was a justified exception, because it respected a transcendent justice.[33] His alleged request for deification in the Greek cities makes the position no clearer; there is no agreement even that the request was made, let alone about what, if any, political significance it had.[34]

Alexander's last important action that concerned the Greeks was his decision, not carried out, to substitute Craterus for Antipater as regent of Macedonia and Hegemon of Greece.[35] This move may have been intended to meet Greek grievances, but it is evident that opposition to Macedonian rule, especially at Athens, was more fundamental than mere discontent with the way in which the settlement of 338/337 had been carried out by Antipater. Many Greeks were far from convinced by the battle of Chaeronea that their special form of political existence had been extinguished. In the theoretical field Aristotle continued to think only in terms of the city-state; and in practice at Athens (the only city, as often, about which much is known at this period) the anti-Macedonian politicians, especially Lycurgus, worked hard to renovate strength for another war. When Lycurgus said that Greek liberty was buried with the dead of Chaeronea,[36] he did not mean that it could never be resurrected, but that phantoms appearing in Macedonian guise should be known for what they were. To cherish hopes of true freedom was not folly. Athens had not been taken; Philip indeed must have been glad to avoid the necessity of a siege. Alexander had hesitated to extract the ten orators by force. When Alexander crossed to Asia, the Persians became for a few years possible allies; then, as he pushed further and further eastwards, it must have seemed increasingly probable that he would be killed or his empire fall to pieces behind him.[37] In 324 Harpalus nearly succeeded in detaching the Athenians from loyalty to Alexander;[38] they and the Aetolians, it is said, had special reasons for being displeased with the Exiles Decree,[39] while the assistance given to the Spartans in 331 is evidence of unrest in the Peloponnese.[40]

The news of Alexander's death in 323 was the signal for a widespread and confident uprising. The Athenians and the Aetolians formed an alliance of Greek cities, which overthrew the treaty, and began to expel Macedonian garrisons, though they did not succeed in winning universal support.[41] Antipater, who was legally regent of the young king, Philip Arrhidaeus, suppressed this movement, but he could hardly have punished the offending cities through the synhedrion – as Alexander had punished the Thebans, and as he himself had been willing to punish the Spartans – for they were too numerous. Indeed, though he did not, as far as is known, formally dissolve the settlement of 338/337, he did not reconstitute the synhedrion and took what measures he thought fit to prevent further trouble.

Notes

1 Cf. Hammond, *History of Greece*, pp. 570 ff.
2 On the character of Philip's settlement in general – simply a Common Peace with no alliance between him and the Greeks – see Appendix X [in Ryder, *Koine Eirene*].
3 Cf. Hampl, *Die griechischen Staatsverträge*, p. 92, on the difference between the value of this Peace to Philip and that of the King's Peace to the Spartans, who exploited it to try to win control of Greece.
4 Tod 177, vv. 19–23; Ps.-Dem. xvii. 6, 8 and 19; and see Appendix X [in Ryder, *Koine Eirene*].
5 Tod 177, vv. 19–23; Ps.-Dem. xvii. 15; and see Appendix X [in Ryder, *Koine Eirene*].
6 See Appendix X [in Ryder, *Koine Eirene*].
7 Tod 177, vv. 22–23; and see Appendix X [in Ryder, *Koine Eirene*].
8 Cf. Diod. xvii. 9. 5 (Alexander's proclamation to the Thebans) and 14. 1 (his commission of their punishment to the synhedrion).
9 Cf. Diod. xvii. 73. 5 (punishment of Spartans entrusted to the synhedrion); Aesch. iii. 254 ('those who transgress the Common Peace') probably refers to the Spartans.
10 Tod 177, vv. 9–11; Ps.-Dem. xvii. 19; on something like this clause in the Peace of Philocrates cf. Accame, *La lega ateniense*, pp. 207 ff.
11 Tod 177, vv. 14–15; Ps.-Dem. xvii. 10, 15–16.
12 Boeotia – Paus. ix. 1. 8; confederacy – Paus. i. 25. 3; cf. Accame, *La lega ateniense*, pp. 222 ff.
13 The Boeotians and the Arcadians dealt as states with Alexander in 336 – Arrian i. 7. 11; Diod. xvii. 3. 4; κοινοὶ σύλλογοι of Boeotians, &c. in Hyperides, *c. Dem.* 18.
14 Oropus – Paus. i. 34. 1; Spartans – Polyb. ix. 33. 11–12, who talks of a 'common judgement from all the Greeks'. C. Roebuck, 'The Settlements of Philip II of Macedon with the Greek States in 338 BC', *Class. Phil.* xliii (1948), 73 ff., takes this to mean the *de iure* confirmation in the treaty or by the synhedrion of transfers of territory carried out earlier by Philip; I. Calabi, 'Il sinedrio della lega di Corinto e le sue attribuzioni giurisdizionali', *Riv. di filol.* lxxviii (1950), 63 ff., disagrees and suggests a separate arbitrating tribunal set up by Philip before the meeting at Corinth.
15 Tod 179.
16 Tod 177, vv. 4–5.
17 See Appendix X [in Ryder, *Koine Eirene*].
18 Diod. xvi. 89. 3, &c.
19 Diod. xvii. 4; Arr. i. 1. 2; cf. Larsen, 'Representative Government in the Panhellenic Leagues', *Class. Phil.* xx (1925), 316, n. 3.
20 Diod. xvii. 8. 3 ff.
21 Diod. xvii. 9. 5 and 14. 1 ff.
22 Aesch. iii. 161.
23 This very vexed question seems to allow no probable solution; cf., for instance, F. Miltner, 'Die staatsrechtliche Entwicklung des Alexanderreiches', *Klio*, xxvi (1933), 39 ff.; E. Bickermann, 'Alexandre le grand et les villes d'Asie', *Rev. d'étud. grec.* xlii (1934), 346 ff.; V. Ehrenberg, *Alexander and the Greeks* (Oxford, 1938), pp. 1 ff.; T. Lenschau, 'Alexander der grosse und Chios', *Klio*, xxxiii (1940), 201 ff.; W. W. Tarn, *Alexander the Great*, ii (Cambridge, 1948), 199 ff. Ehrenberg also denied the inclusion of many islands in the League, but did not convince Lenschau or Tarn.
24 Tod 192, vv. 14–16 (Alexander's proclaimed intention to send wrongdoers to the synhedrion) and Arr. iii. 2. 5 ff. (his own judgement of them) could be interpreted otherwise; cf. Ehrenberg, *Alexander and the Greeks*, pp. 23 ff.; Lenschau, art. cit., *Klio*, xxxiii (1940), 204 ff., and Tod's commentary on 192.
25 Diod. xvii. 62. 6 ff., 73. 5.
26 Cf. E. Badian, 'Harpalus', *J.H.S.* lxxxi (1961), 28.
27 Cf. Badian, art. cit., pp. 28 ff.

28 Diod. xvii. 109. 1, xviii. 8. 2 ff.; Hyper, *c. Dem.* 18; Dinarchus, *c. Dem.* 81 ff.; Plut. *Moralia*, 221A; Justin xiii. 5. 2; Curtius x. 2. 4 ff.

29 Tod 202.

30 Cf. Heuss, art. cit., *Hermes*, lxxiii (1938), 135 ff., for the strongest condemnation. On possible role of the synhedrion cf. H. Bengtson, *Die Strategie in der hellenistischen Zeit*, i (Munich, 1937), 46 ff.

31 Ps.-Dem. xvii. 16.

32 As Heuss, l.c., implies.

33 Exile 'contrary to the cities' established laws' was also prohibited in the treaty – Ps.-Dem. xvii. 15.

34 The story is found to be false by J. P. V. D. Balsdon, 'The "Divinity" of Alexander', *Historia*, ii (1950), 383 ff.; on possible political implications contrast esp. Tarn, *C.A.H.* vi. 419, and Balsdon, art. cit., pp. 386 ff.

35 Arr. vii. 12. 4.

36 *c. Leocr.* 50.

37 On all this cf. A. W. Gomme, 'The End of the City-State', *Essays in Greek History and Literature* (Oxford, 1937), pp. 204 ff.; Ps.-Dem. xvii gives a fair idea of the attitude of the anti-Macedonian politicians to the treaty.

38 Cf. Badian, art. cit., *J.H.S.* lxxxi (1961), 31 ff.

39 Diod. xviii. 8. 6; Justin xiii. 5. 1 and 6.

40 Diod. xvii. 62. 7.

41 The extent of the alliance is given by Diod. xviii. 11. 1 ff.; the battle-cry was Greek freedom – cf. ibid. 9. 5 and 10. 2–3.

RELATIONS WITH THE GREEK STATES

N.G.L. Hammond and F.W. Walbank

Relations between an island state and Alexander were based either on membership of the Common Peace or on a treaty of alliance (e.g. at Arr. 2. 1. 4 κατὰ συμμαίαν in the case of Mytilene). In consecutive chapters Arrian gives an example of each, Tenedos having its agreement 'with Alexander and the Greeks', and Mytilene in Lesbos simply 'with Alexander' (2. 2. 2 and 1. 4).[1] These agreements carried different obligations. For example, offenders from Chios as a member of the Common Peace were tried by the Court of the Common Peace (*GHI* 192, 15). On the other hand, some Lesbian offenders were tried by the court of their own state in the island (3. 2. 7; C. 4. 8. 11–13), others by Alexander (*GHI* 191, 99), and others under an agreed procedure which stemmed from Alexander's *diagramma* (191, 129–30 and *SEG* 12. 1 and 16, being lines 20 and 28 of Heisserer 123 f.). Again in Lesbos Alexander rewarded Mytilene with money and 'a large grant of territory' (C. 4. 8.13). This land was taken probably from the king's territory on the mainland. Such a grant of land was not within the competence of the Council of the Common Peace.

During the struggle between Macedonia and Persia the faction strife which was already endemic in many states of the eastern Aegean took on a new impetus. With each change a new faction took power. Thus Chios had fought against Macedonia in 341/0; but in 335, if not earlier, it was a member of the Common Peace and, as such, a member of a common alliance with Macedonia. Then in 333 it resisted Memnon, but fell through betrayal from within and became an ally of Persia (2. 1. 1). Finally the popular party invited the help of Hegelochus, in 332, who defeated the Persian garrison and took over the island. The regulations which were made then by Alexander as *hegemon* have survived (*GHI* 192).[2] There was to be a democratic constitution, a new code of laws, and a banishing of those responsible for betraying the island to Persia from all Common Peace territories. Further, any persons so responsible, but still in Chios, were to be tried 'before the Council of the Greeks', and any such elsewhere were to be liable to arrest 'in accordance with the decree of the Greeks'. Any dispute arising between those in Chios and the returning exiles was to be tried by Alexander, and the drafted code of laws was to be submitted to him. Here we see Alexander as *hegemon* trying to check victimization through discriminatory verdicts and laws. Those of the pro-Persian leaders who were subsequently caught by the Macedonian fleet were imprisoned that winter at Elephantine in Egypt, probably until they could be sent safely through the Aegean to the Greek mainland for trial by the Council of the Greeks. For Alexander insisted on the establishment of law and proper legal procedures, and he put a stop to lynching and persecution (as we see at Ephesus, 1. 17. 12). In a second letter to Chios he called a halt to indictments on the charge of Medism and requested honourable treatment for a Chian citizen whom he regarded as a personal friend and as a sincere patriot (*SEG* 22. 506).[3]

There had been faction strife also in Eresus, a city-state on the island of Lesbos, with which Alexander made a treaty of alliance, as with Mytilene. Here between *c.* 350 and *c.* 340 a tyranny headed by three brothers had been in power, and it had been succeeded by a democracy which set up altars to Zeus Philippius, presumably because Philip had had a hand in promoting the change. Its life was short; for before the agreement was made between Alexander and the Greeks in late 336 there was already another set of tyrants in power ([Dem.] 17. 7). They fled in 334, only to return with Memnon in 333, whereupon they committed a number of atrocities against their fellow citizens. In 332 the Macedonians gained control of Lesbos and brought the leader of the Eresus tyrants, Agonippus, to Alexander in Egypt, by whom he was sent back to be tried by a court of the restored democracy. He and his colleague were executed.[4] In accordance with normal Greek practice, reprisals were taken against the families of the condemned tyrants, and the relatives of both sets of tyrants were duly exiled. At an unknown date Alexander asked the democracy to consider in its court whether the descendants of the first set of tyrants should be restored or continue in exile; the verdict was the latter. The relatives of the second set were exiled by a judgement of Alexander, and this judgement was confirmed later by Philip Arrhidaeus. In the inscriptions which give us this information we can see that Alexander insisted on the democracy following legal procedures and instituting trials with a secret ballot.

Mytilene as an ally of Alexander defied Memnon in 333. When it was compelled to submit, Pharnabazus installed a garrison, made a restored exile tyrant, banished the previous leaders, and exacted a heavy financial penalty; and perforce the state allied itself with Persia and accepted the 'Peace of Antalcidas', a fossil some fifty years old (Arr. 2. 1. 2–5). A year later Mytilene was liberated by Hegelochus and was rewarded for its loyalty [. . .]. The exiles were recalled, the tyrant (if he survived) was tried in the local court and a democracy was set up. Alexander issued a *diagramma* which was expressly designed to bring the two factions of the Mytileneans into concord (Heisserer 123 ll. 28–30, with his restoration).

We may assume that Rhodes yielded to Memnon in 333; for we should have learnt from Arrian, were it otherwise. Then in 332 during the siege of Tyre ten Rhodian triremes made their way to Alexander (2. 20. 2), and after the fall of Tyre the city of Rhodes surrendered itself and its harbours into Alexander's hands (C. 4. 5. 9). Here too there must have been changes of faction, and probably a *diagramma* was issued by Alexander in favour of reconciliation; for a garrison was placed there, as at Chios, and it was removed later, probably after the end of the actions in Crete (C. 4. 8. 12). There is no sign that Rhodes became a member of the Common Peace. It simply remained an ally of Alexander, to the mutual satisfaction of both parties.

Greek cities on the Asiatic mainland formed a separate category. They were not admitted to membership of the Common Peace, and there is no evidence that the question of admission ever arose. Modern scholars have expressed surprise or disapproval, because they have associated liberation from Persian rule with membership of the Common Peace.[5] Greeks of the 330s probably had no such expectations. Athens and Sparta had 'liberated' Greek cities from Persian rule, not in order that they should become free members of the Hellenic League or the Peloponnesian League, but in order that they should enter the power system of the 'liberator'. So now the 'liberated' Greek cities entered Alexander's power system, the Kingdom of Asia, as subjects of the King, but by his grace with a preferential status, paying a 'contribution' for the war and not 'tribute' and dealing directly with the King. Such was the status of Aspendus, for instance. But when Aspendus went back on its obligations, it was made tributary both to Alexander as King of Asia and to Macedonia and also made subject to the orders of Alexander's deputy, the satrap; and at the moment it had to pay an indemnity, provide hostages for good conduct, and accept Alexander's ruling in a border dispute (Arr. 1. 27. 4). Athens had done no less to an 'ally' who broke her agreement in the 450s, and Alexander's methods now served as a model for the treatment of Greek cities within a kingdom.

The Greeks of the islands and of the Asiatic mainland preferred the rule of Alexander to the rule of Persia,[6] particularly because Alexander favoured democracy, while Persia relied on cliques or tyrants, and because the restored democratic leaders obtained the general support of the electorate. The real centre of disaffection was on the Greek mainland, at Sparta, which stood outside the Common Peace and had good reason to hate Macedonia. Philip had had her excommunicated by the Amphictyonic Council in 346, had thwarted her attempts to reconstitute an alliance in the Peloponnese, and had finally deprived her of some border territories and maintained the independence of Messene and Megalopolis. When Sparta refused to recognize Philip, Alexander, and the Common Peace, she was left in proud, but impotent, isolation. When her hated rival, Thebes, was in danger, Sparta did not go to her aid either in 338 or in 335; and when she decided in 333 to side with Persia against Macedonia, she was too late to affect the course of the war at sea, as we have seen, but she did obtain what she had lacked, a large enough subsidy of Persian gold to hire eventually 10,000 Greek mercenaries (Dinarch. 1. 34) and maintain her own army on a war footing.

In the last months of 331 Sparta faced a difficult choice. More than a year of war in alliance with Persia against the forces of the Greek League and Macedonia at sea had ended in utter failure. Prudence might now have advised capitulation. But some factors seemed to favour the continuation of war, not at sea, but on the Greek mainland. Most important of all, Sparta had the military means; for her forces were more than twice as large as they had been for some generations thanks to the Persian subsidy, which would however become a wasting asset if they delayed. On the other hand, the forces of Macedonia were widely dispersed and over-strained: the army of Antipater, drained by the sending of 6,500 Macedonians to the East, was now at a low ebb, and Alexander himself was far away in Mesopotamia. The news of Memnon's large-scale rising in Thrace [. . .] seemed to promise that Antipater's army would be further depleted and pinned down in the north. There were also political changes in some Peloponnesian states whereby anti-Macedonian leaders were coming into the ascendancy, and this might be a token that Greek opinion generally was moving towards a war of 'liberation' (D.S. 17. 62. 3–6). Yet Sparta must have realized that she had irreconcilable enemies in the Peloponnese – Messenia, Megalopolis, and Argos (cf. Isoc. 5. 74) – and that north-eastern Greece from Boeotia to Thessaly was likely to support the Common Peace and Macedonia. Much would depend upon the attitude of Athens and Aetolia, as at the time of Thebes' rising, and it was discouraging for Sparta that Athens had recently congratulated Alexander on his victories and he had released Athenian prisoners of war, captured at the Granicus river.

The news of Alexander's victory at Gaugamela on 1 October 331 and of his advance to Babylon may have contributed to the decision of the Spartan people; for it was clear he would not turn back to Greece. So they marched under the command of Agis and engaged the forces of the Macedonian commander Corragus, which represented the Greek League and Macedonia as keepers of the Common Peace. Sparta's full levy and her 10,000 mercenaries were completely victorious, and her success brought two states into alliance with her, Elis and Achaea apart from Pellene [. . .]. These states renounced their membership of the Common Peace, laid themselves open to attack by members of the Common Peace (*GHI* 177, 20 f.), and accepted the hegemony of Sparta, as in the days of the Peloponnesian League. Their example was followed later by Arcadia apart from Megalopolis. Elsewhere Sparta's approaches were rejected, and in particular Athens did not move from her membership of the Common Peace and her alliance with Macedonia.[7]

Early in 330 Sparta did not deploy the forces of her coalition against the Macedonian garrison of Acrocorinth or show the flag in central Greece, but instead she and her allies laid siege to Megalopolis, which was of particular concern to Sparta herself. Her strategy suited Antipater admirably. Having come to terms with Memnon and received a huge sum of money from Alexander (3. 16. 10), he reinforced his relatively small Macedonian army of some 1,500 cavalry and 12,000 phalanx infantry (D.S. 17. 17. 5) with perhaps some Balkan troops and certainly large numbers of Greeks, loyal to the Common Peace, who were willing to serve (Athenians not among them). It was probably April or May of 330 when Antipater led an army, reputedly of 40,000 men, into the Peloponnese (D.S. 17. 63. 1) and won near Megalopolis a hard-fought, but decisive, victory over an army numbering 2,000 cavalry, 20,000 citizen troops, and 10,000 mercenaries.[8] In particular the Macedonian pikeman outfought the Spartan hoplite, and Agis died fighting heroically. Losses of the Spartan coalition were 5,300 killed, and of Antipater's coalition 3,500 killed according to D.S. 17. 63. 3, but 1,000 and very many wounded according to C. 6. 1. 16. It was, in the words of Alexander 'a battle of mice'.[9]

Antipater, who had acted as deputy of the *hegemon*, now asked the Council of the Greek League to decide on the fate of the insurgents. Was Sparta to be destroyed, as Thebes had been? The Council imposed an indemnity of 120 talents on Elis and Achaea, which was to be paid to Megalopolis, arrested the ringleaders of the revolt in Tegea and probably other Arcadian cities (D.S. 17. 73. 5–6; C. 6. 1. 20), and referred the decision about Sparta to the *hegemon* himself, to whom Sparta was ordered to send fifty leading Spartiates to be held as hostages and also envoys to plead her case (Aeschin. 3. 133). Alexander showed surprising clemency; for he pardoned Sparta. It was also a sound piece of statesmanship, as Philip had realized [. . .]. For the course of the war had shown that the existence of Sparta was a source of disunity among those Greek states which might otherwise combine against him. On her side Sparta had shown more courage than intelligence in her continuation and conduct of the war; and Elis and Achaea were fortunate in escaping with a fine, as compared with what had happened to Thebes. It is probable that all three states and the Arcadian states were admitted to the Common Peace, Sparta for the first time.[10]

The failures of Greek resistance to Macedonia can be epitomized in the words 'united we stand, divided we fall.' Only a few mainland states fought at Chaeronea in 338, and none of them except Achaea fought again in 331/0. Thebes was abandoned even by the few states which had intended to help her in 335. Other Greek states fought against the resisting states in 335 and in 331/0. This situation was due to the long traditions of inter-state rivalry and warfare on the mainland and to the internal politics of individual states. Thus in 330, although Athens had not moved to help either side, Lycurgus in prosecuting Leocrates claimed that 'the freedom of Greece' was buried with the fallen at Chaeronea, and Aeschines failed to win even a fifth of the votes in his attack on the policy of Demosthenes. In fact, though not in spirit, the only form of unity lay still in the Common Peace.

Although Alexander could not command the allegiance of the Greek states to the spirit of the Common Peace, he could and, as far as we can tell, did respect the letter of the Agreement (*syntheke*) which he had made in 336 as *hegemon*. This was demonstrated particularly by the poor case which the speaker of the pseudo-Demosthenic speech, *On the Articles of Agreement with Alexander*, put forward late in 331. The omissions are highly significant. There was no raising of points which modern scholars might raise: the right of Macedonia to hegemony, the position of Alexander as *hegemon*, the destruction of Thebes, the disbanding and the recall of the Greek fleet, the non-admission of 'liberated' Greek states on some islands and in Asia to the Common Peace, and Alexander's treatment of pro-Persian Greeks, e.g. from Chios. We may conclude that in all these matters Alexander had not acted *ultra vires*. The charges actually made are trivial. They were based on the more or less tacit assumption that the *hegemon* was bound to observe the rules and regulations imposed on the member states by the Charter of the Common Peace. But the assumption was false; for the *hegemon* clearly had emergency powers. Thus just as he approved a change of government from oligarchy to democracy at Ambracia (D.S. 17. 3. 3), so he or his deputy approved or facilitated changes of government at Messene and Pellene, which the speaker represented, not necessarily with truth, as becoming close oligarchies or tyrannies ([Dem.] 17. 4 and 10).[11] As events were quickly to prove, these changes of government were in the interest of the Common Peace; for they were among the factors which kept Messene and Pellene loyal during the war of Agis.

As allies of Macedonia in the joint war against Persia, the members of the Common Peace had no grounds for complaint. Alexander was personally correct in his treatment of 'the Greeks'. Spoils were dedicated in the names of 'Alexander and the Greeks'; captured works of art were restored to their Greek owners; and large bounties were given to the allies at the end of their service in 330 (Arr. 1. 16. 7; 3. 16. 7–8 and 19.5). The war of revenge for the profanation of the Greek temples by Xerxes which 'the Greeks' had declared (D.S. 16. 89. 2) was brought to a dramatic conclusion by the burning of the Persian palace at Persepolis.

The dealings of Alexander with the Greek states did not begin or end with the members of the Common Peace. They began with the states of the Amphictyonic League. A list of the 'temple-building' delegates in 327 is remarkable for the large number of states which were represented; this surely indicates a high degree of reconciliation and co-operation. Argos had nine delegates out of forty-five. She may have taken a lead as the rival of Sparta and as the homeland of Alexander's family. Alexander's contacts with Greek states went far beyond those of the Common Peace. He was in treaty with probably all Greek states east of the Ionian and Sicilian Seas. While Alexander dealt with the Council of the Common Peace on all matters which fell within its competence, he did not use it as a channel of communication with Greek states in general. In his attempts to check the excesses of political faction and in his proposal that the Greek states should each recall and reinstate its own exiles, he preferred rightly to address the Greek states directly. For he was concerned with a problem which was not particular to the members of the Common Peace and did not fall within the sphere of competence of the Council of the Common Peace.

The announcement (*diagramma*) of Alexander's request that Greek states should recall all their exiles and restore to their exiled owners any confiscated territory, except for men under a curse and those exiled from Thebes, was made first at Susa to the army and later at Olympia to an audience at the Olympic festival which included more than 20,000 exiles. Alexander chose these occasions because he was addressing his request not to the members of the Common Peace alone, as Tarn and others have supposed, but to all states within his sphere of influence.[12] The announcement was not an 'order', as hostile critics suggested (e.g. Hyp. *Dem.* 18, *epitagmata*) but the starting-point for a dialogue, during which envoys were sent to Alexander, for instance at Babylon (D.S. 17. 113. 3).

Who would benefit from this restoration of exiles? It has sometimes been suggested that the return of the exiles would strengthen the pro-Macedonian parties in the states.[13] But a moment's reflection shows that this was not so. For those who had been exiled since the rise of Macedonia to power were not the supporters, but the enemies, of Macedonia. For example, the men in exile from Tegea had supported Sparta against Alexander. Yet, as we know from an inscription (*GHI* 202, 57–66), special steps were taken by Alexander to protect them from any victimization by loyal citizens of Tegea on their return; for his *diagramma* laid down strict principles which attest his humane concern for exiles (ibid. 2–3, 10–11, etc.). How greatly the modern world would benefit from such a measure! The reaction of the Greek world at the time may be summed up in the words of D.S. 18. 8. 6 (tr. R. M. Geer): 'people in general welcomed the restoration of exiles as a good thing', i.e. 'for a good purpose' (ὡς ἐπ' ἀγαθῷ γινομένην; cf. LSJ[9] s.v. ἐπί B III 2).

The restoration of confiscated territory to a dispossessed population (such as the Palestinian Arabs today) was likely to be resisted by the current owners. In particular Athens had expelled the population of Samos in 365 and seized the territory for her own citizens; and the Aetolians had acted similarly at Oeniadae in Acarnania. It would be absurd to suppose that the gratitude of the dispossessed would weigh more than the enmity of Athens and the Aetolian League in terms of power politics. That Alexander was prepared to incur that enmity is a measure of his sincerity and of his determination to establish more settled conditions in the Greek world of city-states. We do not hear of any attempt by Alexander to restore the survivors of Olynthus and Galepsus within the Macedonian kingdom to their original territories.[14] But it is probable that they had already been settled in new towns founded by Philip and Alexander.

Although Athens resented Alexander's plan, she behaved correctly in the matter of Harpalus. As one of Alexander's treasurers, this Macedonian officer had relieved a famine at Athens by sending shipments of grain, and for this he had been made an Athenian citizen. During Alexander's absence in India Harpalus embezzled funds and in the summer of 324 he fled with 6,000 mercenaries, thirty ships, and 5,000 talents to Sunium in Attica. The Assembly refused, on the recommendation of Demosthenes, to grant him asylum, and he moved on with his forces to Taenarum in the Peloponnese. From there he returned with the money but in a single ship, hoping to buy support. Once again he was disappointed. Indeed the Athenians arrested him, as the Macedonians had requested. However, he escaped and fled to Crete, where he met his death. These events at Athens took place between the announcement at Susa and the announcement at Olympia.[15]

In this year, 324, Alexander addressed two further requests to the Greek states in general. First, he asked that they should establish cults in honour of his dead friend Hephaestion as 'hero'. Such heroization of a dead man had been granted voluntarily in the past, for instance to Brasidas and Timoleon. Alexander's request was accepted.

Some cults were established in 323. Second, he asked that he himself should be granted 'divine honours'. Precedents were rare; but one was apposite for the would-be liberator of Samos, for his predecessor in that role, Lysander, had been worshipped at Samos *c.* 404. Moreover, some Greek cities in Asia in 334/3 and Thasos and Rhodes later had on their own initiative granted Alexander divine honours and established a cult with its own shrine, sacrifices, and games. But it was unique that the request was made by the would-be recipient. What were Alexander's motives? His chief motive was the desire for glory: to be recognized by the Greeks as a benefactor of exceptional degree.[16] To this may be added a political motive. A request from so powerful a person was likely to be accepted by many as a veiled order, and the general acceptance of him as a god would enhance his authority in the Greek world. This request, then, may be seen as a first, perhaps tentative step on the road towards establishing a ruler cult in the Greek world.

As Alexander had no doubt anticipated, the Greek states granted him 'divine honours', sometimes with sarcasm (e.g. Demosthenes at Athens remarking 'Let him be a son of Zeus . . . or Poseidon, for all I care') and sometimes no doubt with real gratitude. In 323 worship of him was inaugurated with shrines, altars, and statues (e.g. at Athens, Hyp. 1. 31, 6. 21), and games were held in his honour (by the Ionians, Str. 644).[17] Envoys came 'from Greece' to greet Alexander as a god. They were crowned and they crowned Alexander with golden crowns, as 'sacred envoys come to honour a god' (Arr. 7. 23. 2).[18] That was in Babylon shortly before his death. Had he lived to fulfil his plans, he would have built three great temples in Delos, Dodona, and Delphi and three more in Macedonia, all in honour of the leading gods whom Greeks and Macedonians shared. For whether he himself was recognized as a god or not, his duty to the Greek gods was his first priority, as he showed in his hearing of embassies at Babylon (D.S. 17. 113. 4). They repaid him in true Greek fashion: he died young.

Notes

1 The clear difference is obfuscated by E. Badian's assumption in 'Alexander the Great and the Greeks in Asia' in *Ancient Society and Institutions* (Oxford, 1966) 50 that Arrian's distinction is 'probably mere inaccuracy', or Bosworth's idea that the omission of 'and the Greeks' is a 'stylistic variation' (*C* 181). It is then easy for them to argue that A. broke his obligations to the Common Peace by using different methods of trial for persons from Chios and persons from Mytilene, for instance, as in Badian 53. Brunt, L. 124 n. 2, thinks Arrian mistaken. There is a better understanding of these passages in V. Ehrenberg, *Alexander and the Greeks* (Oxford, 1938) 20 ff., against whom Tarn's arguments were weak in 2. 201. n. 6. We do not know why some islanders joined the Common Peace and others did not, but it was probably due to preference on both sides and to opportunity when the Persian fleet was controlling most of the Aegean Sea. The verb ἐπανάγεσθαι in line 14 of *GHI* 192 is best explained like ἐπαναφέρεσθαι πρὸς Ἀλέξανδρον in line 7 as meaning 'be referred to A.', who was on the way to, or already in, Egypt.

2 This dating by Tod is preferable to that proposed by Heisserer 79–95, namely 334. Heisserer's view that Memnon took Chios in 335 (his pp. 83 and 93) overlooks the fact that Memnon campaigned only on land (D.S. 17. 7. 3 and 8–10); and if a Macedonian garrison was placed there in 334 and Chios was captured despite it in 333, as Heisserer supposes, Arrian would surely have mentioned that garrison, since he mentioned the garrison of A. at Mytilene (2. 1. 4). On my view Memnon 'won it over' (D.S. 17. 29. 2) through treachery from within (2. 1. 1) in 333. Thus from A.'s point of view Chios was then guilty of 'revolt' (*apostasis* 3. 2. 5) from the Common Peace.

3 Well discussed by Heisserer 96–116.

4 The order and the dating of events are disputed. Tod (*GHI* 191) has the above order, except that he puts the installation of the second set of tyrants early in A.'s reign (despite [Dem.] 17. 7, unless he means at the very start). Griffith in Volume II. 720 f. has the same order and dating down to the installation of the second set. Heisserer 27–78 carries the first down to 334, and introduces the second set in 333 (despite [D.] 17. 7). Bosworth 179 f. has tyrants continuously until they meet with trouble in 332; this requires them to change political horses rapidly with impunity, which seems very unlikely.

5 In this controversial matter Ehrenberg, *Alexander and the Greeks* makes a better case than E. Badian in *Ancient Society and Institutions* (Oxford, 1966) 37 f.

6 As a change from enslavement to autonomy; see *SIG* 278. 3, Priene marking the new era with the words αὐτονόμων ἐόντων Πριηνέων.

7 The sequence of events is clearly given in Aeschin. 3. 165 and Dinarch. 1. 34, and there is no reason to rearrange them, as Tarn did in *CAH* 6. 445. For Athens' hostility to Sparta in the war see *IG* ii². 399 with *BSA* 79 (1984) 229 ff.

8 For the mercenaries see Dinarch. 1. 34; they are omitted by D.S. 17. 62. 7–8. The meaning of the latter passage is uncertain. If Diodorus' phrase 'most of the Peloponnesians' does not include the Lacedaemonians, then we may add Sparta's forces *pandemei*. This makes a total of almost 40,000. Berve 2. 9, much followed by others, is mistaken in putting Agis' forces at 22,000 in all; for he included the 10,000 mercenaries in the figure of 20,000 soldiers expressly recruited by 'most of the Peloponnesians' in D.S. 17. 62. 7. Thus the view of R. Lane Fox, *Alexander the Great* (London, 1973) 252, that the odds were 'two to one' in numerical strength in favour of Antipater, seems to be incorrect. For the size of Antipater's army we may compare that of Epaminondas, namely 40,000 hoplites, when he invaded the Peloponnese.

9 P *Ages* 15. 4 'myomachia', being contrasted with A.'s own epic fight against Darius, just as the 'batrachomyomachia' was contrasted with the Homeric epic.

10 The chronology of the war is much disputed, because Diodorus and Curtius are at variance. The *terminus post quem* is given by the arrival of Macedonian reinforcements between Babylon and Susa in November/December 331, they having set out before trouble broke out, and the *terminus ante quem* by the imminent journey of the Spartan envoys when Aeschines made his remark in 3. 133 in August 330. Diodorus is probably right in putting the final decision of Sparta after the news of Persia's defeat at Gaugamela (17. 62. 1). For various views see E. Badian, 'Agis III', *Hermes* 95 (1967) 190 f.; E. N. Borza, 'The end of Agis' revolt', *CP* 66 (1971) 230 f.; G. L. Cawkwell, 'The crowning of Demosthenes', *CQ* 19 (1969) 171 f.; Brunt, L 1. 480 ff.; G. Wirth, 'Alexander zwischen Gaugamela und Persepolis', *Historia* 20 (1971) 617 f. For the final settlement see E. I. McQueen in *Historia* 27 (1978) 53–8.

11 As regards the tyrants at Eresus in [Dem.] 17. 7 see p. 82.

12 A. Heuss, 'Antigonos Monophthalmos u. d. griech. Städte', *Hermes* 73 (1938) 135, accepts as genuine A.'s letter which was read out at Olympia (D.S. 18. 8. 4). It was addressed to τοῖς ἐκ τῶν Ἑλληνίδων πόλεων φυγάσι, i.e. to the exiles from the Greek states in general and not merely to those which participated in the Common Peace. That phrase may be genuine; but I do not think that A. would have committed himself and Antipater to the use of compulsion in advance (as the last sentence of the letter does). J. 13. 5. 2 had the exiles from all Greek states in mind: 'omnium civitatum exsules'.

13 As alleged in D. 18. 8. 2.

14 This point was hinted at by Demosthenes in speaking at Olympia (P *Demosth* 9. 1).

15 The chronology is in doubt. See D.S. 17. 108. 6–8; C. 10. 2. 2–4; P *Demosth* 25; and the discussion by E. Badian, 'Harpalus', *JHS* 81 (1961) 41 ff.

16 His desire to see Olympias deified after death (C. 9. 6. 26; 10. 5. 30) was to give her glory, not political power. Habicht 35 and C. F. Edson in *CP* 53 (1958) 64 stress A.'s desire for glory in this connection.

17 The second passage in Hyperides refers probably, but not necessarily, to Athens (see Habicht, *Studien* 28 f. and 246 f.) The people of Ephesus wrote of A. as 'a god' (Str. 641). A cult of A. as a god, son of Ammon, was probably established at Megalopolis in 323 before A.'s death (Paus. 8. 32. 1); see E. Fredricksmeyer, 'Alexander's deification', *AJAH* 4 (1979) 1 f. The

evidence is well assembled by Berve 1. 96 ff. Lucian, *DMort* 391, said that some added A. in his life to the twelve gods, built him temples, and made sacrifice to him.

18 See Fredricksmeyer, op. cit. 3–5. The expression 'from Greece' takes its meaning from the context, namely Greece in general as A. was at Babylon (Arr. 7. 23. 2) rather than the Greek mainland in particular as Habicht *Studien* 22 argues ('die festländische Städte'). But Greece in general here did not include Asia Minor, parts of which were mentioned in Arr. 7. 23. 1.

References

A. = Alexander the Great.

Berve = H. Berve, *Das Alexanderreich auf prosopographischer Grundlage* (Munich: 1926).

Bosworth = A.B. Bosworth, *A Historical Commentary on Arrian's History of Alexander* (Oxford: 1980–).

Brunt, L. = P.A. Brunt, *Arrian, History of Alexander*, Loeb Classical Library 1 (Cambridge, MA and London: 1976).

Griffith = N.G.L. Hammond and G.T. Griffith, *A History of Macedonia* 2 (Oxford: 1979).

Habicht, *Studien* = C. Habicht, *Studien zur Geschichte Athens in hellenistischer Zeit* (Göttingen: 1982).

Heisserer = A.J. Heisserer, *Alexander the Great and the Greeks* (Norman, OK: 1980).

THE HARPALUS AFFAIR AND THE GREEK
RESPONSE TO THE MACEDONIAN HEGEMONY

Ian Worthington

The period of relative tranquillity amongst the Greek states during the later 330s and most of the 320s was shattered by the death of Alexander III of Macedonia in 323. Antagonism between Greece and Macedonia was nothing new: it had characterized virtually the whole of the reign of Philip II, manifesting itself not only in the oratory of Demosthenes and others but also in open warfare. Then in 337, a year after the decisive battle of Chaeronea, Philip set up the League of Corinth, all Greece except Sparta fell under the hegemony of Macedonia, and plans for a Persian invasion with Philip at the head of the united Greeks were announced. The last was not a new idea; Isocrates had been advocating such a course for years, but not as the result of an enforced union of the states. After Philip's murder in 336 the Greek states had revolted, a revolt backed by Persia, but quickly terminated the following year by the new king Alexander III, who then ordered the razing of Thebes. This catastrophic event was to send shock-waves throughout the Greek world and be remembered in vivid terms in oratory years later (for example, Aes. 3. 133 ff., Din. 1. 18 ff.). In 334 Alexander left for Persia, never to return to Greece, leaving behind his tried and trusted general Antipater to hold Macedonia and Greece in check during his absence. Apart from an abortive attempt by the Spartan king Agis III in 331 to stir up the Greeks against the Macedonian power, Greece for the most part remained subservient – perhaps the lesson of Thebes had been learned. Yet the tone of our sources presents us with Greeks who in spirit were anti-Macedonian, Greeks who were ready to seize the first chance to revolt, holding out against this enemy power for as long as they could, irrespective of past defeats and future punishments if unsuccessful, and for a stirring ideal: to regain for their *poleis* the autonomy and liberty which had fallen with their dead at Chaeronea. This conception of the Greek attitude to the Macedonian hegemony and indeed the ability even of the Greek states to revolt still largely prevails: in a rather extreme form it can be found in a paper by A. W. Gomme entitled 'The End of the City-State' in his *Essays in Greek History and Literature*.[1] However, things are not always what they seem, and that our contemporary sources are oratorical (given the problems raised by oratory as historical source material), should put us immediately on our guard.

Perhaps unsurprisingly, Alexander's death on 10 June 323 heralded a widespread revolt against the Macedonian hegemony.[2] However, the Exiles Decree and the events of the Harpalus affair of 324/3 would seem to have tested the subservience of the Greeks to Macedonia before the king's death. Alexander's return from India in 324 after his conquests in the more exotic regions of the world took many by surprise, especially those who had indulged in political intrigues and extortion whilst he had been absent. Such culprits were now faced by royal retribution of the direst kind, regardless of their position.[3] Thus the corruption and political liaisons of the imperial treasurer Harpalus made him a prime candidate: there would be no royal reprieve this time,[4] and so, in keeping with his track-record, he again fled from his master. Together with a powerful force and a large amount of treasure, he sought asylum in Athens. There the Assembly ordered the *strategos* Philocles to deny him entry ([Plut.]

X. *Or.* 846a), and he made for the mercenary base at Taenarum. Obstinately, and with a much reduced force and allegedly 700 talents, he returned to Athens, this time as a suppliant, and was admitted into the city by Philocles. Thus begins the controversial Harpalus affair, set as it is against the background to the final struggle against Macedonian hegemony.

The general belief today is that Harpalus fled to Athens to instigate a revolt against Alexander, especially as Athenian – and Greek – anger had been aroused by the Exiles Decree. For the Athenians, the decree called not only for the return of the city's exiles but also, by implication, the surrender of the island of Samos, which would have to be returned to its native owners. News of the decree was known in advance (cf. Din. 1. 82, Hyp. 5. 18),[5] but despite the resentment it must have caused Demosthenes advised the Athenians against using Harpalus' force in a revolt against the king. The Athenians took his advice and Harpalus' plan of rebellion was rejected. In a nutshell I call this synopsis of the situation the orthodox view.[6] Recently, in 'The Lamian War – A False Start?', *Antichthon*, 17 (1983), 47–63, N. G. Ashton has questioned that view, and argued that *prior* to Harpalus' entry into the city the Athenians were bent on military resistance, primarily because of the Exiles Decree, and that Harpalus' sudden arrival interrupted an Athenian-led revolt in 324. In other words, Harpalus did not try to instigate a Greek revolt since war between Athens and Alexander was imminent over the decree, and this revolt was common knowledge when Harpalus fled.

The issue is important, for by extension I believe it has implications for the Greek attitude to the Macedonian hegemony – in this respect I would argue that it is possible to equate the attitude of Athens with that of the Greeks. Questions are raised such as how long the Greeks were prepared to remain passive under Antipater's watchful eye or whether they were planning a revolt before mid-June 324 (when I believe Harpalus entered Athens),[7] to be led by Athens. Was the Exiles Decree, which so blatantly disregarded the autonomy of the Greek states, the final straw which forced the Greeks into overt resistance, or was Alexander's unexpected death really the rallying-point? Considerations such as these lead us to reassess how completely Greece was dominated by Macedonia. I start with the Harpalus affair, and in this I am not concerned with the question of Demosthenes' guilt or innocence in it,[8] but with the Ashton vs. orthodox debate (as I call it), and the implications from it for these questions.

Dr Ashton rightly and importantly stresses that the Harpalus affair is not merely an episode in the disintegration of Alexander's regime in his last years, but needs to be treated against the background of Athenian history in the crisis caused by the promulgation of the Exiles Decree. However, I find myself in disagreement with his overall thesis, and thus I lean towards the orthodox view.

Ashton's theory that preparations for an Athenian-led revolt were in progress when Harpalus arrived in Greece is based on several ancient sources, and I would like to deal with each in turn. He attaches particular importance to a passage of Hyperides' prosecution speech against Demosthenes ('Lamian War', 52–3). The passage, Hyperides 5. 19, which follows a lacuna, is as follows:

ταῦτα σὺ πα[ρεσκεύ]ακας τῶι ψηφ[ίσματι], συλλαβὼν τὸ[ν Ἅρπα]λον,
καὶ τοὺς μὲ[ν Ἕλ]λη[ν]ας ἅπαντας [πρεσ]βεύεσθαι πεπ[οίη]κας ὡς

'Αλέξανδ[ρον], οὐκ ἔχοντας ἄλλ[ην] οὐδεμίαν ἀποσ[τρο]φήν, τοὺς δὲ
σ[ατράπας], οἳ αὐτοὶ ἂν ἡκο[ν ἑκόν]τες πρὸς ταύτη[ν τὴν] δύναμιν,
ἔχοντες τὰ χρήματα καὶ τοὺ[ς] στρατιώτας ὅσους ἕκ[α]στος αὐτῶν εἶχεν,
τούτους σύμπαντας οὐ μόνον κεκώλυκας ἀποστῆναι ἐκε[ί]νου τῇ συλλήψει
τῇ Ἁρπάλου, ἀλλὰ καὶ . . . καστον . . .

You [Demosthenes] have brought about this situation by having Harpalus
arrested under the terms of your decree. You have caused all the Greeks to
send embassies to Alexander since they had no other resort. You have not
only stopped the satraps who themselves would willingly have joined together
in this force, each of them having money and so many troops, from revolting
from him by the arrest of Harpalus, but also . . .

Another lacuna then occurs, followed by the sort of rhetorical invective against
Demosthenes we would expect in oratory. 'This situation' is in the Greek the straightforward neuter plural ταῦτα, but we have no idea to what it refers since it is preceded
by a lacuna, and before that lacuna Hyperides is talking about Nicanor's arrival in
Greece with the Exiles Decree and some order affecting at least the Achaeans,
Arcadians, and Boeotians. The specific context of ταῦτα has been lost. Rather than
to the period prior to Harpalus' arrest, as Ashton argues ταῦτα ('this situation')
refers, the passage surely refers to the effect in Greece (not to mention Athens) of the
whole Harpalus incident.[9] At the time of Demosthenes' trial in mid-March 323
the Athenians were faced with the return of their exiles and the question of Alexander's
deification. Neither of these had ever faced them before – or faced any other Greek
state, for that matter. The Exiles Decree in particular demonstrated the extent of
Alexander's power, despite the terms of the League of Corinth, and that he was not
afraid of exercising it. Demosthenes and Phocion, and perhaps also Lycurgus, who
generally dominated Athenian affairs in the 330s and 320s, had pursued a cautious
policy in relations with Macedonia. Since the battle of Chaeronea Demosthenes
had only twice opposed Alexander: the first time probably in 335, when the king
requested Athenian ships ([Plut.] X. Or. 847c, 848e, Plut. Phocion 21. 1),[10] and the
second in 323, when Alexander desired divine recognition (although later
Demosthenes apparently acquiesced in that demand). He had of course initially advised
support for the revolt of Thebes in 335, against Phocion's advice, and indeed it seems
the Athenians had supplied arms to the Thebans, but later the Athenians in Assembly
reversed this policy.[11]

Demosthenes' caution does not mean that as he grew older so he changed his attitude towards Macedonia; he was merely less 'open' in his opposition in these years.
However, his actions were not enough to placate the more overtly militant element
of the anti-Macedonians at Athens, headed by Hyperides (cf. Hyp. 5. 17–19 and 31),
which would have been anxious to seize the opportunity for revolt afforded by Harpalus
and his force and money. It had been thwarted of this by Demosthenes' counsel at a
meeting of the Assembly when Harpalus first appeared off Athens, and that Assembly
had forbidden his entry ([Plut.] X. Or. 846a). When Harpalus finally entered Athens,
the caution of Demosthenes was again victorious: he had Harpalus arrested and
proposed an embassy to Alexander to decide what to do with him. Later Demosthenes
was probably responsible for his flight from the city, which, along with the news that

half of the allegedly 700 talents Harpalus had brought with him to Athens was missing, was to cause such uproar and suspicion. And during all this time the Greek exiles were poised to return to their various states, and everywhere Alexander's apotheosis loomed large as an issue. It is hardly surprising that a flurry of diplomatic activity to the king was underway.[12]

The effect, then, of the Harpalus incident is the force of the Hyperides passage (5.19): if Demosthenes had seized the chance of Harpalus' arrival and force to revolt, and not had him arrested, the Greeks might not then (at the time of Demosthenes' trial in 323) have had to send envoys to Alexander over the implementation of the Exiles Decree and in the process to recognize his divinity. The passage refers to the situation at the time of Demosthenes' trial, not to several months before. It would be good to know who were these enigmatic satraps, to which Hyperides refers, and it is well worth pointing out that the word is almost completely restored.[13] I believe the restoration is almost certainly correct, in which case Hyperides may well be guilty of rhetorical exaggeration. This throws greater doubt on the possibility of the passage alluding to any premeditated revolt in the period in question – even on its general veracity. Thus I do not consider that we can take the passage as an indication that the seizure of Harpalus upset a Greek revolt which was well beyond the planning stage.

As further evidence that war between Athens and Alexander over the Exiles Decree was imminent, and had been planned for some time, Ashton ('Lamian War', 54–6) takes Pseudo-Plutarch, *Moralia* 531a, Curtius 10. 2. 2, and Athenaeus 12. 538b (the last of these drawing on Ephippus, *FGrH* 126 F 5). The passage from the *Moralia* is as follows:

τῶν γὰρ Ἀθηναίων ὡρμημένων Ἁρπάλῳ βοηθεῖν καὶ κορυσσομένων ἐπὶ τὸν Ἀλέξανδρον.

The Athenians were resolved to help Harpalus and were preparing themselves against Alexander . . .

I quite agree with Ashton that the Loeb translation of this passage is misleading and that the two participles have only a temporal, not causal, connection, so that to interpret this statement as evidence that Harpalus instigated an attempted revolt is incorrect. However, Ashton takes the passage to be genuinely implying that at the same time as the Athenians were offering Harpalus refuge they were planning a conflict with Alexander. Perhaps by Athenians Pseudo-Plutarch refers to the 'war-hawks' led by Hyperides, who were more openly militant (the overt anti-Macedonian faction). Out of context the passage may indeed appear to refer to a planned conflict, but the purpose of the passage and what precedes and, especially, follows it (the sudden arrival of Alexander's governor Philoxenus) are important. At this point of the *Moralia* Pseudo-Plutarch discusses how firmness is sometimes better than compliancy, and to illustrate his point uses an anecdote of Demosthenes' reaction to Philoxenus' arrival at Athens. Assuming the context is the Macedonian demands for Harpalus' surrender, the historical accuracy of the anecdote is doubtful, for elsewhere Pseudo-Plutarch names envoys from Antipater (X. Or. 846b). More importantly, Hyperides 5. 8 specifically excludes Philoxenus' presence by saying that envoys came from him (οἱ παρὰ Φιλοξένου). The reliability of oratory is suspect, a point which cannot be emphasized enough, but I cannot see why Hyperides would have falsified a fact which could only have lent weight to his case against Demosthenes. Moreover, Philoxenus' presence in Greece at this time is puzzling, for as the financial governor of Western Asia Minor he was based at Sardis: what could he have been doing in Greece? Pausanias (2. 33.4–5) tells us that he was on Rhodes soon after the flight of Harpalus, where he arrested the latter's administrator, but Pausanias' account has many problems, especially chronological, and should be discounted.[14] It appears unlikely, then, that Philoxenus did appear off the Attic coast, as Pseudo-Plutarch would have him do, and perhaps this author has had an undue influence on Pausanias' anecdote. Thus, if Pseudo-Plutarch erred about Philoxenus' appearance and Demosthenes' reaction to it in order to support his argument at this part of his work, he could equally well have made another mistake by saying that the Athenians were planning a revolt against Alexander. The accuracy of *Moralia* 531a must therefore be rejected.

I now turn to Curtius 10. 2. 2, which is as follows:

> [Alexander] Harpalo Atheniensibusque iuxta infestus, classem parari iubet, Athenas protinus petiturus.

> [Alexander] was furious equally towards Harpalus and the Athenians. and ordered a fleet to be prepared, and was resolved to go immediately to Athens.

The passage does not support the belief, as Ashton would argue, that war between Alexander and Athens was imminent before Harpalus' arrival, nor that the conflict centred on the Exiles Decree. Alexander was angry with the Athenians and decided to send a force against them because they were dealing favourably with Harpalus – thus Curtius here. Again, we must not take the passage out of context, for as Curtius goes on to tell us at 10. 2. 3–4, the king abandoned his plan when he found out that the Athenians had rejected Harpalus' offer and that he had subsequently fled to Crete and been murdered. Ashton ('Lamian War', 55 with n. 34) is right to point out that Curtius, despite his chronological inaccuracy, shows that the Athenians were resolved to resist the Exiles Decree (10. 2. 5–7; cf Justin 13. 5. 7), but there is no indication they would resist by warfare. Furthermore, since Alexander knew of events in Athens (Curt. 10. 2. 2–3), it is hard to understand why he decided to abandon his mission against that city if the Athenians were indeed planning to revolt over the Exiles Decree. That was the sort of news difficult to keep secret: can we really expect Alexander to have known about it but not done anything?[15] Again, these arguments make an Athenian-led Greek revolt prior to Harpalus' arrival highly unlikely.

Finally, Athenaeus 12. 538b (= Ephippus, *FGrH* 126 F 5), which is as follows:

> Γόργος ὁ ὁπλοφύλαξ ᾿Αλέξανδρον ῎Αμμωνος υἱὸν στεφανοῖ χρυσοῖς τρισχιλίοις, καὶ ὅταν ᾿Αθήνας πολιορκῇ, μυρίαις πανοπλίαις καὶ τοῖς ἴσοις καταπέλταις καὶ πᾶσι τοῖς ἄλλοις βέλεσιν εἰς τὸν πόλεμον ἱκανοῖς.

> Gorgus, the custodian of arms, gave 3,000 gold pieces to Alexander son of Ammon, and whenever he should besiege Athens, he would give 10,000 panoplies and as many catapults and all the other types of missiles as were sufficient for the war.

I agree with Ashton that this passage may be linked to Curtius 10. 2. 2, and seems to indicate that Alexander had a punitive expedition against Athens on hand. Ashton connects it with *SIG*[3] 312, in which the Samians honoured Gorgus of Iasus for his later help in recovering Samos from Athens, and thus he sees the above passage as referring to an impending conflict between Alexander and Athens over the Exiles Decree and occupation of Samos before Harpalus had been admitted into Athens.[16] Again, though, this is not necessarily the case, Alexander must have expected discontent once he issued the Exiles Decree, and the request for deification (whether it came from the king or not) may also play a role here. In order to counter any resistance, at the end of the Exiles Decree he inserted a clause ordering Antipater to coerce any unwilling city into receiving back its exiles (Diod. 18. 8. 4):

γεγράφαμεν δὲ ᾿Αντιπάτρῳ περὶ τούτων, ὅπως τὰς μὴ βουλομένας τῶν πόλεων κατάγειν ἀναγκάσῃ.

We have written to Antipater about this, so that if any of the cities are unwilling to restore you, he may compel them to do so.

Curtius has told us that the Athenians resisted the Exiles Decree (10. 2. 6–7), and Harpalus had fled to Athens because it represented the last real threat to Macedonia (see below). It comes as no surprise, then, for Alexander and his retinue to have anticipated a situation which could have led to potential warfare, with Athens at the forefront, hence Gorgus' extravagant offer ὅταν ᾿Αθήνας πολιορκῇ ('whenever he should besiege Athens'). But again all of this was to take place long after Harpalus had departed Athens – in fact, after Alexander's own death. Interpreted in this way, the passage takes on a new light whereby prominent members at least of Alexander's retinue were encouraging the king to wage war on Athens, and by extension on the Greeks. It is also not necessary to link *SIG*[3] 312 with the passage.

Dr Ashton further argues that the circumstances surrounding Harpalus' reception – his initial failure, then his entry into the city – also help to show that the Athenians were then planning a revolt. Harpalus, according to Ashton, was initially refused entry into Athens because of the size of his accompanying force.[17] However the refusal was primarily because the Athenians thought he was on a punitive mission from Alexander, who knew of their desire to rebel over the Exiles Decree. For his evidence in support Ashton takes Dinarchus 2. 4:

ἀποκτείνατε τοῦτον [Aristogeiton], ὃς παρ᾿ ᾿Αρπάλου λαβεῖν χρήματ᾿ ἐτόλμησεν, ὃν ᾔσθεθ᾿ ἥκειν καταληψόμενον τὴν πόλιν ὑμῶν κτλ.

Kill him [Aristogeiton], who dared to take money from Harpalus who he knew came to seize your city . . .

In other words, Harpalus came to enforce its acceptance by military means. Certainly the size of his force was a determining factor: Diodorus (17. 108. 6) says that when Harpalus fled from Babylon he collected along the way 6,000 men, and Curtius (10. 2. I) tells us he had 30 ships, which is a formidable force to appear off Cape Sunium. But to interpret Dinarchus 2. 4 in this way is stretching the Greek too much. The same goes for another passage in Dinarchus (3. 1), which Ashton uses as additional evidence in support of his theory:

[Philocles] φάσκων κωλύσειν Ἅρπαλον εἰς τὸν Πειραιᾶ καταπλεῦσαι, στρατηγὸς ὑφ' ὑμῶν ἐπὶ τὴν Μουνιχίαν καὶ τὰ νεώρια κεχειροτονημένος κτλ.

[Philocles] promised that he would prohibit Harpalus from sailing into the Piraeus when he had been elected by you as *strategos* of Munychia and the dockyards . . .

Philocles was brought to trial for disobeying the express directive of the Assembly in allowing Harpalus into the city (and for accepting a bribe from him): that is the context of this passage, and what precedes and follows it supports the context.[18] I cannot see how the passage may be linked to Dinarchus 2. 4 to the effect that Harpalus' arrival was connected to that of Nicanor, and that both had come to enforce the Exiles Decree.

It is more plausible that the Athenians were about to send an embassy to Alexander over the Exiles Decree – as other states were doing[19] – and so refused to grant Harpalus asylum in case this jeopardized the chances of success of that embassy. Moreover, in quoting the text of the Exiles Decree, Diodorus expressly says that Antipater had been empowered by Alexander to enforce the terms of the decree on any unwilling city (Diod. 18. 8. 4). Why would (or should) the Athenians think that the imperial treasurer had also been given this authority? One would not connect that office with such wide-sweeping military power.[20] That Harpalus succeeded in entering Athens at the second attempt was not, as Ashton considers, because the Athenians recognized that he was a true fugitive after all from Alexander rather than spearheading a force against the city, but because he arrived with a significantly reduced number of ships and men and as a suppliant. The last point is important, for to deny a suppliant access to a city of which he was a citizen was unthinkable.[21] It is very likely that he also bribed Philocles to let him in, for Philocles did disobey the Assembly's directive which was still in force,[22] hence his later prosecution (Dinarchus 3).[23]

It is well to point out that the very nature of our evidence means that we cannot arrive at a precise understanding of the affair, and any theory will meet its critics – as Dr Ashton rightly and succinctly remarks: 'With the evidence as it is, incontestable solutions . . . are not to be expected' ('Lamian War', 50). In the present case, I believe that the sources cannot be interpreted as Ashton has argued, and thus there are reasons for doubting his thesis. This takes us back to the orthodox view of the Harpalus affair, and in support of the *communis opinio* we may now return to Harpalus and the situation facing the Athenians after Harpalus had effected his entry into the city.

To begin with, why did Harpalus rest his hopes on either a Greek revolt or his being sheltered by the Athenians rather than, as might seem prudent, simply fleeing as far away as possible from Alexander – say to the West?[24] Harpalus does not strike one as the sort of person who would deliberately disregard his own well-being for a greater cause! The king's return from India and his accomplishments to date, unparalleled as they were, must have shell-shocked the Greeks: what could be expected next – and where? Alexander seems to have set his eyes on Arabia (a plan abandoned on his death),[25] but perhaps even the West, a potential place of refuge for Harpalus, was possible. It is my opinion that Harpalus would not have felt safe anywhere, and so for self-security reasons (now and in the future) he had to go to Athens in the hope of defeating the king by force. Moreover, Athens was the logical place to go, and not only because of her traditional enmity with Macedonia. With Sparta cowed after Agis' abortive war in 331, Athens represented the last place on the Greek mainland which could offer real opposition to Macedonia. Harpalus' force and money could be deployed for war against Macedonia if necessary, as indeed was the case when the king died (Diod. 18. 9. 4), and Harpalus probably hoped this would secure his protection. Finally, he had received Athenian citizenship for his gift of corn to the city in the recent famine,[26] not to mention the other links he had with the city from his two Athenian mistresses, Pythionice and Glycera, who had lived with him at his court,[27] and with Phocion's son-in-law Charicles.[28]

If the Athenians had a revolt in hand, then it is hard to understand why they denied Harpalus entry, given the resources he had at his disposal as well as the contacts he had. Indeed, that the Athenians had no such intention to revolt at that time is supported by some consideration of Harpalus' motives in surprisingly going back to Athens after his initial refusal, and of his conduct when there. By returning as a suppliant he evidently expected to gain entrance. This was not because he was now fully aware that Athens intended to rebel over the Exiles Decree and so had even greater cause to seek refuge there, hence his much reduced force, as Ashton argues ('Lamian War', 57–8). I suggest that Harpalus hoped to offset the influence of the moderates Demosthenes and Phocion by appealing to those Athenians who could be incited to revolt (the 'war-hawks', to call them that), a task demanding time and money. But he did not get the necessary time to instigate an immediate or 'direct' revolt, in which he himself played the role of *agent provacateur*, because of the arrival of Macedonian envoys from Philoxenus (Hyp. 5. 8), Olympias (Diod. 17. 108. 7), and probably Antipater too ([Plut.] X. Or. 846b) seeking his extradition, and his subsequent arrest and imprisonment. He had the opportunity to use some of the money which he had brought with him, but although he may have won over less influential men he was ultimately unsuccessful.

By the time of his arrest Harpalus must have realized that his plans for inciting an immediate revolt had fallen through and that retribution at the hands of Alexander for all his misdeeds loomed imminent. However, instead of fleeing from Athens he stayed in jail for what I believe are a few weeks after his arrest.[29] Why? One plausible explanation is that he knew he would not be allowed to remain in the city unmolested for the rest of his life, and so hoped that his continued presence might engineer what I call an 'indirect' revolt. In other words, as a suppliant he hoped that the Athenians would give him continued shelter in defiance of any Macedonian extradition order. This in turn would lead to increased friction between the Athenians and Alexander, opening up the way for organized resistance and leaving Harpalus comfortably out of Alexander's reach. If the Athenians were bent on leading a Greek revolt at this time, then the imprisonment of Harpalus was pointless and a farce, as, more importantly, was the embassy to Alexander about him.

What the Athenians themselves made of Harpalus' emergence on the Greek scene may be used as support for the case that no rebellion had been planned in advance of his arrival. Clearly the Athenians were in a quandary, but they were cautious.

An Assembly was held, and Demosthenes carried a decree providing for the arrest of Harpalus, the confiscation of his money (allegedly 700 talents), and the despatch of an embassy to the king seeking his directive on the affair.[30] In this way he decreased the apparent defiance of the Macedonian demands for Harpalus' extradition, relieved the immediate tension, and, perhaps for the good of the Athenians' moral considerations, also parried any criticism levelled against him or the Athenians about betraying a suppliant.

That Assembly meeting which discussed the Harpalus issue is, in my opinion, crucial to our perception of the affair and of the Athenian attitude to Macedonian rule in this period – and plausibly by extension, of the Greek attitude (cf. below). Given the political significance of having Harpalus in Athens the Assembly that debated what to do with him would probably have been filled by a capacity crowd – anything up to some 13,400 citizens densely packed, perhaps even more.[31] Demosthenes was urging the Athenians not to surrender Harpalus but at the same time attempting to dissuade them from taking advantage of his offer of rebellion. No doubt he also had in mind Harpalus' use as a potential supplier of arms and money, and possibly as a useful bargaining tool in his own forthcoming political negotiations with Nicanor at Olympia over the Exiles Decree. After all, Demosthenes usually saw two sides to every situation, and exploited whichever was necessary. The enforced return of the Greek exiles struck hard at the individual autonomy of the Greek states, but for the Athenians the Samian issue was equally crucial and analogous to their attitude over Amphipolis in the reign of Philip II. They had no intention of giving up that island (Diod. 18. 8. 7), which had been seized by Timotheus from Persian rule in 366/5, was then peopled by Athenian cleruchs, and had been reconfirmed an Athenian possession by Philip II after the battle of Chaeronea (Diod. 18. 56. 7).[32] If Athenian diplomatic negotiations with both Nicanor (at the hands of Demosthenes) and Alexander (at the hands of the embassy) went badly for the Athenians, then Harpalus and his resources were still on hand and could be deployed.

Hyperides too would have spoken against the surrender of Harpalus, but for different reasons: here was the opportunity for immediate revolt and the chance to be rid of the Macedonian masters. Demosthenes, despite his advice (and cautious policy), would not have been upset to see the end of Macedonian rule – neither the Athenians nor Alexander could have been in any doubt about Demosthenes' true attitude towards the Macedonian hegemony. However, it was only after Alexander's death, at the time of the so-called Lamian War, that his anti-Macedonian policy became more overt. In 324 and 323, then, Alexander presented a threat to the Athenians and their interests, a threat which Demosthenes recognized, as is reflected in his actions.

To return to the Assembly meeting debating the Harpalus case. The clash between Demosthenes and Hyperides hinged on the issue of war with Alexander. Ultimately Demosthenes' proposal was accepted, and by a very clear majority since a vote was estimated by the number of hands raised (*cheirotonia*) rather than an actual count.[33] It is plausible, then, that Athenian public opinion followed a cautious bent at this time. Enough Athenians had supported Demosthenes in forbidding Harpalus' entry into Athens the first time, and their attitude was to remain the same when he finally got in thanks to his bribery. Only when Demosthenes had been sufficiently discredited for his role in the Harpalus affair were Hyperides and the 'war-hawks' able to come to the fore and Athenian policy took on a new turn. I further suggest that the vote in Demosthenes' favour shows that other states were not then harbouring militant feelings, otherwise Hyperides may have been able to counter Demosthenes' arguments by alluding to states willing to join Athens in rebellion. Rather, the other states were following a diplomatic course over the Exiles Decree. That is why we find a number of embassies journeying to the king over this issue, and why only one state, Tegea, actually implemented the decree before his death.[34] At the time of the Harpalus affair the Athenians were not bent on military resistance, nor does it plausibly seem were the other states, which were largely quiet and which, despite a diversity of attitudes, would have looked to Athens for leadership.

The presence of Harpalus in Athens represented a significant factor in the success or failure of her diplomatic mission – all the more so if he happened to be in collusion with Hyperides and the overtly militant opponents of the Macedonian hegemony, as was suggested before. Whilst Harpalus was in prison Demosthenes had gone to Olympia to discuss there the terms of the Exiles Decree with Nicanor, who brought the decree to Greece, presumably to try to modify its terms or at least achieve a stay of execution. Soon after he returned from Olympia Harpalus left Athens.[35] Perhaps even demands for his surrender had again been made, this time from the powerful Antipater, which further increased the pressure on the Athenians.[36] If the Athenian embassy which was due to leave for Alexander's court was able to take news that Harpalus was no longer sheltered in Athens, and that the Athenians had recognized the king's divinity – for on his return from Olympia Demosthenes advocated this course[37] – then the hope was that Alexander would deal favourably with the Athenian plea over Samos and the non-return of the city's exiles. After all, when Alexander had demanded the surrender of leading Athenian statesmen in 335 he had relented in that demand as a result of diplomacy.[38] Why might he not adopt a similar course again over the exiles and Samian issues, especially as Alexander, like his father, had generally treated the Athenians well? It mattered little what happened to Harpalus after his departure: the important fact was that the Athenians no longer harboured a fugitive whose connections and resources made him – and by implication themselves – politically dangerous to Alexander. In this I agree with Ashton ('Lamian War', 59–60) that Demosthenes spoke against Harpalus because he did not want Athens to become embroiled in a war purely over him as opposed to the Exiles Decree, in which Athens would be seen as the wronged party. Ashton bases his view quite credibly on Plutarch, *Demosthenes* 25. 3; what I cannot accept is that the passage can be used as corroborating evidence that a military revolt led by Athens was imminent.

With the Athenians' mission so dangerously in the balance military rebellion against the Exiles Decree, and thus Macedonian rule, does not seem an option at this time – indeed, such a course would verge on the foolhardy. However, following up Ashton's arguments, could the effects of the Exiles Decree have prompted the Athenians – and the Greeks – to armed resistance at any stage in 324? Certainly the sequence of events in the Harpalus affair pivots on the promulgation of the decree. Not only did the decree ride roughshod over any relative autonomy the Greeks enjoyed, but also we can imagine that in the smaller states especially the return of the exiles would have led to *stasis*. In the two decrees we have governing the return of exiles in this period we note the emphasis placed on reconciling those who stayed with those who returned, usually by the swearing of an oath.[39] Sources exist which hint at the possibility of the Athenians' resisting the Exiles Decree,[40] and they did refuse to receive back their exiles (Curt. 10. 2. 6–7), who had gathered at Megara (Din. 1. 58 and 94).[41] Indeed, contacts of a military nature had been maintained throughout the 320s (for example, alliances between Athens and the Aetolians, Phocians, and Locrians),[42] and in connection with this, and the military power of a potential Athens-led coalition of Greek states once the full political and social implications of the decree were realized, Nicanor may even have brought another directive from Alexander forbidding the joint-muster of a force, as I have argued elsewhere.[43] Then there is Badian's theory, based on Hyperides 5. 13, that Demosthenes took money from Harpalus to help support a mercenary force of some 8,000 at Taenarum, headed by the *strategos* Leosthenes, for a revolt against Alexander. For a number of reasons the theory is exploded: the sum involved was too small (twenty talents); the Athenians were unwilling to risk a leak and endanger their chances of diplomatic success; and the state at this time simply could not afford the upkeep.[44]

Thus, whilst all these factors would make military mobilization understandable, none points to planned hostilities before Harpalus' arrival or even before Alexander's death became known, and nothing was implemented. What influence did Alexander's proposed apotheosis play in Greek resentment becoming more overtly militant? Whether the request to recognize Alexander's divinity came from the king or not, our sources indicate that there certainly was some debate amongst the Greeks over his deification in the later 320s.[45] Public opinion at Athens evidently did not allow the Exiles Decree to be accepted without a fight, but not so the deification issue. What did it matter to call Alexander a god if he ruled in the Athenians' favour? Demades hit the nail on the head with his remark, if it may be connected to the Samian issue, that the Athenians were so concerned about heaven that they stood to lose the earth (Val. Max. 7. 2. 13). Heaven could wait if more practical issues were pressing. Once, however, the king had ruled against Athens in her claim to Samos, which he did (hence the later war against the Samians culminating in the arrest of prominent Samians and the intervention of Antileon of Chalcis),[46] the situation was a different matter, but by then Harpalus had been out of Athens for several months.[47] I follow Malcolm Errington's arguments that the Samian directive was made only when the Athenian embassy met Alexander at Babylon, as opposed to the generally accepted date at Susa simultaneous with Nicanor's despatch to Greece.[48] There is no reason to think, in the light of the evidence that we have, that Athens had been selected for individual treatment when Alexander conceived the Exiles Decree. His response more logically stems from an embassy on the matter.

Furthermore, it took the Areopagus six months to enquire into those accused of complicity in the Harpalus affair and to publish its results (Din. 1. 45), a period of time which is too much of a coincidence, for at about that time the embassy to Alexander returned home with the news of the Athenians' diplomatic failure over Samos. At his trial Demosthenes himself pleaded that he had been sacrificed to please the king (Hyp. 5. 14), and since no evidence against him was given and the background to that trial (and to the trials of the others accused of complicity, for that matter) is equally controversial, it is plausible that the Athenians were still hoping to get into Alexander's good books by finding Demosthenes guilty: he thus becomes a scapegoat.[49] A diplomatic, not military, solution to the Exiles Decree and the Samian issue thus rears its head again.

If the Athenians, and by extension the Greeks, were not planning a revolt in 324, had one been planned before Alexander died (as Ashton argues)? The Harpalus affair was over and done with by the time Alexander breathed his last, and was not the flashpoint which triggered organized resistance, as the mood of the Athenians shows. Nor was the Exiles Decree, as the diplomatic flurries by the states indicate, even though shock and resentment must have been high. What then did lead to the so-called Lamian War and what can we say, as a result, about the Greek response to Macedonian domination?

It is my opinion that the Greeks were pretty soon and completely cowed into military submission by the Macedonians, especially by Antipater after Agis' abortive war.[50] Once Alexander unexpectedly died they realized in the confusion which followed – for there was no strong successor to the Macedonian throne as there had been in 336 – that the time had come to do something about their situation, and they seized it. Other factors then combined with this *kairos*, especially Alexander's disregard of the League of Corinth as seen in the Exiles Decree. The terms of the Common Peace League of Corinth of 337 were not so unduly harmful for the Greeks, especially the Athenians, and certainly allowed them the right to make their own domestic decisions.[51] Greece may well have come to accept a Macedonian rule which thus allowed it relative autonomy and the chance for some peace and prosperity. But the Exiles Decree changed all that. No doubt Alexander's increasing megalomania, as revealed in his activities in Asia and his push towards deification in Greece, also played a role. That such a widespread revolt took so long to break out is a tribute to Antipater, who deserves double credit for also keeping Macedonia powerful and united under his regency, so much so that there was economic growth, and education and military training, for example, remained at a high standard.[52]

The situation in 324/3, then, as a result of Alexander's orders, reveals growing dissatisfaction, but not organized rebellion, as the diplomatic moves show. The turning-point came with Alexander's unexpected death. But it is not just Greece which reveals growing dissatisfaction. Macedonia too in this period provides interesting insights into the Macedones' attitude to their king – something of a 'balance' to the Greek attitude.[53] The reaction of the Macedones at home to Alexander's conquests, his long absence, and especially his adoption of Asian customs and use of Asians and Orientals in the administration and army reveals an increasing dissatisfaction which may well have placed in jeopardy the unity of that state achieved by Philip II. Nor should we underestimate the effect of his setbacks at the hands of his own men (the Hyphasis and Opis mutinies, for example), news of which would hardly fill the people back home with confidence. It is significant that of the bronze coins minted at Amphipolis none mentions Alexander's Asian conquests nor uses the title ΒΑΣΙΛΕΥΣ.[54] Moreover, when the Macedones in Asia refused to bestow on Alexander the divine honours which had been granted to Philip II (Curt. 4. 7. 31, 8. 5. 5, 10. 5. 11), the Macedones at home may well have followed suit, thus bringing matters to a head.[55] That Alexander did not endear himself to his own people has interesting implications for his ultimate objectives and how he saw himself – his attitude to his own divinity is an obvious example,[56] but the move to establish a kingdom of Asia and not a Macedonian empire in Asia is equally significant.[57] Had he not died in 323 a potentially explosive situation might well have developed at home, jeopardizing the Macedonian hegemony more than any Greek revolt, and testing Antipater's leadership abilities to the utmost.

In conclusion, the Harpalus affair plays an important role in Greek history, and for that it and its implications deserve close attention. I have argued that the 'orthodox' view on the Harpalus affair is to be preferred since it is unlikely that an Athenian-led Greek revolt over the Exiles Decree was interrupted by the arrival of Harpalus and resumed in the so-called Lamian War.[58] At the same time, I make the qualification that the events connected with the affair are more intimately linked to the Exiles Decree than has previously been seen. The implications of the affair and the decree for how the Macedonian hegemony was viewed by the Greeks are wide-sweeping: instead of our seeing the Greeks as ready to seize the first chance to revolt against their Macedonian masters, especially over something as shocking as the Exiles Decree – and the request for deification – a different picture emerges, one which sees the Greeks as subservient and more willing to resort to diplomacy than to revolt. The picture thus indicates an acceptance of Macedonian rule. The problems associated with the aftermath of Philip's death and the accession of Alexander called for drastic and immediate remedies as Macedonian rule was reinstated. Hence the example made of Thebes, which did the trick of keeping the states quiet, and the moves forming the basis of the allegations in [Demosthenes] 17, allegations which are in keeping with exhorting a call to arms in this unsettled period.[59] Once Macedonian rule had been re-established life under it was not so harsh, and Alexander generally had been responsive to the Greeks, particularly the Athenians. Hence when there are problems affecting the Greek states the first reaction to combat them is diplomacy. At the same time, the real power wielded by Macedonia over Greece is demonstrated, and it is total. This is supported by the fact that when the conflict between Alexander's successors ended it was not Greek but Macedonian power which ultimately triumphed. Although the spirit of Greek autonomy might not have been beaten, and the Hellenic War of 323–2 would prove that, until the time of the Chremonidean War Greek liberty in effect had ended on the field at Chaeronea.

Notes

The topic of the Greek attitude to the Macedonian hegemony has attracted attention in various works from virtually the fourth century BC onwards, and thus an immediate reaction to my title is that another treatment is unjustified. Yet there are grounds, in my opinion, for another exploration of the Greek response, one which is intended to reassess the Greek attitude by drawing on the implications of the Harpalus affair. To embark on this subject, given Nicholas Hammond's unparalleled expertise in matters Greek and Macedonian, has taken no small amount of courage, and it is with no small degree of nervousness that I dedicate this chapter to him.

I am indebted to Professors Ernst Fredricksmeyer, Bob Milns, and Frank Walbank, and to Dr Norman Ashton, for their comments on a draft of this paper – I should point out that Dr Ashton is unconvinced by my arguments. A short version of this paper was delivered at the Second Australian International Symposium on Ancient Macedonia, held at the University of Melbourne in July 1991, and will appear (as delivered) in the Proceedings. I am grateful to the Academic Committee for allowing me to improve and enlarge that paper for publication now.

1 Oxford, 1937, at pp. 204–48.
2 On relations between Alexander and the Greek states see N. G. L. Hammond and F. W. Walbank, *A History of Macedonia*, iii (Oxford, 1988), 72–85, and R. M. Errington, *A History of Macedonia* (Berkeley, Calif., 1990), 93–7.
3 See E. Badian, 'Harpalus', *JHS* 81 (1961), 16–25 (= G. T. Griffith, ed., *Alexander the Great: The Main Problems* (Cambridge, 1966), 206–15); S. Jaschinski, *Alexander und Griechenland unter*

dem Eindruck der Flucht des Harpalos (Bonn, 1981), 18–22; A. B. Bosworth, *Conquest and Empire: The Reign of Alexander the Great* (Cambridge, 1988), 148–50.

4 On Harpalus' first flight from Alexander in 333 see Ian Worthington, 'The First Flight of Harpalus Reconsidered', *G&R*[2] 31 (1984), 161–9, to which add E. D. Carney, 'The First Flight of Harpalus Again', *CJ* 77 (1981), 9–11, and B. M. Kingsley, 'Harpalos in the Megarid (333–331 BC) and the Grain Shipments from Cyrene', *ZPE* 66 (1985), 165–77.

5 Diod. 18. 8. 5 tells of 20,000 who gathered at Olympia to hear the announcement of the decree – clearly these had pre-knowledge.

6 Cf. e.g. A. W. Pickard-Cambridge, *Demosthenes* (London, 1914), 451–2; Badian, 'Harpalus', 16–25 (= Griffith, *Main Problems*, 206–15); T. T. B. Ryder, *Koine Eirene* (Oxford, 1965), 108–9; Peter Green, *Alexander of Macedon* (Harmondsworth, 1974), 461–3, cf. his *Alexander to Actium* (Berkeley, Calif., 1990), 10; N. G. L. Hammond, *Alexander the Great*[2] (Bristol, 1989), 257–8, and *Macedonia*, iii, 107–9; Bosworth, *Conquest and Empire*, 215–16 and 225 ff.

7 On chronology see Ian Worthington, 'The Chronology of the Harpalus Affair', *SO* 61 (1986), 63–76.

8 I believe that Demosthenes was the victim of a political conspiracy, and argue this in my *A Historical Commentary on Dinarchus: Rhetoric and Conspiracy in Later Fourth-Century Athens* (Ann Arbor, Mich., 1992), 41–77. (In that book I have been able to make reference only to the conference paper cited in the opening note of this chapter.)

9 Cf. Badian, 'Harpalus', 37 (= Griffith, *Main Problems*, 227).

10 R. Develin, *Athenian Officials* (Cambridge, 1989), 387, dates the request and opposition of Demosthenes and Hyperides to 332/1.

11 For discussion see Worthington, *Commentary on Dinarchus*, ad 1. 21. I took the view that at that stage Athens would have supported any potential rebel, an attitude soon to change, as evidenced by the lack of support to Agis III in his war (see below, n. 50).

12 On the embassies see Arr. 7. 19. 1 and 23. 2, Diod. 17. 113, Pliny, *NH* 3. 57, Justin 12. 13. 1–2; cf. Arr. 7. 15. 4–6 and Hyp. 5. 19, with the discussions of W. W. Tarn, *Alexander the Great*, ii (Cambridge, 1948), 374–8, and P. A. Brunt, *Arrian: Anabasis*, ii. Loeb Classical Library (London, 1983), 497–8.

13 On this see the remarks of Ashton, 'Lamian War', 53 n. 28 and 61 n. 61. Diod. 17. 111. 1–2 says that Persian satraps also collected at Taenarum, but the validity of this has been questioned by both Goukowsky in the Budé edition of Diodorus 17 at pp. 269–70 and Ashton, 'Lamian War', 53 n. 28.

14 Ian Worthington, 'Pausanias II, 33. 4–5 and Demosthenes', *Hermes*, 113 (1985), 123–5.

15 Indeed, Ashton, 'Lamian War', 60 (with n. 55), negates his argument on 54–5 to a large extent by stating: 'Also, Athens' decision to arrest Harpalus must have allayed many of Alexander's suspicions regarding the polis.'

16 On this see further below, with n. 46.

17 Ashton, 'Lamian War', 56–9; cf. Badian, 'Harpalus', 31 with n. 106 (= Griffith, *Main Problems*, 221), Bosworth, *Conquest and Empire*, 216.

18 See Worthington, *Commentary on Dinarchus*, ad loc.

19 Ashton, 'Lamian War', 51, Bosworth, *Conquest and Empire*, 221–2. See also n. 12 above.

20 Harpalus' alleged lameness (Arr. 3. 6. 6) too may have precluded him from active military campaigning, but on Harpalus' physical defect note the reservation of A. B. Bosworth, *A Historical Commentary on Arrian's History of Alexander*, i (Oxford, 1980), 283.

21 Professor Hammond made the point at the Macedonian conference (above opening note (the uncued one)) that a force of 6,000 mercenaries in Athens would have disastrous consequences for security, and therefore the Athenians denied Harpalus access. I agree, but the religious implications of Harpalus' suppliant status must not be forgotten.

22 I quite agree with Ashton ('Lamian War', 58) that Harpalus used his money to sway influential people (see further below), but not that he had 'to procure the right to remain resident in the polis', for he was already an Athenian citizen (see below, with n. 26).

23 This point was missed by L. Tritle in his *Phocion the Good* (London, 1988), 119, who says that it was the Athenians [in Assembly] who decided to admit Harpalus.

24 I thank Gene Borza for the (oral) genesis of this line of thought.

25 See Hammond, *Alexander the Great*[2], 245 and 282 (with n. 307) for references and discussion.

26 Athen. 13. 586d and 596a–b; Tod, *GHI*, no. 196, esp. line 5; M. J. Osborne, *Naturalization in Athens*, iii (Brussels, 1983), T82.

27 Plut. *Phocion* 22. 1–2; Paus. I. 37. 5: Athen. 13. 586c–d (drawing on Theopompus, *FGrH* 115 FF 253 and 254 and Cleitarchus, *FGrH* 137 F 30) and 594d–596b (drawing on a variety of earlier sources).

28 According to Plutarch, *Phocion* 22. 2, Harpalus' daughter was later adopted by Phocion and Charicles.

29 On chronology see Worthington, 'Chronology of the Harpalus Affair', 66–8.

30 Din. 1. 70 and 89 (cf. 90), Dion. Hal. *Dinarchus* 11 and *Demosthenes* 57; cf. Hyp. 5. 9 and [Plut.] *X Or.* 846b.

31 I accept this attendance figure for Pnyx III as put forward by M. H. Hansen, 'Political Activity and the Organization of Attica in the Fourth Century BC', in *The Athenian Ecclesia*, ii (Copenhagen, 1989), 73–91.

32 See further C. Habicht, 'Samische Volksbeschlüsse der hellenistischen Zeit', *MDAI(A)* 72 (1957), 156–64.

33 On this see M. H. Hansen, 'How Did the Athenian Ecclesia Vote?', in *The Athenian Ecclesia*, i (Copenhagen, 1983), 103–21. There is no evidence to suggest that a special count was made at this meeting: see further, on this debate and the implications of the vote, Worthington, *Commentary on Dinarchus*, 46–8.

34 For arguments that *IG* xii 2. 6 = Tod, *GHI*, no. 201 (the decree of Mytilene) belongs not to 324 but to 332 see A. J. Heisserer, *Alexander the Great and the Greeks: The Epigraphic Evidence* (Norman, Okla., 1980), 118–41, and my 'Alexander the Great and the Date of the Mytilene Decree', in *Acta of the University of New England International Seminar on Greek and Latin Epigraphy*, Ian Worthington, ed. (Bonn, 1990), 194–214 – also published in *ZPE* 83 (1990), 194–214. On Tegea see too Worthington, 'The Date of the Tegea Decree (Tod ii 202): A Response to the *Diagramma* of Alexander III or of Polyperchon?', *AHB* 7 (1993), 59–64.

35 Diod. 17. 108. 7 has it that Harpalus was forced to slip away (διέδρα καὶ κατῆρεν), echoed to a very large extent by Plutarch, *Demosthenes* 25. 6, who adds a note of compulsion: the Athenians sent Harpalus away from (ἀπέπεμψαν) the city.

36 Bosworth suggests (*Conquest and Empire*, 217) that perhaps Harpalus was forced to escape to save Alexander the embarrassment of extraditing and condemning his boyhood friend; I find this unlikely.

37 A *volte face* which not unnaturally provoked suspicion: Din. 1. 94, Hyp. 5. 31–2.

38 Diod. 17. 115, Arr. 1. 10. 4–6, Plut. *Demosthenes* 23. 4, *Phocion* 17. 2, [Plut.] *X. Or.* 841e, 847c, 848e, Justin 11. 4. 10–11; cf. Aes. 3. 161 and Din. 1. 82, and on this episode cf. the discussion of Bosworth, *Commentary on Arrian*, i. 92–6.

39 From Mytilene (Tod, *GHI*, no. 201) and Tegea (Tod, *GHI*, no. 202). The Tegean Decree may be placed in 324, in the context of the Exiles Decree, but the Mytilenean Decree should be dated to 332: see above, n. 34 with bibliography there cited.

40 Athen, 12. 538b drawing on Ephippus (*FGrH* 126 F 5); cf. Diod. 18. 8. 7.

41 Cf. also Hyp. 5. 18–19, Curt. 10. 2. 5–7, Justin 13. 5. 1–6. The core of the problem, as Ashton rightly points out in his article, was the Samian issue. On the impact of the Exiles Decree cf. also the remarks of Errington, *History of Macedonia*, 95–7.

42 See Ian Worthington, '*IG* ii[2] 370 and the Date of the Athenian Alliance with Aetolia', *ZPE* 57 (1984), 139–44, for full references and dates.

43 'Hyper. 5 *Dem*. 18 and Alexander's Second Directive to the Greeks', *C&M* 37 (1986), 115–21.

44 Dinarchus' scare at 1. 68, asking what would happen if Alexander demanded back the money stolen by Harpalus, may not just be rhetoric. The Athenians often ran short of money until the taxes were collected (Dem. 20. 115 and 24. 98), and finances must have been considerably drained by Eubulus' military ventures and Lycurgus' building programme. Indeed, during the latter's administration loans from private individuals were used to meet unforeseen expenditure ([Plut.] *X. Or.* 852b; *SIG*[3] 289. 29), and some building costs were offset by gifts: for example, *IG* ii[2] 351 + 624 (= *SEG* xxiv 99 = *SIG*[3] 288 = Tod, *GHI*, no. 198 = C. Schwenk, *Athens in the Age of Alexander: The Dated Laws and Decrees of the 'Lykourgan Era'* (Chicago, 1985), no. 48), *c*. 330/29, honouring Eudemus, son of Philourgus of Plataea, for supplying 1,000 oxen

for the building of the Stadium and Theatre of Dionysus. See further, on the Badian hypothesis, my *Commentary on Dinarchus*, 66–9.

45 Cf. Bosworth, *Conquest and Empire*, 288–9. Polybius 12. 12b. 3, [Plut.] *Moralia* 219e, and Aelian, *VH* 5. 12 show that the Greek states had attempted to resist Alexander's deification. Demades, who proposed Alexander's deification, was later fined ten talents – probably early in the Lamian War: J. M. Williams, 'Demades' Last Years, 323/2–319/8 BC: A "Revisionist" Interpretation', *Ancient World*, 19 (1989), 23–4. For a different interpretation on Alexander's deification, see George Cawkwell [in *Ventures into Greek History*, Ch. 14; reprinted in Chap. 9 of this Reader].

46 Cf. E. Badian, 'A Comma in the History of Samos', *ZPE* 23 (1976), 289–94. G. Shipley, *A History of Samos* (Oxford, 1987), 166–8.

47 *Contra* Ashton, 'Lamian War', 62–3, and Bosworth, *Conquest and Empire*, 215 and 221. See further below.

48 R. M. Errington, 'Samos and the Lamian War', *Chiron*, 5 (1975), 51–7: *contra* Ashton, 'Lamian War', 62–3, and Bosworth, *Conquest and Empire*, 215 and 221. The Persians may well have used Samos as a supply-base with the Athenian cleruchs' permission, hence Alexander's decision (Shipley, 165–6).

49 This point is argued in greater detail in my *Commentary on Dinarchus*, 63–5.

50 Note the lack of widespread active support for Agis and, significantly, the extent of Athenian opposition to involvement from the outset (Worthington, *Commentary on Dinarchus*, ad 1. 34–5 with bibliography cited). This was very different from the Athenians' initial support for the Thebans only a few years previously (cf. above, with n. 11). On Agis' war see now E. Badian [in *Ventures into Greek History*, Chap. 13].

51 See C. Roebuck, 'The Settlements of Philip II with the Greek States in 338 BC', *CPh* 43 (1948), 73–92, with 80–2 on Philip's dealings with the Athenians; J. R. Ellis, *Philip II and Macedonian Imperialism* (London, 1976), 204–9; N. G. L. Hammond and G. T. Griffith, *A History of Macedonia*, ii (Oxford, 1979), 623–46.

52 Antipater is a worthy (and neglected) figure for a detailed study – and thus Elizabeth Baynham's contribution to this volume is particularly welcome (below, Ch. 16). On Antipater's power in Greece see also Hammond's remarks in *Macedonia*, iii. 89, and Errington, *History of Macedonia*, 92–4.

53 On Macedonia during Alexander's absence and especially the disunity, potential and otherwise, see Hammond and Walbank, *Macedonia*, iii. 86–94: cf. Errington, *History of Macedonia*, 104 and 114–15. On the apparent decline in Macedonian manpower see A. B. Bosworth, 'Alexander the Great and the Decline of Macedon', *JHS* 106 (1986), 1–12, but against this see now Badian, [in *Ventures into Greek History*, Chap. 13].

54 Hammond in *Macedonia*, iii. 92.

55 Cf. Hammond, *Macedonia*, iii. 93–4. Philip's divinity is based on Diodorus 16. 91. 4–92. 5 and 16. 95. 1 (the wedding of his daughter Cleopatra at which a statue of Philip was carried in procession with those of the twelve gods): see further on the issue, Hammond and Griffith, *Macedonia*, ii. 692–5, and E. N. Borza, *In the Shadow of Olympus: The Emergence of Macedon* (Princeton, NJ, 1990), 249–51.

56 There is a vast bibliography on this issue: see, for example, J. Seibert, *Alexander der Grosse* (Darmstadt, 1972), 116–25 and 148–62; Bosworth, *Conquest and Empire*, 71–4, 282–3, and 278–89; E. Badian, 'The Deification of Alexander the Great', in *Ancient Macedonian Studies in Honor of C. F. Edson*, H. J. Dell, ed. (Thessaloniki, 1981), 27–71; and see also George Cawkwell [in *Ventures into Greek History*, Ch. 14; reprinted in Chap. 9 of this Reader].

57 On this issue cf. the remarks of Errington, *History of Macedonia*, 111–14.

58 On the Hellenic ('Lamian') War see especially Hammond and Walbank, *Macedonia*, iii. 107–17; cf. N. G. Ashton, 'The Lamian War – *stat magni nominis umbra*', *JHS* 104 (1984), 152–7.

59 The speech seems to be roughly contemporary with the events of 336–5; for a date of 331 see W. Will, 'Zur Datierung der Rede Ps.-Demosthenes XVII', *RhM* 125 (1982), 202–13.

5

ALEXANDER
AND ASIA

Alexander invaded Persia in 334 with about 32,000 infantry and 5,000 cavalry (but note Sources 17 and 18). This force grew to 50,000 when it linked with an advance force (Arr. 1.17.11). He crossed the Hellespont, but rather than immediately engage any Persian forces he went to Troy to sacrifice to Achilles and Ajax.[1] Soon after Alexander defeated a Persian force at the Granicus river (cf. Sources 40 and 41).[2] This was not a Persian army proper but a hastily levied contingent and the Great King, Darius III, was not present. A detour to Gordium, where he untied (in controversial fashion) the famous Gordian knot, followed (Sources 42 and 43): this was an important action, for it was written that whoever cut the knot would conquer Asia. Alexander then journeyed down the coast of Asia Minor, freeing Greek cities there from Persian rule in accordance with one of the declared reasons for the invasion. In Priene in either 334 or 330 he dedicated the newly constructed temple of Athena Polias (Source 21).[3] It is likely that these cities then joined the League of Corinth.[4]

In 333, the invaders again met the Persians, led by the Great King himself, in battle at Issus (Sources 44–46, 85). Alexander's strategy won the day, and Darius fled the battlefield, leaving behind his wife and daughters, whom Alexander treated with respect (cf. Source 48). Issus was a turning point for Alexander, for after it he began to regard himself as King of Asia (although Darius was still alive), and the battle was quickly taken up by Alexander's propaganda machine.[5] Rather than pursue Darius, Alexander announced his intention to go to Egypt, which he reached in late 332 after being distracted for some time by the siege of Tyre (Sources 51 and 52; cf. 86). Egypt welcomed him with open arms, and while there he laid the foundations of the great city of Alexandria, which became so important in the Hellenistic and Roman periods (Source 49). He also visited the oracle of Zeus Ammon at Siwah (see Sources 92–97), a visit which was the turning point in the belief in his own divinity.[6]

Despite Alexander's preoccupation with the Asian campaign he did not neglect the Greeks, nor they him, and in the 330s and 320s epigraphical evidence attests to various issues which they brought to his attention and his willingness to adjudicate at all levels. In Source 33, which may be dated shortly after his return from Siwah, the 'little sea' (wherever that was) would hold no interest for Alexander, yet he appreciated that it was an important issue for the people of Iasus (south of Miletus on the coast of Asia Minor). Source 34, from the same period or 330, from Priene, deals with the freedom of Prienians living at Naulochum (probably the harbour of Priene). See Chapter 4 for other inscriptional evidence.

Darius was still alive, and had managed to regroup his forces. In spring 331, Alexander left Egypt and engaged Darius in battle at Gaugamela on 1 October 331 (Sources 47, 53 and 54), waging this battle as a son of Zeus (Source 98).[7] It was another Issus, except that Darius was not allowed to remain King for very long, and was murdered the following year. He was succeeded by Bessus, who proclaimed himself Artaxerxes V, but in reality Persia was now Alexander's – the deliberate (as opposed to perhaps accidental after a drunken orgy; cf. Source 55) burning of Persepolis, the great summer palace of the Persian kings, in mid-330 showed that.[8] However, Alexander could not ignore Bessus, who had mustered troops against him, and so he moved east, into central Asia, towards Bactria against Bessus, who was captured and executed in 329 (cf. Sources 56 and 57). A revolt of Bactria and Sogdiana, both in the northernmost parts of the old Persian empire, followed which took until 327 for Alexander to end it.

During the Asian campaign, Alexander's appearance and personality underwent drastic changes – hardly a surprise given not only his successes but also the wealth and splendour of the Persian court (see Sources 37 and 38). After his visit to Siwah in 331 he called himself son of Zeus, which caused dissatisfaction with his men, and his attempt to introduce *proskynesis*, perhaps to be connected to his own divinity at his court in Bactra in 327, was resisted (Sources 87 and 88).[9] Alexander's wearing of Persian dress, adoption of Persian customs, and integration of Persians into his army and administration also caused dissatisfaction. Although the Persian satraps he set up in various regions were never in control of the army or treasury,[10] Alexander's 'orientalism' distanced himself from his men. Because of conspiracies against him,[11] of which that of the Pages in 327 was the most serious (see Sources 102–104), and his growing paranoia, Alexander grew suspicious of those who were close to him. For example, at Phrada in 330 he had Philotas executed and his father Parmenion assassinated (Source 101), and in 328 after a drunken quarrel he killed Cleitus at Maracanda for his undue (in Alexander's opinion) praise of Philip (Source 58).

In 327, Alexander was at the farthest limits of the old Persian empire: he had travelled vast distances, and as a general he had won spectacular successes.[12] The mandate of the League of Corinth was accomplished, and it was time to return to Greece. Alexander had no such intention: exotic India beckoned (cf. Sources 61–64).[13]

Alexander's military exploits are less controversial than the questions they raise. Why did Alexander not want to return to Greece? What were his aims now?[14] How did he see himself, as Macedonian king, Great King, or some combination of both? Again, the nature of our sources and their presentation of Alexander pose problems.

Ancient sources

33 Since Gorgus and Minnion, sons of Theodotus, have been good and noble men concerning the public affairs of the city,[15] and in private they have benefited many of the citizens, and after speaking with King Alexander about the little sea,[16] they recovered and restored (it) to the people, freedom from taxation and the front seats[17] shall be bestowed on to them and their descendants for all time. The decree shall be inscribed on the vestibule in front of the record office (Tod, no. 190).

34 From King Alexander. Of those living in Naulochum, as many as are Prienians are to be independent and free, possessing the land and all the houses in the city and the countryside, just like the Prienians themselves ... but the Myrseloi ... and the countryside I consider to be mine.[18] Those living in these villages are to pay tribute, and I discharge the city of the Prienians from its taxes, and the garrison ... to lead in ... the trials ... law court ... (Tod, no. 185).

35 As we pass from Europe to Asia in our geography, the northern division is the first of the two divisions to which we come; and therefore we must begin with this. Of this division the first portion is that in the region of the Tanais River, which I have taken as the boundary between Europe and Asia. This portion forms, in a way, a peninsula, for it is surrounded on the west by the Tanais River and Lake Maeotis as far as the Bosporus and that part of the coast of the Euxine Sea which terminates at Colchis; and then on the north by the Ocean as far as the mouth of the Caspian Sea; and then on the east by this same sea as far as the boundary between Albania and Armenia, where empty the rivers Cyrus and Araxes, the Araxes flowing through Armenia and the Cyrus through Iberia and Albania; and lastly, on the south by the tract of country which extends from the outlet of the Cyrus River to Colchis, which is about three thousand stades from sea to sea, across the territory of the Albanians and the Iberians, and therefore is described as an isthmus. But those writers who have reduced the width of the isthmus as much as Cleitarchus has, who says that it is subject to inundation from either sea, should not be considered even worthy of mention. Poseidonius states that the isthmus is fifteen hundred stades across, as wide as the isthmus from Pelusium ... 'And in my opinion,' he says, 'the isthmus from Lake Maeotis to the Ocean does not differ much therefrom' (Cleitarchus, *FGrH* 137 F 13 = Strabo 11.1.5).

36 Parthia's capital, Hecatompylos itself, is 133 miles distant from the Caspian Gates. Thus the kingdom of the Parthians also is shut out by these passes. As soon as one leaves these gates one meets the Caspian nation; this extends to the shores ... from this nation back to the river Cyrus the distance is said to be 225 miles; if we go from the same river to the Caspian gates, it is 700 miles. It was these Gates that they made the central point of Alexander's marches, setting down the distance from the Gates to the frontier of India as 15,680 stades; to the city of Bactra, which they call Zariasta, as 3,700 stades; from there to the river Iaxartes, as 5,000 stades. But, in order that the topography of the region may be understood, we are following Alexander the Great's tracks. Diognetus (*FGrH* 120 F 1) and Baeton, the surveyors of his expeditions, have written that from the Caspian Gates to Hecatompylos, the city of the Parthians, there are as many miles as we have said; from there to Alexandria of the Arii, a city which Alexander founded, the distance is 575 miles; to Prophthasia, a city of the Drangae, 199 miles; to the town of the Arachosii, 565 miles; to Hortospanus, 175 miles; from there to Alexander's town, 50 miles – in certain copies different figures are found – and this city is placed at the foot of the Caucasus itself; from it to the river Cophes and to Peucolatis, a town of India, 237 miles; from there to the river Indus and the town of Taxila, 60 miles; to the famous river Hydaspes, 120 miles; to the Hyphasis, a river no less famous, 390 miles – which was the terminus of Alexander's marches, although he crossed the river and dedicated altars on the opposite side (Baeton, *FGrH* 119 F 2a = Pliny, *Natural History* 6.44–45, 61).

37 But Chares of Mytilene, in the fifth book of his *History of Alexander*, says: 'The Persian kings had come to such a pitch of luxury, that at the head of the royal couch there was a supper-room laid with five couches, in which there were always kept five thousand talents of gold; and this was called the King's pillow. And at his feet was another supper-room, prepared with three couches, in which there were constantly kept three thousand talents of silver; and this was called the King's footstool. And in his bedchamber there was also a golden vine, inlaid with precious stones, above the King's bed' – and this vine, Amyntas says in his *Stages* (*FGrH* 122 F 6),[19] had bunches of grapes, composed of most valuable precious stones – 'and not far from it there was placed a golden bowl, the work of Theodorus of Samos' (Chares, *FGrH* F 2 = Athen. 12.514e–f).

38 Perhaps also the following, mentioned by Polycleitus, is one of their customs. He says that in Susa each one of the kings built for himself on the acropolis a separate habitation, treasure houses, and storage places for what tributes they each exacted, as memorials of his administration; and that they exacted silver from the people on the sea board, and from the people in the interior such things as each country produced, so that they also received dyes, drugs, hair, or wool, or something else of the kind, and likewise cattle; and that the king who arranged the separate tributes was Darius, called the Long-armed, and the most handsome of men, except for the length of his arms, for they reached even to his knees; and that most of the gold and silver is used in articles of equipment, but not much in money; and that they consider those metals as better adapted for presents and for depositing in storehouses; and that so much coined money as suffices their needs is enough; and that they coin only what money is commensurate with their expenditures (Nicobule, *FGrH* 127 F 3a = Strabo 15.3.21).

39 Now in early times the Sogdians and Bactrians did not differ much from the nomads in their modes of life and customs, although the Bactrians were a little more civilized; however, of these, as of the others, Onesicritus does not report their best traits, saying, for instance, that those who have become helpless because of old age or sickness are thrown out alive as prey to dogs kept expressly for this purpose, which in their native tongue are called 'undertakers', and that while the land outside the walls of the metropolis of the Bactrians looks clean, yet most of the land inside the walls is full of human bones; but that Alexander broke up the custom (Onesicritus, *FGrH* 134 F 5 = Strabo 11.11.3).

40 Of the Barbarians, we are told, twenty thousand footmen fell (at the Granicus), and twenty-five hundred horsemen. But on Alexander's side, Aristobulus says there were thirty-four dead in all, of whom nine were footmen (Aristobulus, *FGrH* 139 F 5 = Plut. *Alex.* 16.15).

41 They fight. Fearing then that they might some time be rebuked as having betrayed the cause to Alexander, they stayed and made ready for battle. Now Alexander encamped on the edge of the Granicus and the Persians on the side opposite. When they joined in battle, Alexander won. He took much booty from the Persians and sent it to Greece, astounding the Greeks even in this manner; he also sent gifts to his mother Olympias. After this he proceeded to the next region (*Anonymous History of Alexander*, *FGrH* 151 F 1).

42 When Alexander arrived at Gordium, he was seized with an ardent desire to go up into the citadel, which contained the palace of Gordius and his son Midas. He was also desirous of seeing the wagon of Gordius and the cord of the yoke of this wagon. There was a great deal of talk about this wagon among the neighbouring population. It was said that Gordius was a poor man among the ancient Phrygians, who had a small piece of land to till, and two yoke of oxen. He used one of these in ploughing and the other to draw the wagon. On one occasion, while he was ploughing, an eagle settled upon the yoke, and remained sitting there until the time came for unyoking the oxen. Being alarmed at the sight, he went to the Telmissian soothsayers to consult them about the sign from the deity; for the Telmissians were skilful in interpreting the meaning of Divine manifestations, and the power of divination has been bestowed not only upon the men, but also upon their wives and children from generation to generation. When Gordius was driving his wagon near a certain village of the Telmissians, he met a maiden fetching water from the spring, and to her he related how the sign of the eagle had appeared to him. As she herself was of the prophetic race, she instructed him to return to the very spot and offer sacrifice to Zeus the king. Gordius requested her to accompany him and direct him how to perform the sacrifice. He offered the sacrifice in the way the girl suggested, and afterwards married her. A son was born to them named Midas. When Midas was grown to be a man, handsome and valiant, the Phrygians were harassed by civil discord, and consulting the oracle, they were told that a wagon would bring them a king, who would put an end to their discord. While they were still deliberating about this very matter, Midas arrived with his father and mother, and stopped near the assembly, wagon and all. They, comparing the oracular response with this occurrence, decided that this was the person whom the god told them the wagon would bring. They therefore appointed Midas king; and he, putting an end to their discord, dedicated his father's wagon in the citadel as a thank-offering to Zeus the king for sending the eagle. In addition to this the following saying was current concerning the wagon, that whosoever could loosen the cord of the yoke of this wagon, was destined to gain the rule of Asia. The cord was made of cornel bark, and neither end nor beginning of it could be seen. It is said by some that when Alexander could find out no way to loosen the cord and yet was unwilling to allow it to remain unloosened, lest this should exercise some disturbing influence upon the multitude, he struck it with his sword and cutting it through, said that it had been loosened. But Aristobulus says that he pulled out the pin of the wagon-pole, which was a wooden peg driven right through it, holding the cord together. Having done this, he drew out the yoke from the wagon-pole. How Alexander performed the feat in connection with this cord, I cannot affirm with confidence. At any rate both he and his troops departed from the wagon as if the oracular prediction concerning the loosening of the cord had been fulfilled. Moreover, that very night, the thunder and lightning were signs of its fulfilment; and for this reason Alexander offered sacrifice on the following day to the gods who had revealed the signs and the way to loosen the cord (Aristobulus, *FGrH* 139 F 7a = Arr. 2.3).

43 And after he had taken the city of Gordium, reputed to have been the home of the ancient Midas, he saw the much-talked-of wagon bound fast to its yoke with bark of the cornel tree, and heard a story confidently told about it by the Barbarians, to the effect that whosoever loosed the fastening was destined to become king of the whole world. Well, then, most writers say that since the fastenings had their ends concealed, and were intertwined many times in crooked coils, Alexander was at a loss how to proceed, and finally loosened the knot by cutting it through with his sword, and that when it was thus smitten many ends were to be seen. But Aristobulus says that he undid it very easily, by simply taking out the so-called 'hestor' or pin, of the wagon-pole, by which the yoke-fastening was held together, and then drawing away the yoke (Aristobulus, *FGrH* 139 F 7b = Plut. *Alex.* 18.2–4).

44   Of the Persians[20] were killed Arsames, Rheomithres, and Atizyes, three of the men who had commanded the cavalry at the Granicus. Sabaces, viceroy of Egypt, and Bubaces, one of the Persian dignitaries, were also killed, besides about 100,000 of the private soldiers, among them being more than 10,000 cavalry. So great was the slaughter that Ptolemy, son of Lagus, who then accompanied Alexander, says that the men who were with them pursuing Darius, coming in the pursuit to a ravine, passed over it upon the corpses (Ptolemy, *FGrH* 138 F 6 = Arr. 2.11.8).

45   I mean Alexander's battle with Darius in Cilicia. Callisthenes tells us that Alexander had already passed the narrows and the so-called Cilician Gates, while Darius had marched through the pass known as the Gates of Amanus and had descended with his army into Cilicia. On learning from the natives that Alexander was advancing in the direction of Syria he followed him up, and when he approached the pass, encamped on the banks of the River Pinarus. The distance, he says, from the sea to the foot of the hills is not more than fourteen stades, the river running obliquely across this space, with gaps in its banks just where it issues from the mountains, but in its whole course through the plain as far as the sea passing between steep hills difficult to climb. Having given this sketch of the country, he tells us that Darius and his generals, when Alexander turned and marched back to meet them, decided to draw up the whole phalanx in the camp itself in its original position, the river affording protection, as it ran close past the camp. After this he says they drew up the cavalry along the sea shore, the mercenaries next them at the brink of the river, and the peltasts next the mercenaries in a line reaching as far as the mountains. It is difficult to understand how they posted all these troops in front of the phalanx, considering that the river ran close past the camp, especially in view of their numbers, for as Callisthenes himself says, there were thirty thousand cavalry and thirty thousand mercenaries. . . . Where, then, were the mercenaries posted, unless indeed they were drawn up behind the cavalry? This he tells us was not so, as they were the first to meet the Macedonian attack. We must, then, of necessity, understand that the cavalry occupied that half of the space which was nearest to the sea and the mercenaries the half nearest the hills, and from this it is easy to reckon what was the depth of the cavalry and how far away from the camp the river must have been. After this he tells us that on the approach of the enemy, Darius, who was halfway down the line, called the mercenaries himself from the wing to come to him . . . Lastly, he says that the cavalry from the right wing advanced and attacked Alexander's cavalry, who received their charge bravely and delivering a counter-charge fought stubbornly. He forgets that there was a river between them and such a river as he has just described. Very similar are his statements about Alexander. He says that when he crossed to Asia he had forty thousand foot and four thousand five hundred horse, and that when he was on the point of invading Cilicia he was joined by a further force of five thousand foot and eight hundred horse. Suppose we deduct from this total three thousand foot and three hundred horse, a liberal allowance for those absent on special service, there still remain forty-two thousand foot and five thousand horse. Assuming these numbers, he tells us that when Alexander heard the news of Darius' arrival in Cilicia he was a hundred stades away and had already traversed the pass. In consequence he turned and marched back through the pass with the phalanx in front, followed by the cavalry, and last of all the baggage-train. Immediately on issuing into the open country he re-formed his order, passing to all the word of command to form into phalanx, making it at first thirty-two deep, changing this subsequently to sixteen deep, and finally as he approached the enemy to eight deep. These statements are even more absurd than his former ones. From all this it is quite plain that when Alexander made his army sixteen deep the line necessarily extended for twenty stades, and this left all the cavalry and ten thousand of the infantry over.

After this he says that Alexander led on his army in an extended line, being then at a distance of about forty stades from the enemy ... A single one mentioned by Callisthenes himself being sufficient to convince us of its impossibility ... For he tells us that the torrents descending from the mountains have formed so many clefts in the plain that most of the Persians in their flight perished in such fissures. But, it may be said, Alexander wished to be prepared for the appearance of the enemy ... But here is the greatest of all his mistakes. He tells us that Alexander, on approaching the enemy, made his line eight deep ... But he tells us that there was only a space of less than fourteen stades, and as half of the cavalry were on the left near the sea and half on the right, the room available for the infantry is still further reduced. Add to this that the whole line must have kept at a considerable distance from the mountains so as not to be exposed to attack by those of the enemy who held the foothills. We know that he did as a fact draw up part of his force in a crescent formation to oppose these latter ... It would be too long a story to mention all the other absurdities of his narrative, and it will suffice to point out a few. He tells us that Alexander in drawing up his army was most anxious to be opposed to Darius in person, and that Darius also at first entertained the same wish, but afterwards changed his mind (Callisthenes, *FGrH* 124 F 35 = Polybius 12.17–22).

46 (3) When he reached Cilicia and passed over the Cilician Taurus Range, he encamped at Issus, a narrow spot in Cilicia and hard on the cavalry because it is rough ground. (4) Darius was not willing to wait for Alexander in Persia nor to risk all his power. He therefore raised an army and came to meet him. When he heard that Alexander was in camp at Issus, he realized well how unsuitable for battle the place was. But he did not want to appear as if he were choosing his ground, so with Persian vain-glory he came to the Issus himself and pitched his camp there. The armies met in battle and Alexander won the day. (5) Darius despairing for his safety fled, leaving his dearest ones behind him. Alexander caught his wife prisoner, his mother, his daughters Stateira and Drypetis and his son Ochus. Darius wished to ransom them and sent envoys to Alexander asking for a truce and peace and offering him all the lands within the River Halys and whichever one of his daughters Alexander might choose to marry and a dowry of 20,000 talents. But Alexander rejected the offer and went on, subjugating the barbarian nations next in his course (*Anonymous History of Alexander*, *FGrH* 151 FF 3–5).

47 However, it is thought that he [Darius] would not then have made his escape, had not fresh horsemen come from Parmenion summoning Alexander to his aid, on the grounds that a large force of the enemy still held together there and would not give ground. For there is general complaint that in that battle Parmenion was sluggish and inefficient, either because old age was now impairing somewhat his courage, or because he was made envious and resentful by the arrogance and pomp, to use the words of Callisthenes, of Alexander's power. At the time, then, although he was annoyed by the summons, the king did not tell his soldiers the truth about it, but on the grounds that it was dark and he would therefore remit further slaughter, sounded a recall; and as he rode towards the endangered portion of his army, he heard by the way that the enemy had been utterly defeated and was in flight (Callisthenes, *FGrH* 124 F 37 = Plut. *Alex.* 33.9–11).

48 Nor did he treat the mother, wife, and children of Darius with neglect; for some of those who have written Alexander's history say that on the very night in which he returned from the pursuit of Darius, entering the Persian king's tent, which had been selected for his use, he heard the lamentation of women and other noise of a similar kind not far from the tent. Enquiring therefore who the women were, and why they were in a tent so near, he was answered by someone as follows: 'O king, the mother, wife, and children of Darius are lamenting for him as slain, since they have been informed that thou hast his bow and royal mantle, and that his shield has been brought back.' When Alexander heard this, he sent Leonnatus, one of his Companions, to them, with injunctions to tell them: 'Darius is still alive; in his flight he left his arms and mantle in the chariot; and these are the only things of his that Alexander has.' Leonnatus entered the tent and told them the news about Darius, saying, moreover, that Alexander would allow them to retain the state and retinue befitting their royal rank, as well as the title of queens; for he had not undertaken the war against Darius from a feeling of hatred, but he had conducted it in a legitimate manner for the empire of Asia. Such are the statements of Ptolemy and Aristobulus (*FGrH* 139 F 10). But there is another report, to the effect that on the following day Alexander himself went ... (Ptolemy *FGrH* 138 F 7 = Arr. 2.12.3–6).

49 In his desire to overtake Darius he started in his pursuit. But again he came to Egypt and saw a site naturally suited for the erection of a city. He wanted to build one; at once he ordered his architects to trace the circuit of the city to be founded. But as they had no clay to do so, he happened to see a threshing-floor with wheat on it and ordered them to place the grains around and use them instead of clay in marking the circuit. They did so. The following night fowls came and picked up the grain. This seemed to be a sign: some said it portended ill (the city to be founded would be captured); Alexander, however, said it was a good omen (though it was made clear that many would be fed by that city) and at once built a large city there, which he called Alexandria, after his own name. Then he advanced in pursuit of Darius (*Anonymous History of Alexander*, *FGrH* 151 F 11).

50 While he was still in Cilicia, he fell sick of a very serious attack of illness for the reason following: The River Cydnus flowed through the middle of Tarsus, a city of Cilicia. Its waters are crystal clear and its flow perfectly calm. On account of the heat Alexander plunged in and was swimming more than he should, when for this very reason he was seized with convulsions and fell sick and after the seventh day all despaired of his life. The doctors saved him with difficulty (*Anonymous History of Alexander*, *FGrH* 151 F 6).

51 But Tyre he besieged for seventh months with moles, and engines-of-war, and two hundred triremes by sea. During this siege he had a dream in which he saw Heracles stretching out his hand to him from the wall and calling him. And many of the Tyrians dreamed that Apollo told them he was going away to Alexander, since he was displeased at what was going on in the city. Whereupon, as if the god had been a common deserter caught in the act of going over to the enemy, they encircled his colossal figure with cords and nailed it down to its pedestal, calling him an Alexandrist. In another dream, too, Alexander thought he saw a satyr who mocked him at a distance, and eluded his grasp when he tried to catch him, but finally, after much coaxing and chasing, surrendered. The seers, dividing the word 'satyros' into two parts, said to him, plausibly enough, 'Tyre is to be thine'. And a spring is pointed out, near which Alexander dreamed he saw the satyr (Chares, *FGrH* 125 F 7 = Plut. *Alex.* 24.5–9).[21]

52 When he was out of Cilicia and came to Sidon, he attacked Tyre, a city of Sidon, and laid siege to it. Because he could not take it after a long siege, he was in a dilemma: neither did he wish to leave it unconquered nor to wait in his hurry to over-take Darius. He formed a plan as follows: Along the wall he saw a place constructed of several stones built in together. He ordered his subordinates to dig under them and when the place was dug through he and his army entered the city. In this manner he became master of Tyre and indignant for the Tyrians' long resistance he had in mind to kill all from the youth upwards. After the death of some he ceased this excessive cruelty, both due to his friends' intercession and to his reverence for Heracles, who was preeminently honoured by the Tyrians (*Anonymous History of Alexander*, *FGrH* 151 F 7).

53 But those authors who make Arbela most distant say that it is 600 stades away from the place where Alexander and Darius fought their last battle, while those who make it least distant, say that it is 500 stades off. But Ptolemy and Aristobulus (*FGrH* 139 F 16) say that the battle was fought at Gaugamela near the River Bumodus. As Gaugamela was not a city, but only a large village, the place is not celebrated, nor is the name pleasing to the ear; hence, it seems to me, that Arbela, being a city, has carried off the glory of the great battle (Ptolemy, *FGrH* 138 F 10 = Arr. 6.11.5).

54 (12) After his defeats in two battles[22] Darius was preparing for a third engagement. He mustered all the hosts under his sway, till they aggregated one million. A large portion of his army was cavalry and archers, especially since the barbarians had not trained themselves in Greek war-practice. He also had elephants brought to him from India, the equipment of which was as follows: wooden towers suitably fashioned were placed on their backs, from which men fought with weapons, the result being that opponents were destroyed both by the men in the towers with their arms and by the elephants that trod them underfoot. Besides these Darius had scythe-bearing chariots drawn by four horses each and built as follows: On their wheels in the felloes were fashioned scythes, so that when these chariots rolled forward the ranks would break up and the men who fell would meet a most horrible death; because, with the motion of the scythes, some were caught by the arms, others by their legs and others by their armour and were dragged a long way till they were killed. (13) When they engaged in the fight Alexander devised the following weapon against the elephants: he had bronze caltrops made of extreme sharpness and cast on the ground where the animals were. The elephants would be pricked and would not come forward; they were pinned by the caltrops and fell. The scythe-bearing chariots ... (*Anonymous History of Alexander*, *FGrH* 151 FF 12–13).

55 And did not the great Alexander keep Thais about him, who was an Athenian courtesan? And Cleitarchus speaks of her as having been the cause that the palace of Persepolis was burnt down (Cleitarchus, *FGrH* 137 F 11 = Athen. 13.576d–e).

56 After passing over the River Oxus, he made a forced march to the place where he heard that Bessus was with his forces; but at this time messengers reached him from Spitamenes and Dataphernes, to announce that they would arrest Bessus and hand him over to Alexander if he would send to them merely a small army and a commander for it; since even at that very time they were holding him under guard, though they had not bound him with fetters. When Alexander heard this, he gave his army a rest, and marched more slowly than before. But he dispatched Ptolemy, son of Lagus, at the head of three regiments of the Companion cavalry and all the horse-javelin-men, and of the infantry, the brigade of Philotas, one regiment of 1,000 shield-bearing guards, all the Agrianians, and half the archers, with orders to make a forced march to Spitamenes and Dataphernes. Ptolemy went according to his instructions, and completing ten days' march in four days, arrived at the camp where on the preceding day the barbarians under Spitamenes had bivouacked. Here Ptolemy learned that Spitamenes and Dataphernes were not firmly resolved about the betrayal of Bessus. He therefore left the infantry behind with orders to follow him in regular order, and advanced with the cavalry till he arrived at a certain village, where Bessus was with a few soldiers; for Spitamenes and his party had already retired from thence, being ashamed to betray Bessus themselves. Ptolemy posted his cavalry right round the village, which was enclosed by a wall supplied with gates. He then issued a proclamation to the barbarians in the village, that they would be allowed to depart uninjured if they surrendered Bessus to him. They accordingly admitted Ptolemy and his men into the village. He then seized Bessus and returned; but sent a messenger on before to ask Alexander how he was to conduct Bessus into his presence. Alexander ordered him to bind the prisoner naked in a wooden collar, and thus to lead him and place him on the right-hand side of the road along which he was about to march with the army. Thus did Ptolemy. When Alexander saw Bessus, he caused his chariot to stop, and asked him, for what reason he had in the first place arrested Darius, his own king, who was also his kinsman and benefactor, and then led him as a prisoner in chains, and at last killed him? Bessus said that he was not the only person who had decided to do this, but that it was the joint act of those who were at the time in attendance upon Darius, with the view of procuring safety for them-selves from Alexander. For this Alexander ordered that he should be scourged, and that the herald should repeat the very same reproaches which he had himself made to Bessus in his enquiry. After being thus disgracefully tortured, he was sent away to Bactra to be put to death. Such is the account given by Ptolemy in relation to Bessus; but Aristobulus (*FGrH* 139 F 24 = Source 57) says that Spitamenes and Dataphernes brought Bessus to Ptolemy, and having bound him naked in a wooden collar betrayed him to Alexander (Ptolemy, *FGrH* 138 F 14 = Arr. 3.29.6–30.5).

57 But Aristobulus says that Spitamenes and Dataphernes brought Bessus to Ptolemy, and having bound him naked in a wooden collar betrayed him to Alexander (Aristobulus, *FGrH* 139 F 24 = Arr. 3.30.5).

58 Aristobulus does not say whence the drunken quarrel originated, but asserts that the fault was entirely on the side of Cleitus, who, when Alexander had got so enraged with him as to jump up against him with the intention of making an end of him, was led away by Ptolemy, son of Lagus, the confidential bodyguard, though the gateway, beyond the wall and ditch of the citadel where the quarrel occurred. He adds that Cleitus could not control himself, but went back again, and falling in with Alexander who was calling out for Cleitus, he exclaimed: 'Alexander, here am I, Cleitus!' Thereupon he was struck with a long pike and killed (Aristobulus, *FGrH* 139 F 29 = Arr. 4.8.9).

Modern works

In the first extract, M.M. Austin, Reader in Ancient History at the University of St Andrews, examines how the ancient sources treated the causes and objectives of Alexander's invasion of Persia, what their views were on it both as a war and as a motive for warfare. Then N.G.L. Hammond, formerly Professor of Greek at the University of Bristol, examines Alexander's attitude to the Persian throne and sees it and the invasion as a different form of imperialism from that under Philip.

1   M.M. Austin, 'Alexander and the Macedonian Invasion of Asia', in J. Rich and G. Shipley (eds.), *War and Society in the Greek World* (London: 1993), pp. 197–223.[23]
2   N.G.L. Hammond, 'The Kingdom of Asia and the Persian Throne', *Antichthon* 20 (1986), pp. 73–85.[24]

Additional reading

(See also the Modern Works in Chapter 3.)

E. Badian, 'The Administration of the Empire', *Greece and Rome*[2] 12 (1965), pp. 166–182.

—— , 'Alexander in Iran', *Cambridge History of Iran* 2 (Cambridge: 1985), pp. 420–501.

—— , 'Agis III: Revisions and Reflections', in Ian Worthington (ed.), *Ventures into Greek History, Essays in Honour of N.G.L. Hammond* (Oxford: 1994), pp. 258–292.

E.A. Fredricksmeyer, 'Alexander, Zeus Ammon, and the Conquest of Asia', *Transactions of the American Philological Association* 121 (1991), pp. 199–214.

—— , 'Alexander the Great and the Kingship of Asia', in A.B. Bosworth and E.J. Baynham (eds.), *Alexander the Great in Fact and Fiction* (Oxford: 2000), pp. 136–166.

J.R. Hamilton, 'Alexander's Iranian Policy', in W. Will and J. Heinrichs (eds.), *Zu Alexander d. Gr. Festschrift G. Wirth* 1 (Amsterdam: 1988), pp. 467–486.

N.G.L. Hammond, 'The Archaeological and Literary Evidence for the Burning of the Persepolis Palace', *Classical Quarterly*[2] 42 (1992), pp. 358–364.

A.J. Heisserer, *Alexander the Great and the Greeks* (Norman: 1980).

W.E. Higgins, 'Aspects of Alexander's Imperial Administration: Some Modern Methods and Views Reviewed', *Athenaeum* 58 (1980), pp. 129–152.

F.L. Holt, 'Alexander's Settlements in Central Asia', *Ancient Macedonia* 4 (Institute for Balkan Studies, Thessaloniki: 1986), pp. 315–323.

—— , '*Imperium Macedonicum* and the East: The Problem of Logistics', *Ancient Macedonia* 5 (Institute for Balkan Studies, Thessaloniki: 1993), pp. 585–592.

—— , *Alexander the Great and Bactria* (Leiden: 1988).

—— , *Thundering Zeus: The Making of Hellenistic Bactria* (Berkeley and Los Angeles: 1999).

Notes

1 Diod. 17.17.3, Arr. 1.12.1, Plut. *Alex.* 15.7–8, Justin 9.5.12.
2 Diod. 17.19–21, Arr. 1.13–16, Plut. *Alex.* 16; cf. Curt. 2.

3   For another of Alexander's dealings with Priene, see Source 34.
4   Cf. Chapter 4.
5   On sources, see Chapter 1.
6   See Chapter 9.
7   Diod. 17.56–61, Arr. 3.11–15, Plut. *Alex.* 31–33, Curt. 4.14–16.
8   Diod. 17.70–72, Arr. 3.18.10–12, Plut. *Alex.* 37.6–38, Curt. 5.7.3–11.
9   See further, Chapter 9.
10 Cf. Chapter 8.
11 See Chapter 10.
12 On Alexander as a general, see Chapter 7.
13 See Chapter 6.
14 Cf. Chapter 3.
15 Iasus; the inscription bestows honours on these two brothers for their diplomacy with Alexander. See also Source 24 for other honours bestowed on the two brothers.
16 The precise location is unknown; perhaps it was an inland lake connected to the sea, and an important fishing ground: see the discussion by Heisserer, *Alexander the Great and the Greeks*, pp. 174–177.
17 At the public festivals.
18 Thus, Alexander claims some of the land as his own, and exempts only the Prienians and Priene itself from taxation (the tribute paid for membership of the League of Corinth).
19 'In this bedroom above the bed was a golden vineyard set with precious stones – and Amyntas says in his *Stages* that it has grape-clusters consisting of the most precious gems' (= Athen. 12.514f).
20 The context of this source and the following one is the Battle of Issus in 333.
21 For what comes after this passage, see Source 86.
22 This is incorrect, for Darius was not present at the battle of the Granicus river.
23 Reprinted with the permission of Routledge and of the author.
24 Reprinted with the permission of Mrs M. Hammond.

ALEXANDER AND THE MACEDONIAN INVASION OF ASIA: ASPECTS OF THE HISTORIOGRAPHY OF WAR AND EMPIRE IN ANTIQUITY

Michel Austin

The focus of this paper is primarily historiographical rather than historical. It seeks to relate some current views on the causes and objectives of war as presented by ancient writers to the specific case of the Macedonian invasion of Asia under Alexander.[1] I do not wish to suggest that historiographical and historical aspects can be entirely disso-ciated. But there are numerous questions about the invasion beyond the purely historiographical, some of which are touched on below, that deserve fuller investiga-tion than can be given here. Perhaps I should add that the emphasis in what follows on the material motives for the invasion of Asia by the Macedonians is not meant to imply that no other motives were present (such as the search for glory, at least on the part of the kings). I simply wish to react against the tendencies in some writers to underplay this aspect (e.g. Ducrey 1968, 159; 170; 1985, 228) or to draw a distinc-tion between 'political' and 'economic' motives for wars that is perhaps artificial (cf. Garlan 1975, 183; 1989, 33–6). This approach may derive ultimately from state-ments in some of the ancient sources, which stress Alexander's lack of interest in wealth and self-indulgence, as compared with his pursuit of glory and his generosity to others, and draw a (perhaps artificial) contrast between him and his friends and followers).[2]

Before the invasion

Preliminaries to the war

> No single topic occupies more attention in ancient history, more space in print, than the preliminaries leading to a war. . . . Yet it is neither mischievous nor perverse to suggest that there is no topic on which we are less well equipped to express any views at all.

Thus M. I. Finley in his chapter on 'War and empire'; and he then went on to suggest (1985b, 80; 81) that 'ancient wars can normally be examined concretely only after they have got under way'. Although Finley was chiefly concerned with the wars between the republican states of antiquity, in Greek and Roman history, and had little to say about royal wars of the hellenistic or other periods, these statements apply particularly well to the Macedonian invasion of Asia initiated by Philip and carried out by Alexander. It is striking how little the extant sources have to say about the preliminaries leading to the expedition, and its possible aims and motives before it was launched.

The fullest extant ancient statement appears to be the sensible, but brief remarks of Polybios in relation to his discussion of the differences between the causes, pretexts, and beginnings of wars (3. 6). According to Polybios, the 'causes' of the war were the march of the Ten Thousand (in 400–399) and the expedition of Agesilaos to Asia Minor (in 396–394), which convinced Philip of the weakness of the Persians and revealed the rich rewards to be gained. The 'pretext' was Philip's proclaimed intention to avenge the injuries inflicted by the Persians on the Greeks. The 'beginning' of the war was Alexander's crossing into Asia. Brief as Polybios' remarks are, they are far more informative than any of the principal extant sources for the Macedonian expedition.

Of those sources, Diodoros presents Philip as thinking of the war against the Persians already by the time of the peace of Philokrates in 346 BC (16. 60). In 336 Philip, about to launch the war, was confident of overthrowing the Persian king and making Asia a captive of the Macedonians (16. 91–2). But Diodoros gives no further analysis or explanation for the decision. Similarly, Arrian presents Alexander's wish to invade as self-evident from the start and in no need of comment.[3] So, too, Plutarch portrays Alexander as very interested in the Persian empire and anxious from an early date to get on with conquest (*Alexander*, 5), but does not feel the need to provide any further explanation. (How Quintus Curtius presented the decision to invade is unknown, since his first two books are lost.)

Nor are we much informed about the debates that led to the decision to invade Asia. No extant ancient source enables us to date precisely when and why Philip formed the plan of invading the Persian empire (see below). As for Alexander's own decision after his accession, all we have is a brief and tantalizing report in Diodoros (17. 16) of a debate involving Alexander, his officers, and his leading friends on the timing and handling of the invasion. Antipater and Parmenion urge Alexander to provide heirs to the throne before undertaking the invasion, but Alexander is anxious to make a start and argues successfully for immediate action.

Concerning the expectations of the mass of the army at the start of the invasion, we would have no direct information at all but for Justin, of all sources, who provides in a few lines (11. 5) the only concrete picture of the mood of the Macedonian rank and file, avid for rich plunder from the Persian empire and oblivious, according to him, of their families at home.

With this general dearth of information concerning the beginnings of one of the most momentous wars in the history of the ancient world, compare for example the extensive contemporary reporting by Thucydides of the debates at Athens that led to the launching of the Sicilian expedition in 415 BC (6. 8–26), and his vivid description of the contrasted hopes and fears of the various participants as they set out on their journey (6. 30–1).

Discussing the 'causes of wars' was in fact a favourite pastime of ancient authors, as may be seen from Herodotos on the Persian wars, Thucydides on the Peloponnesian war, the Oxyrhynchus historian on the Corinthian war, Polybios on the second Punic war, and others (Momigliano 1966). Why, then, the apparent dearth of such discussion in the sources for the war of the Macedonians against the Persians? The short answer may be simply that we do not have a Thucydides or a Polybios for this war. The historians of Alexander, whether the original writers, starting with Kallisthenes, or the later derivative sources, had other purposes, literary or moral in character rather than historical, and were not primarily concerned with analysing the background of the invasion.

It may also be suggested that the sources felt little need to discuss the causes and aims of the war, precisely because it was so conspicuously successful and the material benefits for the victors so self-evident, at least from the time of the battle of Issos in 333, the turning-point of the invasion. Unlike all the many ancient wars that ended in failure (the Persian wars – from the point of view of the invaders – the Peloponnesian war, the Sicilian expedition, and many others), this one left no *Kriegsschuldfrage* to be debated retrospectively.

It might also be mentioned that the actual beginning of the war was less clear-cut than Polybios suggested. The plan of the war had been initiated and put into action by Philip in 336, and early campaigns had been waged by Attalos and Parmenion in advance of Philip's projected assumption of the command. His assassination in 336 delayed the campaign, and the disturbances that resulted from the death of Philip postponed the start of Alexander's own campaign until 334.[4] When Alexander did eventually take over, he was clearly anxious to make the expedition his own and to place his personal stamp on it.

The pretext for the war

What the extant sources do tell us about specifically, and in some detail, is of course the pretext put forward, first by Philip and then by Alexander. The expedition was meant to be a panhellenic war of revenge against the Persians. Philip, and then Alexander, were supposedly leaders of a united Hellenic expedition which aimed at exacting retribution from the Persians for the harm they had done, and for their burning of the temples of Athens during the Persian wars.[5] Whether liberation of the Greek cities of Asia was also part of the original propaganda motive, as only Diodoros asserts (16. 91. 2 on Philip's advance invasion; 17. 24. 1 on Alexander in Asia Minor), is uncertain.[6]

On this well-known subject I shall simply list without discussion some familiar points. The propaganda posture was aimed clearly at the Greek world, and was of no direct interest to the Macedonians themselves. It was felt necessary by the Macedonian kings to make this claim, because they needed status in relation to the Greek world. Pretensions at leadership over other Greeks had to be cloaked and justified in terms of the championship of a Greek cause (Perlman 1976). The Greekness of the Macedonians, long a matter of doubt, had become a subject of renewed argument and propaganda. The Athenians in the time of Demosthenes were presenting their resistance to Macedon as a re-enactment, on behalf of the Greeks, of their resistance to the Persians in the fifth century (Habicht 1961; Thomas 1989, 84–6). Failure on the part of the Macedonian rulers to answer this with their own counter-claim, that of leadership of the Greeks, would mean that they were conceding by default the Athenian view. As for the theme of revenge, wars in the Greek world in the classical period, whatever their real motives, needed to be justified in terms of the requital of harm done by the enemy in the past.[7] Unprovoked raids had once been not merely acceptable, but a matter of glory, as in the Homeric poems (as Thucydides remarked, 1. 5): but this had long ceased to be the case (Jackson 1985).

Possible motives

The sources thus leave unanswered many questions about the most fundamental aspects of the Macedonians' decision to invade Asia. Historians are still uncertain as to the point at which Philip conceived his plan to turn away eventually from the Greek world and to invade Asia. Was the plan conceived early, by the time of the peace of Philokrates in 346 or perhaps even before this, as many believe? Or was it only a late decision that did not take shape until the time of the battle of Chaironeia in 338?[8] We do not know for sure, and are reduced to arguing over a small number of allusions or statements in contemporary (Demosthenes) or later sources (Diodoros), and speculating about how far Isokrates' writings may or may not have influenced Philip's plans.

While there is no such problem in the case of Alexander, the respective war aims of Philip and Alexander at the start of the invasion remain a matter of conjecture.[9] The silence of the ancient sources on the preliminaries to the invasion has had the effect of discouraging modern discussion. It is striking how, in all the prolific modern literature on Philip and Alexander, down-to-earth questions about the initial motives for the invasion rarely receive extended treatment.[10] On the other hand, Alexander's alleged future aims for his Asiatic conquests – in terms, for example, of a 'civilizing mission', a 'policy of fusion', or the so-called 'Last Plans' – are raised explicitly in some of the ancient sources, and consequently receive much attention in modern writing.

A number of obvious suggestions can be made. The material advantages to be expected by the Macedonians from an invasion of Asia can easily be conjectured. The notion that the Persian empire was a soft target, and a suitable object for profitable aggression, antedated the fourth century and all the Greek propaganda of that age (Starr 1976, 48–61). It was not Xenophon, Isokrates, and others who first argued the point; it is already found in essentials in Herodotos, whose *Histories* read like a forecast before the event of the downfall of the Persian empire over a century later (see below). This is seen in a number of passages, notably in the advice Aristagoras of Miletos reportedly gave to Kleomenes I of Sparta in 499 when trying to enlist support from the mainland Greeks for the Ionian revolt (5. 49). Aristagoras dangles before Kleomenes prospects of an easy and lucrative invasion: gold, silver, fine embroideries, beasts of burden, and slaves are all there for the taking.[11] Aristagoras' advice is evidently anachronistic, and reflects Greek experiences in their encounters with the Persians during and after the Persian wars; but that does not matter here. Subsequently, by the middle of the fifth century, the era of profitable aggression by the Greeks against the Persians in practice came to an end (see de Ste. Croix 1972, 312, for this formulation). Relations between the two began to take on new forms, which involved political, diplomatic, and financial intervention instead of military confrontation.

In the early fourth century, ideas of Greek aggression revived. The expedition and return of the Ten Thousand, as presented by Xenophon in his *Anabasis* (see esp. 3. 2. 26), were a powerful stimulus. Not long afterwards, the campaigns of Agesilaos in Asia Minor (396–394) showed what might be achieved in terms of conquest, and provided a possible model for Philip and Alexander in the early stages of their expedition.[12] All this fed the negative views of fourth-century Greek writers on the (alleged) weakness and degeneracy of the contemporary Persian empire. Modern historians of Persia have emphasized the shallowness of these views.[13] The point is taken, though the fact remains that this was a widely expressed Greek conception of the Persian empire at the time, which may conceivably have influenced the Macedonian rulers.

To this view of the Persian empire as a suitable target for profitable aggression should be added the evidence for contemporary Greek attitudes to wars between Greeks, and to empire exercised at the expense of other Greeks. Though Greeks continued to fight each other with undiminished zest, the idea had been growing since at least the fifth century that this was somehow disreputable and unnatural, and that Greeks ought not to enslave other Greeks.[14] Besides, wars between Greeks were not always very profitable, compared to what might be expected from a successful attack on Asia.[15] On the subject of empire, one of the by-products of the fifth-century Athenian experience was that *phoros* (tribute), a word probably initially neutral in colouring (Powell 1988, 15), came to acquire a pejorative connotation, as the history of the second Athenian naval confederacy illustrates.[16] Again, levying of tribute from barbarians was another matter (cf. Jason of Pherai's boast, Xen. *Hell*, 6. 1. 12).

All this was of particular relevance to the Macedonian rulers, since the Greekness of the Macedonians had become a matter of intense political propaganda. The expansion of Macedonian power in the earlier years of Philip, down to the peace of Philokrates in 346, involved the capture and destruction of some Greek cities, the dispersal or actual enslavement of their populations, and the redivision of their territory for the benefit of Macedonian settlers; this is true at least of Methone in 354[17] and Olynthos in 348,[18] and perhaps of others as well. Though Demosthenes' rhetoric magnified the numbers and distorted the character of these 'destructions', they were nevertheless a stigma. As his career progressed, Philip came to appreciate more and more the sensitivity of Greek public opinion, as did the later hellenistic dynasties. One may compare the changing Roman attitude to the Greek world from the first to the second Macedonian war. Philip's defeat of the sacrilegious Phokians, and his consequent admission to the Amphiktyonic Council, marked a breakthrough in this respect (cf. Diod. 16. 60; Just. 8. 2. 5–9). Greeks had to be treated with some care, hence the need to redirect Macedonian energies against the Persian empire and try to enlist Greek support. This did not mean that Greek recalcitrance against the Macedonians would not still be met with violence, as Alexander showed in his sack of Thebes in 335. In the initial stages of the invasion before Alexander took over, Parmenion did sack a small Greek city in Asia Minor, Gryneion, and sold its inhabitants into slavery.[19]

While the value of a Macedonian invasion of Asia from Philip's point of view is obvious enough, the aim should not be discussed purely in terms of the ruler alone. Too much attention can be devoted to the leader, too little to the influence of his followers and their own demands (see Austin 1986, 461–5, for the general point). The approach of the ancient sources, which focus upon the kings, obscures this point. Among recent writers, Ellis (1976, esp. 6–13; 219–22; 227–34) has put particular emphasis on the need to see the development of Macedonian society and military power in the time of Philip as a process of interaction between leaders and. followers. Philip brought together the Macedonians by developing the army and the Companion class, and by providing them with profitable military objectives. This created an expansionist momentum, almost independent of the ruler himself, that had to be supplied with fresh objectives. The notion of a powerful, but impersonal, 'war machine' may have a somewhat too modern ring (cf. Errington 1981, 85–6, against Ellis); it also begs questions about how much influence different sections of Macedonian society actually had on royal decisions under Philip. This may be impossible to assess, since evidence on this subject is so scarce for Philip's reign as compared with Alexander's. Nevertheless, this seems a fruitful line of explanation, as valid for Alexander as for Philip.

Nor is it difficult to see why Alexander should have been in such a hurry after his accession to move against the Persian empire, as soon as he had consolidated his position in Macedon, the Balkans, and Greece. Whether his ultimate conquest aims coincided with or diverged from those of Philip, Alexander, to put it crudely, needed a great war of his own. He needed it to prove his leadership inside and outside Macedon, to counteract the influence of possible rivals, to establish his personal hold over his followers and the Macedonian army by distributing to them the spoils of successful warfare, and to replenish the Macedonian finances, which were reportedly in a depleted state at the end of Philip's reign (Arr. 7. 9. 6; Plut. *Alex.* 15). There were limits to how far expansion could profitably be pursued on the European mainland. An invasion of Asia was the only viable course of action available, once control of the Balkans and of the Greek world had been enforced.

The invasion itself

Ancient sources on wars for self-enrichment

At this point it may be appropriate to quote from Momigliano's celebrated and influential paper on the causes of war in ancient historiography. He wrote (1966, 120), 'The Greeks came to accept war as a natural fact like birth and death about which nothing could be done. They were interested in the causes of wars, not in causes of war as such.' The statement has been frequently cited with commendation (e.g. Finley 1985b, 68–70; Garlan 1989, 22–3); yet it now appears to be increasingly in need of modification. Recently Garlan (1989, 21–40) has shown in detail that Plato and Aristotle had clear views about the causes of war in general, and took for granted that wars aimed at material self-enrichment at the expense of one's enemies. A few years ago, Cobet took issue with Momigliano, arguing that both Herodotos and Thucydides had implicit or explicit views about why wars were fought (Cobet 1986, 2–3; cf. also Gould 1989, 114–15). 1 would like to take these remarks further, and apply them specifically to the case of the extant historians of the Macedonian invasion of Asia. While, as we have seen, these historians, for the most part, say little explicitly about what were the aims and motives for launching the invasion in the first instance, they all take for granted in varying degrees that once the expedition was under way, material profit was the name of the game.

Ancient sources frequently refer to the doctrine that the persons and property of the defeated belong to the victor by right of conquest.[20] Indeed, the frequency of such references is in itself suggestive. One wonders whether they did not feel the need to keep reminding themselves that the brutality of war was simply a universally accepted convention that had to be accepted with a shrug of the shoulders – just like slavery, one of the concomitants of ancient wars.

In the extant Alexander sources there are a number of references to this doctrine of the right of appropriation through victory. In Diodoros (17. 17; cf. Just. 11. 5) Alexander, before landing in Asia, casts his spear onto the land to signify that he is taking possession of it at a stroke as 'spear-won' (*doriktetos*) territory. This was a notion with a long history behind it, as far back as Homer, which was explicitly appealed to by the successors of Alexander in their struggles for power and control of territory (cf. Schmitthenner 1968; Mehl 1980–1; Hornblower 1981, 53).[21] In Arrian (2. 14. 9) Alexander, in correspondence with Darius after Issos, tells Darius to regard him as master of all his possessions: 'if you claim the kingship (*basileia*), stand your ground and fight for it.' Later (2. 25. 3) Alexander refuses an offer of money and territory from Darius, 'for the money and the country all belonged to him'. After Gaugamela, Babylon and Susa are described as 'the prize (*athlon*) of war' (3. 16. 2). In Plutarch (*Alex*. 20. 12), after Issos and the plundering of the Persian camp, Alexander decides to go and have a wash in Darius' bath, at which one of his Companions exclaims that it is Alexander's bath; 'the conqueror takes over the possessions of the conquered and they should be called his'.

The same point is made in different forms in many of the sources on Alexander. Plutarch (*On the Fortune or Virtue of Alexander the Great*, 2.336 a) quotes the view of Antisthenes: 'we should pray that our enemies be provided with all good things, except courage; for thus these good things will belong, not to their owners, but to those that conquer them'. Again, compare the fourth saying of Alexander in Plutarch's *Sayings of Kings and Commanders* (*Moralia*, 179 e–f); Alexander can offer frankincense and cassia to his tutor Leonidas, now that he is master of the land that produces these. In the fifth saying, before the battle at Granikos, Alexander urges his troops to eat without stint, since on the next day they will dine from the enemy's stores. In Polyainos (4. 3. 6) Alexander refuses a request from Parmenion, at the battle of Gaugamela, to protect the camp and baggage train, on the grounds that, 'if defeated, they would not need them, and if victorious they would have their own and that of the enemies'. A final example: on the looting of Darius' belongings after his death, Quintus Curtius comments that this was done 'as though in accordance with the laws of war' (*quasi belli iure diripitur*, 5. 12. 17).

The idea of the succession of empires

At this stage I would like to open a digression, though one related to the topic under discussion.

One of antiquity's views of ancient history was that, in political and military terms, it could be seen as a succession of empires. These were empires exercised by collective peoples, not by individual monarchical figures – even though the various imperial peoples who formed part of the scheme, until the coming of the Romans, were all peoples living under monarchies. In this scheme, a sequence of imperial peoples held sway, one at a time, over part or all of the known world, eventually to be defeated and superseded by another, stronger people. The subject has received much discussion; modern writers debate whether the notion was originally of eastern, perhaps specifically Persian, origin (Swain 1940, 7–8; 11–12; Flusser 1972, esp. 153–4, 172–4; Gruen 1984, 329 n. 53), or whether it was from the beginning yet another invention of Greek historiography, subsequently taken over by the Romans and the Jews – a view which is at present gaining ground (Mendels 1981; Momigliano 1982; Kuhrt, in Kuhrt and Sherwin-White (eds) 1987, 47–8).

The scheme was susceptible of numerous variations in detail, and could be adapted for a variety of political and propaganda purposes. It appears for the first time in Herodotos, in the sequence of the ruling peoples who held power in Asia: first the Assyrians, then the Medes, and finally the Persians (1. 95–6 and 130). In the fourth century, the fall of the Persian empire prompted contemporaries to add the Macedonians to the list, as we know from the remarks of Demetrios of Phaleron (*FGH* 228 F 39) quoted by Polybios (29. 21), as well as from references to the scheme in some of the sources for the Macedonian invasion (see below). It is also known that the Seleukids are frequently referred to as 'the Macedonians who ruled Asia' in sources of the imperial period, notably Strabo, Justin (summarized from Trogus Pompeius), and many others as well.[22] Subsequently, with the downfall of the hellenistic monarchies, the Romans were to take over from the Macedonians, and were themselves added to the scheme (Alonso-Nunez 1983; Gruen 1984, 329; 339–40).

Does this conception of a succession of empires merely register mechanically a sequence of historical events, without seeking to explain it? Or does it imply some causal mechanism for the process? I suggest the latter may be the case, though I put this forward as a tentative hypothesis which may not work systematically in every case. To reconstruct a 'model' of how the succession of empires may have worked involves speculative extrapolation, since the relevant ancient writers provide at best only implicit views, not an explicitly argued scheme. But the essentials of that scheme are already there in Herodotos, and are to be seen in at least two of the Alexander sources: Justin (from Pompeius Trogus) and Quintus Curtius. I shall now outline the main steps in the argument in a schematic form.

First, wealth. Wealth consists essentially of land, all its products, whether vegetable or mineral, and all the life that the land sustains, whether animal or human. The consequence of this conception is that the total wealth to be found in the world is, in practice, finite. It is already there, and new wealth cannot be created, except for the discovery and exploitation of new resources previously untapped, such as mines of precious metals, or the bringing into productive use of land not hitherto exploited.

Second, the ownership of wealth. It follows from the view just outlined that existing wealth is already, for the most part, distributed among the various peoples of the world. Some people inhabit poorer territories and so are poor, others inhabit richer lands and so are better off. Richest of all are those who control the lands of others and the peoples who live there. From these they can draw rich revenues in the form of tribute or services from dependent peoples. Hence the principal way for peoples who are not themselves rich to acquire wealth is for them to take it from those who control existing wealth. Since those who have wealth cannot be expected to give it up without a struggle, wealth will usually have to be seized by superior force. Since wealth is assumed to be intrinsically desirable, the possession of wealth therefore makes a people an automatic target for possible attack. Conversely, poor people are assumed to be protected from aggression on the grounds that it is simply not profitable for any aggressor to want to attack them. The assumption is, therefore, that successful wars ought normally to be profitable.

Third, the moral and physical characteristics attached to poor and wealthy peoples.[23] Poor peoples are by definition tough and warlike, able to defend themselves against attack and to attack others; wealthy peoples, on the other hand, are soft and unwarlike, and hence an object of contempt (cf. Austin 1986, 459, on this notion); they are unable to defend themselves adequately against poorer but tougher peoples, and this makes them an obvious target for aggression. The trouble is, on this view of things, that people may not in fact be well advised to covet the wealth of others. Poor people who attack and seize the wealth of rich people make themselves vulnerable to attack in their turn. By becoming wealthy they are in danger of losing their original national characteristics; they take on those of the people they defeated, and so become softened and an object of contempt. Their newly acquired wealth encourages further aggression by others, who will dispossess them in their turn. Hence, perhaps, the cycle of rising and falling imperial peoples. Hence also, perhaps, the ever-recurring consciousness in ancient authors of the fragility and evanescence of empires, even at the height of their prosperity and success.

All these views are already found in essentials in Herodotos. He takes it for granted that successful wars ought to be profitable, and that there is therefore no point in attacking poorer people. At 1. 71 Croesus of Lydia is warned by a wise Lydian not to attack the (then) poor, hardy Persians, since if he is victorious there will be nothing worth taking from them, while if he is defeated the Persians will then covet the wealth of the Lydians themselves. At 1. 126 Cyrus graphically makes the point to the Persians that being ruled means a life of poverty and toil, whereas ruling others means plenty and enjoyment. Conversely, after the battle of Plataea, the Spartan Pausanias is astonished at the sumptuous lifestyle of the defeated Persian commander Mardonios, and comments on the madness for such a wealthy man of attacking the poverty-stricken Greeks (9. 82). Mardonios, in urging Xerxes to invade Greece, emphasizes its wealth, fit for a king, and minimizes the Greeks' military ability (7. 5. 3; 7. 9). Demaratos the Spartan gives the lie to this: Greece is poor and the Greeks defend their independence (7. 102). Hence the Greek view, which may have originated at this time if not earlier, that if the Greeks were sensible they would stop fighting unprofitable wars between themselves and turn instead to the far more lucrative business of attacking Asia, as is argued (in Herodotos) by Aristagoras to Kleomenes in 499 (5. 49, discussed above).

The concluding chapter of the whole work repeats the theme that if poor people acquire wealth they risk being softened and becoming liable to attack (9. 122). The Persian Artembares is there said to have advised Cyrus, now that the Persians had achieved hegemony, to move them from their barren, rocky land to better territory in order to increase their status. To this Cyrus is made to answer that if they did so, they would become ruled instead of rulers. 'Soft countries', Cyrus says, 'produce soft men; the same land cannot produce both wonderful crops and warlike men.' Hence, says Herodotos, 'the Persians preferred to inhabit poor land and rule, rather than cultivate the plain and be slaves to others.' The statement is loaded with irony, since Herodotos otherwise portrays the Persians as having fully discovered the material pleasures of life, as the aftermath of the battle of Plataea revealed to the astonished Greeks (9. 82).

The views outlined above are in fact commonplaces about war and the rise and fall of empires in ancient writings, and a large anthology could no doubt be compiled. How are they presented in the Alexander sources?

Arrian

Arrian is familiar with the notion of the 'succession of empires', which he refers to at 2. 6. 7: 'It was destined that the Persians should forfeit the sovereignty of Asia to the Macedonians. just as Medes had lost it to Persians, and Assyrians even earlier to Medes.' But for Arrian it seems to be merely a familiar cliché, mechanically applied without further reflection. He is also familiar with the idea that the possession of wealth is in itself an inducement to aggression from outsiders, while poverty normally protects against attack. At 3. 24. 2 (on 330 BC) he remarks that 'no one had invaded the country [of the Mardians] for a long time, owing to the difficulty of the terrain, and because the Mardians were not only poor, but warlike'. Similarly, at 4. 1. 1, he says of the Scythians who live in Asia 'they are independent (*autonomoi*), chiefly through their poverty and their sense of justice' (see also 6. 23. 1–3 on the poverty of Gedrosia). Conversely, at 5. 25. 1–2, 'the country beyond the Hyphasis was reported to be fertile. . . . These people also had a far greater number of elephants than the other Indians, and the best for size and courage. This report stirred Alexander to a desire for further advance.' Similarly, in relation to the projected Arabian expedition of Alexander, Arrian comments (7. 20. 2–3):

> The prosperity of the country was also an incitement, since he [Alexander] heard that cassia grew in their marshes, that the trees produced myrrh and frankincense, that cinnamon was cut from the bushes, and that spikenard grew self-sown in their meadows. Then there was also the size of their territory, since he was informed that the sea-coast of Arabia was nearly as long as that of India, and that there were many islands off-shore and harbours everywhere in the country, enough to give anchorages for his fleet, and to permit cities to be built on them, which were likely to prosper.

In general, Arrian is perfectly aware that the invasion of Asia had resulted in massive enrichment for the invaders. This is the view given in general terms in the speeches of Alexander and Koinos at the Hyphasis in 326 BC (5. 26. 7–8 and 27. 6–8), and in Alexander's speech at Opis in 324 BC (7. 10. 3–4).

Yet beyond this there are significant differences between the presentation by Arrian of the material gains of the expedition and that put forward by the other sources, especially Justin and Quintus Curtius.

First, Arrian does not seem to reproduce the idea that the acquisition of wealth by the conquerors is likely to have a debilitating effect on them in turn. He is aware of the idea that poverty toughens while wealth softens, as is shown by his reference to the Mardians (above). Similarly, at 2. 7. 4, before Issos Alexander is made to contrast Macedonian fitness with the long habit of luxury of the Medes and Persians. What Arrian does not do, however, is to apply this notion to the future and suggest that the Macedonians in their turn may be affected by the same process. In so far as the rapid acquisition of conquered wealth had any effects on the Macedonians at all, it merely stimulated others at home in Macedon to join the expedition in order to enjoy the same benefits (note the speeches at the Hyphasis, 5. 27. 7–8, and at Opis, 7. 8. 1). All this may reflect Arrian's primary focus on Alexander and his lack of interest in the Macedonians.[24]

Second, Arrian's detailed reporting of the material gains made and distributed during the expedition appears incomplete and understated when compared with all the other extant Alexander sources. What Arrian seems to present is a rather bland, 'sanitized' version of the expedition. It hardly makes clear the essential role, played in the expedition by the forcible acquisition and redistribution of wealth. It does not dwell on all the brutalities involved, and fails to convey what the presence of an invading army must have meant to the local populations. Several examples may illustrate this.

(1) Arrian's reporting of the sequels to the major battles against the Persians – first Issos and the capture of the Persian camp (2. 11. 9–10), then Gaugamela (3. 15. 4–6)

and the captures of Babylon (3. 16. 3–5), Persepolis, and Susa (3. 16. 6–7) – is consistently sketchier than that of all the other sources, and neutral in tone. In the case of Persepolis he manages to obscure the facts that the army stayed there for four months, and that Alexander gave the city to his army to plunder (see 3. 18. 10–12; Bosworth 1980, 329–33).

(2) Arrian underplays the gift-giving by Alexander that played a major part in the expedition, and about which there is much evidence from many sources (Berve 1926, i. 195; 304–6; 311–13; cf. esp. Plut. *Alex.* 39). Alexander was one of the most prodigal rulers in antiquity, and was in a good position to be so, thanks to the captured wealth of the Persian empire. His gift-giving had obvious functions: to assert his hold over his followers, and to present himself as the supreme dispenser of wealth in competition with other possible rivals, such as Attalos at the start of his reign (Diod. 17. 2; Berve 1926, no. 182), and later Philotas (Plut. *Alex.* 48; Berve 1926, no. 802), both of them described simultaneously as generous in their gift-giving and popular with the army. There is much less evidence in Arrian on all this than in other sources. For example, we know from Plutarch (*Alex.* 15) that at the start of the expedition Alexander made lavish gifts to his friends, evidently to confirm them in their loyalty to him. There is no mention of this in Arrian, and only a belated and oblique reference (at 7. 9. 6) to the debts of Philip and Alexander at the start of the expedition, which does not make clear what had happened in 334. Again, Arrian's account (7. 5. 1–3) of the settling of the army's debts, which amounted to 10,000 talents, at Susa in 324 leaves many questions unanswered. It does not make clear how and why those debts had been contracted, nor to whom the soldiers were in debt (perhaps members of the Macedonian élite? cf. *Plut. Eumenes*, 2, for their lending of money to Alexander). Nor does it make clear that by settling the debts of his soldiers Alexander was in effect cutting the bond that tied them to their creditors and putting them under obligation to himself.

(3) Arrian virtually ignores the important, though rather neglected, role in the expedition that was played by women. I am not referring here to the conspicuous royal figures – Alexander's mother Olympias, the Persian royal ladies captured after Issos, or Roxane – about whom the sources all have much to say. I mean the very numerous ordinary captives seized as a result of victories at major stages of the expedition, distributed to the soldiers as spoils of war, or perhaps sometimes simply snatched by them along the way in more or less irregular fashion. Something is known about them; but chiefly from sources other than Arrian (see Berve 1926, i. 172–3). No mention from him, for instance, of Thais the mistress of Ptolemy, who may have incited the burning of the palace of Persepolis (Plut. *Alex.* 38; Berve 1926, no. 359); or of Antigone, mentioned in Plutarch as one of the captives made after Issos, who fell to the share of Philotas and became his mistress (Plut. *Alex.* 48–9; Berve 1926, no. 86). In 324, in relation to the marriages of Alexander and the leading Macedonians with noble Persian women, Arrian mentions casually (7. 4. 8) that 'there proved to be over ten thousand Macedonians who had married Asian women; Alexander had them all registered, and every one of them received a wedding gift'. But he provides no explanation of how those 'marriages' were supposed to have come about.

It is clear, therefore, that Arrian's reporting of the material and acquisitive sides of the expedition is incomplete. It is interesting to compare him in this respect not only with the other Alexander sources, who all provide more detail, but also with

Xenophon's *Anabasis*. Arrian explicitly refers to this as a literary model (1. 12. 3),[25] and cites the expedition of the Ten Thousand as a precedent for the Macedonian invasion (see Alexander's speech before Issos, 2. 7. 8–9). Yet the character of the two narratives, as accounts of military history, could hardly be different. Where Xenophon's account gives us a view from within the army itself, albeit from the vantage point of an officer with an itch for leadership, Arrian allows us very little insight into the mood and reactions of the army. Where Xenophon is disarmingly frank about all the raiding and snatching of captives performed by the army, and about how these captives were disposed of, Arrian is again bland and uninformative, even though the quantities of booty and captives seized by the Macedonians vastly exceeded anything the Ten Thousand could have dreamt of.

Justin and Trogus Pompeius: Quintus Curtius

It is unfortunate that the account of Trogus can only be divined through the meagre summary of Justin; for Trogus was one of the most interesting of ancient writers on the subjects of war and empire. In Trogus, the ideas that are left implicit in Herodotos seem to have been brought out explicitly, and his debt to Herodotos is extensive, as numerous echoes show. He adopts and systematizes the scheme of the succession of empires as the framework for his view of history, from the Assyrians via (among others) the Medes, Persians, and Macedonians to the Romans (see notably Just. 1. 1, 3, 6; 6. 9 and 7. 1; 9. 15. 2; 30. 4. 1–4; 41. 1).

Of particular interest is his hostility to aggressive imperialism as such (cf. Momigliano 1982, 91–2), at least in so far as imperialism was motivated by material greed and not just glory. This idea runs through his work, and is most clearly expressed in relation to the 'Scythians', who act in Trogus as the noble savages, an object-lesson to supposedly civilized peoples who indulge in wars for profit and empire. They are introduced (at 2. 2) as a people who are just because they are poor. They despise gold and silver, which others covet, and do not grasp after what their neighbours have. Greed for the wealth of others is the cause of wars, says Trogus, and we ought to imitate the example of the Scythians, who are wiser than the Greeks and all their philosophers. They did, it is true, conceive the ambition to exercise empire over Asia on three occasions. But, for one thing, they remained themselves largely unconquered even by the Romans (2. 3), unlike so many imperial peoples who eventually fell subject to others. For another, they did not seek material profit from empire, only glory; and when they reduced Asia they only imposed a modest tribute, as a token of power rather than as a reward for victory (2. 3). Other would-be conquerors came to grief against them, starting with Darius (2. 5; cf. 37. 3; 38. 7). Later Philip of Macedon made an unprovoked plundering raid upon them (339BC), which resulted in the capture of (reportedly) 'twenty thousand' prisoners and countless cattle. But Philip found out to his dismay that the Scythians had no gold and silver, and he himself lost some of his spoils through an attack by the Triballi (9. 1–3). The moral of the story is obvious.

It is unfortunate that Justin's summary does not make clear how Trogus presented the story of Alexander's relations with the Scythians. An indication, however, comes from the mention of the activities of Zopyrion (Berve 1926, no. 340). He was appointed governor in 'Pontus' (Thrace, rather) by Alexander, was anxious for personal exploits, and made an unprovoked invasion of the Scythians, but was defeated and paid the penalty for his rash attack on an innocent people (12. 2; cf. 37. 3; 38. 7).

For the Scythians in relation to Alexander, we have to turn to the account of Quintus Curtius (7. 8. 12–30), who makes the point explicit. The Scythian envoys, whose speech Curtius promises to report accurately (7. 8. 11), are made to rebuke Alexander at great length, and with a wealth of rhetorical flourishes, for his insatiable greed which leads to ever more wars; all the Scythians want is to be left in peace, neither slaves nor masters of anybody. The presentation is identical in spirit to that in Trogus, and Curtius may have drawn on him directly or indirectly. It is interesting to contrast this highly pointed and 'thematic' presentation of the Scythians with Arrian's brief and neutral account of Alexander's decision to attack them (4. 1. 1–2).

If the Scythians are the noble savages who disdain material wealth and wish neither to dominate others nor to be dominated by anybody, then the Macedonians are to be reckoned among the imperial culprits. They start off from humble beginnings (7. 1), but then under their kings Philip (books 7–9) and Alexander (books 11–13) they turn to aggression for material gain. They pay the penalty in becoming themselves corrupted by greed and luxury (30. 1; 36. 1; 38. 10). This results in attacks by others (24. 6; 25. 1), strife between themselves (13. 1; 14. 5–6; 15. 4; 17. 1; 27. 2–3; 39. 5), and internal dynastic conflict, a persistent theme in Trogus (14. 5–6; 15. 2; 16. 1; 24. 2–3; 26. 3; 27. 1; 30. 2; books 35 and 39–40). Hellenistic history, as presented by Trogus, is the story of the decline of the Macedonians as a direct consequence of their imperial success, and reflects Roman preoccupations with their own decline.

Quintus Curtius' presentation of the motive for the invasion, and of its effects on the Macedonians, is similar to that of Trogus, though his focus is primarily on Alexander himself and his evolution into an 'oriental despot' rather than on the Macedonians collectively (cf. e.g. 6. 6. 1–10). Although the first two books are lost, we can imagine how the Macedonians were presented as initially a hardy and poor people. 'Do not think that they are motivated by a desire for gold and silver', says the Athenian Charidemos to Darius before Issos; 'until now their discipline has been maintained by poverty's schooling'.[26] Darius believes otherwise (4. 13. 14; 5. 1. 4–6), and the narrative of the campaign gives the lie to him. Curtius draws an elaborate and colourful picture of all the material gains of the victors, for which they invade Asia, and of the debilitating effects these have on them.[27] After Alexander's death the Macedonians fall out between themselves, unable to be satisfied with what they have already gained (10. 10. 6–8).

Conclusions

To sum up. The sources for the Macedonian invasion all show, in their different ways, definite views, implicit or explicit, about the motives for war in general, as well as for the Macedonian invasion in particular. No one would claim profundity for these views; still less would one wish to suggest that 'softness' and 'luxury' are necessarily useful analytical tools for the study of the fall of ancient empires, though 'greed' may be for their rise. Nor does the schematic division between rich and poor peoples work very well in practice – certainly not in the case of the Macedonians. At the end of the reign of Philip the Macedonians could no longer be described as a poor people,[28] but had already started to enjoy the material benefits of successful military expansion, and so had both the taste for more and the means of acquiring it.[29] Successful warfare in the world of the fourth century needed financial resources, as all Greek states found out, and that was something the Macedonians did already possess at home in the shape of their mines.

But at least the sources have a view of sorts, which takes for granted that wars are fought for material gain, and that therefore wealth by itself attracts aggression. This is a view so common in many ancient writers over a long period of time that it has to be taken seriously.[30] One may repeat here the important observation of Finley, that the richest and most prosperous states in antiquity were conquest states who owed their wealth to the fruits of superior military power, whatever precise form that took (Finley 1983, 61–4; 109–16; 1985a, 204–7). It should be added that wealth in the ancient world was not a matter of invisible bank accounts and the like, but was generally highly visible and concrete. Wealth consisted of good land, agricultural stores, flocks and cattle, human beings, and precious metals stored in one form or another, all of which were there for the taking by an aggressor.

A few general points in conclusion. What of the attitudes to war and empire revealed by these sources? There seems to be no wholly favourable endorsement of the Macedonian invasion of Asia, apart from Plutarch's in his *De Alexandri Magni fortuna aut virtute*; but for all the considerable historiographical importance of this work as the starting-point of many an idealized modern view of Alexander, from Droysen onwards, it can hardly be regarded as a realistic source on Alexander. Otherwise, ambivalence seems to be the keynote, in that no source is wholly free from some note of doubt.

Diodoros, like Quintus Curtius, reproduces pathetic descriptions of the brutalities of the soldiery after Issos (17. 35–6) and at the sack of Persepolis (17. 70). This probably follows Kleitarchos, who relished the opportunity for colourful writing. Arrian carefully avoids this particular theme; but for all his avowed admiration for Alexander and the general blandness of his account, he does nevertheless introduce a note of censure against the restless conqueror who is unable to stand still, vain as his exertions will ultimately be in the face of inevitable mortality (4. 7. 5; 7. 1–2; cf. Bosworth 1988b, 72–4; 148–9). This is a common theme in ancient writers, found for example in Plutarch's portraits of Alexander (ch. 64, where the Indian gymnosophists put him in his place) and Pyrrhos (ch. 14, the confrontation between the wise Kineas and the king; on Pyrrhos compare also Just. 17. 3–18. 1; 25. 3–5). Plutarch's *Pyrrhos* also carries a sweeping condemnation of the insatiable aggressiveness of the Successors (ch. 12; so, too, Justin in books 14–17).

What of the Roman imperial writers? They provide an apparent critique of war and empire in the form of the theme of 'Alexander the brigand', a theme that appears peculiar to them. This is the view found in Quintus Curtius, but also in a number of other authors, notably Seneca, Lucan (see the splendid outburst at the beginning of book 10 of his *Pharsalia*, lines 20–45), and St Augustine (in a famous and much-quoted passage from the *City of God*, 4. 4). To this theme Plutarch's *De Alexandri Magni fortuna aut virtute* might seem to be a reply, in its explicit denial that Alexander was a brigand who devastated Asia (333 d).

Yet how far does this critique of empire really go? Cobet (1986) argues that despite all the negative presentation of war and its attendant suffering in many passages of

Herodotos and Thucydides, at the end of the day there seems to be a positive acceptance of the inevitability of war and empire. The same may be largely true, in varying degrees, for the Alexander sources.

Diodoros endorses the invasion as a whole (17. 1; 17. 117), and so does Arrian (1. 12. 2–4; 7. 28–30); they both regard it as an outstanding achievement.[31] As for Plutarch in his *Parallel Lives*, his real regret is that the invasion should have been carried out not by the Greeks, but by Macedonians, whom Plutarch, espousing the Athenian democratic view of Demosthenes, does not consider to be authentic Greeks (*Alex.* 37 and 56; contrast *Kimon*, 19; and *Agesilaos*, 15). In the Roman writers the negative presentation of Alexander is inspired by republican-minded opposition against Roman incarnations of 'oriental despotism' – Caesar, Mark Antony, and some Roman emperors (see Rufus Fears 1974; Ceausescu 1974; Vidal-Naquet 1984, 333–5; 371–3) – and this opposition was directed more against a certain style of political behaviour on the part of rulers than against war and empire as such. Even the condemnations of acquisitive imperialism, as voiced by Trogus Pompeius and Quintus Curtius, may not mean as much as they appear to. In practice there was no alternative. A parallel may be drawn between slavery and empire; as we saw above, attitudes to war and attitudes to slavery frequently converge. Just as ancient writers could only imagine a world without slaves by placing it in the utopian setting of a mythical golden age before civilization (Vogt 1974, 26–38; Finley 1975, 178–92; Garlan 1988, 130–8), so too the only peoples to reject imperialism motivated by greed had to be an imaginary people like the mythical Scythians, who remained outside the confines of the civilized world and so could manage to stay untainted by its corruption.

Notes

1 My thanks are due to the participants at seminars in St Andrews and Leicester, and to the editors of this volume; their comments and suggestions have helped to improve the original, though the responsibility for any remaining errors and omissions remains my own.

2 E.g. Arr. 7. 28. 3, cf. Bosworth 1988b, 137; 139; Plut. *Alex.* 5; 39–40.

3 Brunt 1976–83, i, pp. li–lv (paras 39–42); ii. 567 (para. 30).

4 Cf. Badian 1966, 39–41, on the campaigns before Alexander's takeover.

5 See Brunt 1976–83, i, p. lii (para. 40), for the sources.

6 Brunt 1976–83, i, p. li (para. 39); Seager 1981, 106–7. Isokrates (5. 123) had suggested to Philip the liberation of the (Greek) cities of Asia as a minimum objective.

7 On revenge in Greek thought and practice see Gehrke 1987, esp. 144 on Philip, Alexander, and Persia.

8 See Errington 1981, esp. 77–83, who argues for the latter against other recent views; *contra*, Borza 1990, 229–30.

9 See, e.g., Fredericksmeyer 1982 for a maximalist view of Philip's aims, with references to earlier work.

10 Among many, see Berve 1926, who apparently gives no systematic discussion of the question; Tarn 1948, i. 8–9; Brunt 1965, 205–8; Seibert 1972, 70–8, who has nothing on the subject in his survey of Alexander's early years down to the start of the expedition; Hamilton 1973, 38–9 (Philip); 46, 50–1 (Alexander); Lane Fox 1973, chs 3–4; Hammond and Walbank 1988, 66–7; Errington 1990, 87–9 (Philip); 103–5 (Alexander); Borza 1990, 226; 228–30. Even Bosworth (1988a, 17–19; 34; 38–9; 43; 50; 54; 179) provides no systematic treatment of the question. Rather fuller on Philip are Hammond and Griffith (1979, 458–63; 631–4) and Fredericksmeyer (1982).

11 The Persian kings' vast treasures of uncoined gold and silver were a special temptation; cf.

de Callatay 1989, 260–4, for an attempt to quantify the amounts of precious metals captured by the Macedonians from the Persians.

12 See Xen. *Hell.* 6. 1. 12; *Ages.* 1. 36, cf. 7. 7; Isoc. 4. 144; Plut. *Ages.* 15; cf. Cartledge 1987, 212–18.

13 See e.g. Momigliano 1975, 132–6; Starr 1976, 1977; Cartledge 1987, 184–5; Sancisi-Weerdenburg (ed.) 1987, 33–45, on Ktesias; ibid. 117–31, on Xenophon's *Cyropaedia*; Kuhrt 1988, 60–1.

14 For some passages see Garlan, in Finley (ed.) 1987, at pp. 13–15 (= Garlan 1989, 83–4); Garlan 1988, 50–2; cf. also Xen. *Hell.* 3. 2. 22.

15 See explicitly Hdt. 5. 49, and cf. Xen. *Hell.* 3. 2. 26; cf. also Xenophon's comment on the inconclusive outcome of the Battle of Mantineia (362), *Hell.* 7. 5. 27.

16 Tod ii. 123, line 23; Theopompos, *FGH* 115 F 98; Plut. *Sol.* 15; cf. Wilson 1970.

17 Diod. 16. 34, with Hammond and Griffith 1979, 361–2.

18 Diod. 16. 53, with Hammond and Griffith 1979, 324–8; 365–79 (Chalkidike); see also McKechnie 1989, 48–51.

19 Diod. 17. 7. 9; see Badian 1966, 40; 44–5; Seager 1981, 106–7.

20 For some examples see Garlan, in Finley (ed.) 1987, at p. 8; Garlan 1989, 75–6.

21 I have not see Instinsky 1949, 29–40.

22 See Edson 1958, though the conclusions he draws about the nature of the Seleukid monarchy do not necessarily follow.

23 On this section, and on 'soft' and 'hard' peoples in Hdt., see Redfield 1985, 109–18; Gould 1989, 58–60.

24 See notably Arrian's final evaluation of Alexander (7. 28–30), with Bosworth 1988b, ch. 6.

25 Cf. Bosworth (1988b), 25–6; 138–9; index, s.v. Xenophon.

26 3. 2. 15: *ne auri argentique studio teneri putes, adhuc illa disciplina paupertate magistra stetit.*

27 See esp. 3. 11. 20–2 and 3. 13. 2–11, 16–17 (Issos); 5. 1. 36–9 (at Babylon); 5. 6. 1–8 (Persepolis, Pasargadae); 6. 6. 14–17 (destruction of booty); 8. 8. 9 and 12 (before the invasion of India); 9. 1. 1–3 (after the Hydaspes); 9. 10. 12 (in Gedrosia).

28 Cf. Arr. 7. 9. 1–5 (Alexander at Opis, on Philip).

29 Cf. Theopompos, *FGH* 115 F 224–5, on the Companions of Philip.

30 See e.g. Cassius Dio, 39. 56. 1–2 (Gabinius) and 40. 12. 1 (Crassus), on Roman motives for attacking the Parthians.

31 Cf. Bosworth 1988b, 156: 'Arrian had a thoroughly conventional view of the desirability and glory of conquest.'

Bibliography

Alonso-Nunez, J. M. (1983), 'Die Abfolge der Weltreiche bei Polybios und Dionysios von Halikarnassos', *Historia*, 32: 411–26.

Austin, M. M. (1986), 'Hellenistic kings, war and the economy', *CQ* 80 (n.s. 36): 450–66.

Badian, E. (1966), 'Alexander the Great and the Greeks of Asia', in *Ancient Society and Institutions. Studies presented to V. Ehrenberg* (Oxford), pp. 37–69.

Berve, H. (1926), *Das Alexanderreich auf prosopographischer Grundlage* (Munich).

Borza, E. N. (1990), *In the Shadow of Olympus: The Emergence of Macedon* (Princeton).

Bosworth, A. B. (1980), *A Historical Commentary on Arrian's History of Alexander*, i: *Commentary on Books I–III* (Oxford).

—— (1988a), *Conquest and Empire: The Reign of Alexander the Great* (Cambridge).

—— (1988b), *From Arrian to Alexander: Studies in Historical Interpretation* (Oxford).

Brunt, P. A. (1965), 'The aims of Alexander', *G&R* 12: 205–15.

—— (1976–83), *Arrian: History of Alexander and Indica* (Loeb Classical Library; Cambridge, Mass.).

Cartledge, P. (1987), *Agesilaos and the Crisis of Sparta* (London).

Ceausescu, P. (1974), 'La double image d'Alexandre le Grand à Rome: essai d'une explication politique', *Studii Clasice*, 16: 153–68.

Cobet, J. (1986), 'Herodotus and Thucydides on war', in I. S. Moxon, J. D. Smart, and A. J. Woodman (eds), *Past Perspectives: Studies in Greek and Roman Historical Writing* (London), pp. 1–18.

de Callatay, F. (1989), 'Lea trésors achéménides et les monnayages d'Alexandre: espèces immobilisées et espèces circulantes?', *REA* 91: 259–74, with comments on pp. 274–6, 334.

de Ste. Croix, G. E. M. (1972), *The Origins of the Peloponnesian War* (London).

Ducrey, P. (1968), *Le Traitement des prisonniers de guerre dans la Grèce antique* (Paris).

—— (1985), *Guerre et guerriers dans la Grèce antique* (Fribourg, Switzerland).

Edson, C. F. (1958), '*Imperium Macedonicum*: the Seleucid empire and the literary evidence', *CP* 53: 153–70.

Ellis, J. R. (1976), *Philip II and Macedonian Imperialism* (London).

Errington, R. M. (1981), 'Review discussion: four interpretations of Philip II', *AJAH* 6: 69–88.

—— (1990), *A History of Macedonia* (Berkeley, etc.).

Finley, M. I. (1975), *The Use and Abuse of History* (London).

—— (1983), *Politics in the Ancient World* (Cambridge).

—— (1985a), *The Ancient Economy* (2nd edn, London).

—— (1985b), 'War an empire', in *Ancient History: Evidence and Models* (London), pp. 67–87.

—— (ed. 1987), *Classical Slavery* (London).

Flusser, D. (1972), 'The four empires in the fourth Sibyl and in the book of Daniel', *Israel Oriental Studies*, 2: 148–75.

Fredericksmeyer, E. A. (1982), 'On the final aims of Philip II', in W. L. Adams and E. N. Borza (eds), *Philip II, Alexander the Great and the Macedonian Heritage* (Lanham, etc.), pp. 85–98.

Garlan, Y. (1975), *War in the Ancient World: A Social History* (London).

—— (1988), *Slavery in Ancient Greece*, trans. J. Lloyd (Ithaca).

—— (1989), *Guerre et économie en Grèce ancienne* (Paris).

Gehrke, H. (1987), 'Die Griechen und die Rache: ein Versuch in historischer Psychologie', *Saeculum*, 38: 121–49.

Gould, J. (1989), *Herodotus* (London).

Gruen, E. (1984), *The Hellenistic World and the Coming of Rome* (Berkeley).

Habicht, C. (1961), 'Falsche Urkunden zur Geschichte Athens im Zeitalter der Perserkriegen', *Hermes*, 89: 1–35.

Hamilton, J. R. (1973), *Alexander the Great* (London).

Hammond, N. G. L., and Griffith, G. T. (1979), *A History of Macedonia*, ii: *550–336 BC* (Oxford).

—— and Walbank, F. W. (1988), *A History of Macedonia*, iii: *336–167 BC* (Oxford)

Hornblower, J. (1981), *Hieronymus of Cardia* (Oxford).

Instinsky, H. (1949), *Alexander der Grosse am Hellespont*.

Jackson, A. H. (1985), review of W. Nowag, *Raub und Beute in der archaischen Zeit der Greichen*, *Gnomon*, 57: 655–7.

Kuhrt, A. (1988), 'The Achaemenid empire: a Babylonian perspective', *PCPS* 214 (n.s. 34): 60–76.

—— and Sherwin-White, S. (eds 1987), *Hellenism in the East* (London).

Lane Fox, R. (1973), *Alexander the Great* (London).

McKechnie, P. (1989), *Outsiders in the Greek Cities in the Fourth Century BC* (London).

Mehl, A. (1980–1), '*Doriktetos chora*: kritische Bemerkungen zum "Speererwerb" im Politik und Völkerrecht der hellenistischen Epoche', *Ancient Society*, 11–12: 173–212.

Mendels, D. (1981), 'The five empires: a note on a propagandistic topos', *AJP* 102: 330–7.

Momigliano, A. (1966), 'Some observations on the causes of war in ancient historiography', in *Studies in Historiography* (London), pp. 112–26; = *Secondo contributo alla storia deglia studi classici* (Rome, 1960), pp. 13–27.

—— (1975), *Alien Wisdom: The Limits of Hellenization* (Cambridge).

—— (1982), 'The origins of universal history', *Annali della Scuola Normale Superiore di Pisa, classe delle lettere e filosofia*, series 3, 12(2): 533–60; = *Settimo contributo all storia degli studi classici e del mondo antico* (Rome, 1984), pp. 77–103.

Perlman, S. (1976), 'Panhellenism, the polis and imperialism', *Historia* 25: 1–30.

Powell, A. (1988), *Athens and Sparta: Constructing Greek History* (London).

Redfield, J. (1985), 'Herodotus the tourist', *CP* 80: 97–118.

Rufus Fears, J. (1974), 'The Stoic view of the character and career of Alexander the Great', *Philologus*, 118: 114–30.

Sancisi-Weerdenburg, H. (ed. 1987), *Achaemenid History*, i: *Sources Structures and Synthesis* (Leiden).

—— and Kuhrt, A. (eds 1987), *Achaemenid History*, ii: *The Greek Sources* (Leiden).

Schmitthenner, W. (1968), 'Über eine Formveränderung der Monarchie seit Alexander dem Grossen', *Saeculum*, 19: 31–46.

Seager, R. (1981), 'The freedom of the Greeks of Asia: from Alexander to Antiochus', *CQ* 31: 106–12.

Seibert, J. (1972), *Alexander der Grosse* (Erträge der Forschung, 310; Darmstadt).

Starr, C. G. (1976, 1977), 'Greeks and Persians in the fourth century BC: a study in political contacts before Alexander', *Iranica antiqua*, 11: 39–99; 12: 49–116.

Swain, J. W. (1940), 'The theory of the four monarchies: opposition history under the Roman empire', *CP* 35: 1–21.

Tarn, W. W. (1948), *Alexander the Great* (Cambridge).

Thomas, R. (1989), *Oral Tradition and Written Record in Classical Athens* (Cambridge).

Vidal-Naquet, P. (1984), 'Arrien entre deux mondes', in *Arrien: Histoire d'Alexandre* (trans. P. Savinel; Paris), pp. 311–94.

Vogt, J. (1974), *Ancient Slavery and the Ideal of Man* (Oxford).

Wilson, C. H. (1970), 'Athenian military finances, 378/7 to the peace of 375', *Athenaeum*, 48: 302–26.

THE KINGDOM OF ASIA AND THE PERSIAN THRONE*

N. G. L. Hammond

1 The Kingdom of Asia

In order to appreciate the originality of Alexander in his policy in Asia, we may note that the actions of Philip in the Balkan area were described in terms of traditional Greek imperialism. 'Philip made Macedonia mistress of many great tribes and city-states', wrote Diodorus in a Proem which was probably an abbreviated form of the Proem of Ephorus XXVIII[1] (Diod. 16.1.3 παραλαβὼν τὴν Μακεδονίαν δουλεύουσαν Ἰλλυριοῖς πολλῶν καὶ μεγάλων ἐθνῶν καὶ πόλεων κυρίαν ἐποίησε). In 349 B.C. Demosthenes remarked that 'the Paeonian, the Illyrian and in a word all those folk, it should be realised, would gladly be self-governing and free rather than be slaves (δοῦλοι);[2] for they are unaccustomed to being anyone's subject' (1.23). In addressing the Macedonians at Opis, Alexander pointed out that thanks to Philip the Macedonians had become masters and not slaves and subjects of those very barbarians who used to plunder their possessions and carry off their persons; and that Philip 'added to Macedonia the greater part of Thrace' (Arr. *An.* 7.9.3).[3]

Diodorus was drawing very probably on Ephorus when he wrote that Philip compelled the Paeonians 'to obey the Macedonians' (16.4.2) and made all the people up to Lake Lychnitis 'subjects' (16.8.1 ὑπηκόους).[4] When he was perhaps using a very short Hellenistic account like *POxy* 1 no. 12, he reported that Philip compelled the three kings (Thracian, Paeonian and Illyrian) to 'take the side of the Macedonians' and later 'ordered the defeated barbarians (Thracians) to pay tithes to the Macedonians' (16.22.3 and 16.71.2).[5] When Alexander campaigned against Balkan tribes, Diodorus – now probably using Diyllus – wrote of him making them 'subject' and compelling them to be 'subordinated' (17.3.6 and 8.1).[6] Thus the Macedonians ruled over subject peoples, as the Athenians ruled over their Greek subjects. It was a national empire.

Philip reduced some Greek city-states in the Balkan area (as distinct from the Greek peninsula) to subjection (Diod. 16.31.6 and 52.9). Others he razed to the ground (Potidaea, Methone, Zereia, Olynthus, Stageira, Galepsus and Apollonia east of the Strymon mouth), appropriated their lands to Macedonia, and either sold their population into slavery or settled them in other parts of Macedonia or Macedonia's possessions.[7] He behaved as Athens had done at Samos in 366 and 361 B.C., for instance; but he did not massacre the adult males, as she had done at Sestus in 353 B.C.

It was expected by Isocrates and no doubt by Aristotle that Philip would establish his rule over as many barbarian peoples in Asia as possible (Isoc. *Philippus* 154).[8] Liberation was to be for the Greek city-states in Asia (Diod. 16.91.2), but only if they fought against Persia; for when Gryneum defected to Persia it was captured and destroyed by Parmenio in the course of 335 B.C. (Diod. 17.7.9).[9] He was operating in the manner of Philip, and the lands of Gryneum were no doubt confiscated by Parmenio in the names of Macedonia and the Greek League.

A new attitude to Asia and its peoples was initiated by Alexander on his first setting foot on Asiatic soil. He courted publicity by his personal actions and he certainly had his official historian, Callisthenes, publish these actions and his words at the start of the great campaign. Ptolemy and Aristobulus, who were being used by Arrian at 1.11.5, wrote of Alexander's sacrifice to Protesilaüs and presumably of his landing on the Asiatic side after the sacrifice; and they mentioned the taking of the shield of Trojan Athena from the temple, for 'the sacred shield from Ilion' was mentioned later in a passage dependent on those two writers (Arr. *An.* 6.10.2). Arrian turned to other authors also in 1.11.6. The fullest accounts, it seems, came from Callisthenes and from authors who used Callisthenes; for that would explain why Arrian preferred not to continue with Ptolemy and Aristobulus alone but to give what he called 'the majority account' (ὁ πλείων λόγος),[10] presumably because he thought that account to be as trustworthy as the accounts of Ptolemy and Aristobulus.

His actions and his words on being first to land fully armed on Asiatic soil (Arr. *An.* 1.11.7) are described by Diodorus and Justin (epitomising Trogus, a younger contemporary of Diodorus). They were clearly using a common source which was very detailed.[11] Diod. 17.17.2 καταπλεύσας πρὸς τὴν Τρῳάδα χώραν πρῶτος τῶν Μακεδόνων ἀπὸ τῆς νεὼς ἠκόντισε μὲν τὸ δόρυ πήξας δὲ ἐς τὴν γῆν καὶ αὐτὸς ἀπὸ τῆς νεὼς ἀφαλλόμενος corresponds closely with the conciser wording of Justin 11.5.10 *cum delati in continentem essent, primus Alexander iaculum velut in hostilem terram iecit armatusque de nave tripudianti similis prosiluit.* 'Casting his spear into the soil' was to suit the act to the words he uttered: 'from the gods I accept Asia, won by the spear' (17.17.2 παρὰ τῶν θεῶν ἀπεφαίνετο τὴν 'Ασίαν δέχεσθαι δορίκτητον) and Justin loc. cit. 'with the prayer that those lands should not be unwilling in accepting him as their king' (*precatus ne se regem illae terrae invitae accipiant*). It was a proleptic but none the less confident claim, to be by gift of the gods King of Asia, which he will win with the spear but of which the people will accept him as king not unwillingly.[12] The gods he had in mind were not only the gods of Macedonia and Greece but the gods also of Asia, especially Trojan Athena (Arr. *An.* 1.11.7; Diod. 17.18.1; Plu. *Alex.* 15.7). He makes it clear that this is to be a personal kingdom,[13] and that he is to win the consent of the peoples of Asia to his kingship. He is not conquering new lands for Macedonia and Greece, and he is not reducing the peoples of Asia to be subject to the Macedonians and the Greeks.

This new attitude is borne out by a series of actions in the months which followed. The army was forbidden to ravage Asia (Justin 11.6.1), peasants who came down from the hills to submit to servitude were sent back 'each to their own property' (Arr. *An.* 1. 17.1; cf. Hdt. 1.63.2, i.e. not to be dispossessed), he gave proper burial to the Persian officers who fell at the Granicus river (1.16.6),[14] he let the Lydians use their own laws and be free (1.17.4), he accepted adoption by Ada and made her ruler of Caria (1.23.8) and he took into his service those who survived the first two battles and willingly joined his forces (2.14.7). Before the battle of Issus he had had confirmation of the gods' grant of Asia. For he had not only demonstrated by undoing the knot at Gordium that he would 'rule Asia' in accordance with the legend (2.3.6; Justin 11.7.4 *tota Asia regnaturum*), but he had also sacrificed to the gods who had shown him how to undo the knot and had marked the fulfilment of the legend by sending thunder and lightning that very night (Arr. *An.* 2.3.8). His prayer that the peoples of Asia would willingly accept him as their king was answered; for as he advanced the Phoenician cities except Tyre, the kings of Cyprus and the Lycian ship-captains joined him and were not blamed for having served with Persia (2.20.3).[15]

He claimed to be liberating both the Greek cities in Asia (Diod. 17.24.1) and the Asian peoples from despotic rule by Darius, unjustly King of Persia (Arr. *An.* 2.14.5). As he needed money to do so, he raised the same taxes. For the Greek cities he called the tax 'a contribution' (as Athens had done). One city, Aspendus, accepted liberation on these terms, but then it reneged. When it yielded under threat, it was punished by being made subject to the satrap (unlike other liberated Greek cities in Asia) and subject to 'the Macedonians' in that it had to pay them an annual tribute (1.27.4 φόρους ἀποφέρειν ὅσα ἔτη Μακεδόσι). This is the one and only instance of a city or people in Asia being made subject to Macedonia.[16]

The claims which Alexander had made on landing in Asia were reiterated in his reply to Darius in the winter of 333–332 B.C. (Arr. *An.* 2.14.7–9). 'The land I hold by the gift of the gods to me'; and 'I take care of all who were your soldiers . . . they are now with me not against their will, but of their own free will they are serving with me.' As King of Asia Alexander issued orders to Darius. 'Come to me, since I am Lord of all Asia (ἐμοῦ τῆς 'Ασίας ἁπάσης κυρίου ὄντος) . . . and in future in sending to me send to me as the King of Asia' (ὡς πρὸς βασιλέα τῆς 'Ασίας πέμπε).' Arrian was able to quote Alexander's letter (not verbatim but in substance), because he found it in one or both of his chosen sources, Ptolemy and Aristobulus; and there was no doubt a record of it in *The King's Journal*, to which in my view Ptolemy had access.[17] When Darius made a second approach to Alexander, the reply included similar claims according to Arrian (2.25.3).[18] After his victory at Gaugamela Alexander was formally proclaimed 'King of Asia' (Plu. *Alex.* 34.1 βασιλεὺς δὲ τῆς 'Ασίας ἀνηγορευμένος);[19] that was by the Macedonians in his army. His original claim seemed now to be justified; accordingly he gave thanks to the gods with magnificent sacrifices. In particular he made to Athena of Lindus in Rhodes a dedication on which his own words are preserved: 'King Alexander, having mastered Darius in battle and having become Lord of Asia, made sacrifice to Athena of Lindus in accordance with an oracle' (*FGrH* 532 F 1.38).[20]

By proclaiming Alexander King of Asia the Macedonians had committed themselves to making that claim good, and on several occasions they undertook to carry the campaign through to the end at Hecatompylus (Diod. 17.74.3; cf. Plu. *Alex.* 47. 1–4, Justin 12.3.2–4, and Curt. 6.4.1); in Bactria (Curt. 7.5.27); and after the battle of the Hydaspes (Curt. 9.1.1–3 *totam Asiam*).[21] It was only at the Hyphasis river that the army refused to go further. Alexander himself intended to conquer all Asia as he had stated in his reply to Pharasmanes, king of Chorasmia (near the Caspian Sea), which was that if he reduced India he would indeed 'hold all Asia' (Arr. *An.* 4.15.6 τούτους γὰρ καταστρέψαμενος πᾶσαν ἂν ἤδη ἔχειν τὴν 'Ασίαν).[22] At the Hyphasis river he wished to go on and conquer 'the rest of Asia' (5.24.8, 25.2 and 26.6 and 8). When he agreed to turn back, he built twelve altars as a thanksgiving to the gods who had brought him so far in victory (5.29.2). No doubt he continued to call himself 'King of Asia' by divine consent; for at Arr. *Ind.* 35.8 he was quoted (ultimately by Nearchus) as saying he had won all Asia, and in 323 B.C. the envoys who came from Libya congratulated him on being 'King of Asia' (7.14.4 ἐπὶ τῇ βασιλείᾳ τῆς 'Ασίας). In the division of administrative responsibilities which was made after his death a clear distinction was made between two spheres: the Macedonian Kingdom with its Balkan empire and the Kingdom of Asia (including Egypt). The latter sphere was to be administered in its entirety by Perdiccas (*FGrH* 156 Arrian F 1.3 τῆς ξυμπάσης βασιλείας).[23]

The same distinction is apparent in the coinage of Alexander. In Macedonia and Europe Philip, like his predecessors, had not put the title 'King' on their coins, and Alexander did not put that title on the coins which he minted at Pella, the Macedonian capital. But a year or so after the battle of Gaugamela he placed ΒΑΣΙΛΕΩΣ on the coins which were minted in Cilicia and were intended primarily for Asia; for they thereby proclaimed him 'King of Asia'.[24] Similarly the first undeniable use of the title 'King' on an inscribed dedication is at Lindus, when he was 'King' and 'Lord of Asia'.[25] Coins minted at Babylon, the chief mint in Asia, carried sometimes the letter M, an abbreviation for Μητρόπολις in the sense not of foundress but of capital city of the Kingdom of Asia.[26] The last acts of Alexander before his death, such as the excavation of dockyards and a harbour for a thousand ships at Babylon, made it clear that his Asian capital, like his Macedonian capital, was to be on a navigable river in the centre of the realm.

In this wealth of documentation on the Kingdom of Asia there is no mention whatsoever of Alexander being King of Persia and no indication that he intended to make the Persian capital Susa his capital. What he does mention is the overthrow of Persian imperial power as the prelude to his becoming in fact King of Asia: at the end of his reply to Darius 'if you dispute the kingship (of Asia, which he had just mentioned), stand and fight'; and in the dedication at Lindus 'having mastered Darius in battle and having become Lord of Asia'.[27] Plutarch made the same point after the victory of Alexander at Gaugamela. 'The battle having had this result, the empire of the Persians seemed to be utterly dissolved, and Alexander having been proclaimed King of Asia made sacrifice etc.' (*Alex.* 34.1).

Little attention has been paid to the two facts that in our sources of information Alexander attached such great importance to 'the Kingdom of Asia' from the very start to the finish of his campaigns in Asia, and that he made his winning of that kingdom the test of divine favour towards himself. And the question why he did so seems not to have been asked. We may attempt to answer it under three headings. The manpower of Macedonia was so limited that even with Greek help she could not hold down by force a further empire of great size in Asia. What Alexander offered to his Macedonians was not such an extension of empire but a great and glorious undertaking, the winning of all Asia by the Macedonian spear.[28] Secondly, the Greek city-states in Asia, having been abused in the name of 'liberation' by Athens and Sparta and so having lost any taste they may have had for union with the Greek mainland, were to be accorded a privileged position politically and great economic opportunities in a Kingdom of Asia, which might become for them a new centre of loyalty.[29] The third aspect was the most important, namely to devise a framework within which the Asian peoples would govern themselves and participate in the projects of Alexander. For this purpose it was not enough to become Pharaoh of Egypt and King of Babylon. He needed to subsume all the peoples of Asia, from Troy itself to the kingdom of Porus, into a single unity, the Kingdom of Asia.

2 THE PERSIAN THRONE

We must consider one thing which Alexander did not do, and his reasons for not doing it. 'Alexander did not proclaim himself King of Kings' (Plu. *Demetr.* 25.3 οὐδὲ αὑτὸν ἀνεῖπε βασιλέων βασιλέα),[30] that is he did not proclaim himself King of Persia in the style of Darius the Great βασιλεὺς βασιλέων Δαρεῖος (Meiggs-Lewis *GHI* no. 12). His reasons are not difficult to imagine. In the eyes of the Macedonians and the Greeks alike the Great King, the King of Kings, was the symbol of oriental despotism and tyrannical oppression. The expedition of the Macedonians and the Greeks was undertaken expressly to avenge the wrongdoings of Darius and Xerxes in Macedonia, which they had occupied for some thirty years, and in Greece, where they had committed atrocities against gods and men. Alexander placed that purpose in the forefront of his letter to Darius (Arr. *An.* 2.14.4). The Greeks in Asia, the Egyptians, the Babylonians and no doubt many other peoples hated the names of the Great Kings who had deprived them of their liberty and violated their religious shrines.[31] Alexander had the best of reasons for not proclaiming himself 'King of Kings', the successor of Darius Codomannus on the Persian throne.

Yet that is precisely what Alexander is alleged nowadays to have done. If we go back no further than this century, J. B. Bury described Alexander as 'the successor of Darius' in the first edition of *A History of Greece* (London 1900), and that is still the case in the fourth edition of 1975. All writers, I think, have taken this view,[32] and I did so myself in *A History of Greece*[2] (Oxford 1967), 621. But in *Alexander the Great King, Commander and Statesman* (New Jersey and London 1980), 305 I advanced a different opinion, that which I am developing in this article.

Why was Alexander thought to have succeeded Darius on the throne of Persia? One reason was that the Persian kings claimed the rule over all Asia, e.g. in Hdt. 9.116.3 or Isoc. 5.66 and 76, and that Alexander claimed it too. The deduction was then made that Alexander was a Persian king. On reflection it is a *non sequitur*. Just as Midas claimed to rule over all Asia and was a Phrygian king, so too Alexander claimed to rule over all Asia and was a Macedonian king. In other words the claim to be King of Asia was not a monopoly of a Persian king. When Alexander claimed on the shore of the Troad to be accepting Asia from the gods, he was speaking as King of Macedon. He intended to combine that Kingship with the Kingship of Asia.[33]

Another reason was a misinterpretation, as I understand it, of Alexander's dealings with Darius and the members of his family. The usual view has been that Alexander was aiming to usurp the Persian throne and was fortunate in finding Darius dead when he overtook him. 'It was Alexander's one piece of mere good fortune; he was saved the embarrassment of dealing with his rival.'[34] But the sources indicate that Alexander had a different purpose. It is revealed first in the reports of offers by Darius and replies by Alexander.

When Darius made his first offer to Alexander, the reply included this statement. 'Do you come to me, because I am Lord of all Asia . . . and when you come to me, ask from me and receive from me your mother, your wife, your children and anything else you want' (Arr. *An.* 2.14.8). The significance of the last words is made apparent in Diod. 17.54.6, which described Alexander's response to a later offer by Darius: either Darius should stand and fight or 'let him carry out the orders of Alexander and be king, ruling over other (kings),[35] through the goodness of Alexander who grants him the authority (i.e. to rule over other kings)'. αὐτὸς μὲν ᾽Αλεξάνδρῳ ποιείτω τὰ προσταττόμενα, ἄλλων δὲ ἄρχων βασιλευέτω, συγχρουμένης αὐτῷ τῆς ἐξουσίας ὑπὸ τῆς ᾽Αλεξάνδρου χρηστότητος. Thus Alexander offered to leave Darius on the Persian throne as King of Persia, βασιλεὺς βασιλέων, but he was to be subject to Alexander, the Lord of all Asia, who would as such take over the lands outside Media and Persia which we call the Persian Empire.

What is the value of this passage? Diodorus obtained it almost certainly from Cleitarchus, who paid more attention to Persian affairs than Ptolemy and Aristobulus did, to judge from the reflection of them in Arrian's narrative.[36] As Goukowsky has pointed out,[37] in detail the second offer by Darius in Diodorus 17.54 (but not the timing of it)[38] corresponds with the second offer reported by Arrian at *An.* 2.25.1–3; and, we may add, with the second offer in the description by Justin at 11.12.3. The reply of Alexander in Arrian is given in a brief summary ending with the words: 'he ordered Darius to come, if he wanted to find any generous treatment at the hands of Alexander'. Justin says: 'he ordered Darius to come as a suppliant and to entrust decisions about his kingdom to the victor (i.e. to Alexander) (*iussitique supplicem venire, regni arbitria victori permittere*). As Ptolemy and. Aristobulus were being used by Arrian, and a different author – most probably Cleitarchus – by Justin,[39] there is considerable support for the report that Alexander either hinted or stated that, if Darius would accept the overlordship of Alexander, Darius would be allowed by Alexander to stay on the throne of Persia. That is expressly stated in Diod. 17.54.6, quoted above.

There are other indications. Alexander offered to return his captives – the mother, the wife and the heir of Darius (a boy of 6 years of age in the winter of 333–332 B.C.) and other children – not in exchange for thousands of talents but on condition that Darius should 'come to him', i.e. accept submission. They had their own court, retinue and titles.[40] He treated them as royalty. He intended them to be royalty, if Darius yielded to his offer. When Alexander learnt that Darius had been arrested by his own officers and was obviously in danger of being killed by them, he made extraordinary efforts to capture Darius but just failed to take him alive. If he had succeeded he would probably have taken Darius to Susa. There he had left the mother and the heir Ochus;[41] and his intention would surely have been to keep Darius on the throne of Persia, even as he did continue Porus in his kingship.

In the event Alexander made other arrangements for Media and Persia. Certainly, to win the cooperation of the Medes and Persians, he paid honour to the Achaemenid dynasty, repairing the tomb of Cyrus, burying Darius in the royal cemetery at Persepolis and mounting a lavish funeral for his queen when she died in captivity. He appointed as his satraps in Media and Persia Persians loyal to the Achaemenid house.[42] Sisygambis, the queen mother, and Ochus, heir to the throne, lived in royal state at Susa, and the grief of Sisygambis when Alexander died was a sign that they had been treated as royalty up to the end. Being sixteen[43] in 323 B.C., Ochus would be of age to act as king in 321 B.C. If Alexander had usurped the throne of Persia, would he have brought up the natural heir in such a way at Susa? Or would he have thought of resigning in 321 B.C. and giving his throne to Ochus? The answer surely is that Alexander did not occupy the throne of Persia and did intend that Ochus should do so. In the meantime the highest organ of government in Persia was 'the meeting of Medes and Persians' at Ecbatana, before which the pretender Bessus was taken and executed for high treason against the Achaemenid house.[44]

Why did Alexander show such respect for Persian feelings? The reason was certainly that he needed to use the Persians in his military and administrative services, and he could only do so if he showed respect for them and their abilities. This need led him to adopt Asiatic dress for some ceremonial occasions at his court. The nature of the dress and the purpose of Alexander are interpreted in different ways in our sources.

Plutarch reported that he did not wear the upright tiara or the dress of a King of Persia but a mixture of Median and Persian features which were of his own devising; and that his purpose was to win approbation from the Asian peoples. Plutarch's source was most probably Eratosthenes, an eminent scholar writing a century or so after Alexander's death. This account, then, commands respect.[45] It shows that Alexander was not operating as the successor of Darius on the Persian throne.

We have three other accounts (Diod. 17.77.4; Justin 12.3.8; Curt. 6.6.4) which are derived from a common source, most probably Cleitarchus.[46] In them Alexander wore the dress of a Persian king, stamped letters he wrote 'for Asia' with Darius' signet-ring, enjoyed the favours of Darius' three hundred and sixty concubines, indulged himself with herds of eunuch-prostitutes and forced the leading Macedonians to dress up as Persians. These excesses were attributed to the moral deterioration of Alexander, and his purpose was said to be to humiliate his own Macedonians. Arrian (*An.* 4.9.9), probably took from the same source the 'story' (λόγος)[47] that in this matter of dress Alexander was showing a higher regard for Persian ways (than for Macedonian ways). These accounts are clearly inferior to the account in Plutarch.

Our distrust of the three accounts from a common source is heightened by the fact that in each case they were immediately preceded by the absurd story of the Amazon queen bedding with Alexander for thirteen days to satisfy her desire and become pregnant (e.g. Curt. 6.5.32 *in obsequium desiderii*). This story, which was expressly denied by Ptolemy and Aristobulus, probably came from Cleitarchus, a notorious romancer,[48] and it and the items which followed it are worthless for historical reconstruction. Yet U. Wilcken leant heavily on Curt. 6.6.6, which says that Alexander used two signet-rings – his old one for Europe and Darius' one for Asia – 'so that it became obvious that no single mind was equal to the fortune of two (sc. kingdoms)'. The idea of two rings, rather impractical in itself, is refuted by the emphasis laid on Alexander's ring (clearly a single one) which was mentioned in the last stage of his life and in the succeeding troubles: 'the ring with which he was wont to seal the affairs of his kingdom and his empire' (Curt. 10.6.5 *anulum quo ille regni atque imperii res obsignare erat solitus*).[49] And we can see that the story at Curt 6.6.6 was designed to make the point on which Curtius played later, that the burden was too great for one man to carry (10.5.37 *maior moles erat quam ut unus subire eam posset*). Wilcken's reliance on two rings to show Alexander was King of Macedonia and King of Persia is clearly misplaced.[50]

Tarn, following G. F. Hill,[51] made deductions from a lion-gryphon, mistakenly in my opinion. After the battle of Issus in 333 B.C. Alexander struck gold coins with a head of helmeted Athena, the war goddess, and on the reverse a standing Nike to celebrate his victory.[52] Relevant emblems and decorations were added. One of them was a gryphon on the bowl of Athena's helmet. Hill noted that the great majority of these gryphons were bird-headed in the usual Greek fashion, but some were lion-headed. He then pointed out that Greek artists usually represented the lion-gryphon 'as in conflict with Persians . . . as the enemy *par excellence* of the Persians'. To me it was now clear that the lion-gryphon on Athena's helmet indicated the hostility of the war-goddess to Persia, just as the Nike indicated Alexander's victory over Persia. But to my surprise Hill concluded quite the reverse. The lion-gryphon 'advertises Alexander's Persian sovereignty' and 'is a manifesto of his claim to the sovereignty of Persia'. Tarn accepted this conclusion. To me it is unjustified.[53]

If Alexander had become King of Persia, he would have acted in that capacity (even as he had acted in Egypt and Babylon) during the last eighteen months of his life, when he was in and close to Persia. He would have presided at religious ceremonies, sat in splendour under the sacred emblem of Ahuramazda, received tribute-bearing subjects or driven a chariot of Nesaean greys. And our sources would have informed us of these acts; for they are just what interested many of them. But no, there is not a shred of evidence that he ever acted so. Two things happened at Pasargadae, both in connection with Cyrus the Great, who was honoured by Greek writers and who was regarded by Alexander as a predecessor and a rival. When Alexander came to Pasargadae, he distributed money to Persian women there (Plu. *Alex.* 69.1), a practice instituted by Cyrus and maintained by Persian kings,[54] and he saw to the repair of the damaged tomb of Cyrus. In these acts he seems to have paid honour to Cyrus as 'founder of the Persian empire' and as 'King of Asia' (Arr. *An.* 6.29.8), and to have acted for his own part as 'King of Asia' rather than as King of Persia.[55]

There were certainly Greeks who in their own homeland thought of Alexander as a Great King, and there were others who deliberately misrepresented him as such. His short-lived attempt to persuade some Macedonians and some Greeks, including Callisthenes, to follow his Asiatic courtiers in the practice of *proskynesis* gave both groups suitable material. Stories gained circulation which portrayed Alexander in the role of a Persian King and added a touch of mockery. Thus, when Alexander captured Susa, he sat himself on the throne of Darius but found that his legs were too short to reach the ground, and a eunuch wept to see the sight and so on (Diod. 17.66.3–7 and Curt. 5.2.13).[56] In his extreme old age Demaratus came to see Alexander sitting on the throne of Darius and was himself moved to tears and died soon afterwards (Plutarch liked the anecdote so much that he told it twice, at *Alex.* 27 fin. and 56).[57] Darius, outdone in generosity, prayed pathetically that Alexander should sit on the throne of Cyrus (Plu. *Alex.* 30 fin.), and in another version that he should inherit Darius' power as King of Asia (Arr. *An.* 4.20.3, citing it as a *logos*).[58] Finally, in the tremendous lamentation which followed the death of Alexander, the Persians mourned him as 'their most righteous and most gentle master' and as 'the most righteous king of their race' (Curt. 10.5.9 and 17). These passages have all the signs of having been made up after the events and do not provide any basis for maintaining that Alexander was King of Persia.

A portent foreshadowing the death of Alexander was reported by Arrian as it had been described by Aristobulus (Arr. *An.* 7.24.1–3). During a military parade of the Macedonian troops in 323 B.C. Alexander and his retinue of Companions left 'the royal throne' and the couches on the platform, and an obscure person went up to the throne and sat on it. This person passed through the eunuchs to reach the throne. 'However, in accordance indeed with some Persian custom the eunuchs did not make him quit the throne but rent their clothes and beat their breasts and faces as at a great disaster.' This was clearly a Macedonian occasion, at which the new troops were being drafted into the existing Macedonian units. I take it that the royal throne was that used by the Macedonian king. By this time Alexander was often attended by Asians as well as by Macedonians,[59] and on this occasion the eunuchs acted as attendants. Having been trained in Persian ceremonial, they did not dare to interfere with the throne. That is the significance of the phrase 'in accordance indeed with some Persian custom', κατὰ δή τινα νόμον Περσικόν.[60]

Notes

* The following abbreviations are used. Atkinson *C* = J.E. Atkinson, *A Commentary on Q. Curtius Rufus' Historiae Alexandri Magni Books 3 and 4* (Amsterdam 1980). Bosworth *C* = A.B. Bosworth, *A Historical Commentary on Arrian's History of Alexander* 1 (Oxford 1980). Brunt *L* = P. A. Brunt, Loeb ed. of Arrian 1 (London 1976) and 2 (1983). Goukowsky *D* = P. Goukowsky, Budé ed. of Diod. XVII (Paris 1976). Hamilton *C* = J. R. Hamilton, *Plutarch Alexander: a Commentary* (Oxford 1969). Hammond *AG* = N. G. L. Hammond, *Alexander the Great: King, Commander and Statesman* (New Jersey and London 1980). Hammond *Sources* = idem, 'The sources of Diodorus Siculus XVI', *CQ* 31 (1937), 79 ff. and 32 (1938), 137 ff. Hanunond *THA* = idem, *Three Historians of Alexander the Great: the so-called Vulgate authors, Diodorus, Justin and Curtius* (Cambridge 1983).

1 Hammond *Sources* 1937. 81 and 1938. 149. Ephorus was contemporary with Philip.
2 'Slaves', i.e. subjects; cf. Thuc. 1.98.4 for the verb in this sense.
3 'The greater part' is a rhetorical exaggeration, even though Thrace started east of the Axius river, Chalcidice being ἐπὶ Θρᾴκης. See Hammond and Griffith, *A History of Macedonia* 2 (Oxford 1979), 656 f. The speech probably contains the sense of the original. *Contra* Brunt *L* 2.532 ff.; his n.7 on p. 236 (cf. 533) is mistaken, since the main army's 'return to Susa' through the lowlands (6.28.7) marked the end of the campaign of conquest which had started with the conquest of Persia. This 'return to Susa' does not mean the place of mutiny.
4 See Hammond *Sources* 1937.81 and 85.
5 Ibidem 90.
6 For the use of Diyllus of Athens see Hammond *THA* 31 ff.; for his qualities 33 ff. and *Sources* 1937. 89 f.
7 See Justin 8.6.1; by contrast Athens simply ejected the Samians.
8 In *Ep.* 3.5 Isocrates wanted the barbarians reduced to serfdom to the Greeks: ὅταν τοὺς μὲν βαρβάρους ἀναγκάσῃς εἱλωτεύειν τοῖς Ἕλλησι.
9 Both passages were probably based on Diyllus *Syntaxis* II and *Syntaxis* III; see Hammond *Sources* 1937. 89 f. and 1938. 150 and *THA* 33.
10 So translated by Brunt *L* 2.259 with n.3 (differently in 1.49 and 231), rather than as in Bosworth *C* 100 'consensus', which implies unanimity. Brunt *L* 1.49 n.5 '"Vulgate" to end of ch.' overlooks the likelihood that 'the majority' included Ptolemy and Aristobulus. See Hammond *THA* for the argument that 'Vulgate' is a misleading umbrella term.
11 Probably Diyllus, whom I suggested for Diodorus here, whereas I made no suggestion for Justin. See Hammond *THA* 35 f., 91, 96 and 113.
12 These passages in Diodorus and Justin are overlooked by Brunt *L* 1.lxiii 'although Alexander was bent on conquest from the start we have no evidence that he hoped to subdue "Asia" (n.64) before the incident at Gordium.'
13 So Goukowsky *D* 178 'il affirmait surtout le caractère strictement personnel des conquêtes à venir'. See also H. U. Instinsky, *Alexander der Grosse am Hellespont* (Godesberg 1949), 29 ff.
14 Arrian probably mentioned only one instance of what was Alexander's general practice; see Curt. 3.12.13 and Plu. *Alex.* 21.4 for burial after Issus.
15 So too Pitane, which was besieged by Parmenio at the time he captured Gryneum, was probably pardoned by Alexander; for if there had been a destruction Strabo 614 would surely have mentioned it.
16 The terms are probably cited originally from a treaty; see my comments in *CQ* n.s. 30 (1980), 461 f. and Hammond *AG* 85. Bosworth *C* 1.168 does not comment on the payment. The alternative, that Arrian wrote 'Macedonians' mistakenly for 'Alexander' seems to me less likely.
17 See Hammond *AG* 1 and 295 f. and *THA* 5–10 for citations from *The King's Journal* by Arrian, Plutarch and other writers (J. Moles' remark in reviewing the latter, that the existence of a king's journal 'is little more than an assumption' overlooks such citations), and for arguments that *The King's Journal* which they used was not a fake, as most scholars maintain, but genuine.
18 It has been argued in Hammond *THA* 42, 45 and 122 that Arrian's accounts of the negotiations are to be preferred to those of Diod. 17.39.1–2 and 54.1–6, which were derived probably from Cleitarchus. For a summary of the problems see Bosworth *C* 1.227 ff. His conclusion on p.233 that 'the whole correspondence reads much better as contemporary propaganda than as

an authentic extract from the archives' overlooks the fact that Alexander's missives were intended both to be propaganda and to go into the archival *King's Journal*.

19 The Greek words are translated by Justin at the corresponding moment as *Asiae imperium* (11.14.6); cf. *omne imperium Asiae ad se redegisse credidit in Alex. M. Macedonis epitomae r.g.* (ed. P. H. Thomas, 1966) 1.1.

20 Athena was the goddess to whose favour he ascribed his success – Athena Alcidemus in Macedonia and Athena of Troy in Asia – and it was the head of Athena which appeared on his first issue of gold coins after the battle of Issus (see Hammond *AG* 284 (a)).

21 For the probable sources see Hammond *THA* 58 (being for Diod. Diyllus), 134 (for Curtius 6.4.1 being Diyllus), 141 (for Curt. 7.5.27 being Aristobulus), and 152 (for Curt 9.1.1–3 being Diyllus); cf. 102 (no offer for Justin). Arrian did not mention these occasions; he had to cut a lot to keep his *Anabasis* to the length he wanted.

22 For Alexander's geographical assumptions see my *History of Greece to 322 B.C.*[2] (Oxford 1967), 627 and Fig. 33.

23 Described later by H. Bengtson, *Die Strategie in der hellenistischen Zeit*[2] (Munich 1964), 18 and 89, 'die gesamte asiatische βασιλεία Alexanders, wozu auch Ägypten gehörte.'

24 See C. Seltman, *Greek Coins* (London 1933), 207, 211 and Fig. 9. The mint at Amphipolis seems to have served both kingdoms; for some of its coins have 'king' and others do not.

25 By contrast the spoils sent to Athens after the battle of the Granicus river were dedicated by 'Alexander, son of Philip' (Arr. *An.* 1.16.7), not by King Alexander.

26 Seltman, op. cit. 211.

27 Arr. *An.* 2.14.9 and *FGrH* 532 F 1.38.

28 The appeal to the martial spirit of the Macedonian soldiers is a constant theme of the speeches in Arrian and other historians, and their record especially in siege warfare shows that they responded. It is only for rhetorical effect that Alexander is made to speak of 'your empire' and 'your possessions' at Arr. *An.* 7.9–10.

29 That this did happen is clear from the honours which many of these city-states paid to Alexander; see Hammond *AG* 250 and 253.

30 This passage seems to have been missed by those who have written standard works on Alexander.

31 For instance, Cambyses in Egypt (Hdt. 3.29) and Xerxes in Babylonia (Arr. *An.* 7.17.2), at least in popular belief.

32 Bury 785 and 794, and Meiggs-Bury 472 and 477. W. W. Tarn in *CAH* 6.387 'Alexander was now Great King'. U. Wilcken tr. G. C. Richards, *Alexander the Great* 149 'Alexander regarded himself as his (Darius') heir and lawful successor on the Persian throne'. Brunt *L* 2.515 'the role Alexander was about to assume as the rightful successor of Darius'. Bosworth *C* 270 'Alexander's claims to be the legitimate King of Persia'. F. Schachermeyr, *Alexander der Grosse* (Vienna 1949), 247 'da war er selbst gleichsam zum Grosskönig, zum Achaimeniden, zum Perser gewesen'. P. Bamm, *Alexander* (Zurich 1965), 317 'Erben des Thrones der Grosskönige'.

33 The King of the Medes too had claimed to be King of Asia (Arr. *An.* 5.4.5), before Cyrus acquired the title for the Persians (Arr. *An.* 6.29.8). To be King of a country and Lord of Asia were separate offices. They could be and sometimes were combined as in the case of Darius. For instance in Arr. *An.* 4.20.1–3, related as a *logos*, and Curt. 4.10.34 Darius speaks of 'his rule over the Medes and Persians' (his *regnum* in Curt.) and of his being 'King of Asia' (*Asiae rex* in Curt.). The common source behind the two passages was not Ptolemy or Aristobulus; see Atkinson *C* 395. Hammond *THA* 100 and 122 suggested that the source was Cleitarchus. The contest which Alexander stressed was not for the throne of Persia but for the rule of Asia, claimed unjustly by 'the kings of the Medes and Persians' (Arr. *An.* 7.1.3) and justly by himself (Arr. *An.* 2.12.5).

34 So Tarn in *CAH* 6.386.

35 The phrase is so understood by Goukowsky *D* 79.

36 See Hammond *THA* 130 f., for instance.

37 Goukowsky *D* 208 ff.

38 Goukowsky *D* 209 notes that the source is 'vraisemblablement Clitarque' and that the change of timing to early summer 331 B.C. may have been due to his desire for dramatic effect. *Contra* Bosworth *C* 1.256, invoking 'the vulgate tradition', which is here, in my opinion, a euphemism for the notoriously unreliable Cleitarchus. See Hammond *AG* 120 and *THA* 26. In this context

I am concerned only with the substance of the reply. Alexander's orders to the Great King had been foreshadowed by Isocrates, *Ep.* 3.5 ο τι ἀν σὺ προστάττης.

39 Arrian gave the *logos* concerning Parmenio but put the offer and the reply in narrative verbs, that is, from his main sources; see Hammond *THA* 100 for the source of Justin.

40 Arr. *An.* 2.12.5, citing Ptolemy and Aristobulus as well as others unnamed as his authorities, is clearly trustworthy. Court and retinue also are in Curt. 3.12.12, Diod. 17.38.1, and Plu. *Alex.* 21.4; the title 'queens' appears in them and in Justin 11.9.15. As the sexual restraint of Alexander is the main interest of the sources, the son and heir came in for less attention; but the statement in Diod. is important: 'Alexander promised that he would bring the boy up as his own son and he would hold him worthy of royal status (βασιλικῆς τιμῆς ἀξιώσειν)'. For discussion see Atkinson *C* 252 ff., Bosworth *C* 220 ff. and Hamilton *C* 54, who pay little or no attention to the son of Darius.

41 Curtius gave his name in two speeches at 4.11.6 and 4.14.22. He was left at Susa according to Diod. 17.67.1 and Curt. 5.2.18. It was the capital of the Persian kingdom.

42 Arr. *An.* 3.18.11 and 4.18.3. Before Darius' death he had appointed a man hostile to Darius (Arr. *An.* 3.20.3); but he soon removed him and adopted his new policy.

43 In Curt. 10.5.18 'the region nearest to Babylon' was clearly Persia, and the grandson is mentioned at 10.5.24. He disappeared thereafter from the record.

44 Arr. *An.* 4.7.3. The numbers are not known. 'Meeting' rather than 'council' or 'assembly', both of which Brunt *L* uses in translating this section.

45 Plu. *Alex.* 45.2 with Hamilton *C* 120, and Plu. *Mor.* 329 f – 330 d. Alexander wanted the loyalty (εὔνοιαν in *Mor.* 330 a) not only of the governing class but also of the military elements; for in 323 B.C. he had more than 50,000 Asian infantrymen under arms (Arr. *An.* 7.6.1 and 7.23.1) and thousands of cavalry. 'The upright tiara' or *kidaris* was the special mark of Persian kingship. When the pretenders Bessus and Baryaxes wore it, they 'assumed the title of the King of the Medes and Persians' (Arr. *An.* 3.25.3 and 6.29.3). Bessus went on to claim to be 'King of Asia' in Arr. *An.* 3.25.3.

46 See Hammond *THA* 59 and 136.

47 The source, being other than Ptolemy and Aristobulus, was very probably Cleitarchus; see Hammond *THA* 136. Arrian was probably recalling this 'story' when he censured Alexander for wearing the Persian *kidaris*, and proposed reasons for Alexander wearing Persian dress (*An.* 4.7.4 and 7.29.4); in each case he was giving his own ideas, not those of any source.

48 See Hammond *THA* 26, 59, 102 and 135 f. for ancient estimates of Cleitarchus.

49 *Res* is an emendation for *vires*. The ring occurs also at Curt. 10.5.4, Diod. 17.117.3 and Justin 12.15.12, always in the singular. Curtius may use *imperii* here for the Kingdom of Asia; cf. Justin 11.14.6 *Asiae imperium*.

50 Wilcken (above, n. 32) 246, where he is far from clear in his deductions. Darius had only one seal at Curt. 6.6.6.

51 'Alexander the Great and the Persian lion-gryphon', *JHS* 43 (1923), 156 ff.

52 See Hammond *AG* 156 f., 284 (a) and Fig. 35. A different interpretation in M. J. Price, *Coins of the Macedonians* (London 1974), 24 f. with Pl. 11, 60. *CAH Plates* 2.8 *o* shows a coin with the lion-gryphon.

53 That other explanations may be possible is clear from the gryphons which appear to have different heads including that of a lion, on the fringe of the frescoes in the first (plundered) tomb at Vergina. See M. Andronikos, *The Royal Graves at Vergina* (Athens 1978) 8.

54 See Hamilton *C* 191.

55 Alexander gave gifts to the Arimaspians as Cyrus had done (Diod. 17.81.1–2), and he was thought to have wished to outdo Cyrus in crossing the Jaxartes river and the Gedrosian desert.

56 The source of both passages was probably Diyllus; see Hammond *THA* 55 and 130. Curtius himself may have added the offence against the *hospitales deos*.

57 Also in his *Ages.* 15.4 and at *Mor.* 329 d. See Hamilton *C* 99.

58 The variations in the timing of Stateira's death and in its relation to an offer by Darius do not inspire confidence; see Hamilton *C* 78.

59 When acting as a judge in an Asian court as opposed to a Macedonian court of justice, Alexander was attended by very large numbers of élite Macedonian troops and élite Asian (mainly Persian) troops 'in Bactria, Hyrcania and India' (Polyaen. 4.3.24).

60 An early form of this paper was given to seminars at the Australian National University and the University of Queensland in autumn 1984. I am most grateful for comments then, and for the comments of Mr. G. T. Griffith and Prof. F. W. Walbank, who have read and improved the final version.

6

ALEXANDER, INDIA AND
THE FINAL YEARS

Introduction

Alexander did not face the same types of military problems in India as in Persia,[1] and there was only the one great battle at the River Hydaspes in 326 (Sources 73 and 74).[2] After his victory against Porus' elephant corps, he incorporated elephants into his army. Of especial importance during Alexander's Indian campaign are his encounter with the Brahman philosophers (one of them, Calanus, accompanied him until his death, by ritual burning; Sources 66–69), and Nearchus' great voyage around India, with its fascinating description of the geography and peoples. The longer fragments from Nearchus' work deal with this expedition, the basis of the full account of Arrian's *India*.

In spring 327 Alexander marched from Bactra through the Hindu Kush and advanced towards the plain of the Indus. He split the invasion force into two, one half under the command of Hephaestion and Perdiccas, which was to march to the Indus via the Hindu Kush and secure the main communications route, and the second under himself, which marched east through Laghman into the Swat. In the spring of 326 the two forces met at the Indus, and after bridging it (cf. Source 1) Alexander moved to the capital Taxila.

When news came that a neighbouring prince, Porus, refused to yield to Alexander, the king set out immediately to meet him and the two sides did battle at the Hydaspes river. Alexander effected a brilliant river crossing when faced with adversity (cf. Source 19), and decisively defeated Porus. This was a momentous victory, although propaganda exaggerated it, and Alexander celebrated it by founding two new cities, Nicaea and Bucephala, after his horse Bucephalus, who had died from exhaustion following the battle (Arr. 5.19.4–5, Plut. *Alex.* 61.1): see Sources 75 and 76. He also struck special commemorative coinage at the mint in Babylon. Porus was confirmed king of his subjects but as a vassal to Alexander, and his elephant corps integrated into the Macedonian army.

The battle of the Hydaspes was the high point of Alexander's campaign in India. Rather than return to Taxila to wait for the monsoon rains to pass, he continued eastwards. By the time he reached the Hyphasis river, some 390 miles from the Hydaspes (Baeton, *FGrH* 119 F 2a = Source 36),[3] it had been raining for 70 days (Diod. 17.94.3; cf. Source 61); the men had had enough, and led by Coenus they refused to go further (Arr. 6.2.1, Curt. 9.3.20): Source 77. Alexander was forced to turn around, and by late September 326 he was back at the Hydaspes. Rather than return west by the same route, he chose to emulate and outdo certain predecessors by marching as they had done across the Gedrosian desert, a major tactical blunder which cost him dearly in manpower because of the harsh environment, lack of food and water, and sudden flash flooding (see Sources 78–81).

Alexander's belief in his own divinity never abated but intensified in the last years of his reign (see Source 99), and in March 324 when Alexander reached Susa he issued his Exiles Decree,[4] which some have connected with his deification.[5] While in Susa the mass marriage was held in which he and 91 members of his court married Persian noble women (see Sources 90 and 91), an event that has often been seen as an attempt to unite the races together.[6] Not long after, Alexander left Susa, and by summer he was at Opis, where he was faced with another mutiny, which he ended with his banquet of reconciliation and prayer for concord.[7] From there he marched to Ecbatana and then to Babylon, arriving in early 323 (cf. Sources 82, 83 and 108). At the end of May Alexander developed a fever, which soon confined him to his bed; after lapsing into a brief coma he died on 10 June 323, at the age of thirty-two years and eight months (Source 84). Typhoid has been suspected or liver collapse given Alexander's drinking habits (see Sources 7–13, 68, 103, 109), perhaps even a combination of both; the true reason will never be known.[8]

Ancient sources

59 Ctesias the Cnidian says that India is equal to the rest of Asia, but he talks nonsense; and so does Onesicritus (*FGrH* 134 F 6 = Source 60), saying that it is the third part of all the earth. Nearchus says that it is a journey of four months through the plain alone of India. To Megasthenes the distance from the east to the west ... He says that where it is shortest it extends 16,000 stades, and that from north to south ... it extends 22,300 stades, where it is the narrowest (Nearchus, *FGrH* 133 F 5 = Arrian, *Indica* 3.6, Strabo 15.1.12).

60 Ctesias ... says that India is equal to the rest of Asia, but he talks nonsense; and so does Onesicritus, saying that it is the third part of all the earth (Onesicritus, *FGrH* 134 F 6 = Arrian, *Indica* 3.6, Strabo 15.1.12).

61 Aristobulus says that only the mountains and their foothills have both rain and snow, but that the plains are free alike from rain and snow, and are inundated only when the rivers rise; that the mountains have snow in the winter-time, and at the beginning of spring-time the rains also set in and ever increase more and more, and at the time of the Etesian winds the rains pour unceasingly and violently from the clouds, both day and night, until the rising of Arcturus; and that, therefore, the rivers, thus filled from both the snows and the rains, water the plains. He says that both he himself and the others noted this when they had set out for India from Paropamisadae, after the setting of the Pleiades, and when they spent the winter near the mountainous country in the land of the Hypasians and of Assacanus, and that at the beginning of spring they went down into the plains and to Taxila, a large city, and thence to the Hydaspes river and the country of Porus; that in winter, however, no water was to be seen, but only snow; and that it first rained at Taxila; and that when, after they had gone down to the Hydaspes river and had conquered Porus,[9] their journey led to the Hypanis[10] river towards the east and then back again to the Hydaspes, it rained continually, and especially at the time of the Etesian winds; but that when Arcturus rose, the rain ceased; and that after tarrying while their ships were being built on the Hydaspes river, and after beginning their voyage thence only a few days before the setting of the Pleiades, and, after occupying themselves all autumn and winter and the coming spring and summer with their voyage down to the seacoast, they arrived at Patalene at about the time of the rising of the Dog Star; that the voyage down to the seacoast therefore took ten months, and that they saw rains nowhere, not even when the Etesian winds were at their height, and that the plains were flooded when the rivers were filled, and the sea was not navigable when the winds were blowing in the opposite direction, and that no land breezes succeeded them.

Now this is precisely what Nearchus (*FGrH* 133 F 18) says too, but he does not agree with Aristobulus about the summer rains, saying that the plains have rains in summer but are without rains in winter. Both writers, however, speak also of the risings of the rivers. Nearchus says that when they were camping near the Acesines river they were forced at the time of the rising to change to a favourable place higher up, and that this took place at the time of the summer solstice; whereas Aristobulus gives also the measure of the height to which the river rises, forty cubits, of which cubits twenty are filled by the stream above its previous depth to the margin and the other twenty are the measure of the overthrow in the plains. They agree also that the cities situated on the top of mounds become islands, as is the case also in Egypt and Aethiopia, and that the overflows cease after the rising of Arcturus, when the waters recede; and they add that although the soil is sown when only half-dried, after being furrowed by any sort of digging instrument, yet the plant comes to maturity and yields excellent fruit. The rice, according to Aristobulus, stands in water enclosures and is sown in beds; and the plant is four cubits in height, not only having many ears but also yielding much grain; and the harvest is about the time of the setting of the Pleiades, and the grain is winnowed like barley; and the rice grows also in Bactria and Susis, as also in Lower Syria (Onesicritus, *FGrH* 134 F 15).

Aristobulus, comparing the characteristics of this country that are similar to those of both Egypt and Aethiopia, and again those that are opposite thereto, I mean the fact that the Nile is flooded from the southern rains, whereas the Indian rivers are flooded from the northern, enquires why the intermediate regions have no rainfall; for neither the Thebais as far as Syene and the region of Meroe nor the region of India from Patalene as far as the Hydaspes has any rain. But the country above these parts, in which both rain and snow fall, is cultivated, he says, in the same way as in the rest of the country that is outside India; for, he adds, it is watered by the rains and snows. And it is reasonable to suppose from his statements that the land is also quite subject to earthquakes, since it is made porous by reason of its great humidity and is subject to such fissures that even the beds of rivers are changed. At any rate, he says that when he was sent upon a certain mission he saw a country of more than a thousand cities, together with villages, that had been deserted because the Indus had abandoned its proper bed, and had turned aside into the other bed on the left that was much deeper, and flowed with precipitous descent like a cataract, so that the Indus no longer watered by its overflows the abandoned country on the right, since the country was now above the level, not only of the new stream but also of its overflows (Aristobulus, *FGrH* 139 F 35 = Strabo 15.1.17–19).

62 All the Indians wear their hair long and dye it with a sable or saffron colour. Their particular luxury is gems. They make no display at funerals. Besides, as has been made known in the works of Kings Juba and Archelaus, the dress is as varied as the customs of the people. Some dress in linen robes, others in woollen ones; some are nude, others cover their private parts only and several are just girded with flexible bark fibres. Some tribes are so tall that with a very easy leap they clear an elephant as they would a horse. Many are wont neither to kill an animal nor to eat meat; most of them subsist on fish alone and depend on the sea for food. There are some who kill their parents and nearest kin just as they would victims of sacrifice, before age or disease emaciate them; then they banquet on the entrails of the slain; this is not considered a crime there, but an act of piety. There are even those who on falling sick withdraw into hidden places far from other people and wait for death with equanimity (Archelaus, *FGrH* 123 F 1 = Solinus 52.18–23).

63 The Indians use linen clothing, as says Nearchus, made from the flax taken from the trees, about which I have already spoken. And this flax is either whiter in colour than any other flax, or the people being black make the flax appear whiter. They have a linen frock reaching down half-way between the knee and the ankle, and a garment which is partly thrown round the shoulders and partly rolled round the head. The Indians who are very well off wear earrings of ivory; for they do not all wear them. Nearchus says that the Indians dye their beards various colours; some that they may appear white as the whitest, others dark blue; others have them red, others purple, and others green. Those who are of any rank have umbrellas held over them in the summer. They wear shoes of white leather, elaborately worked, and the soles of their shoes are many-coloured and raised high, in order that they may appear taller. The Indians are not all armed in the same way; but their infantry have a bow equal in length to the man who carries it. Placing this downward to the ground and stepping against it with the left foot, they discharge the arrow, drawing the string far back. Their arrows are little less than three cubits long; and nothing can withstand one shot by an Indian archer, neither shield nor breast-plate nor anything else that is strong. They carry on their left arms targets of raw ox-hide, narrower than the men who carry them, but not much inferior in length. Others have javelins instead of arrows. All wear a sword which is broad, and not less than three cubits in length. When the battle is at close quarters, a thing which very rarely happens to be the case between Indians, they bring this sword down upon the antagonist with both hands, in order that the blow may be a mighty one. The cavalry have two darts, like the darts called *saunia*, and a target smaller than that of the infantry. Their horses are not saddled or bridled like those of the Greeks or Gauls; but a piece of raw ox-hide stitched is fastened right round the front of the horse's mouth, and in this there are brass or iron spikes not very sharp, turned inwards. The rich men have ivory spikes. In the mouth their horses have a piece of iron, like a spit, to which the reins are attached. When therefore they draw the rein, the spit curbs the horse and the spikes which are fastened to it prick him and do not allow him to do anything else than obey the rein. The Indians are spare in body and tall and much lighter than other men. Most of the Indians ride camels, horses, and, asses, and those who are well off, elephants. For among the Indians royal personages ride on elephants. Next to this in honour is the four-horsed chariot, third camels. It is no honour to ride on horseback. Their women who are very chaste and would not go astray for any other reward, on the receipt of an elephant have communication with the donor. The Indians do not think it disgraceful for them to prostitute themselves for an elephant, and to the women it even seems an honour that their beauty should appear equal in value to an elephant. They marry, neither giving nor receiving any dowry, but the fathers bring forward the girls who are of marriageable age and station them in a public place for the man who wins the prize for wrestling, boxing, or running, or who has been adjudged winner in any manly contest, to make his choice. The Indians are bread-eaters and agriculturalists, except those who live in the mountains. These live upon the flesh of wild animals. I have copied the very well-known statements made by Nearchus and Megasthenes, two esteemed authors (Nearchus, *FGrH* 133 F 11 = Arrian, *Indica* 16–17).

64 Crates of Pergamus calls the Indians, whose age exceeds one hundred years, by the name of Gymnetae; but not a few authors style them Macrobii. Ctesias mentions a tribe of them, known by the name of Pandare, whose locality is in the valleys, and who live to their two hundreth year … On the other hand, there are some people joining up to the country of the Macrobii, who never live beyond their fortieth year … This circumstance is also mentioned by Agatharchides, who states, in addition, that they live on locusts, and are very swift of foot. Cleitarchus and Megasthenes give these people the name of Mandi, and enumerate as many as three hundred villages which belong to them. Their women are capable of bearing children in the seventh year of their age, and become old at forty (Cleitarchus, *FGrH* 137 F 23 = Pliny, *Natural History* 7.28–29).

65 And Chares of Mytilene, in his *Records of Alexander*, tells us how to keep snow, when he recounts the siege of the Indian capital Petra. He says that Alexander dug thirty refrigerating pits which he filled with snow and covered with oak boughs. In this way, he says, snow will last a long time (Chares, *FGrH* 125 F 16 = Athen. 3.124c).

66 They [the Brahmans] never jump into the fire. Onesicritus, Alexander's pilot, saw Calanus burn himself and, according to him, when the pyre has been made ready, they stand motionless, resting in front of it. Then they climb on top and there they sit, smouldering away in a dignified manner (Onesicritus, *FGrH* 134 F 18 = Lucian, *De mort. Peregr.* 25).

67 As soon as the men to whom the duty had been assigned set fire to the pyre (of Calanus), Nearchus says the trumpets sounded, in accordance with Alexander's order, and the whole army raised the war-cry as it was in the habit of shouting when advancing to battle. The elephants also chimed in with their shrill and warlike cry, in honour of Calanus (Nearchus, *FGrH* 133 F 4 = Arr. 7.3.6).

68 Chares of Mytilene, in his *Tales of Alexander*, says of Calanus … that he threw himself on a funeral pyre which he had built, and so died, and he says that at his tomb Alexander got up a contest in athletic games and in a musical recital of his praises. 'He,' Chares says, 'because of the love of drinking on the part of the Indians, also instituted a contest in the drinking of unmixed wine, and the prize for the winner was a talent, for the second-best thirty minas, for the third ten minas. Of those who drank the wine, thirty-five died immediately of a chill, and six others shortly after in their tents. The man who drank the most and came off victor drank twelve quarts and received the talent, but he lived only four days more; he was called "Champion"' (Chares, *FGrH* 125 F 19a = Athen. 10.437a–b).[11]

69 Onesicritus says that he himself was sent to converse with these sophists; for Alexander had heard that the people always went naked and devoted themselves to endurance, and that they were held in very great honour, and that they did not visit other people when invited, but bade them to visit them if they wished to participate in anything they did or said; and that therefore, such being the case, since to Alexander it did not seem fitting either to visit them or to force them against their will to do anything contrary to their ancestral customs, he himself was sent; and that he found fifteen men at a distance of twenty stades from the city, who were in different postures, standing or sitting or lying naked and motionless till evening, and that they then returned to the city; and that it was very hard to endure the sun, which was so hot that at midday no one else could easily endure walking on the ground with bare feet. Onesicritus says that he conversed with one of these sophists, Calanus, who accompanied the king as far as Persis and died in accordance with the ancestral custom, being placed upon a pyre and burned up (*FGrH* 134 F 18 = Source 66). He says that Calanus happened to be lying on stones when he first saw him; that he therefore approached him and greeted him; and told him that he had been sent by the king to learn the wisdom of the sophists and report it to him, and that if there was no objection he was ready to hear his teachings; and that when Calanus saw the mantle and broad-brimmed hat and boots he wore, he laughed at him and said: 'In olden times the world was full of barley-meal and wheaten-meal, as now of dust; and fountains then flowed, some with water, others with milk and likewise with honey, and others with wine, and some with olive oil; but, by reason of his gluttony and luxury, man fell into arrogance beyond bounds. But Zeus, hating this state of things, destroyed everything and appointed for man a life of toil. And when self-control and the other virtues in general reappeared, there came again an abundance of blessings. But the condition of man is already close to satiety and arrogance, and there is danger of destruction of everything in existence.' And Onesicritus adds that Calanus, after saying this, bade him, if he wished to learn, to take off his clothes, to lie down naked on the same stones, and thus to hear his teachings; and that while he was hesitating what to do, Mandanis, who was the oldest and wisest of the sophists, rebuked Calanus as a man of arrogance, and that too after censuring arrogance himself; and that Mandanis called him and said that he commended the king because, although busied with the government of so great an empire, he was desirous of wisdom; for the king was the only philosopher in arms that he ever saw, and that it was the most useful thing in the world if those men were wise who have the power of persuading the willing, and forcing the unwilling, to learn self-control; but that he might be pardoned if, conversing through three interpreters, who, with the exception of language, knew no more than the masses, he should be unable to set forth anything in his philosophy that would be useful; for that, he added, would be like expecting water to flow pure through mud ... (Onesicritus, *FGrH* 134 F 17a = Strabo 15.1.63–64).

70 That Dionysus fought and defeated Indians is told by Dionysius and Aristodemus in the first of the Theban epigrams and by Cleitarchus in the *History of Alexander*, who adds to the account that there is a Mt. Nysa in India and a plant similar to ivy is planted there, called scindapsos ... (Cleitarchus, *FGrH* 137 F 17 = Scholiast on Apollonius, *Argonautica* 2.904).

71 Among the Malli Alexander was wounded with an arrow two cubits in length, that went in at his breast and came out at his neck, as Aristobulus relates (Aristobulus, *FGrH* 139 F 46 = [Plut.] *Mor.* 341c).

72 Alexander himself also was wounded with an arrow under the breast through the breast-plate in the chest, so that Ptolemy says air was breathed out from the wound together with the blood (Ptolemy, *FGrH* 138 F 25 = Arr. 6.10.1).

73   But Ptolemy, son of Lagus, with whom I agree, gives a different account. This author also says that Porus dispatched his son, but not at the head of merely sixty chariots; nor is it indeed likely that Porus hearing from his scouts that either Alexander himself or at any rate a part of his army had effected the passage of the Hydaspes, would dispatch his son against him with only sixty chariots. These indeed were too many to be sent out as a reconnoitring party, and not adapted for speedy retreat; but they were by no means a sufficient force to keep back those of the enemy who had not yet got across, as well as to attack those who had already landed. Ptolemy says that the son of Porus arrived at the head of 2,000 cavalry and 120 chariots; but that Alexander had already made even the last passage from the island before he appeared. Ptolemy also says that Alexander in the first place sent the horse-archers against these, and led the cavalry himself, thinking that Porous was approaching with all his forces, and that this body of cavalry was marching in front of the rest of his army, being drawn up by him as the vanguard. But as soon as he had ascertained with accuracy the number of the Indians, he immediately made a rapid charge upon them with the cavalry around him. When they perceived that Alexander himself and the body of cavalry around him had made the assault, not in line of battle regularly formed, but by squadrons, they gave way; and 400 of their cavalry, including the son of Porus, fell in the contest. The chariots also were captured, horses and all, being heavy and slow in the retreat, and useless in the action itself on account of the clayey ground (Ptolemy, *FGrH* 138 F 20 = Arr. 5.14.5–15.2)

74   Aristobulus says that the son of Porus arrived with about sixty chariots before Alexander made his later passage from the large island, and that he could have hindered Alexander's crossing, for he made the passage with difficulty even when no one opposed him, if the Indians had leaped down from their chariots and assaulted those who first emerged from the water. But he passed by with the chariots and thus made the passage quite safe for Alexander; who on reaching the bank discharged his horse-archers against the Indians in the chariots, and these were easily put to rout, many of them being wounded. Other writers (Ptolemy, *FGrH* 138 F 20 = Source 73) say that a battle took place … (Aristobulus, *FGrH* 139 F 43 = Arr. 5.14.3).

75   The horse of King Alexander was called 'Bucephalas' because of the shape of his head. Chares wrote that he was bought for thirteen talents and given to King Philip … It seemed a noteworthy characteristic of this horse that when he was armed and equipped for battle, he would never allow himself to be mounted by any other than the king. It is also related that Alexander in the war against India, mounted upon that horse and doing valorous deeds, had driven him with disregard of his own safety, too far into the enemies' ranks. The horse had suffered deep wounds in his neck and side from the weapons hurled from every hand at Alexander, but though dying and almost exhausted from loss of blood, he yet in swiftest course bore the king from the midst if the foe; but when he had taken him out of range of the weapons, the horse at once fell, and satisfied with having saved his master breathed his last, with indications of relief that were almost human. Then King Alexander, after winning the victory in that war, founded a city in that region and in honour of his horse called it 'Bucephalon' (Chares, *FGrH* 125 F 18 = Gellius 5.2.1–5).

76   After the battle with Porus, too, Bucephalas died – not at once, but some time afterwards – as most writers say, from wounds for which he was under treatment, but according to Onesicritus, from old age, having become quite worn out; for he was thirty years old when he died (Onesicritus, *FGrH* 134 F 20 = Plut. *Alex.* 61.1).

77 Having said this, Alexander retired into his tent,[12] and did not admit any of the Companions on that day, or until the third day from that, waiting to see if any change would occur in the minds of the Macedonians and Grecian allies, as is wont to happen as a general rule among a crowd of soldiers, rendering them more disposed to obey. But on the contrary, when there was a profound silence throughout the camp, and the soldiers were evidently annoyed at his wrath, without being at all changed by it, Ptolemy, son of Lagus, says that he none the less offered sacrifice there for the passage of the river, but the victims were unfavourable to him when he sacrificed. Then indeed he collected the oldest of the Companions and especially those who were friendly to him, and as all things indicated the advisability of his returning, he made known to the army that he had resolved to march back again (Ptolemy, *FGrH* 138 F 23 = Arr. 5.28.3–5).

78 They say that Alexander pursued this route,[13] not from ignorance of the difficulty of the journey – Nearchus, indeed, alone says that he was ignorant of it – but because he heard that no one had hitherto passed that way with an army and emerged in safety, except Semiramis, when she fled from India. The natives said that even she emerged with only twenty men of her army; and that Cyrus, son of Cambyses, escaped with only seven of his men. For they say that Cyrus also marched into this region for the purpose of invading India, but that he did not effect his retreat before losing the greater part of his army, from the desert and the other difficulties of this route. When Alexander received this information he is said to have been seized with a desire of excelling Cyrus and Semiramis. Nearchus says that he turned his march this way, both for this reason and at the same time for the purpose of conveying provisions near the fleet (Nearchus, *FGrH* 133 F 3a = Arr. 6.24.2).

79 If, however, one should dismiss these accounts and observe the records of the country (India) prior to the expedition of Alexander, one would find things still more obscure. Now it is reasonable to suppose that Alexander believed such records because he was blinded by his numerous good fortunes; at any rate, Nearchus says that Alexander conceived an ambition to lead his army through Gedrosia when he learned that both Semiramis and Cyrus had made an expedition against the Indians, and that Semiramis had turned back in flight with only twenty people and Cyrus with seven; and that Alexander thought how grand it would be, when those had met with such reverses, if he himself should lead a whole victorious army safely through the same tribes and regions. Alexander, therefore, believed these accounts. But as for us, what just credence can we place in the accounts of India derived from such an expedition made by Cyrus or Semiramis? And Megasthenes virtually agrees (Nearchus, *FGrH* 133 F 3b = Strabo 15.1.5).

80 Most of the historians of Alexander's reign assert that all the hardships which his army suffered in Asia were not worthy of comparison with the labours undergone here. They say that Alexander pursued this route, not from ignorance of the difficulty of the journey – Nearchus (*FGrH* 133 F 3a = Source 78), indeed, alone says that he was ignorant of it – but because he heard ... The scorching heat and lack of water destroyed a great part of the army, and especially the beasts of burden; most of which perished from thirst and some of them even from the depth and heat of the sand, because it had been thoroughly scorched by the sun. For they met with lofty ridges of deep sand, not closely pressed and hardened, but such as received those who stepped upon it just as if they were stepping into mud, or rather into untrodden snow. At the same time too the horses and mules suffered still more, both in going up and coming down the hills, from the unevenness of the road as well as from its instability. The length of the marches between the stages also exceedingly distressed the army; for the lack of water often compelled them to make the marches of unusual length. When they travelled by night on a journey which it was necessary to complete, and at daybreak came to water, they suffered no hardship at all; but if, while still on the march, on account of the length of the way, they were caught by the heat, the day advancing, then they did indeed suffer hardships from the blazing sun, being at the same time oppressed by unassuageable thirst.

The soldiers killed many of the beasts of burden of their own accord; for when provisions were lacking, they came together, and slaughtered most of the horses and mules. They ate the flesh of these, and said that they had died of thirst or had perished from the heat. There was no one to divulge the real truth of their conduct, both on account of the men's distress and because all alike were implicated in the same offence. What was being done had not escaped Alexander's notice; but he saw that the best cure for the present state of affairs was to pretend to be ignorant of it, rather than to permit it as a thing known to himself. The consequence was, that it was no longer easy to convey the soldiers who were suffering from disease, or those who were left behind on the roads on account of the heat, partly from the want of beasts of burden and partly because the men themselves were knocking the wagons to pieces, not being able to draw them on account of the depth of the sand; and because in the first stages they were compelled on this account to go, not by the shortest routes, but by those which were easiest for the carriages. Thus some were left behind along the roads on account of sickness, others from fatigue or the effects of the heat, or from not being able to bear up against the drought; and then was no one either to lead them or to remain and tend them in their sickness. For the expedition was being made with great urgency; and the care of individual persons was necessarily neglected in the zeal displayed for the safety of the army as a whole. As they generally made the marches by night, some of the men also were overcome by sleep on the road; afterwards rousing up again, those who still had strength followed upon the tracks of the army; but only a few out of many overtook the main body in safety. Most of them perished in the sand, like men getting out of the course at sea. Another calamity also befell the army, which greatly distressed men, horses, and beasts of burden; for the country of the Gadrosians is supplied with rain by the periodical winds, just as that of the Indians is; not the plains of Gadrosia, but only the mountains where the clouds are carried by the wind and are dissolved into rain without passing beyond the summits of the mountains. On one occasion, when the army bivouacked, for the sake of its water, near a small brook which was a winter torrent, about the second watch of the night the brook which flowed there was suddenly swelled by the rains in the mountains which had fallen unperceived by the soldiers. The torrent advanced with so great a flood as to destroy most of the wives and children of the men who followed the army, and to sweep away all the royal baggage as well as all the beasts of burden still remaining. The soldiers, after great exertions, were hardly able to save themselves together with their weapons, many of which they lost beyond recovery. When, after enduring the burning heat and thirst, they lighted upon abundance of water, many of them perished from drinking to excess, not being able to check their appetite for it. For this reason Alexander generally pitched his camp, not near the water itself, but at a distance of about twenty stades from it, to prevent the men and beasts from pressing in crowds into the river and thus perishing, and at the same time to prevent those who had no control over themselves from fouling the water for the rest of the army by stepping into the springs or streams.

Here I have resolved not to pass over in silence the most noble deed perhaps ever performed by Alexander, which occurred either in this land or, according to the assertion of some other authors, still earlier, among the Parapamisadians. The army was continuing its march through the sand, though the heat of the sun was already scorching, because it was necessary to reach water before halting. They were far on the journey, and Alexander himself, though oppressed with thirst, was nevertheless with great pain and difficulty leading the army on foot, so that his soldiers also, as is usual in such a case, might more patiently bear their hardships by the equalization of the distress. At this time some of the light-armed soldiers, starting away from the army in quest of water, found some collected in a shallow cleft, a small and mean spring. Collecting this water with difficulty, they came with all speed to Alexander, as if they were bringing him some great boon. As soon as they approached the king, they poured the water into a helmet and carried it to him. He took it, and commending the men who brought it, immediately poured it upon the ground in sight of all. As a result of this action, the entire army was reinvigorated to so great a degree that anyone would have imagined that the water poured away by Alexander had furnished a draught to every man ... The following adventure also occurred to the army in that country. At last the guides declared that they no longer remembered the way, because the tracks of it had been rendered invisible by the wind blowing the sand over them. Moreover, in the deep sand which had been everywhere reduced to one level, there was nothing by which they could conjecture the right way, not even the usual trees growing along it, nor any solid hillock rising up; and they had not practised themselves in making journeys by the stars at night or by the sun in the daytime, as sailors do by the constellations of the Bears – the Phoenicians by the Little Bear, and other men by the Greater Bear. Then at length Alexander perceived that it was necessary for him to lead the way by declining to the left; and taking a few horsemen with him he advanced in front of the army. But when the horses even of these were exhausted by the heat, he left most of these men behind, and rode away with only five men and found the sea. Having scraped away the shingle on the sea-beach, he lighted upon water fresh and pure, and then went and fetched the whole army. For seven days they marched along the sea coast, supplying themselves with water from the shore. Thence he led his expedition into the interior, for now the guides knew the way (Aristobulus, *FGrH* 139 F 49a = Arr. 6.24).

81 But Alexander was in great distress throughout the whole journey, since he was marching through a wretched country; and from a distance, likewise, he could procure additional supplies only in small quantities and at rare intervals, so that his army was famished; and the beasts of burden fagged out, and the baggage was left behind on the roads and in the camps; but they were saved by the date palms, eating not only the fruit but also the cabbage at the top. They say that Alexander, although aware of the difficulties, conceived an ambition, in view of the prevailing opinion that Semiramis escaped in flight from India with only about twenty men and Cyrus with seven, to see whether he himself could safely lead that large army of his through the same country and win this victory too.

In addition to the resourcelessness of the country, the heat of the sun was grievous, as also the depth and the heat of the sand; and in some places there were sand-hills so high that, in addition to the difficulty of lifting one's legs, as out of a pit, there were also ascents and descents to be made. And it was necessary also, on account of the wells, to make long marches of two hundred or three hundred stades, and sometimes even six hundred, travelling mostly by night. But they would encamp at a distance from the wells, often at a distance of thirty stades, in order that the soldiers might not, to satisfy their thirst, drink too much water; for many would plunge into the wells, armour and all, and drink as submerged men would; and then, after expiring, would swell up and float on the surface and corrupt the wells, which were shallow; and others, exhausted by reason of thirst, would lie down in the middle of the road in the open sun, and then trembling, along with a jerking of hands and legs, they would die like persons seized with chills or ague. And in some cases soldiers would turn aside from the main road and fall asleep, being overcome by sleep and fatigue. And some, falling behind the army, perished by wandering from the roads and by reason of heat and lack of everything, though others arrived safely, but only after suffering many hardships. And a torrential stream, coming on by night, overwhelmed both a large number of persons and numerous articles; and much of the royal equipment was also swept away; and when the guides ignorantly turned aside so far into the interior that the sea was no longer visible, the king, perceiving their error, set out at once to seek for the shore; and when he found it, and by digging discovered potable water, he sent for the army, and thereafter kept close to shore for seven days, with a good supply of water; and then he withdrew again into the interior (Aristobulus, *FGrH* 139 F 49b = Strabo 15.2.5–7).

82   When Alexander had crossed the River Tigris with his army, and was marching to Babylon, he was met by the Chaldaean philosophers; who, having led him away from his Companions, besought him to suspend his march to that city. For they said that an oracular declaration had been made to them by the god Belus, that his entrance into Babylon at that time would not be for his own good. But he answered their speech with a line from the poet Euripides to this effect: 'He is the best prophet that guesses well.' But the Chaldaeans said: 'O king, do not at any rate enter the city looking towards the west nor leading the army advancing in that direction; but rather go right round towards the east.' But this did not turn out to be easy for him, on account of the difficulty of the ground; for the deity was leading him to the place where entering he was doomed soon to die (Aristobulus, *FGrH* 139 F 54 = Arr. 7.16.1).

83   Having thus proved the falsity of the prophecy of the Chaldaeans, by not having experienced any unpleasant fortune in Babylon, as they had predicted, but having marched out of that city without suffering any mishap, he grew confident in spirit and sailed again through the marshes, having Babylon on his left hand. Here a part of his fleet lost its way in the narrow branches of the river though want of a pilot, until he sent a man to pilot it and lead it back into the channel of the river. The following story is told. Most of the tombs of the Assyrian kings had been built among the pools and marshes. When Alexander was sailing through these marshes, and, as the story goes, was himself steering the trireme, a strong gust of wind fell upon his broad-brimmed Macedonian hat, and the band which encircled it. The hat, being rather heavy, fell into the water; but the band, being carried along by the wind, was caught by one of the reeds growing near the tomb of one of the ancient kings. This incident itself was an omen of what was about to occur, and so was the fact that one of the sailors swam off towards the band and snatched it from the reed. But he did not carry it in his hands, because it would have been wetted while he was swimming; he therefore put it round his own head and thus conveyed it to the king. Most of the biographers of Alexander say that the king presented him with a talent as a reward for his zeal, and then ordered his head to be cut off; as the prophets had expounded the omen to the effect that he should not permit that head to be safe which had worn the royal head band. However, Aristobulus says that the man received a talent; but also received a scourging for placing the band round his head. The same author says that it was one of the Phoenician sailors who fetched the band for Alexander; but there are some who say it was Seleucus, and that this was an omen to Alexander of his death and to Seleucus of his great kingdom. For that of all those who succeeded to the sovereignty after Alexander, Seleucus became the greatest king,[14] was the most kingly in mind, and ruled over the greatest extent of land after Alexander himself, does not seem to me to admit of question (Aristobulus, *FGrH* 139 F 55 = Arr. 7.22).

84 Alexander died in the hundred and fourteenth Olympiad, in the archonship of Hegesias at Athens. According to the statement of Aristobulus, he lived thirty-two years, and had reached the eighth month of his thirty-third year (Aristobulus, *FGrH* 139 F 61 = Arr. 7.28.1).

Modern works

In these extracts, A.K. Narain, formerly Principal of the College of Indology at Banaras Hindu University, deals with Alexander's Indian campaign as a whole, making observations on Alexander's aims, battles, and accomplishments, and A.B. Bosworth, Professor of Classics at the University of Western Australia, examines a specific and enormous problem that Alexander encountered: how to administer India.

1   A.K. Narain, 'Alexander and India', *Greece and Rome*[2] 12 (1965), pp. 155–165.[15]
2   A.B. Bosworth, 'The Indian Satrapies under Alexander the Great', *Antichthon* 17 (1983), pp. 37–46.[16]

Additional reading

E. Badian, 'The Administration of the Empire', *Greece and Rome*[2] 12 (1965), pp. 166–182.

A.B. Bosworth, *Alexander and the East* (Oxford: 1995).

—— , 'Calanus and the Brahman Opposition', in W. Will (ed.), *Alexander der Grosse: Eine Welteroberung und ihr Hintergrund* (Bonn: 1998), pp. 173–203.

P.A. Brunt, *Arrian, History of Alexander*, Loeb Classical Library 2 (Cambridge, MA and London: 1983), Appendix XVI, 'Dionysus, Heracles and India', and Appendix XVII, 'Indian Questions', pp. 435–474.

W.E. Higgins, 'Aspects of Alexander's Imperial Administration: Some Modern Methods and Views Reviewed', *Athenaeum* 58 (1980), pp. 129–152.

A.N. Oikonomides, 'The Real End of Alexander's Conquest of India', *Ancient World* 18 (1988), pp. 31–34.

R. Stoneman, 'Naked Philosophers: The Brahmans in the Alexander Historians and the *Alexander Romance*', *Journal of Hellenic Studies* 105 (1995), pp. 99–114.

Notes

1 See Chapter 5.
2 Diod. 17.87–89.3, Arr. 5.14–18, Plut. *Alex.* 60, Curt. 8.13–14. On Alexander as a general, see Chapter 7.
3 On distances, see Sources 2 and 36; cf. Sources 59 and 60.
4 See Chapter 4.
5 See Chapter 9.
6 See Chapter 8.
7 Arr. 7.8.1–12.3, Diod. 17.109.2–3, Plut. *Alex.* 71.2–9, Curt. 10.2.3 ff., Justin 12.11; see also Chapter 8.
8 The controversy surrounding Alexander's death is not dealt with in this book: see A.B. Bosworth, 'The Death of Alexander the Great: Rumour and Propaganda', *Classical Quarterly*[2] 21 (1971), pp. 112–136.
9 The Battle of the Hydaspes river in 326.
10 The Hyphasis river, at which Alexander's men mutinied and forced him to turn back.
11 On drinking, see Sources 7–13, 58, 68, 103 and 109.
12 The context is the mutiny at the Hyphasis river in 326.
13 The Gedrosian Desert.
14 The founder of the Seleucid dynasty, which was the most powerful and the largest kingdom in the hellenistic period.
15 Reprinted with the permission of Oxford University Press.
16 Reprinted with the permission of the author.

ALEXANDER AND INDIA

A.K. Narain

No army leader has become more famous in history than Alexander. He has been praised and admired as well as blamed and cursed. But even if blemishes can be found in his career and character, no one can deny his 'daemonic' strength of will and leadership, which alone are sufficient to mark him out as one of the greatest generals history has seen. Opinions may, however, differ as to whether he was more than that.

We are told Alexander's invasion of Persia was a pan-Hellenic war of revenge and he was elected as the leader of the League of Corinth for the purpose. It is said he was influenced by Isocrates' *Philippus*; if so, he should have envisaged the conquest of Asia Minor only. And Tarn would have us believe that Alexander did not cross the Dardanelles with any definite design of conquering the whole of the Persian empire (Tarn, i. 9). But when it comes to Alexander's invasion of India, he states, 'India had been part of the empire of Darius I; and Alexander's invasion was only the necessary and inevitable completion of his conquest of that empire. It had nothing to do with any scheme of world conquest; indeed it could not have, for in the far East the 'world', like 'Asia', only meant the Persian empire; nothing else was known' (ibid. i. 86–87). He goes one step further and adds, 'possibly the Beas [= Hyphasis] had been the boundary of Darius I; it would agree with what happened. For at the Beas the army mutinied and refused to go farther' (Tarn, i. 98). Tarn would not like Alexander to dream of more than he actually achieved. For nothing succeeds like success and a fulfilled dream is the perfection of success.

But Alexander was certainly more ambitious than that; perhaps his ambition had no end. Describing the return march of Alexander, when he reached the Pasargadae and Persepolis, Arrian pauses to remark 'that Alexander had no small or mean conceptions, nor would ever have remained contented with any of his possessions so far, not even if he had added Europe to Asia, and the Britannic islands to Europe; but would always have searched far beyond for something unknown, being always the rival if of no other, yet of himself'.[1] Even if Alexander dreamt of more than Isocrates recommended he might very well have stopped with the collapse of the power of Darius III or when the latter died, and he would still be remembered as the glorious Captain of the League who succeeded not only in avenging the prestige of Hellas but also in bringing the Achaemenid era to an end. But he did not stop. He dragged his war-weary army to Sogdiana and the Punjab. He could have even taken them beyond the Beas, but he was fortunate, as he was in his death (cf. Tarn, i. 121), that the army refused to listen to him.

Of course, it serves no purpose to speculate what would have happened if Alexander had not retreated from the Beas, just as it does not help to discuss what would have happened if Napoleon had not marched into Russia. But certainly there is no evidence to extend the empire of Darius I east of the Indus and certainly not as far as the Beas. Even if it was Alexander's *mission* to conquer the whole of the Persian empire, whether to Hellenize it or for *Homonoia*, he had no justification in crossing the Indus, for 'the Indus river was the boundary between India and Ariana, which latter was situated next to India on the west and was in the possession of the Persians at that time'.[2] Doubtless therefore Alexander did nourish an ambition to conquer India, perhaps even to reach the Eastern ocean' (Tarn, i. 99). Otherwise the crossing of the Indus was meaningless. Of course, Alexander hardly invaded India within its present boundaries because the point he reached at the Beas is only a few miles within the Indian Union. India, as his contemporaries knew it, did not end at the Beas either, and it was reported to him that the main power of India was really beyond this river. But the conquest of India remained an unfulfilled dream of Alexander. However, even what remains of Alexander's story would be shorn of all its romance and glory if his campaigns in Sogdiana and the Punjab were deleted and if there were no Spitamenes and Porus, Scythians and the Malloi.

It is beyond the scope of the present paper to give a detailed account of Alexander's conquest. But we can make a summary review of Alexander's march from Kabul to the Beas and from the Beas to the lower Indus. Alexander took almost two years to cover this area, which is proportionately a longer time for a lesser space than in his other campaigns, and the battles fought were as dangerous, as glorious, as full of bravery and adventure.

It was early summer of 327 when Alexander recrossed the Hindu Kush and divided his army. He sent Hephaestion and Perdiccas with the baggage and part of the army through the Khyber pass to the Indus and himself followed the old route through Laghman, ascended the Kunar river, and crossed into Swat. The people of these mountain tracts were called the Aspasians, Gouraians, and Assakenians by Arrian (iv. 23. 1). They were brave people and it was hard work for Alexander to take their strongholds, of which Massaga and Aornus need special mention. At Massaga, Alexander massacred 7,000 mercenaries because they refused to join him against their own countrymen (A. iv. 27.3 ff.; D. 84). What makes this massacre 'a foul blot on Alexander's martial fame'[3] is his treachery to the mercenaries who had capitulated, and the account given by Diodorus of the desperate fight which both the men and the women gave to meet a glorious death 'which they would have disdained to exchange for a life with dishonour'[4] is really heart-rending. At Aornus, the fighting was at once fierce and dangerous. Ptolemy, who had taken a vantage point at the far end of the fortress by surprise, was cut off there for two days and hard pressed before the main body under Alexander could break through to him (A. iv. 29). The valley of the Swat was thus subjugated.

After these prodigious encounters, Alexander had a pleasant relief when he reached Nysa. The leader of the Nysaeans, Acuphis, not only offered submission but claimed kinship on account of their Greek origin and traditional association with the mythical Dionysus (A. v. 1–2; C. viii. 10. 7 ff.). It pleased the fancy of Alexander and his army. The Nysaeans were left undisturbed in their rule and Alexander gave his army licence to fraternize and enjoy Bacchanalian revelry.

Alexander joined Hephaestion at the Indus. Hephaestion had already bridged the river at Ohind, sixteen miles above Attock.[5] He crossed the Indus and was welcomed by Ambhi and lavishly entertained in Taxila for three days. Alexander also made return presents to Ambhi, enjoyed the hospitality there and allowed Ambhi and those who were unable to defend themselves to live in peace.[6] But the ambition of the impetuous and aggressive Alexander as well as the brave warrior in him did not wander so far only to enjoy stale luxury in the company of cowards and those who did not value freedom. He appointed Philippus as a satrap and left a garrison there (A. v. 8. 3) and proceeded to the Jhelum (= Hydaspes) without wasting more time, for he was getting restive to meet Porus, perhaps more because he wanted to test his mettle than to help Ambhi in his designs.

Alexander had learnt that Porus was ready at the far side of the Hydaspes with all his army, determined to prevent his crossing or at least to attack him, should he attempt it.[7] Although hemmed in by enemies, cowards, and traitors, both in front and rear, the undaunted spirit of Porus refused to submit. We are told, when envoys went to him to summon him to meet Alexander, he proudly replied that he would indeed meet him, but at his frontiers and in arms.[8] This was a sufficient challenge for Alexander and he reached the Jhelum in early June 326. He found Porus ready with his forces on the opposite bank [. . .]. Both sides made active preparation for the inevitable war, of which the details of strategy and movements are so well known that we need not repeat them.[9] The part played by the rains also need not be gainsaid. Porus fought bravely, and even when he saw his army had almost perished, 'he did not copy the example of the great king Darius and set his own men an example of flight, but so long as any part of the Indian troops held their ground in the fight, so long he battled bravely', but having been wounded in the right shoulder 'he wheeled his elephant and retreated'. 'Alexander having seen him play a great and gallant part in the battle desired to save him' (A. v. 18). First Ambhi was sent with Alexander's message, but, when Porus saw him coming, he once again turned his elephant and rode up to pierce him with a javelin and Ambhi could save himself only with great difficulty and returned. Alexander sent others in relays and finally Meroes who had long been a friend of Porus. 'But Porus, hearing Meroes' message, and being also much distressed by thirst, halted his elephant and dismounted; and after drinking, and recovering his strength, bade Meroes conduct him at once to Alexander. Porus was then conducted to Alexander, who, learning of his approach, rode a horse and met him in advance of the line with a few of the Companions; then halting his horse, he admired the great size of Porus, who was over five cubits in height, and his handsomeness, and the appearance he gave of a spirit not yet tamed, but of one brave man meeting another brave man after an honourable struggle against another king for his kingdom.'[10] We need not repeat again the very well known conversation between Alexander and Porus. Porus was not only reinstated but further territories were added to his kingdom. Alexander thus became greater in peace than in war; according to Indian codes he acted as a *Dharmavijayi*[11] like Samadragupta, the great king of the Magadhan empire, who behaved in this way towards the kings of South India in the middle of the fourth century A.D.[12]

Alexander then proceeded further and crossed the Chenab and the Ravi (= Acesines and Hydraotes) and on the way defeated another Porus[13] and also obtained the submission of Abhisares.[14] He then crossed the Ravi and entered the country of the Cathaeans (Kathas),[15] who were among the best fighters of the Punjab and first among 'the self-governing Indians'; they gave Alexander some of the toughest experiences of his campaign.[16] He did capture Sangala, the hill fortress of the Kathas, by assault in which 'there perished some seventeen thousand of the Indians, and over seventy thousand were captured, with three hundred waggons, and five hundred horsemen'; however, Alexander had at one time to leap down from his horse and lead the Phalanx on foot, and over twelve hundred, including several of the officers and Lysimachus, were seriously wounded besides those who were slain (A. v. 24. 5–8). Alexander razed the city of Sangala to the ground and advanced towards the Beas.

Phegeus, a near-by king who submitted to Alexander without resistance in order that his subjects might attend to the cultivation of their fields according to their needs, told Alexander about the extent and power of the Nanda empire east of the Beas, and Porus also confirmed his statements.[17] Of course, such statements whetted Alexander's eagerness to advance further; but his troops, especially the Macedonians, had begun to lose heart at the thought of the distance they had travelled from their homes, and the hardships and the dangers they had been called upon to face after their entry into India. Alexander's exhortations and the reply of Coenus, which form a classic dialogue between a general and his army, are well known.[18] The army mutinied and refused to march further. It was a severe blow to Alexander. He saved his face by offering a sacrifice preliminary to crossing the river, and, finding the omens unfavourable, as expected, he proclaimed his decision to return.[19] The army received the announcement with tears of joy and grateful shouts. They hardly realized what was still in store for them. For Alexander had yet to fight some of his fiercest and most dangerous battles. From the bank of Beas he returned to the Jhelum, handed over all the country between the Jhelum and the Beas to Porus, and sailed down the Jhelum on his return journey.

Below the confluence of the Jhelum and the Chenab the armies of Alexander camped and he prepared for his last important campaign against the Malloi (Malavas).[20] Unlike the monarchical states of the Punjab, the 'republican' states had the sense to unite against the common aggressor. The spectacle of Alexander's success did not deter them. The Cathaeans fought alone and failed. The Malloi therefore made a confederacy with the Oxydracae (Kshudraka) and planned to defend themselves together. But by his quick movements Alexander prevented the Oxydracae from joining the Malloi[21] and the latter had to face the aggression alone, and it is clear from the accounts that they fought bravely. In fact, among Alexander's campaigns this is unique in its dreadful record of mere slaughter. Indeed, it was the least creditable of the campaigns, and the deep wound Alexander got in his chest as a result of his desperate expedient in the fight with the Malloi left him weakened and indirectly hastened his end. The Oxydracae, who could not join the Malloi, had no alternative but to submit after the collapse of their confederates the Malloi.

'The progress of the flotilla down the Chenab and the Indus cannot be traced, nor the places mentioned be identified, because all the rivers, more especially the Indus, have since altered their course many times' (Tarn, i. 103). But obviously more 'peoples' and kings fought with him. The most important among them were the Brahmanas and a king called Musicanus.[22] About the end of July 325, Alexander reached Patala. Here the Indus bifurcated and Alexander halted to prepare for the last stage of his journey out of India and back to Hellas (Tarn, i. 104).

How did contemporary India react to his invasion? The following information about 'the wise men' and 'philosophers' of ancient India is significant in this connexion:

Arrian refers to Indian wise men, some of whom, the story goes, were found by Alexander in the open air in a meadow, where they used to have their disputations, and who, when they saw Alexander and his army, did nothing further than beat with their feet the ground on which they stood. Then when Alexander inquired by interpreters what this action of theirs meant, they replied: 'O king Alexander, each man possesses just so much of the earth as this on which we stand; and you being a man like other men, save that you are full of activity and relentless, are roaming over all this earth far from your home troubled yourself, and troubling others. But not so long hence you will die, and will possess just so much of the earth as suffices for your burial' (A. vii. 1.5 ff.).

Plutarch says that, 'the philosophers gave him (Alexander) no less trouble . . . because they reviled the princes who declared for him and encouraged the free states to revolt from his authority. On this account he hanged many of them'.[23]

Plutarch[24] also refers to a certain Indian 'philosopher', Kalanus, as showing Alexander a symbol of his (Alexander's) empire. Kalanus threw down on the ground a dry and shrivelled hide and planted his foot on the edge of it. But when it was trodden down in one place, it started up everywhere else. He then walked all round it and showed that the same thing took place wherever he trod, until at length he stepped into the middle, and by doing so made it all lie flat. This symbol was intended to show Alexander that he should control his empire from its centre, and not wander away to its distant extremities.

There is again a reference[25] to the capture of ten of the 'gymnosophists', who had been principally concerned in persuading Sabbas (?) to revolt and who had done much harm to the Macedonians in other ways. They were all to be executed for this, but before their execution they were asked certain questions. One of them was asked for what reason he had induced Sabbas to revolt. He answered, 'Because I wished him to live with honour or die with honour.'[26]

The contemporary Indian observations made above are at once philosophical and patriotic. They indicate two things. First, there was an emotional love of freedom and a patriotic sense of honour. Second, India, with her peculiarly philosophical attitude, was not at all overawed by the greatness of Alexander and not only regarded the Indian campaign as most unjustifiable, but also anticipated its futility. The astute Brahman politician Chanakya[27] and the youthful Kshatriya commoner Chandragupta,[28] who seems to have had a first-hand view of Alexander's campaign in the Punjab, and who had perhaps met and offended Alexander (J. xv. 4), understood the Indian pulse of reaction correctly. Even while Alexander was in Gedrosia, the only alien satrap appointed by him in India was murdered[29] and when Alexander was dying in Babylon, Chandragupta and Chanakya, perhaps with the help of Porus,[30] were liberating and unifying the Punjab as a prelude to the final overthrow of the great Nanda power of the Ganges valley, which the army of Alexander dreaded so much that the latter was forced to withdraw from the Beas. Alexander's campaign in India was therefore certainly not a political success. And it is also true that it left no permanent mark on the literature, life, or government of the people. The name of Alexander is not found in Indian literature. Certainly, Alexander did not intend his conquests in India to be as meaningless as this. But it was so.

One Indian historian[31] feels that 'the adventure was no doubt highly creditable, but cannot be regarded as a brilliant military achievement, as he had never been brought face to face with any of the great nations of Hindusthan'. The same historian makes a note of 'the untold sufferings inflicted upon India – massacre, rapine, and plunder on a scale till then without a precedent in her annals, but repeated in later days by more successful invaders like Sultan Mahmud, Tamerlane, and Nadir Shah. In spite of the halo of romance that Greek writers have woven round the name of Alexander, the historians of India can regard him only as the precursor of these recognized scourges of Mankind'.[32] This may be an extreme statement. But so is the statement that Alexander 'proclaimed for the first time the unity and brotherhood of mankind'.[33] If the Indian historian suffers from sentiment, the western historian suffers from guilt; if one sees in Alexander's campaign an unjustified aggression, the other sees a justification for his mission, and neither of them needs to be blamed for his attitude. Shorn of these overstatements, Alexander's image remains that of an admirable army leader who suffered no defeat before he died, an image of a youthful person full of ambition and adventure curbed only by death, and above all an image of a human being who could commit crimes and atrocities and yet feel remorse and sympathy. Alexander will no doubt remain 'great', but not because of historians seeing more in him than what he actually was, but just for what he actually was.

But when all is said, we must admit two indirect results of Alexander's raid. People of the North-West, perhaps, realized that 'emotional love of independence was no match to the disciplined strength of a determined conqueror';[34] and it was felt that the existence of small states was not in the wider interests of the country. Chandragupta had probably himself witnessed the spirit of resistance, which the freedom-loving people of the Punjab had shown. He organized a disciplined army out of them and unified the Punjab and later the whole of Northern India after overthrowing the Nandas; he even added territories in the south and within a few years the first big Indian empire was established.[35] To this empire were also added the four satrapies of Aria, Arachosia, Gedrosia, and Paropamisadae, which were ceded by Seleucus to Chandragupta only a few years after the death of Alexander.[36] Seleucus I sent Megasthenes as an ambassador to the Mauryan court of Chandragupta.[37] We have no evidence to tell us whether Chandragupta sent a return embassy to Seleucus. But stray references do indicate the continuance of diplomatic exchanges between the Hellenistic kingdoms and India. Athenaeus tells us, on the authority of Hegesander, that Amitrochates, king of the Indians, wrote to Antiochus I of Syria asking that monarch to buy and send him sweet wine, dried figs, and a sophist. The Syrian king replied, 'We shall send you figs and the wine, but in Greece the laws forbid a sophist to be sold' (Ath. xiv. 652 ff.). Diodorus testifies to the great love of the king of Palibothra, apparently a Mauryan king, for the Greeks (D. ii. 60). Strabo refers to the sending of Deimachus to the court of Allitrochades, son of Sandrokottos (ii. 1. 9. 70c). Pliny mentions another envoy, Dionysius, from Ptolemy II of Egypt (NH vi. 58). Asoka's friendly relations with the Yavanas of Western Asia and Egypt are well known. The thirteenth Rock Edict, a version of which has also been found in Greek recently at Kandahar,[38] refers to the Dhammavijaya of Asoka in the kingdoms of Antiochus II of Syria, Ptolemy Philadelphus II of Egypt, Antigonus Gonatas of Macedonia, Magas of Cyrene, and Alexander of Corinth.[39] Asoka arranged for the medical treatment of men and cattle in the dominions of Antiochus II and his neighbours.[40] It is not unlikely that his description of himself as Devanampriya Piyadassi is an echo of the deification of kings current among Alexander's successors in the Hellenistic East,[41] although the style of his edicts is clearly influenced by edicts of Darius.[42] These stray references do give a cumulative impression of a continuous contact of India with the Hellenistic world. The very fact that both Megasthenes and Kautilya refer to a state department run and maintained specifically for the purpose of looking after foreigners,[43] who were mostly Yavanas and Persians, testifies to the impact created by these contacts. It also explains the occurrence of such finds as the fragmentary handle of a terra-cotta vase recovered from Taxila,[44] showing Alexander's head in lion's skin, or random finds from the Sarnath, Basarh, and Patna regions of terra-cotta pieces of distinctive Hellenistic appearance or with definite Hellenistic motifs and designs.[45] [. . .].

The second indirect result was the rise of the Yavana power in Bactria and its ultimate expansion and rule over what is now known as Afghanistan and Western Pakistan for about one hundred and fifty years.[46] I have shown elsewhere that these 'Greeks' were not necessarily Hellenistic Greeks, but mostly the descendants of earlier settlers preserving their traditions but much intermixed with the Iranian peoples and in some measure reinforced by the newcomers, the veterans of Alexander or colonists of the Seleucids. But they no doubt got their chance owing to the invasion of Alexander and the resultant dismemberment of the Achaemenid empire. There are as many as forty-one names of men who ruled this Yavana kingdom known from coins alone.[47] It is to these kings that Strabo referred when he mentioned that 'more tribes were subdued by them (i.e. the Indo-Greeks) than by Alexander – mostly by Menander (at least if he actually crossed the Hypanis towards the east and advanced as far as the Imanus), for some were subdued by him personally and others by Demetrius, the son of Euthydemus. the King of the Bactrians . . .'. I have shown elsewhere that Menander was the most powerful among the Indo-Greek kings.[48] He is the only king who has survived in Indian literature and tradition [. . .]. He is known to have become a Buddhist and a tradition connects with Menander the origin of the most famous statue of Buddhism in Indo-China, the statue of Buddha of the Emerald, which Menander's Indian teacher Nagasena materialized out of a magic emerald by supernatural power.[49] The discussions between Menander, who is known as king Milinda in the Pali-Buddhist literature, and Nagasena are embodied in a book called *The Questions of King Milinda*. Plutarch (*Moralia* 821D–E) says that when Menander died the cities celebrated his funeral in other respects as usual, but in respect of his remains they put forth rival claims and divided the ashes equally to erect monuments on the relics, which is typical of the Buddhist custom. Numismatists believe that the occurrence of the wheel on some coins of Menander is the *Dharma Çakra*, the wheel of righteousness connected with Buddhism.[50] We also know from an inscription engraved on a Garuda pillar [. . .] found at Besnagar near Bhilsa (in the state of Madhya Pradesh) that an inhabitant of Taxila named Heliodorus, son of Dion, came as an envoy from Antialcidas, an Indo-Greek king, to the court of the Indian king, Bhagabhadra, and that Heliodorus was a follower of the Bhagawat sect of Hinduism.[51] We also know from later evidence about Greeks who adopted not only Indian religions but also Indian names. The Indo-Greeks were more influenced by Indian religion and thought than was any Hellenistic king by the faith and ideas of the land in which he lived and ruled. No Seleucid ever put Iranian or Babylonian legends on his coinage, no Ptolemy ever used Egyptian, but the Indo-Greeks introduced Indian legend in Indian scripts on their money [. . .]. They came, they saw, but India conquered.

Notes

1 A. vii. 1. 4 (Loeb translation).
2 Strabo, xv. 1. 10 (Loeb translation).
3 K.A. Nilakanta Sastri, *The Age of the Nandas and Mauryas* (Banaras, 1952), 50.
4 D. xvii. 84; see R. C. Majumdar, *The Classical Accounts of India*, 163. Majumdar has reproduced the extract from McGrindle, *The Invasion of India by Alexander the Great as described by Arrian, Quintus Curtius, Diodorus, Plutarch and Justin* (London, 1896).

5 A. v. 3. 5; D. xvii. 86. 3; C. viii. 11. 4 ff.

6 A. v. 3. 5; 8. 2 ff. ('Mophis'); all the Diodorus references are to Book xvii unless otherwise stated; C. loc. cit. ('Omphis').

7 A. v. 8. 4; D. 87; C. viii. 12.

8 C. loc. cit.

9 [. . .].

10 A. v. 18. *fin.*–19, *init.* (Loeb translation); cf. C. viii. 14; P. 60.

11 Dharmavijayi means 'conqueror through righteousness'.

12 Samadragupta was the fourth king of the Gupta dynasty. He was a great conqueror and Smith thought of him as the Indian Napoleon. An account of the campaigns of the king is inscribed on an Asokan pillar found at Allahabad. It refers to the defeat of several kings of South India whose names are given and it says that the king reinstated all those kings after their defeat, having obtained only their allegiance. He did not annex their territories.

13 Arrian (v. 21. 2 ff.) refers to him as 'Porus, the bad one', because he was reported to have left his own province and fled. Some sources believe that this Porus was a cousin of the great Porus; cf. D. 91. 1.

14 A. v. 20. 5; C. ix. 1. 7 ff.; cf. D. 90. 4.

15 A. v. 22. 1; D. 91. 2 ff.

16 A. v. 20. 5–6; 24. 2; D. 91. 4. Cathaeans had a non-monarchical form of government and they were the 'republics' of ancient India, like the Malloi (Malavas), Oxydracae (Kshudraka), and others.

17 C. ix. 1. 36 ff.; D. 93. 1.

18 A. v. 25 ff.; C. ix. 2–3; cf. D. 94, *fin.*; P. 62.

19 Ibid.

20 A. vi. 3–11; D. 97 ff.; C. ix. 4. 15 ff.; P. 63.

21 A. vi. 11. 3 (Loeb translation): '. . . they (the Mallians) had determined to join the Oxydracae and to fight together, but Alexander reached them too quickly . . .'. A different account in D. 98; confused in C.

22 A. vi. 16; D. 102–3; C. ix. 8. 8 ff. ('the Musicani').

23 P. 69; see R. C. Majumdar, op. cit. 200.

24 Ibid. 65; Majumdar op. cit. 201–2.

25 Ibid. 64; Majumdar op. cit. 200–1.

26 Ibid.

27 Chanakya was a Brahman scholar of Taxila (?), who was offended by the Nanda king. He later became the Chief Minister of Chandragupta after having helped him to overthrow the Nandas. He wrote the famous treatise on Polity known as Kautalya's *Arthasastra*.

28 According to the Buddhist sources, Chandragupta was born in a self-governing Kshatriya tribe known as the Moriyas in the Nepalese Terai.

29 Philippus: A. vi. 27. 2; C. x. 1. 20.

30 According to Indian literary sources, Chandragupta and Chanakya were helped in their bid to overthrow the Nanda power by a certain Indian king named Parvartaka who ruled in the Punjab and who may be identified with Porus.

31 Radha Kumud Mukherjee, *The Age of Imperial Unity* (Bombay, 1951).

32 Ibid.

33 Tarn i. 147 cf. ii, Appendix 25. Against this, however, E. Badian, *Historia* vii (1958), 425 ff.

34 K. A. Nilakanta Sastri, op. cit. 79.

35 His empire is definitely known to have included an area from Aria to Bengal and from Kashmir to Mysore. This empire over which the Mauryas ruled up to the time of Asoka was never ruled again by any single king or power in Indian history.

36 The discovery of an Asokan inscription in Greek characters in Kandahar should dispel whatever lurking doubts some scholars might have had in this regard.

37 Strabo, ii. 1. 9, 70 c; xv. 1. 36, 702 c; A. v. 6. 2; Pliny, *NH* vi 58; Clem. Alex. *Strom.* i. 72. 5.

38 D. Schlumberger, L. Robert, etc., *Une bilingue gréco-araméenne d'Asoka* (Paris, 1958).

39 See the text of Rock Edict XIII; Hultzsch, *Inscriptions of Asoka* in *Arch. Sur. Ind.* (Calcutta and Oxford, 1925).

40 K. A. Nilakanta Sastri, op. cit. 354.
41 Ibid.
42 Ibid. 358.
43 Ibid.; see Kautilya's *Arthasastra*, ed. and trans. by Shama Sastri.
44 Marshall, *Taxila* (Cambridge, 1951), ii. 433, iii. Pl. 130.
45 L. Bachhofer, *Early Indian Sculpture* (Paris, 1929), i. Pl. 13.
46 See A. K. Narain, *The Indo-Greeks* (Oxford, 1957).
47 Ibid. 181.
48 Narain, op. cit. 97.
49 *Bulletin de l'École française d'Extrême-Orient*, xxv (1925), 112; xxxi (1931), 448.
50 Marshall, *Taxila*, i. 33–34.
51 Narain, op. cit. 118.

THE INDIAN SATRAPIES UNDER
ALEXANDER THE GREAT

A. B. Bosworth

Alexander's administrative arrangements in India are an obscure and somewhat neglected subject. The obscurity is due to a crucial lacuna in the narrative sources, which take us to a crisis in government but say nothing of its resolution. Late in 325 the satrap of northern India, Philip son of Machatas, was assassinated by some of his native mercenaries. In his place Alexander appointed the native prince Taxiles to govern the territory along with Eudamus (the officer commanding the satrapal army of Thracians) until such time as he sent out a new satrap from court.[1] Nothing more is heard of a replacement or of India. The sources foreshadow an administrative change but never report the outcome. Instead we have to wait for the reports of the satrapal distributions of Babylon and Triparadeisus, in which the division of the Indian provinces is sensibly different from what it had been in Alexander's day. The change may be due to the king himself or to his successors. Both views have been stated, but the issue has never been fully argued and it is worth reopening. It has important implications for Alexander's view of empire in his last years and for the status of India in his imperial plans.

Down to late 325 B.C. Alexander's administrative acts in India are clearly reported and easy to follow.[2] When he entered India in the summer of 327, he ensured that the strategic line of communication along the Cophen valley was strongly garrisoned. Its tribal centres were placed under native hyparchs, some of them former refugees who had been at loggerheads with the previous rulers.[3] The administrative head of the area was a Macedonian satrap, Nicanor, who had general oversight between the borders of Parapamisadae and the Indus.[4] Beyond the Indus a second satrapy was established, comprising the area of the Punjab between the rivers Indus and Hydaspes and extending as far south as the confluence with the Acesines. Its nucleus was the principality of Taxiles, Alexander's most constant local ally. This second satrapy was governed by Philip son of Machatas, who had a formidable garrison force which included the entire Thracian contingent.[5] For a time at least the western satrapy also formed part of his competence. Nicanor, it seems, was assassinated by his subjects in the Cophen valley late in 326. Philip was sent to restore order there, and after a successful punitive campaign he was vested with the territory west of the Indus as far as Parapamisadae.[6] For the moment the lands between the Hindu Kush and the Acesines were in the hands of a single satrap.

Beyond the Hydaspes was the territory of Porus. Defeated in battle in the spring of 326, he attracted the conqueror's favour and benefactions by his heroism, and his realms were systematically expanded. In early 325 Porus was made vassal king of all the lands between the Hydaspes and the Hyphasis,[7] an area which Alexander had overrun but was unwilling to keep under direct Macedonian control. He may have had the technical title of satrap[8] but he was in fact plenipotentiary, exercising power without Macedonian troops or Macedonian officials. To the south of the Acesines was another Macedonian satrap, Peithon son of Agenor, who was in charge of the territory as far as the Indian Ocean.[9] The Indus and the Hydaspes now formed a continuous river frontier, its defence and administration shared between two

Macedonian satraps, and there was an extensive buffer zone across the Punjab under the control of a native prince. That was the situation at the end of 325 when Philip was assassinated in the north.

The evidence begins again after Alexander's death, and it will be convenient to deal first with the reports of the distribution at Triparadeisus in 321. We have parallel narratives in Photius' digest of Arrian's *History of the Successors* and in Diodorus Siculus, which are clearly taken from the same ultimate source.[10] They list the same appointments in the same geographical order and use very similar terminology. Diodorus is the less efficient excerptor, briefer and much more careless, and his description of the Indian satrapies is perplexing at first sight: the satrapy contiguous to Parapamisadae was conferred upon Peithon, son of Agenor, while the neighbouring kingdoms were given to native rulers, that along the Indus to Porus and that along the Hydaspes to Taxiles, 'for it was not possible to move them without a royal army and a first-rate general' (Diod. 18.39.6). This account is paradoxical in several ways. Porus' territory under Alexander did not impinge on the Indus, and Peithon's satrapy had been southern India, not the western province. The problem, however, is largely relieved by the fuller excerpt of Photius/Arrian. This agrees on Peithon's appointment in the north-west and it defines the native kingdoms more explicitly: the satrapy extending along the Indus to Patala, the greatest city of the region, was ceded to Porus, that along the Hydaspes to Taxiles, 'for it did not seem easy to remove them, seeing that they had received their realms at Alexander's hands and maintained considerable armies'.[11] There are two additions of importance. Porus' territory extended to Patala and both kings owed their position to Alexander. Now Patala was at the mouth of the Indus, Nearchus' departure point for his Ocean voyage, and it marked the southern limit of Peithon's old satrapy. If we accept this explicit record, it follows that Peithon was at some stage transferred to western India while Porus' realms were enlarged to include his old satrapy. This reorganization, so Photius' digest implies, took place under Alexander.

This evidence has been very variously treated in modern times. Benedictus Niese accepted Photius/Arrian at face value, but Beloch bluntly dismissed the report as incredible ('ganz unglaublich') and deterred most subsequent scholars from accepting the evidence of the sources.[12] In 1937 Helmut Berve criticized Beloch's dogmatism, based as it was upon wholly subjective criteria, and modified his own earlier treatment of the Indian satrapies, accepting the evidence of Photius/Arrian and drawing the necessary conclusion of a reorganization at the end of Alexander's life. Unfortunately his discussion was embodied in a little-read article in Pauly-Wissowa and has been generally overlooked.[13] Meanwhile Tarn returned to scepticism, arguing that Peithon only received the western satrapy at the time of the Triparadeisus distribution: between 324 and 321 Taxiles ruled the territory from Parapamisadae to the Indus and Porus his old realm between the Hydaspes and Hyphasis.[14] If the critics are correct, a gross error has been committed. Either Photius or Arrian is mistaken in asserting that the situation ratified at Triparadeisus dates back to Alexander's reign.

The easiest assumption would be garbling by Photius, either an explanatory gloss or an incompetent contraction of the original text. Fortunately we can test his technique by comparison with his treatment of a similar passage from the *History of Alexander* (cod. 91). There Photius gives a detailed summary of Arrian's list of the bridal partners at Susa. He virtually transcribes Arrian,[15] retaining his vocabulary for the most part but varying the word order. The result is a reasonably faithful rendering of the original, the last few sentences almost verbatim reproduction. Textual variants are rare, one major (Ἀρσινόη for Βαρσίνη) and one trivial (Ἀρτώνην for Ἄρτωνιν). There are a number of omissions, most of them involving peripheral detail. The father of Rhoxane is not named and Photius does not give Arrian's explanation of the choice of Hephaestion's bride.[16] The only structurally serious omission is the sentence recording Perdiccas' marriage to the daughter of Atropates, which is a slip rather than deliberate excision. We may conclude that the excerpt is a fairly reliable reproduction. The original is pruned but not drastically, and, most importantly for our purposes, there are no glosses or intrusive explanations. In that case there is every reason to believe that his account of the Triparadeisus settlement is an accurate rendering of the original and that Arrian did in fact attribute the Indian reorganization to Alexander.

Arrian himself may be in error but there is no *a priori* reason to think so. There is also some corroborative evidence. The geographical survey of Asia at the beginning of Diodorus 18 has long been accepted as an account of the administrative divisions of the empire at the time of Alexander's death. Almost certainly it is part of a *mise en scène* which Hieronymus placed at the beginning of his history and as such is contemporary evidence.[17] This survey begins with a description of India, starting with the eastern territories and moving to the portion conquered by Alexander, the land of the five rivers. In that area, says Diodorus (18.6.2), were many kingdoms, including the realms of Porus and Taxiles, through which it happens that the Indus flows (ἥ τε τοῦ Πώρου καὶ Ταξίλου δυναστεία, δι' ἧς συμβαίνει ῥεῖν τὸν Ἰνδὸν ποταμόν). The passage seems to envisage the domains of Porus and Taxiles as a single entity covering the length of the Indus, and it is exactly the position described by Photius/Arrian.

Paradoxically Tarn used this evidence to support his conclusion that Peithon was not in western India until 321 B.C., but he could only do so by selective quotation: 'the Indus river happens to run through the realm of Taxiles'.[18] Having omitted Porus he was able to argue that Taxiles' domains covered both sides of the Indus and so included the western satrapy. This presses Diodorus' vague terminology very uncomfortably. Even if the Indus merely formed the western boundary of Taxiles' realm it would be possible to say in so general a context that the river flowed through it. In any case, if Taxiles did occupy land west of the Indus, there is no proof that his holdings included the whole of the western satrapy as far as Parapamisadae. But once we read the complete text the argument founders irretrievably. There are two alternatives. If Porus' domains comprised territory on the Indus, they extended to south India and Peithon had been replaced as satrap. If the passage is wrong about Porus there is no conceivable reason to suppose that it is right about Taxiles. Tarn cannot have it both ways. On the contrary, as it stands, Diodorus' text agrees with the situation in 321 as described by Photius/Arrian. It may be a retrojection of the later position but there is no compelling reason to believe so. Otherwise the list is perfectly compatible with the situation at Alexander's death, and the inclusion of Susiane in Persis (18.6.3) must date to the period before Triparadeisus, when Susiane had a satrap of its own once again.

The reports of the Babylon settlement are not as unanimous as those of Triparadeisus. Photius' digest of Arrian says nothing of the eastern satrapies, implying that they remained under their former rulers. That information is provided in another digest of Arrian, that of Dexippus, who wrote a *History of the Successors* on the same lines as Arrian but with a more complete record of satrapies. He states that Taxiles and Porus ruled all the Indians, Porus the peoples between the Hydaspes and the Indus and Taxiles the rest. Peithon controlled the territory bordering on theirs, except for Parapamisadae.[19] That is a repetition of the distribution of territories at Triparadeisus, except that the digest has Porus in Taxiles' kingdom – an inversion most probably due to Dexippus' own carelessness.[20] Otherwise the two native rulers control all the Indian territories except for the western satrapy, which is already in Peithon's hands. There is no explicit reference to a satrapy of south India and no note of a Macedonian commander in that area.

The other sources are even less helpful. Justin gives a typically competent satrapy list which has a similar note that the Indian and Bactrian commanders were confirmed in office. He then reports Taxiles' domains correctly as the lands between the Hydaspes and Indus, omits Porus altogether and states that Peithon son of Agenor was placed over the colonies founded in India.[21] There is a fair degree of garbling here, and the reference to the colonies is particularly difficult, for there are no known foundations in western India. Berve argued that Peithon was stationed in western India as his primary base but maintained supervision of the cities newly founded in the south of the Indus valley.[22] That would be an extraordinary division of authority between two wholly disparate areas several hundred kilometres apart. It is more likely that there is an error of contraction. Justin's list gives some indication that Pompeius Trogus (the author he abridges) annotated the bare record of appointments with historical details. Nearchus is anachronistically assigned to Lycia and Pamphylia, from which he was in fact withdrawn in 329;[23] and we can only make sense of the report if we assume that Trogus mentioned that Lycia and Pamphylia, which (as all other sources attest) were included in Antigonus' satrapy in 323, had been governed by Nearchus in the past. Justin then carelessly placed Nearchus' original appointment in the Babylon distribution and omitted the rest of the note. In the same way Trogus might first have referred to Peithon's original commission in southern India, which was to populate the cities recently fortified by Alexander,[24] and then proceeded to his appointment at Babylon. Justin then operated in his usual slovenly manner and recorded only the preliminary details. If that is true, we have no way of knowing where Trogus actually located Peithon's satrapy at the time of the Babylon settlement.

There remains Diodorus (18.3.2–3), whom many have taken to be the most reliable source for the satrapy distribution. He retains the division between eastern and western satrapies, agreeing that no change was made in the east. Like Dexippus he lists the unchanged appointments and begins with the Indian satrapies. Unfortunately the text is corrupt. The notice of the confirmation of Taxiles' and Porus' kingdoms has been displaced by seventeen lines; it occurs after Seleucus' appointment to the cavalry *agema* at a stage in the list when it is irrelevant and ungrammatical. Kallenberg's transposition is necessary and unavoidable.[25] But the corruption probably needs further surgery. Diodorus goes on to describe the western Indian satrapy, and his language is most peculiar as it is transmitted: τούτων δὲ τὴν συνορίζουσαν σατραπείαν τοῖς περὶ Ταξίλην βασιλεῦσι συνεχώρησε. Tarn took this to mean that Taxiles received the western satrapy and he has been generally followed. Unfortunately this can only be sustained by translating 'he conceded the satrapy bordering on them (sc. Porus and Taxiles) to Taxiles'. That is ungrammatical. Elsewhere συνορίζειν takes the dative,[26] and the genitive τούτων can only be interpreted as possessive: 'the contiguous satrapy which belonged to them'.[27] That is not only clumsy to the last degree but also nonsensical, implying that Taxiles and Porus had some mysterious joint-ownership of western India. Given the textual disruption at this point it is fair to posit additional corruption. The traditional emendation, Πείθωνι δέ for τούτων δέ, at least restores grammar and provides a double dative construction which coheres with Diodorus' usage elsewhere.[28] The text now reads: 'he conceded to Peithon the satrapy which bordered on Taxiles' and is in exact agreement with Dexippus. Unfortunately Peithon's name depends on emendation and Diodorus cannot be taken as complete corroboration. He does, however, indicate that Porus and Taxiles had kingdoms in India proper and that there was no Macedonian control of southern India. And the most natural interpretation of the text implies that western India was under a separate command.

The only full and explicit evidence for the division of the satrapies remains that of Dexippus, who is certainly not contradicted by any other source and suggests that the situation ratified at Triparadeisus was already in force at the time of Alexander's death. It is a theoretical possibility that he has anticipated Peithon's appointment at Triparadeisus, as he seems to have done with Seleucus' appointment to Babylon.[29] But, if that were the case, we should have to assume that Peithon remained in south India, his appointment recorded in none of the sources for the Babylon settlement, except conceivably Justin. That cannot be technically disproved, but it is overwhelmingly more probable that, as Photius/Arrian implies, the southern Indian satrapy was attached to Porus' kingdom during Alexander's reign and Peithon was transferred to western India. That arrangement was approved, together with Alexander's other eastern appointments, at Babylon and again at Triparadeisus.

Alexander's final settlement amounted to a withdrawal of Macedonian control. The Indian territories were now virtually ceded to the two native princes. In fact the whole history of the Indian campaign had been turbulent and unsatisfactory. On the northwest frontier the tribes of the Cophen valley had been hard to conquer and they remained recalcitrant. The death of Nicanor had proved that their administration would be costly and dangerous. Similarly the conquest of southern India had been marked by repeated insurgency and massacre, and the pacification achieved was superficial. Even at Patala, where the Macedonian fleet was stationed, there was trouble. As soon as the king departed for the west the local tribesmen renounced his royal authority and attacked Nearchus, forcing him to take to sea prematurely.[30] Once Nearchus and the fleet were gone, the unfortunate satrap would have been in a confused vortex of hostile peoples, his writ unenforceable outside the region where his army happened to be. It was only in the northern satrapy that conditions had been relatively peaceful, under the influence of Alexander's faithful ally and subject, Taxiles, but even here the Macedonian satrap was murdered late in 325. By 324, then, it would have been painfully obvious to Alexander that India could only be fully subjugated if he returned there with his royal army and subjected it to the vicious punitive campaigns and forced resettlement that he had inflicted on the peoples of Bactria and Sogdiana. But now his military ambitions were focused on the west, with preparations for the Arabian campaign under way,[31] and a return to India was wholly unacceptable.

The alternative was reorganization – and contraction. Peithon was withdrawn from the Indus delta and transferred to the north-western satrapy. His army probably went with him, together with any European settlers left in southern India.[32] Now direct

Macedonian rule was restricted to the narrow corridor between the central Hindu Kush and the Indus valley. This was garrisoned strongly, as it had been before, and governed by a Macedonian satrap with a mercenary army. It was a relatively small area, where the army could in time hope to contain and subject the local tribesmen; and it provided automatic entry into the Punjab, if Alexander should ever wish to renew his campaigns in India. To the east was a bridgehead between the Indus and Hydaspes, governed by a native prince of proven loyalty with a European army under a Macedonian commander.[33] On its frontiers were the new cities founded by Alexander, Nicaea and Bucephala on opposite sides of the Hydaspes and an Alexandria at the great confluence of the Acesines and the Indus, now garrison centres marking the limit of empire. Beyond the Hydaspes was a vast buffer zone from the foothills of the Himalayas to the Indian Ocean, all under the nominal rule of Porus. In that territory even Porus' control may have been largely theoretical outside his own domains, and the peoples of southern India were in effect left to their own devices. This was a tactical retreat without parallel in the reign. Alexander tacitly recognized that his conquests were untenable. He retained nominal suzerainty, but over vast tracts of India he abdicated any attempt to maintain military control. For all the ostensible victories and all its dreadful carnage the campaign in India had proved a failure in the end.

Notes

1 Arr. 6.27.2; Curt. 10.1.20-1.
2 Cf. P. Julien, *Zur Verwaltung der Satrapien unter Alexander dem Grossen* (Leipzig 1914), 44–50; H. Berve, *Das Alexanderreich auf prosopographischer Grundlage* (Munich 1926), 1.268–73. There is a good short account by E. Badian, *Greece & Rome* 12 (1965), 178–80.
3 Cf. Arr. 4.22.8 (Sangaeus); Arr. 4.30.4 (Sisicottus).
4 Arr. 4.28.6. Nicanor had come fresh from his supervision of Alexandria in Caucaso, the new foundation in neighbouring Parapamisadae.
5 Arr. 5.8.3; 6.15.2. For full references see Berve (above, n. 2) 2.384–5, no. 780.
6 Arr. 5.20.7: a report from Sisicottus, 'satrap' of the Assaceni, that the tribesmen had killed their hyparch. The victim is not named, but he is usually identified as Nicanor, who disappears from history after 326 and is replaced by Philip son of Machatas by the time of the Indus voyage (Arr. 6.2.3). Arrian's terminology is very loose. Sisicottus, previously attested garrison commander at Aornus (Arr. 4.30.4), is here termed satrap and we must assume that Nicanor, previously attested satrap, is the unnamed hyparch. There are parallels. Arrian often uses hyparch as a synonym of satrap (cf. Bosworth, *CQ* 24 [1974], 56–7) and occasionally refers to city commanders as satraps (cf. 7.6.1: οἱ σατράπαι οἱ ἐκ τῶν πόλεων). But the exchange of titles at 5.20.7 is perverse and misleading, and the text may be garbled.
7 Arr. 5.29.2; 6.2.1.
8 So Plut. *Alex.* 60.15. B. Niese, *Geschichte der griech. und mak. Staaten* (Gotha 1893), 1.502, accepted the statement but found little support. It makes no difference what Porus' official title was. To his subjects he remained their monarch and to Alexander he was a vassal.
9 Arr. 6.15.4; cf. Berve (above, n. 2) 2.310, no. 619; *RE* 19.219.
10 This has been generally agreed since Kallenberg, *Philologus* 36 (1877), 318–21. E. Will, *AC* 29 (1960), 376–86, concedes that there is a common source but modifies the theory considerably, arguing that Arrian conflated two different traditions. His argument is excessively complex and has evoked dissent: cf. F. Bizière, *REG* 87 (1974), 369–74; J. Hornblower, *Hieronymus of Cardia* (Oxford 1981), 51–3.
11 Phot. 71 b 40 ff. = Arr. *Succ.* F 1.36 (Roos): τὴν μὲν παρὰ τὸν Ἰνδὸν ποταμὸν καὶ Πάταλα, τῶν ἐκείνῃ Ἰνδῶν πόλεων τὴν μεγίστην, Πώρῳ τῷ βασιλεῖ ἐπεχώρησε, τὴν δὲ παρὰ τὸν Ὑδάσπην ποταμὸν Ταξίλῃ.

12 Niese (above, n. 8) 1.505. For the rebuttal see J. Beloch, *Griechische Geschichte* 4².2.316, who seems to believe that Porus was never given the south Indian satrapy and airs the possibility of confusion in the common source. Julien (above, n. 2) 49–50 accepted Beloch's general argument but suggested that Peithon had a dual command, in north-west India and in the Delta.

13 *RE* 19.219 (Peithon [2]). Berve's earlier treatment (above, n. 2) had avoided the question of Alexander's final reorganisation, and his biographies of Peithon (no. 619) and Porus (no. 683) briefly endorsed Beloch's views, retaining Peithon in southern India until Alexander's death. It does not seem to have been noticed that he changed his mind; the later treatment was apparently unknown to H. Schaefer when he wrote the Pauly article on Porus (*RE* 22.1228).

14 W. W. Tarn, *Alexander the Great* (Cambridge 1948), 2.310–13, briefly accepted by Badian (above, no. 2) 180 with references to Berve's unmodified views.

15 Phot. 68 b 5–18 = Arr. 7.4.4–6.

16 Photius also excises the brief reference to the offices of Ptolemy and Eumenes (68 b 12); and, more importantly, he omits Arrian's note (7.4.4) that Aristobulus was his authority for Alexander's second marriage at Susa. The same occurs at 68 b 37–9, where a reference to Aristobulus is the only omission in an otherwise verbatim excerpt of Arr. 7.28.1. Any citation of sources in the *History of the Successors* is likely to have been automatically suppressed by Photius.

17 See now Hornblower (above, n. 10) 80–7, rightly rejecting Tarn's view that the geography is taken from a contemporary gazetteer.

18 Tarn (above, n. 14) 2.310. The passage is fully quoted somewhat earlier (2.276 n. 1), where Diodorus' 'additions' are printed in square brackets. Porus' name does not appear in parenthesis.

19 Phot. 64 b 10–11 = *FGrH* 100 F 8: ἦσαν δὲ ἄρχοντες Ἰνδῶν μὲν ἁπάντων Πῶρος καὶ Ταξίλης· ἀλλ' ὁ μὲν Πῶρος οἵ ἐν μέσῳ Ἰνδοῦ ποταμοῦ καὶ Ὑδάσπου νέμονται. Ταξίλης δὲ τῶν λοιπῶν. Πείθων δέ τις τούτοις ὁμόρων ἡγεῖτο πλὴν Παρ<οπ>αμισαδῶν.

20 The error recurs at *Metz Epitome* 121, whereas the Alexander Romance proper seems to have the facts right (cf. R. Merkelbach, *Die Quellen des gr. Alexanderromans* 249).

21 Justin 12.4.20: *terras inter amnes Hydaspen et Indum Taxiles habebat, in colonias in Indis conditas Pithon mittitur.*

22 Berve, *RE* 19.219 (this is in fact a revival of Julien's suggestion of a divided satrapy [see above, n. 12]).

23 Justin 13.4.15. For Nearchus' earlier command and recall see Arr. 3.6.6; 4.7.2. The historical notes on the appointments may be ultimately derived from Hieronymus himself. Eumenes' assignment in Cappadocia is usually reported with a brief note on the area's history under Alexander (Diod. 18.3.3; Plut. *Eum.* 3.3; Curt. 10.10.3) and the résumé presumably derives from the common source, Hieronymus, who was evidently interested in Cappadocia (App. *Mithr.* 8.25 = *FGrH* 154 F 3).

24 Arr. 6.17.4, 20.2. Niese (above, n. 8) 1.504 n.6 had already seen the connexion.

25 Hornblower (see above, n. 10) 96 has argued for the retention of the tradition, suggesting that Diodorus rearranged the appointments and became muddled doing so. This does not explain the disruption of grammar and the lone intrusive infinitive (ὁμοίως εἶναι).

26 18.3.1: Εὐμένει δὲ Παφλαγονίαν . . . καὶ πάσας τὰς συνοριζούσας ταύταις χώρας. 18.39.6: τῆς δὲ Ἰνδικῆς τὰ μὲν συνορίζοντα Παροπανισάδαις Πείθωνι.

27 Goukowsky's Budé translation reads: 'quant à la satrapie limitrophe de ces royaumes, il l'accorda au roi Taxile.' That is ambiguous, leaving it undecided whether or not the satrapy was part of the kingdoms.

28 Another approach, which is perhaps preferable, is to retain τούτων as a partitive genitive referring to the totality of the satrapies mentioned in the previous sentence and to add Peithon's name at the end of the clause (συνεχώρησε <Πείθωνι>): 'it was resolved to leave the satrapies under the same commanders (likewise that Taxiles and Porus should be masters of their own kingdoms, as Alexander himself had ordained). Of these satrapies he assigned to Peithon the one contiguous with Taxiles''.

29 *FGrH* 100 F 8.6 (Archon of Pella was actually satrap of Babylonia in 323). Carmania is also falsely attributed to Neoptolemus instead of Tlepolemus, perhaps through scribal error. The supposed muddle over Susiana (cf. Tarn 2.313 ff.) is a red herring; the manuscript reading is

Σογδιανῶν and the traditional emendation to Σουσιανῶν is wholly unjustified (cf. *CP* 78 [1983], 160).

30 Strabo 15.2.5 (721) = *FGrH* 133 F 1a.

31 The preparation of the fleet for Arabia was well under way by the spring of 323 (Arr. 7.19.3–6; Strabo 16.1.11 [741]). Tarn's view (2.394–6) that the expedition was for exploration not conquest is at total variance with the sources and has only curiosity value. Interestingly Tarn stresses Alexander's ceding of territory to Porus as a crucial turning point, the move from conquest to exploration, and somewhat contentiously states: 'those who wish to rule the world do not of themselves give away hard won provinces' (2.398). 'Of themselves' is the vital point. Alexander's renunciation of territories in India was an acknowledgement that he could not hold them with his present forces and present ambitions. He had certainly not given up imperial aspirations elsewhere. *Reculer pour mieux sauter* is the best description of his final arrangements in India.

32 There is no evidence that the embryonic foundations at the Indus mouth continued their existence (for the scanty testimonia see V. Tscherikower, *Die hellenistischen Städtegründungen* [*Philologus* Suppl. 19: Leipzig 1927], 109). Tarn (above, n. 14) 2.239 went so far as to dispute whether Alexander founded any cities as such in southern India.

33 Eudamus remained in India until 317, when he returned to the war in the west, taking with him the 120 elephants acquired by his assassination of Porus (Diod. 19.14.8).

7

ALEXANDER
AS GENERAL

Introduction

Alexander's military exploits extended the Macedonian empire as far east as India. There is no question that he was a spectacularly successful general, and that he had a demonstrated brilliance for battle and siege tactics (cf. Sources 51 and 52 on Tyre). His own willingness to fight rather than hold back until battles were over was both commendable in a general and an inspiration to his troops; Alexander always led the charge, and was always to be found in the thick of fighting. That meant that he, too, was often wounded (cf. Sources 6, 71, 72, 85). He was quick to identify with his men, and to suffer the same hardships as they did (see Source 80), nor would he abandon them, often risking great personal danger (cf. Sources 85, 86). Although Alexander battled against various tribes and people on many occasions, some of which were minor and nothing more than skirmishes, four major or 'set' battles from his reign are usually considered especially important and represent his military prowess at its best. These are the three battles against the Persians at Granicus (334), Issus (333) and Gaugamela (331),[1] and the battle against the Indian prince Porus at the Hydaspes river (326).[2]

However, the Homeric nature of the battles and magnitude of the military victories that we associate with Alexander may be questioned, and they were perhaps the products of his own propaganda. He very likely told the court historian Callisthenes of Olynthus what to say about his victory over Darius III at the battle of Issus in 333,[3] after which he started to call himself King of Asia. Yet, he allowed Darius to escape from the battle, and rather than pursue him to consolidate his gains he pushed south into Egypt (cf. Source 49), allowing Darius to regroup his forces and bring Alexander to battle again at Gaugamela in 331. After the defeat of Porus Alexander had struck a commemorative coinage that exaggerated his victory, for while he effected a brilliant river crossing in reality Porus was outnumbered and outclassed by the superbly drilled Macedonian phalanx, and he and his army never stood a chance. Finally, we ought to note that Alexander's men twice mutinied on him (326 and 324), hardly a sign of confidence in a general and a king.[4]

Ancient sources

85 At Issus he (Alexander) was run through the thigh with a sword by Darius (as Chares relates), who encountered him hand to hand. Alexander also himself, writing the truth with all sincerity to Antipater, said, that it was my fortune to be wounded with a poniard in the thigh, but no ill symptoms attended it either when it was newly done or afterwards during the cure (Chares, *FGrH* 125 F 6 = [Plut.] *Mor.* 341c).

86 While the siege of the city was in progress,[5] he made an expedition against the Arabians who dwelt in the neighbourhood of Mount Antilibanus. On this occasion he risked his life to save his tutor, Lysimachus, who insisted on following him, declaring himself to be neither older nor weaker than Phoenix. But when the force drew near the mountains, they abandoned their horses and proceeded on foot, and most of them got far on in advance. Alexander himself, however, would not consent to abandon the worn and weary Lysimachus, since evening was already coming on and the enemy were near, but sought to encourage him and carry him along. Before he was aware of it, therefore, he was separated from his army with a few followers, and had to spend a night of darkness and intense cold in a region that was rough and difficult. In this plight, he saw far off a number of scattered fires which the enemy was burning. So, since he was confident in his own agility, and was ever wont to cheer the Macedonians in their perplexities by sharing their toils, he ran to the nearest camp-fire. Two barbarians who were sitting at the fire he dispatched with his dagger, and snatching up a fire-brand, brought it to his own party. These kindled a great fire and at once frightened some of the enemy into flight, routed others who came up against them, and spent the night without further peril. Such, then, is the account we have from Chares (*FGrH* 125 F 7 = Plut. *Alex.* 24.10–14).

Modern works

In the modern extract below, Major General J.F.C. Fuller deals generally with Alexander's military prowess. I would especially recommend the articles by A. Devine, cited in the additional reading, which deal not only with Alexander's strategy but also with the nature of the sources.

J.F.C. Fuller, *The Generalship of Alexander the Great* (New Brunswick: 1960), pp. 284–305.[6]

Additional reading

A.R. Burn, 'The Generalship of Alexander', *Greece and Rome*[2] 12 (1965), pp. 140–154.

A.M. Devine, 'Grand Tactics at Gaugamela', *Phoenix* 29 (1975), pp. 374–385.

—— , 'The Strategies of Alexander the Great and Darius III in the Issus Campaign (333 BC)', *Ancient World* 12 (1985), pp. 25–38.

—— , 'Grand Tactics at the Battle of Issus', *Ancient World* 12 (1985), pp. 39–59.

—-, 'The Battle of Gaugamela: A Tactical and Source-Critical Study', *Ancient World* 13 (1986), pp. 87–115.

—— , 'The Battle of Hydaspes: A Tactical and Source-Critical Study', *Ancient World* 16 (1987), pp. 91–113.

—— , 'A Pawn-Sacrifice at the Battle of the Granicus: The Origins of a Favorite Stratagem of Alexander the Great', *Ancient World* 18 (1988), pp. 3–20.

—— , 'Alexander the Great', in J. Hackett (ed.), *Warfare in the Ancient World* (New York: 1989), pp. 104–129.

D. Engels, *Alexander the Great and the Logistics of the Macedonian Army* (Berkeley and Los Angeles, CA: 1978).

N.G.L. Hammond, 'The Battle of the Granicus River', *Journal of Hellenic Studies* 100 (1980), pp. 73–88.

R.D. Milns, 'The Army of Alexander the Great', in E. Badian (ed.), *Alexandre le Grand, Image et Réalité*, Fondation Hardt, *Entretiens* 22 (Geneva: 1976), pp. 87–136.

P. Romane, 'Alexander's Siege of Tyre', *Ancient World* 16 (1987), pp. 79–90.

—— , 'Alexander's Siege of Gaza', *Ancient World* 18 (1988), pp. 21–30.

W.W. Tarn, *Alexander the Great* 2 (Cambridge: 1948), Appendices 1–6, 'Military', pp. 135–198.

Notes

1 On Alexander in Persia, see Chapter 5.
2 On Alexander in India, see Chapter 6.
3 On the problem of the sources, see Chapter 1.
4 On this aspect, see Chapter 11.
5 The siege of Tyre; for what comes before this passage, see Source 51.
6 © 1960 by John Frederick Charles Fuller. Reprinted by permission of Rutgers University Press.

ALEXANDER AS STRATEGIST

J.F.C. Fuller

At the opening of the eighteenth century the word 'strategy' – 'the art of the general (*strateges*)' – was added to the military vocabulary to denote the methodical manoeuvres, marches and counter-marches prevalent in the age of strictly limited wars. Today, in most dictionaries, it is defined as the science or art of projecting and directing military movements, and after the Napoleonic wars, which, unlike the wars of the twentieth century, were still simple enough to bear some resemblance to Alexander's, Clausewitz defined strategy as follows:

> Strategy is the employment of battle to gain the end in war; it must therefore give an aim to the whole military action, which must be in accordance with the object of the war; in other words, strategy forms the plan of the war, and to this end it links together the series of acts which are to lead to the final decision, that is to say, it makes the plan for the separate campaigns and regulates the combats to be fought in each.

He adds that at its highest point 'strategy borders on political science, or rather . . . the two become one'.[1]

Alexander was as fully aware as Clausewitz that strategy employs the battle to gain the end in war. But where he profoundly differs from him is in the definition of the end – that is, in the aim or object of the war. In Clausewitz's days the twentieth-century democratic conception that the object is to annihilate the enemy, not only militarily, but politically, economically and socially as well, had not yet fuddled man's mind. To Clausewitz war was a clash between armed forces which protected their respective civil populations; each contended for a political aim, and when one side gained a decisive victory, the vanquished automatically sued for peace, and the victor's political aim was gained in a negotiated treaty. But Alexander's aim was not to bring Darius to terms, it was to appropriate his empire, and, were his conquest to be of profit to him, he had not only to defeat the Persian army but win his acceptance in the eyes of the Persian peoples. There was no question of suing for peace, which after his crushing defeat at Issus Darius vainly attempted to do, nor of a negotiated treaty, because Alexander's aim was conquest, and at the minimum expenditure of force and the minimum dislocation and damage of the Persian empire: his policy limited and moderated his strategy.

This limitation is noticed by Polybius in a citation he makes from a speech delivered by Alexander Isius concerning Philip V of Macedon (221–179 B.C.). The orator said that Philip avoided meeting his enemies face to face, and instead employed his time in burning and plundering cities.

> Yet [he added] former kings of Macedonia had not adopted this plan, but one exactly the reverse: for they were continually fighting with each other in the open field, but rarely destroyed and ruined cities. This was shown clearly by Alexander's war in Asia against King Darius; and again in the contentions between his successors . . . they had been prompt to war against each other

in the open field, and to do everything they could to conquer each other in arms, but had spared the cities, that they might rule them if they conquered, and be honoured by their subjects. But that a man should abandon war, and yet destroy that for which the war was undertaken, seemed an act of madness, and madness of a very violent sort.[2]

It was because Alexander's aim was conquest, and not vengeance or spoliation, that, according to Justin, when 'marching forward in quest of the enemy, he kept the soldiers from ravaging Asia, telling them that "they ought to spare their own property, and not destroy what they came to possess"'.[3] Wilcken points out that 'his extensive money gifts to his army were a compensation for the prohibition of plundering the conquered districts, which for political reasons he thought necessary'.[4] While the aim of his strategy was to win great battles, the aim of his policy was to pacify and not antagonize his enemy, so as to limit the number of battles he would have to fight. In idea it was not far removed from the policy which Themistocles recommended to the Athenians after Salamis: 'I have often myself witnessed occasions, and I have heard of many more from others where men who had been conquered by an enemy, having been driven quite to desperation, have renewed the fight, and retrieved their former disasters.'[5] The same advice was given by Jason of Pherae to the Thebans after Leuctra. 'It behoves you to reflect', he said, 'that the Lacedaemonians, if they be forced to relinquish the hope of life, will fight with desperation; and the divine powers, as it seems, often take delight in making the little great, and the great little.'[6]

It was because Alexander's aim was to achieve, as far as it was possible, a bloodless conquest, that he drew so distinct a line between the Persian army and the Persian peoples; the defeat of the army was his strategical aim; the winning over of the peoples his political aim. The first was the means to attain the second, because, as long as the Persian army held the field, there was no certain assurance that the people would willingly accept him. Alexander needed no telling that 'war is only a part of political intercourse, therefore by no means an independent thing in itself'.[7]

After he had defined strategy, Clausewitz turned to the more important strategical principles, and these are worth quoting because they show that, had Clausewitz enumerated them in the fourth century B.C., Alexander would have had little to learn from them; in fact he might have tendered the German military theorist some useful advice.

> There are three principal objects [he writes] in carrying on war:
>
> (*a*) to conquer and destroy the enemy's armed forces.
>
> (*b*) to get possession of the material elements of aggression, and of the other sources of existence of the hostile army.
>
> (*c*) To gain public opinion.[8]

The first object calls for no comment: to remember the battles of the Granicus, Issus, Arbela, and the Hydaspes is sufficient.

The second needs none either, because once Alexander had seized the Persian treasure at Susa and Persepolis, he deprived Darius of his most important means of recruiting another army, and it prevented Darius from fomenting rebellions in his enemy's rear by bribery. Gold and silver, and not 'principal towns, magazines and great fortresses', were the chief 'material elements' in Alexander's day.

The third object – public opinion – is, according to Clausewitz, 'ultimately gained by great victories, and by the possession of the enemy's capital'. Although in the eighteenth and nineteenth centuries the occupation of the enemy's capital more frequently than not brought war to an end,[9] in classical times, except for Rome,[10] strictly speaking there were no capital cities; instead there were city-states, or royal residences, such as Babylon, Susa and Persepolis.[11] With the exception of war between two city-states, because the occupation of cities and royal residences did not bring war to an end, as has several times been pointed out in these pages, Alexander substituted the ultra-modern conception of subversion of the enemy's people. Russia is today the leading exponent of this.

Clausewitz next lays down five strategical principles.

The first, and in his opinion the most important, is: 'to employ *all* the forces which we can make available with the *utmost* energy'.

'The second is to concentrate our force ... at the point where the decisive blows are to be struck, to run the risk even of being at a disadvantage at other points, in order to make sure of the result at the decisive point. The success at that point will compensate for all defeats at secondary points'.

'The third principle is: not to lose time.... By rapidity many measures of the enemy are nipped in the bud, and public opinion is gained in our favour'.

The fourth is surprise: '... it is the most powerful element of victory'.

And the last is: 'to follow up the success we gain with the utmost energy. The pursuit of the enemy when defeated is the only means of gathering up the fruits of victory.'[12]

After what we have recorded on Alexander's generalship, and because these principles will be discussed in the next section, it is unnecessary to point out here that the value of utmost energy, concentration at the decisive point, rapidity of movement, surprise and pursuit were as clearly apparent to Alexander as they were to Clausewitz.

In all strategical problems which embrace war, either in its entirety or in part, there are two outstanding strategical factors – the establishment of secure bases and secure communications. The first may be compared with the foundations of a house, they must be sufficiently substantial to bear the weight of the superstructure; the second is the scaffolding, which enables the builders to maintain contact with the ground (base), and progressively feed the masons with the materials they require. Should the foundations sink, the superstructure will be imperilled; should the scaffolding collapse, its erection cannot be continued until the scaffolding is restored.

When a war or campaign is compared with the superstructure, the importance of the base – its starting point – at once becomes apparent, and no general has understood this better than Alexander. First he established a secure home base – that is, his initial or main base – by his Danubian campaign and the destruction of Thebes. The Danubian campaign was a strategical operation, the establishment of a secure northern frontier; the destruction of Thebes a political operation, the establishment of a quiescent inner front. They were complementary; one removed a danger that might have been exploited by anti-Macedonian factions within Greece, the other resulted in the paralysis of these factions, and thereby deprived the Thracian and

Illyrian tribesmen of all hope of being able to take advantage of revolt within Greece. Together they secured the Macedonian home base throughout Alexander's reign.

Next, Alexander established his base of operations against Persia on the eastern coast of the Aegean, which, before he moved eastward, he secured by his victory on the Granicus. It did not secure the sea-link between his base of operations and his home base, because naval command was in his enemy's hands. That was why, because there was no Persian army west of the Halys which could impede his advance, his strategy was to strike at his enemy's naval bases, the more important of which lay in Phoenicia and Cyprus. This strategy is so clearly revealed in his speech to his generals immediately before the siege of Tyre, that it is worth reverting to it. With his home base in mind, it will be remembered that Alexander said: 'I am apprehensive lest, while we advance with our forces toward Babylon and in pursuit of Darius, the Persians should again conquer the maritime districts, and transfer the war into Greece.' The offer of non-belligerence made to him by the Tyrians was insufficient; it was imperative that Tyre and Egypt should be occupied, for then, as he said, 'no anxiety about Greece and our land will any longer remain'. He also saw that, when the Phoenician cities were threatened, the high probability was that the Phoenician fleets would come over to him and give him 'absolute sovereignty of the sea'. The aim of his strategy, then, was not only to deprive his enemy of his sea power, but simultaneously to acquire it and thereby win the command of the eastern Mediterranean, and secure his home base and his conquests in Asia Minor for good and all. Only then did he consider that he would be free to renew his land operations against Darius.

Again, when he reached Arbela, he abandoned his pursuit to strike at the 'material' base of his enemy's military power; first he occupied Babylon, and next seized the treasure stored at Susa and Persepolis. With that in his hands, he was in a position of strength such as the French would have been in if, in 1940, they had decisively defeated the Germans, and, instead of pursuing them, had occupied the Ruhr – the material base of the German fighting forces. Here again, it will be seen that Alexander's strategy led to the augmentation of his own power, not by destroying the foundations of his enemy's power, but by appropriating them. As the Persian fleet had passed into his hands, so did the Persian treasure. He became financial master of Asia, and Darius a bankrupt.

After the death of Darius his first action was not to pursue the usurper Bessus, but to secure his rear – his most advanced base – by subduing the tribesmen of the Elburz mountains. As soon as this had been done, he set out after Bessus; but directly he learnt of the revolt of Satibarzanes, he broke off the chase to re-establish his authority over his rear before he continued. In Sogdiana he followed an identical strategy. After the capture of Bessus, suddenly he found himself in an extraordinary predicament; the revolt of Spitamenes not only threatened his base at Maracanda, but deprived him of Cyropolis and his frontier posts on the Jaxartes. He was between two forest fires – which should he extinguish first? Should he turn on Spitamenes, the leader of the revolt? No, he must first secure his base of operations against him, and this meant the reoccupation of Cyropolis, and the defeat of the Scythians. Once this had been done his rear was secure, and he was free to deal with Spitamenes. Later, the same basic strategy was followed. When he had occupied the tribesmen's cities in the Swat valley, he did not march on their stronghold at Aornus, but moved southward into the Peshawar valley to establish a firm base of operations from which he could operate against Aornus without imperilling his communications. Soon after this he established his advanced base at Taxila before proceeding against Porus.

It is important to remember that the means Alexander used to make secure the more important bases, that covered extensive territories, were more political than military. Their administration was carefully organized, peaceful conditions were restored, trade was stimulated, and the garrisons left in them were police forces and colonists rather than armies of occupation. As his conquests extended, his empire progressively took form; he won his peace as he waged his war,[13] and bound the whole into one by means of his communications.

Strategy today is so intimately related to communications – road, rail, river, canal, sea and air – that it is difficult to picture a strategical problem in which there are no maps, and movements are limited to a few caravan routes and an unknown number of pack-ways and trails connecting village with village.[14] In Greece there were no made-up roads, except in the vicinity of important sanctuaries, and no road-construction is recorded during the reigns of Alexander and his successors.[15] But, as described in chapter 4, [in Fuller], since the days of Darius I a number of main roads had existed in the Persian empire, and it was possible to travel by road from Ephesus, on the Aegean, by way of Sardes, Babylon, Ecbatana and Bactra to Taxila. This great thoroughfare was the axis of Alexander's communications – a kind of trans-Siberian railway.

In addition to this road, and a number which branched from it, Alexander had the sea, and at the beginning of the war it was one of Antipater's tasks to keep open the passage of the Dardanelles. After the fall of Tyre, when the threat to the Aegean was eliminated, this responsibility was delegated to Philoxenes who, according to Plutarch, was appointed 'governor of the coast-line of Asia Minor',[16] or what would seem a more appropriate title – Base Commandant. His headquarters were at Ephesus–the western terminus of the axial road–and there he collected supplies and reinforcements coming from Macedonia and Greece, and when required dispatched them in convoys to Alexander. When Susa was occupied, Alexander placed Menes, son of Dionysius, in command of sea communications between Phoenicia and the west,[17] and when the Thessalians' service was terminated, he was instructed to arrange for their transit by sea from Syria to Euboea.[18] Finally toward the close of his reign, Alexander was engaged on opening a sea-way from Patala on the Indus to Babylon on the Euphrates, to help him to hold India.

From west to east, with the axial road as its backbone, Alexander divided his land communications into sections, each under a responsible officer. The most westerly section included Asia Minor, and was allotted to Antigonus with his headquarters at Celaenae in Phrygia. East of it and to some undefined point eastward – possibly Meshed or Herat – came the next section, first under Parmenion and later under Cleander, with headquarters at Ecbatana. Then there was probably the Bactrian section, and possibly east of it the Indian, but of these sections nothing is known.

Although we have no details of the organization of Alexander's communications, because of the ease with which reinforcements constantly reached him, it is not difficult to supply them. Depots, at which supplies were collected from the surrounding country, and staging camps, each a day's march from the other, must either have been established or taken over from the Persians in each section along the axial road. Further, it would appear that the Persian postal relay system was retained and improved upon, because we are told by Plutarch that, when Alexander was at

Samarkand, 'some people came bringing Greek fruit to the king from the sea-board'[19] – a distance of well over 3,000 miles. Incidentally, this fruit was the indirect cause of the death of Cleitus, because Alexander was so struck with its 'beauty and perfection' that he asked him to share some with him at the fatal supper.

In only one of his Asiatic campaigns did Alexander lose touch with his home base, and then only for twenty-four hours before the battle of Issus; only once is it recorded that his supply system broke down, and that was during his march across Gedrosia.[20] This is sufficient proof of the superb staff work of his headquarters.

His lack of maps was made good by what must have been a highly organized intelligence service. He always tried to obtain advance information about the country he decided to conquer, and there was nothing adventurous in his movements. Like Napoleon and Wellington, whenever possible he saw things for himself, and from his actions it may be judged that he held with Napoleon that, 'A general who has to see things through other people's eyes will never be able to command an army as it should be commanded.' And he could, with truth, have said with Wellington: 'The real reason why I succeeded . . . is because I was always on the spot. I saw everything, and did everything myself.' When this was not possible, as happened repeatedly, he stepped into his enemy's shoes, looked at the situation through his enemy's eyes, and fathomed his intentions. Although he was one of the most audacious generals in history, the risks he accepted were seldom left to chance; they were carefully weighed and calculated probabilities.

As tactician

As a tactician, Alexander's greatest asset was the army he inherited from his father; without it, and in spite of his genius, his conquests would be inconceivable – it was an instrument that exactly suited his craft. Its composition has been dealt with in Chapter 2 [in Fuller], here its organization will be briefly examined, because it was from its organization that Alexander was able to develop his tactics.

On the opening page of his great work *On War*, Clausewitz makes a very simple yet profound remark. It is, that 'War is nothing but a duel on an extensive scale', and he likens it to a struggle between two wrestlers; between two pugilists would be a more apt comparison. If so, then the primary elements of tactics are to be seen in their simplest form in a fight between two unarmed men. They are: to think, to guard, to move and to hit.

Before a bout opens, each man must consider how best to knock out his adversary, and though as the fight proceeds he may be compelled to modify his means, he must never abandon his aim. At the start he must assume a defensive attitude until he has measured up his opponent. Next, he must move under cover of his defence towards him, and lastly by foot-play, and still under cover of his defence, he must assume the offensive and attempt to knock him out. In military terms, the four primary tactical elements are: the aim or object, security, mobility and offensive power.

If the two pugilists are skilled in their art, they will recognize the value of three accentuating elements. They will economize their physical force, so as not to exhaust themselves prematurely; they will concentrate their blows against the decisive point selected, the left or right of their opponent's jaw, or his solar plexus, and throughout will attempt to surprise him – that is, take him off-guard, or do something which he does not expect, or cannot guard against. In military terms these accentuating elements are: economy of force, concentration of force, and surprise.

With this elementary picture in mind, Philip's tactical organization can be considered. It was threefold, not merely a phalanx with protective bodies of cavalry on its flanks, as was then customary, but a phalanx with two fighting arms, each of which was more mobile than the trunk, each of which could be used either to guard or to hit, and of which the right was the more powerful, because Philip decided to concentrate his punching-power in it. His army – whether intentionally, accidentally, or experimentally does not matter – was a gigantic pugilist, and in the hands of a skilled leader it could fight as such.

The only extraneous point worth making is that, although in the inter-city wars the punching had been done almost entirely by infantry, Philip decided that it should be done by cavalry; not only because cavalry was more mobile than infantry, and so could be concentrated more rapidly against the point of decision, but also because throughout history there has been something irresistible and terrifying in the cavalry charge, and the foot soldier has always dreaded being trampled by horsemen – hence the value of mounted over foot police. In other words, provided that cavalry could charge, the moral effect produced by the combination of two living creatures – man and horse – coupled with mobility, was greater than anything the foot soldier could produce.

In most military text books, more particularly in those known as *Field Service Regulations,* a list of the principles of war will be found. Five, as propounded by Clausewitz, have already been given. There are several versions of these so-called principles, but they are no more than pegs on which to hang our tactical thoughts. There is nothing irrevocable about them; sometimes they may be discarded with impunity; but as a study of military history will show, they should only be discarded after deep consideration. They are very important guides rather than principles, and in the writer's opinion the simplest and most useful are derived from the seven tactical elements mentioned above – aim or object, security, mobility, offensive power, economy of force, concentration of force, and surprise. Further, they are as applicable to strategy (operations in plan) as to tactics (operations in action), two terms which should never be separated by a bulkhead, because their components flow into each other and together constitute the art of war, which, incidentally, was cleverly defined by Captain Cochegrue when he said: 'In great battles, he endeavoured always to give blows without receiving them, which is, and always will be, the only problem to solve in war.'[21] It is illuminating to examine the military activities of Alexander by applying to them, in turn, the seven principles cited.

The principle of the maintenance of the aim

'To conquer is nothing, one must profit from one's success' – Napoleon.

The first point to note in all Alexander's tactical operations is, that they were invariably subordinated to the strategical aim of their respective campaigns. For example, when he acceded to the throne of Macedonia and when Greece was in turmoil, because he planned war with Persia, his strategical aim was to establish his authority as rapidly and peacefully as he could, and he did so with such lightning-like speed, that a display of tactical force was sufficient to attain it without bloodshed. Soon after this, when the Thebans revolted, because his aim was still the same, he offered terms of surrender; but when they refused them, to paralyse their allies he obliterated Thebes, and attained his aim at the cost of one city. Again, after his victory at Issus, he abandoned his pursuit and laid siege to Tyre in order to maintain his strategic aim, which was then the elimination of his enemy's naval power. After Arbela, again he sacrificed pursuit in order to occupy Babylon and seize Susa and Persepolis, because the treasure stored in these cities was the mainstay of Persian political and military power. In all his campaigns it was the same; his strategical aim was subordinated to his political aim, and his tactical aim to his strategical aim, and the result was systematic and methodical conquest.

In each of his four great battles his aim was to assault from a secure base and annihilate his enemy's power of resistance; his base was his order of battle which, except in the battle of the Hydaspes, he never varied. With the phalanx as his chest, his left arm was his left wing, which he used defensively; and his right arm his right wing, used offensively to break through the enemy's front, and thereby disrupt his organization. Penetration was his tactical means, and he held fast to it in all his great battles. At the Granicus, he broke through the Persian cavalry at the head of his Companion cavalry; at Issus, he broke through the Persian infantry, and at Arbela he broke through a gap in the Persian front. Only at the Hydaspes, his most skilfully fought battle, did he make use of his phalanx to deliver the knock-out blow, and that was because his cavalry horses would not face the Indian elephants.

During the heat of the battle he never lost sight of his tactical aim. At the Granicus, once he had effected a penetration, he turned on the Greek mercenary infantry; he did the same at Issus; at Arbela, first – as assumed – he came to the help of his hard-pressed right wing, and then – as is known – he set out to rescue his left wing, which was hard pressed by Mazaeus, that is, where the battle was still in doubt. At the sieges of Tyre, Gaza and Aornus, once he had made up his mind, the tenacity with which he held fast to his tactical aim is remarkable. But he was not a pigheaded general. When he decided to capture the island of Peuce in his Danubian campaign, and he found that it would be both costly and difficult, he substituted for its capture a more profitable operation; at the Persian Gates he did the same, and when in his campaign against the Malli, with cavalry alone he attacked the Indians who were holding the opposite bank of the Ravi, directly it became apparent to him that they intended to stand up to his assault, he broke off the engagement, surrounded them with his horsemen, and awaited the arrival of his infantry. Although he was always ready to attempt the seemingly impossible, he was just as ready to avoid the obviously unprofitable.

The principle of security

'The whole art of war consists in a well-reasoned and extremely circumspect defensive, followed by rapid and audacious attack' – Napoleon.

Unfortunately, little has been recorded of the security measures adopted by Alexander while at rest, on the line of march, or in battle. Now and again it is recorded that he fortified his camp, ordered entrenchments to be dug, and picketed the road along which he marched, as he did in the Elburz mountains. On that occasion, Arrian writes, whenever he thought there was danger along the road, he posted pickets on its flanks to protect the marching troops from the hillmen on the heights above them.[22] Also, he frequently resorted to night movements to hide his intentions or to surprise his enemy, and notably so before the battles of Arbela and the Hydaspes and during the Persepolis campaign. The probable reason for the lack of information is that, unlike Julius Caesar, Alexander was not an entrenching general; the tactical conditions of his campaigns did not require him to be so, because the Persians seldom assumed the offensive, and the tribesmen he conquered did not indulge in night attacks.

In battle, the security of his army was guaranteed by its organization, coupled with its usual oblique approach. Its centre was impenetrable as long as the phalanx maintained its dressing, and its mobile wings, composed as they were of infantry and cavalry, were self-protective; they could adapt themselves to attack or defence as occasion demanded. Although reserves were hitherto unknown, at Issus Alexander is said to have held the Greek mercenaries in reserve, and because at Arbela the Macedonian front was far outflanked by the Persian, to secure his front from an attack in flank and rear he drew up a second, or reserve, phalanx behind it, which, when the two wings on the flanks of the forward phalanx were drawn backward, enabled a hollow square to be formed, a formation which offered all-round defence. Yet it is strange that, neither at Issus nor Arbela, did he attempt to overcome the one great danger to his phalanx. It was that, due to its oblique approach and the speed of his assault on its right, it was liable to break in half, as it did in both these battles. To rectify this, all that was necessary was to withdraw one battalion of the phalanx and post it in rear of the centre of the others, so that, should a gap occur in the ranks in front, it could at once be filled by the battalion in rear.

Of the various protective means used by Alexander, the most interesting is his use of the catapult as field artillery. Though for long used as a siege weapon, until his campaign in Illyria it had never been brought into the field. It was then that for the first time in the history of war catapults were deployed to cover a river crossing, as again they were in the battle with the Scythians on the Jaxartes. Also, they were used with considerable effect to cover the assaults on Aornus and elsewhere. Wherever Alexander went his field artillery accompanied him, and after his death, in the hands of his successors it became a recognized arm in every well-organized army, and remained the artillery of the world until the introduction of cannon. Alexander has the distinction of being the first field gunner in history.

The principle of mobility

'In the art of war, as in mechanics, velocity is the grand element between weight and force' – Napoleon.

Except for Napoleon, probably no other general appreciated as fully as Alexander the value of mobility in war. From the opening of his career until its close, speed dominated all his movements, and the result was that, by increasing the time at his disposal, in any given period he could proportionately accomplish more than his opponent.

In his first campaign his enemies were so completely paralysed by the rapidity of his advance that they were not allowed time enough to assemble their forces; in his advance on the Cilician Gates, although it was reported to Arsames, who held the pass, Arsames was so unhinged by his enemy's speed that he abandoned it. The dividends paid by speed, whether against an organized enemy on the plains, or hillmen in the mountains, were a long series of surprises, which enabled Alexander to accomplish with a fraction of his forces what at a slower pace might have demanded his whole army.

He was the first general in history to understand that the fruits of a great battle are to be gathered in the pursuit. At the battle of Arbela, directly he had assured himself of the safety of his left wing, he turned about his Companion cavalry, and in spite of their exhausted horses followed Darius, and pressed on to Arbela, thirty miles east of the battlefield. Alter his defeat of Ariobarzanes at the Persian Gates, in spite of a most fatiguing night march and the exertions of the battle, he pressed on to Persepolis, some eighty to 100 miles away, and reached it at dawn on the following morning. Also, in the heat of a Persian summer and in a region largely devoid of water, his pursuit of Darius was kept up for seven days at the average daily speed of either thirty or thirty-six miles. As Tarn observes: he taught the West a lesson his successors did not forget, 'that in warfare distance was no longer a prohibitive factor'.[23] Also he taught the West the advantage of marching in two divisions; one composed of a selected body of troops marching light, and the other of the slower moving troops and the impedimenta.

That the velocity of his movements on occasion led him into difficulties is understandable. It seems to have done so during his Illyrian campaign, when Glaucias came up on his rear, and it certainly did so at Issus, when he lost his communications and was surprised. But during his twelve years of campaigning the exceptions are so rare that they prove the rule that he who can move twice as fast as his opponent doubles his operative time and thereby halves it for his opponent. As a winner of time Alexander has few equals.

The principle of the offensive

'In short, I think like Frederick, one should always be the first to attack'
– Napoleon.

The reason why all the great Captains were offensively-minded was not only because battle is the tactical aim in war but also because, as Moltke pointed out in his *Instructions for the Commanders of Large Formations*: 'The offensive knows what it wants', whereas 'the defensive is in a state of uncertainty'. In other words: the initiative is more readily gained by offensive than by defensive action; not only does it enable a general to develop his plan, select his point of attack, and surprise his adversary, but it exalts the spirit of his troops – as Frederick said: 'To conquer is to advance'. Though Napoleon was forced on the defensive at Leipzig, La Rothière and Arcis, he never once set out to fight a defensive battle; nor did Alexander, and all his offensive battles were successful.

What is remarkable about them is, that he overcame his several opponents by a tactics shaped to fit each occasion. Thus, with same certainty with which he attacked his known opponents – Greek mercenaries or Persian cavalry – he overcame opponents who before he fought them were entirely unknown to him; the Scythians, Indian hillmen, and Porus with his elephants. In his many battles his tactical genius is apparent in the lightning-like speed with which he adapted his actions to novel circumstances; he never copied his former successes, and this was the main reason why success followed success.

Although in his great battles he relied on his Companion cavalry as his main offensive arm, he never brought it into action until he was certain that its assault would prove decisive. At the Granicus, because of the faulty deployment of the Persian cavalry, directly his feint against the Persian left began to tell, he charged instantly, and the battle was virtually won before the rest of his troops had crossed the river. At Issus he held back his assault until he had cleared his right flank, then in a headlong charge he burst through the Persian infantry; and at Arbela he fought a protracted defensive engagement with his right flank guard, which drew his enemy in and thereby created the opportunity for his decisive cavalry charge. When it came, in a flash he seized the initiative, and swept through the gap in the Persian front. The timing was perfect, and as Napoleon once said. 'The fate of a battle is a question of a single moment, a single thought . . . the decisive moment arrives, the moral spark is kindled, and the smallest reserve force settles the argument.'[24] And again: 'There is a moment in engagements when the least manoeuvre is decisive and gives the victory; it is the one drop of water which makes the vessel run over.'[25] The last reserve in his right wing was his Companion cavalry, and its assault was decisive, as was the assault of his phalanx at the battle of the Hydaspes.

The principles of economy and concentration of force

'The art of war consists in bringing to bear with an inferior army a superiority of force at the point at which one attacks or is attacked' – Napoleon.

These two principles are closely related and their application is largely governed by the depth of the forces engaged. Today, it may run to many miles, with the bulk of the troops in reserve; because of this the battle is usually prolonged, and is decided by the reserves. Consequently, economy of force – the judicious expenditure of the reserves – is of vital importance. But when all troops are concentrated in the battle front, with no reserves in rear of them, economy of force is restricted to the troops immediately at hand, and in Alexander's day it was restricted to cavalry and light infantry because, when once engaged, the heavy infantry were unable to manoeuvre. Few better examples of this restricted form of economy of force are to be found than his handling of the right flank guard at Arbela. By judiciously feeding his light cavalry, squadron by squadron, into the action, he progressively enticed his enemy to denude his left wing of its main cavalry forces, and so to create the fatal gap that led to his ruin. Another and equally notable example is to be seen at the battle of the Hydaspes. Because the elephants forbade Alexander his usual cavalry assault, he was compelled to rely on his phalanx to penetrate his enemy's front. But, in order to secure its advance, it was first necessary to draw in the whole of the Indian cavalry, to prevent it from attacking the phalanx in flank or rear. This he did by a most skilful economy of his own cavalry.

When Clausewitz wrote that 'the greatest possible number of troops should be brought into action at the decisive point',[26] he had in mind the battles of the Napoleonic wars, in which the depths of the contending armies were already considerable. But in battles of the classical age depths were seldom more than 100 paces, and frequently no more than that of a phalanx; so thin that, when a front was broken, it usually fell to pieces, and its men took to their heels. But to make certain of breaking a front, it was as necessary then as in Napoleon's day – and it still is necessary – to bring a superiority of force against the decisive point; but superior in quality rather than in quantity. Alexander did this by means of his superb Companion cavalry, coupled with his oblique order of approach, which automatically brought his offensive right wing opposite to the point in his enemy's front that he intended to penetrate, while his centre and left wing, though refused, were sufficiently close to the enemy's centre and right wing to threaten or hold them. Should the enemy attempt to overwhelm Alexander's left wing, which he could only do with cavalry, then he would have fewer cavalry to hold back Alexander's right wing. And should he concentrate the bulk of his cavalry against Alexander's right wing, he would risk penetration or envelopment of his own right wing by the Thessalian cavalry, who numerically were as powerful as the Companion cavalry and little inferior to them.

The only way out of this dilemma was to seize the initiative and attack first, and this Darius did at Arbela; he was frustrated by Alexander's application of the principle of economy of force. Coupled with the initiative, Alexander's oblique order of approach enabled him to concentrate a superiority of force against the decisive point, and at the same time, until he struck, economize – virtually hold in reserve – the rest of his army. First, the battering-ram assault, then '*tout le monde à la bataille*'. The assault preceded the general attack, a tactics which was reintroduced by the tank at the battle of Cambrai in 1917, and which characterizes so many of the tank offensives of the Second World War.

The principle of surprise

'The art of war is no more than the art of argumenting the chances which are in our favour' – Napoleon.

According to Clausewitz, 'surprise lies at the foundation of all [military] undertakings without exception', and of the means at the disposal of the general it is the most effective in attaining either physical or moral superiority. 'Without it', he writes, 'the preponderance at the decisive point is not properly conceivable'.[27] But where is the decisive point?

Throughout the history of war its position has remained constant; it is the will of the commander as expressed in his plan, coupled with the will of his soldiers to carry it out. All other points of decision should be related to this ultimate goal, because they are no more than stepping-stones toward it. Therefore the question: 'Where should the decisive point be sought?' does not arise; the question is, 'How best can a preponderance of force be brought against the enemy's will?'

There are two answers to this question: to do something which the enemy cannot prevent, and to do something which he does not suspect. The first action may be compared to surprising a man with his eyes open, in the other, the man has his eyes shut. At the Granicus, Issus and Arbela, the Persians were the victims of the first of these modes of surprise, because they were unprepared to counter Alexander's great cavalry assaults; at the Persian gates and the battle of the Hydaspes, Ariobarzanes and

Porus respectively were victims because their eyes were shut. Though the battle of the Persian Gates was a rapidly improvised manoeuvre, and the Hydaspes a methodically prepared operation, both were based on a common factor, the fixing of the enemy's attention, therefore of his will, in a direction other than the one in which surprise was to be sought. In all these surprisals, whether the approach was direct and visible, or indirect and invisible, Alexander paralysed the will of his enemy by shattering his plan. But it should be remembered that, in the warfare of his age, the will of the commanding general was far more his personal property than it is now,[28] when he shares his responsibilities with his General Staff, and to a lesser extent with his subordinate commanders; therefore it was vastly more sensitive in Alexander's day.

As is to be expected, Alexander's small wars abound with surprisals, because – then as now – though tribesmen are adepts at ambushes and ruses, their lack of discipline and submission to authority make them particularly susceptible to surprisals. Alexander drew the Triballians into battle by a ruse; surprised the Getae by an unexpected crossing of the Danube; threw Glaucias off guard by a ceremonial parade; captured Pelion by an unlooked-for night attack; surprised the Uxian hillmen while asleep in their villages; re-took Cyropolis at an unsuspected point; lured the Scythians into battle by an inviting bait; captured the Sogdian Rock by scaling its most precipitous side; drew the Assacenians into battle by a feint withdrawal; and fell upon the Malli unexpectedly by crossing a waterless desert. Further, whenever it was possible, he attacked the hillmen during the winter months, when the snow kept them in their villages. The economy of force derived from these surprisals was enormous; without them his army would have rapidly melted away.

As leader

Battles now are so vast, so complex, and so dependent on the handling of reserves, that a general-in-chief can no longer lead his army into action; he directs it from an elaborately organized headquarters, which may be 100 or more miles behind the battle front, and the leadership of his men is delegated, not to his more senior, but to his most junior officers.

In battles of the classical age the duties of the general and the subaltern coincided, and in consequence the personal leadership of the general-in-chief was of paramount importance. When Alexander took the field, he was both the thinking and fighting head of his army. In battle he invariably set his men an example of supreme personal bravery; on the line of march there was no toil that he did not share with them; in his sieges he laboured with them, and it was his presence among them that fired their imagination and awoke in them the mystical faith that led them to accept without question that there was nothing he would not dare, and nothing he could not do – to them, as to the priestess of Delphi, he was ΑΝΙΚΗΤΟΣ – the Invincible. There are many examples of this in the preceding chapters; here, that side of his leadership which won the devotion of his officers and the affection of his men will be considered.

The Macedonian army cannot have been easy to lead, particularly because the prestige it had won under Philip divided its officers into two age-categories: the elder, who had shared his successes, and the younger – the boyhood companions of Alexander – who at the outset of the war still had their spurs to win. This division led to the growth of what may be called the Parmenion and Alexander factions: the stubborn-minded

Philippians, and the more liberal-minded Alexandrians, men like Hephaestion, Nearchus and Ptolemy, who had been Alexander's playmates. Because of the constitution of the Macedonian monarchy, elimination of jealousies was no easy task. The monarchy was still partly of the heroic type, in which the idea of the kin survived. The king was the hereditary military chief of the Macedonian tribes; he was acknowledged by the assembly of the armed people – the army – and limited in power by the other 'kings', the heads of the aristocracy, who were his kin or companions. According to Macedonian usage, the army, not the king and his council, was the supreme court before which capital charges, such as murder or treason, were brought, as happened with Philotas. Alexander, though an autocrat, was not a despot who could do exactly as he liked.

In spite of this limitation of power, Alexander treated his followers impartially, and his attitude towards them was seldom one of suspicion. In Egypt, when it was alleged that Philotas was implicated in a somewhat similar conspiracy to the one which led to his death, because of the long friendship between them Alexander did not believe it to be possible; when word was brought to him by Ephialtes and Cissus that Harpalus had absconded with 5,000 talents, he threw them into prison, because he could not believe it of Harpalus, who had been a friend of his boyhood. Invariably, it would appear, he treated all his followers alike, and lavished honours and presents upon them so extravagantly, that his mother complained that he made them the equals of kings. But at all times he was their master, and when in India a quarrel arose between Craterus and Hephaestion, he publicly called Hephaestion a fool and a madman for not knowing that without his favour he was nothing, and in private he sharply reproved Craterus. 'Then he brought them together and reconciled them, taking an oath . . . that he loved them most of all men; but that if he heard of their quarrelling again, he would kill both or at least the one who began the quarrel.'[29]

This was no idle threat, for he would not tolerate any infringement of his authority. 'For instance', writes Plutarch, 'when a certain Menander, one of his companions, who had been put in command of a garrison, refused to remain there, he put him to death.'[30] And, at the close of his reign in Babylon when Cassander, one of Antipater's sons, saw Persians doing obeisance to him, and burst out laughing, Alexander was so enraged that with both hands he clutched him by the hair and dashed his head against the wall.

> And in general [writes Plutarch], as we are told, Cassander's spirit was deeply penetrated and imbued with a dreadful fear of Alexander, so that many years afterwards, when he was now king of Macedonia and master of Greece, as he was walking about and surveying the statues at Delphi, the sight of an image of Alexander smote him suddenly with a shuddering and trembling from which he could scarcely recover, and made his head swim.[31]

Whether on the battlefield or in camp, Alexander dominated his companions. Through his overmastering personality and his genius for war he won their trust and devotion, and many of them were outstanding personalities, among whom Cassander was not the least.[32] When it is remembered that the Macedonians were a truculent and semi-barbaric people, not a few of whose kings had perished by the knife, it redounds to Alexander's leadership that, in spite of his pro-Persian policy, which was so deeply resented by Philip's old veterans, he was able to carry out his conquests with so few internal dissensions as those recorded.

To his men he was not only their king but their comrade in arms, and on the battlefield one of them. Their devotion to him and reliance on him are touchingly described by Arrian in the scene which followed his wounding in the assault on the Mallian citadel. His extreme heroism, coupled with the hesitation of his men to mount the wall, must have awakened in them a sense of guilt and rage, which is to be seen in their indiscriminate slaughter of the unfortunate Malli and Oxydracae. When rumours spread through the camp that Alexander had succumbed to his wound, they were thrown into the depths of fear and despair; surrounded as they were by warlike tribes, without him how could they hope to return to their homes? Next, a rumour was circulated that he was alive, but their despair was so great that they would not believe it, and as soon as his wound permitted, Alexander had himself carried to the river, placed on a boat and conveyed to the camp. But his soldiers still would not believe that he was alive until he raised his hand toward them, when a great shout bunt from their lips. He was carried ashore and raised on to his horse, and when he dismounted at his tent and his men saw him walking, 'they all ran towards him from this side and that, some touching his hands, some his knees, some his garments; others just looked on him from near at hand, and with a blessing upon him went their way; some cast wreaths upon him, some such flowers as the country of India bare at that time'.[33]

This devotion was roused, not only by his heroism, but also by his daily concern in their welfare and happiness, and because of his deep understanding of how to stir their hearts. Before battle, he would ride down the ranks, and call aloud by name, not only the generals, but also those men who in previous battles had performed conspicuous deeds of valour; at such a moment to call a soldier by name is to electrify every soldier within hearing. After battle, his care for the wounded won the affection of all his men; 'and the dead he gathered together and gave them a splendid military funeral, the whole army marshalled in their finest battle array'. Then 'he praised all who, by his own personal witness, or by the agreed report of others, he knew had done valorous deeds in the battle; these men and all he honoured by a devotion suitable to their desert'.[34] At a prolonged halt, or after a notable success, he held games and festivals of all sorts to celebrate the prowess of his army.

What appealed to his men probably more than anything else, were his unexpected kindnesses toward them; such as when, after the capture of Halicarnassus, he sent his newly married men home to spend the winter with their families; the care with which he prepared the return journey of his Thessalians from Ecbatana; and when after the great reconciliation at Opis he not only rewarded his departing veterans in a princely way, but 'also ordained that the orphan children of those who had lost their lives in his service should receive their father's pay'.[35]

He never asked his men to do what he would not do himself. When, before he set out on his march to India, he found that the army train was cumbered with booty, he first ordered the contents of the wagons which belonged to him and his companions to be burnt. Also, he always placed the needs of his men before his own. When he led his men on foot to set an example to them during the march through Gedrosia, he was distressed by thirst and some of the light-armed troops found a little water in a water-hole and carried it in a helmet to the king.

He received it [writes Arrian], and thanked those who had brought it; and taking it poured it out in the sight of all his troops; and at this action the whole army was so much heartened that you would have said that each and every man had drunk that water which Alexander thus poured out. This deed of Alexander's above all I commend most warmly as a proof both of his endurance and his excellence as a general.[36]

Incidents such as these bound his men to him with invisible and unbreakable moral ties. They endowed them with particles of his invincible will, and, under his leadership, they obliterated dangers, smoothed away adversities, and enabled him to lead them to what for them appeared to be the ends of the world.

Notes

1 *On War*, vol. I, pp. 164, 167.
2 Polybius, XVIII, 3.
3 Justin, XI, vi.
4 *Alexander the Great*, p. 243.
5 Herodotus, VIII, 109.
6 Xenophon's *Hellenics*, VI, iv, 23. Aeneas Tacticus (xxxviii, 1–5) says much the same thing: 'But he who acts in a harsh and savage manner, immediately after becoming master of a city . . . makes other cities hostile, so that the war becomes laborious for him and victory difficult to attain . . . For nothing makes men so brave as to fear of what ills they will suffer if they surrender.' And Rabelais (bk. I, chap. XLIII) makes Gargantua proffer the following words of wisdom to Gymnast: '. . . according to right military discipline, *you must never drive your enemy unto despair*. For that such a streigth doth multiply his force, and increase his courage, which was before broken and cast down. Neither is there any better help for men that are out of heart, toiled and spent, than *to hope for no favour at all.*'
7 Clausewitz, *On War*, vol. III, p. 121.
8 Ibid., vol. III, p. 209.
9 Though the occupation of Paris in 1870 failed to do so, in 1940 it immediately led to the capitulation of France.
10 Had Hannibal after the battle of Cannae (216 B.C.) occupied Rome, the probability is that he would have brought the second Carthaginian war to an end.
11 The occupation of Athens by Xerxes in 480 B.C. did not bring war to an end, nor did Alexander's occupation of Babylon, Susa, and Persepolis.
12 Ibid., vol. III, pp. 210–11
13 In the Civil War in Spain (1936–9) General Franco did the same; directly a district was won it was placed on a peace footing.
14 In recent times much the same difficulty faced the British command in the South African War of 1899–1902. Roads were not more than cart tracks, approximately shown on unreliable maps, and footpaths were known only to the local inhabitants. Only what may be called bee-line strategy was possible.
15 From an early date the Romans were aware of the importance of roads, but it was not until 312 B.C. that the earliest of the main roads, the Via Appia, which linked Rome and Capua, was built.
16 Plutarch's *Moralia*, 'On the Fortune of Alexander', 333A.
17 Arrian, III, xvi, 9.
18 Ibid., III, xix, 6.
19 Plutarch's 'Alexander', L.
20 Due largely to Apollophanes, who failed to forward supplies.
21 *Balzac's Droll Stories* (English trans. illustrated by Gustave Doré, 1874), 'The Devil's Heir', p. 111.

22 Arrian, III, xxiii, 3. Compare 'crowning the heights' in present-day mountain warfare.
23 *Hellenistic Military and Naval Developments*, p. 41.
24 *Mémorial de St Hélène*, Las Cases (1823), vol. II, p. 15.
25 *Correspondence de Napoléon Ier*, 'Précis des guerres de J. César', vol. XXXII, p. 27.
26 *On War*, vol. I, p. 194.
27 *On War*, vol I, p. 194.
28 An example of this is the conquest of Peru by Pizarro and 183 men. The Inca power was so highly centralized that when Atahualpa was eliminated the whole country was rapidly subdued.
29 Plutarch's 'Alexander', XLVIII.
30 Ibid., LVII.
31 Ibid., LXXIV.
32 He rebuilt Thebes, founded Cassandreia and Thessalonica (Salonika), was the slayer of Alexander's mother, son and widow, and had friends among the Peripatetics.
33 Arrian, VI, xiii, 3.
34 Ibid., II, xii, I.
35 Plutarch's 'Alexander', LXXI. Cf. Arrian, VII, xii, 2.
36 Arrian, VI, xxvi, 2–3. Plutarch ('Alexander', XLII) attributes this incident to the pursuit of Darius, and ends his account as follows: 'But when they beheld his self-control and loftiness of spirit, they shouted out to him to lead them forward boldly . . . declaring that they would not regard themselves as weary, or thirsty, or as mortals at all, so long as they had such a king.'

8

ALEXANDER AND THE 'UNITY OF MANKIND'

Introduction

Certain events in Alexander's reign involving non-Macedonians have sometimes been cobbled together and taken as something akin to a 'policy' of the fusion of races or brotherhood of mankind. Actions and events which have been singled out in particular are Alexander's integration of foreigners into his army and administration, the attempt in 327 to introduce *proskynesis* (genuflection) at Bactra (see Sources 87 and 88),[1] the mass marriage in 324 at Susa (see Sources 90 and 91), at which Alexander and 91 of his court married Persian noblewomen (Alexander taking two wives) in a Persian ceremony which lasted for five days,[2] and the banquet of reconciliation and prayer for concord amongst the races (Arr. 7.11.9) after the mutiny at Opis in 324.[3] Consequently, Alexander has been viewed as a philosophical idealist, striving to create a unity of mankind, and so even more worthy of being called 'Great'.[4]

However, there was no fusion of the words 'policy'. Alexander rarely integrated foreigners into his army, and when he used them in his administration it was for their local knowledge and linguistic expertise to aid his administration, for Macedonians and Greeks significantly always controlled the army and the treasury. Pragmatics rather than idealism influenced Alexander. His attempt to adopt the Asian custom of *proskynesis* (a long-standing social act which involved subjects prostrating themselves before their king in an act of subservience) may be seen as a way of uniting his own men and foreigners in a common social protocol. However, given the religious connotations associated with the act which he knew his men could not accept, it is more likely that the attempt should be connected with his belief in his own divinity.[5]

Too much has also been read into the mass wedding at Susa, for no Macedonian or Greek women were brought out from the mainland to marry Persian noblemen, and the marriages were forced on his men (cf. Arr. 7.6.2). Furthermore, after Alexander's death all but one of the men divorced their wives. Most likely is that Alexander could not afford these noblewomen to marry their own races and thus provide the potential for revolt, something mixed marriages with his own court might offset. As for the reconciliation banquet at Opis and prayer for harmony, it is important to note that in order to end the mutiny Alexander played on the hatred between the Macedonians and the Persians, and that it was the Macedonians who were seated next to him at the banquet in order to emphasize their racial superiority. In any case, we would also expect a prayer for future harmony after a mutiny and as a prelude to further expansion, including a projected invasion of Arabia (cf. Source 100).

Ancient sources

87 Chares of Mytilene says that once at a banquet Alexander, after drinking, handed the cup to one of his friends, and he, on receiving it, rose up so as to face the household shrine, and when he had drunk, first made obeisance to Alexander, then kissed him, and then resumed his place upon the couch. As all the guests were doing this in turn, Callisthenes took the cup, the king not paying attention, but conversing with Hephaestion, and after he had drunk went towards the king to kiss him; but Demetrius, surnamed Pheido, cried: 'O King, do not accept his kiss, for he alone has not done thee obeisance.' So Alexander declined the kiss, at which Callisthenes exclaimed in a loud voice: 'Well, then, I'll go away the poorer by a kiss' (Chares, *FGrH* 125 F 14a = Plut. *Alex.* 54.4–6).

88 The following account has also been given: Alexander drank from a golden goblet the health of the circle of guests, and handed it first to those with whom he had concerted the ceremony of prostration. The first who drank from the goblet rose up and performed the act of prostration, and received a kiss from him. This ceremony proceeded from one to another in due order. But when the pledging of health came to the turn of Callisthenes, he rose up and drank from the goblet, and drew near, wishing to kiss the king without performing the act of prostration. Alexander happened then to be conversing with Hephaestion, and consequently did not observe whether Callisthenes performed the ceremony completely or not. But when Callisthenes was approaching to kiss him, Demetrius, son of Pythonax, one of the Companions, said that he was doing so without having prostrated himself. So the king would not permit him to kiss him; whereupon the philosopher said: 'I am going away only with the loss of a kiss' (Chares, *FGrH* 125 F 14b = Arr. 4.12.3–5).

89 But Alexander ... neither laid hands upon these women, nor did he know any other before marriage, except Barsine. This woman, Memnon's widow, was taken prisoner at Damascus. And since she had received a Greek education, and was of an agreeable disposition, and since her father, Artabanus, was son of a king's daughter, Alexander determined, at Parmenion's instigation as Aristobulus says, to attach himself to a woman of such high birth and beauty (Aristobulus, *FGrH* 139 F 11 = Plut. *Alex.* 21.7–9).

90 And Chares, in the tenth book of his *History of Alexander*, says: 'When he took Darius prisoner, he celebrated a marriage feast for himself and his companions,[6] having had ninety-two bedchambers prepared in the same place. There was a house built capable of containing a hundred couches; and in it every couch was adorned with wedding paraphernalia to the value of twenty minae, and was made of silver itself; but his own bed had golden feet. And he also invited to the banquet which he gave, all his own private friends, and those he arranged opposite to himself and the other bridegrooms; and his forces also belonging to the army and navy, and all the ambassadors which were present, and all the other strangers who were staying at his court. And the apartment was furnished in the most costly and magnificent manner, with sumptuous garments and cloths, and beneath them were other cloths of purple, and scarlet, and gold. And, for the sake of solidity, pillars supported the tent, each twenty cubits long, plated all over with gold and silver, and inlaid with precious stones; and all around these were spread costly curtains embroidered with figures of animals, and with gold, having gold and silver curtain-rods. And the circumference of the court was

199

four stades. And the banquet took place, beginning at the sound of a trumpet, at that marriage feast, and on other occasions whenever the king offered a solemn sacrifice, so that all the army knew it. And this marriage feast lasted five days. And a great number both of barbarians and Greeks brought contributions to it; and also some of the Indian tribes did so. And there were present some wonderful conjurors – Scymnus of Tarentum, and Philistides of Syracuse, and Heraclitus of Mitylene; after whom also Alexis of Tarentum, the rhapsodist, exhibited his skill. There came also harp-players, who played without singing – Cratinus of Methymne, and Aristonymus the Athenian, and Athenodorus the Teian. And Heraclitus the Tarentine played on the harp, accompanying himself with his voice, and so did Aristocrates the Theban. And of flute-players accompanied with song, there were present Dionysius of Heraclea, and Hyperbolus of Cyzicus. And of other flute-players there were the following, who first of all played the air called The Pythian, and afterwards played with the choruses – Timotheus, Phrynichus, Caphesias, Diophantus, and also Evius the Chalcidian. And from this time forward, those who were formerly called Dionysio-colaces, were called Alexandro-colaces, on account of the extravagant liberality of their presents, with which Alexander was pleased. And there were also tragedians who acted – Thessalus, and Athenodorus, and Aristocritus; and of comic actors there were Lycon, and Phormion, and Ariston. There was also Phasimelus the harp-player. And the crowns sent by the ambassadors and by other people amounted in value to fifteen thousand talents (Chares, *FGrH* 125 F 4 = Athen. 12.538b–539a).

91 In Susa also he celebrated both his own wedding and those of his companions. He himself married Barsine, the eldest daughter of Darius, and according to Aristobulus, besides her another, Parysatis, the youngest daughter of Ochus (Aristobulus, *FGrH* 139 F 52 = Arr. 7.4.4).

Modern works

The belief in a unity of mankind 'policy' was put forward by W.W. Tarn, a lawyer by profession and a brilliant scholar of Alexander, in the first extract. Tarn was influenced by a rhetorical work on Alexander attributed to Plutarch centuries after Alexander's life, *On the Fortune or Virtue of Alexander*.[7] The attack on Tarn began properly with E. Badian, in his classic article of 1958 (see Additional reading). However, in striving to obtain an objective evaluation of Alexander the unity of the races is still a subject of discussion as the second extract by A.B. Bosworth, Professor of Classics at the University of Western Australia, indicates.

1   W.W. Tarn, *Alexander the Great* 1 (Cambridge: 1948), Chapter II, 'The Conquest of the Far East', 'the Susa wedding', pp. 110–111, 'the mutiny at Opis', pp. 115–117, Chapter III, 'Personality, Policy and Aims', 'the policy of fusion', pp. 137–138 and 145–148.[8]
2   A.B. Bosworth, 'Alexander and the Iranians', *Journal of Hellenic Studies* 100 (1980), pp. 1–21.[9]

Additional reading

E. Badian, 'Alexander the Great and the Unity of Mankind', *Historia* 7 (1958), pp. 425–444.

——— , 'Alexander the Great and the Loneliness of Power', in E. Badian, *Studies in Greek and Roman History* (Oxford: 1964), pp. 192–205.

H.C. Baldry, *The Unity of Mankind in Greek Thought* (Cambridge: 1965), pp. 113–140.

W.W. Tarn, 'Alexander the Great and the Unity of Mankind', *Proceedings of the Cambridge Philological Society* 19 (1933), pp. 123–166.

——— , *Alexander the Great* 2, Appendix 25, 'Brotherhood and Unity', Sec. VI 'Alexander at Opis', (Cambridge: 1948), pp. 434–449.

C.G. Thomas, 'Alexander the Great and the Unity of Mankind', *Classical Journal* 63 (1968), pp. 258–260.

R.A. Todd, 'W.W. Tarn and the Alexander Ideal', *The Historian* 27 (1964), pp. 48–55.

Notes

1 Arr. 4.10.5–7, Plut. *Alex.* 54.3–6, Curt. 8.5.9–12.
2 Arr. 7.4.1–8, Diod, 17.107.6, Plut. *Alex.* 70.3, Justin 12.10.9–10.
3 Arr. 7.8.1–12.3, Diod, 17.109.2–3, Plut, *Alex.* 71–.2–9, Curt. 10.2.3 ff., Justin 12.11.
4 On his justifying the title, see Chapter 11.
5 On which, see Chapter 9.
6 At Susa in 324; cf. Chapter 6.
7 On the sources, see Chapter 1.
8 © Cambridge University Press 1948. Reprinted with the permission of Cambridge University Press.
9 Reprinted with the permission of Council of the Society for the Promotion of Hellenic Studies.

THE SUSA WEDDING

W. W. Tarn

At Susa too a great feast was held to celebrate the conquest of the Persian empire, at which Alexander and 80 of his officers married girls of the Iranian aristocracy, he and Hephaestion wedding Darius' daughters Barsine and Drypetis. It was an attempt to promote the fusion of Europe and Asia by intermarriage. Little came of it, for many of the bridegrooms were soon to die, and many others repudiated their Asiatic wives after Alexander's death; Seleucus, who married Spitamenes' daughter Apama, probably an Achaemenid on her mother's side, was an honourable and politic exception. At the same time 10,000 of the troops married their native concubines. Alexander undertook to pay the army's debts, and invited all debtors to inscribe their names. It is significant of the growing tension between him and his men that they at once suspected that this was merely a trick to discover those who had exceeded their pay; he thereon paid all comers in cash without asking names. But the tension grew from another cause. The governors of the new cities came bringing for enrolment in the army the 30,000 native youths who had received Macedonian training; this inflamed the discontent already aroused among the Macedonians by several of Alexander's acts, the enrolment of Asiatic cavalry in the Hipparchies and of Persian nobles in the *agemā*, and the Persian dress worn by himself and Peucestas. Alexander, they felt, was no longer their own king, but an Asiatic ruler.

THE MUTINY AT OPIS

W. W. Tarn

It was soon afterwards, at Opis, that the discontent in the army came to a head. Alexander was not trying to oust the Macedonians from their ancestral partnership with him, but they thought he was; he only wished to take it up into something larger, but they distrusted the changes entailed by a new world, and especially his Persian policy. The occasion was his proposal to send home with Craterus any veterans past service. The Macedonians took this to mean that he intended to transfer the seat of power from Macedonia to Asia, and the whole army except his Guard, the *agēma* of the Hypaspists, broke into open mutiny; all demanded to go home, and told him to go and campaign with his father Ammon. Alexander's temper rose; after ordering his Guard to arrest the ringleaders, he passionately harangued the troops[1] and ended by dismissing the whole army from his service. 'And now, as you all want to go, go, every one of you, and tell them at home that you deserted your king who had led you from victory to victory across the world, and left him to the care of the strangers he had conquered; and no doubt your words will win you the praises of men and the blessing of heaven. Go.' Then, after shutting himself up for two days, he called the Persian leaders to him and began to form a Persian army, whose formations were to bear the old Macedonian names.[2] This broke down the Macedonians; they gathered before his quarters, crying that they would not go away till he had pity on them. He came out and stood before them, with tears running down his face; one began to say 'You have made Persians your kinsmen', and he broke in 'But I make you all my kinsmen.' The army burst into wild cheers; those who would kissed him; the reconciliation was complete. Those veterans who desired (10,000) were then sent home with large presents under Craterus' leadership.

But before they went, Alexander's reconciliation with the army had been followed by a greater reconciliation.[3] He made a vast banquet – traditionally there were 9,000 guests – to celebrate the conclusion of peace; at his own table there sat Macedonians and Persians, the two protagonists in the great war, together with representatives of every race in his Empire and also Greeks, who were part of his world though not under his rule. The feast ended, all at his table drew wine for the libation from a huge silver crater which had once belonged to Darius, the crater which Eratosthenes or his informant was to figure as a loving-cup of the nations, and the whole 9,000 made libation together at the sound of a trumpet, as was Macedonian custom, the libation being led by Greek seers and Iranian Magi. The libation led up to, and was followed by, Alexander's prayer, in which the ceremony culminated. A few words of summary, and a brief allusion, are all that have reached us; but he prayed for peace, and that Macedonians and Persians and all the peoples of his Empire might be alike partners in the commonwealth (i.e. not merely subjects), and that the peoples of the world he knew might live together in harmony and in unity of heart and mind – that *Homonoia* which for centuries the world was to long for but never to reach. He had previously said that all men were sons of one Father, and his prayer was the expression of his recorded belief that he had a mission from God to be the Reconciler of the World. Though none present could foresee it, that prayer was to be the crown of his career; he did not live to try to carry it out.

Notes

1 On the genuineness of the essential parts of this speech, notably the conclusion, see Appendix 15 [in Tarn].
2 There is nothing to show that such an army was ever formed.
3 This paragraph is a brief summary of App. 25, vi [of Tarn], to which I refer.

THE POLICY OF FUSION

W. W. Tarn

Next, Alexander's policy of the fusion of races. It was a great and courageous idea, which, as he planned it, failed. He might indeed fairly have supposed that his experiment in mixed marriages would be successful, for he only applied it to Asia and it only meant marriage between different branches of the white race. Greek blood had once been mixed with Anatolian with good results in Miletus and many other cities, as with Libyan (Berber) blood in Cyrene; Herodotus and Themistocles were half-breeds, while the intermarriage of Macedonian and Iranian was to produce that great organiser Antiochus I; but speaking broadly, the better-class Greeks and Macedonians now refused to cooperate.[1] And it is doubtful whether, even had he lived, he could have carried out his idea of a joint commonwealth; for his system of Iranian satraps had broken down before he died. Of eighteen appointed, two soon died, one retired, and two are not again heard of; but ten were either removed for incompetence or executed for murder of subjects or treason, and were replaced by Macedonians. The three who alone held office when Alexander died were doubtless good men; nevertheless Atropates certainly, and Oxyartes possibly,[2] ended by founding independent Iranian kingdoms, while from Phrataphernes' satrapy of Parthia-Hyrcania came later the main Iranian reaction. In fact, Alexander had come into conflict with the idea of nationality, which was exhibited, not merely in the national war fought by Sogdiana, but in the way in which, even during his lifetime, independent states like Cappadocia and Armenia under Iranian rulers arose along the undefined northern limits of his empire. But of course, owing to his death, his policy never had a fair trial. The Seleucid kings indeed, half Sogdian in blood, were a direct outcome of that policy, and they did carry out parts of it; they transferred Europeans to Asia, employed, though sparingly, Asiatics in high position, and produced a marvellous mixture of east and west. But it was not done on Alexander's lines or in his spirit; the Macedonian meant to be, and was, the dominant race. What Alexander did achieve was again done through the cities, both his own and those which he inspired Seleucus to found, and it was a great enough achievement; the cities radiated Greek culture throughout Asia till ultimately the bulk of the upper classes over considerable districts became partially hellenised, and Demetrius of Bactria led Greeks for a second time beyond the Hindu Kush, to succeed for a moment where Alexander had failed and rule northern India for a few years from Pātaliputra to Kathiawar. What Alexander did succeed in ultimately giving to parts of western Asia was not political equality with Greece, but community of culture.

[. . .]

The real impress that he left on the world was far different; for, whatever else he was, he was one of the supreme fertilising forces of history. He lifted the civilised world out of one groove and set it in another; he started a new epoch; nothing could again be as it had been. He greatly enlarged the bounds of knowledge and of human endeavour, and gave to Greek science and Greek civilisation a scope and an opportunity such as they had never yet possessed. Particularism was replaced by the idea of the 'inhabited world', the common possession of civilised men; trade and commerce were internationalised, and the 'inhabited world' bound together by a network both of new routes and cities, and of common interests. Greek culture, heretofore practically confined to Greeks, spread throughout that world; and for the use of its inhabitants, in place of the many dialects of Greece, there grew up the form of Greek known as the *koinē*, 'common speech'. The Greece that taught Rome was the Hellenistic world which Alexander made; the old Greece counted for little till modern scholars re-created Periclean Athens. So far as the modern world derives its civilisation from Greece, it largely owes it to Alexander that it had the opportunity. If he could not fuse races, he transcended the national State; and to transcend national States meant to transcend national cults; men came to feel after the unity which must lie beneath the various religions. Outwardly, this unity was ultimately satisfied in the official worship of the Roman Emperor, which derived from the worship of Alexander after his death; but beside this external form there grew up in men's hearts the longing for a true spiritual unity. And it was Alexander who created the medium in which the idea, when it came, was to spread. For it was due to him that Greek civilisation penetrated western Asia; and even if much of the actual work was done by his successors, he broke the path; without him they would not have been. Consequently, when at last Christianity showed the way to that spiritual unity after which men were feeling, there was ready to hand a medium for the new religion to spread in, the common Hellenistic civilisation of the 'inhabited world'; without that, the conquests made by Christianity might have been as slow and difficult as they became when the bounds of that common civilisation were overpassed.

But if the things he did were great, one thing he dreamt was greater. We may put it that he found the ideal State of Aristotle, and substituted the ideal State of Zeno. It was not merely that he overthrew the narrow restraints of the former, and, in place of limiting men by their opportunity, created opportunities adequate for men in a world where none need be a pauper and restrictions on population were meaningless. Aristotle's State had still cared nothing for humanity outside its own borders; the stranger must still be a serf or an enemy. Alexander changed all that. When he declared that all men were alike sons of one Father, and when at Opis he prayed that Macedonians and Persians might be partners in the commonwealth and that the peoples of his world might live in harmony and in unity of heart and mind,[3] he proclaimed for the first time the unity and brotherhood of mankind. Perhaps he gave no thought to the slave world — we do not know; but he, first of all men, was ready to transcend national differences, and to declare, as St Paul was to declare, that there was neither Greek nor barbarian. And the impulse of this mighty revelation was continued by men who did give some thought to the slave world; for Zeno, who treated his slave as himself, and Seneca, who called himself the fellow-slave of his slaves, would (though Alexander might not) have understood St Paul when he added 'there is neither bond nor free'. Before Alexander, men's dreams of the ideal state had still been based on class-rule and slavery; but after him comes Iambulus' great Sun-State, founded on brotherhood and the dignity of free labour. Above all, Alexander inspired Zeno's vision of a world in which all men should be members one of another, citizens of one State without distinction of race or institutions, subject only to and in harmony with the Common Law immanent in the Universe, and united in one social life not by compulsion but only by their own willing consent, or (as he put it) by Love. The splendour of this hopeless dream may remind us that not one but two of the great lines of social-political thought which until recently divided the world go back to Alexander of Macedon. For if, as many believe, there was a line of descent from his claim to divinity, through Roman Emperor and medieval Pope, to the great despotisms of yesterday, despotisms 'by the grace of God', there is certainly a line of descent from his prayer at Opis, through the Stoics and one portion of the Christian ideal, to that brotherhood of all men which was proclaimed, though only proclaimed, in the French Revolution. The torch Alexander lit for long only smouldered; perhaps it still only smoulders to-day; but it never has been, and never can be, quite put out.[4]

Notes

1 The attitude of the Greeks in Asia to mixed marriages is discussed, Tarn, *Bactria and India*, pp. 34–8.

2 A. de la Fuye, *Revue Numismatique*, 1910, pp. 281 sqq. (Now very doubtful; for a more probable suggestion of what happened to the Paropamisadae, see Tarn, *J.H.S.* LIX, 1939, p. 322, reviewing E. T. Newell, *The coinage of the Eastern Seleucid mints.*).

3 See App. 25, VI, [in Tarn] and pp. 116–17 ante.

4 I have left the latter part of this paragraph substantially as written in 1926. Since then we have seen new and monstrous births, and are still moving in a world not realised; and I do not know how to rewrite it.

ALEXANDER AND THE IRANIANS*

A. B. Bosworth

The last two decades have seen a welcome erosion of traditional dogmas of Alexander scholarship, and a number of hallowed theories, raised on a cushion of metaphysical speculation above the mundane historical evidence, have succumbed to attacks based on rigorous logic and source analysis. The brotherhood of man as a vision of Alexander is dead, as is (one hopes) the idea that all Alexander sources can be divided into sheep and goats, the one based on extracts from the archives and the other mere rhetorical fantasy. One notable theory, however, still flourishes and has indeed been described as one of the few certainties among Alexander's aims.[1] This is the so-called policy of fusion. As so often, the idea and terminology go back to J. G. Droysen, who hailed Alexander's marriage to Rhoxane as a symbol of the fusion (*Verschmelzung*) of Europe and Asia, which (he claimed) the king recognised as the consequence of his victory. At Susa the fusion of east and west was complete and Alexander, as interpreted by Droysen, saw in that fusion the guarantee of the strength and stability of his empire.[2] Once enunciated, Droysen's formulation passed down the mainstream of German historiography, to Kaerst, Wilcken, Berve and Schachermeyr, and has penetrated to almost all arteries of Alexander scholarship.[3] Like the figure of Alexander himself the theory is flexible and capable of strange metamorphoses. In the hands of Tarn it developed into the idea of all subjects, Greek and barbarian, living together in unity and concord in a universal empire of peace.[4] The polar opposite is an essay of Helmut Berve, written in the heady days before the Second World War, in which he claimed that Alexander, with commendable respect for Aryan supremacy, planned a blending of the Macedonian and Persian peoples, so that the two racially related (!) *Herrenvölker* would lord it over the rest of the world empire.[5] On Berve's interpretation the policy had two stages. Alexander first recognised the merits of the Iranian peoples and placed them alongside the Macedonians in his court and army hierarchy. Next came the '*Blutvermischung*', the integration of the two peoples by marriage.[6]

Most scholars have tacitly accepted Berve's definition and take it as axiomatic that Alexander did recognise the merits of the Iranians and did try to integrate them with the Macedonians. The extent of the fusion is disputed, some confining it to the two aristocracies, but few have denied that Alexander had a definite policy. The loudest voice crying in the wilderness has been that of Franz Hampl.[7] Hampl has repeatedly emphasised the arbitrary and speculative nature of most discussions of the subject and the absence of concrete evidence in the ancient sources, and he categorically denies the existence of any policy of fusion. The protest is a valuable warning but in itself it is insufficient. The fact that there is no reliable ancient attestation of the policy of fusion does not prove that no such policy existed; it merely makes the case more complex. The attested actions of Alexander may still be explicable only on the assumption that he had some definite policy of integration. This is a viable hypothesis, but it must be tested rigorously. We need to examine precisely what the ancient sources say and not interpolate them with our own interpretations or wishful thinking; and above all the evidence needs to be treated in its historical context, not thrown together haphazardly to buttress some abstract concept which attracts us for sentimental reasons.

There are two passages in the sources that suggest that Alexander had some ideas of fusing together the Macedonians and Persians. Foremost comes the famous prayer of reconciliation after the Opis mutiny (late summer 324). According to Arrian Alexander held a sacrifice at which all participants, Macedonians, Persians and representatives of other nations, sat around Alexander while he and his entourage poured libations from the same vessel. The king made a prayer whose main burden was 'concord and community in empire for Macedonians and Persians' ὁμόνοιάν τε καὶ κοινωνίαν τῆς ἀρχῆς Μακεδόσι καὶ Πέρσαις).[8] The two concepts, concord and community, are tied together grammatically and contextually. The background of the prayer was mutiny, a mutiny caused in part at least by Macedonian resentment of Persians and crushed by Alexander turning towards his Persians and creating a new court and army structure composed totally of Persians.[9] The stratagem had been entirely successful and the Macedonians capitulated as soon as Alexander began his distribution of army commands to notable Persians. There was certainly Macedonian fear and resentment of the Persians around Alexander and the king played upon these emotions to destroy the mutiny. There was every reason under the circumstances for a ceremony of reconciliation and a prayer for concord. Concord is associated with community in empire, and there is no doubt that Arrian means the sharing of command in Alexander's empire.[10] The terminology is vague and imprecise, as so often with Arrian, but there is no reason to give the prayer a universal significance. Alexander may be referring to the satrapies of the empire which had been and were to continue to be governed both by Macedonians and Iranians.[11] There may even be a reference to the army commands recently conferred upon Persians and a covert threat that he would repeat his action if there were further trouble. The prayer and its context are primary evidence for bad blood between Macedonians and Iranians and Alexander's desire to use some at least of both races in the administration of the empire. They do not give any support for a general policy of fusion.[12]

Diodorus is more explicit. In the context of the notorious *hypomnemata*, the alleged last plans of Alexander presented to the Macedonian army by Perdiccas, came a proposal to synoecise cities and transplant populations from Europe to Asia 'to bring the continents to common unity and friendly kinship' by means of intermarriage and ties of community.[13] We have here two things, a proposal to found cities and transplant populations, and an interpretation of that proposal. The interpretation is unlikely to have been embodied in the original plans submitted by Perdiccas, and like the puerile note a few sentences later (that the Pyramids were accounted among the Seven Wonders) it is most probably a comment either by Diodorus or his source.[14] Now there is little or no evidence that Diodorus had a personal interest in Alexander as an apostle of international unity[15] and the overwhelming probability is that the comment comes from his immediate source, Hieronymus of Cardia.[16] Hieronymus was a contemporary of Alexander but his history was written towards the end of his prodigiously long life and covered events at least to 272.[17] His recollections of Alexander were now distant and his views of the king's motives perhaps affected by fifty years of experience and reflection. He may have considered that Alexander's shifts of population were designed to bring about greater community between races,[18] but nothing suggests that Alexander shared his views. What is more, the authenticity of the *hypomnemata* is a notorious crux. It is certainly possible that Perdiccas included fictitious proposals which he knew would antagonise the army in order to induce them to revoke the whole of Alexander's *acta*.[19] If so, those proposals would have been couched in the most provocative terms. There is, then, no certainty that even the original proposal to transplant populations emanates from Alexander, let alone the parenthetical comment. And the force of the comment is that Alexander envisaged a general spirit of unity among all his subjects, Greek and barbarian; it is not in any sense a plan to combine Macedonians and Persians as a joint ruling class. The only connection with the Opis prayer is the fact that the concept of ὁμόνοια occurs in both passages!

The next relevant observation comes from Eratosthenes, who observed that Alexander ignored advice to treat the Greeks as friends and barbarians as enemies, preferring to welcome all possible men of fair repute and be their benefactor.[20] On the surface Eratosthenes' comment has nothing to do with any policy of fusion: it is merely the just observation that Alexander was catholic in his benefactions and did not treat the conquered peoples with hostility. There is no hint here of a proposed union of races. But discussion has been unforgivably confused by the belief that Eratosthenes lies at the base of Plutarch's exposition in the first of his speeches *de Alexandri fortuna*. As is well known, this essay is the prime source for the view of Alexander as the reconciler of mankind. In a famous passage of rhetoric Plutarch tells of the rejection of Aristotle's advice to treat the Greeks ἡγεμονικῶς; Alexander blended all men together, mixing their lives, marriages and ways of life in a *krater* of friendship and making his only distinction between Greek and barbarian a man's virtue or vice.[21] After the recent analyses by Badian and Hamilton[22] there should be no question that the whole shaping of the passage is Plutarch's own, designed to show that Alexander achieved in fact the single polity which Zeno advocated. He may have drawn on Eratosthenes, but nothing suggests that the passage as a whole is an extract or summary. In particular there is no reason to believe that Eratosthenes used the metaphor of mixing.

There is still a tendency to argue that Eratosthenes described a policy of fusion. Two chapters later Plutarch explicitly cites him on the subject of Alexander's court dress, a mixture of Persian and Macedonian elements.[23] He goes on to explain that the object was to win the respect of the subject peoples and further the aim of a single law and polity for all mankind. But there is nothing to suggest that Plutarch's interpretation of the mixed dress comes from Eratosthenes. The whole passage is designed to buttress the paradoxical thesis that Alexander was a philosopher in arms and seeking the reconciliation of mankind which was merely preached as an ideal by conventional philosophers. The concrete examples of the Susa marriages and the adoption of mixed court dress are chosen as examples of his achievement of κοινωνία and the choice is Plutarch's own. The reference to Eratosthenes seems thrown in as a passing remark, just as in chap. 3 he interlaces his exposition with casual references to Onesicritus, Aristobulus, Anaximenes and Duris. Eratosthenes, we may be sure, described Alexander's court dress, but we cannot assume that he gave it an ecumenical significance. What matters is Plutarch's mode of procedure. His task is to prove the thesis that Alexander was a philosopher in practice[24] and both the examples and their rhetorical embellishment are carefully geared to that end. His general view may derive ultimately from Onesicritus' story of Alexander and the gymnosophists,[25] but, if so, the original is totally transformed. Onesicritus' view is of an Alexander who still has sympathy for the search for wisdom even in the cares of empire; but for Plutarch Alexander not only sympathises with philosophical theories, he embodies and perfects them in his actions. In the same way the interpretation he gives to the Susa marriages and the assumption of court dress need owe nothing to previous writers. Once he had propounded his theme he was limited in his choice of material and his interpretation was predetermined. Other rhetoricians with other theses to prove would adapt their viewpoint accordingly. One need only compare Aelius Aristides' *Roman Oration*. Here Rome is exalted as Plutarch exalts Alexander. She is the civilising power, breaking down the old distinction of Hellene and barbarian by the conferment of citizenship upon all deserving men. Against that background Alexander can only be presented as a meteoric failure, who acquired empire but had no time to establish a permanent system of law, taxation and civil administration.[26] If Rome was the great reconciler, Alexander could only appear as an ephemeral conqueror. In these pieces of epideictic rhetoric it is the thesis adopted for debate which determines both the choice of material and the interpretation put upon it,[27] and it is a possibility, if no more, that the whole topic of racial fusion in Alexander's reign was a creation of the rhetorical schools of the early Empire. In Plutarch himself there is only one reference in the *Life of Alexander* (47.3) to Alexander's efforts to achieve κοινωνία and ἀνάκρασις, and the examples he chooses are different from those in the earlier speech – the creation of the *Epigoni* and the Marriage to Rhoxane. And there is virtually no reference to racial fusion outside Plutarch. Only Curtius places in Alexander's mouth a speech commemorating the Susa marriages as a device to remove all distinction between victor and vanquished.[28] This speech was allegedly delivered to the Iranian soldiers during the Opis mutiny, and once again the circumstances determine the content of the speech. The subject matter, as often in Curtius, may be derived from his immediate source; but the speech is composed in generalities with none of the interesting points of authentic detail found in other Curtian speeches, and it seems to me that the observations on the fusion of Macedonian and Iranian tradition are most likely to be embellishments by Curtius himself. Even so, it is interesting that the idea of fusion occurred to Curtius as a natural theme for a speech of Alexander during the Opis crisis. The *topos* of fusion existed in the early empire and there were regular *exempla* – court dress, dynastic marriages, and the assimilation of Iranians in the national army. Not surprisingly these are the areas in which modern discussion of the 'policy of fusion' has tended to centre – and there is the possibility that the rhetoricians of the early empire and modern scholarship are correct in their interpretation. But forensic eloquence is no substitute for analytic evaluation of the evidence, and the various *exempla* need to be assessed both in their historical detail and historical context.

We may begin with the assumption of Persian court ceremonial. This is most fully described by the vulgate sources,[29] especially Diodorus who mentions five aspects. Alexander introduced court chamberlains of Asiatic stock (ῥαβδοῦχοι 'Ασιαγενεῖς) and a bodyguard of distinguished nobles including Darius' brother Oxyathres. Secondly he adopted some aspects of Persian court dress – the diadem, the white-striped tunic and the girdle.[30] Next he distributed scarlet robes and Persian harness to his companions, and finally took over Darius' harem of 360 concubines. Curtius has much the same detail but adds that Alexander used Darius' ring for his correspondence in Asia. The sources assess these moves variously. The vulgate sources unanimously regard them as a decline towards barbarian τρυφή as indeed does the normally uncritical Arrian (later he suggests on his own initiative that the adoption of mixed dress was a σόφισμα to win over the barbarians).[31] Plutarch in his life represents the mixed dress as either an adaptation to native custom or anticipation of the introduction of *proskynesis*. It is only in the *de Alexandri fortuna* that he represents it as a means to bring about friendship between victor and vanquished.[32] There is no indication that any of the ancient sources had direct information about Alexander's motives for the innovation.

It should be emphasised that the adoption of Persian court protocol was fairly extensive, not confined to Alexander's choice of a mixed court dress. On the one hand he used Persians in ceremonial positions, but he also issued his ἑταῖροι with the traditional purple robes of the Achaemenid courtiers.[33] The new king had his *purpurati*, but they were Macedonians. As yet there was no attempt to integrate the two nobilities. Diodorus implies quite clearly that they formed separate groups. The Persians might be given posts as chamberlains and selected nobles formed into a corps of δορυφόροι, but Alexander showed clearly by his distribution of purple that the courtiers of the new Great King were his Macedonians.[34] In his dress and court ceremonial Alexander adopted Achaemenid practices but he kept Persians and Macedonians distinct and the Macedonians were in a privileged position.

The date of the innovation is also important. Plutarch states explicitly that Alexander first assumed mixed dress during the rest period in Parthia after the Hyrcanian expedition, that is, in autumn 330.[35] It is precisely at this point that the vulgate sources place the episode, and we cannot doubt the accuracy of the chronology.[36] Now Alexander's claims to be the legitimate king of the Persian empire go back at least to the Marathus correspondence of early 332, when he demanded that Darius acknowledge him as overlord. After Gaugamela he was solemnly pronounced King of Asia and furthered his claims by solemnly occupying the throne of Darius in Susa.[37] It is possible (though it cannot be proved) that Alexander was never formally consecrated in Pasargadae, and he seems never to have used the title 'King of Kings' in his dealings with the Greek world.[38] But his claims to be the legitimate king of the Persian empire were absolute. Yet, even so, Alexander did not adopt Achaemenid court protocol until at least six weeks after the death of Darius. What was the importance of the period in Parthia? The answer is that Alexander now had a rival. It was precisely at the time that he returned to Parthia that Alexander learned that Bessus had declared himself Darius' successor, assuming the jealously guarded royal prerogative, the *kitaris* or upright tiara, and also the regnal name Artaxerxes.[39] The news, according to Arrian, reached Alexander on his return to Parthia and the vulgate sources place Bessus' usurpation in the context of Alexander's new court protocol. Now the threat from Bessus should not be underestimated. He was related by blood to Darius[40] and could be seen by some as his legitimate successor. He also commanded the resources of Bactria and Sogdiana, whose cavalry had retired practically undefeated from the field of Gaugamela. It was also a period at which Alexander's military resources were at a low ebb. The Greek allied troops had been demobilised from Ecbatana, probably at the news of Darius' death.[41] More seriously Alexander had left behind 6,000 of his phalanx troops at the Median border for the escort of his vast bullion train, and they were to remain detached from his main force until he entered Arachosia in early 329.[42] He had also transferred his Thracian troops and a large body of mercenaries for the garrison of Media.[43] Alexander was caught with a greatly reduced army and he suffered for it. Satibarzanes, once a regicide and Alexander's first governor of Areia, immediately revolted and forced Alexander to return from his march on Bactria.[44] His intervention brought only temporary relief. No sooner had he moved south to Drangiana and Arachosia than

Satibarzanes returned with reinforcements from Bessus, and his uprising was not crushed until the summer of 329.[45] At the same time Bessus' forces invaded Parthia and tried to establish a certain Brazane as satrap.[46] The disaffection was widespread and it lasted almost a year. It was late 329 before Bessus was captured and the last rebels were brought from Parthia and Arcia to meet the judgement of Alexander. There had been almost a year of challenge and insurrection, and it is difficult to believe that Alexander did not foresee trouble when he first heard of Bessus' usurpation.

The adoption of court protocol had an obvious propaganda value in these circumstances. Alexander demonstrated that he was genuinely King of Kings, not a mere foreign usurper, and the bodyguard of noble Persians was crucial to his claim. At his court in a position of high honour was none other than Oxyathres, brother of the late king. Not only was Alexander the self-proclaimed successor to Darius, but Darius' brother recognised the claim and supported Alexander's court ceremonial. This had been one of Alexander's assertions as early as 332, when he boasted that the Persians in his encourage followed him out of free choice.[47] At the same time Alexander adopted some items of Persian court dress, not the more obtrusive regalia (the tiara, and the purple trousers and long-sleeved *kandys*) but the diadem, the royal tunic and girdle, which he wore with the broad-brimmed Macedonian hat (*kausia*) and the Macedonian cloak.

Even this caused serious discontent among the Macedonian army – and Macedonian resistance to things oriental is one of the persistent factors of Alexander's reign. All sources stress the hostility to Alexander's adoption of mixed dress and it is prominent in the list of grievances which led to the Opis mutiny in 324.[48] The cleft widened among Alexander's officers, and the disagreements between Craterus and Hephaestion were notorious; Craterus, we are told, steadfastly adhered to Macedonian tradition.[49] Now the popularity of Craterus is one of the best-attested facts of the period after Alexander's death. His short marriage to Phila made the lady a desirable bride for Demetrius.[50] So strong was the devotion of the phalangites that Eumenes in 321 went to extraordinary lengths to conceal the fact that Craterus led the opposing army, in the belief that no Macedonian would fight against him.[51] The reason Plutarch gives (excerpting Hieronymus) is that Craterus often incurred Alexander's hatred by opposing his inclination to Persian excess and protecting ancestral customs from erosion.[52] Now it is notable that in the latter years of Alexander's reign Craterus was sent repeatedly on lengthy missions away from court, almost assuming the mantle of Parmenion. In particular he led the army division of Macedonian veterans first from India to Carmania in 325/4 and then from Opis to the coast.[53] The veterans were the men most closely bound to him but his popularity was universal and the reason was his championship of ancestral custom. Macedonian kings were said to rule by custom rather than force (οὐδὲ βίᾳ ἀλλὰ νόμῳ)[54] and the sight of a Heraclid and Argead in the trappings of the Great King, the paradigm of despotism, must have been deeply shocking. All the more so since the march from Babylon, which had been a triumphal progress, marked by the sacking of Persepolis and the burning of the palace and finally the ignominious death of the last Achaemenid at the hands of his subjects. Now the victor was assuming the protocol of the vanquished, acting the part of Great King and declaring his intentions of remaining as lord of Asia – a matter of weeks after his troops had come near mutiny in their desire to end the campaign and return home.[55]

The autumn of 330 was a time of crisis when Alexander was under strong and conflicting pressures. On the one hand the challenge from Bessus and his temporary shortage of troops forced him to propaganda, demonstrating to his subjects that he was not merely a foreign conqueror but the true Great King, supported by the old nobility of Darius. On the other he could not antagonise his Macedonians by too outrageous a breach of custom. The mixed dress was a compromise, taking on the very minimum of Persian attire compatible with his pretentions: and at the same time Alexander's Macedonian companions were given the purple robes of courtiers. This involved them in some of the odium of breach of custom and at the same time marked them out as the friends and satraps of the Great King. It was a limited experiment, and Diodorus is probably right that Alexander used the new ceremonial fairly sparingly.[56] We hear little of it in the years after 330. The Persian ushers figure among Cleitus' complaints at Maracanda, but only in Plutarch's version and then only as a peripheral attack.[57] The complaints re-emerge in Curtius' speeches on the occasion of the Pages' Conspiracy (327). They are raised briefly by Hermolaus and answered by Alexander.[58] The material may come from Curtius' sources, as do several details in these speeches, but the formulation is vague and consistent with the limited experiment implied by Diodorus. Polyaenus also indicates that Alexander reserved his Persian ceremonial receptions of his barbarian subjects during the campaigns in Bactria, Hyrcania and India,[59] but, as we shall see, his information is garbled to some extent and mostly refers to the last years of the reign. Nothing, however, contradicts the pattern of the evidence, which suggests that Alexander's first introduction of Persian ceremonial was a limited gesture, designed to capture the allegiance of his barbarian subjects at a time of crisis.

The court ceremonial was far more obtrusive after the return from India in 325/4. Alexander's court dress figured prominently in the complaints made by his Macedonian troops before the Opis mutiny, and, far from confining it to his appearances before barbarian subjects, he now wore it every day, the Macedonian cloak with the Persian white-striped tunic and the Macedonian *kausia* with the Persian diadem. The source admittedly is Ephippus of Olynthus, who was markedly hostile to Alexander, but there is no reason to doubt what he says.[60] In any case it is not the day-to-day costume of the king that he is out to pillory but the outrageous charades that he staged at banquets, dressing as Ammon, Hermes, Heracles and even Artemis. Ephippus' evidence moreover fits in well with what is otherwise known of the extravagance of Alexander's court during his last year. There is a famous description, deriving from the third century author Phylarchus, which deals with the day-to-day splendour of Alexander's court. Three versions survive (in Athenaeus, Aelian and Polyaenus) and they are complementary.[61] All these sources indicate that the court scene described was regular in Alexander's later days, but it is clear that the description refers primarily to the five-day period of the Susa marriages. The vast tent with its 100 couches and 50 golden pillars corresponds to the description of the Susa marriage hall provided by Alexander's chamberlain, Chares of Mytilene,[62] and it is hard to see how such a mammoth structure could have accompanied Alexander on all his travels. Similarly Polyaenus refers to a group of 500 dignitaries from Susa who formed a group outside the tent[63] and there is no reason why such a group should have been present when the court was not at Susa. The description, then, refers to a limited period, but the arrangements described are interesting. The court was arranged in concentric circles around Alexander and his σωματοφύλακες, that is, the eight supreme marshals of the Macedonian nobility. The first circle comprised 500 Macedonian *argyraspides*, selected for their physique; next came 1,000 archers in multi-coloured costumes, and on the outer circle of the tent 500 Persian *melophoroi*, the old infantry guard of the Achaemenid court with the distinctive golden apples on their spear butts. Alexander now had two royal guards, one the traditional Macedonian *agema* of hypaspists (the equation with *argyraspides* is certain)[64] and the other the traditional Achaemenid guard, but the two forces were kept distinct – the Macedonians closest to the king and the Persians separated by a girdle of archers. The division was continued outside the tent where the *agema* of elephants was stationed together with 1,000 Macedonians in Macedonian dress and in the final outer circle 10,000 Persians in Persian costume and scimitars. This was a brilliant display of Persian and Macedonian ceremonial, but the two races were kept rigidly separated. There was no attempt at integration – or even of '*Gleichstellung*', for the Macedonians were invariably closer to the king. Again we have no reason to doubt the main details of this description. The arrangement with its concentric circles was clearly imitated in Peucestas' great state banquet at Persepolis in 317 B.C., only here it was the closeness to Philip and Alexander which was emphasised by the division and at the centre Persian dignitaries occupied couches alongside Macedonians.[65]

Some degree of integration had taken place by the end of the reign. After the great mutiny of 324 Alexander introduced 1,000 Persians into the court guard of hypaspists. Both Diodorus and Justin agree on the fact but differ over whether it came after or during the mutiny.[66] Either it was part of Alexander's moves to bring his Macedonians to heel or it was a consequence of the mutiny, a permanent reminder of his threat to recruit his guard from Persians alone. But even so there is no evidence that the two races were intermingled in the guard and some that they were not. The panels on Alexander's sarcophagus portrayed the elaborate progress of the king in the last part of his life. Alexander rode in a chariot, preceded by an advance guard and surrounded by his regular court guard. This guard was divided into two separate bodies, one Macedonian armed in Macedonian style and the other Persian *melophoroi*.[67] Now the two races stood side by side, but they were brigaded in separate and identifiable corps. There was no attempt to integrate them into a unified body; if anything, it looks like deliberate design to balance one against the other.

It is clear that Alexander's court had become much more pretentious in the last two years of his life. The mixed dress was a more permanent feature and there was an increasing use of Persian *melophoroi* as court guards. The pomp and circumstance fits well the increasing megalomania of Alexander's last years which, as is well known, rose to a climax after the death of Hephaestion.[68] The increase in Persian ceremonial was doubtless caused by the fact that in 325/4 Alexander was travelling consistently between the old Achaemenid capitals (Persepolis, Susa, Ecbatana and Babylon) and needed to display himself to his oriental subjects as the new Great King. What is more, his absence in India between 327 and 325 had brought renewed insubordination and insurrection. The satraps of Carmania, Susiana and Paraetacene were executed when Alexander returned to the west and replaced by Macedonians.[69] More seriously, when he reached Persia proper he discovered that Orxines, apparently a lineal descendant of Cyrus the Great who had commanded the Persian contingent at Gaugamela, had established himself as satrap without any authorisation by Alexander.[70] There had also been trouble in the inner satrapies, for Craterus needed to arrest an insurgent,

Ordanes, during his progress through southern Iran; and in Media a certain Baryaxes had assumed the upright tiara and laid claim to the throne of the Medes and Persians.[71] Alexander must have felt that there was widespread reluctance among his Iranian subjects to accept his regal authority,[72] and his parade of all the magnificence of the Achaemenid court including the old bodyguard of *melophoroi* is perfectly understandable. But while Alexander increased the Persian complement in his immediate entourage he appears to have reduced their political influence away from court. The end of the reign saw only three Iranians governing satrapies – Alexander's own father-in-law in distant Parapamisadae, the impeccably loyal Phrataphernes in Parthia/Hyrcania, and Atropates in Media, the satrapy with the most formidable garrison of Hellenic troops. There are many aspects to Alexander's behaviour. We may plausibly argue a desire to flaunt ostentatiously the splendour of his court, to impress his Iranian subjects with his military power and legitimacy as Great King; and there are signs that he used his promotion of Iranians to crush discontent among his Macedonian army. What we cannot as yet assume is any serious policy of assimilating and fusing the two races. The reverse seems the case.

We must now turn to the theme of mixed marriage, which was the original inspiration for Droysen's idea of '*Verschmelzungspolitik*'. For almost the first ten years of his reign Alexander avoided marriage with remarkable success.[73] After Issus the majority of the Persian royal ladies were in his power. Alexander scrupulously cultivated the Queen Mother, Sisygambis as his 'Mother' and promised dowries to Darius' daughters.[74] Taking over Darius' functions as son and father he buttressed his claims to be the genuine King of Asia. But he stopped short of actual marriage, contenting himself with a liaison with Barsine, the daughter of Artabazus and descendant of Artaxerxes II. This liaison was protracted and from it came a son, Heracles, born in 327,[75] but there was no question of marriage until the last days of Alexander's campaign in Bactria/Sogdiana. Then came his meeting with Rhoxane and almost immediate marriage. The circumstances whereby Rhoxane came into his hands cannot be elucidated here, for they involve one of the most intractable clashes of authority between Arrian and the vulgate tradition,[76] but fortunately there is unanimity about the date of the wedding (spring 327) and equal unanimity that it was a love match. There is, however, no suggestion of a policy of fusion. Curtius merely accredits him with a statement that it was conducive to the stability of the empire that Persians and Macedonians were joined in marriage; the arrogance of the victors and shame of the vanquished would both be reduced.[77] This is a far cry from the symbolic union of races which many have seen in the marriage.

There is, however, a point to be stressed. Alexander married Rhoxane whereas he had only formed a liaison with Barsine. If all that was at issue was physical attraction, there was no reason for a formal marriage, unless we believe that Alexander's chivalry had improved since Issus. There were undoubtedly political reasons as well. Rhoxane married Alexander in spring 327 on the eve of his march into India. The previous two years had seen unremitting warfare caused by repeated insurrections inside Bactria/Sogdiana and invasions from the Saka nomads of the steppes. Alexander's response had been increasingly savage repression. During the first stage of the uprising, summer 329, his orders included the massacre of all male defenders of conquered cities and the enslavement of women and children.[78] Later we hear a dark story of the crucifixion of defenders who actually capitulated[79] and the index of Diodorus hints at wholesale massacre.[80] At the same time Alexander founded a network of military settlements with a nucleus of Greek mercenaries and discharged Macedonian veterans together with settlers from the barbarian hinterland.[81] The relationship between Greek and barbarian is hard to elicit in this instance, but both Curtius and Justin suggest that the barbarians involved in the foundation of Alexandria Eschate were survivors from the recently conquered cities, especially Cyropolis.[82] In that case they can hardly have acted in any other role than that of native serfs.[83] Curtius adds that the survivors from the rock of Sogdiana were distributed to the colonists of the new foundations, as additional slaves.[84] Some of the barbarians may have participated as volunteers on a more privileged basis, but the Greek settlers certainly formed a governing élite and their numbers were such that they could keep their barbarian subjects under military control. Outside the colonies the principal fortresses were occupied by Greco-Macedonian garrisons[85] and both colonies and fortresses had commandants directly imposed by Alexander. Finally the satrapy of Bactria/Sogdiana was in the overall control of a Macedonian, Amyntas son of Nicolaus.[86] In no other satrapy of the east was Macedonian military strength so firmly entrenched in the permanent establishment. Though there remained small pockets of independence such as the districts of Sisimithres and Chorienes,[87] Hellenic military settlements dominated the bulk of the countryside and the hierarchy was exclusively Greco-Macdonian.

The marriage to Rhoxane marks the final act of the settlement, and Curtius may be justified in viewing it as an act of conciliation after two years of warfare and devastation. But there is another aspect. The taking of a bride from the Iranian nobility of Bactria underlined Alexander's claims to be the legitimate lord of the area. In 336 he had had a painful object lesson in his wooing of the daughter of Pixodarus of Caria and the result of that episode had been the demonstration that with the princess went the satrapy.[88] He himself had taken care to venerate the elderly Hecatomnid princess Ada as 'Mother' to support his claims to Caria.[89] It was natural that after demonstrating his military supremacy to the Bactrians and Sogdians he married one of their princesses, cementing his rule by the wedding. There is a tradition moreover that Alexander also persuaded some of his friends to marry Bactrian ladies.[90] If it is true (and there is no contrary evidence), his fellow bridegrooms may well have been the satrap and garrison commanders left behind after the march on India. The new lords of the region would now have native wives.

Finally we come to the palladium of Alexander's alleged policy of fusion – the mass marriage at Susa at which Alexander and 91 of his Companions took Iranian brides. The weddings were celebrated with the utmost splendour in the Iranian mode[91] and Alexander commemorated the event by distributing gifts to Macedonian soldiers who had taken native wives, to the number of 10,000.[92] Without doubt this was a ceremony of unparalleled pomp with important political implications, but the sources leave us totally uninformed of those implications. In the speech *de Alexandri fortuna* Plutarch represents the marriage as a means of uniting the two imperial peoples, as does Curtius in the speech he attributes to Alexander;[93] but, as we have seen, both statements reflect the rhetorical interpretations of the first century A.D. rather than any authentic tradition from the time of Alexander. But if we look at the recorded facts, one feature stands out starkly—so starkly that it is incredible that it was first noted by Hampl in 1954.[94] The marriages were totally one-sided. Persian wives were given to Macedonian husbands, but there is no instance of the reverse relationship.

Admittedly Alexander's court was not well endowed with noble ladies of Greek or Macedonian extraction, but, if his aim was really to place the two imperial races on an equal footing, it would have been relatively easy for him to import the necessary brides from mainland Greece and delay the ceremony until they arrived. In fact there is nothing attested except Persian women married to Greco-Macedonian men.[95] The names as recorded are striking. Alexander and Hephaestion both married daughters of Darius, Craterus a daughter of Darius' brother, Oxyathres. The other wives whose names are recorded came from prominent satrapal families – daughters of Artabazus, Atropates of Media, and even Spitamenes, the leader of the insurgent Sogdians during 329 and 328.[96] This was an integration of sorts, but its effect was to mark out Alexander's Companions as the new rulers of the Persian Empire. They already had the scarlet robes of Persian courtiers; now they were married into the most prominent satrapal families. Nothing could have made it clearer that Alexander intended his Macedonians to rule with him as the new lords of the conquered empire.

It is also debatable how far Alexander intended his Macedonians to be assimilated into Persian ways. The traditional view is that Alexander wished the Macedonian nobles to adapt themselves to Persian customs but was frustrated by the Macedonians' tenacious adherence to their ancestral tradition. This theory rests primarily upon Arrian's account of Peucestas' installation as satrap of Persis in early 324. As soon as he was appointed he affected Median dress and became the only Macedonian to do so and learn the Persian language. Alexander commended him for his actions and he became popular with his Persian subjects, correspondingly unpopular with the mutinous Macedonian rank-and-file.[97] Peucestas' adoption of Persian customs is an unchallengeable fact, but it remains to be seen whether his behaviour was unique. In the first place he was not the only person in Alexander's entourage to learn an oriental language. We are told explicitly that Laomedon of Mytilene (brother of Erigyius) was a bilingual, or at least could understand Semitic script, and Eumenes could concoct a letter in Aramaic, the *lingua franca* of the eastern world.[98] If Arrian's credit be retained, we must assume either that Peucestas was the only foreigner to learn Persian (as opposed to Aramaic) or that he excluded the Greeks and referred only to true Macedonians. But Diodorus gives another perspective when he explains Peucestas' popularity with his subjects in 317 B.C. Alexander, so it was said, made a concession. Only Peucestas was *allowed* to wear Persian dress, so that the favour of the Persians could be secured.[99] If we accept the text as it stands (and nothing in Arrian contradicts it) we must conclude that as a general rule Macedonian nobles were not permitted to assume the full Persian dress.[100] The satrap of Persis was the one exception Doubtless Alexander had laid to heart the lesson of Orxines' usurpation and concluded that in Persis his satrap had to conform and be seen to conform to the local *mores*. And in the case of Peucestas there was no reason to suspect his personal loyalty; he had saved the king in the Malli town and owed his promotion to Alexander's favour.[101] He could therefore be encouraged to adapt himself to Persian tradition and ingratiate himself with his subjects. In other satrapies Alexander might have felt it prudent to drive a wedge between the satraps and their subjects. The rulers were marked out by their dress as aliens and were accordingly most unlikely to develop the accord with their subjects which they would need to revolt from the central authority. The evidence of Diodorus suggests that Peucestas was not meant to be a paradigm for other governors but rather an exception to the general rule.

It is difficult to trace any admission of Persian nobles into the Macedonian court hierarchy. Before 324 the only certain example is Oxyathres, brother of Darius, who was admitted to the ranks of the ἑταῖροι immediately after his brother's death.[102] It is hazardous to argue from silence, given the defective nature of all Alexander histories, but there is some evidence that Persians were initially excluded from the court hierarchy. In 329 Pharnuches, apparently an Iranian domiciled in Lycia,[103] found himself in titular command of a force of mercenaries thanks to his competence in the local dialects. When his force was ambushed, he attempted (so Aristobulus claimed) to cede his command to Macedonian officers on the grounds that he was a barbarian while they were Macedonians and ἑταῖροι of the King. The account in general is confused and tendentious, but the clear distinction between barbarians and ἑταῖροι is fundamental to it.[104] Admittedly the text does not state that there were no barbarian ἑταῖροι, but it does support the argument from silence. Nearchus' list of trierarchs for the Indus fleet takes us further. The Macedonians of Alexander's court are listed according to their domicile, as are the Greeks. There are two representatives of the regal families of Cyprus, and finally one solitary Persian – Bagoas, son of Pharnuches.[105] The rarity of the patronymic virtually guarantees that Bagoas was the son of the Lycian Pharnuches. Unlike his father, he achieved a status commensurate with the Macedonian ἑταῖροι, and he was probably the Bagoas who entertained Alexander at Babylon.[106] But at the time of the Indus voyage he was the only Persian among the ἑταῖροι (Oxyathres had retired to Ecbatana to supervise Bessus' execution); otherwise it is inconceivable that his fellow Iranians did not compete as trierarchs.

By 324 there were more Iranians among the ἑταῖροι. Arrian gives the names of nine nobles who were drafted into the élite cavalry *agema*, the king's guard. The list is intended to be exhaustive, and what makes the first impression is its brevity.[107] Not only is the list short but the families are well known – a group selected by Alexander for especial distinction. There is a son of Artabazus, two sons of Mazaeus, two of Phrataphernes and finally Itanes, brother of Alexander's wife Rhoxane.[108] The fathers were all satraps and their loyalty was impeccable throughout the reign. Two names, Mithrobaeus and Aegobares, are totally unknown,[109] but the leader of the group, Hystaspes of Bactria, was connected by marriage to the house of Artaxerxes III Ochus, and he may have been a descendant of the son of Xerxes who ruled Bactria in the fifth century.[110] The lineage of these nobles was beyond reproach and, given their small numbers, one may assume that Alexander was forming an élite within the Persian nobility. One can only guess at his motives, but there were two clear results from his actions. The small group of nobles incorporated in the *agema* were effectively isolated from their father's satrapies. They were trained and armed in Macedonian style and doubtless identified with the conquerors by their people. At the same time they acted as hostages for their parents, as did the Macedonian pages around Alexander's person.[111] These adlections to the *agema* seem a parallel phenomenon to Alexander's satrapal appointments. The Iranian satraps were reduced to a handful – Phrataphernes, Oxyartes and Atropates – and their sons were attached to Alexander's own court, separated by distance and culture from their roots in the satrapies.

The evidence so far has produced little or nothing that suggests any policy of fusion. Alexander's actions when viewed in their historical context seem rather to indicate a policy of division. There was no attempt to intermix the Macedonian and Persian nobilities, if anything an attempt to keep them apart. In particular the Macedonians seem to have been cast as the ruling race. It is they who monopolise the principal commands, civil and military, they who marry the women of the Persian aristocracy, they who dominate court life. Even when Alexander adopted Persian ceremonial his Macedonians were marked out as his courtiers and his chiliarch (or grand vizier) was no Persian but his bosom friend Hephaestion. By contrast apart from a small, carefully chosen élite the Persians had no positions of power at court and the Iranian satraps were inexorably reduced in numbers as the reign progressed. The factor which dominated everything was Alexander's concept of personal autocracy. From early 332 to the end of his life he declared himself King of Asia. He acknowledged no equal and all were his subjects. Against that background the traditional recalcitrance of the Iranian satraps was totally unacceptable and, I believe, Alexander's actions can largely be explained as a demonstration of the fact of conquest. His court ceremonial underlined that he alone was the Great King and the mass marriages made it patently obvious that he and his nobles were the inheritors of the Achaemenids. As for the Persians, they were gradually extracted from the satrapies in which they had been prematurely confirmed in the years after Gaugamela and only a small group was left, tied by marriage to the Macedonian conquerors and with sons virtual hostages at court. This is a far cry from any policy of fusion. The only counter evidence comes from the Opis mutiny, when Alexander turned to his Iranians in order to crush disaffection among the Macedonians. Afterwards Alexander was able to pray for community of command, but the prayer was demonstrably affected by the recent events. In effect there is no hint that Alexander gave positions of power to Iranians during his last year; the hierarchy of command remained stubbornly Macedonian.

If there is no trace of any planned integration of the Macedonian and Persian aristocracies, it might be thought that the fusion took place at a lower level. By the end of his reign Alexander certainly possessed a mixed army, in which Persians and Macedonians fought side by side both in the phalanx and Companion cavalry. But did the mixture come about by policy or by military necessity? And how rigorous was the fusion? Were the two races divided into separate sub-units or did they fight side by side in integrated companies and with common weaponry? These questions are fundamental and once again require close examination of the evidence.

According to orthodox dogma Alexander began to use oriental cavalry at an early stage. In his description of the Hyrcanian campaign (late summer 330) Arrian notes that the king now had a body of mounted javelin-men (ἱππακοντισταί).[112] These troops were used repeatedly in the campaign in central Iran and Bactria, and it is universally assumed that they were a select Iranian squadron, recruited to give extra flexibility to his cavalry.[113] But there is no hint in any of the ten references in Arrian that these troops were Iranians. In fact they are invariably grouped with regular units of the Macedonian army, the Agrianians, and the Companions. What is more, ἱππακοντισταί formed the nucleus of the garrison of Areia in 330 and they were massacred during Satibarzanes' first revolt.[114] It is surprising that Iranians were chosen for such an exposed position, more surprising that they remained loyal. One should certainly admit the possibility that these troops were Macedonians. Now one of Alexander's principal cavalry units, the Scouts (πρόδρομοι) is not mentioned after the pursuit of Darius. Instead the ἱππακοντισταί appear precisely in the role formerly cast for the Scouts,[115] and in Sogdiana they are used alongside σαρισσοφόροι, who previously belonged to the Scouts.[116] It is possible that Alexander reorganised the

Scouts in the year after Gaugamela and turned them into two formations, one using the ponderous *sarisa* and the other light missile javelins.[117] At Gaugamela the Scouts had been mauled by the cavalry of the eastern satrapies, and Alexander perhaps thought it prudent to variegate his cavalry before moving east. The year 330 was one of reorganisation, the year that hipparchies are first mentioned in Ptolemy's campaign narrative,[118] and it is perfectly credible that Alexander trained some of his Scouts as a unit of javelin-men.[119] There is no reason to assume that he was using an Iranian squadron in conjunction with his Macedonian troops as early as 330.

The first unequivocal reference to use of oriental troops comes in the Sogdian revolt of 328/7, when we are told that Bactrians and Sogdians fought in the satrapal forces of Amyntas.[120] When he left Bactria for India Alexander had with him large numbers of Iranian cavalry, from Bactria, Sogdiana, Arachosia and Parapamisadae. There were also Saka cavalry from the northern steppes.[121] These troops fought alongside the Macedonians at the Hydaspes but they were brigaded in separate formations and outside the battle narrative they are not individually mentioned. There is one exception, the squadron of horse-archers (ἱπποτόξοται) which first emerges during the march on India and is mentioned repeatedly in Arrian's campaign narrative.[122] The horse-archers are usually employed alongside Macedonian units in relatively light formations, performing the same functions, it seems, as did formerly the Scouts and ἱππακοντισταί (who are mentioned once only after the invasion of India). These horse-archers seem to have been recruited from the Dahae, who are specifically designated the horse-archers at the Hydaspes,[123] and it looks as though they formed a *corps d'élite* corresponding to the Agrianians in the infantry. The first appearance of these Iranian troops is significant. After the protracted campaign in Bactria/Sogdiana Alexander was leaving the area altogether and moving to invade India. The Iranian cavalry were being employed outside their home territory where there was little chance of disaffection. Alexander could safely draw upon them to strengthen his own cavalry, and at the same time they served as a great pool of hostages, exactly as had the troops of the Corinthian League during the first years of the campaign. They fought in national units and there was as yet no attempt to combine them with his Macedonian troops.

The combination took place, in the cavalry at least, after Alexander's return to the west in 325. The only evidence unfortunately is a single passage of Arrian which is at best unclear and most probably corrupt. In his list of Macedonian grievances at Susa Arrian gives superficially detailed information about the use of barbarians in the cavalry (vii 6.2–5); this he summarises two chapters later as an admixture of heterogeneous cavalry into the ranks of the barbarians.[124] What kind of admixture is meant? Arrian divides the Macedonians' grievance into three parts. In the first place he mentions that certain Iranians, selected for their social distinction and physique, were assigned to the Companion cavalry. There were three categories, carefully marked off: first Bactrians, Sogdians and Arachosians; next Drangians, Areians and Parthyaeans; and finally an obscure group of Persians termed the 'Euacae'. As Brunt saw, these groups correspond to the cavalry taken from Bactria in 327, the troops which arrived in Carmania in late 325, and finally cavalry levied in Persis in early 324.[125] The incorporation of the last two groups was a relatively recent occurrence, but it is possible that the Bactrian cavalry had been integrated with the Companions as early as the campaign in Southern India. The verb Arrian used to describe the incorporation (καταλοχισθέντες) is unfortunately flexible. In its technical sense it denotes the division of an amorphous body of troops into distinctive files or λόχοι,[126] but it is most often used in the most general sense as a synonym of καταλέγειν. What it does not mean is assignment of extra troops to existing units.[127] Arrian makes the situation clearer in his next phrase. Besides these Iranians assigned (καταλοχισθέντες) to the Companion cavalry there was a fifth hipparchy which was not entirely barbarian. The phrase implies clearly that there were four hipparchies consisting wholly of Iranian cavalry,[128] and a fifth which was only partially so. It must be emphasised that the passage says nothing about the number of Macedonian hipparchies at this period (although it has frequently been taken to do so).[129] What is at issue is the reaction of the Macedonians to Persian involvement in the Companion cavalry, and their grievances are presented in ascending order. First comes the objection that the Iranians were organised in separate hipparchies within the cavalry body, next the more serious complaint that there was a mixed hipparchy, in which Iranians and Macedonians served together and finally the crowning outrage that there was a troop of Persian nobles inside the élite *agema*. The organisation of the Macedonians was irrelevant to the grievances, and we must assume that there was an unspecified number of Macedonian hipparchies *in addition to* the four Persian hipparchies and the mixed hipparchy.[130] The total number at this period cannot even be guessed at.

Arrian says virtually nothing about the process of infiltration. He merely adds an obscure parenthesis remarking that the fifth mixed hipparchy had originated at a time when the entire cavalry body was expanded. The date of the expansion is not given, but it is a reasonable (and popular) assumption that it came after the crossing of the Gedrosian desert, which certainly caused great loss of life and greater loss of livestock, especially horses.[131] Probably Alexander reformed his cavalry during his stay in Persis, regrouping the Macedonians and adding the recent arrivals from central Iran. The supernumeraries, both Macedonian and Iranian, were grouped together in a single hipparchy, the only unit apart from the *agema* in which the two races were combined. The basic reorganisation, then, seems to have occurred in 325/4, but there is a possibility that the Bactrians and Sogdians had served inside the Companion cavalry before this date. We have noted that they fought at the Hydaspes in separate national units and it is a striking fact that they are never again mentioned in the campaign narrative for Southern India. Once more it is possible that the omission is purely fortuitous, but there is nothing against the hypothesis that some of the Iranian cavalry had been brigaded in hipparchies as early as 326.

If the evidence of Arrian is strictly interpreted, it indicates that, apart from one hipparchy, Macedonians and Iranians served in separate units within the body of the Companion cavalry. In other words, the Iranian cavalry shared the title of ἑταῖροι. This has often been doubted, but Arrian's terminology seems unambiguous: they were assigned to the Companion cavalry. Alexander's actions at Opis are not contrary evidence. There he began to create new formations of Persians bearing the Macedonian names, including a fresh cavalry *agema* καὶ ἡ τῶν ἑταίρων ἵππος.[132] This does not imply that all Companions had previously been Macedonians, rather that in future he intended to have a corps of Companions who were exclusively Persian. That is quite compatible with a situation before the mutiny in which Macedonians and Iranians served together in a single body of Companions. And the single reference in Arrian to Macedonian Companions does not exclude there having been Persian Companions also.[133] A curious picture therefore emerges. The Iranian cavalry largely served in separate hipparchies, and they retained their national weapons (it is only the group of nobles in the *agema* who are said to have exchanged their javelins for Macedonian lances). Nevertheless they served in the Companion cavalry and presumably bore the title ἑταῖροι. It would seem that Alexander was using the traditional policy of Macedonian kings. The title *pezhetairoi* (Foot Companions), as a name for the entire phalanx infantry, appears to have been introduced as a deliberate measure to place the infantry on terms of equality with the cavalry.[134] The King named all his infantry his Companions and emphasised their close ties to him, thus setting them up as a group parallel and opposed to the aristocratic cavalry, the group which had previously monopolised the title of Companion. Alexander, it seems, did the same with his cavalry, establishing a body of Iranian Companions in the same organisation as the Macedonians. This development fits well into the period after the Hyphasis mutiny, when Alexander was faced with disaffection or, at best, lack of enthusiasm among his own troops. The admission of Iranian Companions made it clear that he was not limited to his Macedonians and could find support elsewhere. It was an implicit threat, which was nearly fulfilled at Opis. There is, then, no trace of a policy of fusion. Once again the tendency seems to have been to keep Iranians and Macedonians separate and even mutually suspicious. Each served as a check and balance on the other.

The pattern is further exemplified in Alexander's use of Iranian infantry. First and foremost is the formation of 30,000 *Epigoni*, Iranian youths armed in Macedonian fashion and trained in phalanx discipline. All sources agree that the *Epigoni* arrived during Alexander's stay in Susa and aroused the jealousy and fear of the Macedonians by their brilliant display.[135] Plutarch alone says that the institution was designed to promote a mixture (ἀνάκρασις) and harmony;[136] the vulgate sources see much more sinister motives. For Diodorus the formation was Alexander's reaction to the recalcitrance of his Macedonian troops ever since the Hyphasis mutiny (he speaks of the Ganges!). The king needed an ἀντίταγμα for his Macedonian phalanx. Pierre Briant has recently elucidated the sense of ἀντίταγμα; it was a counter-army, 'face à une phalange macédonienne et contre elle'.[137] Elsewhere Diodorus uses the word to describe the force of mercenaries raised by Thrasybulus of Syracuse to counter his citizen forces and Plutarch describes as an ἀντίταγμα the force of cavalry which Eumenes in 322/1 built up to counter and crush the phalanx infantry of Neoptolemus.[138] When applied to Alexander's *Epigoni* the word has a sinister ring. Alexander intended the Persians not only to balance his Macedonian forces but also to be thrown against them if necessary.

Curtius describes the origins of this new counter-infantry, claiming that Alexander gave orders for the levy of 30,000 youths before he left Bactria in 327, intending them to be conveyed to him when trained, to act as hostages as well as soldiers.[139] His order is presented as a security measure – a measure against the Iranians not the Macedonians. Some of this coheres with other evidence. Arrian claims that the *Epigoni* were raised by satraps from the newly-founded cities and the rest of the conquered territories.[140] His terminology is loose, using σατράπης to refer to the city commandants whom he elsewhere terms ὕπαρχοι,[141] but it is clear that the new foundations of the east were the prime recruiting grounds for the *Epigoni*. These foundations were concentrated most densely in Bactria/Sogdiana and, as we have seen, the conquered peoples formed a large pool of second-class citizens. They were an obvious area for recruits; young men were closely concentrated and it would be a prudential step to remove those who were outstanding and most likely to be discontented with their lot. Originally, then, Alexander's intention might have been to skim away the most outstanding youths of the central satrapies, train them in effective infantry tactics and then isolate them from their cultural background. As the morale and obedience of his Macedonians declined he saw the potential of his new infantry phalanx and deliberately used the new force to balance and intimidate his Macedonians. It was essential that the two infantry bodies were kept distinct – an obvious and permanent exception to any policy of fusion.

According to Justin there was a second body of *Epigoni*, the offspring of mixed marriages between Macedonian soldiers and Asiatic wives. Justin states that Alexander began to encourage these unions in 330, at the time when he first adopted Persian dress. Two motives are given – to reduce his troops' longing for domestic life in Macedonia and to create an army of mixed race whose only home was the camp.[142] Justin is fuller than usual and not apparently garbled; and there is corroborative evidence. Arrian agrees that more than 10,000 mixed marriages had been contracted by the time of the celebrations at Susa and the veterans of Opis had produced a fair number of offspring by their native wives, enough for Alexander to retain them, promising to train them in Macedonian style and to reunite them with their fathers when they reached manhood.[143] The evidence is consistent and indicates that Alexander had long- and short-term objectives. In the first place the legitimisation of his troops' liaisons with native women gave them an inducement to remain in Asia which was stronger than mere concubinage and politically desirable in 330, when there was agitation in the army to conclude the campaign and return to Macedonia.[144] The ultimate aim, however, was to produce a corps of troops without roots in Europe or permanent home in Asia, the janissaries of the new Empire, whose loyalty would be to Alexander alone.[145] The two bodies of *Epigoni* were alike in their close attachment to the court and their training in Macedonian discipline. In both cases Alexander was attempting to create a supra-national army, but his motives were grounded in practical politics and military considerations were paramount.

So far the evidence has indicated that Alexander kept Iranians and Macedonians separated in both cavalry and infantry and that he used the two races to counterbalance each other. There is, however, one instance of a combined force of Persians and Macedonians. Shortly before Alexander's death Peucestas arrived in Babylon with a force of 20,000 Persians, reinforced with mountaineers from the Zagros and Elburz.[146] The king commended this new force and assigned them to the Macedonian ranks (κατέλεγεν ἐς τὰς Μακεδονικὰς τάξεις). The details of this reorganisation are given, for once, and they are interesting. This new composite infantry was organised into files (δεκάδες) of sixteen, twelve Persians to four Macedonians. Each file was commanded by a Macedonian, backed by two other Macedonians in second and third place. The Persians then filled out the centre of the phalanx and a Macedonian brought up the rear. The four Macedonians were armed in traditional style (with the *sarisa*) and were given preferential rates of pay, whereas the Persians retained their native bows and javelins. The result was a curiously heterogeneous phalanx, packed with Persians untrained in Macedonian discipline. The Macedonians formed an élite, the first three ranks using *sarisae* and bearing the brunt of any attack. Even in the old phalanx there was hardly space for more than the first three ranks to use sarisae in couched position. In Polybius' day, when *sarisae* were longer, only the first five ranks were able to thrust with their weapons; the rest added weight and held their *sarisae* vertically as a screen against missiles.[147] The Persians in the new phalanx added weight and numbers and no doubt they were intended to shoot arrows and javelins over the heads of the Macedonian ranks, much in the same way as the λογχοφόροι were to operate in Arrian's legionary phalanx of A.D. 135.[148] This new phalanx could only be used in frontal attacks. There was no possibility of complex manoeuvres or changes of front and depth on the march which had been the hallmark of the old Macedonian phalanx and had been displayed so prominently in the Illyrian campaign of 335 and the approach to Issus.[149] This reorganisation was in fact a means to make the best use of untrained manpower and also to husband the trained Macedonian phalangites. It is strong *prima facie* evidence that Alexander's native Macedonian troops were in short supply by 323.

There is every reason to believe that the main army was drained of Macedonians. Curtius (x 2.8) implies that Alexander was thinking of leaving a moderate holding army in Asia after the departure of Craterus' veterans, an army comprising 13,000 infantry and 2,000 cavalry. These are superficially high figures, but none the less misleading. There is no reason to think that only Macedonians are understood.[150] The explicit context is the size of the force to be left in Asia (he had recently threatened to attack Athens and the Arabian expedition was in preparation);[151] it is specifically a holding force and presumably contained a relatively small proportion of Macedonians.[152] After Opis Alexander deliberately drained his infantry forces, sending with Craterus 6,000 of the veterans present at the Hellespont in 334 and 4,000 of the troops conveyed in later reinforcements.[153] There is no statement how many remained, but one may assume that the fighting in India and the Gedrosian desert march took a heavy toll of life, and there is little trace of reinforcements. Only Curtius speaks of 8,000 *Graeci* sent to Sogdiana in 329/8 and 5,000 cavalry (*sic*) sent from Thrace in 326.[154] There is no trace in the sources of Macedonian reinforcements and it seems that Antipater did not have the necessary manpower resources to cater for Alexander's demands. Diodorus says explicitly that Macedonia was drained of national troops in 323 because of the numbers of reinforcements sent to Asia, so that he could not cope with the initial crisis of the Lamian War.[155] The forces who remained in Babylon can only be guessed at. The *argyraspides*, 3,000 in number, were present in Perdiccas' invasion force in 321, and, since their baggage train contained their wives and children, we can assume that they were not sent with Craterus' column in 324.[156] Alexander must have retained them in Babylon together with an unspecified number of phalingites.[157] They were also veterans for the most part. The evidence for the *argyraspides* is unanimous that they had all fought through the campaigns of Philip and Alexander. The statement that the youngest of the corps were sixty years old may be an exaggeration, but it is common to Diodorus and Plutarch and presumably derives from Hieronymus.[158] And we should not forget the exploits of Antigonus at Ipsus and Lysimachus and Seleucus at Corupedium: *in hac aetate utrique animi iuveniles erant*.[159] It seems then that Alexander was left with a nucleus of Macedonian veterans. He had ordered Antipater to bring prime troops from Macedonia to replace Craterus' army column but they could not be expected for some time after Craterus reached Macedon – and he was travelling with prudent slowness.[160] But Alexander was about to embark on the Arabian expedition, and shortly before his death the advance orders for the departure of both land and naval forces had been given.[161] There was no alternative but to make the best of his Macedonian veterans – to distribute them among the front-rank positions and fill up the phalanx in depth with Persian infantry. The mixture was patently forced upon Alexander by military necessity. Had the fresh levies from Macedon ever arrived, he would certainly have removed the Iranian rank and file and replaced them with the trained manpower from Macedon.[162]

Nothing remains of the policy of fusion. As regards his military organisation Alexander was reacting to a series of problems. To begin with, his use of Iranians from the central satrapies was determined by his need for auxiliaries in the Indian campaign and the obvious desirability of removing crack fighting men from their native satrapies, where they would be fuel for any revolt against his regal authority. The next stage was to use his Iranian auxiliaries as a counter-weight to his increasingly mutinous Macedonian troops, and finally, when the Macedonians were decimated and cowed, they were used as a pool of manpower to supplement the trained Macedonian cadres. There is nothing here remotely resembling a deliberate policy to fuse together the two peoples into a single army. If there is any policy it is *divide et impera*. We have seen Alexander at work at two levels. Firstly the continuous and traditional recalcitrance of his Iranian nobles forced him to proclaim his pretensions as the heir of the Achaemenids with increasing pomp and splendour and to make it increasingly obvious that his Greco-Macedonian nobles had in fact supplanted the Iranians as a ruling class. On the other hand the increasing disaffection of his Macedonian rank and file forced him to rely more on Iranian infantry and cavalry. If there is any consistent element it is Alexander's categorical claim to personal autocracy and the reciprocal demand for total obedience from his subjects at all levels of society. The resistance to that claim appeared in different forms and Alexander's response was accordingly different. There is little that can be said to approximate to careful premeditated policy: rather Alexander seems to have reacted promptly to the various challenges confronting him during his reign. The result is piecemeal and certainly less romantic than a visionary policy of fusion and conciliation but it is far truer to the evidence as it stands.

Notes

* This paper was delivered at the annual meeting of the American Association of Ancient Historians, held at Boulder, Colorado in May 1978, and at seminars in Berkeley and Oxford. I am grateful for the comments made on those occasions and acknowledge liability for the remaining errors.

1 G. T. Griffith, *JHS* lxxxii (1963) 74.

2 J. G. Droysen, *Geschichte des Hellenismus* i² (Gotha 1877) 2.83 f.=i³ (Basel 1952) 307; i² 2.241 f.=i³ 404.

3 For a bibliographical survey see J. Seibert, *Alexander der Grosse* (Darmstadt 1972) 186–92. The references which are definitive for German scholarship are J. Kaerst, *Geschichte des Hellenismus* i³ (Berlin/Leipzig 1927) 471; U Wilcken, *Alexander the Great*, ed. E. N. Borza (New York 1967) 248 f.; F. Schachermeyr, *Alexander der Grosse: Das Problem seiner Persönlichkeit und seins Wirkens (SÖAW Wien* cclxxxv: 1973) 355, 472, 479–83 (exposition unchanged from the first edn: Graz 1949). For recent statement of orthodoxy see F. Altheim–R. Stiehl, *Geschichte Mittelasiens in Altertum* (Berlin 1970) 212 ff., esp. 217; H. E. Stier, *Welteroberung und Weltfriede im Wirken Al. d. Gr. (Rhein.-Westfäl. Akad. Wiss.* Vorträge G 187: 1972) 38–41. For the diffusion of the idea outside its German context see G. Radet, *Alexandre le Grand* (Paris 1931) 342 f.; W. W. Tarn, *Alexander the Great* (Cambride 1948) 1 111, 137 f.; J. R. Hamilton, *Alexander the Great* (London 1973) 105, 163.

4 *Op. cit.* (n. 3) ii 399–449 (the definitive statement). Tarn separated the two ideas of brotherhood and fusion, but he used precisely the same evidence to argue for universal brotherhood that others had used to support the policy of fusion. For the counter-arguments, which are conclusive, see E. Badian, 'Alexander the Great and the Unity of Mankind', *Historia* vii (1958) 425–44 with P. Merlan, *CPh* xlv (1950) 161–6.

5 H. Berve, 'Die Verschmelzungspolitik Alexanders des Grossen', *Klio* xxxi (1938) 135–68. Berve took his view to extreme lengths, even arguing that the concubines in Alexander's army train were exclusively Iranian (158 f.)

6 *Cf.* Berve (n. 5) 136 for the full definition.

7 F. Hampl, 'Alexander der Grosse und die Beurteilung geschichtlicher Persönlichkeiten', *La Nouvelle Clio* vi (1954) 115–23; cf. *Studies presented to D. M. Robinson* ii (Washington 1953) 319 f. For some pragmatic recent views which I would largely endorse, see E. Badian, *Studies in Greek & Roman History* (Oxford 1964) 201; P. Green, *Alexander of Macedon* (1974) 446.

8 Arr. vii 11.8–9. For the grammatical structure see the discussion of Badian (n. 4) 430 f.

9 For the Macedonian resentment see Arr. vii 6.1–5; 8.2. For the crushing of the mutiny see Arr. vii 11.1–4; Curt. x 3.5–6; Diod. xvii 109.3; Plut. *Al.* 71.4; Justin xii 12.1–6.

10 Cf. Arr. iii 21.5: καὶ διασῴζειν ἐς τὸ κοινὸν τὴν ἀρχήν (the regicides with Bessus).

11 For examples of ἀρχή as a synonym of satrapy see Arr. i 17.7, 23.8; vi 29.1. In Arrian ἀρχή implies rule over subjects (*cf.* iv 20.3 where the Persian empire is described as Περσῶν τε καὶ Μήδων τὴν ἀρχήν, rule *over* Persians and Medes). I cannot see how the Opis prayer can imply anything other than that the Persians and Macedonians were to rule jointly over subject peoples. The distinctions hitherto made between ἀρχή as 'rule' and ἀρχή as 'realm' are meaningless: Tarn (n. 3) ii 443 f.; F. Wüst, *Historia* ii (1953) 429; *cf.* Badian (n. 4) 431.

12 Arrian makes it clear that the participants at the feast were clearly divided by their national origins. Far from intermingling the Persians and Macedonians were separated from each other and the Macedonians alone were in the king's entourage (ἀμφ' αὐτὸν μὲν Μακεδόνων, ἐν δὲ τῷ ἐφεξῆς τούτων Περσῶν). *Cf.* Badian (n. 4) 429 f.

13 Diod, xviii 4.4: ὅπας τὰς μεγίστας ἠπείρους . . . εἰς κοινὴν ὁμόνοιαν καὶ συγγενικὴν φιλίαν καταστήσῃ.

14 So Badian, *HSCP* lxxii (1968) 194–5. Even if the proposals did contain statements of intent, those statements were transmitted by Perdiccas and cannot be directly attributed to Alexander himself. *Cf.* Schachermeyr, *Alexander in Babylon (SÖAW Wien* cclxviii. 3: 1970) 192: 'natürlich hat Perdikkas am Heer nicht ganz Schriftsätze vorgelesen, sondern das meiste einfach paraphrasiert'.

15 At xvii 110.2 he refers to the mixed phalanx of Persians and Macedonians as κεκραμένην καὶ ἁρμόζουσαν τῇ ἰδίᾳ προαιρέσει, but there is no other reference to any deliberate policy of fusion.

16 *Cf.* Schachermeyr, *JÖAI* xli (1954) 120–3; Badian (n. 14) 183 ff., both conclusive against Tarn (n .3) ii 380.

17 *Cf.* F. Jacoby, *RE* viii 1542 f.; Schachermeyr (n. 14) 106 f.

18 *Cf.* R Andreotti, *Saeculum* viii (1957) 134, arguing that Hieronymus may have had a pacifist ideology after his experience of the devastation wrought by the Successors (but *cf.* Schachermeyr [n. 14] 194 n. 188). If so, he may have placed a romantic interpretation upon Alexander's projected colonisation in order to preach a sermon to his own generation.

19 *Cf.* Badian (n. 14) 198 f., 203 f. Schachermeyr (n. 14) 193 f. places too much faith in the incorruptibility of Eumenes and takes it for granted that Hieronymus both had inside information and revealed nothing but the truth. Perdiccas read the *hypomnemata*, but he acted on a group decision and, if there were forgeries, Eumenes would have been privy to them and acquiesced.

20 Strabo i 4.9 (66).

21 Plut. *de Al. for.* i 6 (329a–c). The attribution to Eratosthenes began with E. Schwartz, *RhM* xl (1885), 252–4: briefly and dogmatically stated but subsequently accepted as dogma (*cf.* Tarn (n. 3) ii 437).

22 Badian (n. 4) 434–40; J. R. Hamilton, *Plutarch Alexander* (Oxford 1969) xxix–xxxiii. See now P. A. Brunt, *Athenaeum* lv (1977) 45–7.

23 *de Al. for.* i 8 (330a) = *FGrH* 241 F 30.

24 The thesis to be proved is expounded at i 4 (328b), and it is regularly pointed by contrasts between philosophical principle and Alexander's actions in practice (328c–e, 329a–b, 330c).

25 Strabo xv 1.64 (715) = *FGrH* 134 F 17; *cf.* Hamilton (n. 22) xxxi.

26 For the characterisation of Alexander see Ael. Arist. xxvi (εἰς Ῥώμην) 24–7. By contrast under Rome there is no distinction of Europe and Asia (60), ἀλλὰ καθέστηκε κοινὴ τῆς γῆς δημοκρατία ὑφ' ἑνὶ τῷ ἀρίστῳ ἄρχοντι καὶ κοσμητῇ, and there has developed a single harmonious union: καὶ γέγονε μία ἁρμονία πολιτείας ἅπαντας συγκεκληκυῖα (66).

27 One may compare the orations of Dio of Prusa. In the first Alexander appears briefly as the type of an immoderate ruler, in the second he is the defender and emulator of an idealised Homeric kingship, and in the fourth he is presented as the youthful interlocutor of Diogenes, basically sound but in need of Cynic deflation. See A Heuss, *Antike und Abendland* iv (1954) 92 f.

28 Curt. X 3. 12–14: cf. 14, 'omnia eundem ducunt colorem. Nec Persis Macedonun morem adumbrare nec Macedonibus Persas imitari decorum. Eiusdem iuris esse debent qui sub eodem victuri sunt' (the continuation is lost in a lacuna).

29 Diod. xvii 77.4–7; Curt. vi 6.1–10; Justin xii 3.8–12; *Metz Epitome* 1–2. Cf. Plut. *Al.* 45.1–4; Arr. iv 7.4–5. For full discussion see H.-H. Ritter, *Diadem und Königsherrschaft* (*Vestigia* vii: 1965) 31–55, superseding Berve (n. 5) 148–52.

30 Arrian iv 7.4 (and the derivative *Itinerarium* 88) claim that Alexander adopted the upright tiara (*kitaris*) of the Persian king. Berve (n. 5) 148–50 therefore argued that Alexander alternated full Persian dress with a more conservative mixed costume, and scholars have been reluctant to reject Arrian's statement. But there is no corroboration (apart from the passing remark of Lucian, *Dial. Mort.* 14.4), and it conflicts with the explicit statements of the other sources. In fact Arrian's report of the Persian costume is a parenthesis, a further example of Alexander's barbarism tacked onto the punishment of Bessus, and Arrian may have added it from his own memory – in which case he could easily have made a slip (*cf.* iii 22.4 where he refers casually to the battle of 'Arbela' despite his fulminations at vi 11.4). Certainly his passing comment cannot stand against the rest of the tradition (so Ritter [n. 29] 47).

31 Arr. iv 7.4; *cf.* vii 29.4.

32 Plut. Al. 45.1; cf. *de Al. for.* i 8 (330a).

33 The Achaemenid courtiers are regularly termed φοινικισταί or *purpurati*; *cf.* Xen. *Anab.* i 2.20; 5.7–8; Curt. iii 2.10; 8.15; 13.13 f. M. Reinhold, *Purple as a Status Symbol in Antiquity* (Coll. Latomus cxvi: 1970) 18–20.

34 The lesson was underlined when Alexander selected as his chiliarch or Grand Vizier (Persian *hazarapatis*) his closest friend, Hephaestion: Berve, *Das Alexanderreich* (Munich 1926) ii 173 no. 357; Schachermeyr (n. 14) 31–7. The date of this appointment is not known, but it presumably followed his elevation to the command of the Companion cavalry in late 330 (Arr. iii 27.4), some time after Alexander first introduced Persian court ceremonial.

35 Plut. *Al.* 45.1; *cf.* Diod. 77.4; Curt. vi 6.1, etc.

36 Arrian places it in his narrative of 329/8, but the context is a timeless digression (above n. 30) and there is no basis for chronological arguments: *cf.* Ritter (n. 29) 47–9.

37 Arr. ii 14.8–9; Curt. iv 1. 1–14; Plut. *Al.* 34.1 (cf. *FGrH* 532 F 1. C 38); Plut. *Al.* 37.7, 56.2; *de Al. for.* 329d; Diod. 66.3; Curt. v 2.13. Altheim (n. 3) 195–202 is totally unconvincing when he argues that Alexander had no pretentions to be king of Asia before the death of Darius.

38 The arguments of Ritter (n. 29) 49 ff.

39 Arr. iii 25.3; *cf.* Curt. vi 6.12–13; *Metz Epit.* 3. For the royal monopoly of the upright tiara see Ar. *Birds* 487 with scholia; Xen. *Anab.* ii 5.23; Plut. *Artax.* 26.4 and, in general, Ritter (n. 29) 6 ff.

40 Arr. iii 21.5, 30.4; *cf.* Diod. 74.1.

41 Arr. iii 19.5–6; Plut. *Al.* 42.5; Diod. 74.3–4; Curt. vi 2.17; Justin xii 1.1. *Cf.* Bosworth, *CQ* xxvi (1976) 132–6 for the chronology.

42 Arr. iii 19.7–8. For the reunification in Arachosia see Curt. vii 3.4. R. D. Milns, *GRBS* vii (1966) 165 n. 34 (so R. Lane Fox, *Alexander the Great* [London 1973] 532) has argued that the whole army was united in Parthia, but the argument rests on a misinterpretation of Arr. iii 25.4. The forces there said to be united are patently the several army columns used separately

during the Elburz campaign (*cf.* iii 22.2, 24.1). It is clear that even the cavalry from the Median contingent only caught up when Alexander was on his way to Bactra (iii 25.3); the infantry must have followed at a considerable interval.

43 *Cf.* Arr. iii 19.7. The mercenaries and Thracians commissioned to Parmenion were earmarked for the abortive Cadusian expedition, but they clearly remained as the garrison of Media. Parmenion's lieutenants and murderers are known to have held commands over mercenary troops and Thracians: cf. Berve (n. 34) nos 8, 422, 508, 712.

44 Arr. iii 25.5–7; Diod. 78.1–4; Curt. vi 6.20–34. The vulgate tradition is fuller and more credible than Arrian.

45 Arr. iii 28.2–3; Diod. 81.3; Curt. vii 3.2 (renewed revolt when Alexander was in Ariaspian territory: Jan. 329); Diod. 83.4–6; Curt. vii 4.32 ff. (revolt crushed before Alexander reached Bactra: summer 329).

46 Arr. iv 7.1: Brazanes and his fellow rebels were captured by Phrataphernes and conveyed to Bactra/Zariaspa during the winter of 329/8. At the same time Arsaces, Alexander's second satrap of Areia, was arrested for connivance in Satibarzanes' revolt: ἐθελοκακεῖν at iii 29.5 implies dereliction of duty (*cf.* iv 18.3; *Tact.* 12.11 – the word is Herodotean) rather than actual rebellion (Berve [n. 34] nos 146, 179). There was trouble in the central satrapies apparently as late as 328/7, when Alexander felt it necessary to dismiss his satraps in Drangiana and Tapuria (Arr. iv. 18.3; Curt. viii 3.17; *cf.* x 1.39). The details and chronology of these dismissals are obscure, but the fact is certain.

47 Arr. ii 14.7 (at this stage the only Persian noble known to have been with Alexander was Mithrines: Berve [n. 34] no. 524).

48 Diod. 77.7; Curt. vi 6.9–12; Justin xii 4.1; *cf.* Arr. vii 6.2, 8.2.

49 *Cf.* Plut. *Al.* 47.7–12; *de Al. for.* ii 4 (337a).

50 Plut. *Demetr.* 14.2: διὰ τὸ προσυνωκηκέναι Κρατέρῳ τῷ πλείστην εὔνοιαν αὐτοῦ παρὰ Μακεδόσι τῶν Ἀλεξάνδρου διαδόχων ἀπολιπόντι.

51 *Cf.* Plut. *Eum.* 6–7; Nepos *Eum.* 3.4–5; Arr. *Succ.* F 1.27 (Roos) (*cf.* F 19=Suda s.v Κράτερος, contrasting Craterus' popularity with the unpopularity of Antipater).

52 Plut. *Eum.* 6.3 This explicit statement has been queried (cf. Berve [n. 34] ii 226; Hamilton [n. 22] 131), mainly on the strength of Alexander's farewell at Opis (τὸν πιστότατόν τε αὐτῷ καὶ ὄντινα ἴσον τῇ ἑαυτοῦ κεφαλῇ ἄγει). But the king had given an equally moving (and permanent) farewell to Coenus shortly after his determined opposition at the Hyphasis (Arr. vi 2.1; Curt. ix 3.20; *cf.* Badian, *JHS* lxxxi [1961] 25), and in the case of Craterus the public statement of confidence and friendship does not exclude there having been bitter wranglers in private. Curtius describes Craterus as *regi carus in paucis* (vi 8.2), but the comment comes in the context of Philotas' trial, before there can have been concerted opposition to Alexander's Medism.

53 See the detailed exposition of Berve (n. 34) ii 222–4 (no. 446).

54 *Cf.* Arr. iv 11.6: the context is Callisthenes' speech against *proskynesis*, which presumably owes much to Arrian's own shaping, but the sentiment is convincing enough.

55 Curt. vi 2.15 ff.; Diod. 74.3; Justin xii 3.2–4. The episode is omitted by Arrian, probably because his sources were reluctant to stress the discontent in the army.

56 Diod. 77.7: τούτοις μὲν οὖν τοῖς ἐθισμοῖς Ἀλέξανδρος σπανίως ἐχρῆτο, τοῖς δὲ προυπάρχουσι κατὰ τὸ πλεῖστον ἐνδιέτριβε.

57 Plut. *Al.* 51.2; *cf.* 71.3.

58 Curt. viii 7.12: *Persarum te vestis et disciplina delectat: patrios mores exosus es.* Cf. viii 8.10–13.

59 Polyaen. iv 3.24.

60 *FGrH* 126 F 5 (Athen. xii 537e–f). His description of the mixed dress coheres with the other evidence, particularly that of Eratosthenes (nn. 23, 29), and Aristobulus seems to confirm that Alexander wore the *kausia* with the diadem as his day-to-day dress (Arr. vii 22.2 = *FGrH* 139 F 55). *Cf.* Ritter (n. 29) 57–8, accepting the material from Ephippus despite his misgivings about the value of the source.

61 Athen. xii 539d = *FGrH* 81 F 41; Ael. *VH* ix 3; Polyaen. iv 3.24.

62 *FGrH* 125 F 4: 100 couches and 20 cubit pillars covered with gold and silver leaf.

63 ἐπὶ τούτοις πεντακόσιοι Σούσιοι πορφυροσχήμονες. This group of 500 is also mentioned by Athenaeus, but Polyaenus alone says that they came from Susa.

64 *Cf.* Diod. 57.2; Curt. iv 13.27 with Arr. iii 11.9. According to Justin xii 7.5 the name originated in 327 when Alexander began his march into India and had his men's shields silvered for the occasion – and Harpalus allegedly sent 25,000 items of equipment chased with silver and gold (Curt. ix 3.21). The *argyraspides* also appear in the list of units named at the Opis mutiny in the place of the hypaspists (Arr. vii 11.3). This evidence cannot be dismissed as fantasy and anachronism (*pace* R. D. Lock, *Historia* xxvi [1977] 373–8. After the Indian campaign the hypaspists could also be known as *argyraspides*. The fact that the famous corps of Teutamus and Antigenes is called solely *argyraspides*, never hypaspists, is easy to explain. After Alexander's death the Successors set up their own bodyguards of hypaspists (Polyaen. iv 6.8; Diod. xix 28.1; Polyaen. iv 9.3) and hypaspist was no longer an exclusive title. Accordingly the veterans of Alexander used their second title *argyraspides* to distinguish themselves from the hypaspists of the other generals, who had not served under Alexander.

65 Diod. xix 22.2.

66 Diod. 110.1 f. (after the mutiny); Justin xii 12.4 (during). Both sources conflate the expansion of the guard with the formation of a mixed phalanx, which only occurred in mid 323 (p. 224). The common source (Cleitarchus) may well have given a summary of Alexander's various experiments with mixed infantry forces and tacked them onto the report of the great mutiny. Arr vii 29.4 speaks in the most general terms of the admixture of μηλοφόροι into the Macedonian ranks, corroborating the fact but giving no indication of chronology.

67 Diod. xviii 27.1: περὶ τὸν βασιλέα μία μὲν ὑπῆρχε θεραπεία καθωπλισμένη Μακεδόνων, ἄλλη δὲ Περσῶν μηλοφόρων.

68 *Cf.* J. R. Hamilton, *CQ* iii (1953) 156 f.; Schachermeyr (n. 3) 514 f.

69 Curt. ix 10.21, 29 (Carmania); Arr. vii 4.1; Plut. *Al.* 68.7 (Susiana/Paraetacene). See further Badian (n. 52) 17; Bosworth, *CQ* xxi (1971) 124; Schachermeyr (n. 3) 477 f.

70 Arr. vi 30.1–2; Curt. x 1.24 ff. For Orxines' lineage see Curt. iv 12.8. Curtius states that he had the overall command of the Persians at Gaugamela; Arrian (iii 8.5) gives him the command of the forces of the Red Sea, but there is almost certainly a lacuna in his text – all reference to the Persian national contingent is omitted.

71 Arr. vi 27.3; 29.3. Curtius ix 10.19 mentions two rebels, Ozines and Zariaspes, who were arrested by Craterus; the former at least seems identical with Arrian's Ordanes: Droysen (n. 2) i² 2.199 n. 1; but *cf.* Berve (n. 34) no. 579.

72 Plut. *Al.* 68.3: καὶ ὅλως διέδραμε σάλος ἁπάντων καὶ νεωτερισμός; *cf.* Curt. x 1.7.

73 Note the wrangle with Antipater and Parmenion in 335 (Diod. 16.2); the story is circumstantial and there is no reason to doubt it.

74 Diod. 37.6; Curt. iii 12.24 f.; *cf.* Diod. 38.1; 67.1; Curt. v 2.18 ff.; Arr. ii 12.5.

75 Plut. *Al.* 21.7; *Eum.* 1.7; Diod. xx 20.1; 28.1; Justin xi 10.2 f.; xii 15.9; Tarn's attempt to disprove the existence of the captive Barsine and her son Heracles (ii 330–7) is now a mere historical curiosity; *cf.* Schachermeyr (n. 14) 22 n. 32a; P. A. Brunt, *RFIC* ciii (1975) 22–34; R. M. Errington, *JHS* xc (1970) 74.

76 Arrian iv 18.4 says that the family of Oxyartes was captured on the rock of Sogdiana in spring 327. Curtius says nothing about Oxyartes and his family in the context of the Sogdian rock, whose capture he dates to spring 328 (vii 11.1). Rhoxane first appears in a banquet given by 'Cohortandus' in spring 327 (viii 4.21–30). That is the order of events in the index of Diodorus (the narrative proper is lost) and the *Metz Epitome* (15–18, 28–31). Strabo xi 11.4 (517) claims that Alexander met Rhoxane not on the rock of Sogdiana but on the rock of Sismithres, the next to be captured. The source conflict is obstinate and can only be settled by careful analysis of all sources in context, with particular emphasis on chronology. Fortunately all sources place the actual marriage immediately before the march on India.

77 Curt. viii 4.25; *cf.* Plut. *Al.* 47.7 with Hamilton (n. 22) 129 f.

78 Arr. iv 2.4: οὕτως ἐξ Ἀλεξάνδρου προστεταγμένον; 3.1; Curt. vii 6.16.

79 Curt. vii 11.28 (*Metz Epit.* 18 has a variant); the story is omitted by Arrian but not contradicted (*cf.* iv 19.4).

80 Diod. xvii index κγ' (p. 3 Budé; 110 Loeb): ὡς Ἀλέξανδρος ἀποστάντας τοὺς Σογδιανοὺς κατεπολέμησε καὶ κατέσφαξεν αὐτῶν πλείους τῶν δώδεκα μυριάδων.

81 Cf. Arr. iv 4.1. At Alexandria in Caucaso there were 7,000 locals to 3,000 Hellenic troops (Diod. 83.2; Curt. vii 3.23). There is no indication that the number of settlers or the racial proportion was consistent throughout Alexander's foundations.

82 Curt. vii 6.27; Justin xii 5.12 f. *Cf.* P. Briant, *Klio* lx (1978) 74–7.

83 So Berve (n. 34) i 299. The excavations at Aï Khanoum are illustrating with ever increasing fullness the stubbornly Hellenic nature of that foundation. *Cf.* Seibert (n. 3) for bibliography, to which add Sir M. Wheeler, *Flames over Persepolis* (London 1968) 75 ff. and the successive reports by P. Bernard in *CRAI* 1974–6. Note particularly the new discoveries relating to the theatre and theatrical performances: *CRAI* 1976, 307–22.

84 Curt. vii 11.29: *multitudo deditorum incolis novarum urbium cum pecunia capta dono data est.*

85 Arr. iii 29.1 (Aornus); *Metz Epit.* 7–8; Arr. iv 5.2 (Maracanda), 16.4–5; Curt. viii 1.3 (Attinas, phrurarch of an unknown fortress).

86 Berve (n. 34) no. 60. He was appointed satrap either in winter 328/7 (Arr. iv 17.3) or in summer 328 (Curt. viii 2.14).

87 For Sisimithres see Curt. viii 2.32; 4.20; *Metz Epit*, 19; for Chorienes *Metz Epit.* 28; Curt. viii 4.21 (Alde's emendation Oxyartes for 'Cohortandus' is unacceptable). Arrian (iv 21.9) conflates the two figures.

88 For the story of Pixodarus see Plut. *Al.* 10.1–5; *cf* Badian *Phoenix* xvii (1963) 244 ff. with Hamilton (n. 22) 24 ff. For the outcome of the episode see Arr. i 23.8; Strabo xiv 2.17 (657).

89 Plut. *Al.* 22.7; Arr. i 23.8. For the eastern tradition of descent through the female line see H. Gelzer, *RhM* xxxv (1880) 515–17.

90 *Metz Epit.* 31; Diod. xvii index λ': τῶν φίλων πολλοὺς ἔπεισε γῆμαι.

91 Arr. vii 4.6 (*cf.* Plut. *Al.* 70.3; *de Al. for.* 7 [329d–e]; Diod. 107.6; Justin xii 10.10; Chares *FGrH* 125 F 4). The Persian ritual was what irked the Macedonian rank and file (vii 6.2); the marriage to Rhoxane had been celebrated in Macedonian mode according to Curtius (vii 4.27), and there is no reason to dispute his statement (*cf.* M. Renard and J. Servais, *Ant. Class.* xxiv [1955] 29–50).

92 Arr. vii 4.8; Plut. *Al.* 70.3. See further p. 224.

93 Plut. 329e: κοινωνίαν συνιοῦσι τοῖς μεγίστοις καὶ δυνατωτάτοις γένεσι; *cf.* Curt. x 3.11–14.

94 *Cf.* Hampl (n. 7) 119.

95 Artabazus (Berve [n. 34] no. 152) had married a sister of Mentor and Memnon of Rhodes but that marriage had taken place by 362: Dem. xxiii 154, 157; *cf.* Brunt, *RFIC* ciii (1975) 25.

96 Arr. vii 4.5–7. For the role of Spitamenes see iii 28.10, 29.6; iv 3.6 ff.; 17.7. Full references in Berve (n. 34) ii 359–61 (no. 717).

97 Arr. vi 30.2 f.; vii 6.3, 23.3.

98 Arr. iii 6.6 (Laomedon); Diod. xix 23.1–3; Polyaen. iv 8.3 (Eumenes). Note, however, the use of an Iranian interpreter in Sogdiana (Arr. iv 3.7).

99 Diod. xix 14.5: φασὶ καὶ τὸν Ἀλέξανδρον αὐτῷ μόνῳ Μακεδόνων συγχωρῆσαι Περσικὴν φορεῖν στολήν, χαρίζεσθαι βουλόμενον τοῖς Πέρσαις καὶ διὰ τούτου νομίζοντα κατὰ πάνθ' ἕξειν τὸ ἔθνος ὑπήκοον.

100 Arrian states that one of Peucestas' qualifications to govern Persis was his general sympathy with the barbarian life-style (τῷ βαρβαρικῷ τρόπῳ τῆς διαίτης; vi 30.2). This does not imply that he had already adopted Persian dress. Leonnatus, for instance, is said to have attached himself to the lifestyle of the conquered peoples in Alexander's lifetime; he only assumed items of Persian dress after the king's death: Suda s.v. Λεόννατος = Arr. *Succ.* F 12 (Roos).

101 Peucestas was trierarch with his brother in 320 (Arr. *Ind.* 19.8), but at the Malli town he is merely styled 'one of the hypaspists' (Diod. 99.4; but *cf.* Arr. vi 9.3). He seems to have held no position of command before his elevation to the Bodyguard in Carmania (Arr. vi 28.3). See further Berve (n. 34) no. 634.

102 Plut. *Al.* 43.7; Curt. vi 2.11. He remained at court for a little over a year, returning to Ecbatana to supervise the execution of Bessus (Diod. 83.9; Curt. vii 5.40; Justin xii 5.11).

103 Arr. iv 3.7. For the persistence of Iranian families in southern Asia Minor throughout the Hellenistic and Roman periods see L. Robert, *Opera Minora Selecta* iii (Amsterdam 1969) 1532 ff.; *CRAI* 1975, 326–30. For the specifically Lycian evidence see E. Benveniste, *Titres et noms propres en iranien ancien* (Paris 1966) 101–3.

104 Arr. iv 6.1 = *FGrH* 139 F 27. For the general bias of this account see L. Pearson, *The Lost Histories of Alexander the Great* (1960) 167 f. Curtius vii 6.24, 7.34 ff. says nothing about Pharnuches and makes Menedemus sole commander (so *Metz Epit.* 13).

105 Arr. *Ind.* 18.8 = *FGrH* 133 F 1a.

106 Ael. *VH* iii 23 = *FGrH* 117 F 2a. Berve (n. 34) no. 195 and Badian, *CQ* viii (1958) 156, prefer to identify this Bagoas as the notorious eunuch.

107 Arr. vii 6.4–5. For the textual problems (not relevant here) see the *Appendix*, [below, pp. 234–5].

108 Some had already given service to Alexander: Cophes had negotiated the surrender of Ariomazes (Curt. vii 11.22 ff.), Phradasmenes had brought succour to the army in Carmania (Arr. vi 27.3) and Artiboles had played a role in the pursuit of Darius (iii 21.1; but *cf.* Curt. v 13.11; Berve (n. 34) nos. 82, 154).

109 There is a possibilbity that they are the sons of Atropates, the third Iranian satrap surviving in 324 (Berve (n. 34) no. 124); his two colleagues, Phrataphernes and Oxyartes, had supplied sons for the *agema*, and he had visited Alexander at Pasargadae, shortly after the arrival of Phradasmenes and Phrataphernes (Arr. vi 29.3; *cf.* 27.3).

110 *Cf.* Curt. vi 2.7, adding that Hystaspes was both a relative of Darius and a military commander under him. For the fifth-century Hystaspes see Diod. xi 69.2. Given his Bactrian connexions and his relationship to Darius there is some chance that he was a relative of Bessus!

111 Arr. iv 13.1; Curt. viii 6.2–6; *cf.* Berve (n. 34) i 37–9.

112 Arr. iii 24.1; *cf.* 25.2–5, 29.7; iv 4.7, 23.1, 25.6, 26.4, 29.7; vi 17.4.

113 Berve (n. 34) i 151; Brunt, *JHS* lxxxiii (1963) 42; Griffith, *JHS* lxxxiii (1963) 69 f.

114 Arr. iii 25.2, 5. The remaining ἱππακοντισταί were used on Alexander's punitive expedition (25.6).

115 Compare Arr. iii 25.6 with 20.1.

116 Arr. iv 4.6–7. *Cf.* Brunt (n. 113) 27 f.; R. D. Milns, *JHS* lxxxvi (1966) 167; M. M. Markle, *AJA* lxxxi (1977) 337.

117 It is possible that even before 330 the σαρισσοφόροι used their special weapon only in pitched battle (Arr. i 14.1; Curt. iv 15.13); it would have been an unnecessary encumbrance: *cf.* Markle (n. 116) 334–6.

118 Arr. iii 29.7. The date and nature of the reorganisation is disputed (*cf.* Brunt (n. 113) 28–30; Griffith (n. 113) 70–73) and the subject badly needs a thorough investigation. But the year 330 was undoubtedly a time of military innovation: *cf.* iii 16.11 (cavalry *lochoi*), iii 18.5 (a mysterious and unique cavalry *tetrarchia*).

119 The javelin was a traditional weapon of the Macedonian cavalry, illustrated on the coinage of Alexander I (*cf.* Markle (n. 116) 337 n. 59); the Companions may have fought with a javelin as well as their thrusting lance (Diod. 60.2; Arr. i 2–6; but *cf.* i 15.6).

120 Arr. iv 17.3; *cf.* Griffith (n. 113) 69.

121 Arr. v 11.3 (cavalry from Arachosia and Parapamisadae serving alongside Craterus' hipparchy); v 12.2 (Bactrians, Sogdians and Saka, including Dahian horse archers).

122 Arr. iv 24.1, 28.8; v 14.3, 15.1, 16.4, 18.3, 20.3 22.5; vi 5.5, 6.1, 21.3, 22.1.

123 Arr. v 12.2 καὶ Δάας τοὺς ἱπποτόξοτας. They were apparently 1,000 strong (v 16.4); see further Altheim (n. 3) 210 f.

124 vii 8.2: ἀνάμιξις τῶν ἀλλοφύλων ἐς τὰς τῶν ἑταίρων τάξεις. Griffith (n. 113) 68, 72 f., made absurdly heavy weather of this passage and denied that Arrian is summarising his previous exposition. Instead he argues that Arrian refers to a reorganisation during the Indian campaign, in which Orientals were added to the hipparchies; see the convincing rebuttal of Badian, *JHS* lxxxv (1965) 160.

125 Brunt (n. 113) 43. For the arrival of Drangians, Areians and Parthyaeans see Arr. vi 27.3. The Euacae are only known from Arrian, but they may be a picked unit, the cavalry equivalent of the *Kardakes* of the infantry (Arr. ii 8.6; Nepos *Dat.* 8.2; Hsch. s.v.; Tarn (n. 3) ii 180–2 should be discounted).

126 So Arr. *Tact.* 5.2–4: πλῆθος ἀνθρώπων ἀθρόον καὶ ἄτακτον ἐς τάξιν καὶ κόσμον καταστῆσαι – τὸ δ' ἔστιν καταλοχίσαι τε καὶ ξυλλοχίσαι. Compare Arr. vii 24.1 where he describes the division of Peucestas' Persians into phalanx files; at vii 23.3 he uses καταλέγειν as a synonym (*cf.* Diod. xviii 70.1).

127 So Griffith (n. 113) 72: his second interpretation 'one λόχος of each *ile* now became a λόχος of picked Iranians' is not impossible, but again it reads too much into the wording. The word anticipates κατελέγησαν and προσκαταλεγέντες immediately below and, as at vii 24.1, it is used as a conscious variant in the most general sense.

128 I do not understand how Brunt (n. 113) 44 can say that it 'might mean that it was more or less Oriental than the other four'.

129 E.g. Berve (n. 34) i 111 f.; Tarn (n. 3) ii 164 f.; Brunt (n. 113) 43 f.; Griffith (n. 113) 72–4.

130 There were eight hipparchies in addition to the *agema* between 328 and 326 (*cf.* Arr. iv 24.1 with 22.7, 23.1; vi 6.4 with 7.2 and 6.1; Brunt [n. 113] 29 has miscalculated by one). There must have been serious losses in Gedrosia but we have no basis for speculation.

131 For the casualties see H. Strasburger, *Hermes* lxxx (1952) 486 f. (15,000 survivors out of 60,000/70,000). For the livestock see Arr. vi 25.1: τῶν ἵππων τοὺς πολλοὺς ἀποσφάζοντες.

132 Arr. vii 11.3; *cf.* Griffith (n. 113) 72: 'this must imply that hitherto its members have been all Macedonians'.

133 Arr. vi. 17.3; vi 14.4 does not explicitly exclude Iranians.

134 Anaximenes *FGrH* 72 F 4; on which see most recently P. A. Brunt, *JHS* xcvi (1976) 150–3; R. D. Milns in *Entr. Hardt* xxii (1976) 89 ff.

135 Arr. vii 6.1; Diod. 108. 1–3; Plut. *Al.* 71.1.

136 Plut. *Al.* 47.6.

137 P. Briant, *RÉA* lxxiv (1972) 51–60, esp. 55 – an excellent summary, but slightly misleading in that Briant (57) seems to think that Alexander actually conferred the title *pezhetairoi* upon his Iranian infantry at Opis. Arrian suggests that Alexander made a threat only; there is not hint that he fully carried it out.

138 Diod. xi 67.5 (*cf.* Plut. *Cleom.* 23.1); Plut. *Eum.* 4.2–3: *pace* Briant (n. 137) 58 it does not appear that Eumenes created an ἀντίταγμα against his own troops. After the victory against Ariarathes Neoptolemus was left to continue operations in Armenia with a large nucleus of Macedonian troops (Briant, *Antigone le Borgne* [Paris 1973] 152 n. 8). According to Plutarch Perdiccas had his suspicions of Neoptolemus' loyalty and commissioned Eumenes to control him – hence the need for the Iranian cavalry to be used against Neoptolemus' phalanx (*Eum.* 4.3, *cf.* 5.4). There is no indication that Eumenes had Macedonians of his own in any numbers (*cf.* Diod. xviii 29.5).

139 Curt. viii 5.1: *obsides simul habiturus et milites.* Justin xii 4.11 dates the formation of the *Epigoni* to the same period but conflates them with the soldiers' children who were also trained in Macedonian style (*cf.* Arr. vii 12.2).

140 vii 6.1: οἱ σατράπαι οἱ ἐκ τῶν πόλεων τῶν νεοκτίστων καὶ τῆς ἄλλης γῆς τῆς δοριαλώτου. At v 20.7 Sisicottus, previously named phrurarch of Aornus (iv 30.4), is termed satrap. For the interchangeability of the terms satrap and hyparch see Bosworth, *CQ* xxiv (1974) 55–7.

141 E.g. iv 22.4.

142 Justin xii 4.2–10: Berve (n. 5) 157–9 valiantly attempts to prove that the women of these marriages were predominantly Iranian.

143 Arr. vii 4.8 (*cf.* Plut. *Al.* 70.3); vii 12.2.

144 Diod. xvii 74.3; Curt. vi 2.15–4.1; Justin xii 3.2–4; Plut. *Al.* 47.1–2.

145 *Cf.* Badian (n. 7) 201: 'his purpose, ultimately, was the creation of a royal army with no fixed blood or domicile – children of the camp who knew no loyalty but to him'.

146 Arr. vii 23.1–4; *cf.* Diod. 110.2 (wrongly assigned to Susa 324).

147 Plb. xviii 30.1–4; *cf.* Arr. *Tact.* 12.10.

148 Arr. *Ect. c. Alanos* 15–17, 26 f. For full discussion see Bosworth, *HSCP* lxxxi (1977) 238–47.

149 Arr. i 6.1–3; ii 8.2 (*cf.* Plb. xii 19.5 f.; Curt. iii 9.12).

150 So Brunt (n. 113) 38; Griffith, *G&R* xii (1965) 130–1 n. 4. Berve (n. 34) i 134, was more cautious (Curtius gives a total of Macedonians *and Greeks* without giving their relative proportions).

151 *Cf.* Curt. x 2.2; Justin xiii 5.7 (Athens). For the Arabian expedition see Schachermeyr (n. 3) 538–46.

152 Even so the possibility of being chosen led to panic (Curt. x 2.12).

153 Diod. xviii 16.4. The figure 10,000 is standard; Arr. vii 12.1; Diod. xvii 109.1; *cf.* Justin xii 12.7 (11,000, presumably including the 1,500 cavalry).

154 Curt. vii 10.11 f.; ix 3.21. Alexander had sent a recruiting expedition from Sogdiana in winter 328/7 (Arr. iv 18.3) but there were no results before 323, when the cavalry with Menidas at Babylon *may* have come from Macedonia (vii 23.1; *cf.* Berve [n. 34] no. 258, Badian [n. 52] 22 n. 39). Justin also suggests that the shortage of Macedonians was becoming apparent by 327 (xxii 4.5).

155 Diod. xviii 12.2. *Pace* Griffith (n. 150) 130 f., the forces of Antipater in 323 cannot be estimated from Diodorus' figures, for Μακεδόνες at 12.2 patently means 'the forces on the Macedonian side', doubtless including Illyrians and Thracians as well as mercenaries: *cf.* M. Launey, *Recherches sur les armées hellénistiques* (Paris 1949) 292 f. We should remember that Antipater was in similar difficulties at the time of Agis' War yet was able to raise a force of 40,000: Diod. 63.1; cf. *Phoenix* xxix (1975) 35–8. Similarly we have no idea how many of the 20,000 foot raised by Leonnatus (Diod. xviii 14.4–5) were native Macedonians. The only thing certain is that the forces with Craterus in 321 were 20,000 in number and 'mostly Macedonians' (Diod. xviii 30.4; *cf.* 24.1), but, once again, the nucleus must have been the veterans he had brought from Opis.

156 For their presence with Perdiccas see Arr. *Succ.* F 1.35 (Roos) and for their famous ἀποσκευή see Diod. xix 43.7; Plut. *Eum.* 16; Justin xiv 3.3 ff.

157 Peithon in 323 had 3,000 infantry and 800 cavalry selected by lot from the Macedonians (Diod. xviii 7.3) and Neoptolemus had an unspecified number of Macedonians in Armenia (above, n. 138); but we have no criteria for calculating the total. Berve's estimate of 4,000–5,000 (i 185) is the merest guess (see also Schachermeyr [n. 14] 14 f: 5,000–6,000 phalangites and hypaspists).

158 Diod. xix 30.6, 41.1–2; Plut. *Eum.* 16.7–8.

159 Justin xvii 2.10 f.; for Antigonus see Hieronymus, *FGrH* 154 F 10.

160 Arr. vii 12.4; on this matter see Badian (n. 52) 38 f.; Bosworth (n. 69) 125.

161 Arr. vii 25.2 (from the *Ephemerides*); *cf.* Plut. *Al.* 76.3 with Hamilton's notes.

162 Contrast Berve (n. 5) 157: 'Und es kann kaum einem Zweifel unterliegen, dass Alexander auch den aus Makedonien zu erwartenden Nachschub mit iranischen Elementen . . . in ähnlicher Weise zu verbinden beabsichtigte.'

APPENDIX: ARRIAN VII 6.4

καὶ πέμπτη ἐπὶ τούτοις ἱππαρχία προσγενομένη, οὐ βαρβαρικὴ ἡ πᾶσα, ἀλλὰ ἐπαυξηθέντος γὰρ τοῦ παντὸς ἱππικοῦ κατελέγησαν ἐς αὐτὸ τῶν βαρβάρων.

'. . . and a fifth hipparchy added in addition to these, not entirely barbarian (but partially), for when the entire cavalry was expanded some barbarians were assigned to it.'

The difficulty is in the parenthesis. It purports to explain the existence of the fifth hipparchy but instead talks of the entire cavalry. The fact that some barbarians were assigned to the cavalry is a mere summary of the preceding phrases not an explanation of the formation of the fifth mixed hipparchy. There have been two recent attempts at emendation:

(i) Brunt, *JHS* lxxxiii (1963) 44, deletes the following phrase (τῷ τε ἀγήματι προσκαταλεγέντες) as a gloss and emends ἐς αὐτὸ to ἐς αὐτήν. The effect of this is to identify the fifth hipparchy as the *agema* (or rather, to remove the *agema* altogether) and contrast a fifth, barely infiltrated, hipparchy with four more heavily Oriental hipparchies. The gloss presupposed is difficult. Explanatory glosses in Arrian are usually rudimentary, whereas here we have a very sophisticated inference by the scribal commentator, identifying the fifth hipparchy with the *agema*. Nor is the τε 'curiously unemphatic'; it is the regular connective used to denote the last item in a series (Denniston, *Greek Particles*[2] 500 f.)–and the reorganisation of the *agema* is patently the last of the Macedonians' grievances.

(ii) Badian, *JHS* lxxxv (1965) 161, suggests the simple supplement <μόνον> οὐ βαρβαρικὴ ἡ πᾶσα. This creates the impression that the fifth hipparchy contrasted with the other four by its preponderance of barbarians. But the parenthesis remains curiously unhelpful. The idiom ἀλλὰ . . . γὰρ is extremely frequent in Arrian and in all cases it combines an adversative with an explanation (*cf.* e.g. v 13.2: οὐκ ἐς βέβαιον χωρίον ἐκβὰς . . . ἀλλὰ ἐς νῆσον γὰρ – 'not onto sure ground but the reverse, for it was an island'). The negative prepares the way for the explanation and cannot be emended away.

The difficulty lies in ἐς αὐτό, which is pleonastic and vacuous. What is needed is an explanation why the fifth hipparchy was not wholly barbarian, as opposed to the four wholly Iranian hipparchies. Any attempt to solve the problem involves quite drastic surgery, but I would tentatively suggest ἐς <τ>αὐτό, or more explicitly ἐς <τ>αὐτό <τοῖς Μακεδόσι> and translate 'not entirely barbarian but partially, for when the entire cavalry was expanded some barbarians were assigned to the same unit as Macedonians'. (For Arrian's use of ἐς ταὐτό see v 25.3; *Ind.* 3.9; 10.9.) But, whatever the original sense of the parenthesis, Arrian's presentation of the Macedonian grievances is clear and logical; first the existence of hipparchies comprised wholly of Iranians and then, much worse, the fifth hipparchy in which they served with the barbarians.

9

ALEXANDER
AND DEIFICATION

Introduction

One of the most controversial aspects of Alexander's reign is his apparent belief in his own divinity. The figure of the Macedonian king was semi-divine while alive,[1] and it is possible that Philip II was deified on his death in 336. As Alexander's reign progressed he strove to outdo his father's achievements, and deification while alive was clearly one way to do so. Perhaps at first Alexander sought to be recognised as a god in an effort to maintain the conquered people's unity and loyalty to him. However, as his megalomania grew in the later part of his reign, he seems to have held the belief that he was divine, dressing in imitation of various deities, having incense burned in honour of him (Source 99), and even thinking that his exploits outstripped those of Dionysus (Source 100).

The road to Alexander's deification began in winter 332 when he visited the oracle of Zeus Ammon in the oasis of Siwah in Egypt, guided there in miraculous fashion (Sources 92–97).[2] Here, the priests apparently told him (we have only Alexander's word for it, for he met with them in private) that he was a son of Zeus. This was the turning-point in his belief, and from then on he referred to himself in this way (for example, before the Battle of Gaugamela in 331: Source 98).

In 327, he tried to have the Asian custom of *proskynesis* (prostrating oneself before the person of the king in an act of subservience) adopted by his men at his court in Bactra (Sources 87 and 88).[3] To them, prostration before a ruler was tantamount to worship, hence blasphemous, and they resisted. Alexander was forced to abandon the attempt. While his aim may have been to create a form of social protocol common to Macedonians, Greeks and Persians,[4] he must have been aware of the religious connotations associated with the act and the reaction it would provoke among his men. Another possible explanation, then, is that his measure was a means of having his divine status recognised by all men in public (Arr. 4.9.9, Curt. 8.5.5).

Then in 323 the Greeks of the mainland were discussing divine honours for Alexander,[5] although there was resistance to it.[6] It has sometimes been thought that by this stage Alexander wanted all Greeks to worship him and issued a decree ordering this, but that seems unlikely. Equally mistaken is the view that Alexander claimed divinity because his Exiles Decree, which flouted the autonomy of the Greek cities, would be rejected by the League of Corinth as an unconstitutional measure – but not if it came from a god!

Alexander's deification had repercussions for him and his kingship. The Greeks accepted that Alexander was a descendant of Zeus through Heracles, but descendant of Zeus was different from Alexander calling himself an actual son of Zeus, and this the people did not accept. The *proskynesis* attempt caused widespread dissatisfaction of the army with him, which Alexander must have anticipated but chose to ignore. Certainly, the wishes and beliefs of his men meant little to him for a year later he was back to claiming divine status (Arr. 7.2.3), and during the Opis mutiny his men mocked their king's association with Zeus Ammon (Arr. 7.8.3). Finally, there was widespread resistance to Alexander's proposed deification among the Greeks and even more significantly among the Macedonians on the mainland, Alexander's own people.[7]

Ancient sources

92 Hence the oracle of Ammon, which was formerly held in great esteem, is now nearly deserted. This appears chiefly from the historians who have recorded the actions of Alexander, adding, indeed, much that has the appearance of flattery, but yet relating what is worthy of credit. Callisthenes, for instance, says that Alexander was ambitious of the glory of visiting the oracle, because he knew that Perseus and Heracles had before performed the journey thither. He set out from Paraetonium, although the south winds were blowing, and succeeded in his undertaking by vigour and perseverence. When out of his way on the road, he escaped being overwhelmed in a sand storm by a fall of rain, and by the guidance of two crows, which directed his course. These things are stated by way of flattery, as also what follows: that the priest permitted the king alone to pass into the temple in his usual dress, whereas the others changed theirs; that all heard the oracles on the outside of the temple, except Alexander, who was in the interior of the building; that the answers were not given, as at Delphi and at Branchidae, in words, but chiefly by nods and signs, as in Homer: 'the son of Kronos nodded with his sable brows', the prophet imitating Zeus. This, however, the man told the king, in express terms, that he was the son of Zeus. Callisthenes adds (after the exaggerating style of tragedy) that when Apollo had deserted the oracle among the Branchidae, on the temple being plundered by the Branchidae (who espoused the party of the Persians in the time of Xerxes) and the spring had failed, it then reappeared (on the arrival of Alexander); that the ambassadors also of the Milesians carried back to Memphis numerous answers of the oracle respecting the descent of Alexander from Zeus, and the future victory which he should obtain at Arbela,[8] the death of Darius, and the political changes at Sparta. He says also that the Erythraean Athenais, who resembled the ancient Erythraean Sibyl, had declared the high descent of Alexander. Such are the accounts of the historians (Callisthenes, *FGrH* 124 F 14a = Strabo 17.1.43).

93 . . . ravens appeared and assumed direction of their march, flying swiftly in front of them when they followed, and waiting for them when they marched slowly and lagged behind. Moreover, what was most astonishing of all, Callisthenes tells us that the birds by their cries called back those who straggled away in the night, and cawed until they had set them in the track of the march (Callisthenes, *FGrH* 124 F 14b = Plut. *Alex.* 27.3–4).

94 Ptolemy, son of Lagus, says that two serpents went in front of the army, uttering a voice, and Alexander ordered the guides to follow them, trusting in the divine portent.

He says too that they showed the way to the oracle and back again. But Aristobulus (*FGrH* 139 F 14 = Source 96), whose account is generally admitted as correct, says that two ravens . . . (Ptolemy, *FGrH* 138 F 8 = Arr. 3.3.5).

95 Alexander then was struck with wonder at the place, and consulted the oracle of the god. Having heard what was agreeable to his wishes, as he himself said, he set out on the journey back to Egypt, by the same route, according to the statement of Aristobulus (*FGrH* 139 F 15 = Source 96); but according to that of Ptolemy, son of Lagus, he took another road, leading straight to Memphis (Ptolemy, *FGrH* 138 F 9 = Arr. 3.4.5).

96 After these transactions, Alexander was seized by an ardent desire to visit Ammon in Libya, partly in order to consult the god, because the orade of Ammon was said to be exact in its information, and Perseus and Heracles were said to have consulted it, the former when he was despatched by Polydectes against the Gorgon, and the latter, when he visited Antaeus in Libya and Busiris in Egypt. Alexander was also partly urged by a desire of emulating Perseus and Heracles, from both of whom he traced his descent. He also deduced his pedigree from Ammon, just as the legends traced that of Heracles and Perseus to Zeus. Accordingly he made the expedition to Ammon with the design of learning his own origin more certainly, or at least that he might be able to say that he had learned it. According to Aristobulus, he advanced along the sea shore to Paraetonium through a country which was a desert, but not destitute of water, a distance of about 1,600 stades. Thence he turned into the interior, where the oracle of Ammon was located. The route is desert, and most of it is sand and destitute of water. But there was a copious supply of rain for Alexander, a thing which was attributed to the influence of the deity; as was also the following occurrence. Whenever a south wind blows in that district, it heaps up sand upon the route far and wide, rendering the tracks of the road invisible, so that it is impossible to discover where one ought to direct one's course in the sand, just as if one were at sea; for there are no landmarks along the road, neither mountain anywhere, nor tree, nor permanent hills standing erect, by which travellers might be able to form a conjecture of the right course, as sailors do by the stars. Consequently, Alexander's army lost their way, as even the guides were in doubt about the course to take. Ptolemy, son of Lagus (*FGrH* 138 F 8 = Source 94), says that two serpents went in front of the army . . . But Aristobulus, whose account is generally admitted as correct, says that two ravens flew in front of the army, and that these acted as Alexander's guides . . .

The place where the temple of Ammon is located is entirely surrounded by a desert of far-stretching sand, which is destitute of water. The fertile spot in the midst of this desert is not extensive; for where it stretches into its greatest expanse, it is only about forty stades broad. It is full of cultivated trees, olives and palms; and it is the only place in those parts which is refreshed with dew. A spring also rises from it, quite unlike all the other springs which issue from the earth. For at midday the water is cold to the taste, and still more so to the touch, as cold as cold can be. But when the sun has sunk into the west, it gets warmer, and from the evening it keeps on growing warmer until midnight, when it reaches its warmest point. After midnight it goes on getting gradually colder: at daybreak it is already cold; but at midday it reaches the coldest point. Every day it undergoes these alternate changes in regular succession. In this place also natural salt is procured by digging, and certain of the priests of Ammon convey quantities of it into Egypt. For whenever they set out for Egypt they put it into little boxes plaited out of palm, and carry it as a present to the king, or some other great man. The lumps of this salt are large, some of them being longer than three fingers' breadth; and it is clear like crystal. The Egyptians and others who are respectful to the deity use this salt in their sacrifices, as it is clearer than that which is procured from the sea. Alexander then was struck with wonder at the place, and consulted the oracle of the god. Having heard what was agreeable to his wishes, as he himself said, he set out on the journey back to Egypt by the same route, according to the statement of Aristobulus; but according to that of Ptolemy, son of Lagus (*FGrH* 138 F 9 = Source 95), he took another road, leading straight to Memphis (Aristobulus, *FGrH* 139 FF 13–15 = Arr. 3.3–4).

97 On arriving at the shrine and finding out that there was an oracle in it, Alexander wished to consult it. The priest and the prophet said that it was impossible for them to give out an oracle on that day. Alexander insisted. To his pressing demand the seer replied: 'Lad, you are irresistible.' At this Alexander was delighted. Then the seer at once told him that he was not Philip's son but the son of Zeus Ammon himself. Alexander recalled the account of his mother Olympias that a dragon once prevailed over her just about the birth of Alexander. So he trusted oracles all the more and prospered the most by these acts of his (*Anonymous History of Alexander, FGrH* 151 F 10).

98 On this occasion[9] he made a very long speech to the Thessalians and the other Greeks, and when he saw that they encouraged him with shouts to lead them against the Barbarians, he shifted his lance into his left hand, and with his right appealed to the gods, as Callisthenes tells us, praying them, if he was really sprung from Zeus, to defend and strengthen the Greeks (Callisthenes, *FGrH* 124 F 36 = Plut. *Alex.* 33.1).

99 And Ephippus tells us that Alexander used to wear even the sacred vestments at his entertainments; and sometimes he would wear the purple robe, and cloven sandals, and horns of Ammon, as if he had been the god; and sometimes he would imitate Artemis, whose dress he often wore while driving in his chariot; having on also a Persian robe, but displaying above his shoulders the bow and javelin of the goddess. Sometimes also he would appear in the guise of Hermes; at other times, and indeed almost every day, he would wear a purple cloak, and a tunic shot with white, and a cap which had a royal diadem attached to it. And when he was in private with his friends he wore the sandals of Hermes, and the petasus on his head, and held the caduceus in his hand. Often also he wore a lion's skin, and carried a club, like Heracles … And Alexander used to have the floor sprinkled with exquisite perfumes and with fragrant wine; and myrrh was burnt before him, and other kinds of incense; and all the bystanders kept silence, or spoke only words of good omen, out of fear. For he was a very violent man, with no regard for human life; for he appeared to be a man of a melancholic constitution.

And on one occasion, at Ecbatana, when he was offering a sacrifice to Dionysus, and when everything was prepared in a most lavish manner for the banquet, and Satrabates the satrap, feasted all the soldiers … But when a great multitude was collected to see the spectacle, says Ephippus, there were on a sudden some arrogant proclamations published, more insolent even than Persian arrogance was wont to dictate. For, as different people were publishing different proclamations, and proposing to make Alexander large presents, which they called crowns, one of the keepers of his armoury, going beyond all previous flattery, having previously arranged the matter with

Alexander, ordered the herald to proclaim that 'Gorgos, the keeper of the armoury, presents Alexander, the son of Ammon, with three thousand pieces of gold; and will also present him, when he lays siege to Athens, with ten thousand complete suits of armour, and with an equal number of catapults and all weapons required for the war' (Ephippus, *FGrH* 126 F 5 = Athen. 12.537e–538b).

100 The common report is that he heard that the Arabs venerated only two gods, Uranus and Dionysus; the former because he is himself visible and contains in himself the heavenly luminaries, especially the sun, from which emanates the greatest and most evident benefit to all things human; and the latter on account of the fame he acquired by his expedition to India. Therefore he thought himself quite worthy to be considered by the Arabs as a third god,[10] since he had performed deeds by no means inferior to those of Dionysus (Aristobulus, *FGrH* 139 F 55 = Arr. 7.20.1).

Modern works

In the first extract, the Alexander scholar W.W. Tarn argues the point that Alexander proclaimed himself a god for political reasons associated with the issuing of the Exiles Decree. Tarn's view was persuasively attacked by J.P.V.D. Balsdon (see Additional reading). In the second extract, E. Badian, John Moors Cabot Professor Emeritus at Harvard University, considers influences on Alexander, specifically divine honours for previous Macedonian kings and for Persian kings, as well as what form Alexander's divinity took in 324. Finally, G.L. Cawkwell, formerly Lecturer in Ancient History at Oxford, argues that in 324 Alexander issued no deification decree and that it was the Greeks who initiated the moves to recognise him as a god. The differing views on this question and others, such as Alexander's reason for introducing *proskynesis*, for example, well illustrate the controversy that surrounds the study of Alexander.

1   W.W. Tarn, *Alexander the Great* 2 (Cambridge: 1948), pp. 370–373.[11]
2   E. Badian, 'Alexander the Great between Two Thrones and Heaven: Variations on an Old Theme', in A. Small (ed.), *Subject and Ruler: The Cult of the Ruling Power in Classical Antiquity* = *JRA* Suppl. 17 (1996), pp. 11–26.[12]
3   G.L. Cawkwell, 'The Deification of Alexander the Great: A Note', in Ian Worthington (ed.), *Ventures Into Greek History: Essays in Honour of N.G.L. Hammond* (Oxford: 1994), pp. 293–306.[13]

Additional reading

E. Badian, 'The Deification of Alexander the Great', in H.J. Dell (ed.), *Ancient Macedonian Studies in Honour of C.F. Edson* (Institute for Balkan Studies, Thessaloniki: 1981), pp. 27–71.
J.P.V.D. Balsdon, 'The "Divinity" of Alexander', *Historia* 1 (1950), pp. 363–388.
A.B. Bosworth, 'Alexander and Ammon', in K. Kinzl (ed.), *Greece and the Ancient Mediterranean in History and Prehistory* (Berlin: 1977), pp. 51–75.
——— , *Conquest and Empire: The Reign of Alexander the Great* (Cambridge: 1988), pp. 278–290.
——— , 'Alexander, Euripides and Dionysos: The Motivation for Apotheosis', in W. Wallace and E.M. Harris (eds), *Transitions to Empire: Essays in Honor of E. Badian* (Norman, OK 1996), pp. 140–166.

L. Edmunds, 'The Religiosity of Alexander', *Greek, Roman, and Byzantine Studies* 12 (1971), pp. 363–391.

E.A. Fredricksmeyer, 'Three Notes on Alexander's Deification', *American Journal of Ancient History* 4 (1979), pp. 1–9.

—— , 'On the Background of the Ruler Cult', in H.J. Dell (ed.), *Ancient Macedonian Studies in Honour of C.F. Edson* (Institute for Balkan Studies, Thessaloniki: 1981), pp. 145–156.

—— , 'On the Final Aims of Philip II', in W.L. Adams and E.N. Borza (eds.), *Philip II, Alexander the Great, and the Macedonian Heritage* (Lanham, MD: 1982), pp. 85–98.

—— , 'Alexander, Zeus Ammon, and the Conquest of Asia', *Transactions of the American Philological Association* 121 (1991), pp. 199–214.

A.N. Oikonomides, 'The Deification of Alexander in Bactria and India', *Ancient World* 12 (1985), pp. 69–71.

W.W. Tarn, *Alexander the Great* 2 (Cambridge: 1948), Appendix 22, 'Alexander's Deification', pp. 347–369.

Notes

1 On the powers of the Macedonian kingship and Alexander's relations with Philip II, see Chapter 2.
2 Strabo 17.1.43, Arr. 3.3–4, Plut. *Alex.* 27.8–10; cf. Diod. 17.51, Curt. 4.7.25, Justin 11.11.2–12.
3 Arr. 4.10.5–7, Plut. *Alex.* 54.3–6, Curt. 8.5.9–12; see Chapters 5 and 8.
4 See Chapter 8.
5 Athen. 12.538b; cf. Hyp. 5.31–32, Diod. 18.8.7, Curt. 10.2.5–7, Justin 13.5.1–6. On Alexander and the Greeks, see Chapter 4.
6 Polybius 12.12b3, [Plut.] *Mor.* 219e, 804b, 842 and Aelian, *Varra Historia* 5.12.
7 On this, see Chapter 11.
8 The Battle of Gaugamela in 331: see Chapter 5.
9 Before the Battle of Gaugamela.
10 Alexander seems to have planned an invasion of Arabia; cf. Source 112.
11 © Cambridge University Press 1948. Reprinted with the permission of Cambridge University Press.
12 Reprinted with the permission of the *Journal of Roman Archaeology*.
13 © G. L. Cawkwell 1994. Reprinted by permission of Oxford University Press.

ALEXANDER'S DEIFICATION

W. W. Tarn

324 B.C.

In 324, at Susa, Alexander was faced by a new problem. In old Greece there was a mass of exiles from every city, many of them democrats exiled by Antipater or his governments. Some had taken service as mercenaries with Alexander's satraps while he was in India; when he made the satraps disband their private armies, they had returned to Greece with their arms and without occupation. The position in that over-crowded country had become difficult; at best the exiles were a focus for every kind of discontent, at worst a possible menace. Alexander saw that, if he were to have the peace in his world (not merely in his Empire, for Greece was not in his Empire) which soon after he was to pray for at Opis, the exiles must be restored to their cities and their cities must receive them. But his difficulty was that the cities were those of the League of Corinth, and as its President he had sworn to the Covenant of the League, which forbade him to interfere in the internal affairs of the cities; yet it was very necessary to interfere. In these circumstances he issued to the cities of the League[1] a decree ordering them to receive back their exiles (which he had no constitutional power to issue) and also a request for his own deification (which probably came first); for the Covenant bound Alexander the king but did not, and would not, bind Alexander the god, and he could therefore set it aside without losing his self-respect. To us this may seem a quibble, but no one can say it was a quibble to him, or that his careful observance throughout life of the outer forms of religion meant that they were nothing to him but forms. It has been objected that deification did not actu-ally give him any new powers, but that is not the point; he had all the power he wanted, but he had not the right to use it; and to be a god gave him a juridical standing in the cities which he could not otherwise have got, for there was no place for a king in the constitution of a Greek city. The cities of the League granted his request and deified him[2], thereby (in form) condoning his breach of the Covenant; for while Alexander was thinking of a way of escape from the Covenant which bound him, the cities and States of the League were thinking primarily of the exiles decree which hit some of them hard, notably Athens and Aetolia, and was disturbing to them all; and they were hoping to appease Alexander by granting his request for deifi-cation, which by comparison seemed to them of little importance. Calling him a god did not mean that they were going to worship him; no cult of him was set up anywhere, and in fact there is no sign that, Egypt apart, anybody ever did worship him till after his death; the first known case is that of Eumenes and his Macedonian troops in the Alexander-tent. His request for deification, then, was a limited *political* measure for a purely political purpose, and nothing else. It is well known that some scholars have long believed this,[3] while others have strenuously denied it; I trust that what I have written in this study will show that the view which I follow is not only true but inevitable. His deification showed that he meant to stand above parties and factions, for many of the exiles, banished by Antipater or by the governments he supported, were Macedonia's enemies; it also showed that he had no intention of adopting Aristotle's view that such as he were above the law and that he could break the Covenant of the League at his pleasure. That his deification was purely political seems to be further supported by two facts: one is that he never put his own head on his coinage, as he must have done had he been a god in the sense in which many of the kings who followed him were gods; and the other is that his request for deification did not (so far as is known) extend to the Greek cities of Asia Minor, who were his free allies and who were not members of the League of Corinth.[4] There may have been no exiles problem there; but had there been he could have settled it without being their god, for he was not bound to them by any covenant which forbade him to interfere in their internal affairs. His deification, therefore, in 324 B.C., like his preliminary attempt at Bactra, was entirely a political matter, but this time limited to the cities of the League of Corinth; and it only remains to consider two modern objections to this view.

Professor Berve's pupil A. Heuss has put forward the view,[5] if I understand him rightly, that a political *Herrschaft* – say kingship – was always compounded of two independent elements, a political and a religious, and that you cannot abolish the religious element and make the political element do the work of both. He said there was warrant enough for this view in history, but did not say what it was; as I understand the matter, one need go no further than the Macedonian and Epirote monarchies to see that Heuss' view is untenable, and that there were plenty of kings whose kingship had no religious element; indeed I doubt if one could find any king in Alexander's day and in his sphere whose kingship *had* any religious element, putting aside Egypt and the little priest-kings of Asia Minor. Heuss makes a point that the deified kings (he includes Alexander) never mention their divine powers in their letters to the cities, where one would expect it. Why one should expect it I cannot imagine, seeing that they never mention their temporal powers either, any more than is ever done by kings or presidents to-day.

The other objection is one made in 1931 by Wilcken in his *Alexander der Grosse*. After discarding offhand the view that Alexander's deification in 324 was a political measure (though he had taken the scene at Bactra to be a political measure) he said (p. 201) that both the decree for the recall of the exiles and Alexander's request to the Greek cities of the League for deification had their roots in Alexander's psychology, and that that psychology was not only an outcome of his amazing success but was connected with, or conditioned by, his desire and plans for world-dominion; for he had been conscious for years that he *was* the son of Zeus-Ammon (p. 198) and history will go wrong if it neglects this inner religious experience. I trust I have given full weight to Alexander's inner religious experience (Ammon), fuller, possibly, than, even if not quite in the same way as, my predecessors; but this can have nothing to do with his deification in 324. There are several things to be said about Wilcken's view; the first and most obvious is that he has refuted it himself by his repeated statement that, as was indeed the fact, Alexander's request for deification in 324 was confined to the Greek cities of the League of Corinth, who were not even his subjects; what has that to do with the psychology of world-rule? The second is that, before it is possible to talk of Alexander's plans for world-dominion, some one has got to refute my demonstration (App. 24 [of Tarn 1948]), based on evidence, that his supposed plans in that behalf are a late invention; this has never been done, and I greatly doubt if it can be. As to Alexander's psychology in the matter of deification, I should be sorry to claim exact knowledge; but I have been considering it throughout this study, and as there is no reputable evidence that he ever called himself the son of any god, let alone a god, or that he even alluded to the descent of his line from Zeus, it is only fair to suppose that he did not believe that he was a god or even the son of one; and if those about him called him a son of Zeus, or even intimated that he ought to be a god, that has no bearing on his own thoughts or beliefs. Wilcken made one other point: his deification in 324 cannot have been political, or the Greek cities would never have granted it in the casual way they did. Certainly the cities did not take it to be a political move; but the only sign of casualness, I think, is the contemptuous remark attributed to Demosthenes, which is none too certain (p. 363 n. 2). I have already explained why the cities granted deification; but, quite apart from that, no city could afford to refuse. There was a great struggle at Athens over the proposal, but Demosthenes finally gave in, and those who desired appeasement and peace carried the day; Sparta, bled white at Megalopolis, was helpless; and probably most of the cities, great and small, acted as they did largely through fear of Alexander, for the moment that that fear was removed by his death they tore up the Covenant of the League of Corinth and started war against Macedonia, led by Athens, who punished Demades for having moved the proposal that Alexander should be a god.[6]

Notes

1 To the cities of the League only, for Antipater was to be executant, Diod. XVIII, 8, 4, and he had no authority on the mainland of Asia; see App. 7, 1, p. 202 n. 4 [in Tarn]. The Greek cities of Asia Minor, who were not in the League (App. 7, 11 [in Tarn]), were not affected. See [n. 4].

2 The story that at Athens he became a particular god, Dionysus, has long been exploded; see A. D. Nock, 'Notes on ruler-cult I–IV', *J.H.S.* XLVIII, 1928, p. 21. Some had rejected it before, e.g. Ed. Meyer, *Kleine Schriften*, 1, 1910, p. 331; P. Perdrizet, *R.E.A.* XII, 1910, p. 227 n. 6. There was a good deal of difference between becoming a god and becoming a particular god.

3 Ed. Meyer, *Kleine Schriften*, 1, pp. 283 *sqq.*, 312, 331; W. S. Ferguson, *Amer. Hist Rev.* 1912, p. 32; *Greek Imperialism*, 1913, pp. 147 *sqq.*; *C.A.H.* VII, 15.

4 See App. 7, II [in Tarn]. Wilcken, who so long championed the view that they were in the League of Corinth, finally abandoned it, 1938, p. 302 [7] n. 5, and in doing so he left it open (*ib.*) whether Alexander's request for deification was directed to them also or not. It seems certain that it was not; there is no evidence that the request was sent to any mainland city of Asia Minor, and the reason against it given [. . .] n. 1 *ante* should be conclusive; also no mainland city took any part in the Lamian war.

5 *Stadt und Herrscher des Hellenismus,* Klio, Beiheft XXVI, 1937, pp. 188 *sq.*

6 Athen. VI, 251B; Aelian, *V.H.* v, 12.

ALEXANDER THE GREAT BETWEEN TWO THRONES AND HEAVEN: VARIATIONS ON AN OLD THEME

E. Badian

When I was asked by the organizers of the Edmonton conference to speak on Alexander the Great in connection with divine honours, I could assume that they knew (as our honorand certainly knew) that I had published a long essay on the deification of Alexander some time ago[1] and have since referred to the subject in passing on other occasions. I obviously cannot treat the subject without reference to that earlier essay. On the other hand, it happens that I have in fact changed my mind on at least one major aspect of the problem, and that I have come to recognize that I failed to pay sufficient attention to the background (and especially the Persian background) in that earlier treatment. Thus, although much that was argued there will here be taken for granted and merely referred to, the present discussion should be regarded as superseding the earlier one in some important respects as well as supplementing it.

I. The starting-point

Let us first look at the Macedonian kingship that Alexander inherited. The dynasty of the Argeads, encouraged by that presumably tribal name, claimed descent from Argos, indeed from the Argive Temenids, the senior branch of the Heraclids descended from Zeus. We have no historical evidence of this claim before Alexander I advanced it and had it accepted at the Olympic Games, against the protests of his competitors who were obviously taken by surprise (Hdt. 5.22 ff., 8.137 ff.). That acceptance by the *Hellanodikai* ensured that it was never officially doubted again. The descent from Heracles was obviously important to the Argead kings, and Heracles appears on much of their coinage from the middle of the 5th c. B.C.

Unfortunately we know little about the daily life of those kings: practically nothing before Philip II and very little before the detailed (but obviously time-bound) information provided by the Alexander biographers. Since the move of the administrative capital to Pella by Archelaus (the sacred capital remained at the sanctified site of Aegae), they lived in a palace adorned by the great painter Zeuxis (Aelian, *VH* 14.17); yet by comparison with other kings their lifestyle remained rather simple. At home, the king would hunt, eat, and perhaps above all drink, with his *hetairoi*. In the field he fought at their head, conspicuous (if we may judge by Philip and Alexander) by his splendid arms and attracting the enemy's attack to his person.[2] Under Alexander we find him surrounded by a select bodyguard of seven nobles, who protect him in battle and take turns in guarding access to his quarters.[3] We cannot tell when this group was formed: perhaps only under Philip II. There is at any rate no trace of it in what we hear of Alexander I and of Perdiccas in the 5th c. There was no elaborate ceremonial of approach or address, at least for men of the right class. We cannot be quite sure how the king was addressed by his nobles, since the speeches in our sources are presumably largely fictitious. The usual address was perhaps simply "King" (βασιλεῦ or ὦ βασιλεῦ), as in early Hellenistic times; but the name in the vocative was apparently quite acceptable.[4]

245

This familiarity was no doubt traditional, although clearly attested only under Philip and Alexander. It is confirmed by the Greek cities' references to the Macedonian kings. Not once, either in Herodotus or in the *Corpus Demosthenicum*, is the king of Macedon referred to with "King" before his name: he is regularly referred to by his mere name. And this corresponds to the usage we find in the documents. We have no documents from cities within Macedon. But Athenian documents refer to the king of Macedon by mere name, just as the writers do.[5] And this is not confined to Athens. The alliances of the Chalcidic League with Amyntas III and later with Philip II use bare names, with patronymics added in more formal sections.[6] In what is called the foundation document of the "League of Corinth"[7] Philip's βασιλεία is referred to, but he himself is called plain Philip or, in the introduction to the oath, "Philip the Macedonian".[8] This last item makes quite clear what the evidence in any case suggests: that the omission of the royal title was not a mark of disrespect, but was approved of by (perhaps due to) the kings themselves. The reason for this can only be conjectured. But they were not legitimate Greek kings, like those at Sparta, and so they may have preferred to avoid a title that would seem invidious to Greeks (Isocr. 5.105 f.; cf. 154)[9] and would set them apart from Greek aristocrats, among whom they wanted Greeks to count them. The practice seems to carry on into the early years of Alexander, apparently until after the battle of Issus, when he seems to have regarded himself as King of Asia and, at least potentially, as successor to the Achaemenids. There is no good evidence for any change before early 331.[10]

Yet in the last year of Philip II we find a surprising development.[11] It begins in Asia Minor and just offshore. At Ephesus, after his army had expelled the Persian garrison and the oligarchy it supported, Philip's portrait statue (εἰκών, not ἄγαλμα, cult statue) was set up in the famous temple of Artemis as *synnaos* of the goddess (Arr. 1.19.11). While not deification, this is clearly an extravagant and perhaps unprecedented honour. At Eresus on Lesbos a cult of Zeus Philippios was instituted after a similar "liberation" – again extravagant, but in no way tantamount to deification, as anyone familiar with elementary Greek will recognize: it is a cult of "Philip's Zeus" (i.e., of Zeus as Philip's special protector – a duty that Zeus had assumed in addition to his numerous other special duties), not of Philip *as* Zeus.[12] We do not know whether Philip himself worshipped such a personal Zeus.

This does not amount to deification. But it clearly raised Philip to a status above that of other mortal men, and one unprecedented for a Macedonian king, whose royalty had been of a simple and accessible kind. But worse was to come. It seems that these honours gave Philip the idea of approaching even more closely to the gods. At the celebration of his daughter's wedding at Aegae, in the autumn of 336, he had his own statue carried in the procession among those of the 12 Olympians: he was making himself the *synthronos* of the gods (Diod. 16.92.5).

It was at this point that Philip was assassinated.

II. Hero and god

In the 19th c. it was commonly suggested that Alexander got the idea of deification from the tradition of the Oriental kings whom he superseded. Kaerst[13] thought that the individualized worship of Alexander and his Hellenistic successors differed notably from the veneration of the Oriental (he was thinking especially of the Egyptian) king

246

as "Abbild des Gottes": Kaerst derived it from Greek ideas on the reward of individual achievement, carried to their extreme. This idea – rather to Kaerst's annoyance – was appropriated and spectacularly developed by Eduard Meyer, with whom it remains principally connected.[14] Julius Beloch, on the other hand, continued to see Oriental inspiration: he regarded the deification of the king as the Orient's first reaction visited upon the victorious Greeks.[15]

Meyer was right, of course, in stressing that nowhere in the ancient world, as Alexander found it, was the living king worshipped as a god, with the sole exception of Egypt, even though an aura of divinity normally attached to him. As for Egypt, we must add that it does not count as an example. Alexander of course visited Egypt, but as I have pointed out,[16] we have no justification for suggesting that he was crowned Pharaoh according to Egyptian ritual, either before or after his visit to Ammon. Such a striking and colourful event, had it taken place, could not be missing in the whole of our tradition. The reason for its omission was no doubt political: his Macedonians would not have relished such a ceremony. But he quite probably had no real interest in it. In official art and documents, he of course appears with all the Pharaoh's titles, *inter alia* as son of Amun-Re and a god himself: thus, strikingly, in the Alexander chamber in the temple at Luxor.[17] But if he ever knew what was depicted there (and he quite possibly never heard of it: it may be due to customary practice at a much lower level), it meant nothing to him, except as a device to engage Egyptian loyalty. On the other hand, as also needs to be pointed out, Meyer's use of some passages in Aristotle to support his claim of entirely Greek origins for the deification of kings involved such flagrant misinterpretation of the texts that one must wonder whether he ever read them without a preconceived interpretation. It is hard to see how anyone reading those passages in their context could take any of them as relevant to deification.[18]

There is in fact little in Greek tradition to prepare us for the deification of a living man.[19] We know of only one example of securely attested deification of a mortal before Alexander: the Spartan Lysander; and I have tried to show[20] how little solid reason there is for ascribing it to his lifetime: essentially no more than a single word in a miscellaneous collection of anecdotes in Plutarch. *Heroic* honours after death were quite conceivable: founders of cities got them as a matter of course (see, e.g., Thuc. 5.11.1), and it would be rash to deny that some men may have attained them while still alive, though we seem to have no positive evidence for this.[21] Hagnon's successor as hero-*ktistes* of Amphipolis, at any rate, received that honour only after his death. Nonetheless, the great speech by "Callisthenes" over the *proskynesis* affair, which (as I tried to show) reflects popular religion late in the time of Alexander, does not exclude heroic honours, even for living men: the impassable frontier lies between hero and god. Only a "licensed lunatic" like the physician Menecrates ever called himself a god; and it is worth noting for ancient assessments of Philip that, in an anecdote that of course need not be authentic, it is precisely Philip who makes fun of his pretensions.[22]

Let us now return to Philip. We must now ask: did he claim, or at least wish, to be a god on the level of the Olympians? Had he lived longer, would he have tried to establish a cult of himself in Macedonia and perhaps in Greece? We cannot answer this question with real assurance (though it is clear that ancient tradition never imagined this), but it must be pointed out that such a conclusion does not follow from his action at Aegae; and also, that he must have known how difficult it would have been to impose a cult of himself in Macedonia. However, he had made himself what the Greeks called ἰσόθεος: a mortal in many respects equal to the gods, but always known to differ from them, not least by his acknowledged mortality, and to be subject to them.

In Homer several of the heroes, all of them subject to arbitrary divine intervention, are given this epithet. In epic scansion, it provided a convenient hexameter ending: ἰσόθεος φώς – a combination that in itself stresses the hero's humanity. The word then disappears from our sources[23] until we pick it up in Aeschylus. I need not follow its later history. It is never common. but is used in various senses (e.g. by Plato[24]), not all of them favourable, which have in common the implication that the man thus described is in fact not a god: there is no question of his receiving cult. As A. D. Nock concisely put it, citing an earlier scholar's informal communication, "ἰσόθεος is not θεός."[25]

III. The "godlike" King of Persia

Let us now look at Aeschylus. The word ἰσόθεος appears twice in his surviving works: both times in the *Persae* and both times applied to a Persian King. In its first use, we can see a deliberate assimilation of Xerxes to Homer's heroes. In line 80, Aeschylus uses what one must call the actual Homeric quotation ἰσόθεος φώς, complete with the epic scansion, which Broadhead noted in his commentary on the line. The other reference is to Darius (856), who, in a word reminiscent of Homer (though not used by him), is also called θεομήστωρ (god-like counsellor? – cf. Homer's θεόφιν μήστωρ, of Priam and one or two others), continuing the heroic parallel. We should also, however, note ἰσοδαίμων (634), obviously not Homeric (since it would not scan), but recalling Homer's δαίμονι ἶσος (which could not be used in tragedy) – a word fit for heroes, yet with negative (hubristic) associations (e.g. of Diomedes attacking Apollo: *Il.* 5.438. 459, 884; cf., for Patroclus, 16.705. 786), hinting at a link between the idealized Darius and his son. There is only a single passage where the Kings are explicitly called divine: in lines 157 ff. Atossa, Darius' widow and Xerxes' mother, is called wife and mother to a god (the latter with some qualifications). As has always been seen by commentators (e.g. Broadhead p. 69), this is hyperbolic flattery of the Queen and cannot stand as meant literally against the numerous contrary instances we have noted. The poet's opinion is in any case made quite clear when he describes Darius as having lived *"like* a god" (ὡς θεός).

Much that is reported about the King of Persia in our Greek sources stresses his more than human status.[26] Can this be how Philip got the idea? We cannot be sure. But it is worth noting an important and stimulating essay by D. Kienast[27] that argued, more than 20 years ago, that Philip took much of the organization of his court and his expanded kingdom from Persia, the only obvious model at the time. Some of the detailed suggestions may be exaggerated, but a good deal of the case seems convincing, whatever we think of the actual relations of Philip with the King. Oddly enough, Kienast never mentioned Philip's final pretension to ἰσόθεος status, but we may supply this here. Kienast rightly pointed out that, as an educated man in the Greek tradition, Philip would have read at least Herodotus and Xenophon (p. 269). We may confidently add Aeschylus' *Persae* – obvious reading for one who was preaching a crusade to avenge Xerxes' invasion, whatever Philip's literary and cultural interests.

To put it simply: this step would make him (we may say) the equal of the Persian King whom he was attacking, in the social and the religious sphere. For one who needed to attract support in Asia Minor, the idea had much to commend it. Philip's preparations for the invasion had been careful and rational: we need only mention the contacts with Hermias of Atarneus in northwest Asia Minor[28] and the attempt to seize a chance of establishing a connection with the Carian dynast and satrap Pixodarus, which failed only owing to Alexander's irresponsible interference.[29] After the invasion, we must note the politically profitable establishment of democracy in co-operating Greek cities occupied by his forces – we have commented on Eresus and Ephesus, which we may regard as delineating a more general policy – while most of European Greece was run for him by pro-Macedonian oligarchies, precisely comparable to the pro-Persian ones he was expelling in Asia.[30] As we saw, both Eresus and Ephesus responded by enhancing his status beyond the merely human. The Greek cities of Asia, accustomed to being ruled by a more than human barbarian for 50 years, would find it a natural status for a descendant of Heracles who had freed them from that barbarian. As for the native tribes in the interior and along the southeast coast, such status might well seem an essential prerequisite in one who aimed at defeating the King and ruling them. Agesilaus of Sparta, himself a descendant of Heracles, who would never have countenanced such honours, had shown in years of futile campaigning that being a mere mortal king was not enough.

This is not meant to assert that Philip's motives were wholly rational. After his achievement in raising a barbarian fringe kingdom to the status of the foremost power in Greece and the Aegean in less than 25 years, he seems, in the last year of his life, to have departed from that purposeful rationality on which his achievement had been based. An element of irrationality enters his personal life and ultimately helps to destroy him: as the biographer Satyrus later put it in a famous passage (quoted by Athenaeus 13.557b ff.), the man who had always married for political and strategic profit in the end made the mistake of marrying for love (ἐρασθείς) and thus "confounded his whole life". It cannot be denied that, whatever good political reasons there might have been for his calling himself more than human and demonstrating the claim by conspicuous symbolic actions, it is not the act of a wholly rational man. In the end we cannot really conjecture what Philip's motives may have been in the religious sphere, any more than we can conjecture what limits he had set for his campaign in Asia – another issue much debated in the 19th and early 20th c., with Meyer and Beloch again on opposite sides.[31] Leaving aside what A. Demandt has called "ungeschehene Geschichte" (the historian's equivalent of science fiction), we can now turn to Alexander with a better understanding of his background.

IV. The road to kingship

What I have been trying to disengage is that a precedent (a *domesticum exemplum*) had been set for Alexander. If he wanted to equal his father – and he surely wanted to surpass him – he would from the start have to aim at becoming ἰσόθεος. For the moment, succeeding to his father's throne in highly suspicious circumstances, he would have to establish his right to it by acting like a traditional Macedonian monarch: like his father, he would dine, drink and hunt with his *hetairoi*; and he led his army with speed and decision, himself fighting in the front rank. This was how he would earn the confidence of his men, on whom his success ultimately depended. But Homeric reminiscence was stressed right from the start of the invasion of Asia, in the sacrifice to Protesilaus (Arr. 1.11.5) – also, of course, recalling the blood-curdling incident that concludes Herodotus' account of the victory of Hellas over Asia (Hdt. 9.116–22), which Alexander must have known. The romanticizing tradition that we call the Alexander Vulgate found a good deal more to add to the Homeric theme: Arrian did not usually find it in his main sources and added it for additional colour. We find such choice items as his taking from Athena's temple the very arms surviving from the Trojan War and henceforth having them carried before him by hypaspists in his battles – a picture hard to imagine, even if we grant the postulate that the original arms survived, for the centuries since the Trojan War (whatever it was). The "sacred shield from Ilium" makes an appearance in the hands of Peucestas in the battle at the town of the Malli (Arr. 6.9.3, 10.2). In Curtius (9.5.17–18) Peucestas has only his own shield, which he uses to protect Alexander as long as he can. In Diodorus (17.18.1; cf. 21.2) Alexander merely takes the best of the armour dedicated to Athena and uses it himself: there is no mention of Troy. Since this elaboration is confined to Arrian (and obviously was unknown to Clitarchus), we may suspect Aristobulus of having introduced it. Perhaps he (rather than Callisthenes, as has been suspected[32]) is responsible for such items as the sacrifice to Priam, with the plea that Priam should not take vengeance on the descendant of Neoptolemus (who had killed him), and various Homeric reminiscences, culminating in the *proskynesis* of the Pamphylian Sea to its lord, as in Homer the waves bow to Poseidon. Much of this is patent fiction, though modern biographers tend to believe all or most of it.[33] Plutarch, who was no fool, ignored it all, except for the very plausible honours for Alexander's ancestor Achilles (*Alex*. 15.8).

We need not follow Alexander's campaign in detail.[34] One or two items may be of interest to this enquiry, thus his dealing (in whatever way) with the Gordian knot – which he was compelled to do once its significance was explained to him.[35] Nowhere in Asia Minor, as far as our information goes, did he either demand or receive superhuman honours; and for at least two cities it can be proved that he did not receive any, as we shall soon see. After defeating the royal Persian army under Darius' leadership at Issus and capturing his family, he occupied Egypt without meeting any resistance (332). By then some negotiations between him and Darius had certainly been going on, for Darius was willing to give up a great deal (on terms ultimately favourable to himself) to get his family back But we cannot know the details, since the various communications cited in our sources[36] must be dismissed as fictitious, like nearly all speeches and letters in ancient historians.[37] As we have seen, coronation as Pharaoh can be confidently excluded, although Alexander sacrificed to Apis and no doubt other native gods. He then designated the site of the city of Alexandria, which would at least guarantee him the heroic honours (if only posthumous) of a City Founder. The ritual act of foundation had to wait for the approval of Ammon, whose oracle, respected in Greece for generations, Alexander decided to visit in person. The foundation of Alexandria was the first cautious step on the road to superhuman status, a road that his father had taken before him.[38]

The visit to Ammon, one of the crucial events in Alexander's life, need not be treated in detail, for far too much has been written about it and we simply cannot tell exactly what happened: only conjectures are possible.[39] That he was hailed as son of Zeus-Ammon is certain; and Callisthenes did not delay in proclaiming this to the world. The result was immediate: two Ionian cities, Miletus and Erythrae, sent messengers to Alexander (they met him in Memphis where he spent the winter after his return from Ammon) informing him of divine communications proclaiming him the son of Zeus. This, of course, is proof positive, at least for these two cities and presumably for all Greek cities in Asia, that nothing of the sort (let alone deification) had occurred to them before, e.g. on his first dealings with them. Recognition of the new fact of Alexander's divine sonship, although now respectably confirmed, was not imposed on Macedonians and Greeks, for the Macedonians (in particular) still cherished Philip's memory. It was presumably voluntary, and appreciated by him: perhaps confined to the Greeks of Asia Minor and to "flatterers" at his court. Even so, it did not go down well with Macedonians, although they had to hold their peace. Many years later, Macedonian soldiers still regarded Alexander's divine filiation with what appears to be sarcastic irritation. (See Arr. 7.8.3.)

Philotas is said by Curtius (6.9.18 *et al.*) to have been frank in expressing his opinion. As the son of Parmenio, and himself commander of the *hetairoi* cavalry, he no doubt thought he could afford it. But the result of his lack of caution was that Alexander set Philotas' mistress to spy on him and the elaborate conspiracy against him, which ultimately led to his death and to Parmenio's, began to take shape. Plutarch (*Alex.* 49) first suggested the connection, which ought to be accepted, despite the interval.[40] Alexander did not forgive open objection to his newly-won heroic status, although we cannot be sure how he interpreted it.[41] But Ammon must in some sense have confirmed in his own mind a story put about, apparently well before this time, by Olympias, that his birth had been the result of a divine visit to her bed, apparently by Zeus, with whom Ammon was identified. Plutarch (*Alex.* 2.6 ff.; cf. 3.2) relates the story and cites Eratosthenes (surely no mere gossip) for the fact that Alexander was told about this before he left for Asia. After the visit to Ammon, Alexander is reported to have written to Olympias that the secret revealed to him there was for her ears alone (ibid. 27.8): we are entitled to conclude that the secret was in fact confirmation of the story, and that this may have been one of the questions that Alexander wanted to ask Ammon; but he did not want to entrust the response to a letter. It would not be safe for him to be discovered denying Philip's physical paternity.

He now advanced across the desert and Mesopotamia and on October 1, 331, destroyed Darius' army at Gaugamela. Darius fled to Ecbatana, while Alexander took over Babylon, Susa and (by January 330) Persepolis, collecting thousands of talents from the royal treasuries and appointing eminent Persians to govern the central lands of the kingdom. He now regarded himself, and obviously meant the Iranian aristocracy to regard him, as the successor to the Achaemenids. At some point the army formally acclaimed him King (Plut., *Alex.* 34.1). At Susa and/or Persepolis (the story is told about both) he ceremonially took his seat on the royal throne of Persia.[42] Yet the town of Persepolis was handed over to his soldiers, who had had no major reward, for plunder (Curt. 5.6.1–10; Diod. 17.71.3). Alexander was between two worlds and already had difficulty reconciling them. When taking his seat on the throne, he would naturally have put his feet on the royal footstool (as we see it in the Persepolis audience scenes), for the King, on ceremonial occasions, was not allowed to touch the ground with his feet. Being short in stature, he could not reach it, and a royal table had to be substituted. (The story is slightly garbled by our Greek sources, who probably did not know about the taboo.[43]) Alexander was announcing to the world that he was now the lawful King. As we saw, the Greek cities had already begun to refer to him as such.

There is a surprising reflection of his change in style in an unexpected place. Cicero, writing to Atticus on May 26, 45, complains that he has been asked to write a symbouleutic letter to Caesar and does not know how to set about it. He thinks of Alexander (*Att.* 13.28.3): "quid? tu non vides ipsum illum Aristoteli discipulum, summo ingenio, summa modestia, postea quam rex appellatus sit superbum crudelem immoderatum fuisse?" That this is based on Clitarchus, whom both Cicero and Atticus had read,[44] is clear from what Curtius writes about Alexander not long after Darius' death, straight after the tale of the Amazon Queen, certainly from Clitarchus (6.6.1): "hic vero palam cupiditates suas solvit continentiamque et moderationem. ... in superbiam ac lasciviam vertit. .. *Persicae regiae par deorum potentia fastigium aemulabatur.*" The Greek source commented on the ἰσόθεος status that Alexander had reached by becoming Persian King, "postea quam rex appellatus sit": the results are described in recognizably similar language, as remodelled by two Latin stylists. For some Greeks, the claim to Achaemenid pseudo-legitimacy was the turning-point in Alexander's career and character.

V. From Persepolis to *proskynesis*

We do not hear much about Pasargadae at this point. We know that Alexander collected the royal treasure there (it did not amount to much), as he had all the others (Art. 3.18.9; Curt. 5.16.10) and that at his request Aristobulus honoured Cyrus' tomb there. He probably went there straight after the capture of Persepolis (just possibly only on his thirty-day campaign before he moved on: Curt. 5.6.12–20). Pasargadae was the sacred capital, the place where the "mysteries" of the King's coronation took place (Plut., *Artax.* 3.1: τὴν βασιλικὴν τελετήν – surely from Ctesias, an author, incidentally, whom Alexander must have read). Did he consider a "legitimate" coronation? If he did, the time was not right. For one thing, the duly crowned King, Darius, was still alive at Ecbatana; the Macedonian soldiers had just been allowed to plunder Persepolis, as the enemy's capital; and in Greece the war against Agis, which we know the King took very seriously, was still going on. He could not afford to antagonize Macedonians and Greeks by a gesture they could not but resent, no matter how well it might have fitted into his personal plans.[45] Ammon had been bad enough. All that he could now do was to see to the safety of Cyrus' tomb, which, as we shall see, may have played an important part in the coronation. That would leave the future open.

Not long after he decided, in one of his best-known acts, to destroy the palace area at Persepolis: an action that must have annihilated any chance he might have had of having the legitimacy of his Kingship recognized by the Persian nobility and far beyond their circle. I have tried to point out[46] that this puzzling step can be rationally explained only as a return to the slogan of the "Hellenic crusade" no doubt due to his anxiety over the war in Greece. That worry was over by the time he reached Ecbatana: he had heard of Agis' defeat and death. The Greek allies could now be sent home and Alexander had to think about how to make up for what had turned out to be a devastating error. There was just one chance: if he could capture Darius alive, the King might be persuaded to pay homage to him. This is clearly what Darius' noble companions in his flight feared. They respectfully bound him in golden fetters and, before Alexander could reach him, stabbed him and left him to die. Bessus, no doubt an Achaemenid and perhaps no less entitled to rule than the man who called himself Darius, assumed the name of Artaxerxes and the royal insignia.[47] Alexander would have to live with the consequences of Persepolis.

He now had to make the best of it. The details are not clear and we cannot go into them here. But he assembled a Persian court, complete with bodyguards, harem and eunuchs, in addition to his Macedonian court, dressed his *hetairoi* in purple and himself adopted a modified style of Achaemenid dress, combining it with Macedonian in ways that may have changed over the years.[48] He continued to pardon and receive Persian nobles, even if they joined him only after Darius' death, including Artabazus, who had been loyal to Darius to the end, and even Nabarzanes, Darius' "chiliarch" (*hazarapatiš*), who had actually taken part in the murder but now voluntarily surrendered. Bessus, who had actually committed the murder and had then assumed the royal title and style, could not be pardoned. He was punished with traditional Persian cruelty. (Berve, *s.vv.*, gives the details.) Roughly contemporary with these events was the elimination of Philotas, Parmenio and Clitus: this is only marginally relevant here, in that it reassured Alexander that he could count on the unquestioning support of his army whatever he did.[49] Before long he married Roxana, daughter of a Persian baron in Sogdiana, according to what may have been a mixed Persian-Macedonian rite. Whatever the technical defects of his claim to royalty, there was no one to challenge him.

It was at this time that he tried to introduce *proskynesis* to himself for Greeks and Macedonians.

The outline of that story is clear enough: I set it out in my earlier essay and I have seen no reason to change my mind.[50] What I must reconsider, however, is the implication. That it was merely a homogenization of court ceremonial (for his Oriental subjects had been performing it as a matter of course) and had no religious implications is a view that is popular with those who construct an entirely "rational" Alexander, and it will inevitably be revived from time to time.[51] That it is a totally unacceptable view will be clear to anyone who can allow that the Greeks (or most of them) took their religion seriously. (See 1981, 52 f.) On the other hand, the view found by Arrian and Curtius in their sources, that the main point at issue (in Arrian between "Anaxarchus" and "Callisthenes") was Alexander's deification – that view, taken over by many scholars (including at one time myself), now seems to me clearly mistaken: it is based, in our sources, on an anachronistic interpretation due to the time of composition, a time when Alexander was indeed seeking, or had recently sought, divinity. As far as the *proskynesis* affair is concerned, that interpretation is premature.

What I missed was the main fact that I have tried to make clear in this paper: that the Greeks never considered *proskynesis* before the King an act of divine worship and that they well knew that the King was not a god but ἰσόθεος, which was far from divine. It is likely that authors who witnessed the actual event and later recorded it got it right, unlike the authors of the set debate, who had not been with Alexander. Arrian (4.9.9), in what he presents as his own view, but what is presumably based on his main sources, makes Alexander's attempt a consequence of his belief that he was the son of Ammon (i.e., a hero). Curtius, detailing (as we have seen) Alexander's deterioration after he was proclaimed King, leads up to the demand for deification (as he considers *proskynesis*: see 8.5.5), "iacere humi venerabundos ipsum ... expectabat," by referring to his ἰσόθεος status as Persian King (6.6.2). Unfortunately Diodorus' account of the incident, which would be a useful control of the Clitarchan tradition, is missing.

The convenience of unifying court ceremonial was certainly a factor, and Alexander would want to do it at the higher level: he could not abolish the custom for Orientals, since that would impugn his claim to legitimacy. But in addition there was the expected ratification of his status as ἰσόθεος. His Oriental subjects (except for those still fighting him) had been forced to recognize him as King, even though he was not qualified for that position by birth and ancestry and was not prepared to submit to the taboos. He was also close to such recognition in the case of those Greeks who acknowledged him as the son of Ammon. But the Macedonians, and probably most of the Greeks at his court, kept stubbornly aloof. If he wanted to equal the status reached by Philip before his death, he could now best do so by means of *proskynesis*, approaching the issue in a way that had not been open to Philip. That all this had nothing to do with actual deification should be obvious. But the failure of the attempt to impose *proskynesis* meant the victory of those who refused to see Alexander as anything but the son of Philip and the king of Macedon.

VI. Pasargadae and legitimation as ἰσόθεος

The failure in India and the disastrous march back through the desert had a serious effect both on him and on his subjects. Both his own belief and theirs in his invincibility, in his control of nature as well as of men, had been profoundly shaken, and he took immediate steps to compensate. That is largely a different *logos*, which I have pursued elsewhere.[52] What we must do here is to consider his return to the Persian homeland against this background.

We have seen that his first visit to Pasargadae had been brief and inconspicuous. This time he made straight for Pasargadae, even though it was well away from the direct route to Susa, where he planned to celebrate the conclusion of the campaign and his "victory". He had taken particular care to honour and safeguard the tomb of Cyrus: we must note that he had never shown any interest in the tomb of Darius I, not far from Persepolis, even though that King had been his ancestor's suzerain and benefactor.[53] He now found Cyrus' tomb desecrated. It had been broken into and robbed of most of its contents. Its appearance, both before the desecration and after, was described by Aristobulus, whom in this instance we have no reason to distrust. He is reproduced, somewhat inaccurately, both by Arrian (6.29) and by Strabo (15.3.7. 730C). The versions combine to give an interesting picture. Cyrus' body lay in a gold sarcophagus, between a couch with golden feet (or a golden couch) and a table with cups on it. There is mention of rich carpets, Babylonian tapestries and Cyrus' clothing, jewellery and sumptuous arms. All that could be moved was now gone. The body had been taken out of its sarcophagus and thrown on the ground – an apparently pointless act of vandalism, since the sarcophagus obviously could not be removed.

It is difficult to believe that the tomb had been thus stripped without the knowledge of the magi who had the full-time task of guarding it. The work could hardly be done in an hour or two, especially since the stone door made access to the tomb difficult. The magi denied any knowledge, even under torture (so Arrian tells us). A favourite of Alexander's charged the satrap Orxines with responsibility: he had assumed office in Alexander's absence in India without Alexander's commission, and the charge made a good pretext for eliminating him.[54]

I should like to suggest that the objects in Cyrus' tomb may have been connected with the initiation mystery (see above, [p. 252]) of the coronation. Plutarch (*Artax.* 3.1. f., from Ctesias) sets this in an implausible temple of a warrior goddess identified with Athena. Excavators found no trace of such a temple and it cannot be reconciled with anything we know of early Achaemenid religion (for the rite must be traditional).[55] Among the buildings actually found on the site (fig. 1),[56] the tomb of

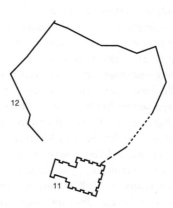

1. The Tomb of Cyrus
2. Gate R
3. Palace S
4. Palace P
5. Stone water channels
6. Pavilion A
7. Pavilion B
8. The Bridge
9. The Zendan
10. The Sacred Precinct
11. The Tall-i Takht
12. The outer fortification of Tall-i Takht

N

0   500 m

Figure 1. Pasargadae. Plan of the principal Achaemenian monuments (reproduced from
D. Stronach, *Pasargadae* [Oxford 1978] by permission of the Oxford University Press).

Cyrus seems the most plausible location,[57] isolated as it was in its own grove. The use of the cups and the donning of Cyrus' cloak are mentioned by Plutarch-Ctesias as parts of the ritual; but little was known in detail about that "mystery". The magi assigned to the tomb were presumably the priests in charge of the ceremony. That Pasargadae, rather than Persepolis, remained the site for it makes it very likely that Cyrus, the Founder, was meant to impart his spirit to his successor.

This must remain speculation. But if it is accepted, it follows that the sacred objects were abstracted by the magi or with their connivance: they certainly had unlimited opportunities. (Whether the satrap was involved we cannot tell.) We know, better than the Greeks did, that torture is not a reliable means of eliciting truth. Many have confessed to crimes they did not commit, others (documented both in antiquity and above all in our own generation) have stood firm and continued to refuse any information or confession. To a religious (and indeed to any patriotic) Mede or Persian the ritual coronation of a Macedonian invader as King would be an act to be prevented at all personal costs. To the magi it would be supreme sacrilege. The casting of Cyrus' body on the floor now becomes explicable: it would produce ritual contamination of the site and make it unusable for a religious ceremony.

We have seen that Alexander could not have risked a formal coronation at Pasargadae on his first visit. The care devoted to Cyrus' tomb (and not to any other building, or to the tomb of any other King) suggests that he considered it a possibility for the future. On his return, visiting the sacred site and holding court there, he certainly had the power to enforce it. We are within a few weeks of the Susa celebrations, involving the marriages to Iranian wives forced upon Greeks and Macedonians of high standing, and of the dismissal of the Macedonian veterans at Opis. The Greeks, by now, were merely remote subjects, whose opinion would count for little. A formal coronation at Pasargadae would have been a fitting prelude to the festivities planned for Susa – a fitting climax to the long campaign whose victorious conclusion was to be celebrated. Had he succeeded, he would have acquired the right to insist that Greeks and Macedonians perform *proskynesis* to him: he would have been recognized as ἰσόθεος.

VI. Forward to divinity

By this time there were probably some cults of Alexander as a god in Asia Minor: that much of Habicht's thesis remains probable.[58] One city that honoured Alexander as a god was Ephesus. It was there, in the Artemisium, that Apelles' famous portrait of him wielding the thunderbolt was set up (Pliny, *NH* 35.92). We cannot really know when it was put there, but certainly not before 331, as follows from our discussion, and probably much later, towards the end of his life. I once suggested that Alexander's offer to pay for rebuilding the temple of Artemis and dedicate it in his name was made when he first passed through the city, in 334.[59] This cannot be so. At that time, no matter how optimistic he felt about the future, he could not have foreseen that he would be able to pay for the construction. (That only became possible by late 331.) And if we consider the Ephesians' reply, that it would not be fitting for a god to make offerings to a god, to be authentic (as we probably should, on the authority of Artemidorus), the incident must be moved down to a time when a cult to him had been set up at Ephesus and the portrait with the thunderbolt stood in the Artemisium: in fact, not long before the end of his life. In 334 there had been no question of calling him a god, even in extreme flattery.[60]

When Hephaestion died, at Ecbatana, in the winter of 324–323, Alexander sent to Ammon, to ask what honours would be appropriate for his dead friend. "Some" (according to Arrian) said that he hoped for divine honours (7.14.7). However, he could be sure his "father" would approve at least a hero cult, which (as we have seen) was not all that extraordinary. In fact he at once made preparations for it. The god indeed allowed only heroic honours.[61] These honours are firmly attested at Athens (Hyp., *Epitaph*. 20 f.): the cult was still celebrated in the middle of the Lamian War, no doubt because of Ammon's sanction, for Ammon was much revered.[62] The same passage of Hyperides attests some divine cults (no doubt of Alexander) in Greek cities, presumably in Europe: θυσίας μὲν ἀνθρώποις γ[ιγνο]μένας . . . , ἀγάλμ[ατα δὲ] καὶ βωμοὺς καὶ ναοὺς τοῖ[ς μὲν] θεοῖς ἀμελῶς. τοῖς δὲ ἀνθρώ[ποις] ἐπιμελῶς συντελούμενα. Although it does not (strictly speaking) tell us whether there had been (but was no longer) one in Athens, it makes it clear that there was not one at the time: had there been one that was abolished after Alexander's death, the orator could be expected to have had something to say about this as at least relative liberation.

Hyperides also (*Dem*. 31) cites Demosthenes as agreeing that Alexander should be addressed as son of Zeus (i.e., Ammon) in what appears to be early 323[63] – which shows that this had not been done up to that time. It was now a hotly debated question. Dinarchus (*Dem*. 94) charges that Demosthenes, after proposing a decree that no gods other than the traditional ones should be recognized, then changed his mind and said that the People must not question Alexander's "honours in heaven" (οὐ δεῖ τὸν δῆμον ἀμφισβητεῖν τῶν ἐν οὐρανῶι τιμῶν Ἀλεξάνδρωι). Demosthenes had clearly changed his mind in the light of Demades' remark that the Athenians must not lose the earth over their concern for heaven (Val. Max. 7.2, ext. 13). That is the context in which the remark belongs, as the coincidence in wording helps to show. And these sources are contemporary: they cannot (as Athenian orators were given to doing) have made up or distorted what was still remembered by everyone. The fate of Samos was at stake, and "honours in heaven" were the only way to save Athens' claim.[64] But how was it to be done?

We may now inspect Hyperides' further report (*Dem*. 32), in an unfortunately lacunose passage, that someone proposed that a portrait statue (εἰκών, not ἄγαλμα) be set up to Alexander, "King and God Invincible" (στῆσαι εἰκό[να Ἀλεξάν]δρου βασιλ[έως τοῦ ἀνι]κήτου θε[οῦ . . .). It was in any case likely that the proposer of this was the man attacked in the speech: Demosthenes is the subject of the statement just before the lacuna, which comprises about 10 lines of about 15 letters. We can now knit the primary evidence together into an explanation of what form Alexander's deification took in Athens.

When Demades made it clear (no doubt from his private contacts at the court) that Alexander, although he had not demanded deification, would greatly welcome it and generously reward such an offer, Demosthenes, who had been firmly opposed to "recognizing any gods other than the traditional ones", opposed setting up a cult, but agreed that "honours in heaven" would in some form have to be granted for the sake of the city. He therefore proposed (or perhaps merely supported) a motion that seemed a reasonable compromise: the city would set up a portrait statue on which Alexander would be *described* as divine, but it would avoid actual cult. We do not know whether that recognition satisfied him, since we do not know his final decision on Samos – but that is a subject too vast to be treated here.

There is indeed no evidence for an order by Alexander demanding deification, even at a time when he was apparently dressing up in a variety of divine costumes in order to identify himself with various gods. (Thus Ephippus *ap.* Athen. 12.537d ff.) But Bickerman's insight remains valid, against what rationalizing historians of Alexander keep reiterating: the debate in Athens amply makes clear what Alexander really wanted in the last months of his life – and what Athens had up to a point to concede, while weaker cities had to grant it in full measure, as Hyperides' comment after Alexander's death reveals. Having failed to achieve universal recognition of ἰσόθεος, he now wanted to prod the Greeks into much more: into what Greek cities in Asia seem to have spontaneously offered him. Perhaps encouraged by Ammon,[65] he came to long for the genuine article, at least in the Greek world, where it was feasible if enough pressure was applied, even if not in the Persian, where religion utterly forbade it and where he had to remain content with an insecure claim to the heritage of the Achaemenids. If it was indeed Ammon who had led him along this path, his prophecy for once stopped short of fulfilment: Alexander was never universally recognized as a god, nor even universally as "equal" to one.

Notes

1 "The deification of Alexander the Great" in *Ancient Macedonian studies in honor of Charles F. Edson* (Thessaloniki 1981) 27–71. It is a special pleasure for me to dedicate this paper to Duncan Fishwick since he had in fact shown an interest in that earlier article.

2 For Philip's wounds see G. T. Griffith in N. G. L. Hammond and G. T. Griffith, *History of Macedonia* II (Oxford 1979) 473 f.

3 See H. Berve, *Das Alexanderreich auf prosopographischer Grundlage* (Munich 1926) I 27 f.

4 We find this used by Parmenio (Arr. 1.13.3); by Coenus, in a fictitious speech which presumably nonetheless preserved the correct forms (Arr. 5.27.2 ff.); and by an obscure person (Arr. 7.11.6). Thus also by Nearchus in his own report as rendered by Arrian (*Ind.* 20.5, 35.6). Clitus, in the episode that ends with his death, uses ὦ Ἀλέξανδρε (Arr. 4.8,7 and 9), explicitly from Aristobulus, therefore authentic. One might think it an example of provocative familiarity, were it not for the fact that Isocrates, in his formal address to Philip (5.1), similarly uses ὦ Φίλιππε.

5 This although the Athenians were occasionally willing to name kings of Thrace with the royal title (Tod, *GHI* II 117, lines 11 f., 23 f.; but not in Tod 151 or 157) and might even give it to a kinglet in Upper Macedonia (*IG* I³ 89 line 69; II² 190).

6 Tod 111, 158.

7 Tod 177.

8 There is a possible exception, it has been claimed. At Lebadeia a king who may be Amyntas son of Perdiccas may be called βασιλεύς Μακεδόνων (*IG* VII 3055), and much has been made of this by some historians, since he never actually became king. That phrase as such would not be extraordinary even in an Athenian author: note that he is not called Βασιλεύς Ἀμύντας, which would indeed be unparalleled. It must be noted that any restoration of this text is based on two unsatisfactory old copies (by Pococke and Leake) and, if it is to make sense, must stray quite far from those copies. The text is discussed (with adventurous historical conclusions) by J. R. Ellis, "Amyntas Perdikka, Philip II and Alexander the Great," *JHS* 91 (1971) 15 ff.

9 Cf. E. Badian, "Greeks and Macedonians" in *Macedonia and Greece in Late Classical and Early Hellenistic times* (Studies in the History of Art 10, Washington 1982) 42 with n.69.

10 The details are too complex for full discussion here. On Priene, see A. J. Heisserer, *Alexander the Great and the Greeks* (Norman, OK 1980) 145 ff. It has since been shown that the actual

inscription of Alexander's edict, which uses the title, must be dated well after his death (S. M. Sherwin-White, "Ancient archives. The edict of Alexander to Priene, a reappraisal," *JHS* 105 [1985] 69 ff.). The Chios letter (Heisserer 79 ff.) presents the puzzle of the use of the royal title in the prescript and its omission in the text (line 7). Heisserer's involved argument trying to explain this does not seem to succeed. (His attempt to move the date from the usual 332 to 334 has not found much support.) On his reconstruction, the Chians called Alexander king while one of his generals uses the bare name in the text. The former would itself need explanation, in view of the fact that no Greek city uses the title with the name of a Macedonian king (see above and, for further discussion, Badian, "A reply to Professor Hammond's article," *ZPE* 100 [1994] 389 f.). The contrast is best explained in the usual way, by the hypothesis that the prescript was engraved somewhat later, when the royal title had come into use. (As we have seen, the descriptive use of the title, in Ἀλεξάνδρου τοῦ βασιλέως, presents no difficulty and can readily be accepted at any time.) The third relevant document, the Eresus file, is too complicated to be treated in detail. But Heisserer's version, putting "Section 1" (which calls Alexander king) first, followed by Sections 2 and 3, where he is plain Alexander, is quite implausible. The traditional reconstruction inserts his "Section 1" between parts of "Section 3" so that Alexander is given his plain name first and the royal title after. (For this, see Tod 191.) The dossier now needs renewed checking.

11 It may have been foreshadowed by Philip's calling cities after himself, except that we cannot be sure precisely when he began to do so. Philippopolis (Plovdiv) was presumably named soon after he had conquered the area (*c*.340). Philippi, on the site of Crenides, is unlikely to have been renamed at once (356): such arrogance at that early time is hard to believe and would have harmed Philip's cause in his dealings with Greek cities. (He could claim to have defended Crenides against barbarian Thracians.)

12 It seems incredible that any scholar knowing elementary Greek could have taken this as a cult of Philip himself. Yet even A. B. Bosworth (*Conquest and Empire* [Cambridge 1988] 322) describes it as "cult honours for Philip" at Eresus; as sole argument he produces the suggestion (p. 281) that "the sacrifices made to Zeus were also *in a sense* offered to Philip" (my emphasis). He does not explain the "sense" and I find it difficult to do so. The statement contrasts with Bosworth's careful and sensible treatment of other aspects of this question. Nock, *Essays* I 156 f. did not know this text.

13 *Geschichte des hellenistichen Zeitalters* I (Leipzig and Berlin 1901) 383 ff.

14 First in an essay in *International Quarterly*, then in an expanded version in *Kleine Schriften* I 307 ff. See my discussion of this in W. M. Calder III and A Demandt (edd.), *Eduard Meyer: Leben und Leistung eines Universalhistorikers* (Leiden 1990) 8 ff., 20 ff.

15 He described it as the first step on the road to "Byzantium", which he regards as the Orient's revenge on the West (see my discussion cited in the preceding note, p. 21).

16 Art. cit. (supra n.1) 45. See, however, infra n.65 for a possible remote relevance.

17 See Mahmud Abd el-Rasiq, *Die Darstellungen und Texte des Sanktuars Alexanders des Großen im Tempel von Luxor* (Mainz 1984) passim.

18 The few relevant passages are frequently misrepresented and even mistranslated. Bosworth (supra. n.12) 279 f. gets it essentially right, but shows some lack of clarity, stating that Aristotle envisages a situation in which one man would be so superior as to appear a god among men. Against this common misinterpretation of *Pol.* 3.8.1284a etc. see my treatment (op. cit. n.14, 20 with n.30). Aristotle is saying that if there is a man or a number of men of outstanding *arete,* he or they cannot be part of an ordinary *polis,* for such a man would be like a god among men; however (Aristotle takes care to add), if there are enough of them, they can form a *polis* by themselves. Nothing could be farther removed from thoughts of deification. In *Rhet.* 1.1361a34 ff., which Bosworth treats very well, he lists outstanding honours awarded for εὐεργεσίαι: they consist of θυσίαι, μνῆμαι ... γέρα, τεμένη, προεδρίαι, τάφοι, εἰκόνες, τροφαὶ δημόσιαι (some barbarian customs intervene) and highly prized gifts. The reference to εἰκόνες (not ἀγάλματα), portrait statues (not cult statues), almost suffices to show that deification is not envisaged. Honours for the living and the dead (as for Greeks and barbarians) are intermingled, and it is probably the latter that may include heroic honours, e.g. sacrifices, perhaps also τεμένη, although the latter may be taken in a purely secular sense, as in Homer: see *LSJ s.v.* and cf. the Loeb translation. There is no good reason for taking the heroic honours as refer-

ring to living men, although we do not know whether living men could reach heroic status. (Cf. infra n.21)

19 I have discussed this (supra n.1, 31–44), dealing with the supposed examples.

20 Op. cit. n.19. Duris is nowhere cited as saying that the divine honours for Lysander were awarded in his lifetime: that conclusion hinges on a single word (Λυσάνδρεια) in Plutarch's collection of miscellaneous anecdotes, we do not know from what sources; the word is Plutarch's own.

21 Thucydides 5.11.1 does not clearly say whether the honours received by Hagnon as founder of Amphipolis (τὰ Ἁγνώνεια) included heroic honours or cult.

22 Supra n.1, 32 n.11. Bosworth appears to believe that Clearchus, the eccentric tyrant of Heraclea, imposed worship of himself as a god on his subjects (supra n.12, 280). That tale turns up only in the Byzantine Suda, and even the less outrageous anecdote that he used a thunderbolt for his sceptre appears as late as Plutarch's Moralia – evidence for what could be believed of him rather than for historical fact. The historian of Heraclea, Memnon (FGrHist 434 F 1.1), knows nothing of this. (Bosworth's statement that he corroborates it is false.)

23 Except apparently for a snippet of Pindar, which we have without context: Paean. 7(a)5 Sn.

24 Phaedr. 255A (applied to the beloved), 258C (the lawgiver and writer); Rep. 2.360C, 8.568B (of irresponsible and tyrannical power).

25 Nock, Essays (supra n.12) II, 841 et al. citing Hepding. The reference given is to Nilsson's Geschichte der griechischen Religion, which was not accessible to me in the edition Nock seems to have used. The (probably) corresponding passage in the third edition (II³ 141 n.1) cites Hepding without an actual reference, among many other scholars for whom references are given. I do not know where Hepding's statement is to be found. It should be added that in the Hellenistic period the word ἰσόθεος (as in ἰσόθεοι τιμαί) comes to be confused with "divine" – a process usefully studied by Nock. It is worth mentioning that a 2nd-c. A.D. papyrus equates βασιλεύς with ἰσόθεος, and that we find ἰσοδαίμονος βασιληίδος ἀρχᾶς in Ariphron of Sicyon (ap. Athen. 15.702a).

26 See the sources collected by S. K. Eddy, The King is Dead: Studies in Near-Eastern Resistance to Hellenism, 334–31 B.C. (Lincoln, NE 1961) ch. 2: to be used with caution in detail.

27 D. Kienast, Philipp II von Makedonien und das Reich der Achaimeniden (Abh. der Marburger Gelehrten Gesellschaft 6, 1971 [1973]).

28 See especially Dem. 10.32 with scholia (1.152 Dilts) and Didymus 8.26 ff. (pp. 29 f. P.-S.).

29 See Plut., Alex. 10.1–3 (the only source), with Badian, "The death of Philip II," Phoenix 17 (1963) 244 ff. Much has been written on this since, but not to much effect. For sound evaluation see Bosworth (supra n.12) 22 n.55.

30 Rightly stressed by Bosworth (supra n.12) 192.

31 See (briefly) Badian (supra n.14) 18 ff.

32 See L. Pearson, The Lost Histories of Alexander the Great (New York 1960) 40 ff., with critical assessment.

33 Surprisingly, Bosworth (supra n.12) 38 f. seems to accept it all without much warning. He expands the reported expiatory offering to Priam into a piece of powerful fiction: "The descendants of Achilles and Priam would now fight together against the common enemy."

34 Bosworth's is now the best-informed and most readable account. See also Badian, Cambridge History of Iran II (Cambridge 1985) ch. 8.

35 For a plausible motive for his going so far out of his way from the coast see E. A. Fredricksmeyer, "Alexander, Midas and the oracle at Gordium," CP 56 (1961) 160 ff.

36 See Bosworth, A Historical Commnentary on Arrian's History of Alexander I (Oxford 1980) 227 ff. for a complete collection of sources, with discussion 228 ff.

37 For an obvious parallel from a better historian, see the treasonable correspondence of Pausanias quoted in Thuc. 1.128.7–129. That these letters cannot be genuine was conclusively proved by C. W. Fornara, "Some aspects of the career of Pausanias of Sparta," Historia 15 (1966) 263 ff.

38 For Philip's foundations see supra n.11. For Alexander's first city, Alexandropolis (never heard of again), see Plut. Alex. 9.1 (with Badian, "Alexander the Great and the unity of mankind," Historia 7 [1958] 442). He founded it in his 16th or 17th year, when put in charge of the kingdom while Philip was away fighting in Thrace. It must have been founded at Philip's suggestion and with his approval. It is presumably to this time that Alexander's reported victory

over the "Illyrians" (perhaps Thracians?) in Philip's absence should be assigned (Curt. 8.1.25). The foundation precisely coincides with Philip's foundation of Philippopolis and was no doubt meant to build up Alexander as heir apparent to the throne. Bosworth (supra n.12) 246, suggests that Alexander may have renamed the city after his accession. This seems unlikely. Quite apart from the chronological coincidence with Philippopolis, we should be left to explain why he founded no other cities for over five years after this; and he was hardly secure enough for such an act of conspicuous arrogance.

39 Supra n.1, 44 ff. with some discussion and references, also for Miletus and Erythrae; for a further conjecture, ibid. 65 f.

40 See Badian, "The death of Parmenio," *TAPA* 91 (1960) 326 ff. for the final form of the conspiracy, and Bosworth (supra n.12) 101 ff. for further discussion and references.

41 It seems to be only much later that we find him denying Philip's paternity: see Plut., *Alex.* 28.2, with the convincing discussion by J. R. Hamilton, "Alexander and his 'so-called' father," *CQ* n.s. 3 (1953) 151 ff. Even then, of course, he would use it when it was politically necessary, e.g. in his address to his mutinous soldiers (Arr. 7.9.2 ff.) – obviously not his actual words, but we can take it that praise of Philip was appropriate to the occasion and was presumably used.

42 Plut., *Mor.* 329d, Diod. 17.66.3, Curt. 5.2.13 (Susa); Plut., *Alex.* 37.7 (Persepolis.) We do not know what made Plutarch change his mind from the former (obviously in the vulgate) to the latter, but he is normally better informed in the biography. The story of the footstool can only have applied to one occasion.

43 In the anecdote (Curt. and Diod., see preceding note) Alexander is too short for his feet to reach the ground and this is the reason for the production of the royal table. For the audience scenes, see, e.g., the reproduction in *Camb. Hist. Iran* (supra n.34) Plate 23, between pp. 814 and 815. That the king was never allowed to touch the ground is popular misrepresentation. Thus the pretender Cyrus, considering himself lawful King, is reported by Ctesias (who must have known of the taboo) as having walked after being wounded, and Artaxerxes himself marched at the head of his troops (Plut., *Artax.* 11.8, 24.10). The taboo must have been confined to formal, especially ritual, occasions.

44 For Cicero, see *Leg.* 1.7 and (facetiously) *Fam.* 2.10.3 (to Caelius). The latter corresponds to *Att.* 5.20.3, where Clitarchus is not named. Atticus is presumed to know the allusion, no doubt also from Clitarchus: as far as I know, there is no evidence of any other Alexander historians being known to Cicero.

45 Bosworth (supra n.12) 154 n.399, impugns the authenticity of Aristobulus' first visit to Pasargadae, as reported by Strabo 15.3.7 730C. I see no good reason for doing so, since Arrian's account (see [pp. 254–6]) is summary and cannot be shown to be more accuarate than Strabo's. Presumably Strabo had read Aristobulus on this, as on matters of geography.

46 Most recently in Ian Worthington (ed.), *Ventures into Greek History* (Oxford 1994) 258–92, revising earlier statements.

47 See my account in *Camb. Hist. Iran* (supra n.34) 488 ff., with the sources.

48 See Bosworth, "Plutarch, Callisthenes and the peace of Callias," *JHS* 110 (1990) 8 for an attempted reconstruction. The vulgate sources and Aristobulus (*ap.* Arr. 7.22) report him as wearing the diadem. In an earlier passage Arrian, citing no sources, says he wore the upright tiara (4.7.4). There is no reason to disbelieve this. He may have changed his style over the years, or he reserved the wearing of the tiara for formal and ritual (Persian) occasions, as indeed the King himself may have done.

49 See Curtius' perceptive comment (8.4.30): "post Cliti caedem libertate sublata".

50 Badian 1981 (op. cit. n.1) 48 ff. Bosworth (supra n.12, 285), in one of his few unfortunate interpretations of sources, tries to reconcile Chares' tendentiously falsified account (aiming at robbing Callisthenes of the glory of opposition) with the main account in Arrian and Curtius by assuming two ceremonies, one and only one of them described in each version. This stock device of making each of two conflicting sources partly right and partly wrong will not work. It is clear that Plutarch, who had seen all the sources and knew (but does not tell) the main account, gives the version of Chares as an alternative account of the same banquet (ἐν τῷ συμποσίῳ). He also fortunately documents Chares' attempt to denigrate Callisthenes on another occasion: in ch. 55, "some say" that Callisthenes was executed by hanging, "others" that he was put in chains and died of illness (both of which can document Alexander's cruelty), but

Chares reports that he was kept in chains for seven months "so that he should be tried before the Synedrion (of the Hellenic League) in the presence of Aristotle, but that he died in India of obesity and lice" – the most undignified end reported. (The other versions were probably those of Ptolemy and Aristobulus respectively: see Arr. 4.14.3.)

51 Thus most recently by G. L. Cawkwell in a very useful article in the collection cited supra n.46, *obiter* on p. 294. My discussion (loc. cit. p. 9) disproved such a view (I hope) for unprejudiced readers. As I there wrote (p.47): "Rationalist historians will have come to terms with the mystical element in Alexander."

52 Most fully Badian, "Harpalus," *JHS* 81 (1961) 16–43.

53 On Alexander I and his relations with the Persians see most recently my essay in S. Hornblower (ed.), *Greek Historiography* (Oxford 1994) 107 ff. Basic discussion appears in the standard histories of Macedonia.

54 For the court background to this, with the methodological questions concerned, see Badian, "The eunuch Bagoas. A study in method," *CQ* n.s. 8 (1958) 147 ff.

55 It is impossible to hold that Ctesias, who had spent many years at the Persian court, could believe, as Herodotus did (1.131), that Mitra was a goddess. Herodotus identifies "her" with the mother goddess Aphrodite, not with a warrior goddess. Ctesias was probably filling out his information with plain fiction.

56 The excavation was splendidly published by D. Stronach, from whose work my illustration of the site is taken. He wrote an extensive summary of the site in *Camb. Hist. Iran* (supra n.34) ch. 20.

57 The mysterious tower called "the Prison of Solomon" has at times been suggested, but is decisively refuted by the fact that Darius I built a similar tower (the "Ka'ba of Zoroaster") near his tomb at Naqsh-i Rustam. See Stronach, *Camb. Hist. Iran* (supra n.34) 848 ff.

58 Supra n.1, 60 ff., with reference to Habicht and discussion.

59 "Alexander the Great and the Greeks of Asia" in *Ancient Society and Institutions: Studies Presented to Victor Ehrenberg on his 75th Birthday* (Oxford 1966) 44 ff.

60 His order to the Ephesians to pay to Artemis the tribute they had been paying to the King (Arr. 1.17.10) was issued before he formulated the policy of freeing the Ionian cities from tribute (ibid. 18.2: see my discussion, op. cit. n.59). Since we are not told it was rescinded, it presumably continued. This was no doubt a way of making sure that the work would in fact be completed – a point not to be taken for granted in major projects undertaken by Greek cities. A later offer to pay for the entire work of construction would be all the more tempting to the Ephesians if they could by then expect a large refund. The Artemidorus cited by Strabo 14.1.22. 640C for the story must be the eminent Ephesian geographer well known to Strabo. He ought to be trusted for an important incident in the fairly recent history of his city.

61 This is the implication of the *logos* reported by Arrian. Most of the sources he saw apparently omitted the story of the embassy to Ammon, but that does not disprove it. Its truth might depend on who the "some" who reported it were: if (as is quite likely) the contemporary Ephippus in his work *On the Deaths of Hephaestion and Alexander,* that would make it credible. Its truth is supported by the fact that the cult of Hephaestion established at Athens was not abolished after Alexander's death: see next note and text.

62 This was pointed out by E. Bickerman, "Sur un passage d'Hypéride, *Epitaphios,* vol. VIII," *Athenaeum* n.s. 41 (1963) 81. No other good reason for the retention of the cult through the Lamian War can be imagined.

63 At the time when the Areopagus had postponed publication of its verdict, in its enquiry that began in autumn 324 – hence at the earliest at the end of 324 or (more probably) early in 323. It is possible that this stage of the debate (over Alexander's divine sonship) may be connected with the letter denying Philip's paternity (see supra n.41); that letter was addressed to the Athenians and concerned Samos (Plut., *Alex.* 28.2).

64 The phrase about "honours in heaven" ascribed to Demosthenes presumably mirrors Demades' warning about the "concern for heaven" leading to the loss of the earth. It quite probably comes from the same debate. It may be relevant that Οὐράνιος is one of the names of Zeus.

65 Supra n.1, 65 ff. This, of course, can only be advanced, as it there was, as reasoned speculation. In this respect only there may be an Egyptian connection: Ammon, in his Egyptian capacity, would be quite accustomed to "introducing" kings to the ranks of the gods. See supra n.17 with text.

THE DEIFICATION OF ALEXANDER THE GREAT:
A NOTE

G. L. Cawkwell

I

The view represented by Hammond has been held by many, including, most recently, A. B. Bosworth, namely that Alexander desired to be recognized as a god and in 324 communicated his desire to the Greeks.[1] Whether this is correct or not will never be decisively settled until there is more evidence than we presently have, but this discussion seeks to support the contrary view, that Alexander communicated no such desire, neither directly nor by anyone acting on his behalf.

One aspect of the matter is plain enough. Alexander did indeed profess to be son of Ammon and, to his own detriment, sought to secure recognition of his sonship.[2] There is no point in further discussing this, nor indeed in speculating on when, how, or why the notion took hold of him. Some would have had it thought that Olympias originated the story, either having dreamt it (Justin 12. 16. 2) or in some mysterious way imagined it (Arr. 4. 10. 2). This cult of Ammon had long flourished in northern Greece (there was in the fourth century a temple to that god at Aphytis, near which Lysander dreamed he was visited by him: Plut. *Lysander* 20.7), and Olympias or Alexander may have picked up the infection in Macedonia itself. But it is as pointless to speculate on such a matter as it would be to dwell on the fact that Clearchus, a tyrant of Heraclea, pronounced himself to be 'son of Zeus' (Justin 16. 5. 8). Alexander likewise pronounced himself son of Ammon. That is a fact. Explanation is neither possible nor necessary.

Equally plain is the complete lack of evidence in the formal accounts of Alexander's life that he sent the Greeks, either collectively to the League of Corinth or separately city by city, any demand to be recognized as a god or even any indication that such recognition would be pleasing to him. The Exiles Decree is formally attested (Diod. 17. 109. Curt. 10. 2. 4–7), as are its later repercussions (Diod. 18. 8. 2–7, Justin 13. 5.2–5). But of any communication concerning divine honours there is not a word. Some have supposed that the lacuna at the end of the twelfth chapter of Arrian Book 7[3] included both a notice about the exiles and another about divine honours, and in view of the reaction the former caused it is hard to believe that Arrian omitted it altogether. It may well be true that neither Ptolemy nor Aristobulus cared about Greek affairs, but other authors certainly did, and it is not to be thought that Arrian entirely omitted matters of such importance. So the Exiles Decree may well have been covered in this lacuna,[4] and if that matter, why not also the other? But there is good reason to suppose that Arrian did not record, let alone discuss, any such thing. When Arrian gave his summation of Alexander (7. 28–30), the only reference he made to what we refer to as 'divine honours' was to Alexander's claim to be son of Zeus, which he declared was a πλημμέλημα (a 'clanger', in English slang usage) 'if it was not perchance a cunning means of impressing his subjects with his majesty' (in which case, Arrian implies, it was no πλημμέλημα at all).[5] Now if Arrian thought it a πλημμέλημα for Alexander to claim divine parentage, he would surely have thought it even more so for Alexander to claim for himself godhead, especially in view of Roman Imperial practice – a number of emperors (including Hadrian in whose reign he wrote) had been titled *divi filius* but the rule enunciated in the last sentence of the fifteenth book of Tacitus' *Annals* stood firm, namely no deification before death.[6] Having censured Alexander's claim to be son of a god, Arrian had no reason not to allude to the major matter, if there had been anything to allude to. The unison of the sources is striking indeed. There is not a word anywhere about Alexander demanding deification. Diodorus and Curtius are, it is true, incompletely preserved, but Plutarch's *Life of Alexander* is before us in its entirety. He not only says nothing, but in the twenty-eighth chapter he discusses Alexander's attitude to 'divine honours' in such terms as exclude any thought that Alexander had sought to have himself recognized as a god. So Plutarch, like Arrian, knew of no such thing.[7]

Indeed there is no good reason to suppose that Alexander was at all concerned with divine honours other than the sonship of Ammon that obsessed him. Of the attempt to introduce *proskynesis* Bosworth has declared: 'it is a much deeper mystery why Alexander attempted to introduce a ceremony which he must have known would be hated and resented. I can only assume that he now believed firmly in his godhead' (*Conquest and Empire*, 286 ff). That is, however, mere explanation. It is notable that Arrian does not appear to draw on either Ptolemy or Aristobulus for the *proskynesis* incident,[8] and the claim that Callisthenes' outspoken criticism was congenial to the Macedonians (Arr. 4. 14. 1) is hardly credible. For one thing they do not seem to have grieved over his fall (Arr. 4. 12. 7) and it must be firmly borne in mind that the whole affair seems to have been concerted by Alexander with some of the Macedonians. At any rate, when Alexander tried to call it all off by sending a message to them, the ceremony still went ahead, and according to some sources, Arrian declared, Hermolaus in his defence in the Pages' Conspiracy asserted that the *proskynesis* plan was not abruptly dropped (4. 14. 2). The whole story has been variously interpreted, but the idea that the introduction of *proskynesis* at court had nothing to do with religion, and was nothing else than an attempt to establish a uniform etiquette for Orientals and Macedonians alike, remains palatable.[9] There is in fact only one point in Arrian's narrative at which Alexander might be supposed to be seeking to show that he was on a par with the gods (7. 20. 1). When he was planning to campaign against the Arabs, 'the story goes that he was being told that the Arabs honour only two gods, Uranus and Dionysus . . . that Alexander did not spurn to be thought a third god by the Arabs . . .'. One might lightly dismiss such a 'story', save that it is to be found in Strabo with the label of Aristobulus (*FGrH* 139 F 56).[10] But how has it come about that Arrian, in apparent contradiction of his professed principle (*Preface*), gives as a 'story' what comes from one of his two main sources? The solution, it may be suggested, is that Aristobulus himself recounted it as a 'story'. If so, it may be regarded as another of Alexander's witticisms concerning 'divine honours' to be set beside the other instances furnished by Plutarch[11] in that chapter which ended thus: 'From what has been said, then, it is clear that Alexander himself was not foolishly affected or puffed up by the belief in his divinity, but used it for the subjugation of others' (*Alexander* 29, translation of B. Perrin).

II

There the matter might rest were it not for various remarks in the Attic orators Hyperides and Dinarchus. In his *Funeral Oration* of 322, i.e. during the Lamian War when Athens was for the while beyond the reach of Macedonian power, Hyperides speaks of what the valour of the fallen had saved Greece from (20ff.):

> It is worth considering too what we think would have happened had these men not fought as was due. Would not the whole world have belonged to a single master, and Greece have been compelled to treat his wishes as law? Would not, in short, Macedonian highhandedness and not the force of justice have prevailed in every city. . . ? This is clear from what we are compelled (ἀναγκαζόμεθα) to put up with even now (καὶ νῦν ἔτι) to *stand by and watch* (ἐφορᾶν), sacrifices being made to men, statues, altars, and temples being completed carelessly for the gods but meticulously for men, and *ourselves* being forced to honour these men's servants as heroes. Where respect for the gods has been destroyed through Macedonian arrogance, what must we suppose would have befallen human rights?

No one disputes that Hyperides is referring to cult being paid to Alexander as a god and to Hephaestion being honoured as a hero, but some have been reluctant to accept that Hyperides was referring to what was happening in Greece during the Lamian War and have followed Tell and Blass in changing ἀναγκαζόμεθα ('we are compelled') to ἠναγκαζόμεθα ('we were compelled') and taking νῦν to mean 'just now' (i.e. very recently).[12] The case for making the change and supposing that Hyperides was referring to a state of affairs no longer existing might be put as follows. He is talking of what the Macedonians would have done had those fighting in the Lamian War not stopped them; his hearers could tell how bad it all would have been when they reflected that the Macedonians had even compelled Greeks to accord divine honours to Alexander and Hephaestion; Leosthenes and the others who had died had to their great glory finished all that. So, it may be argued, ἠναγκαζόμεθα is appropriate and indeed necessary. This, however, should be rejected. The repeated use of the present tense culminating in ἡμᾶς ἀναγκαζομένους ('we ourselves are compelled'), and the final perfect (ἀνήρηται, 'has been removed') suggest that the text as we have it should be retained, that Hyperides was describing what, at the very moment he was speaking, the Athenians were 'being forced to put up with even now'. The text as it stands presents a coherent argument: that the Athenians could realize what the Macedonians would have gone on to do, by reflecting on how far they had actually gone in requiring these divine honours, practices of which the Athenians are all too well aware.

Hyperides drew a line between what was happening in Athens and what Athenians had to put up with happening elsewhere. The latter category we are far from precisely informed about, and evidence from mainland Greece is hardly to be found beyond this passage of Hyperides.[13] But that is not surprising. The evidence for the Greek cities of Asia is almost entirely third-century BC and later, and we have it because the cult of Alexander had been instituted and had persisted for centuries out of genuine gratitude for liberation from Persia.[14] In mainland Greece in so far as such cult was instituted – we know from this passage of Hyperides that it was not at Athens, and there was no precise evidence of its institution elsewhere[15] – what was done would have been done out of calculations of interest, and extravagant honours voted would have been quickly forgotten about. It is not surprising that we know so little when there was so little to know compared with the cities of Asia where the cult of centuries is but sparsely recorded. How widespread such sacrifices, altars, and statues were in mainland Greece there is no telling. Certainly the Exiles Decree evoked expressions of gratitude from the Greeks (*SIG*³ 312. 14, 15) in 324, and in 323 the embassies that arrived in Babylon, crowned and bearing crowns (Arr. 7. 23. 2), may well have been announcing what their cities had done.[16]

That was all outside Athens. It is what the Athenians themselves were forced to do that is challenging. No matter in what circumstances they had begun before the War to accord Hephaestion 'heroic' honours, once the War began one would expect them utterly to abandon them. So how could Hyperides speak of the Athenians being obliged? They may, in effect, have neglected such honours just as two centuries earlier Cleisthenes of Sicyon, unable to get the consent of the Delphic oracle to his 'expelling Adrastus', imported the hero Melanippus, the bitter enemy of Adrastus, and accorded him 'the sacrifices and festivals of Adrastus' (Hdt. 5. 68). But, like Cleisthenes, the Athenians had to keep and honour Hephaestion. What was compelling them? Since in 322 political compulsion was, or seemed, a thing of the past, and since the Athenians can have had no conceivable interest in Hephaestion dead whom they had never heard of alive other than that Alexander had been passionately fond of him, there seems to be only one explanation, viz. that of religion. The god Ammon had long been acknowledged in Greece and consulted, most notably in Boeotia and Sparta.[17] In the middle of the fourth century Athens, it would appear, sent *theoroi* to Ammon (*IG* ii² 1642, 14 ff.) and this evidence of consultation may give a glimpse of long-standing practice.[18] Delphi was the preferred and most prestigious of oracles, but in the middle of the sixth century, according to Herodotus (1. 46. 3), Ammon was famous enough for Croesus to consult; whether he did or not, it must have been familiar to the Athenians of Herodotus' day. Thus the standing of Ammon was such that his oracular utterances counted in the Greek world generally and no less in Athens. Ammon had uttered concerning Hephaestion (Arr. 7. 23. 6, Plut. *Alexander* 72. 2). That would have sufficed to oblige the Athenians.

According to Arrian (7. 14. 7), Alexander gave orders to make offerings, to offer sacrifice to Hephaestion as hero; which must have been after Philippos (Diod. 17. 115. 6) returned with the oracle's response to Alexander's enquiry about how Hephaestion should be honoured (Arr. 7. 23. 6).[19] So the order 'to all' (Diod. 17.115.6) will have gone out in 323, shortly, if we follow Arrian (7. 23), after the second lot of Greek embassies had arrived and as soon as the reply came from Ammon. If the order went 'to all', it went to Greece, arriving there not long before Alexander's death, but the form of the order will have been a communication of the oracle from Ammon. Thus Athens was inescapably obliged by Greek religious attitudes, while Hyperides can speak of it as a measure imposed by the Macedonians.

III

Earlier, perhaps in 324, the Athenian assembly had certainly had before it a proposal by Demades that Alexander should be officially recognized as a god and added to the

Twelve Gods. Dinarchus (1. 94) alludes to the proposal. Sundry sources show that it was Demades who proposed it and was indeed fined a large sum (Athen. 6. 251b, Aelian, *VH*. 5. 12) presumably on a charge of impiety (ἀσέβεια).[20] Why Demades made this proposal can only be conjectured. Demosthenes opposed it (Polybius 12. 12b. 3); according to Dinarchus (1. 94) he proposed a decree expressly forbidding such proposals,[21] which in view of the history of trials for impiety was hardly necessary. It is a reasonable guess that this startling proposal of Demades was made to help dissuade Alexander from implementing the Exiles Decree in the case of Samos; though it had been generally accepted by the Greeks (cf. *SIG*[3] 312), it was a disaster for Athens (Diod. 18. 8. 7). When the Athenians did not accept his idea of how to avert it, Demades is said (Val. Max. 7. 2. 13) to have remarked 'see that in keeping heaven safe you don't lose your land (*terram amittatis*)', the land in question being perhaps the territory of Samos.[22] Whether the Athenians were amongst the embassies that came before Alexander on his way back to Babylon in early 323 is unclear, but it is likely enough; those who 'disputed the return of the exiles' were heard last (Diod. 17. 113. 4) and since the only states known to us to have refused to accept were Athens and Aetolia (Diod. 18. 8. 6), Athenian ambassadors were probably involved.

This debate was referred to by Dinarchus in a passage where he was railing against Demosthenes' inconstancy. 'At one time' (τότε μέν) he opposed the city recognizing Alexander as a thirteenth god; 'at another' (τότε δέ) he took what Dinarchus represented as a quite inconsistent line: he declared that the people ought not to wrangle about 'heavenly honours' (τῶν ἐν τῷ οὐρανῷ τιμῶν). Now there is no reason to suppose that these seemingly inconsistent attitudes were expressed in the same debate, and indeed it is very unlikely that Demosthenes would so shortly after opposing divine honours have seemed to give his consent. Some other occasion must be sought.

It is reasonable to suppose that that occasion was the debate whether to accord heroic honours to Hephaestion. Not that there could have been much real debate. No matter how much Macedonian domination was resented, the expression of the will of Ammon had to be obeyed. Unfortunately we can only guess the terms in which it was conveyed, but if in communicating the oracle of Ammon Alexander described himself as son of Ammon, Demosthenes' comment 'let him be the son of Zeus too if he wishes and the son of Poseidon' (Hyp. 5. 31) would have been apt. Both Hyperides and Dinarchus (1. 94) speak as if Demosthenes was *agreeing* with Alexander: 'The *demos* must not dispute with Alexander the divine honours' (Dinarchus) and 'conceding to Alexander' (Hyperides) are suitable terms for the situation envisaged. As Hyperides' *Epitaphios* shows, Athens did not deify Alexander but it did 'heroise' Hephaestion, and it must have been in connection with this that Demosthenes expressed what Hyperides chose to treat as a change of policy, which it would not have been. They had to accept the command of Ammon; Alexander's posturing was irrelevant.

IV

The precise date of the trial of Demosthenes, in the course of which Hyperides attributes these words to him, is unsure,[23] but for it to be correct that Demosthenes uttered them as comment on the terms used by Alexander to communicate the oracle of Ammon touching 'heroic' honours for Hephaestion, that communication has to be dated before the trial and indeed quite long enough before the trial for Hyperides and Dinarchus to sound as if they were not referring to a debate that happened yesterday. Hephaestion died in the second half of 324,[24] and the response of Ammon to Alexander's question as to how Hephaestion was to be honoured reached Babylon after the Greek embassies had been dealt with (Arr. 7. 23. 1 and 6), and this was the last event recorded by Arrian before the death of Alexander.[25] So one might wonder whether there was enough time for the presupposed sequence, namely a message to Greece, a debate in Athens and, at some interval, the trial of Demosthenes. The message, however, could have reached Greece as quickly as, under Persian rule, a message from Susa reached Sardis, if the Persian Royal Post had been maintained.[26] That could be very swift, and there is no reason to suppose that the Macedonians did not maintain it. No doubt Alexander forwarded the oracle as swiftly as he could, and if the message was sent to Menes, or whoever replaced him in control of Syria, Phoenicia, and Cilicia (Arr. 3. 16.9) envoys could have been on their way to the Greek mainland by trireme (cf. Arr. 3. 19. 6).[27] Alexander died on the night of 10–11 June 323.[28] The news, or at any rate rumours, of his death will have reached Greece in the later days of that month. If the oracle of Ammon was communicated to Athens in the first half of May, there is ample time for Athens to have the debate in which Demosthenes made the comment attributed to him by Hyperides and, at an interval, the trial of Demosthenes in which both Dinarchus and Hyperides alluded to it.

The embassies recorded by Arrian in 323 had nothing to do with Hephaestion, and, to return whither we set out, nothing to do with divine honours for Alexander at Athens. As has been remarked,[29] 'no doubt in his more summary narrative Diodorus grouped all embassies together', but it is clear that the embassies were all from individual cities. After Issus the League of Corinth had sent one embassy on behalf of all to congratulate Alexander on his victory (Diod. 17. 48. 6). In 324 the embassies[30] came on a wide variety of business, which Ptolemy and Aristobulus chose not to record (Arr. 7. 19. 1), but which Diodorus declared that Alexander dealt with in various categories (17. 113. 3 ff.). In the first category were those who had come about the business of the Hellenic sanctuaries, namely Eleans, Ammonians, Delphians, and Corinthians, in the next category those coming 'about the gifts', then those in dispute with their neighbours, then individuals on their own business, lastly those opposing the return of the exiles. There seems no room here for divine honours. But perhaps Diodorus misleads us. He has perhaps omitted the set of embassies who came in Arrian (7. 23. 2) crowned and crowning, a surprising omission in view of the fullness of Diodorus' discussion in Chapter 113, but, if improbable, not inconceivable. It is, however, sure that if these latter-reported embassies from Greece included an Athenian embassy, it was not there to greet Alexander as a god. Hyperides' *Funeral Oration* 21 makes plain that Athens had not itself gone in for that sort of thing

Nor, we may presume, had Sparta. Indeed, if Alexander ever had sought deification for himself, he would have known better than to approach the one state that would have no truck with Macedonia. The oracle of Ammon was a different matter. It had long been respected at Sparta, certainly since the days of Lysander and perhaps much earlier,[31] and the instruction to treat Hephaestion as a hero would be binding on Spartans too. It would have been communicated to Sparta, again by 'the son of Ammon'. In answer to the instructions (τὰ ἐπισταλέντα παρὰ τοῦ Ἀλεξάνδρου), Damis declared, in words reminiscent of Hyperides, 'We concede to Alexander to be *called* a god if he wishes'. That is Plutarch's version (*Moralia* 219e), for by his time the nice distinction between 'Ammon' and 'son of Ammon' was blurred.[32] They conceded to Alexander a title, but they did not vote him divine honours.

As Patroclus to Achilles, so Hephaestion to Alexander, 'who had from boyhood emulated Achilles' and who behaved over the corpse of Hephaestion in a manner evocative of the grief of Achilles (Arr. 7. 14.4, Homer, *Iliad* 18. 22 ff.). Alexander moved in his imagination in the world of Homeric heroes. He did not seek deification. That came from others and mostly after his death.

Such at any rate is the contribution I dare to dedicate to the *Fest* of one who himself has walked in the mountains of Macedonia and is himself a not unheroic soldier and scholar.

Notes

The debate over 'divine honours' for Alexander is a long-fought contest, and I trust that the scholar to whom these pages are dedicated will not be put out to discover that one who greatly respects and admires him dares to dissent from him even as he seeks to honour. In any case Nicholas Hammond is hardly one to blench at any arguments I can muster. Long may he continue to fight his corner in the history of Greece.

Simon Hornblower made helpful comments on a draft of this paper, for which I am duly grateful.

1 Cf. N. G. L. Hammond and F. W. Walbank, *A History of Macedonia*, iii (Oxford, 1988), 82, and A. B. Bosworth, *Conquest and Empire: The Reign of Alexander the Great* (Cambridge, 1988), 278 ff.

2 Cf. A. B. Bosworth, 'Alexander and Ammon', in *Greece and the Eastern Mediterranean in Ancient History and Prehistory*, K. H. Kinzl, ed. (Berlin, 1977), 51–75. Only D. G. Hogarth, 'The Deification of Alexander the Great', *English Historical Review*, 2 (1887), 317–29, in the spirit of brisk no-nonsense that pervades that justly celebrated article, has gone so far as to deny that Alexander was concerned to pass himself off as son of Ammon.

3 *Pace* Bosworth, *Conquest and Empire*, 288 ('the text of both Arrian and Curtius is riddled with lacunae at this juncture and their silence is not significant'), apart from Arrian 7.10. 1, where there is a very minor lacuna, there is in Arrian only this lacuna seriously to be considered. We know from the epitome of Photius (Budé text, ii, p. 19, ed. R. Henry) that it contained a notice of the flight of Harpalus. The missing portion is quite large, but, quite apart from Harpalus, there are other matters which must have been there and which could well have taken quite a lot of space. Cf. P. A. Brunt, *Arrian: Anabasis,* ii, Loeb Classical Library (London, 1983), Appendix XXIII at 506.

4 Bosworth, *Conquest and Empire*, 221, supposed that the Exiles Decree was recorded in 'the great *lacuna*'. It must be remarked that if it was, it was put in the narrative long after Alexander had sent Nicanor to Greece. The date of the Olympic Festival is debatable (cf. K. S. Sacks, 'Herodotus and the Dating of the Battle of Thermopylae', *CQ²* 26 (1976), 234 ff.), but even supposing it was in September and not July, Nicanor would have had to be despatched to Greece probably while Alexander was at Susa, for, although messages could travel fast, individual persons would take quite a long time, not of course the three months which Herodotus asserted (6.50.2) were required by the Royal Road, but even by the reverse of the route followed in 395 by Conon, viz Cilicia, Thapsacus, the Euphrates to Babylon (Diod. 14.81.4), probably a good two months to reach Olympia from Babylon. This might make one doubt that the Exiles Decree was in Arrian, but although his main sources may have passed it by (as they appear to have passed by the *proskynesis* ceremony), the Greek sources of the Vulgate regarded it as so important that Arrian is very likely to have included it.

5 7.29.3: ὅτι δὲ ἐς θεὸν τὴν γένεσιν τὴν αὑτοῦ ἀνέφερεν, τῇδὲ ϱοῦτο ἐμοὶ δοκεῖ μέγα εἶναι αὐτῷ τὸ πλημμέλημα, εἰ μὴ καὶ σόφισμα ἦν τυχὸν ἐς τοὺς ὑπηκόους τοῦ σεμνοῦ ἕνεκα: 'As to his referring his birth to a god, not even this seems to me to be a great fault of his, if indeed it was not, perchance, merely a cunning way of increasing his majesty before his subjects.'

6 'Nam deum honor principi non ante habetur quam agere inter homines desierit': 'For a Princeps does not receive divine honours until he has ceased to act amongst men.'

7 Plut. *Alexander* 28.1: καθόλου δὲ πρὸς μὲν τοὺς βαρβάρους σοβαρὸς ἦν καὶ σφόδρα πεπεισμένῳ περὶ τῆς ἐκ θεοῦ γενέσεως καὶ τεκνώσεως ὅμοιος, τοῖς δὲ Ἕλλησι μετρίως καὶ ὑποφειδομένως ἑαυτὸν ἐξεθείαζε ('in general while he was haughty towards the barbarians and like a man who was very much persuaded of his divine birth and generation, towards the Greeks he was moderate and sparing in his divine claims') – i.e. the only sense in which Alexander ἑαυτὸν ἐξεθείαζε was his claim to being son of Ammon.

8 L. Pearson, *The Lost Histories of Alexander the Great* (New York 1960), 170.

9 Cf. J. P. V. D. Balsdon, 'The "Divinity" of Alexander', *Historia* 1 (1950), 371–82.

10 Cf. P. Högemann, *Alexander der Grosse und Arabien* (Munich, 1985), 130: 'Arrian führt das Motiv mit den Worten λόγος δὲ κατέχει ein, um seinen Lesern zu signalisieren, dass er im folgenden eine zwar glaubhafte aber doch nicht zweifelsfrei Nachricht bieten will.'

11 At least one of which was to be found in Aristobulus (*FGrH* 139 F 47).

12 G. Colin in his Budé text of 1946 followed Blass in his Teubner edition of 1894 in printing ἠναγκαζόμεθα, but Jensen in the Teubner edition of 1917 reverted to what is on the papyrus, ἀναγκαζόμεθα. Professor Bosworth is strongly in favour of the Colin text (as he has informed me by letter). I follow E. J. Bickerman, 'Sur un passage d'Hypéride', *Athenaeum,* 41 (1963), 71 ff., who points to the use of the perfect (ἀνήρηται) in § 22.

13 The evidence is presented by C. Habicht, *Gottmenschtum und griechische Städte*² (Munich, 1970), 17–36, hardly a formidable array. See E. Badian, 'The Deification of Alexander the Great', in *Ancient Macedonian Studies in Honor of C. F. Edson,* H. J. Dell, ed. (Thessaloniki, 1981), 59 ff. Habicht is persuaded that the Hyperides passage shows that Athens established a cult of Alexander with which the cult of Hephaestion is inseparably linked (*Gottmenschtum,* 30–4). This seems to me to be quite contrary to what Hyperides says, drawing a contrast between what the Athenians are obliged to observe others doing and what they are obliged to do themselves.

14 Cf. Habicht, *Gottmenschtum,* 25.

15 Pausanias 8. 32.1 tells of a statue of Ammon, shaped like the Herms at Athens, outside a house, 'the property of a private citizen in my time', which the Mantineans 'made for Alexander'. W. M. Calder, 'Alexander's House (Pausanias 8.32.1)', *GRBS* 23 (1982), 281–7, supposes that Pausanias was deceived by the owner, probably rightly. A house is not a temple, and it seems unlikely that the Mantineans were preparing in case the great man happened to call! It is not to be excluded that the Herm-like statue had been put up long before the reign of Alexander.

16 On the whole I prefer Badian's interpretation of Arrian's notice ('Deification', 55 ff.), but there may well have been some states reporting progress on the building work suggested by Hyperides, *Funeral Oration* 21 (still going on in 322) or announcing that they recognized Alexander as a god.

17 Cf. C. J. Classen, 'The Libyan God Ammon in Greece before 331 B.C.', *Historia,* 8 (1959), 349–55.

18 Cf. A. M. Woodward, 'Athens and the Oracle of Ammon', *BSA* 57 (1962), 5–13.

19 Arrian 7. 14 is a chapter summing up how Alexander reacted to Hephaestion's death. It should not be inferred from §7 that Alexander ordered the 'heroization' of Hephaestion before he had the reply from Ammon. At 7. 23. 6 Arrian says that when the reply came, Alexander 'rejoiced in the oracle and from then on (τὸ ἀπὸ τοῦδε) gave him heroic honours'. Similarly in Diodorus' account (17. 115. 6) the arrival of Philippos with the oracle is given as the explanation of why Alexander issued instructions to all (προσέταξε ἅπασι κτλ.).

20 Cf. E. Derenne, *Les process d'impiété intentés aux philosophers à Athènes au I^{ière} et au IV^{icme} siècles au J. C.,* Bibliothèque de la Faculté de Philosophie et Lettres de 'Univ. de Liège, XLV (Liège and Paris, 1930), 188, and K. M. T. Atkinson, 'Demosthenes, Alexander, and *Asebeia*', *Athenaeum,* 51 (1973), 310–35.

21 γράφων καὶ ἀπαγορεύων μηδένα νομίζειν ἄλλον θεὸν ἢ τοὺς παραδεδομένους ('proposing a decree which forbade treating as a god anyone older than the traditional ones'). Atkinson, 312, claims that 'the words γράφων καὶ ἀπαγορεύων are evidently a hendiadys, and mean 'forbidding through an indictment (γραφή)'. A passage a little further on in the same speech makes it clear that Demosthenes is represented here as merely threatening indictment: it is not implied that he was the actual accuser of Demades. But 'forbidding by proposing a decree' is just as

acceptable a meaning, and there is no evidence to support the idea that Demosthenes prosecuted Demades.

22 Cf. V. de Falco, *Demade Oratore²* (Naples, 1954), 24 ff. The version in the *Gnomologium Vaticanum* (L. Sternbach, 'De Gnomologio Vaticano inedito', *Wiener Studien*, 10 (1888), 221) reads δέδια, φησίν, ὦ ἄνδρες, ὑπὲρ ὑμῶν, μὴ τοῦ οὐρανοῦ φθονοῦντες Ἀλεξάνδρῳ τὴν γῆν ἀφαιρεθῆτε ὑπ' αὐτοῦ ("'fear for yourselves, gentlemen," he says, "lest envying Alexander heaven you are deprived by him of the earth"') – a good remark if 'the land' was Samos. On the background and potential attitude of the Athenians to Alexander see Ian Worthington, Ch. 15 [in Worthington, *Ventures into Greek History*]).

23 E. Badian, 'Harpalus', *JHS* 81 (1961), 43: There appears to be no *terminus ante quem* in our evidence, short of the end of the archon year.' The discussion of Ian Worthington, 'The Chronology of the Harpalus Affair', *SO* 61 (1986), 63–71, which argues for an earlier date for the trial of Demosthenes than is here presupposed, seems only to underline the looseness of any precise chronological scheme. Bosworth, *Conquest and Empire*, 291 ff., seeks to fix the date of Harpalus' escape from Athens by reference to the narrative of Thibron's campaign in Cyrenaica. He argues that Thibron was dead by the end of 322, but it is to be noted that Perdiccas' death in Egypt ended a reign of three years (Diod. 18. 36. 7) and so the failure of his expedition should be put in 321/0; which is not surprising – considering the pattern imposed by the inundation of the Nile, at Cairo (in those times) at its maximum in the early days of October and its minimum in mid-June, invasion had to be made as the Nile fell and completed before it rose very far. So Thibron may still have been alive in early 321, and Bosworth's timetable is to be rejected. However, whatever the date of Harpalus' escape from Athens, it is unclear how long an interval there was before Demosthenes carried his proposal for the Areopagus to investigate the matter of the missing talents, but interval there was (cf. Plutarch, *Demosthenes* 25 ff., which shows that some time was spent in searching before the Areopagus took over). Precise dates for Athens within 324/3 elude us and, as Aristotle remarked, 'the same degree of precision is not to be sought in all subjects'.

24 According to H. Berve, *Das Alexanderreich auf prosopographischer Grundlage,* ii (Munich 1926), 173, Hephaestion died in October, but there seems no good reason to pick one month rather than another. If the date of Alexander's departure from Opis could be fixed, Diodorus 17.110 could be brought in to play, but no precise timetable can be established for the events of 324.

25 As far as I am aware, the universal presumption has been that whatever communication the Greek states received from Alexander arrived in 324 or very early in 323. Cf. the discussion of G. de Sanctis, 'Gli ultimi messaggi di Alessandro ai Greci, I: La richiesta degli onori divini', *Riv. Fil.²* 18 (1940), 6, who regards the arrival in Babylon of the embassies recorded in Arrian 7. 23. 2 as the *terminus ante quem*. But since according to both Arrian (7. 23. 6) and Diodorus (17. 115. 6) Alexander called for the 'heroization' of Hephaestion *after* the response came from Siwah, this will not do unless one is prepared to cast aside Arrian's order of events.

26 For the speed of communications in the Persian Empire, see D. M. Lewis, *Sparta and Persia* (Leiden, 1977), 56 ff.: 'The most optimistic calculations that I know of for Susa to Sardis bring them within 7 days of each other, but I suspect that this is a little on the low side.'

27 Conon travelled to Babylon to see Artaxerxes in 395 by way of Cilicia and Thapsacus (Diod. 14. 81. 4), and that route, or a similar route from the Levant, may have become the regular route for embassies (cf. the Athenian honours for Strato of Sidon who had 'seen to it that the ambassadors whom the People sent journeyed as comfortably as possible to the King', Tod, *GHI*, no. 139, and cf. also Damastes (*FGrH* 5 F 8), which at least shows the ambassadors did not have to trudge the length of the Royal Road). Lewis is of the view that there was probably only the one road provided with way-stations (σταθμοί), but one would expect the King to secure himself the means of speedy communication with the fleet. The obvious route was by way of Tadmor, the later Palmyra. If such a route was used for sending a message to Greece, a huge saving of time would be made (compared to the Royal Road). Of course, Nicanor may have taken the more leisurely route in 324, when he carried the Rescript about the Exiles to Olympia to read it out himself, but the reply of Ammon about Hephaestion in 323 was no doubt treated by Alexander as urgent, and a number of envoys could have been sent off to various parts of Greece from the satrapal court in Phoenicia.

28 Cf. A. E. Samuel, *Ptolemaic Chronology* (Munich 1962), 46 ff.

29 Brunt, *Arrian: Anabasis,* ii. 495.

30 In Arrian there are two, and only two, lots of embassies from Greece (7. 19. 1, 23. 2–7. 14. 6, a chapter which reviews the whole topic of Alexander's extravagant grief, is not another embassy – *pace* Brunt, *Arrian: Anabasis*, ii. 495 – but merely anticipates those of 7–19. 1 just as 7. 14. 7 anticipates 7. 23. 6, a sign of two different sources, since 7. 14. 6 speaks of Alexander being *en route* for Babylon and 7. 19. 1 speaks of him being already in Babylon; perhaps the source of 7. 14. 6 was confusing the embassies of 7. 15. 4 and those of 7. 19. 1). Diodorus has only one lot of embassies (17. 113), thus conflating both those of Arrian 7. 15. 4 and Arrian's two sets of Greek embassies, which are separated in Arrian by Alexander's trip to the Pollacopas. It is curious that Arrian asserted that neither Ptolemy nor Aristobulus explained what the business of the various embassies of 7. 19. 1 was and did not add the details from the sources drawn on by Diodorus in 17. 113: perhaps Arrian was beginning to weary of *onerosa collatio*. It would be more striking, if fashionable theories about divine honours for Alexander were correct, that Diodorus has nothing to report of such a topic when he has so fully discussed other matters of embassies' business.

31 Lysander's consultation of Ammon is familiar, and his family's connection with the Libyan king (Diod. 14. 13. 5 ff.) suggests that Lysander's father may have been a devotee. Indeed the 'ancient oracle' of Plutarch, *Lysander* 25, may be the explanation of how Cleomenes spurned Delphi when he set off on his Libyan venture (Hdt. 5. 42. 2).

32 Even more by Aelian's time (cf. *VH* 2. 19).

10

ALEXANDER
AND CONSPIRACIES

Introduction

Alexander was subject to several conspiracies during his reign, and he himself was not above engineering conspiracies against others. We might expect the latter to be directed against those whom he suspected might challenge his power or authority as king, and hence enable Alexander to maintain his power – here, perhaps the most notorious example involved Philotas and his father Parmenion (see Source 101).[1] However, there are some grounds for implicating Alexander, when heir apparent, in the plot to assassinate his father Philip II in 336. While there were times in his reign when Alexander had genuine cause to fear conspiracies against him, the result of his increasing 'orientalism' which caused dissatisfaction among his closest advisers and army in general, there were times when his own paranoia came too much to the fore (cf. Source 108). Instances of this may be seen in the lead-up to his murder of Cleitus (Source 58),[2] or in the fate of Coenus, found dead shortly after the Hyphasis river mutiny in 326 (Arr. 6.2.1, Curt. 9.3.20). Alexander suspected conspiracies where they did not exist, and came to distrust those at his court and elsewhere (perhaps even as far afield as Antipater in Greece); it is no surprise to hear from Ephippus, a contemporary source, that everyone lived in almost a state of fear given Alexander's disregard for human life (Source 99).

Again, however, the sources need to be carefully evaluated – as is well shown by the differing primary accounts of those who instigated the Pages' Conspiracy (see Sources 102–104) or the manner of Callisthenes' death (Sources 105–107), who had led the opposition to Alexander's *proskynesis* attempt (Sources 87 and 88).

Ancient sources

101 Here [the palace of the Zarangaeans] also Alexander discovered the conspiracy of Philotas, son of Parmenion. Ptolemy and Aristobulus (*FGrH* 139 F 22) say that it had already been reported to him before in Egypt; but that it did not appear to him credible, both on account of the long-existing friendship between them, the honour which he publicly conferred upon his father Parmenion, and the confidence he reposed in Philotas himself. Ptolemy, son of Lagus, says that Philotas was brought before the Macedonians, that Alexander vehemently accused him, and that he defended himself from the charges. He says also that the divulgers of the plot came forward and convicted him and his accomplices both by other clear proofs and especially because

Philotas himself confessed that he had heard of a certain conspiracy which was being formed against Alexander. He was convicted of having said nothing to the king about this plot, though he visited the royal tent twice a day. He and all the others who had taken part with him in the conspiracy were killed by the Macedonians with their javelins; and Polydamas, one of the Companions, was despatched to Parmenion, carrying letters from Alexander to the generals in Media, Cleander, Sitalces, and Menidas, who had been placed over the army commanded by Parmenion. By these men Parmenion was put to death, perhaps because Alexander deemed it incredible that Philotas should conspire against him and Parmenion not participate in his son's plan; or perhaps, he thought that even if he had had no share in it, he would now be a dangerous man if he survived, after his son had been violently removed, being held in such great respect as he was both by Alexander himself and by all the army, not only the Macedonian, but also that of the Grecian auxiliaries as well, whom he often used to command in accordance with Alexander's order, both in his own turn and out of his turn, with his sovereign's approbation and satisfaction (Ptolemy, *FGrH* 138 F 13 = Arr. 3.26).

102 Aristobulus says that the youths[3] asserted it was Callisthenes who instigated them to make the daring attempt; and Ptolemy says the same. Most writers, however, do not agree with this, but represent that Alexander readily believed the worst about Callisthenes, from the hatred which he already felt towards him, and because Hermolaus was known to be exceedingly intimate with him (Ptolemy, *FGrH* 138 F 16 = Arr. 4.14.1).

103 Some say that Alexander accidentally happened to be drinking until day-break; but Aristobulus has given the following account: a Syrian woman, who was under the inspiration of the deity, used to follow Alexander about. At first she was a subject of mirth to Alexander and his courtiers; but when all that she said in her inspiration was seen to be true, he no longer treated her with neglect, but she was allowed to have free access to him both by night and day, and she often took her stand near him even when he was asleep. And indeed on that occasion when he was withdrawing from the drinking-party she met him, being under the inspiration of the deity at the time, and besought him to return and drink all night. Alexander, thinking that there was something divine in the warning, returned and went on drinking; and thus the enterprise of the Pages fell through (Aristobulus, *FGrH* 139 F 30 = Arr. 4.13.5).

104 Aristobulus says that the youths asserted it was Callisthenes who instigated them to make the daring attempt; and Ptolemy says the same (Aristobulus, *FGrH* 139 F 31 = Arr. 4.14.1).

105 As to the death of Callisthenes, some say (Ptolemy, *FGrH* 138 F 17 = Source 106) that he was hanged by Alexander's orders, others (Aristobulus, *FGrH* 139 F 33 = Source 107) that he was bound hand and foot and died of sickness, and Chares says that after his arrest he was kept in fetters seven months, that he might be tried before a full council when Aristotle was present, but that about the time when Alexander was wounded in India, he died from obesity and the disease of lice (Chares, *FGrH* 125 F 15 = Plut. *Alex.* 55.8–9).

106 Aristobulus says that Callisthenes was carried about with the army bound with fetters, and afterwards died a natural death; but Ptolemy, son of Lagus, says that he was stretched upon the rack and then hanged. Thus not even did these authors, whose narratives are very trustworthy, and who at the time were in intimate association with

Alexander, give accounts consistent with each other of events so well known, and the circumstances of which could not have escaped their notice (Ptolemy, *FGrH* 138 F 17 = Arr. 4.14.3).

107 Aristobulus says that Callisthenes was carried about with the army bound with fetters, and afterwards died a natural death (Aristobulus, *FGrH* 139 F 33 = Arr. 4.14.3).

108 But Alexander's own end was now near.[4] Aristobulus says that the following occurrence was a prognostication of what was about to happen. He was distributing the army which came with Peucestas from Persia, and that which came with Philoxenus and Menander from the sea, among the Macedonian lines, and becoming thirsty he retired from his seat and thus left the royal throne empty. On each side of the throne were couches with silver feet, upon which his personal Companions were sitting. A certain man of obscure condition (some say that he was even one of the men kept under guard without being in chains), seeing the throne and the couches empty, and the eunuchs standing round the throne (for the Companions also rose up from their seats with the king when he retired), walked through the line of eunuchs, ascended the throne, and sat down on it. According to a Persian law, they did not make him rise from the throne, but rent their garments and beat their breasts and faces as if on account of a great evil. When Alexander was informed of this, he ordered the man who had sat upon his throne to be put to the torture, with the view of discovering whether he had done this according to a plan concerted by a conspiracy. But the man confessed nothing, except that it came into his mind at the time to act thus. Even more for this reason the diviners explained that this occurrence boded no good to him (Aristobulus, *FGrH* 139 F 58 = Arr. 7.24.1–3).

Modern works

In the following extract, E. Badian, John Moors Cabot Professor Emeritus at Harvard University, traces and discusses a number of conspiracies – real and imagined – during Alexander's reign as well as his involvement in the murder of his father. By close examination of the controversial source material and brilliant argumentation, we see that Alexander exploited suspicions at his court and in doing so used conspiracies as a means to keep opponents in check. We are thus left wondering whether Alexander's own machiavellian plotting ultimately rebounded on him by fuelling his own paranoia.

E. Badian, 'Conspiracies', in A.B. Bosworth and E.J. Baynham (eds.), *Alexander the Great in Fact and Fiction* (Oxford: 2000), pp. 50–77 (of pp. 50–95).[5]

Additional reading

E. Badian, 'The Death of Parmenio', *Transactions of the American Philological Association* 91 (1960), pp. 324–338.

—— , 'Alexander the Great and the Loneliness of Power', in E. Badian, *Studies in Greek and Roman History* (Oxford: 1964), pp. 192–205.

P.A. Brunt, *Arrian, History of Alexander*, Loeb Classical Library 1 (Cambridge, MA and London: 1976), Appendix XI, 'The Deaths of Philotas and Parmenio', pp. 517–521.

E.N. Borza, 'Anaxagoras and Callisthenes: Academic Intrigue at Alexander's Court', in H.J. Dell (ed.), *Ancient Macedonian Studies in Honour of C.F. Edson* (Institute for Balkan Studies, Thessaloniki: 1981), pp. 73–86.

E. Carney, 'The Death of Clitus', *Greek, Roman, and Byzantine Studies* 22 (1981), pp. 149–160.

W. Heckel, 'The Conspiracy *against* Philotas', *Phoenix* 31 (1977), pp. 9–21.

W.Z. Rubinsohn, 'The "Philotas Affair" – A Reconsideration', *Ancient Macedonia* 2 (Institute for Balkan Studies, Thessaloniki: 1977), pp. 409–420.

W.W. Tarn, *Alexander the Great* 2 (Cambridge: 1948), Appendix 12, 'The Murder of Parmenion', pp. 270–272.

Notes

1 Philotas: Arr. 3.26–27, Diod. 17.79–80, Plut. *Alex.* 48–49, Curt. 6.7.1–7.2.38, Justin 12.5.1–8. Parmenion: Arr. 3.27.3–4, Diod. 17.80.3, Plut. *Alex.* 49.13, Curt. 7.2.11–32.
2 Arr. 4.8.1–9, Curt. 8.19–51, Plut. *Alex.* 50–52.
3 The Royal Pages.
4 On Alexander's death, see Chapter 6.
5 © Oxford University Press 2000. Reprinted by permission of Oxford University Press.

CONSPIRACIES

E. Badian

> Plots, true or false, are necessary things
> To raise up commonwealths and ruin kings.
>
> Dryden, *Absalom and Achitophel*

No age has been a stranger to conspiracies and suspicion of conspiracies, least of all our own. Even in the USA, surely the most open society in history, conspiracies both by and against the government or members of it keep occurring and, at least as often, keep being suspected where they cannot be proved. In our age, in democratic societies, a new motive for allegations of conspiracy has been added to the traditional ones: the hope for lucrative publicity. This may have been one of the motives in charges used by lawyers defending O.J. Simpson to secure their client's acquittal, and certainly (one would think) in a recent conspiracy theory regarding the sinking of the *Titanic* advanced around the release of the successful film.[1] Although that motive did not exist in this form in antiquity, we may compare the desire on the part of some historians to enliven their narratives and appeal to a wider audience by juicy allegations of this kind. Indeed, it sometimes seems that no prominent man was deemed by all who wrote about him to have died a natural death – whether he died relatively young, like Alexander the Great, or in middle age, like Aratus of Sicyon, or in extreme old age, like the Emperor Tiberius.

Dryden's verses were written in the light of his own experience of the Civil War and the 'Popish plots'. The conspirators we shall examine would never (like two of the imaginary ones in Herodotus' 'constitutional debate' among the Persian conspirators: 3. 80 ff.) have thought of 'raising up a commonwealth'; at most they aimed at substituting a better king for one whom they thought worse. Where Dryden was right for all ages, however, even if he intended it satirically, was in stressing that tyrannies cannot be overthrown except through conspiracies. What did not fit into his scheme (although he only had to look at earlier English history to notice it) was that kings can plot against their subjects (any of them whom they think too wealthy or too powerful) and that, from their position of supreme power, they are much more likely to succeed. Conspiracies do not always ruin kings, as we shall see: they often make them more secure.

Under an autocratic regime, which maintains its power in part through its ability to conspire against its subjects, conspiracies are more often formed as 'necessary things' – and often alleged, as pretexts for conspiracies by the ruler. The Emperor Domitian said that no one believes there has been a conspiracy against a ruler unless he is killed (Suet. *Dom.* 21.1). To the extent that this was so, he had only himself to blame, because of his use of allegations of conspiracies in order to carry out his own. Those of us who have lived through the age of Stalin and Hitler will find plenty of examples of this, as well as some of real conspiracies against those rulers – though surprisingly few that can be documented and none that succeeded. One result is that public opinion is likely to suspect conspiracies where in fact there were none. The Reichstag, as it turns out, was indeed set on fire by an unbalanced Dutchman, not by either the Communists (as the Nazi government claimed) or the Nazis themselves (as most of the rest of the world believed), even though neither of these charges was implausible in view of the records of the parties concerned.

This conspiracy theory is unlikely to be revived. But where there is powerful motivation – psychological or, often linked with it, financial – mere evidence will not necessarily allay such theories: witness a commercially successful recent pseudo-historical film on the death of John F. Kennedy; or the continuing allegations, ignoring the evidence provided by the Russian archives, that charges of treason against Alger Hiss or I. F. Stone were conspiracies made up by right-wing enemies.

The historian, trying to arrive at the truth, must follow the hard evidence. Unfortunately the historian of Alexander rarely, if ever, has such hard evidence. He must rely on deductions from character and situations: analysis of an individual situation in the light of parallels that can be adduced to elucidate it – in short, the kind of evidence that can never be conclusive and (it must be stressed) that can in perfectly good faith be differently interpreted by different interpreters.

At this point another consideration must be added, which further confuses judgement. A ruler given to conspiring will be inclined to suspect the existence of conspiracies against him, especially when such suspicions suit his purpose. Hitler no doubt genuinely believed in a conspiracy by international Jewry. Stalin, after ordering the assassination of Kirov, may have believed in a conspiracy (which would not have been unjustified) against him by leading members of the party and by the general staff under Tukhachevski. Yet, did Stalin seriously believe, after the War against Germany, that Zhukov and a dozen other generals were preparing to betray the Soviet Union? Or, later, that Molotov and Voroshilov were, and even some of his own relatives? If he did, what does that tell us about his mental state? As we shall see, these questions are not irrelevant to Alexander.

Alexander, in one known case, did believe in a conspiracy that did not exist, on the part of supporters of Cleitus. Whether he genuinely believed this in some other cases is part of the impenetrable mystery of his psychology. The plotter does seem ultimately to have come to believe that he was surrounded by conspiracies. In some cases, this factor can obviously lead the historian into error. But unless it is well documented, the historian cannot allow for it, but, whether in Stalin's case or in Alexander's, must follow where the evidence of character and previous actions leads. Anyone accused of suspecting conspiracies on the part of Alexander, where some do not see them, can only reply that, like the Emperor Domitian, Alexander has only himself to blame if we approach his claims, as transmitted by court historiography with some suspicion. This may, in individual cases, be mistaken, but I would reject any claim that it is unjustified.

The war of Alexander against Darius III and the continuation of Alexander's campaign is marked by a series of conspiracies, allegations of conspiracy, and attempts to anticipate conspiracy unequalled in any other war I know about. The two protagonists were heirs to a long history of conspiracies in their respective dynasties, and each of them had come to the throne through a conspiracy. Only two of Alexander's predecessors in the fourth century B.C., Amyntas III and Perdiccas III (who died in battle), had not died by assassination, and only three among all the successors and destined successors of Darius I (Artaxerxes I, Darius II, Artaxerxes II) who preceded Darius III. In the Persian case, the monarch who had the longest reign and died peacefully in extreme old age, Artaxerxes II, had had to contend with conspiracies throughout his reign: from the well-supported revolt of his brother Cyrus at its beginning, through the Satraps' Revolts, to the conspiracies near the end of his life that began with that by (or against) his chosen successor and joint King Darius (who should really be called Darius III, had the numeral not become immovably attached to Alexander's opponent) and ended with Artaxerxes Ochus' bloody way to the throne.

Whether Darius III was involved in the conspiracy that led to the murder of his predecessor Artaxerxes Arses we cannot tell for certain. The only positive allegation comes in Alexander's supposed first letter to Darius (Arr. 2. 14.5); and we need not even discuss the question of whether the letter is authentic or a historian's rhetoric to see that it cannot be used as evidence proving Darius' real guilt. In either case, it merely offers *ta deonta* ('what was required by the occasion'). Since our sources are not remiss in attacking Darius' actions and character, I think we may confidently exclude at least any Greek knowledge of his having participated in the removal of Ochus and Arses. However, since he had lived, as one of the King's 'friends', through the time of these plots, he could not fail to learn from the experience, in his case (it seems) a wholly passive one.

That Alexander was involved in the conspiracy that led to the death of Philip II seems to me as clear as when I first wrote about the subject;[2] although we cannot tell whether he initiated and led it. In any case, each of the protagonists had good reason to fear conspiracies – and to anticipate them.

Alexander put his experience to good use right from the start. The sons of Aëropus of Lyncestis were accused of having participated in the plot to kill Philip[3] – an implausible charge, since they had nothing to gain by his death. They were not Argeads, hence had not the slightest chance of seizing the Macedonian throne – and only two of the three were executed. The third, Alexander, who was Antipater's son-in-law and apparently had had warning of what was to happen, at once paid homage to Alexander as king and (although he was guilty, so Arrian states) was not only spared, but entrusted with important commands as long as Alexander was close to Antipater (Arr. and Curt., locc. citt.).[4]

That Antipater had master-minded Alexander's accession, hence must have known about the plot to kill Philip, is not attested by any good source. But it is clear from his prompt action, and even more so from that of his son-in-law – as we noted, the only one of the three sons of Aëropus who was fully prepared for the event. No other source for his foreknowledge is conceivable. Antipater's association with Alexander under Philip is attested: they were both sent by Philip to Athens to conclude peace after Chaeronea (Just. 9.4.5). There is no record of his having sought any contact with Attalus after the domestic coup that brought Attalus to power. (In this he contrasts with Parmenio, who married one of his daughters to Attalus.)[5] It was presumably on the occasion of the mission to Athens that Antipater was made a citizen and *proxenos* of Athens, an unusual combination (Harpocration, s.v. Ἀλκίμαχος, quoting Hyperides, *Against Demades*: we do not know when Alcimachus received the same grants, but perhaps also on a mission to Athens).[6] Antipater's patent involvement, incidentally, is another argument against the view (still sometimes advanced, perhaps on the basis of some of Plutarch's sources) that Olympias was involved in Philip's assassination. Not only was she away in Epirus at the time, but it is difficult to picture her collaborating with Antipater on such a project.

Having disposed of the two sons of Aëropus, Alexander could deal with Attalus. He could not be forgiven for wresting power from Olympias and for an insult to Alexander that had had disastrous consequences for the prince's life. His murder was also justified by a charge of conspiracy (Diod. 17.2.5; cf. Plut. *Demosth.* 23.2), which some modern Alexander worshippers have seen fit to extend far beyond what even the hostile sources allege.[7] It was co-operation with the king in this plot against his own son-in-law that secured Parmenio's position and power under the new king, at the price of setting a precedent that Parmenio would have cause to regret. Alexander's cousin Amyntas, who had real claims to the throne, was also at once eliminated, not surprisingly on a charge of having conspired against Alexander.[8] It is significant that we do not hear of any trials in any of these cases, even where evidence was later alleged. Alexander could not yet trust the army to accept his word and his evidence against the denials of men who had been loyal to Philip. In total control of what was reported to the army, he had, however, shown real genius in using charges of conspiracy to make the elimination of men he feared politically acceptable.[9] This is one of the factors to be borne in mind when we evaluate later charges of conspiracies against him.

I must here repeat my warning that no reconstruction can claim certainty: anyone may believe that some or all of these 'conspirators' did conspire, against either Philip or Alexander. Thus, for example, Berve doubts the conspiracy of the sons of Aëropus, but seems to believe the others; Bosworth believes some but not others; Brunt seems not to believe any of them.[10] There are scholars who will even believe, with Plutarch (*Alex.* 10.8), that Alexander disapproved of the murder of Cleopatra and her daughter.[11] Since I see no reason why the sons of Aëropus should have conspired to kill Philip, and I think it unlikely that Amyntas, with no known backing among the Macedonian nobles (and presumably no support in the army, which would hardly know him), would have tried to kill Alexander, I share Brunt's view and regard these executions merely as early indications of Alexander's methods. They could be refined later, when he could confidently resort to show trials.

The 'conspiracy' of Alexander son of Aëropus fits into this context and follows on smoothly. It was discovered in Asia Minor when Alexander was near Phaselis.[12] We do not have Curtius' actual account. It appears to have been based on a different version from the one we have in our other sources (Arrian, Diodorus, and Justin), but that divergence must arouse our suspicion. Caution is indicated: it may be the same tradition, reworked by Curtius himself.[13]

Arrian gives the only full account: a Persian called Sisines[14] was captured by Parmenio as he carried a letter from Darius to the satrap of Phrygia – a circumstantial detail that ought to be accepted (the obscure Atizyes is named as the satrap) and that shows Arrian's date to be correct: by the time Alexander had reached the area of the Cilician Gates (as in Diodorus) Greater Phrygia no longer had a Persian satrap. Sisines, when interviewed by Parmenio (needless to say, through interpreters), is said to have revealed that his real mission was to contact Alexander the Lyncestian, said to have approached Darius to offer treason, and to promise him the throne of Macedon and 1,000 talents in gold if he assassinated his king.

The story, as it stands, is worthless. Parts of it may even have been excogitated for Alexander's show trial in 330, for which we have no details.[15] In the first place, we must ask: why did Sisines, unlikely to have to save himself from torture or death, reveal the 'plot' instead of confining himself to his prima-facie mission, which was perfectly plausible? Next, it is difficult to believe that Sisines was expected to meet in secret, and hold secret conversations through interpreters, with the commander of the Thessalian cavalry: one might even wonder (though an answer to this is possible) what πίστεις (physical pledges of good faith) Sisines could offer him.[16]

The story of the divine warning, this time transmitted through a swallow, is (as we shall see) not unparalleled in the tales of conspiracies against Alexander. However, the kernel of truth is the capture by Parmenio of an envoy from Darius to his governor of the province about to be invaded by Alexander, and Parmenio's sending him on to Alexander, who would want to hear Darius' message to his governor at first hand. The 'conspiracy of Alexander son of Aëropus' was grafted on to this authentic incident.

I think it was done at the time, not later. The opportunity was too good to be allowed to pass. Alexander had at the start of his reign to accept and even honour Antipater's son-in-law. By now he was far enough away from Antipater, and sufficiently secure in his own power, to remove the man, provided a plausible reason could be found. With his usual genius for recognizing and seizing an opportunity, Alexander at once saw that the capture of a Persian messenger would serve his purpose. We may even conjecture (although this is not a necessary or even a secure hypothesis) that Parmenio was informed of Alexander's plan. However, it was the opportunity of needing interpreters to transmit Sisines' message to Greeks and Macedonians that invited exploitation. It provided a perfect setting. Interpreters could be made to perform as instructed. If they were slaves, they obviously had no choice. If (as is quite possible) Alexander called on Laomedon and his staff (cf. Arr. 3.6.6), there can be no doubt of his devotion to Alexander: after all, he had suffered for that devotion under Philip (Arr. 3.6.5) and he would not let him down on an important occasion. The interpreters would produce the required message, and Sisines would never know about it (there is no reason to think he understood Greek), nor would the Greeks and Macedonians who, even if they heard them, would not understand Sisines' own words.[17] Parmenio's loyalty, whether or not he knew of the plot, was not in doubt: the man who had organized the murder of his own son-in-law would not hesitate to act against the son-in-law of Antipater. From what we know of the Macedonian court, there was probably no love lost between those two: Parmenio had at once joined what appeared to be the winning faction of Attalus, while Antipater had stayed with Alexander, awaiting his chance. Nor need we be surprised at Olympias' letter, which we can accept as genuine. I think it had arrived some time before and could be effectively produced at this point.[18] Olympias' feelings towards Antipater do not need documentation. That in Pella she could have acquired information about a plot by the Lyncestian that was not accessible to Alexander surely does not merit serious discussion. Her letter presumably was based on distrust for Antipater and merely contained an injunction to Alexander to be on his guard against the Lyncestian. At the most, it may have given Alexander the idea of staging his namesake's 'treason'.

The story of the 'conspiracy of Alexander son of Aëropus' is instructive. It adds considerably to our perception of Alexander's methods. The next suspicion of conspiracy, that of Philip the Acarnanian, acts as a foil (Arr. 2.4.7 ff.). Berve has shown that it was at the least novelistically expanded by reminiscences of the 'conspiracy' of Alexander.

Although (as Bosworth has shown, 1980a: 191 f.) not all of Berve's arguments are sound, enough remains. Even as Arrian tells the tale (we do not know from what source), it shows features of dramatic embellishment characteristic of vulgate anecdotes.[19] Arrian at least does not go as far as Curtius (3.6.3)., where the feverish king is made to wait three days before he can take the 'medicine' (surely a duplicate of the three days it later took him to recover) and so has plenty of time, while near death, to do an elaborate cost-benefit analysis regarding confidence in Philip. In Arrian, who implies no long interval, but rather seems to envisage Philip mixing his potion by Alexander's bedside, we dramatically see Alexander drinking the supposedly poisoned cup 'at the same time' as Philip reads Parmenio's warning letter.[20]

Some major questions impose themselves. First, where was Parmenio? In 2.4.4 Arrian has just told us that Alexander's 'whole force' was with him just before this incident. Surely Parmenio is included, and there is no indication of his being at once sent away. On the contrary, at the beginning of the very next sentence after the Philip story (2.5.1), Arrian reports that ἐκ δὲ τούτων ('after this') Alexander sent Parmenio ahead to seize the Gates. Of course, Parmenio might have been somewhere else and then sent on from there. A scenario can easily be constructed ad hoc that puts Parmenio either in advance of the point Alexander had reached or behind. But any such conjecture cannot refute Arrian's account, almost certainly from Ptolemy, and his refusal to vouch for the story. Nor will it do to call the Greek phrase a 'weak transitional phrase' (Bosworth 1980a: ad loc.): even when he uses it as a transitional phrase, Arrian always uses it of temporal sequence.[21] It means, quite simply, that Parmenio, who (at least as Arrian, following Ptolemy, saw it) had been with Alexander throughout this incident, was then sent off on his mission. Arrian's narrative is consistent and based on his main sources (in fact, presumably Ptolemy). Parmenio's presence, as Berve saw, deprives the Philip story of any claim to authenticity: there can have been no letter from Parmenio to Alexander, dramatically handed to the physician to read. Moreover: why, in this story, is the informant anonymous; and why did he not take his story straight to Alexander?

Bosworth rightly noted that Arrian's indirect narration shows (as occasionally elsewhere) that he refused to take responsibility for the tale. As often, he could not resist the temptation of inserting a good anecdote from the vulgate tradition into his basic narrative – especially an anecdote with such a eulogistic conclusion. What is striking, however, is that Arrian retains indirect speech in the conclusion: he would not subscribe even to this in his own person. He has in fact warned the sophisticated reader that he himself did not believe any of it. Possibly Philip did save Alexander's life, perhaps when the other physicians did not dare to try. The rest is fiction, and marked as such.

Coming not long after the story of the Lyncestian and sharing some features with it,[22] it was later completely amalgamated with it.[23] By the time it reached Seneca (De Ira 2.23.2), a letter from Olympias had been substituted for the letter from Parmenio. The original point was presumably to serve as a counterweight to the story of the Lyncestian. If we ignore embellishments added by the vulgate in telling of Alexander's hearing of Philotas' 'treason' or of Harpalus' escape, it is the only story on record that shows Alexander as loyal to his friends under suspicion. I have often argued that the court version of Ptolemy and (in part) Aristobulus should not be regarded as the whole truth and that the vulgate tradition, especially as found in

Curtius, offers much to correct or supplement it. But at some point one must draw the line. A story that, on the face of it, does not make sense even as told in Arrian, and that Arrian refused to authenticate, is perhaps hardly even worth the long treatment I have given it, were there not a tendency to defend it. It is about as authentic as the supposed conspiracy of Parmenio confessed to under torture by Philotas (Curt. 6.11.22) which has also recently acquired a defender. Essentially. Berve was right in his judgement.

One lesson, hinted at above, is that Curtius is given to making up not only speeches (as we all know) but exciting dramatic details, even where, as here, they make no sense. Fortunately, we do not have to believe the story of Alexander's waiting at death's door for three days before receiving his medicine. But I have perhaps been too ready to follow Curtius on other occasions where there is no other source and his dramatic details do not produce obvious nonsense. I am not now as certain as I was that we should fully accept his dramatic account of the arrest of Philotas (6.8.16 ff.). Although it is only distantly related to Tiberius' plots as told by Tacitus (see Atkinson 1994: ad loc.), those well-known incidents may have provided points of departure for Curtius' dramatic imagination, elaborating his information (which I think was essentially correct) on relations at the Macedonian court.[24]

But these details are perhaps not important. What really matters about the next conspiracy we must treat, the 'Philotas affair', is whether there was indeed a plot by Dimnus (whoever he was).

In my treatment of the affair in *TAPhA* 91 (1960) 324–38, I implied, without adequate discussion, that there was no such plot: that there was only a conspiracy *against* Philotas, hatched in his absence from the camp and maturing straight after his return. Perhaps I went too far in my implication. Hamilton's suggestion (1969: 134 f.) that there was a plot by Dimnus (though Philotas was not involved in it and merely did not think it important enough to be worth reporting) and that Alexander, already suspicious of Philotas ever since Egypt, was now persuaded by Philotas' many enemies at the court that Philotas must be its prime mover, does not seem an acceptable alternative.[25] It is not, in fact, 'more in accord with the sources', as he writes, except in so far as most of them report that Dimnus was guilty. The sources show a great deal of variation. In Arrian (from Ptolemy) Dimnus is not mentioned: Philotas admits that he heard of 'some plot being hatched' against Alexander and did not report it. In Diodorus (17.79.5–6) Dimnus is arrested and kills himself in the course of the investigation.[26] In Curtius (6.7) we have the usual dramatic elaboration: Dimnus' death is almost worthy of opera. He tries to kill himself, does not quite succeed, is carried into Alexander's presence, and there lives just long enough to hear Alexander's rhetorical (and quite irrelevant) question whether he thought Philotas more fit to be king than Alexander. The only other account is in Plutarch (*Alex.* 49.7). There Dimnus is said to have been killed while resisting arrest. Plutarch adds that Alexander now thought the explanation had escaped him. It is this that makes him inclined to listen to the charges advanced by Philotas' enemies, especially since he had already been feeling hostile towards him. Inevitably, Plutarch shies away from directly accusing Alexander.

As far as Philotas is concerned, Plutarch knows only of a plot against him, initiated by Craterus in Egypt and taken over by Alexander. Abandoning temporal sequence by a wide margin, he relates the events leading to Philotas' execution in immediate sequence. Plutarch surely knew all the earlier sources we know and many more. He must certainly have known the vulgate account, as we find it in Diodorus and Curtius: that Philotas was told of a plot against Alexander and at the least evaded his duty of passing the information on to the king or allowing the informants to do so. In Plutarch, Philotas never (until his trial, presumably) hears of any plot against Alexander. Of course, even if he did and failed to pass on the information, his alleged explanation, that he did not attach much importance to the matter, would seem credible: the conspirators were unimportant men, the motive (if one was stated) quite probably trivial and the way the matter was said to have been revealed conventional. However, Plutarch did not accept this story at all. He followed a source (we cannot specify it) that reported Cebalinus and Nicomachus as telling Philotas that they had 'very important business' to discuss with Alexander; it was only when they got to see Alexander that they revealed the plot of Dimnus (in Plutarch Limnus), and they did not even then imply that Philotas had known of it.

It is hard to understand why scholars have unanimously (as far as I know) chosen to follow the version found in the vulgate and to ignore the one followed (no doubt deliberately) by Plutarch, without asking why he chose to do so.[27] In Plutarch the 'plot' against Philotas, developed by Alexander in Egypt, turns into what he saw was the plot against Philotas at Phrada. Plutarch never questions the existence of a plot by Dimnus and its effect on Alexander. But, being a better historian than he likes to admit (as is indeed clear from other instances, both in this *Life* and in others), he leaves no doubt that he saw that there was no reason why his source should invent a version that made Philotas innocent, while there was every reason why the version officially propounded at the trial and after should insist that Philotas deliberately suppressed (at least) knowledge of the plot, hence was quite likely a participant in it. However, he could not pursue his case to its obvious conclusion and accuse Alexander of arranging the judicial murder of Philotas as well as the undeniable murder of Parmenio: that would have destroyed the image of Alexander that he tried to convey and made him out to he a despicable tyrant. He therefore links Philotas with the plot of Dimnus by making Philotas' enemies, when poisoning the king's mind against Philotas, imply among 'ten thousand other charges' against Philotas that he had indeed known of the conspiracy by Dimnus and had preferred not to reveal it (*Alex.* 49. 8–10). (On this, see further n. 25 with text.)

In view of the (apparently) brief treatment of the affair by Ptolemy, who merely asserted that there was proof of Philotas' guilt and gave no details (which Arrian would not have suppressed), and the chain of events that I sketched forty years ago, I now think it is advisable for the scholar seeking the truth to follow Plutarch and make the choice that he made among the sources: it follows that the 'conspiracy of Dimnus' offered an opportunity to rid Alexander of the house of Parmenio (what remained of it), which he eagerly seized. With Dimnus dead, he no doubt had full control over what Cebalinus and Nicomachus would state at Philotas' trial, and that would be the only information heard by the army. The case, in fact, shows the full development of the method used in the 'discovery' of the 'conspiracy of Alexander son of Aëropus'.

We are now ready to consider what I described as the most important question: whether there really was a plot by Dimnus – or merely one by Alexander and some of his courtiers against Philotas. In the light of the fuller discussion of the back-

ground, and of Plutarch's testimony, this question requires more careful consideration than I devoted to it forty years ago.

The Philotas affair, as I insisted at the time, comes suspiciously soon after Philotas
had been left as the only one of Parmenio's sons still alive and after he had joined
the camp, having fulfilled his sad duty of burying his brother. There was now an
opportunity for decisive action against Philotas and Parmenio. Alexander had a long
memory: he will not have forgotten Parmenio's at the least eager embrace of the new
order at Philip's court by a marriage alliance with Cleopatra's uncle, clearly directed
against the interests of Olympias and Alexander; nor the traumatic incident of Philotas
accompanying Philip when the latter exploded in anger at Alexander's undercutting
his plans for a marriage alliance with Pixodarus. Plutarch's ἐπετίμησεν ἰσχυρῶς καὶ
πικρῶς ἐλοιδόρησεν ('forcefully rebuked and bitterly abused him': *Alex.* 10.3) vividly
paints the atmosphere at that interview, which preceded Philip's exiling Alexander's
friends and demanding the arrest and extradition of Thessalus; even though Plutarch
accepts what is clearly Alexander's later version of the cause for Philip's incommen-
surate fury, that he merely thought the match was not good enough for Alexander.
Philotas was obviously not one of the 'friends and close companions' of Alexander
(thus Plutarch, again no doubt following the later expurgated version): as Hamilton
(1969: 26) rightly points out, he was not exiled when Alexander's friends were (indeed,
we find him at Philip's side, and Hamilton suggests that he may have alerted Philip
to Alexander's treasonable action); and Philotas' father was the father-in-law (Hamilton
mistakenly writes 'son-in-law') of Alexander's most dangerous enemy.

At the time of his accession Alexander had had to pay Parmenio's price for his and
his family's support. Antagonizing him might have been fatal, but the family's loyal
and distinguished service fully justified the forced decision. However, that memory
would be stored alongside the earlier ones. Even at the time of the action against
Philotas and Parmenio, Plutarch notes that the action was not without danger *(Alex.*
49.2), and Curtius' account of the *coup d'état,* rhetorically enhanced though it may be,
proves him right (Curt. 6.8.9 ff.). But by now he felt strong enough to indulge his
stored-up resentment by swift action. The question is, I now think, whether the plot
by Dimnus provided a lucky opportunity that Alexander eagerly seized (we might
compare the action against the Lyncestian Alexander) or whether Dimnus' plot was
manufactured in order to entrap Philotas. I would not now exclude the former possibility: the parallel, both for Alexander's luck and for his seizing the opportunity to
exploit it, is striking. But the timing, and the care taken in setting the trap, on the
whole still makes me incline to the more sinister interpretation. On this reading,
Dimnus was suborned to be the tool: his telling his young lover of a conspiracy and
warning him not to reveal it would almost ensure that he did so. Everything then
went according to plan: Dimnus, when he saw Alexander's soldiers approaching, knew
he was being sacrificed and either killed himself or was killed before he could reveal
the real plot, and Alexander was safe.

In the light of Alexander's pattern of behaviour, it does not seem impossible, or
even improbable, that he would not hesitate to sacrifice an obscure man like Dimnus
for the sake of a great prize, and that, as I suggested in my earlier discussion, the
whole plot was hatched during Philotas' fortunate absence. As Bosworth has recently
demonstrated, Alexander was soon to show mastery on a more massive scale in making
'the victims . . . become the culprits'.[28] How and by what promises Dimnus may have

been persuaded to become the key figure in the plot, we can of course never know. I have merely been concerned to point out that the fact of his death and the fact that most of our sources (we cannot be sure in Arrian's case) believe in his guilt do not exclude the possibility that he was originally a willing participant.

In any case, an express messenger was now sent to organize the assassination of Parmenio, which I still think was, on either interpretation, the ultimate aim. It was entrusted to Cleander, linked to Parmenio by a brother's marriage and promoted by him. Parmenio, clearly, had never thought of the precedent he was setting when he sacrificed his son-in-law Attalus to Alexander for the sake of his family's power under the new king. We cannot here discuss the trials that followed the death of Philotas. (I discussed them in my earlier article.) But it is worth mentioning that the Lyncestian Alexander was now produced in front of the army and 'tried' for the crime he had been charged with in Asia Minor (Curt. 7.1.5 ff.). His execution could be taken for granted and Alexander no longer had to fear that Antipater might stir up Macedonia against him (cf. Just. 11.7.2).[29]

The next event that deserves a brief mention is Alexander's suspicion of a conspiracy against him in the scene that led to the death of Cleitus.[30] It was clear even to Alexander, once he was sober, that there had been no conspiracy. But he genuinely suspected (it seems) a conspiracy by his *hetairoi* and perhaps even his guard when they tried to prevent him from killing Cleitus in a drunken fit of rage. This gives us a foretaste of what was to come years later. But what is important about the Cleitus affair is what followed *post Cliti caedem* (as Curtius put it: 8.4.30). When Alexander continued to sulk in his tent, in spite of various efforts to 'console' him, the army finally passed a resolution posthumously convicting Cleitus of treason (Curt. 8.2.12) – hardly a spontaneous action, one would think. It is only Curtius who alerts us to it, and to its effect: *libertas* was now *sublata*. Both Alexander and his officers now knew that the army would support him, no matter what.

There is no more talk of conspiracies for about a year, when we reach a very peculiar plot – the conspiracy of the pages, perhaps the first genuine conspiracy of the reign, certainly the first where the sources allow no doubt as to its real existence. The story is told in all the standard works and need not be set out here.[31] It is also often pointed out that the pages involved (only a handful of the corps) did not belong to the nobles most active and eminent at Alexander's court. The death of Cleitus and its aftermath, as Curtius pointed out, had suppressed opposition. It seems that the sons of those who had gained real prominence had been taught to share their fathers' caution.[32] One cannot help wondering whether the reaction of precisely these boys was perhaps due to dissatisfaction with the lack of rewards and advancement their fathers had received (no one above ilarch, it seems) – and perhaps talked about in the safety of their tents or lodgings. Jealousy felt for those who had made names and fortunes for themselves would not be unexpected. For what it is worth, Hermolaus' speech in Curtius blames Alexander for acquiring riches while his soldiers had nothing but their scars to show. This may well in part represent talk picked up among the lower officer ranks, if it is entitled to any belief.

A detail arousing some interest in the story of this conspiracy is the warning by the Syrian prophetess that, according to Aristobulus, persuaded Alexander to go back to his all-night drinking-bout until the pages' guard was changed. Curtius (8.6.14), like Arrian (4.13.6), knows both a version that apparently ascribed his escape to his *fortuna* and one that credited the Syrian; which shows that Aristobulus, at least, did tell the story of the conspiracy. Now, the theme of a supernatural warning of a conspiracy is not unique in the tale of these plots: we noted it in the 'conspiracy' of the Lyncestian Alexander (see p. 280 and n. 13 above). If Aristobulus correctly represents the official version, the ascription to fortune may be an attempt to substitute that well-known concept (compare Plutarch's essay!) for the less than respectable figure of the barbarian seer. If so, it would follow that Alexander knew about the conspiracy (unless we are willing to believe in the divine warning as such) and decided to let it mature and fail, since that was certain to lead to his being fully informed about it. The problem is that Aristobulus, who was determined to deny that Alexander was given to excessive drinking,[33] may have invented the Syrian to 'explain' why Alexander stayed at the party all night. However, he was also given to stressing the favour of gods and fortune for Alexander[34] and, had this been the official version, should have had no hesitation in reproducing it. I am inclined to believe that Alexander did know about the plans, but had no detailed information, and so had recourse to the one way of making sure he would find out.[35]

The execution of the pages was followed by the judicial murder of Callisthenes, fully comparable in method to the judicial murder of the Lyncestian Alexander after the conviction of the 'conspirators' with Philotas.[36] The official version stated that he was not only guilty, but had been denounced (under torture, it seems) by the pages (Arr. 4.14.1). Ptolemy, at least, must have been present at the trial and must have known better. He chose, not for the only time, to support his king's memory. Arrian's sympathy is, at least to some extent, with Callisthenes. Indeed, it must have been hard for one who was by profession a philosopher and by choice a panegyrist of Alexander to find those two influences in such sharp conflict. As Bosworth put it (1995: 97), 'Arrian is clearly uncomfortable, and rightly so'. He does report that most of his sources deny that the boys implicated Callisthenes. He does not seem to have known (or if he did, he ignored) the decisive testimony to the fact that Alexander knew this, just as he had known that Philotas was innocent: the letter quoted by Plutarch in *Alexander* 55.5 f.[37] That Callisthenes was at once executed, as Ptolemy reported, cannot be seriously doubted.[38]

This seems to have been the end of documented conspiracies by Macedonians against Alexander. There were still rebellions by Iranian nobles,[39] but they are not strictly relevant here. The only (probable) Iranian conspiracy I have been able to find is the one we are almost forced to postulate as preventing Alexander from undergoing the ritual initiation as Great King as Pasargadae. I have sufficiently discussed this elsewhere.[40] However, it was by no means the end of Alexander's suspicion of conspiracies, a suspicion fed by the events at the Hyphasis and later by the disastrous march through Gedrosia.

At the Hyphasis, what must have been a nightmare to him came true. Ever since the death of Cleitus had led to the end of freedom (as we have seen), Alexander had been secure against plots by senior officers because of the unquestioning loyalty of the army shown on that occasion. The pages' conspiracy, as we observed, involved no offspring of any senior officer or any man close to Alexander. What happened at the Hyphasis must have been totally unexpected. First, according to the only full and reliable account (Arr. 5.25 ff., probably from Ptolemy, except for the speeches, which are probably Arrian's own additions based on vulgate material), the soldiers started grumbling among themselves and some of them went so far as to say they would not march any farther. The base of Alexander's support was collapsing. The only possible response was to appeal (this time) to the officers, to gain their support by rhetoric and promises, and to hope that they would be able to persuade the men to follow. This road was blocked when Coenus stood up to speak in support of the men. There was real danger in this. Coenus, 'in seiner männlich-einfachen Art' (Berve 1926: 218), had always known which side his bread was buttered on. A son-in-law of Parmenio, he had been instrumental in the plot against Philotas and, at least according to the vulgate, had demanded that Philotas be tortured and had even attacked him at the 'trial' (at length in Curt. 6.8 ff.). His forceful intervention could only be due to his judging that he could attach the army to himself, even against the king – so it must have seemed to Alexander.[41]

In the end, seeing officers and men united against him, Alexander surrendered and did what he could to fasten the blame on the gods. What he clearly could not do was to treat the affair as a mutiny (which is how historians see it): it was impossible to punish a limited number of men as responsible for it, as could be done, for example, at Opis later. What was urgently necessary was to remove the danger from Coenus without arousing the army's suspicion or resentment. Alexander was fortunate, as usual. Not long after, Coenus died, not honourably in battle, but of disease, Alexander could defuse suspicion (if anyone had dared to voice it) by giving him a splendid funeral (Arr. 6.2). The immediate danger was past, and the signal to other prominent nobles would be clear.[42]

Next came the shock at the city of the Malli, where Alexander found his soldiers to be 'sluggish' (βλακεύειν: Arr. 6.9.3) in their attack, rushed to expose himself to the enemy and ended by receiving his almost fatal wound, which for the moment regained the remorseful loyalty of the army. The effect, however, threatened to be undone by the disaster of the march through Gedrosia. There is no point in trying to quantify losses or to discuss their distribution. What mattered was the effect on morale. There is no reason to disbelieve the vulgate on this (see Diod. 17.105.6; with dramatic exaggeration Curt. 9.10.11 ff., esp. 15–16). Alexander had lost his aura of invincibility, of being able (as once at the Hindu Kush) to triumph even over the elements.

The overpowering nature of his suspicion was first shown in his order to the satraps to disband their mercenary armies.[43] Diodorus puts it down to his receiving information that rebellions in his absence had relied on mercenaries. But the overreaction documents a fear approaching panic, though we shall see that Alexander indeed had reason to worry about Iranian rebellions. First, we are not told what alternative ways Alexander had found of keeping order in the satrapies and defending them against raiders and guerrillas. Since he could not spare any of his own men for such duties throughout the kingdom, it is difficult to come up with an answer. Had he lived longer, he would certainly have been forced to attend to this aspect of the problem he had created. If he could not ensure peace, rebellions were bound to follow. Another aspect necessitated immediate action. He cannot have been unaware of the dangerous social, and ultimately political, consequences that would follow the dismissal of tens of thousands of professional soldiers, suddenly deprived of the only way of making a living that they knew and sent to find their way home as best they could. Here an instant solution was found: the decree ordering the Greek cities to readmit all their exiles, most of whom had no doubt, in the manner traditional in the fourth century, enlisted as mercenaries. As I have pointed out, Alexander threw the problem he had created to the cities, on which it imposed intolerable burdens, to solve for him. We do not hear of any effort to assist them in doing so, although Alexander could by now well have afforded it. Moreover, he probably no longer cared about the fact that the decree involved a breach of the oaths sworn between him and the cities on his accession – which they would certainly not have been allowed to ignore with impunity. The extent of his fear could not be more strikingly demonstrated.

The reign of terror after his return from India[44] must in part be due to this same fear; though the element of searching for scapegoats for his failure of leadership in Gedrosia is obvious in the sources. It was not by accident, surely, that the only Macedonian commanders caught up in it were Cleander, brother of Coenus, who had so conveniently died in India, and his no doubt hand-picked officers.[45] Those who had organized the murder of Parmenio could be expected, if a case of conflict arose, to put their own interests above the king's.

This was by no means the end of Alexander's suspicions of conspiracy. He clearly thought that Hephaestion's death had been deliberately brought about by his physician, who was punished with impalement – the traditional Persian punishment for traitors (Plut. *Alex.* 72.5; Arr. 7.14.4),[46] and after this he became obsessed with fear of portents and conspiracies (Plut. 73–5; Arr. 7.22, 24; note 24.3, Alexander's suspicion that the simpleton who sat on Alexander's throne had done so ἐξ ἐπιβουλῆς ('with treasonable design')). As I put it long ago,[47] he finally 'found himself . . . on a lonely pinnacle over an abyss, with . . . security unattainable'.

Notes

I should like to thank Professor Bosworth for searching questions and stimulating suggestions, which have made this essay longer and (I hope) better.

1 Robin Gardner and Dan van der Vat, *The Titanic Conspiracy* (1997): essentially that a damaged ship was made up to look like the 'unsinkable' *Titanic* and put under the command of a captain with a bad record, for financial gain by the owners. It may yet make a film.

2 Badian 1963. The replies, of varying quality, called forth by that article contain nothing to make me change my mind on either my interpretation of the train of events or the conclusions I drew from it. But this cannot be argued here.

3 See esp. Arr. 1.25. 1, cf. Curt. 7.1.6 (on Alexander son of Aëropus). See Berve 1926: no. 1 44 (Arrhabaeus) for balanced discussion, except that he believes Alexander saw them as rivals for the throne (against: Bosworth 1980*a*: 159). What Alexander may have feared was that they would raise Lyncestis against him: it was probably not regarded as certain that Philip's integration of the Upper Macedonian states would survive his death. See Bosworth 1971*c*: 93–105; and 1980*a*: 159.

4 Diodorus' statement that the Lyncestian Alexander was related to Antigonus (17.80.2) is a mistake, but should be left in the text. There is no need to emend, as (e.g.) Goukowsky (in the Budé edition) does, following Freinsheim's old suggestion. Diodorus can confuse the Tigris with the Euphrates (2.3.2 – surely not in Ctesias!).

5 Curt 6.9.17. It is sometimes said (correctly, I must admit) that we do not actually know whether the marriage preceded or followed the elevation of Attalus and his niece-ward. I have assumed the latter. But if the former is true, it creates an even more sinister picture: in that case, it would be difficult to avoid the conclusion that it was Parmenio, Philip's most trusted general and adviser, who engineered Philip's marriage to Cleopatra. Attalus was probably not close enough to Philip to do so on his own, and we can hardly assume that Philip came across a noble girl of marriageable age by pure chance.

6   That Philip was made an Athenian citizen is also attested (Plut. *Demosth.* 22.4). I have not found any attestation that Alexander was, but it may not have been necessary, since the grant to Philip would presumably, in the usual manner, include his descendants. The grant to Philip should be put about the time of the treaty after Chaeronea.

7   See Berve 1926: no. 182 for the modern charge of a treasonable understanding with Memnon, cited with apparent approval. Berve also accepts the charge of treasonable correspondence with Demosthenes, which is at least in the sources, but is implausible for various reasons.

8   See Berve 1926: no. 61, again apparently accepting the accusation, although we hear of no other member of the aristocracy involved in this 'conspiracy'.

9   For the chronology see Bosworth 1980*a*: 159 f. (not accepting the charge against Amyntas).

10 For Berve see above, nn. 7 and 8. Bosworth 1980*a*: 159 f. *et al.* Brunt 1976 (Arrian I, Loeb edn.), p. lxi.

11 e.g. Berve 1926: no. 434, though aware of Just. 12.6.14, putting Cleopatra and her brothers (?) in a list of Alexander's victims.

12 This is where it is placed by Arr. 1. 25 (early 333). The vulgate seems to have agreed with this. Just. 11.7.1 ff. puts the affair between Granicus, followed by fighting and the capture of other cities in Asia Minor, and Alexander's arrival in Gordium. For Curtius, see Atkinson 1980, 78: the account was in book 2, apparently following the fall of Halicarnassus. Diodorus is the odd man out: he puts it (17.32) after the incident involving Philip the physician (17.31). See further, n. 23 below. The view I expressed in Badian 1960, that an interval elapsed between the deposition of Alexander the Lyncestian and his being taken into custody, is not seriously tenable.

13 Diodorus mentions the 'evidence' of Sisines and Olympias' letter; Justin writes of an *indicium captiui* (i.e. clearly Sisines) ignoring the letter; Arrian too has only Sisines' evidence. Curtius' two *indices*, if taken literally, are unparalleled. I suspect, however, that he merely combined Sisines' evidence (as in Justin and Diodorus) with Olympias' letter (as in Diodorus), and, for dramatic effect, changed what might fairly be called two *indicia* to two personal *indices*. The fact that the reference to the two *indices* is repeated (7.1.6, 8.8.6, 10.1.40) merely shows that Curtius remembered what he had written (note *sict supra diximus*, 7.1.6). Although Arr. 1.25.9 makes it just possible, I doubt that the swallow that, in an anecdote reported by Arrian (1.25.6 ff.), warned Alexander of danger facing him would count as an *index*. It is not to be excluded that Curtius told the story (obviously of vulgate origin). The supposed letter of Alexander, proving his guilt, was imported by Hedicke (Teubner) into the text at 8.8.6 by fanciful emendation. (Compare. e.g., Barden (Budé), with much simpler and convincing intervention.)

14 We do not know whether this Sisines is identical with the son of Phrataphernes (Berve 1926: no. 709). Berve's attempt to identify him with the hero of a fanciful story in Curt. 3.7.11. ff., whose existence is difficult to credit (no. 710), is worthless. These are the only three individuals by this name who occur in the Alexander historians. Berve's comment that no. 709 may have been too young in 330, when his father joined Alexander, even to meet the king can only be called 'aus der Luft gegriffen'. We are not told where this Sisines was between 330 and 324, when he entered the *agema* of the Companions, together with his brother, who had joined Alexander only a few months before (Phradasmanes, Berve 1926: no. 812; Arr. 7.6.4). As Berve himself says, 'all' those admitted to the *agema* on that occasion will have been with Alexander 'längere Zeit' (and all will have acquired military distinction (sub no. 526)). Since Phradasmanes clearly had not been with Alexander at all long, we must conclude that it was Sisines who secured his brother's admission along with his own. It follows further that he will not have left Alexander's entourage after joining him in 330. As for military distinction, it is quite likely that he had acquired some: our sources simply do not record the military activities of Persians in Alexander's service (of which there must have been many), except for one or two satraps.

15 See Bosworth 1980*a* 161 ff. (As will appear, I think more of the details authentic than he does.)

16 Robson's Loeb translation (copied by Brunt as usual) certainly mistakes the meaning of πίστεις δοῦναι/λαμβάνειν. But although it always means a physical pledge *confirming* an assurance, it can be weakly used, so that the word may be acceptable here. It may mean only an explicit promise over the King's seal (thus probably Arr. 3.6.7; 1.4.7 is not clear). Xenophon rarely

uses the phrase, but see for an amusing instance *Anab.* 1.2.26 (a 'strong' meaning). For Thucydides Bétant explains it as *fidei pignora*

17 It is relevant to refer to a famous translation scene in comedy: Aristoph. *Acharn.* 100 ff. The Persian there, called 'gibberish' by Sommerstein (agreeing with West 1968: 5–7 ff. with fanciful reconstruction of the OP), has been taken seriously by Iranologists. See Brandenstein and Mayrhofer 1964: 91, with a reference to a more detailed discussion (unknown to the two Hellenists). They produce an acceptable OP original, with minimal textual changes. (Noted already, with speculative discussion, Francis 1992: 337–9.)

18 We cannot tell when Olympias' letter was received. Diodorus' aorist (17.32.1: ἔγραψε is non-specific: either 'Olympias wrote' (without specification of time) or, following a common use of the aorist, 'Olympias had written'. His use of an aorist (συνδραμόντων) for the corroborative evidence prima facie suggests an earlier time. Of course, it may mean that that evidence had become known before Olympias' letter arrived, but the run of the narrative does not suggest this. I am therefore inclined to translate: 'when many other plausible points had come together to support the charge'. The letter would then be pulled out and acted upon when the time seemed right (Welles's addition, in his Loeb translation, that the letter arrived 'at this time', is pure fiction). It is interesting that Alexander did not have his name-sake tried at this time: obviously, that was because he could not. Sisines would have to appear as a witness, and the accusation would not have survived his testimony.

19 Berve 1926: 388 n. 2 is wrong in stating that the story was not in Aristobulus. But he is essentially right in rejecting the story as we have it. The Philotas affair is not a parallel for Arrian's reluctance to use direct speech: he there explicitly tells us (3.26.2) that he is following Ptolemy, hence indirect speech is mandatory. There are no clauses in the indicative, except where the infinitive was precluded by grammar. In 4.8.8 (the Cleitus affair) we do see Arrian briefly changing to direct speech for vivid effect, as Bosworth says. Bosworth is surely right in explaining the indirect narrative of that episode by Arrian's reluctance to counter his encomiastic purpose. It would follow that he would have embraced the story of Philip the physician with open arms, and nowhere more so than in its conclusion. I must suggest that he did not do so because he not only did not find it in his main sources, but realised that Ptolemy's account left no room for it, and perhaps that it contained elements that did not make sense.

20 Plutarch, who has precisely the same story as Arrian (presumably not from Ptolemy but from a vulgate source), adding dramatic detail and wording of his own, describes the scene of the reading of the letter as θαυμαστήν καὶ θεατρικήν ('astonishing and fit for the stage'): here, for once, he did not need to add to the dramatic colouring.

Curtius does not call the remedy a purge, which may be to his credit. For the three days' wait, see Atkinson 1980: ad loc. Rolfe (Loeb) and Bardon (Budé) make nonsense worse by mistranslation: they take *praedixit* to mean that Philip *ordered* Alexander to wait, while near death, for three days before he could take the medicine. In fact, *praedixit* is always used by Curtius to mean 'foretell' (see Thérasse's *Index Verborum*): the doctor is said to have warned Alexander that it would be three days before he could take it. It has been suggested to me that finding and mixing the ingredients might take along as that. This seems to me going too far in defence of Curtius' dramatic invention. Purges were not difficult to come by, and since they have a clearly defined effect, one would be a good as another if effective. Pliny, that repository of medical lore, mentions quite a number of them. As it happens, he nowhere mentions a purge for use against fever or a chill. The nearest I have found is in the uses of dried figs (23.121 f.), which *aluum molliuni* and a decoction of which with fenugreek (again a simple mixture!) will treat pleurisy and pneumonia, which were probably diagnosed even by Greek physicians as being what Alexander had contracted. *De Morbis* 44 ff., a discussion of pleurisy and pneumonia, does not mention purges as treatment. The 'purge', I think, helps to give the story away as fiction: it is just what a layman, familiar with physicians' common practices, would make up, even though it was unsuitable in this case. Nor can I believe that a physician would spend three days on finding and preparing the 'purge'. Only very few infusions have to be left to 'draw' a long as that and I have found none at all appropriate here. We must also bear in mind that court physicians would hardly rely on finding familiar plants in the unknown lands to which they were being taken or on taking the word of potentially hostile natives for the effects of the plants they would find there. Philip, obviously one of the court physicians, must have carried a 'medicine chest' with basic remedies and (e.g.) dried herbs with him to last at least for some time. (The physicians were no doubt used to the duration of Philip's campaigns and had no idea of how long Alexander's would turn out to be.) Most ancient remedies were simple enough.

21 See, e.g. 2.1.1, where there is no doubt that the actions described in that chapter (starting with Memnon's capture of Chios) belong to 333, long after Alexander's arrival at Gordium.

22 But Sisines, whatever he had to say, clearly did come across Parmenio first and said it to him.

23 See Berve 1926: no. 788, concluding that it was 'deutlich eine Dublett'. Diodorus' displacement of the incident, which (as we saw) was concordantly and correctly placed earlier by the other sources, is puzzling. Perhaps he remembered the association of the incidents of an Alexander and a Philip (is the name 'Philip' significant? perhaps, if the story was spun out of whole cloth) and tried to associate them more closely than his source. However, the solution to this puzzle is hardly worth a great deal of effort and ingenuity.

24 That the speeches at Philotas' trial are not authentic does not need to be argued. Even speeches in Arrian should not be lightly regarded as such. But the strand of personal relations among the men around Alexander that Curtius found in one of his sources and that is not reproduced in any other of our surviving sources, except occasionally by Plutarch, does seem to add valuable and acceptable information to the court historiographers and the gossips.

25 I am reluctant to accept it (as well as another scholar's theory that the plot against Philotas was hatched by some of his courtiers and that Alexander himself was entirely innocent) because of what we know about Alexander's personality: he is never demonstrably a simple-minded victim of court intrigue, but (on the contrary) seems to be given to stimulating mutual jealousies (e.g. between Hephaestion and Craterus). In the case of Philotas, Plutarch makes it clear that Alexander, once he had been informed of Philotas' remarks in Egypt, personally took charge of what Plutarch calls the 'plot against Philotas'.

26 That he confessed before doing so, thus giving Alexander the full information (as Hamilton believes), is not a legitimate deduction from the source, where the page (Metron) informed Alexander 'of everything'. (In Curtius the information comes from Cebalinus: 6.7.25.)

27 There is no doubt that Plutarch knew the 'vulgate'; he perhaps assumed that the reader would also know it, so that he needed to state only his divergence from it. The *proskynesis* affair would provide a parallel. There Plutarch omitted the common version of the banquet and opted to tell a (presumably) less known one by Chares; but his allusion to Callisthenes' heroism shows that he both knew the standard version and expected the reader to know it. Here he must surely have seen the implication of the version he followed, that Philotas was innocent and that Alexander knew it.

28 Bosworth 1996a: 165. Atkinson 1994: 224 notes Tiberian parallels to Curtius' narrative and suggests they may have influenced Curtius' presentation. If Curtius wrote later than Atkinson believes, Domitian would also have to be considered (Suet. *Dom.* 11). Curtius may have accentuated some of the resemblances (see my comments p. 283 above), but this is no reason to believe (with, e.g., Berve 1926: 395, citing Schwartz) that Alexander was incapable of deviousness towards his enemies. I should perhaps add to my account of Plutarch that his total rejection of the official version (which, I repeat, he must have known) is shown by his statement (49.7) that Philotas' motive for not taking Cebalinus to see the king remains unknown. For deviousness, see further on Astaspes in the Appendix to this chapter [in Badian, 'Conspiracies'].

29 Habicht 1977: 514–15 has shown that a son of this Alexander, called Arrhabaeus, survived (no doubt protected by Antipater in Macedonia) to be a 'friend' of Alexander's successors.

30 The fear of conspiracy: Arr. 4.8.8, Curt. 8.1.47. *Plut.* Alex. 51.6 – which incidentally shows to most (unfortunately not to all) scholars that the Macedonian dialect was the language of command among Alexander's (and no doubt among Philip's) Macedonian forces.

31 Arr. 4.13, Curt. 8.6 (the speeches in 7 and most of 8), Plut. *Alex.* 55. Diodorus reported the fate of Callisthenes (hence presumably the pages' conspiracy), but his narrative is not in our text (see Diod. *Per.* 17.2). Arrian picked up Hermolaus' speech from a vulgate source; indeed, his whole narrative is a *logos*, hence probably composed from various sources in the form in which he tells it. It differs in significant respects from Curtius' elaborate version: each presents

one or two items the other lacks. However, the general topic is no doubt based on Cleitarchus, whose assessment of Alexander's deterioration is echoed in Cic. *Att.* 13.28.3. (See my analysis in Badian 1996: 20.)

32 For the story as a whole see, e.g., Bosworth 1988*b*: 117 ff. For the interesting prosopographical item of Philotas son of Carsis, a Thracian, among the conspirators, see Berve 1926: no. 801 and Bosworth 1995: ad loc.

33 Arr. 7.29.4 Plut. *Alex.* 75.6: enthusiastically welcomed by Tarn 1948 ii. 41. (See 39 ff. for his idealizing portrait of the faithful Aristobulus, closer to Alexander than the Macedonian nobles. In fact there is no evidence for his being at all close to Alexander; much of his work seems to have been secondary interpretation.) Berve 1926: no. 121 also idealizes, but less blatantly. Pédech 1984: 354 f., in a basically favourable discussion of Aristobulus, fully recognizes his tendency to naive apologia.

34 Passages collected by Berve 1926: 65.

35 In Curtius the boys are aware of the fact that delay would lead to exposure: they want at all costs to avoid waiting seven days for the next opportunity. Actual failure, of course, was likely to lead to *sauve qui peut* reaction, since no one would want to be anticipated. We cannot tell what happened to Epimenes, who actually started the unravelling of the plot. His fate is not mentioned in Arrian. In Curtius he shares in the rewards given to the informers, but this may be fictitious elaboration.

36 See Diod. 17.80.2, Curt. 7.1.5–9 (staged by the king, § 5). Arrian suppresses the story.

37 See Hamilton 1969 ad loc., with the reference to his detailed proof that the letter must be authentic. Bosworth 1995: 98 entertains the possibility that it might have been written by a well-informed forger. I cannot put a name to such a putative person, who was close to Alexander at the time, hostile to him, and likely years later to remember the precise location of the commanders addressed. Curtius is wrong in stating that the pages and Callisthenes were tortured to make execution more painful (8.8.20 f.). He knew quite well that torture was not used for that purpose, but to extract confessions – which he also knew were not at all reliable (6.11.21). But his 'confusion' is deliberate, intended to make the story more graphically appalling. Ptolemy, even in Arrian's summary, can be seen to have separated the torture from the death (Arr. 4.14.3: στρεβλωθέντα καὶ κρεμασθέντα). Bosworth (loc. cit.) is unclear and seems to be wrong: Philotas was tortured to extract new revelations, not to intensify execution.

38 Chares, followed in part by Aristobulus (*ap.* Plut. *Alex.* 55.9 – Plutarch apparently thought they were independent accounts), reported that he was made to accompany the expedition as a prisoner, to be tried by the *synhedrion* at Corinth in the presence of Aristotle(!), but died of a disgraceful disease seven months later, 'at the time when Alexander was wounded in India among the Malli Oxydracae'. ἐν Μάλλοις Ὀξυδράκαις is in all the manuscripts, but universally deleted by editors and commentators in order to save Plutarch's (and often Chares') credit. Even Hamilton 1969: 156, argues that Plutarch 'who had made a special study of Alexander's wounds' (no evidence is given for this except for a German dissertation – there is no such claim in Plutarch) would not have made such an error in chronology. (The time between the pages' conspiracy in Bactria (Arr. 4.22.2, cf. Strabo 11.11.4. C517) and Alexander's attack on the town of the Malli was about two years.) Hamilton 1969: 122 in fact mentions two occasions when Plutarch makes mistakes over Alexander's wounds. Add that *Mor.* 341c, 343d ff. apparently confuses Malli and Oxydracae. This makes it likely that Plutarch added that phrase, to specify the occasion referred to by Chares. But he cannot have made up the 'seven months' and it cannot be held that he misinterpreted Chares: no one referring to Alexander's wounding in India, without specification, as Chares seems to have done, could have meant anything but the famous almost-fatal wound. Chares' story discredits itself in all details. Aristobulus can be more briefly dismissed: he was 'never one to omit an opportunity to whitewash' (Bosworth 1995: 100, which see also for general discussion).

39 For brief discussion, see Appendix [in Badian, 'Conspiracies'].

40 See Badian 1996: 22 ff.

41 See now Carney 1996: 33–7.

42 For discussion of this incident see Badian 1961: 20.

43 Diod. 17.106.3,111.1. For the interpretation see Badian 1961: 25ff.

44 See Badian 1961. There can be no doubt that there was reign of terror. I took care to collect the actual figures and distinguish possible from attested victims. Bosworth 1971*a*: 123 charges me with laying 'excessive stress on the arrival of satraps at court, inferring that a summons to court meant danger to the man invited.' All I argued was that 'such a summons *could* [original emphasis] be the prelude to summary trial and execution' (18) and that those summoned had 'ambiguous prospects' – unless, like Peucestas, they were sure of the king's favour. Bosworth's list of those who suffered no harm can be found on my pp. 18–19. However, I still think that any satrap summoned must have felt twinges of uneasiness, in view of what he had seen and heard about; and that, in view of the king's documented duplicity (Philotas and recently Astaspes!), friendly entertainment after arrival did not offer final reassurance.

45 See Badian 1961. The fact that Cleander and his subordinates were the only Macedonian commanders summoned to the court and (probably all of them) executed can hardly be explained except through the connection with Coenus' outspokenness and death.

46 One is reminded of the authentic story of the physician called in to attend to Stalin on his deathbed: Bena (who, of course, saw his own future as uncertain) screamed at him: 'If he dies, you'll be shot.' I do not know if the threat was carried out.

47 Badian 1964, 204.

References

Atkinson 1980 = J. E. Atkinson, *A Commentary on Q. Curtius Rufus' Historiae Alexandri Magni Books 3 and 4* (Amsterdam: 1980).

Atkinson 1994 = J. E. Atkinson, *A Commentary on Q. Curtius Rufus' Historiae Alexandri Magni Books 5 and 7.2* (Amsterdam: 1994).

Badian 1960 = E. Badian, 'The Death of Parmenio', *TAPhA* 91 (1960), pp 324–338.

Badian 1961 = E. Badian, 'Harpalus', *JHS* 81 (1961), pp. 16–43.

Badian 1963 = E. Badian, 'The Death of Philip II', *Phoenix* 17 (1963), pp. 244–250.

Badian 1964 = E. Badian, 'Alexander the Great and the Loneliness of Power', in E. Badian, *Studies in Greek and Roman History* (Oxford: 1964), pp. 192–205.

Badian 1987 = E. Badian, 'The Ring and the Book', in W. Will and J. Heinrichs (eds.), *Zu Alexander d. Gr., Festschrift für G. Wirth* 1 (Amsterdam: 1987), pp. 605–625.

Badian 1996 = E. Badian, 'Alexander the Great between Two Thrones and Heaven: Variations on an Old Theme', in A. Small (ed.), *Subject and Ruler: The Cult of the Ruling Power in Classical Antiquity* = *JRA* Suppl. 17 (1996), pp. 11–26.

Berve 1926 = H. Berve, *Das Alexanderreich auf prosopographischer Grundlage* (Munich: 1926).

Bosworth 1971a = A. B. Bosworth, 'The Death of Alexander the Great: Rumour and Propaganda', *CQ*² 21 (1971, pp. 112–136.

Bosworth 1971c = A. B. Bosworth, 'Philip II and Upper Macedonia', *CQ*² 21 (1971), pp. 93–105.

Bosworth 1980a = A. B. Bosworth, *A Historical Commentary on Arrian's History of Alexander* 1 (Oxford: 1980).

Bosworth 1988b = A. B. Bosworth, *Conquest and Empire: The Reign of Alexander the Great* (Cambridge: 1988).

Bosworth 1995 = A. B. Bosworth, *A Historical Commentary on Arrian's History of Alexander* 2 (Oxford: 1995).

Bosworth 1996a = A. B. Bosworth, *Alexander and the East* (Oxford: 1996).

Brandenstein and Mayrhofer 1964 = W. Brandenstein and M. Mayrhofer, *Handbuch des Altpersischen* (Wiesbaden: 1964).

Brunt = P. A. Brunt, Arrian, History of Alexander, 2 vols., Loeb Classical Library (Cambridge, MA: 1976 and 1983).

Carney 1996 = E. Carney, 'Macedonians and Mutiny: Discipline and Indiscipline in the Army of Philip and Alexander', *CPh* 91 (1996), pp. 19–44.

Francis 1992 = E. D. Francis, 'Oedipus Achaemenides', *AJPh* 113 (1992), pp. 333–357.

Habicht 1997 = C. Habicht, 'Zwei Angehörige des lynkestischen Königshauses', *Ancient Macedonia* 2 (1977), pp. 511–516.

Hamilton 1969 = J. R. Hamilton, *Plutarch Alexander: A Commentary* (Oxford: 1969).

O'Brien 1992 = J. M. O'Brien, *Alexander the Great: The Invisible Enemy* (London: 1992).

Pédech 1984 = P. Pédech, *Historiens compagnons d'Alexandre* (Paris: 1984).

Tarn 1948 = *Alexander the Great* I–II (Cambridge: 1948).

West 1968 = M. L. West, 'Two passages of Aristophanes', *CR* 18 (1968), pp. 5–8.

11

ALEXANDER:
THE 'GREAT'?

Introduction

Alexander III was known as 'Great' for several reasons: in little more than a decade he journeyed further than any single person before him (on distances, see Sources 2, 35, 36; cf. 59 and 60), he defeated opposing forces on a vast scale, he established a huge empire which stretched from Greece in the west to India in the east, he spread Greek culture and education in that empire, he stimulated trade and the economy, and he died young (Source 84). Even the Romans (apparently) sent an embassy to him in recognition of his achievements and stature (Sources 110 and 111). There is no question that Alexander was a brilliant general and strategist; however, he was not merely a general; he was also a king. As such, it is necessary to consider the entire 'package' of him as king, general and statesman. When we do so, we see there is a downside to Alexander's reign, aspects of which have been outlined in the works of some modern scholars in the preceding chapters, and that there is a great difference between the mythical Alexander, the image we have today, and the historical one.

In part, the mythical Alexander is due to the nature of our sources and Alexander's own propaganda, which make any objective evaluation of him difficult (cf. Source 2).[1] At the same time, there has been a tendency to accept the 'greatness' of Alexander at face value because of what he achieved in the military sphere or was said to have done. Alexander's military abilities are beyond question,[2] but it is important to remember that his army mutinied on him twice (cf. Source 77), that his march through the Gedrosian desert was a dreadful and costly mistake (Sources 78–81), and that he often put himself in peril without thought as to who would lead his army were he to die (Sources 6, 71, 72, 85, 86) – and certainly the Macedonians needed Alexander as leader in the far east (cf. Arr. 6.12.1–3). His preference for constant warfare rather than long-term administration and his failure to provide an heir resulted in confusion as to his successor (cf. Source 13), and his empire exploding on his death in 323. The Macedonian throne then became a prize in the wars of his successors for several decades.

Conspiracies were hatched either against Alexander by others or by him because of his paranoia,[3] and he was held in fear by those with him (Source 99). There was reaction against him among his people on the mainland, especially over his megalomania that led to his belief in his own divinity.[4] Alexander's excessive drinking not only wasted his body but also must have clouded his reason on many occasions (Sources 7–12, 58, 68, 103, 109), and it was a criticism levelled against him by a contemporary author (see Source 109). Did Alexander know anything else but conquering? Was his thirst for fighting, at the core of his continued campaigning (such as his next project, the invasion of Arabia; cf. Sources 100, 112), masked by the reasons given for such campaigning? The legacies of Philip[5] and of Alexander were quite different, and need to be borne in mind in any assessment of Alexander.

Ancient sources

109 The things about Alexander that are not good. They say that on the fifth of the month Dius he drank at Eumaeus', then on the sixth he slept from the drinking; and as much of that day as he was fresh, rising up, he did business with the officers about the morrow's journey, saying that it would be early. And on the seventh he was a guest at Perdiccas' and drank again; and on the eighth he slept. On the fifteenth of the same month he also slept, and on the following day he did the things customary after drinking. On the twenty-fourth he dined at Bagoas'; the house of Bagoas was ten stades from the palace; then on the twenty-eighth he was at rest. Accordingly one of two conclusions must be true, either that Alexander hurt himself badly by drinking so many days in the month or that those who wrote these things lie. And so it is possible to keep in mind henceforth that the group of which Eumenes is a member ... makes such statements (*Ephemerides*, FGrH 117 F 2a = Aelian, *Varra Historia* 3.23).

110 [No Romans have recorded a Roman embassy to Alexander] nor of those who have written an account of Alexander's actions, has either Ptolemy, son of Lagus (*FGrH* 138 F 29), or Aristobulus. With these authors I am generally inclined to agree (Aristobulus, *FGrH* 139 F 53 = Arr. 7.15.6).

111 Of the men who have written the history of Alexander, Aristus and Asclepiades alone say that the Romans also sent an embassy to him, and that when he met their embassy, he predicted something of the future power of Rome, observing both the attire of the men, their love of labour, and their devotion to freedom. At the same time, he made urgent enquiries about their political constitution. This incident I have recorded neither as certainly authentic nor as altogether incredible; but none of the Roman writers have made any mention of this embassy ... nor of those who have written an account of Alexander's actions, has either Ptolemy, son of Lagus (*FGrH* 138 F 29), or Aristobulus (*FGrH* 139 F 53 = Source 110) mentioned it (Aristus, *FGrH* 143 F 2 = Arr. 7.15.5).

112 Aristobulus says that he found at Babylon the fleet with Nearchus, which had sailed from the Persian Sea up the river Euphrates; and another which had been conveyed from Phoenicia ... Near Babylon he made a harbour by excavation large enough to afford anchorage to 1,000 ships of war; and adjoining the harbour he made dock-yards. Miccalus the Clazomenian was despatched to Phoenicia and Syria with 500 talents to enlist some men and to purchase others who were experienced in naval matters. For Alexander designed to colonise the seaboard near the Persian Gulf, as well as the islands in that sea. For he thought that this land would become no less prosperous than Phoenicia. He made these preparations of the fleet to attack the main body of the Arabs, under the pretext that they were the only barbarians of this region who had not sent an embassy to him or done anything becoming their position and showing respect to him. But the truth was, it seems to me, that Alexander was insatiably ambitious of ever acquiring fresh territory (Aristobulus, *FGrH* 139 F 55 = Arr. 7.19.3–6).

Modern works

In the first extract, N.G.L. Hammond, formerly Professor of Greek at the University of Bristol, lauds Alexander and his achievements, and so gives us the image that most people have of Alexander today. While acknowledging Alexander's power and achievements, Ian Worthington, Professor of Greek History at the University of Missouri-Columbia, in the second extract, considers aspects of the downside of Alexander's reign and of his psychology, and argues that the epithet 'Great' gives a false impression of the historical Alexander. In the third extract, F. Holt, Professor of History at the University of Houston, responds vigorously to Worthington, while not going as far as scholars such as Hammond and Tarn. Thus, the debate about the greatness of Alexander continues, and so it should given his influence in his own time and in (and on) the centuries that followed.

1 N.G.L. Hammond, *Alexander the Great: King, Commander and Statesman*[2] (Bristol: 1989), pp. 269–273 and 306.[6]
2 Ian Worthington, 'How "Great" was Alexander?', *Ancient History Bulletin* 13.2 (1999), pp. 39–55.[7]
3 Frank L. Holt, 'Alexander the Great Today: In the Interests of Historical Accuracy?', *Ancient History Bulletin* 13.3 (1999), pp. 111–117.[8]

Additional reading

E. Badian, 'Alexander the Great and the Loneliness of Power', in E. Badian, *Studies in Greek and Roman History* (Oxford: 1964), pp. 192–205.
A.B. Bosworth, 'Alexander the Great and the Decline of Macedon', *Journal of Hellenic Studies* 106 (1986), pp. 1–12.
P.M. Fraser, *Cities of Alexander the Great* (Oxford: 1996), pp. 191–201.
N.G.L. Hammond, 'The Macedonian Imprint on the Hellenistic World', in P. Green (ed.), *Hellenistic History and Culture* (Berkeley and Los Angeles, CA: 1993), pp. 12–23.
N.G.L. Hammond and F.W. Walbank, *A History of Macedonia* 3 (Oxford: 1988), pp. 83–94.
F. Holt, 'The Death of Coenus', *Ancient History Bulletin* 14.1–2 (2000), pp. 49–55.
C. Bradford Welles, 'Alexander's Historical Achievement', *Greece and Rome*[2] 12 (1965), pp. 216–228.
Ian Worthington, 'Alexander the Great and the "Interests of Historical Accuracy": A Reply', *Ancient History Bulletin* 13.4 (1999), pp. 136–140.

Notes

1 On the sources, see Chapter 1.
2 See Chapter 7.
3 See Chapter 10.
4 See Chapter 9; cf. Chapter 8.
5 On Philip, see Chapter 2.
6 Reprinted by permission of Gerald Duckworth & Co. Ltd.
7 Reprinted with the permission of the author.
8 Reprinted with the permission of the author.

ALEXANDER'S PERSONALITY

N.G.L. Hammond

Ancient and modern writers have studied various aspects of Alexander's personality. His sexual life, for instance, has been the subject of wild speculation. Some have supposed that his closeness to his mother and his continence in the presence of Darius' mother, wife, and daughters were signs of sexual impotence; others just the opposite, that he travelled with a harem which provided him with a different girl each night of the year; and others that he had homosexual affairs with herds of eunuchs, Hephaestion, Hector, and a Persian boy. The truth is not attainable nor of much importance; for in the Macedonian court homosexual and heterosexual attachments were equally reputable, and the sexual life of Philip, for instance, seems to have had no effect on his achievements in war and politics. Disappointingly for sensationalist writers Alexander's relations with women seem to have been normal enough for a Macedonian king: three or four wives at the age of thirty-two and two or perhaps three sons – Heracles by Barsine, widow of the Rhodian Memnon and daughter of the Persian Artabazus (P. 21.7–9 and Plut. *Eum.* 1 fin.; C. 10.6.11–13; J. 13.2.7; Suidas s.v. Antipatros); by the Bactrian Roxane a boy who died in infancy (*Epit. Metz* 70) and a boy born after Alexander's death, who became Alexander IV.[1]

Alexander's relations with his parents have been interpreted in differing ways. Some have held him guilty of patricide, planned in advance with the connivance of his mother; others have pictured him publicly disowning his 'so-called father,' Philip; and others have made him praise the services of Philip to his country and plan to raise a gigantic memorial over Philip's tomb. If we consider these matters from the viewpoint not of the twentieth century but of the fourth century BC, we should note that patricide, being the most heinous crime in Greek religion, was hardly conceivable in a man of strong religious faith; that to believe one was the son of a god was not to disown one's human father (whether Amphitryon or Joseph); and that praise of Philip was natural in every Macedonian and not least in the successor to his throne. Indeed if the first unplundered tomb at Vergina is that of Philip, as I believe, its unparalleled splendour is a measure of Alexander's affection for and admiration of his father. He was always loving and loyal to his mother, Olympias. Her tears meant more to him than any triumph, and in taking her side he endangered his own chances of the succession to the throne. When he went to Asia, he made her guardian of the kingship and his representative in the performance of state religion and ceremonial in Macedonia, and he sent to her, partly in that capacity, his regular despatches and a part of the spoils of war. As son and king, he seems to have had full control over her.[2]

In the course of the narrative we have described many facets of Alexander's personality: his deep affections, his strong emotions, his reckless courage, his brilliance and quickness of mind, his intellectual curiosity, his love of glory, his competitive spirit, his acceptance of every challenge, his generosity and his compassion; and on the other hand his overweening ambition, his remorseless will, his passionate indulgence in unrestrained emotion, his inexorable persistence, and his readiness to kill in combat, in passion, and in cold blood and to have rebellious communities destroyed. In brief, he had many of the qualities of the noble savage.

What is left to consider is the mainspring of his personality, his religious sense. The background is essential. Members of the Macedonian royal house worshipped the Olympian gods of orthodox Greek religion in the orthodox way; participated in the ecstatic religions of Orpheus, Dionysus, and the Cabiri (in Samothrace); consulted oracles, apparently with credulity, for instance of Zeus Ammon at Aphytis in Chalcidice, Apollo at Delphi, and Trophonius at Lebadea in Boeotia; and believed in omens and their interpreters. Further, they had at Aegeae and Pella their particular worship of Heracles Patroüs as their heroic ancestor and semidivine exemplar; for Heracles himself was a 'son of god,' even of Zeus.

To emulate, even to surpass his father Philip, or the conquering prototype, Cyrus the Great; to rival the journeys and achievements of Heracles and Dionysus; and in his turn to win 'divine honours', was probably Alexander's youthful ambition. Europe had been the scene of Philip's triumphs, and Italy was to be invaded by the Molossian Alexander; so Asia was the continent for Alexander. But would the gods give it to him? As he landed in the Troad Alexander gave expression to his faith: 'from the gods I accept Asia, won by the spear.' He reaffirmed this after his victory at Gaugamela, when he dedicated spoils as 'Lord of Asia' in thanksgiving to Athena of Lindus and wrote to Darius, 'the gods give Asia to me.' And in the end he was to see himself, and others – even the remote Libyans – were to see him as 'King of all Asia' (A. 7.15.4; *Ind.* 35.8).

But in 334 BC, he must have asked himself whether he was indeed a 'son of god,' capable of such heroic achievement. The answers came unambiguously from oracles and priests in whose words he had belief: in 332 BC the priests of Egypt greeted him as 'Son of Ra'; the priest of Ammon at Siwah probably led him and certainly led others to think he was 'Son of Ammon,' and then the shrines of Didyma and Erythrae declared him to be a 'Son of Zeus.' It was tempting to put such faith to the test, and his prayer at Gaugamela did so. The victory there reassured him that he was indeed 'descended from Zeus.'

Many signs and wonders – some self-evident, others interpreted by seers – showed that the gods were on his side. There is no doubt that he and his men believed in them implicitly. We must remember that Alexander's preferred readings were the *Iliad*, the plays of the three great tragedians, and dithyrambic poetry, in all of which the gods revealed their purposes to men in a variety of ways – signs and wonders being among them.[3] Of those which happened to Alexander Arrian, drawing on Ptolemy and Aristobulus, mentions the following: the swallow at Halicarnassus, the knot at Gordium untied by the future 'ruler of Asia,' the thunder and lightning there, the dream before the attack on Tyre, the bird of prey at Gaza, the grain marking the bounds of Alexandria, the rain and the crows on the way to Siwah, the soaring eagle at Gaugamela, the adverse omen at the Jaxartes, the Syrian clairvoyant in Bactria, the springs of oil and water by the Oxus, and the oracle of Belus (Ba'al) before the entry into Babylon (A. 7.16.5–17.6). Even when death was overshadowing him Alexander might have said, like old Oedipus, 'in all the signs the gods themselves have given me, they never played me false.'

The gods were the authors also of all success in the opinion of Alexander (Plut. *Mor.* 343B), and to them he gave the credit and the thanks. He was constantly engaged in religious acts; he sacrificed every morning of his adult life, on any evening of carousal with his Companions, on starting any enterprise, crossing any river, entering battle,

celebrating victory, and expressing gratitude. He was more self-effacing in his devout-
ness than his father. For example, whereas Philip had portrayed himself on his coins
taking the salute, probably at a victory parade, and advertising his successes at the
Olympic games, Alexander showed gods only on his regular coin issues. In the famous
sculptures of Alexander by Lysippus he was represented with a melting and liquid
softness of the eyes 'looking up towards the heavens,' and this was interpreted at the
time as looking up towards Zeus, from whom his inspiration came. In his early years,
for instance on landing in Asia, he paid special honour to Athena Alcidemus (the
Macedonian war-goddess who protected Philip and Alexander according to Pliny *NH*
35.114),[4] Zeus the King ('of gods and men') and Heracles, ancestor of the royal house;
and throughout his reign he showed them, and them alone, on his gold and silver
coins. It is only on the Porus medallion that the figure of Alexander appeared: diminu-
tive in a symbolic combat. On the reverse his face is not thrown into relief. [. . .]

After the pilgrimage to Siwah he put Zeus Ammon, or Ammon of the Libyans (in
contrast to Ammon at Aphytis), or just Ammon on the same level as Athena, Zeus,
and Heracles in his regard; for instance, on meeting Nearchus he called to witness
'Zeus of the Greeks' and 'Ammon of the Libyans' (*Ind.* 35.8). The thunderbolt which
is carried by Alexander on the Porus medallion was probably the weapon of Zeus
Ammon, with which he had armed Alexander to win the Kingdom of Asia. In the
paintings by Apelles, Alexander was portrayed wielding the thunderbolt, probably as
King of Asia. It was the oracle of Zeus Ammon, not an oracle in Greece, that Alexander
consulted about the honouring of Hephaestion, and at the mouth of the Indus, for
instance, he made two sets of sacrifices with the rituals and to the gods prescribed by
the oracle of Ammon.

He sacrificed occasionally to other non-Greek deities, such as Tirian Melkart (identified with Heracles), Apis and Isis in Egypt, and Belus (Ba'al) in Babylon, whose
temple he intended to rebuild. And his readiness to turn to Greek and non-Greek
gods alike for help is shown by his consulting not only Greek seers but also those of
Egypt, Persia (the Magi), and Babylon (the Chaldaeans). It was no doubt because of
his faith in these divine powers that during his last illness Sarapis was consulted; that
his corpse was embalmed by Egyptians and Chaldaeans; and that the ram's horn, the
emblem of Ammon, was added to the head or Alexander on the coins of Lysimachus.
It is evident that Alexander did not think in terms of his national gods defeating
those of other races, as the Greeks and the Hebrews for instance had done; rather he
was ready to accord respect and worship to the gods of other peoples and to find in
some of those gods an excellence equal to that of the Macedonian and Greek gods.

That Alexander should grow up with a sense of mission was certainly to be expected.
For he was descended from Zeus and Heracles, he was born to be king, he had the
career of Philip as an exemplar, and he was advised by Isocrates, Aristotle, and others
to be a benefactor of Macedonians and Greeks alike. His sense of mission was inevitably
steeped in religious associations, because from an early age he had been associated
with the king, his father, in conducting religious ceremonies, and he was imbued
with many ideas of orthodox religion and of ecstatic mysteries. Thus two observations
by Plutarch (*Mor.* 342 A and F) have the ring of truth. 'This desire (to bring all men
into an orderly system under a single leadership and to accustom them to one way
of life) was implanted in Alexander from childhood and grew up with him'; and on
crossing the Hellespont to the Troad Alexander's first asset was 'his reverence towards

the gods.' Already by then he planned to found a Kingdom of Asia, in which he would rule over the peoples, as Odysseus had done, 'like a kindly father' (*Odyssey* 5.11). He promoted the fulfilment of that plan 'by founding Greek cities among savage peoples and by teaching the principles of law and peace to lawless, ignorant tribes.' When he had completed the conquest of 'Asia' through the favour of the gods and especially that of Zeus Ammon, he went on to establish for all men in his kingdom 'concord and peace and partnership with one another' (*Mor.* 329 F).

This was a practical development, springing from a religious concept and not from a philosophical theory (though it led later to the philosophical theory of the Cynics, who substituted for Asia the whole inhabited world and talked of the brotherhood of all men), and it came to fruition in the banquet at Opis, when he prayed in the presence of men of various races for 'concord and partnership in the ruling' of his kingdom 'between Macedonians and Persians.'

What distinguishes Alexander from all other conquerors is this divine mission. He had grown up with it, and he had to a great extent fulfilled it, before he gave expression to it at the banquet at Opis in such words as those reported by Plutarch (*Mor.* 329 C). 'Alexander considered,' wrote Plutarch, 'that he had come from the gods to be a general governor and reconciler of the world. Using force of arms when he did not bring men together by the light of reason, he harnessed all resources to one and the same end, mixing the lives, manners, marriages and customs of men, as it were in a loving-cup.' This is his true claim to be called 'Alexander the Great': that he did not crush or dismember his enemies, as the conquering Romans crushed Carthage and Molossia and dismembered Macedonia into four parts; nor exploit, enslave or destroy the native peoples, as 'the white man' has so often done in America, Africa, and Australasia; but that he created, albeit for only a few years, a supra-national community capable of living internally at peace and of developing the concord and partnership which are so sadly lacking in the modern world.

Notes

1 See the first edition of this volume n. 114 for ancient evidence for and against Alexander being given to paederasty, which was the normal form of homosexual relationship in Greek antiquity (rather than between consenting adults). Statements about his heterosexual practices varied in ancient authors from near-impotence to gross excess. Modern authors have indulged in similar speculations, notably M. Renault, *The Nature of Alexander* (1975).
2 She probably held the *prostasia*; see Hammond, *A* 474 ff. and *HM* 3.90 f.
3 P. 8.2–3.
4 The head of this Athena was represented on the iron helmet in Philip's tomb at Vergina; see M. Andronikos in *AAA* 10 (1977) 47 and *Vergina* 141.

References

Andronikos, *Vergina* = M. Andronikos, *Vergina: The Royal Tombs* (Athens: 1984).

Hammond, *A* = N.G.L. Hammond, 'Some passages in Arrian concerning Alexander', *CQ*² 30 (1980), pp. 455–476.

Hammond, *HM* = N.G.L. Hammond and F.W. Walbank, *A History of Macedonia* 3 (Oxford: 1988).

HOW 'GREAT' WAS ALEXANDER?[1]

Ian Worthington

Why was Alexander III of Macedon called 'Great'? The answer seems relatively straightforward: from an early age he was an achiever, he conquered territories on a superhuman scale, he established an empire until his times unrivalled, and he died young, at the height of his power. Thus, at the youthful age of 20, in 336, he inherited the powerful empire of Macedon, which by then controlled Greece and had already started to make inroads into Asia. In 334 he invaded Persia, and within a decade he had defeated the Persians, subdued Egypt, and pushed on to Iran, Afghanistan and even India. As well as his vast conquests Alexander is credited with the spread of Greek culture and education in his empire, not to mention being responsible for the physical and cultural formation of the hellenistic kingdoms – some would argue that the hellenistic world was Alexander's legacy.[2] He has also been viewed as a philosophical idealist, striving to create a unity of mankind by his so-called fusion of the races policy, in which he attempted to integrate Persians and Orientals into his administration and army. Thus, within a dozen years Alexander's empire stretched from Greece in the west to India in the far east, and he was even worshipped as a god by many of his subjects while still alive. On the basis of his military conquests contemporary historians, and especially those writing in Roman times, who measured success by the number of body-bags used, deemed him great.[3]

However, does a man deserve to be called 'The Great' who was responsible for the deaths of tens of thousands of his own men and for the unnecessary wholesale slaughter of native peoples? How 'great' is a king who prefers constant warfare over consolidating conquered territories and long-term administration? Or who, through his own recklessness, often endangered his own life and the lives of his men? Or whose violent temper on occasion led him to murder his friends and who towards the end of his life was an alcoholic, paranoid, megalomaniac, who believed in his own divinity? These are questions posed by our standards of today of course, but nevertheless they are legitimate questions given the influence which Alexander has exerted throughout history – an influence which will no doubt continue.[4]

The aims of this paper are to trace some reasons for questioning the greatness of Alexander as is reflected in his epithet, and to add potential evidence dealing with the attitude of the Macedonians, Alexander's own people, in their king's absence. It is important to stress that when evaluating Alexander it is essential to view the 'package' of king as a whole; i.e., as king, commander and statesman. All too often this is not the case. There is no question that Alexander was spectacularly successful in the military field, and had Alexander only been a general his epithet may well have been deserved. But he was not just a general; he was a king too, and hence military exploits form only a percentage of what Alexander did, or did not do – in other words, we must look at the 'package' of him as king as a whole. By its nature this paper is impressionistic, and it can only deal rapidly with selected examples from Alexander's reign and discuss points briefly. However, given the unequalled influence Alexander has played in cultures and history from the time of his death to today, it is important to stress that there is a chasm of a difference between the mythical Alexander, which for the most part we have today, and the historical.

Alexander died in 323, and over the course of time the mythical king and his exploits sprang into being. Alexander himself was not above embellishing his own life and achievements. He very likely told the court historian Callisthenes of Olynthus what to say about his victory over Darius III at the battle of Issus in 333, for example.[5] Contemporary Attic oratory also exaggerated his achievements,[6] and so within a generation of his death erroneous stories were already being told.

As time continued we move into the genre of pulp fiction. In the third or second century BC Alexander's exploits formed the plot of the story known as the *Alexander Romance*, which added significantly to the Alexander legend and had such a massive influence on many cultures into the Middle Ages.[7] Given its life-span, deeds were attributed to Alexander which are unhistorical, such as his encounters with the tribe of headless men, his flying exploits in a basket borne by eagles, and the search for the Water of Life, which ended with his transformation into a mermaid. These stories became illustrative fodder for the various manuscripts of the *Alexander Romance* – one of the most popular episodes is Alexander's ascent to heaven, inspired by the myth of Bellerephon to fly to Mount Olympus on Pegasus, which is found in many Byzantine and later art-works, sculptures and paintings. As a result of the *Romance* Alexander astonishingly appears in the literature of other cultures: in Hebrew literature, for example, he was seen as a preacher and prophet, who even becomes converted to Christianity. In Persian literature he is the hero Sikandar, sent to punish the impure peoples. In the West he appears as a Frank, a Goth, a Russian and a Saxon.

Then there is Plutarch, writing in the late first and second century AD, who has probably done the most damage to our knowing the historical Alexander. In his treatise *On the Fortune or The Virtue of Alexander*, Plutarch was swayed (understandably) by the social background against which he was writing and especially by his own philosophical beliefs, and he portrayed Alexander as both an action man and a philosopher-king, whose mission was to impose Greek civilisation on the 'barbarian' Persians. Plutarch's work is essentially a rhetorical exercise, but as time continued the rhetorical aspects were disregarded in favour of a warrior-king who was more than the stuff legends were made of; this was a warrior who was seen to combine military success with wisdom and unification.[8] And so Alexander emerges as the promoter of the brotherhood of man in Tarn's 1948 biography, which was greatly influenced by what Plutarch wrote.

The Alexander legend was a ready feeding ground for artists throughout the centuries as well. When Alexander invaded Persia in 334 he detoured to Troy to sacrifice at the tomb of his hero Achilles. This was a stirring story, which became a model for heroic piety in the Renaissance, and later periods; thus, for example, we have Fontebasso's painting of Alexander's sacrifice at Achilles' tomb in the eighteenth century. In modern Greece Alexander became both an art-work and a symbol, as seen in the painting by Engonopoulos in 1977 of the face-less Alexander standing with his arm around the faceless Pavlos Melas, a modern hero of the struggle for Macedonian independence.

Thus, we can see how the historical Alexander has faded into the invincible general, the great leader, explorer and king, as time continued, especially in the Middle Ages with its world of chivalry, warriors and great battles: a superb context into which to fit Alexander, even if this meant distortion of the truth, and history subsumed to legend. Indeed, during the Middle Ages he was regarded as one of the four great kings of the ancient world. Let us now consider some specific aspects of Alexander's reign in support of this.

In 334 Alexander III left home for Asia, entrusting to Antipater as guardian (*epitropos*) a stable – for a while – Greece and Macedon (Arr. 1.11.3). The king also unilaterally made Antipater deputy hegemon in the League of Corinth. Alexander's 'mandate' or prime directive, as inherited from his father Philip II and endorsed by the League of Corinth, was to pursue his father's plan of punishing the Persians for their sacrilegious acts of 150 years ago and to 'liberate' (whatever that meant) the Greek cities of Asia Minor. In other words, a panhellenic mandate. After he had fulfilled it, people quite rightly would have expected him to return home. People were wrong: the king would soon disregard the prime directive for personal reasons, causing discontent amongst the army with him and also, even more ominously, with his countrymen back home.

We have a fair amount of information for events in mainland Greece, especially Athens, during the reign of Alexander, however events in Macedon in this period are undocumented and largely unknown. We certainly cannot say that there was a hiatus in Macedonian history, for Antipater kept Macedon powerful and united while Alexander was absent, so much so that there was economic growth, and education and military training, for example, remained at a high standard.[9] However, appearance is not likely to reflect reality. Macedon in this period may well have been fraught with discontent, and it provides insights into the Macedonians' attitude to their king and he to them. At the same time a consideration of the Macedonian background also lends further weight to questioning the aptness of Alexander's title 'Great'.

Alexander's military successes throughout his reign were spectacular to a very large degree – certainly manufactured by the king to be great (see below) – and we should expect his people back home to feel proud of their king at the head of his panhellenic mission of punishment and liberation, and to proclaim his victories to all and sundry. His deeds and the geographical extent of his conquests were certainly known for we have references to them in contemporary Attic oratory.[10] However, the impression which strikes us about the Macedonians themselves is that Alexander was far from their idea of an ideal king. Why might they feel this way? In addressing this, we can begin with the vexed question of Macedonian manpower. Did Alexander's demands for reinforcements from the mainland seriously deplete the fighting strength of the army under Antipater? Did he make these demands regardless of the pressure under which he was putting Antipater and without regard for the lives of his people and the security of his kingdom from external threat? And if so, how did the people feel and how did they react?

I take as my example the abortive war of Agis III of 331. This is the only Greek attempt at the overthrow of the Macedonian hegemony which we know about from the time Alexander left for Persia until his death, and therefore it is significant. It is impossible to determine the fighting strength of Macedon at this time,[11] and Badian's most recent discussion of this complex issue, which effectively rebuts the views of others, will no doubt be itself challenged at some point.[12] While Billows and Badian argue that the fighting strength of Macedon was never depleted to the extent that there was a serious manpower problem, numerical accuracy is not the issue here. It has to be said that Agis III had posed no small threat to Antipater, and that the latter's forces were not at full strength (Diodorus 18.12.2 says that Antipater was short of 'citizen soldiers', i.e. Macedonians proper), and he had just sent 6,500 Macedonians to Alexander. Alexander had left Antipater with only 13,500 Macedonians (12,000 infantry and 1500 cavalry), and when the king needed reinforcements the first year he crossed into Asia he had had to resort to somewhat hastily-levied local troops (Arr. 1.24.2). In 332 Alexander needed more men (Diod. 17.49.1, Curt. 4.6.30), this time from the Greek mainland; in 331, 500 cavalry and 6000 infantry arrived after the battle of Gaugamela (Diod. 17.65.1, Curt. 5.1.40), and as late as 324 Antipater had orders to bring more men to him (Arr. 7.12.4). Antipater was never able to rebuild his manpower significantly. Even in the so-called Lamian War, which broke out on Alexander's death and lasted about a year, he had only 600 cavalry and 13,000 infantry and was forced to recruit soldiers from elsewhere – and we know what a detrimental impact on his forces the desertion of the 2,000 strong contingent of Thessalian cavalry was and how Antipater only just managed to struggle to Lamia for refuge (Diod. 18.12.3–4). Moreover, it was only the timely arrivals of Leonnatus and then Craterus with several thousand Macedonian veterans that saved the day.

Agis III had accepted ten ships and money from Persia to hire 8,000 mercenaries (Diod. 17.48.1, Curt. 4.1.39), with which he occupied Crete, and so in late 331 Sparta was able to mobilise a fairly formidable force. Then in the same year Memnon, the general of Thrace, and in command of a powerful army (Diod. 17.62.5), leagued with some Thracians and rose in revolt, thereby stretching Antipater's own army further. Antipater had to lead all his army into Thrace to put down this rising (Diod. 17.62.6). This episode shows not only the ever-present danger of external threats to the kingdom's security but also the need for an adequate army – something denied to Antipater. Although Antipater dealt with Memnon and with Agis successfully, his manpower reserve had been depleted since he had need of a large sum from Alexander (Arr. 3.16.10) to boost his small force of 1500 cavalry and 12,000 infantry (Diod. 17.17.5), and we later find – in 325 – Memnon leading 5,000 Thracian cavalry to Alexander in Asia since Macedon could not then have raised such a large force of cavalry.

Alexander's money on this occasion had helped to save the day, but money cannot be the answer to solving problems: the king should not have continued to demand troops which could, and did, weaken Antipater's position. Take the Thracian discontent at this time, Agis' insurgence, Peloponnesian stirrings, and throw in a potential revolt of the Greek states (as Agis must have intended) and we have a recipe for disaster.[13] These threats would not have been lost on the Macedonians, and we simply cannot imagine they would not have been worried by them.

Perhaps Alexander relied too much on money buying his way out of trouble. Whilst he may be acclaimed for rewarding his men with high pay, various bonuses, remission of taxes in certain cases, cancellation of soldiers' debts and various signs of royal favour (Arr. 1.16.5, 7.5.1–3, 12.1–2), the argument can be made that such measures were to ensure the loyalty of his men, especially as he pushed further eastwards after defeating the Persians so decisively. And the question is, what happened when money and favour were no longer enough, especially when we consider the 'down side' such as the huge numbers of casualties stemming from Alexander's battles,[14] the numerous demands for reinforcements, and especially the forced settlement from Macedon and Greece to the newly-founded cities at the farthest ends of the world?[15] There was also the worrying news from those who did return home of Alexander's drunken rages which resulted in him killing – either by his own hands or from false implication in conspiracies – some of those close to him, his paranoia, his orientalism, and even his belief that he was divine as a son of Zeus. Another factor too is that his people back home did not know Alexander as a man and a king: he had only been home as king for about two years before he left his country, and he showed no signs of coming back until his men forced the issue with a mutiny (see below). Macedon needed a king, and Alexander was not there.

That Alexander's money and favour proved insufficient and discontent grew are proved by the two mutinies which he faced in 326 at the Hyphasis (Beas) river and in 324 at Opis (on the use of the term 'mutiny' see below). In 326 while at Taxila Alexander heard that the Indian prince Porus was defying him, and so marched to do battle at the Hydaspes river. He was successful, and Porus was defeated. Rather than return to Taxila to recuperate and more importantly sit out the monsoon weather, Alexander ordered his men to continue their advance into India, His *pothos* – personal longing (note again the personal element) – to conquer more territory was frustrated when his men mutinied at the Hyphasis river.[16] Perhaps more than just seventy days of marching endlessly through monsoon rains into more unknown territory was at the heart of the issue. After all, Curtius says (9.2.3) that King Aggrammes (*sic*) was reported to be waiting at the Delhi gap with a force which included 3,000 elephants. Curtius believed this was true, and we know that the Nanda kings of Magadha had a more powerful state than any of the ones Alexander tangled with so far. Thus, another battle loomed, one in which Alexander's men had no desire to participate, and they refused to follow him further. Alexander sulked in his tent like his Homeric hero Achilles for three days, but to no avail. His bluff was called and Coenus, representing the views of the men, prevailed. Alexander was forced to turn back, and by late September 326 he was once again at the Hydaspes. Coenus' defiance of Alexander earned him little in the way of reward as a few days after the Hyphasis mutiny he was found dead in suspicious circumstances (Arr. 6.2.1, Curt. 9.3.20). The coincidence is too much, and, as with others who flouted Alexander (see below), we can see the hand of a furious and spiteful king at work here.

Although Alexander might try to disguise the lack of advance at the Hyphasis river as due to unfavourable omens (Arr. 5.3.6), no one would be unaware that the real reason was that the army *en masse* simply did not want to go further.[17] Again needless risk-taking followed: instead of retracing his steps he went for another route, through the Gedrosian desert.[18] Starvation, heat, little water, and flash flooding had their effects, and as the march continued the baggage animals had to be slaughtered for food (Arr. 6.25.2). Plutarch (*Alexander* 66.4–5) talks of the army reduced to a quarter of its original size; although this is over-exaggeration, there is no doubt that this march was a major logistical blunder on the part of Alexander, and that it unnecessarily cost many lives.

A few years later in 324 Alexander was faced with another mutiny, this time at Opis, not far from Babylon. At Opis Alexander announced that his veteran soldiers and those injured were to be discharged and that he had ordered new blood from Macedon.[19] For some reason the older soldiers saw Alexander's move as tantamount to a rejection of them and of their capabilities, and the remaining soldiers had no wish to remain and fight with Persians and Iranians. For the second time in his reign Alexander was hit with a mutiny, this time over his orientalising policy. Once again,

Alexander sulked in his tent for two days, and then he called his men's bluff by announcing that Macedonian military commands and titles were to be transferred to selected Persians. His men capitulated at once, and the clash was resolved with the famous banquet, in which Macedonian, Greek, Persian and Iranian sipped from the same cup and Alexander prayed for *homonoia* or concord (Arr. 7.11.9).[20]

The term 'mutiny' for the army's resistance to Alexander on both occasions has lately been queried. For example, Bosworth has this to say on the Opis incident: 'This protest can hardly be dignified with the term mutiny that is universally applied to it. The troops confined themselves to verbal complaints, but they were contumacious and wounding.'[21] It is important to look beyond the immediate context of both 'protests' to their full implications. The degree to which the men mouthed insults at the king or criticised his behaviour and plans is irrelevant. The crucial point is that in both instances the army as a whole stood fast against the orders of Alexander. This was outright rebellion against the king and commander; refusal to obey the orders of a superior in this manner is mutiny. The 326 incident ended only when Alexander agreed to his army's demands to turn back. Although Alexander's bluff was successful at Opis, it was only when he cunningly played on the racial tensions that his men capitulated. Until that time they had stood fast against him, and there is no indication of a change of mood until Alexander adopted the strategy he did. The Macedonians might well have needed Alexander in the far east (cf. Arr. 6.12.1–3), but this did not stop them from defying him when they felt the situation demanded it. Both incidents were quite simply mutinies, and as such votes of no confidence in Alexander as a military commander and as a king.[22]

Alexander's generalship and actual military victories may be questioned in several key areas. For example, after the battle of Issus in 333 Darius fled towards Media, but Alexander pressed on to Egypt. He did not pursue Darius, as he surely ought to have done and thus consolidate his gains, especially when so far from home and with the mood of the locals so prone to fluctuation, but left him alone. He was more interested in what lay to the south: the riches of Babylon and then Susa, or as Arrian describes them (3.16.2) the 'prizes of the war'. However, a war can hardly be seen as won if the opposing king and commander remains at large and has the potential to regroup. Alexander's action was lucky for Darius, then, as he was able to regroup his forces and bring Alexander to battle again almost two years later, at Gaugamela (331). It was not lucky for Alexander, though, and especially so for those men on both sides who fell needlessly that day in yet another battle.

We have also the various sieges which Alexander undertook and which were often lengthy, costly, and questionable. A case in point is that of Tyre in 332 as Alexander made his way to Egypt after his victory at Issus. In Phoenicia Byblos and Sidon surrendered to Alexander, as did the island town (as it was then) of Tyre until the king expressed his personal desire to sacrifice in the main temple there. Quite rightly considering his demand sacrilegious, the Tyrians resisted him and Alexander, his ego affronted and refusing to back down, laid siege to the town.[23] The siege itself lasted several months, cost the king a fortune in money and manpower, and resulted in the slaughter of the male Tyrians and the selling of the Tyrian women and children into slavery. There is no question that control of Tyre was essential since Alexander could not afford a revolt of the Phoenician cities, given their traditional rivalries, as he pushed on to Egypt. Nor indeed, if we believe his speech at Arrian

2.17, could he allow Tyre independence with the Persian navy a threat and the Phoenician fleet the strongest contingent in it. However, there was no guarantee that the destruction of Tyre would result in the Phoenician fleet surrendering to him as he only seems to have *expected* it would (Arr. 2.17.3). Moreover, laying siege to Tyre was not necessary: he could simply have left a garrison, for example, on the mainland opposite the town to keep it in check. Another option, given that the Tyrians had originally surrendered to him, would have been the diplomatic one: to recognise the impiety of his demand in their eyes and thus relinquish it, thereby continuing on his way speedily and with their goodwill. Ultimately no real gain came from his siege except to Alexander on a purely personal level again: his damaged ego had been repaired; the cost in time, manpower and reputation mattered little.

Alexander's great military victories over his Persian and Indian foes which have so long occupied a place in popular folklore and been much admired throughout the centuries are very likely to have been embellished and nothing like the popular conceptions of them. A case in point is the battle of Issus in 333. Darius threw victory away at that battle and he was, to put it bluntly, a mediocre commander – the battle might have been very different if Alexander had faced a more competent commander such as Memnon, for example. Alexander was lucky, but this does not come in the 'official' account we have of the battle, probably since he told Callisthenes, the court historian, what to write about it.

Luck again is the principal factor in Alexander's victory at Granicus the previous year (334). His river crossing is commendable, no doubt about that, but against an outnumbered and hastily-levied Persian contingent, and with no Great King present in order to exhort and to lead the troops in person, it comes as no surprise that the Macedonians and their superbly drilled phalanx were victorious. Similarly embellished, perhaps distorted out of all proportion even, is the 'great' battle against Porus in India at the Hydaspes river in 326.[24] Alexander effected a brilliant river crossing against his Indian foe, given the swelling of that river by the seasonal rains and melting of the snow in the Himalayas, but in reality the battle was over before it began. Porus was outnumbered and outclassed, and he and his army never stood a chance. However, we would never know this from our sources or indeed from the commemorative coinage which Alexander struck to mark his defeat of Porus, and which are pure propaganda to exaggerate that defeat.[25]

The king's own men would know. And word would filter through to the Macedonians back home. Alexander's growing orientalism, as seen in his apparent integration of foreigners into his administration and army, was a cause of great discontent as the traditional Macedonian warrior-king transformed himself into something akin to a sultan. He began to change his appearance, preferring a mixture of Persian and Macedonian clothing, despite the obvious displeasure of his troops (Arr. 7.8.2), and he had also assumed the upright tiara, the symbol of Persian kingship (Arr. 4.7.4). Some saw the writing on the wall and duly pandered to the king. Thus, Peucestas, the Macedonian satrap of Persis, was well rewarded by the king for adopting Persian dress and learning the Persian language (Arr. 6.30.2–3). However, he was the only Macedonian to do so according to Arrian.

Significant also was Alexander's attempt to adopt the Persian custom of *proskynesis* – genuflection – at his court in Bactra in 327, and his expectation that his men would follow suit.[26] *Proskynesis* was a social act which had long been practised by the Persians and involved prostrating oneself before the person of the king in an act of subservience, and thereby accepting his lordship. The custom, however, was regarded as tantamount to worship and thus sacrilegious to the Greeks – worship of a god or a dead hero was one thing, but worship of a person while still alive quite another. Callisthenes thwarted Alexander's attempt (Arr. 4.10.5–12.1), something which the king never forgot and which would soon cost Callisthenes his life in sadistic circumstances (Arr. 4.14.1–3, Curt. 8.6.24).

Why Alexander tried to introduce *proskynesis* is unknown. Perhaps he was simply attempting to create a form of social protocol common to Macedonians, Greeks and Persians. However, he would have been well aware of the religious connotations associated with the act and hence its implications for his own being. It was plain stupidity on his part if he thought his men would embrace the custom with relish, and his action clearly shows that he had lost touch with his army and the religious beliefs on which he had been raised. Evidence for this may be seen in the motives for the Pages' Conspiracy, a serious attempt on Alexander's life, which occurred not long after Alexander tried to enforce *proskynesis* on all. A more likely explanation for the attempt to introduce *proskynesis* is that Alexander now thought of himself as divine (cf. Arr. 4.9.9, Curt. 8.5.5), and thus *proskynesis* was a logical means of recognising his divine status in public by all men (see below).

Indeed, Alexander's belief that he was divine impacts adversely on any evaluation of him. History is riddled with megalomaniacs who along the way suffered from divine pretensions, and the epithet 'Great' is not attached to them. Regardless of whether his father Philip II was worshipped as a god on his death,[27] Alexander seems not to have been content with merely following in his footsteps but to believe in his own divine status while alive.[28]

Alexander had visited the oracle of Zeus Ammon in the oasis at Siwah in the winter of 332, shortly after his entry into Egypt, and there he apparently received confirmation from the priests that he was a son of Zeus.[29] From that time onwards he openly called himself son of Zeus as opposed to descendant of Zeus. It is important to stress the distinction since he was technically a descendant of Zeus through Heracles. That sort of association the people would have accepted, but they baulked at Alexander at first setting himself up as a son of a god even though born from a mortal mother. Later, as his megalomania increased, he would believe he was divine while alive. Thus, during the Opis mutiny Arrian indicates that his men mocked their king's association with Zeus Ammon (Arr. 7.8.3). This took place in 324, so obviously over the intervening years the situation had grown from bad to worse, with little or nothing on the part of Alexander to pour oil on troubled waters.

If anything, Alexander ignored the displeasure of his men if his move to introduce *proskynesis* at his court in 327, as noted above, was meant to be a means of recognising his divinity. The setback here was soon forgotten as in 326 Alexander was again adamant about his divine status (Arr. 7.2.3). Moreover, Alexander did not restrict his superhuman status to the army with him; by 324 we know from our sources that the Greeks of the mainland were debating his deification,[30] and that there was widespread resistance to it.[31] Evidently his divine status was a serious source of contention amongst his people back home and those with him, yet Alexander ignored it – hardly the mark of a great king, commander and statesman intent on maintaining the loyalty of his troops and indeed of his people.

As Alexander's army found out, the growing dissatisfaction with its commander was fatal. To take but a few brief examples. In the autumn of 330 at Phrada Alexander had Philotas, the commander of the Companion Cavalry, charged with conspiracy. There is little doubt that there was a conspiracy against the king at this time, but the evidence against Philotas was slight. Despite this, Alexander, in a staged trial before the army assembly (Curt. 6.8.23) had him condemned and then executed by stoning.[32] Alexander did not stop with Philotas' execution: his father Parmenion was also treacherously put to death on the king's orders.[33] Parmenion's reputation was great and he was of course very powerful, however he was just too great a danger for Alexander to allow to roam loose and resentful when questioning Alexander's growing Asian leanings.

Then in late 328 after a defeat of a Macedonian force by Spitamenes, Cleitus, commander of the Royal Squadron of the Companions and one of Alexander's closest friends, criticised Alexander's expansionist plans, his personality cult, and praised his father Philip II. The setting was a drinking party and most of the protagonists had drunk too much, as was the Macedonian wont. Tempers flared, and a furious Alexander again allowed reason to give way to emotion. He grabbed a pike and ran Cleitus through.[34] Finally, in 327, Callisthenes, whose moral victory a short time before in preventing the introduction of *proskynesis* (see above) had him implicated by the king in the serious Pages' Conspiracy and then sadistically executed (Arr. 4.14.1–3, Curt. 8.6.24). Our sources indicate that Callisthenes was not part of the Pages' Conspiracy;[35] all would see, however, that this was how criticism of the king for policies not in keeping with Macedonian custom was punished. It is hardly surprising that the contemporary source Ephippus (*FGH* 126 F5) says that those present in Alexander's court lived in a reign of terror. Alexander's growing paranoia is demonstrated by the events referred to, but he also seems to have suffered increasingly from mood changes and bouts of depression: he was probably, in today's terms, bipolar.

However, while the men in his army might have understood Alexander's reasons because they were *there* with him, not so those back home who could only see a king moving further away from his roots, further away from the traditions his father had fought to uphold, becoming more of a paranoid megalomaniac with each passing day. Moreover, as has been said but is worth repeating, they did not properly know him since he had ruled at home as king for only a short time before he left, and only a mutiny by his army was making him come back. Bewilderment can only have changed to dissatisfaction, then, human nature being what it is, to resentment at his disregard of them.

Certainly, Alexander changed the mandate of the League of Corinth, switching the invasion of Persia from its panhellenic motive to a personal one, to destroy the Persian empire and beyond. But it was one thing to conquer Asia Minor and liberate Greeks there and defeat the Great King, another to want to take over as ruler for according to Plutarch (*Alexander* 34) Alexander was proclaimed 'king of Asia', presumably by the Macedonians in his army. The Greeks also would be questioning what Alexander was up to – he had needed them for his Asian invasion (hence why he treated their revolt in 336 with moderation), and probably a large number of Greeks did support the campaign given its panhellenic sentiments (Diod. 16.89.2). However, the invasion was no longer for its original panhellenic ideal. The move now was not to establish a Macedonian empire in Asia but a kingdom of Asia and even to move the capital from Pella to probably Babylon, perhaps Alexandria.[36] That his people back home in Macedon did not want this is shown by the measures which Alexander took to keep his army at full strength. According to Arrian (7.8.1, 12.1–2), Alexander was generous with pay and bounties to soldiers in order to encourage those at home to join him in Asia. If his people had been united behind him in further conquest there would have been no need of such apparent generosity. What we are dealing with here are bribes since those at home did not want to follow Alexander's *pothos*, and normal pay could not persuade them.

Was Alexander using his own people for his own personal ends now? Philip II risked the lives of his men as well, but for his state's hegemonic position in international affairs, not for his own selfish reasons or a *pothos* which might well jeopardise that position of Macedon. Others saw the danger, even from early in his reign. Thus in 335, after the successful termination of the Greek revolt, which broke out on the death of Philip II, Diodorus (17.16.2) says that Parmenion and Antipater urged Alexander not to become actively involved in Asia until he had produced a son and heir. Alexander opposed them for personal reasons: he could not procrastinate at home waiting for children to be born when the invasion of Asia had been endorsed by the League of Corinth! In the end, says Diodorus (17.16.3), he won them over. Then in 331 Darius III offered *inter alia* to abandon to Alexander all territories west of the Euphrates and to become the friend and ally of the king.[37] Parmenion thought the Persian king's offer to be in the Macedonians' best interests, but Alexander refused to accept it (in a famous exchange in which Parmenion is alleged to have said that if he were Alexander he would accept the terms, and a displeased Alexander is alleged to have replied that if he were Parmenion he would, but instead he was Alexander).

The authenticity of this exchange is probably suspect, and in any case it is hardly surprising that Alexander would have refused such an offer given the difficulties of administering the Euphrates frontier (as the Romans would later learn). However, every story has a kernel of truth, and this particular one indicates that at least some of his generals anticipated trouble and were unsettled by Alexander's cavalier attitude towards the future and especially the succession. The aftermath of his death in 323, the eclipse of Macedonian power, and the ensuing decades of bloody warfare between his successors down to around 301, would prove how unthinking and mistaken he was.

Parmenion's criticism and resistance to Alexander's plans led eventually to his execution (see above), but who could *believe* the reason Alexander gave for it? The same goes for Philotas. And Cleitus' death at the hands of Alexander is hardly an example of a king able to put reason over emotion; all the more dangerous given his tendency to consume vast draughts of alcohol, which further muddled his thoughts and allowed his paranoia, rage, and emotional turmoil to come to the fore. What *must* the people back home have thought when they expected their king to return on completing his mission, only to see him move further east, killing his own men in paranoid or drunken (or both) frenzies along his way, ignoring the welfare and best interests of his people, the long-term administration of his empire, and giving no thought to a son and heir?

Here, Alexander fails miserably in what is expected of a king. The chaos revealed in that short-lived compromise in Babylon in June 323, shortly after the king breathed his last, was not solely owing to the personal ambitions of various generals (and one secretary), but the result of Alexander's neglect of his country and empire. His hyper-activity in putting constant expansion over administration, not to mention not providing an adult heir, cost the empire any unity and chance of surviving him intact. Alexander did not follow a strategy of conquest, consolidation and long-term admin-istration, but was constantly on the move. As a result, and especially as he moved further east, territories behind him revolted almost as soon as he left. This does not show foresight in making and *keeping* an empire. He misjudged the native peoples as he moved across Afghanistan and into modern Pakistan, thinking that defeated in battle meant conquered.

Consider also the outcome if as a result of his foolishness Alexander had died during the siege of Malli, in the lower Punjab in 326.[38] The nomadic Malli tribe had stolen his horse Bucephalus, and Alexander with his army set off to retrieve it. The Malli offered to return it when faced with the might of a Macedonian army, but Alexander, always thirsty for a fight and thinking little of the consequences, besieged the town. There was no need to do this. At this siege Alexander scaled the wall of the town and found himself suddenly cut off from his men when the scaling ladders broke behind him. Leaping down amongst the enemy he fought on, in the process having his right lung punctured by an enemy arrow and almost dying. He was saved by his men storming the town, who then went on an orgy of murder. Who would have taken over as commander and as king if Alexander had died? Only literary heroes jump into the enemy's midst as Alexander did at Malli. There was no heir, and the aftermath of his death showed there was no one undisputed leader.

In 327 at Bazeira Alexander was engaged in a lion hunt in a local forest with several others, including Lysimachus (Curt. 8.1.14–16). The king killed a lion, one that was apparently of extraordinary size (*magnitudinis rarae*; then again, it would have to be in an Alexander story). In the process he rudely treated Lysimachus by taunting him about a wound he received when he had killed a lion in Syria, and no doubt embarrass-ing him in front of the others. Afterwards the army voted (*scivere gentis suae more*) that Alexander should never place himself in such danger again (Curt. 8.1.18). In so doing the army must have been remembering the earlier lion hunt involving Lysimachus, who had suffered wounds which almost cost him his life (8.1.15). Regardless of whether the army passed an official vote or merely a motion requesting that Alexander refrain from endangering his life in the future, his men had very real fears of what would happen were he to die. Alexander's activities at Malli showed how little he heeded his army's fears and pleas in the pursuit of his own personal *gloria*.

The adverse reaction of the army towards Alexander and his policies is further rein-forced by the decision on the part of the Macedonian Army Assembly at Babylon after his death to abandon his future plans (Diod. 18.4.2–6, Justin 13.5.7). Assuming these are authentic, they included the invasion of Arabia during the winter and spring of 323/2[39] and the circumnavigation of the peninsula, the construction of 1000 warships in the South-East Mediterranean larger than triremes, the building of six temples each costing 1500 talents, the erection of a memorial to his father to rival the greatest pyramid, and significantly the transpopulation of 20,000 people from Asia to Europe and *vice versa* for the purposes of racial unity and intermarriage.[40] These projects were abandoned for reasons other than Philip III Arrhidaeus or Perdiccas was inca-pable of leading the Macedonians on them, as Hammond would argue,[41] but because they represented all that the people did not consider properly Macedonian practices, especially the continuation of racial fusion. In other words, they represented all that the people had come to hate in Alexander.

Alexander's autocratic nature and its adverse impact on his army have been illustrated many times, but it extended beyond the men with him to the Greeks back on the mainland. One example is his Exiles Decree of 324, which ordered all exiles to return to their native cities (excluding those under a religious curse and the Thebans).[42] If any city was unwilling, then Antipater was empowered to use force against it (Diod. 18.8.4). The context was no doubt to send home the large bands of mercenaries now wandering the empire and which posed no small military or political danger if any ambitious satrap or general got his hands on them. The decree was technically illegal since it clearly flouted the autonomy of the Greek states, not to mention the principles of the League of Corinth, but Alexander cared little about *polis* autonomy or the feelings of the Greeks. Although the Athenians refused to receive back their exiles (Curt. 10.2.6–7), resistance, to coin a phrase, was futile: Alexander was king, the Macedonians controlled Greece, and the final clause of the decree on coercing Greek cities would not be lost on them. The flurry of diplomatic activity to the king over the decree proves this, even though outright rebellion was not planned at that stage.[43] His death altered the situation dramatically, and only one state, Tegea, actually implemented the decree.[44]

There is no need to deal in great detail with the notion which originates in Plutarch's treatise on Alexander (see above), and has found its way into some modern works (such as Tarn's biography), that Alexander pursued an actual policy to promote a unity of mankind. In other words, that Alexander is deserving of the title 'Great' for these ideological reasons. The belief is 'founded' on such factors as his integration of foreigners into his army and administration, the mass mixed marriage at Susa (324), and Alexander's prayer for concord amongst the races after the Opis mutiny (also 324). The belief is quite erroneous, and Alexander, as with everything else, was acting for purely political/military, not ideological, purposes. For one thing, it is important to note that in the army foreigners were not peppered consistently amongst existing units, and when this did happen the instances are very few and far between. Thus, a few Persians are found incorporated in the *agema* of the Companion cavalry (Arr. 7.6.4–5), and Persians and Macedonians served together in a phalanx at Babylon (Arr. 7.23.3–4, 24.1), but Alexander's motive in both cases was military.

While Alexander did use Persians and Orientals in his administration it was always Macedonians and Greeks who controlled the army and the treasury. For example, at Babylon Alexander appointed as satrap the Persian Mazaeus, who had been satrap of Syria under Darius and commander of the Persian right at the battle of Gaugamela. However, Apollodorus of Amphipolis and Agathon of Pydna controlled the garrison there and collected the taxes (Diod. 17.64.5, Arr. 3.16.4, 7.18.1). In a nutshell, the natives had the local knowledge and the linguistic expertise. The conscious policy on the part of Alexander was to have the different races working together in order to make the local administration function as efficiently as possible, and had nothing to do with promoting racial equality.

Then there is the mass wedding at Susa, also in 324, at which Alexander and 91 members of his court married various Persian noble women in an elaborate wedding ceremony (conducted in Persian fashion too), which lasted for five days.[45] The symbolism as far as a fusion of the races is concerned is obvious, but again too much has been made of this marriage: it is important to note that no Persian men were given honours at Alexander's court or in his military and administrative machinery. Moreover, no Macedonian or Greek women were brought out from the mainland to marry Persian noble men, which we would expect as part of a fusion 'policy'. A closer explanation to the truth is probably that Alexander could not afford these noble women to marry their own races and thus provide the potential for revolt, something mixed marriages with his own court might offset. That the marriages were forced onto his men (cf. Arr. 7.6.2) is proved by the fact that all apart from Seleucus seem to have divorced their wives upon the king's death. Once again, however, Alexander seems to have ignored the displeasure of his men, ultimately at great cost to himself and his empire.

Finally, the great reconciliation banquet at Opis in 324 (after the second mutiny),[46] in which Macedonian, Greek, Persian and Iranian sipped from the same cup, and Alexander significantly 'prayed for various blessings and especially that the Macedonians and Persians should enjoy harmony as partners in the government' (Arr. 7.11.9). Yet, *inter alia* it is important to remember that Alexander had played on the hatred between the Macedonians and the Persians in ending the mutiny, and that the Macedonians were seated closest to him at the banquet, thereby emphasising their racial superiority and power. Moreover, we would expect a prayer to future concord after such a reconciliation since dissension in the ranks was the last thing Alexander needed given his plans for future conquest, which involved the invasion of Arabia in the near future![47] Thus, we may reject the notion of a 'brotherhood of mankind', and divorce it from any objective evaluation of Alexander.

In conclusion, the 'greatness' of Alexander III must be questioned, and the historical Alexander divorced from the mythical, despite the cost to the legend. There is no question that Alexander was the most powerful individual of his time, and we must recognise that. For sheer distance covered, places subdued, battle strategy, and breadth of vision he deserves praise. In just a decade he conquered the vast Persian empire that had been around for two centuries, and he amassed a fortune so vast that it is virtually impossible to comprehend. Alexander also improved the economy of his state (to an extent) and encouraged trade and commerce, especially by breaking down previously existing frontiers (of major importance in the hellenistic period), and an offshoot of his conquests was the gathering of information on the topography and geography of the regions to which he went, as well as new and exotic flora and fauna. However, at what cost? Was the wastage in human lives, the incalculable damage to foreign peoples, institutions, livelihoods, and lands, not to mention the continuation of the dynasty at home, the security of Macedon, the future of the empire, and the loyalty of the army worth it?

That Alexander did not endear himself to his own people, and that they grew discontented with him, has significant implications for his ultimate objectives and how he saw himself. The move to establish a kingdom of Asia with a capital probably at Babylon is significant.[48] Given his disregard of the feelings of his own people (as evidenced by his lack of interest in producing a legal and above-age heir to continue the dynasty and hegemonic position of Macedon), we can only surmise that his belief in his own divinity and his attempts to be recognised as a god while alive – including the attempt at *proskynesis* – are the keys to his actions and motives. As Fredricksmeyer has so persuasively argued,[49] Alexander was out to distance himself as far as possible from the exploits and reputation of Philip II since his attitude to his father had turned from one of admiration and rivalry, from one warrior to another, to resentment. He strove to excel him at all costs and he could not handle praise of Philip (the reaction to Cleitus' taunts about Philip is an obvious indication of this). Military conquest was one thing, but simple conquest was not enough: Alexander had to outdo Philip in other areas. Deification while alive was the most obvious way. Everything else became subordinated to Alexander's drive towards self-deification and then his eventual and genuine total belief in it.

Therefore, it is easy to see, on the one hand, why Alexander has been viewed as great, but also, on the other hand, why that greatness – and thus his epithet – must be questioned in the interests of historical accuracy.

Notes

1 I thank Professor A.B. Bosworth for his comments on an earlier draft of this paper.
2 N.G.L. Hammond, 'The Macedonian Imprint on the Hellenistic World', in *Hellenistic History and Culture*, ed. P. Green (Berkeley and Los Angeles 1993) 12–23.
3 The first attested reference to Alexander as great is found in Platus, *Mostellaria* 775, where Tranio compares himself to Alexander 'the great' (*magnum*) and to Agathocles of Syracuse. The casual, non-explanatory, nature of the exchange here would indicate that Alexander had had this title for some time, and that the audience knew it. Besides, it would be hard to ascribe the start of a tradition to someone like Plautus! When was Alexander saddled with this title? Perhaps during the reign of Ptolemy I, at the time when he kidnapped the funeral cortege of the dead Alexander, which proved so useful in promoting his rule.
4 The most recent biography of Alexander, written by N.G.L. Hammond, is ominously titled *The Genius of Alexander* (London 1996).
5 See D. Golan, 'The Fate of a Court Historian: Callisthenes', *Athenaeum* 66 (1988) 99–120.
6 See L.L. Gunderson, 'Alexander and the Attic Orators', in *Ancient Macedonian Studies in Honour of C.F. Edson*, ed. H.G. Dell (Thessaloniki 1981) 183–92.
7 See for example R. Stoneman, 'The Alexander Romance: From History to Fiction', in *Greek Fiction: The Greek Novel in Context*, edd. J.R. Morgan and R. Stoneman (London 1994) 117–29.
8 The historical accuracy of this work was attacked by E. Badian in his classic article 'Alexander the Great and the Unity of Mankind', *Historia* 7 (1958) 425–44. See more recently S. Schröder, 'Zu Plutarchs Alexanderreden', *MH* 48 (1991) 151–7 and A.B. Bosworth, *Alexander and the East* (Oxford 1996) 2–5.
9 On Macedon during Alexander's absence and especially the disunity, potential and otherwise, cf. N.G.L. Hammond and F.W. Walbank, *A History of Macedonia* 3 (Oxford 1988) 86–94 and R.M. Errington, *History of Macedonia* (Berkeley and Los Angeles 1990) 104 and 114–15.
10 Aes. 3.65, Din. 1.34; cf. Hyp. 5.31–32. On the Dinarchus passage see Ian Worthington, *A Historical Commentary on Dinarchus* (Ann Arbor 1992) *ad loc.*, with references there cited.
11 On troop numbers see the discussion of R. Billows, *Kings and Colonists* (Leiden 1995) 183–212. Billows believes that Macedon did not face a manpower shortage at this time, although I disagree.
12 E. Badian, 'Agis III', *Ventures into Greek History: Essays in Honour of N.G.L. Hammond*, ed. Ian Worthington (Oxford 1994) 259–68, who is right to stress that precise figures will never be known. For an opposing view see A.B. Bosworth, 'Alexander the Great and the Decline of Macedon', *JHS* 106 (1986) 1–12.
13 Though the Greeks may well have come to accept the Macedonian hegemony, at least while Alexander was alive: see Ian Worthington, 'The Harpalus Affair and the Greek Response to the Macedonian Hegemony', *Ventures into Greek History: Essays in Honour of N.G.L. Hammond*, ed. Ian Worthington (Oxford 1994) 307–30.
14 Professor Bosworth cautions me here on the extent of the casualties. He believes that there was regular attrition, no major disaster (except at the Persian Gates), and that the casualty rate may

have been 'as low as 30%. Nearly 20,000 out of 30,000+ seem to have survived' (personal letter). Admittedly, in battles using arrows, sarissas, and short swords, the prediction of dead and wounded is impossible, but for over one third of Alexander's combat troops to have been killed or maimed is hardly a low percentage! If a figure of 30% represents those actually killed, then at least the same would have been wounded, which for an army amounts to an annihilation.

15 On cities founded by Alexander, see now P.M. Fraser, *Cities of Alexander the Great* (Oxford 1996) who limits Alexander's genuine foundations to eight (excluding Alexandria in Egypt).

16 Diod. 17.94.3 ff., Arr. 5.25.2 ff., Curt. 9.3.3–5.

17 See now Philip O. Spann, 'Alexander at the Beas: Fox in a Lion's Skin', in Frances B. Titchener and Richard F. Moorton, Jr. (eds.), *The Eye Expanded: Life and the Arts in Greco-Roman Antiquity* (Berkeley 1999), 62–74, which puts forward the highly unlikely view that Alexander himself encouraged the mutiny because he did not wish to proceed further into India yet had to save face amongst his men. He concludes (p. 69) that the mutiny was a 'perfect piece of public relations bunkum'. Coenus would not be alone in disagreeing with his view!

18 On this march see A.B. Bosworth, *Conquest and Empire: The Reign of Alexander the Great* (Cambridge 1988) 139–146, citing sources and modern bibliography.

19 Arr. 7.8.1–12.3, Diod. 17.109.2–3, Plut. *Alexander* 71.2–9, Curt. 10.2.3 ff., Justin 12.11.

20 On the incident see Bosworth, *Conquest and Empire*, 159–161, citing sources and modern bibliography. See further below for this prayer being mistaken for part of a brotherhood of mankind 'policy'.

21 Bosworth, *Conquest and Empire*, 160; on p. 133, Bosworth's treatment of the Hyphasis mutiny makes it sound like a mere dispute between management and union executive.

22 Bosworth, *Conquest and Empire*, 160, goes on to talk of the Opis 'protest' as a challenge to Alexander's regal authority, yet continues to deny the term mutiny for it! It should be mentioned that Alexander was never faced with a large-scale desertion as had happened to his father following his defeat by Onomarchus at the Battle of Crocus Field in 352 (Diod. 16.35.2). However, Diodorus states specifically that military defeat not any *pothos* or orientalising policy had caused this desertion, and he goes on to imply that Philip soon rallied his men. Their loyalty to him stayed assured after this.

23 Arr. 2.1.5 ff.; Curt. 4.3 ff.; Diod. 17.42 ff.

24 On the battle see Bosworth, *Conquest and Empire*, 126–30, citing sources and bibliography.

25 On this see in detail Bosworth, *Alexander and India*, 6–21.

26 Arr. 4.10.5–7, Plut *Alexander* 54.3–6, Curt. 8.5.9–12.

27 E. Fredricksmeyer, 'On the Background of the Ruler Cult', *Ancient Macedonian Studies in Honour of C.F. Edson*, ed. H.J. Dell (Thessaloniki 1981) 145–56 (arguing for divine honours on Philip II), and E. Badian, 'The Deification of Alexander the Great', *Ancient Macedonian Studies in Honour of C.F. Edson*, ed. H.J. Dell (Thessaloniki 1981) 27–71 (arguing against).

28 On this see further below, with E. Fredricksmeyer, 'Alexander and Philip: Emulation and Resentment', *CJ* 85 (1990) 300–15.

29 Callisthenes, *apud* Strabo 17.1.43, Arr. 3.3–4, Plut. *Alexander* 27.8–10, cf. Diod. 17.51, Curt. 4.7.25, Justin 11.11.2–12. See P.A. Brunt's excellent discussion of this visit in the Loeb Classical Library *Arrian* Vol. 1 (London 1976), Appendix V, 467–80.

30 Athenaeus 12.538b; cf. Hyp. 5.18–19, Diod. 18.8.7, Curt. 10.2.5–7, Justin 13.5.1–6. See E. Badian, 'The Deification of Alexander the Great', in *Ancient Macedonian Studies in Honor of C F. Edson*, ed. H. J. Dell (Thessaloniki 1981) 27–71, G.L Cawkwell, 'The Deification of Alexander the Great: A Note', in *Ventures into Greek History: Essays in Honour of N.G.L. Hammond*, ed. Ian Worthington (Oxford 1994) 293–306, and E. Badian, 'Alexander the Great Between Two Thrones and Heaven: Variations on an Old Theme', in *Subject and Ruler: The Cult of the Ruling Power in Classical Antiquity*, ed. A. Small (Ann Arbor 1996) 11–26.

31 Polybius 12. 12b3, [Plutarch] *Moralia* 219e, 804b, 842 and Aelian, *VH* 5. 12 show that the Greek states had attempted to resist Alexander's deification. Demades, who proposed Alexander's deification in Athens, was later fined ten talents.

32 Arr. 3.26–27, Diod. 17.79–80, Plut. *Alexander* 48–9, Curt. 6.71–7.2.38, Justin 12.51–8. For discussion of this incident and that involving Parmenion which follows, see Bosworth, *Conquest and Empire*, 101–103, citing sources and modern bibliography.

33 Arr. 3.27.3–4, Diod. 17.80.3, Plut. *Alexander* 49.13, Curt. 7.2.11–32.

34 Arr. 4.8.1–9, Curt. 8.19–51, Plut. *Alexander* 50–52. For discussion see Bosworth, *Conquest and Empire*, 114–16, citing modern bibliography.
35 Arr. 4.14.1, Plut. *Alexander* 55.6, Curt. 8.6.24, 8.8.21.
36 On this issue cf. the remarks of Errington, *History of Macedonia*, 111–14.
37 Arr. 2.25.2–3, Plut. *Alexander* 29.7–8, Curt, 4.11.1–18.
38 Arr. 6.11.1, Diod. 17.99.4, Curt. 9.5.20. See Bosworth, *Conquest and Empire*, 135–7, citing sources and modern bibliography.
39 N.G.L. Hammond, *Alexander the Great: King, Commander and Statesman*² (Bristol 1989) 300–1 and n.138.
40 Diod. 18.4.4.
41 *History of Macedonia*, 3.105.
42 Diod. 17.109.1, 18.8.4 (text of the decree, from Hieronymus of Cardia), Curt. 10.2.4, [Plut.] *Moralia* 221a, Justin 13.5.2. On the background see, for example, Bosworth, *Conquest and Empire*, 220–8, citing sources and modern bibliography.
43 See further Worthington, 'The Harpalus Affair and the Greek Response to the Macedonian Hegemony', *Ventures into Greek History: Essays in Honour of N.G.L. Hammond*, ed. Ian Worthington (Oxford 1994) 307–30.
44 Ian Worthington, 'The Date of the Tegea decree (Tod ii 202): A Response to the *Diagramma* of Alexander III or of Polyperchon?', *AHB* 7 (1993) 59–64.
45 Arr. 7.4.1–8, Diod. 17.107.6, Plut. *Alexander* 70.3, Justin 12.10.9–10.
46 See above, with note 17.
47 On the whole issue of a 'unity of mankind' see further, for example, E. Badian, 'Alexander the Great and the Unity of Mankind', *Historia* 7 (1958) 425–44 and A.B. Bosworth, 'Alexander and the Iranians', *JHS* 100 (1980) 1–21.
48 On this issue cf. the remarks of Errington, *History of Macedonia*, 111–14.
49 E. Fredricksmeyer, 'Alexander and Philip: Emulation and Resentment', *CJ* 85 (1990) 300–15.

ALEXANDER THE GREAT TODAY: IN THE INTERESTS OF HISTORICAL ACCURACY?

Frank L. Holt

Alexander the Great is not the man he used to be. The dreamy Boy Scout of W.W. Tarn has become the dreary butcher of A.B. Bosworth and Ian Worthington.[1] To some extent, this radical transformation is salutary and rewards the rigorous source-criticism championed by Ernst Badian some forty years ago in his first challenges to Tarn's beatified Alexander.[2] Driven by strong Victorian values and a relentless disdain for anything unfavorable in the sources, Tarn made it popular to see only the good in his hero. So many fell under the sway of this sentimental approach that, Badian later complained, 'many of us remember a time when it was impossible to get an article questioning that interpretation into a professional journal in this country.'[3] That day, thankfully, has long since passed. The danger now, however, is that the new orthodoxy – a reprehensible Alexander beset by paranoia, megalomania, alcoholism, and violence – may gather a deleterious momentum of its own.

The first casualty of every new consensus is methodology itself, as rigorous criticism becomes merely vigorous criticism. The signs are there for all to see in Alexander Studies. Suddenly, it has become popular and perhaps too easy to assert the worst about Alexander based upon inclination rather than evidence. The finest work of Badian and Bosworth predisposes us now to a negative interpretation of nearly every source, threatening a bias in one direction no less potent than Tarn's was in the other. The ultimate danger is that this unity of thought will encourage carelessness which, worse still, somehow passes unnoticed into print.

Writing 'in the interests of historical accuracy' (p. 55), Ian Worthington builds upon the work of Bosworth and questions the greatness of Alexander on a number of grounds.[4] Worthington himself argues that Alexander needlessly depleted the resources of Macedonia, alienated his own countrymen, took unwarranted risks, triumphed more by luck than skill, drank too much, indulged a boundless ego, and exhibited none of the lofty ideals attributed to him by Plutarch and Tarn. In sum, Worthington's Alexander – foolish (pp. 47, 51–2), sacrilegious (pp. 46–7), bipolar (p. 49), and spiteful (p. 44) – was not much of a commander and considerably less a king or statesman. There is ample evidence, of course, to support some of these claims. Worthington is absolutely right to remind his readers of the growing unrest in Greece, the Gedrosian debacle, the reckless disregard for Macedonian succession, the bitter fate of some of the king's closest friends, and other blemishes on a record which Tarn tried too hard to whitewash. But emboldened by the new orthodoxy, Worthington has no trouble adding to his indictment some specific charges of a very dubious nature. In the interests of historical accuracy indeed, let us consider a few examples.

1. Alexander as killer

We begin with Alexander's criminal record, which has grown steadily through the works of Badian, Bosworth, and now Worthington. Tarn's predilection to pardon Alexander's sins led him to choose his sources uncritically: 'Cleitus (as Aristobulus says) had only himself to thank' for being murdered by the king.[5] This is obviously special pleading; but, equally unfair is to charge Alexander with a crime no source ever claims he committed. The *assumption* that Alexander disposed of Coenus after the so-called Hyphasis Mutiny has become a mainstay of modem scholarship. In one of his first critiques of Tarn, Badian hinted that Coenus was 'mysteriously destroyed' by 'misfortune and miscalculation.'[6] Writing later of Coenus' 'mysterious death in India', Badian acknowledged that the sources themselves do not implicate Alexander: 'we are not given any suggestion that his death was due to the King, though his magnificent funeral and Alexander's grudging grief prove little to a generation that witnessed the death of Rommel.'[7] A few years later, Badian wrote of Coenus in a famous article:

> We cannot be certain as to the circumstances surrounding the death of this sinister man. But those who remember the fate of Rommel are entitled to be cynical . . .[8]

Suggesting that Coenus was 'sinister' and repeating the appeals to a *possible* modern parallel prejudice the case against Alexander even though Badian admits throughout that there are no ancient sources to support the allegation.

In truth, our sources are quite clear on the point: Coenus died of disease.[9] No ancient writer seized the opportunity to add Coenus' name to the list of Alexander's victims. Yet today, Alexander's guilt seems certain whether Coenus died of illness or not. A.B. Bosworth writes that, 'Coenus' death, *accidental* or not, was a warning to the most powerful' that opposition was dangerous.[10] Pushing well past Badian's insinuation that Coenus' death may not have been accidental, Bosworth insists upon something malevolent even if it was. On the basis of what rigorous methodology can such a one-sided conclusion be reached? So strongly has the tide turned against Tarn and his hero that these accusations have become all too easy. Worthington now takes the final step (p. 44):

> Coenus' defiance of Alexander earned him little in the way of reward as a few days after the Hyphasis mutiny he was found dead in suspicious circumstances (Arr. 6.2.1, Curt. 9.3.20). The coincidence is too much, and, as with others who flouted Alexander . . . , we can see the hand of a furious and spiteful king at work here.

As already noted, the sources cited here by Worthington do no even hint that Coenus 'was found dead in suspicious circumstances.' The suspicions are entirely modern, inspired by the admitted cynicism of Badian in the shadow of Rommel's demise. There are no ancient intimations of murder or suicide, nor that Coenus was 'found dead' as if unexpectedly or mysteriously. When we consider Alexander's culpability in other instances (the death of Philip, e.g.), there are at least ancient texts that attest a crime and then express some suspicion about Alexander's involvement. Neither is true here. Of course, we may plead that the incriminating evidence has all been suppressed, giving us license to suppose a crime – but this removes all methodological rigor and allows us to imagine any evil we wish anytime we wish. Why not *assume*, for ·example, that when an Arybbas or Nicanor died, too, of disease that 'we can see the hand of a furious and spiteful king at work here' as well?[11]

The reply may be that, in the case of Coenus, 'the coincidence is too much' and therefore license is warranted. Certainly Alexander was at times a murderer and he may have gotten angry with Coenus; but, this does not mean that Alexander killed Coenus (and somehow concealed the deed as a fatal illness). Any argument that Alexander made a habit of murdering those who 'flouted' him must, in fairness, be met with the countervailing fact that Alexander did *not* kill Leonnatus and others who incensed him.[12] This is not to congratulate the king for his restraint, as Tarn did (above, note 5), but simply to remind us that homicide was no foregone conclusion for those who offended Alexander. Surely *everyone* who crossed Alexander died afterward, and cynicism is not sufficient cause to blame 'a furious and spiteful king.' At some point, the censure of Alexander's conduct must return to a rigorous and fair reading of the existing evidence. Adding Coenus' name to the list of Alexander's victims does nothing to improve 'historical accuracy.'

2. Alexander as king

Alexander sometimes took risks that today may seem reckless and irresponsible for a leader. This 'foolishness', as Worthington terms it, allegedly illustrates Alexander's failure as a king and is exemplified by the senseless attack upon the Malli in India. Worthington writes (p. 51):

> The nomadic Malli tribe had stolen his horse Bucephalus, and Alexander with his army set off to retrieve it. The Malli offered to return it when faced with the might of a Macedonian army, but Alexander, always thirsty for a fight and thinking little of the consequences, besieged the town. There was no need to do this.

In the interests of historical accuracy, it must be noted that Worthington's account is entirely untrue. Anxious to condemn Alexander, Worthington has here put into print a new myth about the Malli campaign which is difficult to pardon. The nomadic horse-thieves were, of course, the Mardi – *not* the Malli.[13] The rustlers lived far to the west, in the Zagros Mountains (Arrian) or near the Caspian Sea (Diodorus, Curtius), not in India. Places and peoples have been carelessly transposed. Furthermore, as is well known, Bucephalus died at the Battle of the Hydaspes and was given a famous burial months before Alexander even reached the territory of the Malli in the southern Punjab.[14] So, making the kinds of textual, geographical, and chronological mistakes we so often lament in a Justin or Plutarch, Worthington produces the wrong explanation for Alexander's attack on the Malli town.[15] The king did *not* risk his life in a needless effort to recover his stolen horse.

A similar error occurs in Worthington's critique of the king's actions after Issus. He writes (pp. 45–6):

> Alexander's generalship and actual military victories may be questioned in several key areas. For example, after the battle of Issus in 333 Darius fled towards Media, but Alexander pressed on to Egypt. He did not pursue Darius, as he surely ought to have done and thus consolidate his gains, especially when so far from home and with the mood of the locals so prone to

fluctuation, but left him alone. He was more interested in what lay to the south: the riches of Babylon and then Susa, or as Arrian describes them (3.16.2) the 'prizes of the war.'

Worthington claims (p. 46) that this ill-advised decision by Alexander caused needless deaths because it allowed Darius 'to regroup his forces and bring Alexander to battle again almost two years later, at Gaugamela (331).' This, of course, is misleading. Arrian 3.16.2 does record Darius' flight toward Media and the Great King's (correct) belief that Alexander would instead move south to Babylon and Susa. But all of this, as Arrian makes perfectly clear, took place *after* the Battle of Gaugamela! These are the consequences of the battle, not its cause. The zeal to de-heroize Alexander's campaigns must not be allowed to distort them.

As for Alexander's decision after Issus to continue his coastal march, Worthington ignores completely the very sound strategic reasons for doing so. Indeed, the best way to 'consolidate his gains' was to forgo his impulse to chase after Darius in order better to nullify the Persian naval advantage, secure his flank, and safeguard his lines of communication. As Badian has noted, this was actually one of Alexander's most brilliant decisions.[16] Too much like Plutarch (called by Worthington, p. 40, the most damaging force in Alexander historiography), Worthington has reduced the entire war to a royal duel, as if Alexander's principal aim must be the death of his opponent (p. 46): 'a war can hardly be seen as won if the opposing king and commander remains at large and has the potential to regroup.' But it was not the *man* Darius that mattered so much as his (or someone else's) *means* to continue the war – the empire's large navy, its rich urban centers, its stockpiled wealth, etc. The eastern Mediterranean coastline after Issus and the heartland of Persia after Gaugamela clearly had greater strategic value than did the capture of Darius himself. In the interests of historical accuracy, the king's actions after Issus and Gaugamela make strategic sense and should not be misconstrued as failures of leadership.

3. Alexander as terrorist

Worthington's heavy reliance upon the work of Bosworth brings us to our third and final example of the danger posed by the new consensus. Wherever Tarn willfully twisted the evidence to support his own view of Alexander, good scholars such as Bosworth have rightly complained:

> . . . such manipulation is not uncharacteristic of Alexander studies. All too often, the concern is to brush aside unpalatable facts, and argue from what the sources should have said.[17]

Taking out of context any evidence, literary *or* material, can seriously undermine the interests of historical accuracy. A recent case involves the so-called Porus coinage of Alexander, which Bosworth and his followers have manipulated into a sinister manifesto that casts Alexander in the worst possible light.

To be brief, Bosworth alleges that these medallions were a propaganda tool specifically designed to terrorize the troublesome Greeks back in the Balkans.[18] He writes emphatically, as if no other interpretation were possible:

In a manner unique in ancient coinage he [Alexander] was sending a message to people who could never hope to witness an Indian army in the flesh. These were the outlandish and formidable forces which he had faced in battle and crushed. Five years might have elapsed since the Persian grand army was humiliated at Gaugamela, but his army had lost none of its frightful efficiency. The story over Porus was proof, and the coinage ensured that its implications were not lost. In the context of the troubles in Greece which followed the Exiles' Decree it would constitute a blunt warning. Beware the consequences of revolt. The army which crushed Porus will easily crush you.[19]

Bosworth's confidence in this chilling scenario ignores more than a century of debate and uncertainty regarding these artifacts; in context, these 'coins' have been considered by experts to be stubbornly cryptic.[20] Nonetheless, Bosworth argues – based upon his own view of Alexander – what this 'coinage' *should* have said and to whom; in doing so, he brushes aside unpalatable facts as readily as did Tarn.

We cannot even be certain that these artifacts are coins at all. They conspicuously lack the normal attributes of Alexander's circulating currency. They exhibit inexplicably poor workmanship, erratic weights on no certain standard, unset die axes, and no identifying ethnic. There is absolutely no evidence that these artifacts were struck in large numbers, nor that they circulated anywhere near Greece, as would be essential to effect the sinister purpose imagined by Bosworth. The smaller 'coins' (variously identified as staters, tetradrachms, or two-shekels) depict only the forces of an Indian army with no indication of a victory or loss. The huge decadrachms, or perhaps five-shekels, show a cavalryman attacking a war-elephant and, on the other side, Alexander crowned by victory as he grasps a lightning bolt. Scholars have been hard-pressed to find a single, coherent propaganda message in these 'mismatched' medallions.

Very large 'coins' such as decadrachms/five-shekels are, in any case, a most unlikely choice for the far-reaching propaganda campaign proposed by Bosworth. These denominations pass above, not through, the general population. An average Athenian might handle the smaller types, should they ever reach Aegean marketplaces, but what obvious message could he infer from their ambiguous, anepigraphic images? Could he guess, without the accompanying large medallions, that *Alexander* issued them to celebrate a victory? If so, would he then recognize these as enemy, rather than (as some modern experts propose) allied Indian forces? If he somehow identified them as *defeated* hostile units, why would he then imagine them to have been particularly 'formidable'? Finally, would our Greek understand all this to be a 'blunt' manifesto aimed directly at him from Babylonia?

To say what Bosworth wants them to say, these medallions must therefore be interpreted out of context and exempted from all the normal rigors of numismatic methodology. We must believe that Alexander intended to send a clear warning to the population of Greece about the frightful efficiency of his army, and that he did so by issuing a relatively tiny number of 'coins' in Mesopotamia, struck on an ambiguous and perhaps even non-Greek standard, of poor manufacture, without inscriptions of any kind, of mixed sizes that would not likely circulate together, with equivocal images, and so far *completely unknown* among all the numismatic hoards and stray finds of the Aegean world. These unpalatable facts stand against Bosworth's interpretation and, in the interests of historical accuracy, must not be brushed aside.

The 'murder' of Coenus, the attack at Malli to 'rescue Bucephalus', and the 'blunt warning' of the so-called Porus Coinage illustrate some of the methodological problems in recent Alexander scholarship. The strong inclination today to de-heroize Alexander has contributed to a new consensus about the king that may be making us careless. Tarn's ideas, in as much as they arose from a prejudiced reading of the sources, have rightly been rejected; but, the corrective back-lash begun so well by Badian has perhaps led us to a new extreme orthodoxy that, too, runs counter to the interests of historical accuracy.

Notes

1 Tarn, *Alexander the Great*, 2 vols. (Cambridge 1948); Bosworth, *Alexander and the East: The Tragedy of Triumph* (Oxford 1996); Worthington, 'How "Great" was Alexander?' *AHB* 13.2 (1999) 39–55.

2 Badian, 'Alexander the Great and the Unity of Mankind', *Historia* 7.4 (1958) 425–44; and 'The Eunuch Bagoas: A Study in Method', *CQ* 8 (1958): 144–57.

3 Badian, 'The Alexander Romance', *The New York Review of Books* 21.14 (September 19, 1974): 9; see also Badian, 'Some Recent Interpretations of Alexander', in Badian (ed.), *Alexandre le Grand: Image et réalité* (Vandœuvres–Genève 1976) 296: 'Public attacks on Tarn's overpowering position in the English-speaking world were slow in coming, since difficult to make acceptable to the academic Establishment.'

4 'How "Great" was Alexander?' *AHB* 13.2 (1999) 39–55. All in-text references to Worthington's opinions are drawn from this particular article.

5 Tarn, *Alexander the Great* I.75; cf. 123 where Tarn seems to commend Alexander's ability to restrain himself from murdering friends more often.

6 Badian, 'Bagoas', 150.

7 Badian, 'Harpalus', *JHS* 81 (1961) 20 and cf. 23.

8 Badian, 'Alexander the Great and the Loneliness of Power', *AUMLA* 17 (1962) 87 = *Studies in Greek and Roman History* (Oxford 1964) 200.

9 Curtius 9.3.20; Arrian 6.2.1. See Badian, 'Alexander in Iran', in I. Gershevitch, ed., *The Cambridge History of Iran*, vol. 2 (Cambridge 1985) 467: 'Coenus shortly after this died of illness.' The comments of W. Heckel are judicious: *The Marshals of Alexander's Empire* (London 1992) 64.

10 Bosworth, *Alexander and the East* 117 (my italics).

11 Arybbas the Bodyguard: Arrian 3.5.5; Nicanor the son of Parmenion: Arrian 3.25.4. Of course, Badian has seen the sudden demise of Nicanor as the triggering opportunity Alexander needed to rid himself once and for all from Parmenion's powerful family; but (rightly) Badian does not suggest that Nicanor himself was a victim of the King ('fortune took a hand with Nicanor's death'): 'The Death of Parmenio', *TAPA* 91 (1960) 330. What is true of Nicanor is also true for Coenus – no murder need be imagined.

12 Arrian 4.12.2 records the anger of Alexander at Leonnatus as a result of the failed attempt at *proskynesis*. Other sources name other offenders (Polyperchon in Curtius 8.5.22 and Cassander in Plutarch, *Alexander* 74.2), creating an interesting scholarly crux. Heckel, *Marshals* 95–8 accepts Leonnatus the Bodyguard, but argues against Badian and Hamilton that the *proskynesis* incident harmed Leonnatus' career; whereas, Bosworth – agreeing with Heckel that Leonnatus suffered no reprisals from Alexander – *therefore* believes Polyperchon the more likely offender because of a possible career slump at this time, and he also accepts the story about Cassander: *Commentary on Arrian's* History of Alexander, Vol. 2 (Oxford 1995) 86–7. Even if the offender, however identified, did harm his own career – which is far from certain – he obviously was not murdered by his annoyed sovereign.

13 Arrian 5.19.6; Plutarch, *Alex.* 44.3–5; Curtius 6.5.18–19; Diodorus 17.76.5–8.

14 On Bucephalus, see A.R. Anderson. 'Bucephalus and his Legend', *AJP* 51 (1930) 1–21.

15 Although Worthington cites (n.38) Bosworth's *Conquest and Empire*, philological method might lead us to suspect a careless reading of Bosworth's *Alexander and the East* 28–9, where an account of the Malli campaign is followed by a reference back to the theft of Bucephalus: 'The killing [as at Malli] was certainly a dreadful constant in the reign, and with it went a distinct lack of respect for life. Alexander had a short way with horse thieves, at least when his favourite stallion, Bucephalus, was stolen . . . '

16 'Alexander in Iran', *CHI* II.432. Such decisions, he adds, distinguish Alexander's greatness above 'mere royal adventurers like Demetrius the Besieger or Pyrrhus, who could probably never have conquered the Achaemenian empire.'

17 *Alexander and the East* 167.

18 *Alexander and the East* 6–8; see also Worthington, 'How "Great" was Alexander?' 47, and the popular M. Wood, *In the Footsteps of Alexander the Great* (Berkeley 1997) 187.

19 *Alexander and the East* 8 and see also 169.

20 I deal at greater length with these problems in a forthcoming article, 'Alexander the Great, India, and the Mediterranean World', *Indian Historical Review*.

INDEX OF
PRIMARY SOURCES

Inscriptional	Number	Page
Tod, no. 183	20	66
Tod, no. 184	21	66
Tod, no. 185	34	107
Tod, no. 190	33	107
Tod, no. 192	22	66
Tod, no. 196	26	69
Tod, no. 201	23	67
Tod, no. 202	25	68
*SIG*³, no. 312	24	68

Literary		
Amyntas, *FGrH* 122 F 6	Chap. 5, n. 19	117
Anonymous History of Alexander, *FGrH* 151 F 1	41	109
Anonymous History of Alexander, *FGrH* 151 FF 3–5	46	112
Anonymous History of Alexander, *FGrH* 151 F 6	50	113
Anonymous History of Alexander, *FGrH* 151 F 7	52	114
Anonymous History of Alexander, *FGrH* 151 F 10	97	239
Anonymous History of Alexander, *FGrH* 151 F 11	49	113
Anonymous History of Alexander, *FGrH* 151 FF 12–13	54	114
Archelaus, *FGrH* 123 F 1	62	150
Aristobulus, *FGrH* 139 F 2b	30	71
Aristobulus, *FGrH* 139 F 3	31	72
Aristobulus, *FGrH* 139 F 4	18	43
Aristobulus, *FGrH* 139 F 5	40	109
Aristobulus, *FGrH* 139 F 7a	42	109
Aristobulus, *FGrH* 139 F 7b	43	110
Aristobulus, *FGrH* 139 F 11	89	199
Aristobulus, *FGrH* 139 FF 13–15	96	238

Aristobulus, *FGrH* 139 F 24	57	115
Aristobulus, *FGrH* 139 F 29	58	115
Aristobulus, *FGrH* 139 F 30	103	274
Aristobulus, *FGrH* 139 F 31	104	274
Aristobulus, *FGrH* 139 F 33	107	275
Aristobulus, *FGrH* 139 F 34	1	2
Aristobulus, *FGrH* 139 F 35	61	149
Aristobulus, *FGrH* 139 F 43	74	154
Aristobulus, *FGrH* 139 F 46	71	153
Aristobulus, *FGrH* 139 F 49a	80	155
Aristobulus, *FGrH* 139 F 49b	81	157
Aristobulus, *FGrH* 139 F 52	91	200
Aristobulus, *FGrH* 139 F 53	110	297
Aristobulus, *FGrH* 139 F 54	82	158
Aristobulus, *FGrH* 139 F 55	83	158
Aristobulus, *FGrH* 139 F 55	100	240
Aristobulus, *FGrH* 139 F 55	112	297
Aristobulus, *FGrH* 139 F 58	108	275
Aristobulus, *FGrH* 139 F 61	84	159
Aristus, *FGrH* 143 F 2	111	297
Baeton, *FGrH* 119 F 2a	36	108
Callisthenes, *FGrH* 124 F 14a	92	237
Callisthenes, *FGrH* 124 F 14b	93	237
Callisthenes, *FGrH* 124 F 35	45	111
Callisthenes, *FGrH* 124 F 36	98	239
Callisthenes, *FGrH* 124 F 37	47	112
Chares, *FGrH* 125 F 2	37	108
Chares, *FGrH* 125 F 4	90	199
Chares, *FGrH* 125 F 6	85	178
Chares, *FGrH* 125 F 7	51	113
Chares, *FGrH* 125 F 7	86	179
Chares, *FGrH* 125 F 14a	87	199
Chares, *FGrH* 125 F 14b	88	199
Chares, *FGrH* 125 F 15	105	274
Chares, *FGrH* 125 F 16	65	152
Chares, *FGrH* 125 F 18	75	154
Chares, *FGrH* 125 F 19a	68	152
Chares, *FGrH* 125 F 19b	9	4

Cleitarchus, *FGrH* 137 F 4	32	72
Cleitarchus, *FGrH* 137 F 11	55	114
Cleitarchus, *FGrH* 137 F 13	35	108
Cleitarchus, *FGrH* 137 F 17	70	153
Cleitarchus, *FGrH* 137 F 23	64	152
Cleitarchus, *FGrH* 137 F 24	5	3
Ephemerides, *FGrH* 117 F 1	15	18
Ephemerides, *FGrH* 117 F 2a	109	297
Ephemerides, *FGrH* 117 F 2b	8	4
Ephemerides, *FGrH* 117 F 2c	7	4
Ephemerides, *FGrH* 117 F 3b	12	4
Ephippus, *FGrH* 126 F 5	99	239
Hegesias, *FGrH* 142 F 3	14	18
Harpocration, *Lexicon*, s.v.		
Ariston	27	70
Marsyas, *FGrH* 135 F 3	28	70
Nearchus, *FGrH* 133 F 3a	78	155
Nearchus, *FGrH* 133 F 3b	79	155
Nearchus, *FGrH* 133 F 4	67	152
Nearchus, *FGrH* 133 F 5	59	149
Nearchus, *FGrH* 133 F 11	63	151
Nicoboule, *FGrH* 127 F 1	10	4
Nicoboule, *FGrH* 127 F 2	11	4
Nicoboule, *FGrH* 127 F 3a	38	109
Onesicritus, *FGrH* 134 F 1	3	3
Onesicritus, *FGrH* 134 F 2	17	43
Onesicritus, *FGrH* 134 F 5	39	109
Onesicritus, *FGrH* 134 F 6	60	149
Onesicritus, *FGrH* 134 F 17a	69	152
Onesicritus, *FGrH* 134 F 18	66	152
Onesicritus, *FGrH* 134 F 19	19	43
Onesicritus, *FGrH* 134 F 20	76	154
Onesicritus, *FGrH* 134 F 27	4	3
Onesicritus, *FGrH* 134 F 38	16	18
Polycleitus, *FGrH* 128 F 7	2	2
Ptolemy, *FGrH* 138 F 3	29	70
Ptolemy, *FGrH* 138 F 6	44	111
Ptolemy, *FGrH* 138 F 7	48	113
Ptolemy, *FGrH* 138 F 8	94	237
Ptolemy, *FGrH* 138 F 9	95	238
Ptolemy, *FGrH* 138 F 10	53	114
Ptolemy, *FGrH* 138 F 13	101	273
Ptolemy, *FGrH* 138 F 14	56	114
Ptolemy, *FGrH* 138 F 16	102	274
Ptolemy, *FGrH* 138 F 17	106	274
Ptolemy, *FGrH* 138 F 20	73	154
Ptolemy, *FGrH* 138 F 23	77	155
Ptolemy, *FGrH* 138 F 25	72	153
Ptolemy, *FGrH* 138 F 26a	6	3
Ptolemy, *FGrH* 138 F 30	13	5

INDEX

Abreas 3,
Achaea 83–4, 92
Acrocorinth 84
Aegae 20, 61
Aetolia 78, 86
Agesilaus 34, 37, 46, 55, 118, 121
Agis III 45, 65, 83, 252, 305–6
Agonippus 82
Ahuramazda 55, 143
Alexander I 245
Alexander II 26
Alexander, III the Great: accession 17, 279;
    death 4–5, 101, 159; deification 9, 42,
    47–9, 66, 87, 100, 107, 198, 206, 236–69,
    300, 310; drinking 4, 286–7, 296–7, 312;
    illnesses and injuries 23, 113, 149, 179,
    195; king of Asia 138ff., 178, 181, 212,
    216, 220, 246, 251–2, 300, 310, 315; king
    of Macedon 23, 25, 84, 194, 243, 245, 303,
    321; military commander 24, 112, 166,
    178ff., 308; orientalizing 42, 50, 101, 107,
    142, 211ff., 309, 314; personality 28,
    299–302; policy 137, 149, 182, 203,
    208ff., 215, 223–4, 253–4, 314; youth
    17ff., 301
Alexander IV 51
Alexander of Epirus 60
Alexander the Lyncestian 279–81, 287
Alexander Romance 1, 142, 304
Alexandria, in Egypt 42, 113, 250, 312
Amazons 2
Ambracia 75, 85
Amminapes 31
Ammon see Temple of Ammon
Amphictyonic Council 30, 32, 83
Amyntas 217, 221
Anaximenes 7
Antigonus 173

Antipater 3, 5, 24, 49, 51, 65–6, 75, 77,
    83–4, 94–5, 101, 119, 179, 225, 242, 279,
    281, 305–6, 314
Arabia 49, 179, 198, 240, 297, 313
Arachosia 166,
Arbela 114, 184,
    Battle of see Gaugamela
Arcadia 76, 92
Archidamus 34
Argos 33, 85
Aria 166
Ariobarzanes 193
Aristobulus 1, 5, 7f.
Aristogiton see Harmodius and Aristogiton
Aristotle 17, 50, 78, 136
Arrian 7f., 13f.
Arrhidaeus see Philip III Arrhidaeus
Arsames 190
Arses see Artaxerxes IV
Artabazus 31, 34, 253
Artaxerxes III, Ochus 37–8, 279
Artaxerxes IV, Arses 38
Artaxerxes V see Bessus
Asia Minor 42, 45, 66, 82, 106, 184–5, 251,
    265
Aspendus 45, 82
Athens 34–5, 61, 242, 244, 246, 265–8, 279,
    305
Athenaeus 1, 8
Atropates 172, 205
Attalus 56, 279–80
Audata 29

Babylon 42, 86, 139, 149, 158, 172, 184,
    213, 312
Bactra 148, 198, 236, 309
Bactria 107, 109, 138, 150, 167, 212, 216,
    221, 223

Bagoas 38
Bagoas son of Pharnuches 219
Barsine 199, 200, 202, 216, 299
Bessus 107, 114–5, 141, 184, 212–13, 253
Boeotia 75–6, 92
Branchidae 48
Bucephalus and Bucephala 148, 154–5, 175,
Byzantium 36,

Calanus 148, 152–3, 165
Callisthenes 1–2, 7–9, 119, 199, 274–5, 287,
    310
Calisthenes of Athens 72
Caria 50, 137
Cassander 194
Cersebleptes 35
Chaeronea, Battle of 18, 31, 36, 55, 75, 78,
    121
Chalcidice 30
Chalcis 75
Chandragupta 165–6
Chares 1, 4
Charidemus 72, 130
Chios 66, 77, 81
Cilicia 111, 189–90, 280
Cleitarchus 1, 3, 7f.
Cleitus (Clitus) 24, 107, 115, 186, 214, 273,
    278, 286, 310, 319
Cleopatra, wife of Philip II 280
Coenus 29, 164, 288, 307, 320–21
coins see numismatics
Common Peace see League of Corinth
Companions 29
Cotys 33
Craterus 78, 194, 203, 213, 218, 225, 283,
    306
Crenides 30
Crete 82, 306
Curtius Rufus, Quintus 7
Cydnus River 113
Cyprus 49, 184
Cyropolis 184, 217

Darius III Codomannus 46, 47, 50, 57,
    106–7, 111, 114, 130, 138ff., 181f., 212,
    250, 279, 308, 312
Dataphernes 114
Deisitheus 66
Demades 267
Demon 72
Demosthenes 30, 35, 45, 50, 66, 72, 84, 86,
    87, 91ff., 120, 136, 244, 257, 267–8

Diodochoi 51
Diodorus of Sicily 7, 11f.
Diopeithes 36
Drypetis 112, 202

Ecbatana 149, 195, 239
Egypt 34, 37, 81, 106, 150, 247
Elimiotis 29
Elis 83–4
Ephemerides 1, 4
Ephesus 18, 246, 249, 256
Ephialtes 72
Ephippus 7, 8
Epicurus 68
Epirus 29, Erigyius 29
Erythrae 48, 251
Eumenes 7, 21, 29, 49, 213, 218, 242
Euripides 4
Eurybotas 70
Exiles Decree 65ff., 85, 91, 149, 236, 242,
    263, 288–9, 314

Ganges River 49
Gaugamela, the Battle of 8, 9, 47, 83, 107,
    114, 127–8, 188, 191
Gedrosia 149, 155–57, 166, 186, 288, 307
Gordium 47, 106, 109
Granicus River, the Battle of 12, 45, 46, 106,
    109, 188, 191, 309
Great King, see Persia

Halicarnassus 45, 195
Harmodius and Aristogiton, statues of 45
Harpalus 66, 78, 86, 90f.
Hegelochus 81
Hellanicus 20
Hephaestion 24, 25, 86, 148, 162, 172,
    194, 202, 213, 215, 218, 220, 257, 268,
    289
hetairoi, see Companions
Hindu Kush 49, 148, 162
Homer 18, 24
Hydaspes (Jhelum) River, 138, 148, 162–3,
    170, 188, 191
Hypaspists see Royal Pages
Hyperides 92–3, 265
Hyphasis (Beas) River 42, 49, 138, 161, 273,
    287–8, 307
Hyrcania 220

Iason, see Jason
Iaxartes see Jaxartes

Illyria 18, 20, 65, 136, 225
India 42, 47, 49, 90: culture 150–52;
    geography 149–50
Indus River 148–50, 162, 170, 172
Ioannes Stobaeus 60
Ionia 49, see also Asia Minor
Ipsus, battle of 7
Isocrates 33, 37, 45–6, 55–6, 136, 161
Issus, the battle of 8–9, 47, 106, 111, 127–8,
    178–9, 188, 191, 225, 308, 321

Jacoby, Felix 7,
Jason of Pherae 37, 55
Jaxartes River, 3
Justin 7

Lacrates 34, 37
Lamian War 265, 305
Laomedon 29, 218
Larisa 32
League of Corinth 37, 42, 54, 56, 65, 75ff.,
    81ff., 106, 107, 161, 242, 246, 268, 305,
    311, 314
Leonidas 124
Leonnatus 3, 113, 306
Leosthenes 100
Lesbos 81, 246
Lycia 50
Lycurgus 72, 78, 84, 92
Lydia 137
Lysimachus 163, 179, 313

Macedonia 17: constitution 30; economy 42,
    46; people 26, 31, 305; women in 25,
Maeotis, Lake 3, 108
Malli 3–4, 152, 164, 188, 195, 288, 313,
    321
Mantinea 68
Maracanda (Samarkand) 186, 214
Marathus 57
Massaga 162
Meda 29
Medeius 4, 32
Megalopolis 34, 83–4
Memnon 81, 82, 83
Menander 167
Mentor of Rhodes 37
mercenaries 30, 37, 45, 46, 55, 77, 162,
    314
Messene 83
Messenia 33–4
Metz Epitome 10

Miletus 45, 251
Moerocles 72
mutinies 49, 149, 155, 164, 178, 203, 209,
    223, 307–9
Mytilene 65, 81

Nabarzanes 253
Nearchus 1, 2, 4, 7ff., 29
Neoptolemus 57, 60
Nicaea in India 148, 175
Nicanor 77, 92, 98, 170, 174
Nicoboule 4, 8
numismatics 1, 139, 142, 167, 178, 301,
    322–3
Nysa 162

Ochus see Artaxerxes III
Ochus River 3
Ochus, son of Darius III 112, 141
Oeniadae 86
Olympia 60, 77–8, 86
Olympias, mother of Alexander 17, 25, 29,
    109, 239, 263, 279, 281, 299
Olynthus 29, 31, 86
Onesicritus 1, 3, 7
Opis 49, 149, 195, 203ff., 209, 220, 222,
    237, 302, 307–9, 315
Oropus 75
Oxus River 3
Oxyartes 205
Oxyathres 211, 213, 219
Oxydracae 164

Paeonia 20, 26, 31, 136
Pages see Royal Pages
Pammenes 34
Pangaeum, Mt. 30
Panhellenism, 33, 37–8, 42, 45–6, 56, 65,
    85, 118–120, 161, 252, 305; see also
    League of Corinth
Parapamisadae 170f.
Parmenion 18, 25, 30, 46, 51, 56, 107, 112,
    119, 124, 136, 273–4, 280–82, 285–6,
    310, 312
Parthia 108, 212
Parysatis 200
Pasargadae 143, 161, 252, 254–6
Patala 174
Patalene 150
Peithon 170f.
Pella 17, 42, 245
Pelusium 37

Perdiccas II 24
Perdiccas III 26
Perdiccas 70, 138, 148, 162, 172, 209, 313
Perinthus 46
Persepolis 45, 85, 107, 114, 128, 161, 184, 251–2
Persian Empire 37, 55, 58, 121:
    cities 183; economy 46; foreign policy 45, 83; geography 185, Great King 30, 54, 60–61, 248; Royal Post 268
Persian Gates 190
Peucestas 3, 202, 218, 224, 250, 275, 309
Pharsalus 32
Phila 29
Philinna 29
Philinus 4
Philip II 17, 21, 28: assassination 42, 57; diplomacy 31, 34–5, 37; invasion of Persia 37–8, 42, 45–6, 54ff., 118–9, 120ff., 131, 246, 249; marriages 23, 25, 29, 249; military reforms 32, 186–7, 193; reign 25, 26, 136, 246–8
Philip III Arrhidaeus 23, 78, 82, 313
Philip son of Machatas 170
Philip, Alexander's physician 281–2
Philippopolis 33
Philocles 90f.
Philocrates, the Peace of 30, 119f.
Philodemus 58
Philotas 21, 25, 107, 115, 251, 273–4, 283–5, 310
Philoxenus 93f.
Phocia 122
Phocion 92
Phoenicia 37, 49, 184
Phrygia 20, 110
Plutarch 7
Polemocrates 29
Polybius 8–9
Polycleitus 3
Polyeuctus 72
Portia 170
Porus 49, 141, 148, 154, 163, 170–72, 184, 193, 309
Potidaea 18
Promachus 4
Ptolemy, Son of Lagus: general 115, 162; primary source 1–2, 3–4, 5,7
Python 5

Quintus Curtius see Curtius Rufus

Rhodes 82
Rhoxane (Roxane) 25, 51, 172, 211, 216–17, 253, 299
Royal Pages 29, 59, 107, 264, 273, 286–7, 310

Sacred War 34
Saka see Scythians
Samarkand see Maracanda
Samos 66, 68, 86, 91, 95, 257–8
Sangala 163
sarisa 32, 221, 224
Satibarzanes 184, 212, 220
Scythians 3, 49, 127, 129–30, 184, 221
Seleucus 5, 159, 166, 202, 205, 315
Seuthes 33
Sidon 37
Sisygambis 141, 216
Sitalces 33
Siwah see Temple of Ammon at Siwah
Social War 35
Sogdiana 107, 109, 184, 193, 205, 220
Sparta 33–4, 77–8, 82, 268
Spitamenes 114, 184
Stateira 112
Strabo 1–2, 7f.
Susa 109, 149, 150, 198, 200, 214, 217–18, 242, 256
Swat Valley 162, 184
Syria 57

Tanais (Don) River 3, 108
Tarn, Sir William W. 45
Taxila 148, 166, 184
Taxiles 49, 170–74
Tegea 65, 69, 83–4, 86, 99
Temple of Zeus Ammon at Siwah 9, 42, 47–8, 106, 236, 250, 310
Tenedos 81
Ten Thousand Immortals, the 46
Thais 128
Thalestria, Queen of the Amazons 2
Theagenes of Thebes 71
Thebes 34, 45, 65, 70, 75, 183, 188
Thermopylae 30
Thessaly 32, 45
Thrace 20, 32–3, 83, 136, 306
Tigris River 158
Timaeus 9
Timagenes 3
Timotheus 98
Triparadeisus 170f.

Trogus, Pompeius 7
Tyre 82, 106, 113–4, 184, 188, 300,
 308–9

Xerxes 45

Yavana 167

Zeus Ammon see Temple of Zeus Ammon at
 Siwah
Zopyrion 129